THE
AMERICAN
MERCURY

THE AMERICAN MERCURY

Facsimile Edition of Volume I

The Issues of January, February, March, April 1924

A MONTHLY REVIEW
Edited by H.L. MENCKEN
& GEORGE JEAN NATHAN

Originally Published by
ALFRED A. KNOPF

Introduction to the Book Edition by
RICHARD K. RUSSELL

Freedeeds Books
(a division of Garber Communications, Inc.)
Blauvelt, New York 10913 U.S.A.

FIRST EDITION
Published in Book Format

Copyright © 1984 by Garber Communications, Inc.

Library of Congress Catalog Card Number:
''The Original Knopf edition of this title
was assigned Library of Congress Catalog
Card Number: 25-11667.''

International Standard Book Number:
0-89345-050-2 (clothbound)

Manufactured in the United States of America

The publication of this book has been made
possible, in part, through the assistance of,
and in association with, Sangraal, Inc.

FOREWORD
TO THE REPRINT EDITION

THE AMERICAN MERCURY belongs to the 1920's. It belongs to the era of Babbits and bootleggers, progressives and Prohibition. Its heyday spread from its first issue, which arrived on the newsstands in December of 1923, to its decline in 1930. 1930 saw the departure of George Jean Nathan. H. L. Mencken, the autocratic center resigned in 1933. Alfred Knopf, the publisher who alternately tolerated and gloried in it, sold it in 1935. It limped along after those defections from publisher to publisher, to end up as a "born again" publication for a "born again" evangelist operating out of Oklahoma City. THE AMERICAN MERCURY, like many things American, rose like a shining star, only to fall as quickly as it rose, a burnt-out meteor. In the halcyon days of the Twenties, however, it was America's critic, America's iconoclast, America's sceptic, a hipflask for the American mind, as much a part of American life as bathtub gin.

THE AMERICAN MERCURY began with the literary partnership of H.L. Mencken and George Jean Nathan, who took over as co-editors of the *Smart Set* magazine in October, 1914. H.L. Mencken was already an acclaimed journalist, author and iconoclast. His writings appeared throughout the country, though his home base was in the *Baltimore Sun*. George Jean Nathan was an acerbic critic of theater who had scathingly roasted most native American theater efforts and had been instrumental in the introduction of such European talent as Ibsen, Shaw and Strindberg to America. Mencken was an American Shaw; Nathan, an American Wilde. The *Smart Set*, however, was never a financial success. A tight budget restricted acquisitions, inferior paper made it somewhat of a joke.

As early as 1912, Mencken began to experiment with the idea of a new monthly magazine, somewhat along the lines of the "Blue Weekly," H.G. Wells' fictitious publication in his novel *The New Machiavelli* and Ford Madox Ford's *English Review*. This projected "Blue Review" was, in Mencken's preliminary thoughts, a Nietzschesque view of American life and world events, a journal of out of season thought. Mencken's initial proposals for this magazine were rejected by the then publisher of *Smart Set*, John Adams Thayer.

In 1914, Nathan and Mencken threw themselves into *Smart Set* and went about changing it into some semblance of the "Blue Review" proposal. The acceptance of it, however, was anything but spectacular. Shortly thereafter, Thayer was compelled to relinquish control of the magazine to Eugene F. Crowe, a paper magnate.

From 1914 to 1923, Mencken and Nathan struggled to keep the magazine solvent. Their budget for material was so meager that they were obliged to write a good deal of the material themselves under some fifteen or twenty pseudonyms. Nonetheless, over nine years *Smart Set* introduced, or at least published, such later successes as F. Scott Fitzgerald, Ben Hecht, Sherwood Anderson, and Eugene O'Neill; corralled such notable names as Theodore Dreiser, James Branch Cabell, and Willa Cather; imported James Joyce, and Aldous Huxley.

The crucible of *Smart Set*, boiling together many talents was the liquid steel out of which THE AMERICAN MERCURY would be formed. While the MERCURY cannot truthfully be said to be the successor of *Smart Set*, it was, quite obviously, a product forged of the experiences of Nathan and Mencken with *Smart Set*. Thus, in early 1923, the molten material lay in the vat waiting for someone to pour it into an appropriate mold. That someone appeared in the form of Alfred Knopf, an idealistic young publisher.

Knopf and Mencken were, by no means strangers. In 1913, Knopf, then at Doubleday, tried to persuade Mencken to act as editor for a proposed edition of the works of Conrad. The association between the two continued through 1923 when Knopf, now heading his own fledgling house, decided he needed a magazine. Many publishers, needing a house review for prestige, literary contacts, and cheap advertising founded magazines about this time. Knopf, one of the most able of the era's publishers, was not slow in entering this field, and his choice to head up the enterprise fell on his old friend H. L. Mencken.

When Knopf approached Mencken with the project in early 1923, Mencken persuaded him to take on Nathan as co-editor, and the MERCURY team was born. The first step taken was an attempt to buy *Smart Set*, but Knopf's bid of $25,000 was topped by William Randolph Hearst. The "Blue Review" was resurrected and dusted off, and Knopf bought everything, but the name. A search was initiated for a name. Over Mencken's objections, Knopf settled on THE AMERICAN MERCURY, a name suggested by Nathan. Thus the work of compiling the new magazine was initiated.

The MERCURY was a handsome magazine. Its Paris green cover decorated with scrolls by Elmer Adler, one of America's best known typographers, was wrapped about a sewn volume that opened like a book. Garamond, a particularly attractive typeface used by Claude Garamond, was the chosen type, and the finest Scotch featherweight paper was used. When the first copies hit the newsstands on Christmas Eve, 1923, the response was enthusiastic. A second printing was ordered on December 28, followed by a third the next day. The first number sold 15,000 copies, 3,000 above the most optimistic projection, Mencken's. Not all of the copies, however, sold to friendly readers. Ernest Boyd's lampoon, "Aesthete: Model 1924," was a clever and elegant attack on the avant-garde and the literary left. Within hours of the MERCURY being placed on sale, the Greenwich Village community of avant-gardists snapped up every available copy. Outraged, they practically imprisoned Boyd in his home for three days. The resultant publicity, of course, assured the success of the next number.

The second number brought about the first editorial crisis of the new magazine. Nathan had been given an advance copy of *All God's Chillun Got Wings*, by his friend, the author, Eugene O'Neill. Nathan considered it an editorial triumph as O'Neill had given him the right to publish it before its stage debut. Mencken, however, disagreed. He found no place in his conception of the MERCURY for a full length play. As per prior arrangement, Alfred Knopf was called in as arbitrator. *All God's Chillun Got Wings* debuted in THE AMERICAN MERCURY, but the relationship between Mencken and Nathan was irreparably damaged.

The rest of 1924 was a trying time for the co-editors and their publisher. Mencken pushed for timely, journalistic contributors. Nathan for fastidiously artistic, literary works of lasting value. Alfred Knopf had to hold the middle path, act as arbitrator, and, in the final analysis as editor. Mencken finally won out, and Nathan was demoted to contributing editor. The first year of the magazine, however, was ensemble art. Three great intellects contributed to it in roughly equal shares.

Mencken's "divorce" from Nathan left him free to mold THE AMERICAN MERCURY into the iconoclastic journal that captured the intelligentsia of the Twenties. Mencken's MERCURY was a marvelous achievement, and cannot be discounted as a major contribution to American letters. The first year, however, was something special, something unique, something wonderful. Of all the volumes of THE AMERICAN MERCURY, the first three stand best the test of time. They are, perhaps, the best example of magazine publishing ever produced, and one can, even in admitting the excellence of the later incarnation, regret that the egos of Mencken and Nathan were too large, and the patience of Alfred Knopf too short, to continue that year for the rest of the MERCURY's life.

This first volume of the MERCURY cannot be approached as the work of Mencken alone, as can the numbers from 1925–1933. In actual fact, Alfred Knopf was more the editor than Mencken or Nathan. It was Knopf who was forced into making a good many of the decisions on what to include and what to exclude. This arrangement, short-lived as it was, produced a uniquely American expression, and revealed a good deal about the American character, due mostly, to the make-up of the three men involved.

H. L. Mencken has long been recognized as the quintessential American journalist. An opinionated, blunt critic of American life, Mencken, nonetheless, had an elegant style of insult. While other journals were strident in their carping, Mencken's iconoclasm had the rapier clean thrust of De Bergerac's nose speech. He was an apostle of realism, a fanatic for libertarianism. He detested the rural rube and shunned the avant-garde intellectual. His idea of fiction was a realistic depiction of the human condition where the author had taken only the liberty of rearranging actual events to form his thesis. He was an American version of George Bernard Shaw, a keen observer

of our foibles, our mass ignorance, and our capacity to accept almost anything wrapped up in a pretty enough package.

George Jean Nathan was a theater critic, and through the theater a critic of the American cultural scene. His reviews were reminiscent of those of Oscar Wilde, dripping with vitriol at the boorishness of his fellow citizens. As Mencken was a critic of American life, Nathan was a critic of American culture. Curiously, Nathan, the culture curator, was more blunt than Mencken. The elegance of Mencken was complimented by the candid plainness of Nathan.

In 1923, Alfred A. Knopf was the boy wonder of American publishing. He straddled the thin line between pulp and literature as few publishers have ever been able to do. He had a sense of what the public would accept without descending to the dime novel level to satisfy it. He imported such writers as Arthur Machen, an exquisite writer of prose, and made his champagne writing pay off in America where it had never done so in Machen's native land. He published Mencken's books on language, Nathan's theater books, Kahlil Gibran, Thomas Mann, and André Gide. His touch sold culture to the masses as few have ever been able to do. He was the perfect arbitrator for the disputes that erupted between the plainspoken man of culture, Nathan, and the elegant, earthy iconoclast Mencken.

The MERCURY team is indicative of much in American life. Our societal critic laureates are journalists. George Bernard Shaw was the best known English societal critic, in France, it was Emile Zola. In America, we eschew the literary profession in this regard in favor of journalists. Mencken was the supreme critic of the society of the Twenties. Today, we make popular television shows our societal arbiters. Our cultural pundits are, likewise, journalists. Where Oscar Wilde was primarily a writer, George Jean Nathan was a critic, merely so, with no pretensions to the status of artist. Knopf, the "editor" who smoothly arbitrated the Shaw and Wilde of American letters, was a publisher, first and foremost a man of business. Thus, instead of the essentially free expressions of artists, we have a rigid professional approach to societal and cultural criticism in America, backed with a cool business mind. Of this type of criticism, no finer or clearer example exists than the first three volumes of THE AMERICAN MERCURY.

The essential differences between Mencken and Nathan are evident in the areas of the magazine that were the personal provinces of each. Mencken, after the first volume, was the sole book reviewer, and the major reviewer in the first volume, though Cabell's review in the first number is a classic, it was shaped by Mencken's editing. "Americana" was also Mencken's province, and it contains, perhaps, the best examples of Mencken's wit and criticism. Nathan was the theater critic and, through 1930, the author of "Clinical Notes," though it should be noted that Mencken had a hand in producing the feature in the first few numbers.

"The Library" came as close as any part of the MERCURY to a Knopf house organ. Knopf books were regularly reviewed, though not always approved. There is a persistent question as to whether or not Mencken was, indeed, a literary critic at all. He rarely mentioned style, emotional impact, or any other facet of literature that would normally be allied to art. Rather, books provided Mencken a springboard from which he could spring into discussions of concepts, philosophy. In this sense Mencken was not a critic of literature, but rather a critic of ideas. "The Library" would regularly devote large blocks of space for obscure works on such subjects as journalistic ethics, or to lampoons of the work of somewhat stuffy college professors. Works that were distinctly mainstream

were either disregarded or mentioned in passing. *The Great Gatsby, Saint Joan,* and other soon-to-be classics received but a few remarks in "The Library." There are several nagging questions raised by Mencken's choice of books to be included in "The Library." Was he simply a poor judge of literature? Did he choose books on the basis of how well he could argue with them, praise their ideas, or lampoon them? Looking at the MERCURY, and the failure of volumes after the third to publish literature that stands up well today, one might conclude that both are somewhat true.

"Americana" was a section that worked on two distinct levels. It was a frothy amusement, a chance for Americans to laugh at themselves, their fads and foibles. More importantly, it built up a picture of America based upon the everyday thought of the average American. No one was more aware of the dual nature of the section than Mencken. In 1925, he collected his "Americana" columns in book form. In his introduction to this collection he said: "But those who see only humor in these fantastic paragraphs see only half that is in them. Fundamentally, nine tenths of them are serious in intent . . ."

In form, "Americana" is, perhaps, the most widely copied magazine feature ever created. *Esquire's* "Dubious Achievement Awards," and *Playboy's* "After Hours" are but two examples of the direct descendants of "Americana." In content, "Americana" is charmingly dated, and yet, somehow relevant. The situations were distinctly timely: a woman arrested for rolling down her stockings in public, a man arrested for kissing his wife in a parked car, literary notes on such authors as Edgar Guest, comments on Arthur Brisbane, Ku Klux Klan, Rotarian and American Legion notes. And yet, dated as the actual clips are, they seem to enfold some universal qualities which might be termed uniquely American. Of all of Mencken's writings,

"Americana" is his closest approach to some form of timeless universal appeal. Curiously, "Americana" consists of no more than a sentence or two introducing a current news item. While it should be the most easily made obsolete of all sections of the MERCURY, it is, on reflection, the most timeless contribution of Mencken.

George Jean Nathan has been approached in many ways. To some observers, he was no more than a satellite of Mencken. For others, he was the finest drama critic ever produced in America. As the critic for "The Theatre" in the MERCURY, he was not as cleverly succinct as Oscar Wilde, or Eugene Field, nor as nastily vitriolic as Alexander Woolcott. His short comments on plays, more often than not, consisted of: "is trash," "fetches the yokels," "hornswaggle at the box office" and other such phrases. Nathan was at his best in longer reviews where he would assiduously list stereotypes, clichés, and stock situations. He was also a master at applying reductio ad absurdium to the plots of shaky and borderline plays. Though Nathan was primarily a theater and culture critic, his style made him a first class humorist. The combination of the two, however, comprise the primary reason that Nathan is disregarded today as both a critic and a humorist. His criticism, in many cases, was too jocular to be taken seriously. His humor was often too serious to be enjoyed for itself. He would follow up a clever review in which he sliced up Noel Coward as ". . . so many goldfish trying heroically to swim the ocean" with a silly critique of a motion picture advertisement dominating his entire column in the succeeding number.

"Clinical Notes" was a much better showcase for Nathan's talents than "The Theatre," though it is doubtful Nathan considered it so. It is indicative of the overshadowing of Nathan by Mencken that some of Nathan's better comments are attributed to Mencken. The definition of Puritanism as "the haunting fear that someone, somewhere, may be happy," is Nathan's and yet is often attributed to Mencken. "Clinical Notes" was much more universal and timeless a feature than any regular department of the MERCURY. Nathan discussed such topics as the Harvard Classics, George Bernard Shaw, and G. K. Chesterton, while Mencken, at his best, in "Americana," was mired in names and situations indigenous to the contemporary situation of the 1920's.

Nathan was a polished elitist with a grasp of idiomatic American language unequalled by anyone, with the one exception of Mencken. As a judge of literature, he had few peers. While at the *Smart Set*, he "discovered" Fitzgerald, O'Neill, Ben Hecht, and Sherwood Anderson. It was on his insistence that *Smart Set* published Cabell's masterpiece *Jurgen*. To Mencken, the MERCURY was a general magazine, with literary concerns subordinated to journalistic interests. Nathan, however, held the idea that "a magazine worth its salt should forego the common editorial preoccupation with journalistic immediacy and devote itself instead to those materials of art and life that are not necessarily bound strictly by the clock and that deepen, whether seriously or lightly, a reader's understanding of his surroundings, of himself, and of his fellows."

It was these two contrasting views, both backed by substantial egos, that Alfred Knopf was forced to harmonize in order to bring out a magazine. As characterized by their provinces within the MERCURY the differences are vast. At *Smart Set*, Nathan had been the senior, but Mencken's more forceful character often won his point. Nathan's position was such, however, that his editorial contributions were included with little friction. At the MERCURY, however, the situation was reversed, as Mencken alone had been Knopf's original choice. Thus, almost from the outset, Knopf was placed in the position of championing Nathan against Mencken. Knopf, as he proved time and time again, was as fine a judge of literature as any American publisher has ever been. No doubt his artistic sympathies lay with Nathan, but his loyalty remained with Mencken. As a business matter, moreover, Mencken's timely approach was more likely to produce a profit than Nathan's. The MERCURY was, in the final analysis, a sideline for Knopf. His dedication to its launching was an admirable bit of business that a less skilled businessman would not even attempt. It was obvious, however, that Knopf's days as the editor-in-fact were not to be continued indefinitely. The house of Knopf, even at that early stage of development, was fast becoming one of America's major publishers. The rapid growth of Knopf's book publishing business pressed him, and thus, having failed to set some compromise in place, he turned the MERCURY over to Mencken and demoted Nathan to contributing editor effective January, 1925, with Volume IV.

The importance of the MERCURY to American letters and American thought has never been fully appreciated. From 1924 until about 1928, it was the best American magazine, and, probably, the most influential. It aided the cause of the realist school of American writers, who were eventually to form the mainstream of American literature. The MERCURY gathered in contributors from all over America, and helped move American literature, for a time, outside of the New York Metropolitan area, and the exile community of Paris. This attitude promoted the Midwest realism of Sinclair Lewis, paving the way for such realists as Booth Tarkington and eventually Saroyan and Steinbeck.

For the most part, the immediate impact of the MERCURY lay in its satirical approach to the Twenties. The creation of boobus americanus gives a distinctly American flavor to Swift's Yahoo. Boobus americanus is the perfect little monster,

easily led, prone to the wiles of demagogues, impressed and often guided by sophomoric slogans. Nor is boobus americanus affected greatly by experience or education, as Mencken declared his opposition to the notion that "a moron run through a university and decorated with a Ph.D. will cease thereby to be a moron." Boobus americanus, as a satirical creation, ranks with the best of the genre. It does so because it is whimsical, even silly, and yet has about it the frightful air of reality.

MERCURY satire cut through the pretensions of Americans on all levels of the American society of the 1920's. It formed a comic collage of the Coolidge years; unfortunately, it could not adapt itself to the new order of the Depression. The New Deal appeared on the surface to be an ideal target for the MERCURY. An idealist in Washington, a popular idol, a liberal leaning toward populism from an aristocratic tradition he willingly abrogated for the sake of his fellow citizens. Roosevelt was perfect for the barbs of Mencken, who once defined an idealist as "one who, on noticing that a rose smells better than a cabbage concludes that it will also make better soup." Mencken, however, had spent too many years dividing mankind into men of honor, aristocrats who had none, and the great unwashed, who had nothing but the capacity to make fools of themselves. In good times, on a full stomach, it was funny, it had meaning. In the very unfunny days of the Depression it was merely irritating.

It is difficult to escape the idea that both Mencken and the MERCURY were praised for the wrong reasons, and then damned for them. Perhaps no story illustrative of this is more indicative than the final segment of "Clinical Notes" in Volume One Number One: "Story Without a Moral."

"A number of years ago, in my newspaper days, I received from what would now be called the Ku Klux Klan a circular violently denouncing the Catholic Church. This circular stated ·that the Church was engaged in a hellish conspiracy to seize the government of the United States and put an agent of the Pope into the White House, and that the leaders of the plot were certain Jesuits, all of them foreigners and violent enemies of the American Constitution. Only one such Jesuit was actually named: a certain Walter Drum, S.J. He was denounced with great bitterness, and every true American was besought to be on the watch for him. Something inspired me to turn to "Who's Who in America"; it lists all the principal emissaries of Rome in the Republic, even when they are not Americans. This is what I found:

> Drum, Walter, S.J.; b. at Louisville, Ky., Sept. 21, 1870; s. Capt. John Drum, U.S.A., killed before Santiago.

"I printed the circular of the Ur-Klansmen -and that eloquent sentence from "Who's Who." No more was heard against the foreigner Drum in that diocese. . . .

"Eight or ten years later, having retired from journalism with a competence, I was the co-editor of a popular magazine. One day there reached me the manuscript of a short story by a young Princeton man, by name F. Scott Fitzgerald. It was a harmless and charming story about a young scholastic in a Jesuit seminary. A few months later it was printed in the magazine. Four days after the number was on the stands I received a letter from a Catholic priest, denouncing me as an enemy to the Church, belaboring the story as blasphemous and worse, and stating that the writer proposed to make a tour of all the Catholic women's clubs in the East, urging their members to blacklist and boycott the magazine. The name signed to the letter was 'Walter Drum, S.J.'

"I offer the story, but append no moral. Perhaps its only use is to show how Christians of both wings have improved upon John XV, 12."

The life and death of the MERCURY is a typically American story. We are the land of the disposable culture. The MERCURY blazed across our cultural horizons and died away. Sixty years ago, it was the height of our cleverness, the peak of our erudition. Now it is an antique, and even as it is praised, it is secretly despised, for it is a better thing than our culture now venerates.

The first volume of the MERCURY is, perhaps, the pinnacle of American magazine publishing. A collaborative effort, it has a range from erudition to whimsy that has never been matched before or since. Only the succeeding numbers of 1925, approach it in terms of excellence. Mencken's opening editorial is less strident than his work would eventually become. It presents a Mencken that is easy to get along with. A Mencken who wants nothing more than to chide America, to expound a few charmingly eccentric ideas, and to share a good laugh. He is not yet the shrill satirist.

Nathan's insistence on the inclusion of *All God's Chillun Got Wings* in the second number makes it an important piece of literature in and of itself. Also in the second number, Sherwood Anderson's story *Caught* cements this appraisal.

In this first volume, the perfect balance between Mencken's timely magazine and Nathan's timeless philosophy has been struck. If one were honest, one would have to give credit to Alfred Knopf for what it is. It moves from the whimsy of Mencken's first experimental steps in Americana, through the literary discussions of James Huneker and Samuel Chew, to the original publication of a Eugene O'Neill play. Even the advertisements provide a picture of American culture and society. Everything about the original MERCURY said elegance, erudition.

Each number of the MERCURY was a small book, the first volume sliding easily into a significant work on America,

Americans, American culture, and the American society of the Twenties. At a time when our magazines are four color monstrosities, where the writing, more often than not, is used to fill space between photo spreads of nearly naked women, the Mercury presents a stark contrast. In the initial volume current news is covered, not in the pseudo objectivism of modern journalism, but rather from a strong overtly stated point of view. Fine literature and intelligent criticism of culture is also present, in contrast to today's best selling hack writers and their fawning sycophants whose mission is not criticism but rather preservation of the cultural status quo. Nathan, perhaps O'Neill's greatest friend, did not hesitate to criticize, sharply, an O'Neill work that missed the mark. The *New York Times* of 1983 carried a book review of Norman Mailer's "Ancient Evenings" that called it, rightly, a disaster. After this evaluation, the *Times* placed it in "Editors Choices" and "New and Recommended," practically guaranteeing it a spot on the "Best Seller" list. The Mercury had an integrity that is missing in modern journalism. Neither Mencken nor Nathan nor their chosen contributors hid behind false faces of objectivism, as modern journalists are prone to do. They were human beings, opinionated, accessible. They placed their ideas, their beliefs on the table, and let us judge them. They did not recommend inferior literature or drama either to help a friend or maintain the status quo in the arts.

It is curious to note that the editorial policy of the Mercury overtly considered the great mass of Americans boobs, hicks, rabble, perfect little monsters of the species boobus americanus, and yet, gave Americans enough credit to overtly state philosophy and facts, giving the great unwashed the opportunity to think and judge. The modern media does not grant modern Americans that privilege. It propounds its philosophy as fact, and considers Americans, ignorant, unin-

formed, or mentally deficient if they question those pronouncements. Perhaps the death of the Mercury is the final and most definitive proof of its editorial policy. In 1983, we get our news in pre-digested doses from television anchorpersons. Our art critics criticize only those who dare to break away from the art establishment. Our literature, at its best, is not quite equal to the better pulp magazines of the Twenties. Short stories exist in our magazines only to help rationalize the fact that they are bought, primarily for the purpose of ogling the naked human form. Our largest magazine, *T.V. Guide*, tells us what we obviously want to know, our major informational interest, when "Dallas" comes on. There were a lot of factors which combined to fell the Mercury, but perhaps major of these was the triumph of boobus americanus over truth, culture, honesty and thought.

It is probably no consolation to the ghosts of H. L. Mencken, George Jean Nathan and Alfred A. Knopf that they were right. One can only assume that they initiated the Mercury adventure either with some hope they were wrong, or in the spirit of domesticating boobus americanus. It is in this same spirit that this facsimile of Volume One of The American Mercury is being published. The publishers realize that, with a public that thinks mink, says it with flowers, and is perpetually hungry for Burger King, this stands no better chance of success than the original. And yet, the attempt is being made. This indicates either that the publishers deserve no better fate than the other inmates of psychiatric wards, or that they have a deep abiding faith in the potential of boobus americanus to actually think original thoughts, and to appreciate honesty, especially when it is well conceived and well written. Whether or not this will be successful will depend, primarily upon the capacity of boobus americanus to understand and laugh at itself.

In many ways The American Mercury is

a homely girl. Interesting because of what it is, uninteresting because it strains our conscience. We would all rather go through the dance of life secure in the belief that we will never have to make a decision as to whether or not we will secure a certain absolution from our sins by waltzing with a wallflower. The world might be an improved place if we could trust our journalists to be belles of the ball. Unfortunately, this world is not the improved model. This being the case, the epitaph Mencken wrote for himself and published in *Smart Set* in 1921 may well be our ticket to heaven:

"If, after I depart this vale, you ever remember me and have thought to please my ghost, forgive some sinner and wink your eye at some homely girl."

"*. . . liberty up to the extreme limits of the feasible and tolerable.*"
— H.L. Mencken

Approximately one third of THE AMERICAN MERCURY during Mencken's tenure as editor was dedicated to expositions of his political philosophy, libertarianism. Libertarianism is the extreme emphasis on individual freedom, and opposition to all laws and restraints save those that are absolutely necessary to preserve liberty and provide a habitable environment. How much or how little this philosophy influenced the decline of the MERCURY is debatable. However, it can be shown that historically, the extreme libertarianism professed by Mencken ceased to be a major political force with the onset of the Depression.

In Mencken's hands, libertarianism was a restrained pessimism. Boobus americanus certainly did not have the wherewithal to govern, but then, neither did the demagogues that so impressed the species. Mencken did not believe in answers so much as he believed in something good shaking out of free, individualistic expression. Thus the MERCURY

went on record as distrusting anyone and everyone who contended that governmental control was in any way beneficial, and used a large portion of each issue to debunk the idea that control in any way could lead to bettering the country.

Libertarianism, in the American sense, was born on the frontier, where a man and his family could be relatively independent of all governmental authority with hard labor and a limited amount of barter. The original American libertarian was probably the Mid-Western and Western farmer. The land and his neighbors provided all he needed, and the intrusion of the government only meant paying for what was considered by the farmer to be his or free for the taking. As the farmer became more deeply involved in American society, he lost some of his self-sufficiency. His life became entangled in commodity exchanges and leveraging his crops. He became a piece of a larger economic/societal scheme. Thus, he banded together with other farmers and became a Populist. Libertarianism ceased, at that point, to be a major, if not the major, American political philosophy. One group, however, remained libertarian, the artists.

Mencken characterized the artist as one who "reacts sharply and in an uncommon manner to phenomena which leave most of us unmoved, or, at most, merely annoy us vaguely. He is, in brief, a more delicate fellow than we are . . ." The artist, however, is not a utopian. He has no scheme to save the world, to improve it, he merely acts annoyed at the shackles society places on his creativity. Thus he is the perfect libertarian. He wishes to be left alone, by government, by society, and, if at all possible, by economics. This was Mencken's position.

The MERCURY did not editorialize in the sense that we might consider editorialization today. Mencken's editorials were more in the nature of criticism of those who did editorialize. There are no libertarian schemes for a perfect world because such a scheme would necessarily involve a controlled environment. Mencken makes it clear that the MERCURY Editors "have heard no Voice from the burning bush. They will not cry up and offer for sale any sovereign balm, whether political, economic or aesthetic, for all the sorrows of the world. The fact is, indeed, that they doubt that any such sovereign balm exists, or that it will ever exist hereafter."

It is inherent in libertarian philosophy to take the position of critic, iconoclast, debunker, because the philosophy itself holds no concrete position on anything other than the absurdity of holding any position but one's own, which is exclusive and not beneficial for general consumption. Thus Mencken could admire the homespun religion of the mountain folk of Tennessee and make it an admirable contrast to the demagoguery on both sides of the Scopes Trial in his article on it.

Libertarianism fails on many accounts, but the chief among them is the necessary interdependence of a complicated society. For an artist to be truly free, he must be independently wealthy or be given his living by a patron who places no attachments on the gift, and so it is with all professions. Mencken was, himself, at liberty only so long as the MERCURY produced a profit, only so long as the public acted as his patron.

Libertarianism, however, is not anarchy. It was, perhaps, expressed best by Thomas Jefferson: "The best government, governs the least." It was once a vital philosophy in America, and perhaps would still be viable, if Americans would stop asking the government to do the things they don't wish to do themselves. Libertarians might ask that the government limit itself to guarding the shores and delivering the mail. This sentiment is the one expressed by the philosophy, and certainly one that would have been embraced by Mencken. Interdependence, however, has, for the time being, relegated it to the fringes of political thought and made it a forgotten philosophy.

Richard K. Russell
January, 1984

The AMERICAN MERCURY

VOLUME I   January 1924   NUMBER 1

TABLE OF CONTENTS

THE LINCOLN LEGEND . . . . .Isaac R. Pennypacker   1
FOUR POEMS . . . . .Theodore Dreiser   8
STEPHEN CRANE . . . . .Carl Van Doren   11
FOUR GENERATIONS . . . . .Ruth Suckow   15
HUNEKER ON HUNEKER . . . . . .James Gibbons Huneker   22
EDITORIAL   27
THE DROOL METHOD IN HISTORY . . . . . . Harry E. Barnes   31
MR. MOORE AND MR. CHEW . . . . Samuel C. Chew   39
AMERICANA   48
AESTHETE: MODEL 1924 . . . . Ernest Boyd   51
THE TRAGIC HIRAM . . . . John W. Owens   57
TWO YEARS OF DISARMAMENT . . . . .Miles Martindale   62
SANTAYANA AT CAMBRIDGE . . . . . . .Margaret Münsterberg   69
CLINICAL NOTES . . . George Jean Nathan and H. L. Mencken   75
THE COMMUNIST HOAX . . . . .James Oneal   79
THE WEAVER'S TALE . . . . John McClure   85
THE ARTS AND SCIENCES:
    The New Sky-Line . . . . C. Grant La Farge   89
    The Pother About Glands. . . . . L. M. Hussey   91
    The Test of English . . . . George Philip Krapp   94
SWEENEY'S GRAIL . . . . .Leonard Lanson Cline   99
THE NEW THOUGHT . . . . Woodbridge Riley   104
ON A SECOND-RATE WAR . . . . X——   109
THE THEATRE . . . . George Jean Nathan   113
THE LIBRARY . . . . .H. L. Mencken   120
ADDITIONAL BOOK REVIEWS:
    Once More, The Immortals . . . . . James Branch Cabell   123
    Brandes and Croce . . . . Ernest Boyd   125
    Brazil From Within . . . . .Isaac Goldberg   126
THE AMERICAN MERCURY AUTHORS   128

Unsolicited manuscripts not accompanied by stamped and addressed envelopes will not be returned and the Editors will not enter into correspondence about them. Manuscripts should be addressed to The Editors and not to individuals. All accepted contributions are paid for on acceptance, without reference to the date of publication. The whole contents of this magazine are protected by copyright and must not be reprinted without permission.

Published monthly at 50 cents a copy. Annual subscription, $5.00; Canadian subscription, $5.50; foreign subscription $6.00. . . . The American Mercury, Inc., publishers. Publication office, Federal and 19th Streets, Camden, N.J. Editorial, advertising and subscription offices, 220 W. 42nd Street, New York. . . . Printed in the United States. Copyright, 1924, by The American Mercury, Inc. . . . Application for entry as second-class matter pending.

Alfred A. Knopf   George Jean Nathan } Editors
    Publisher   H. L. Mencken   }

The American
MERCURY

January 1924

THE LINCOLN LEGEND

BY ISAAC R. PENNYPACKER

AMERICAN fiction has never succeeded in portraying satisfactorily a typical American iron-master of the early period. The type has passed away and is now about forgotten. The early iron furnaces and forges in Virginia, Maryland, Pennsylvania and New Jersey were distant from the seats of the civic authorities. Preliminary to pay day the iron-master drove his horses maybe thirty miles to the nearest bank, and on the following day rode back with the men's wages. He maintained the original company store, a necessity in those remote regions. If the workmen, often turbulent, engaged in riot it fell to him to walk into the battle and by force of character and personal authority restore the peace. If a wife appealed to him when her husband beat her, as wives often did, the culprit was brought to different behavior by means which were perhaps as good for the family and the community as the modern divorce mill. As the community about the forge or furnace grew to a town, it was the iron-master who took the first steps to supply its increasing needs—a burying ground, a bank, a bridge in place of the uncertain ford, a shady playground for the children near the unsheltered school-house. Such an iron-master in such a community, swept by a yellow fever epidemic from which the unstricken fled in a panic of fear, went from house to house, nursed the sick and with his own hands coffined and buried the dead. Good human fibre, thus strengthened and disciplined by responsibility, by calls to meet sudden and unlooked for difficulties and personal danger, did not deteriorate. In a family with such a head or a succession of such heads, precept and example set up standards that the offspring learned must be emulated if they were to be men like their fathers.

Contrary to the prevailing belief, it was from such a family that Abraham Lincoln sprang. As his rail-splitting appealed to the proletariat of his own day more than his Cooper Institute speech could do, so the legend of an origin so lowly that it does violence to the elemental laws of heredity has always been popular with the American people. At least once a year in many thousands of school-houses and from innumerable platforms and pulpits that legend is repeated and the accepted miracle is recounted anew. All of us are taught, year in and year out, that the Lincoln in whom was combined one of the shrewdest of politicians, a philosophical statesman, a master of English and an intellectual aristocrat came out of utter darkness into an effulgence of fame attained by but one other American since the beginning of the nation.

The truth is that the obscurity of Lincoln's father was but an accident in the

1

family history caused by the Indian's rifle which left him fatherless at six years—a child in a wilderness. Wherever the Lincoln family lived, in New England, New Jersey, Pennsylvania, Virginia, its members were people of substance and local prominence. Mordecai Lincoln, the great-great-great-grandfather of the President, established the first furnace and forge for making wrought iron in New England. His sons Mordecai and Abraham went to Pennsylvania by way of New Jersey in or about 1720. The second Mordecai had a one-third interest in a forge and other iron works on French Creek in Chester County, by 1723, and he was the owner of more land than was owned by most of the early "cavaliers" of tidewater Virginia. His son Thomas became Sheriff of Berks County in 1758, owned many acres, wrote a copperplate hand and spelled with conspicuous correctness. Another son, Abraham, was County Commissioner from 1772 to 1779, a sub-lieutenant in Berks County in 1777, and was elected to the Assembly in 1782, 1783, 1784 and 1785. He was chosen to make the address to Washington in Philadelphia after the Revolution and was a member of the Pennsylvania Constitutional Convention of 1789-90. His family record book contains the entry of his marriage with Anna Boone, one of many evidences of close association between the Lincolns and the family of Daniel Boone, and is noticeable for its grammatical and other accuracy; he recorded with great precision that he was 5 months, 15 days and 22 hours "older than he." In the modern American language the entry of a fact so meticulously arrived at would certainly be written "older than her" by the average rural American. Besides his other public duties this early Abraham Lincoln was Road Supervisor and School Commissioner. His administrators, who were his two sons (like their father, skilled penmen), accounted for the considerable sum of £2627, 4s., 6ds., exclusive of his real estate.

Another son of Mordecai the elder was John—"Virginia John", his Pennsylvania relatives called him—the great-grandfather of the President. By his father's will, John was given 300 acres of land in New Jersey, which he sold in 1748 for £200. In the two years 1763 and 1765 he sold 331 acres, 49 perches of land in Pennsylvania for £794 and bought 161 acres for £260, and shortly afterward went to Virginia, where in 1768 he bought for £250 600 acres on Linville Creek in Augusta, now Rockingham, County. His son Abraham, the President's grandfather, in 1779 bought for £500, 52 acres on Linville Creek and in 1780 sold for £5000 250 acres, and with his family, including his son Thomas, the President's father, went to Kentucky, where he purchased 2600 acres. Four years after he had gone to Kentucky and while at work with his boys in a clearing, he was shot by an Indian. Thomas, the President's father, was then six years old. The death of the father and the then existing law of primogeniture, which gave all his real estate to Mordecai, the oldest son, was the cause of the humble condition of Thomas Lincoln. For 39 years —surely a brief period compared with the more than two centuries of family activity and prominence—this obscurity was unbroken. Then, at the age of 23, Abraham Lincoln began his public life, resuming as certainly as the fountain water seeks its former height the earlier family plane.

II

The sponsors of an early Lincoln legend would have avoided their initial error if they had attributed to the conditions of his youth and to his rounds of a rural Illinois circuit his limitations as a war leader instead of seeking in those conditions the matrix which moulded him into greatness. They were estopped from this by the assumption held by nearly all the people of the North that the preservation of the Union was chiefly due to Lincoln. After the war certain enthusiasts even asserted that he was the best general of the Northern armies.

De Amicis wrote that the Dutch abhorred that form of apotheosis which attributes to the individual the merits or vices of the many. General Henry J. Hunt wrote that God Almighty hated unequal weights and balances, but that the American people seemed to love them. It is possible, if one gives consideration to what Lincoln himself said and did in war time, to be left with admiration for his unerring sagacity in gauging mass momentum and at the same time to doubt with Herndon whether he judged the individual as shrewdly as he judged the mass, and further to doubt without Herndon whether as a war leader he was the equal of Jefferson Davis.

Lincoln was a far shrewder politician than Davis. Secretary Chase, after an interview with him, returned to his office and raising his hands above his head exclaimed before his private secretary, "That man is the most cunning person I ever saw in my life!" Lincoln's reasoning processes were far more sure-footed than those of Davis. It is impossible to conceive of Davis delighting in the rustic wit of the stories which Lincoln so often told to Stanton's displeasure, shown by his stalking out of the room and slamming the door. Also, it would have been impossible for Davis, had he been in Lincoln's place, to do as Lincoln did—listen patiently to the demand of a formidable group of New York bankers that he make peace, and then reply with such overwhelming power that they departed from the War Office in the manner of cowed school boys. Davis might have been as determined, but he would have been apt to show more signs of irritation. His reply would probably have been more personal and caustic. The bankers very likely would have gone away defeated, but not convinced. It is difficult to picture Jefferson Davis, punctilious, honorable, high-minded, able as he was, rising so far above the plane of his visitors as to convince them of his mastery and hold them as followers.

As commander in chief of an army and navy in active service Davis had the advantage over Lincoln of being a West Point graduate, of having been Secretary of War, of knowing the character and capacity of army officers. Training and experience gave him the effective method, so necessary to war time leadership, of disregarding to a large extent political and other civil influences. Davis lost, not for lack of men or food, but because the inferior industrial civilization of the South—a civilization which in the industrial sense was primitive—collapsed. With abundance of mere man power, the South could not replace its always inferior railroad lines and motive power; it could not transport the food supplies on which Sherman's army lived in Georgia to the army of Lee in Virginia. Davis knew Lee's ability and character and advanced him when Lee was under a cloud, and press and public were condemning him for his West Virginia failure. Davis declined Lee's offer to resign after Gettysburg; Lincoln, after every failure in the field, selected a new general, one after another, and for a long time a worse one. His selection of corps commanders for McClellan was poor; all of them had to be weeded out. McClellan was right in wanting to give some practical test to generals before selecting corps commanders. Beside Burnside, Hooker and Pope, Lincoln was responsible for other soldiers incompetent for the work assigned them—Halleck, Banks, Sickles, the last lacking in both military ability and character. Lincoln made Burnside commander of the Army of the Potomac just after Burnside's weak failure at Antietam, where he had spoiled McClellan's excellent plan. Burnside continued to fail weakly throughout his military career. Stonewall Jackson's opportunity, which he embraced by defeating one after another of Lincoln's generals, was based on Lincoln's inadequacy to the military prob'em. McClellan's critics find much fault with him, but the Northern cause was in far better shape after McClellan's Peninsular campaign, and again after Antietam, than it was under the Lincoln generals I have named.

By July, 1863, Lincoln had had ample time to learn much of practical warfare. But it did not occur to him, though there was long previous warning of Lee's invasion of Pennsylvania, to gather the many thousands of organized, equipped and disciplined troops scattered along the Potomac and at unimportant places in Virginia and throw them in the rear of Lee, the only method by which Lee's army, defeated at Gettysburg, might have been prevented from returning to Virginia. With a military skill at Washington in 1863 at all comparable with the scientific methods of the Germans in 1870, Lee's venture into Pennsylvania would have ended in his destruction. It is doubtful if Lincoln had the military instinct, in which lack he was like the American people, or, indeed, like all democracies. Witness the American Revolution, when the army at Valley Forge suffered with abundant supplies at Reading, only thirty miles away; the war of 1812; our war with Spain and its scandalous revelations of civilian incompetency. Or witness the poor showing made by the British in the World War, in which they were saved from defeat only by the energy of the most extraordinary propaganda that the world has ever known. So good an authority as General Smuts, on whom England placed so much reliance, has said that in the World War "Hindenburg commanded the only army; Haig and Pershing commanded armed mobs."

But as Lincoln's place in history depended upon success in war, the battles which contributed most to that success must necessarily find place in any competent biography of him, the most important of them, of course, being Gettysburg. Many battles were fought which had no determining influence upon the war and need not detain the biographer, but Meade's victory at Gettysburg, McClellan's at Antietam and Thomas' at Nashville put an end to invasion of the North, and Gettysburg made an end also of the Confederate hope of English and French aid. That biography, if it is ever written, will show that the war during which Lincoln stood for a civilization based on free labor and Davis for one based on slave labor was not a civil war such as that between Charles I and Oliver Cromwell, in which both of two forces struggled for the control of the whole. To call it a "war between the states" as English writers and those Americans who follow them sometimes do, is inexact. Nor was it a war between the North and South, for not all the Southern states undertook to secede. The connection of Ireland with Great Britain, like the connection of the Philippines and Porto Rico with the United States, is involuntary; they are all conquered territory. The connection of the seceding Southern states with the American Union was voluntary. As rebels they united with Northern rebels to destroy England's authority over them, and, succeeding, they helped to draft the Constitution, and when it was perfected their representatives signed it and by separate state action adopted it. It was as rebels again that they fought in 1861-65. The once popular Virginian boast and toast "Washington and Lee—rebels both" expressed a truth with complete accuracy, the distinction between the two Virginians being that one succeeded and the other failed.

III

Herndon and Weik have furnished many instances showing that Lincoln was not an infallible judge of individuals, despite his accurate judgment of men in the mass, and that he was sometimes indifferent to the character and acts of men close to him. Writers still praise him and condemn Simon Cameron in discussing the latter's early retirement from the Cabinet, but they ignore the Lincoln statement that Cameron was no more responsible for the thieving war contractors of the time than the President himself—that the government had practically no war material and was compelled to buy in great haste wherever it could be obtained. The enforced retirement of Cameron to the position of Minister to Russia was therefore a political measure adopted by Lincoln, not with any moral motive, but as a means of avoiding the effects of a public scandal created by the contractors. The purchase by the Navy Department from a relative of the Secretary of the Navy of a defective vessel at an exorbitant price created no furore, and hence did not cost Gideon Welles his head, though that purchase came closer to Welles than the army contracts had come to Cameron.

Of the strong men of Lincoln's Cabinet, Seward and Chase were placed there by existing political conditions. Stanton came from the Buchanan administration, and a rugged war horse he proved to be, making himself disagreeable to thousands of dishonest civilians and to the unfit who were trying to push their military or political fortunes, but thoughtful, considerate and kind to the meritorious in military and civil life who came up to his severe standard of duty. Chase's method raised the money for the war largely through the agency of Jay Cooke of Philadelphia, who once told the present writer that he had placed $3,000,000,000 worth of bonds, vouchers, etc., without a cent of profit. These three members of the Cabinet, Stanton, Chase and Seward, have suffered through the labors of writers seeking to attribute to Lincoln the results of the earnest work of all.

The future biographer of Lincoln will perforce sift, contrast and weigh with due consideration of the character, ability and experience of witnesses the great volume of contradictory evidence relating to the war and Lincoln's fortunes, and avoid the too frequent habit of accepting as uncontrovertible such books as those of Dana, Carl Schurz, and Gideon Welles and the military memoirs of the middle period. The historical difficulty may be illustrated by the opposing accounts of General James H. Wilson and General Horace Porter of the same incident. Both were present on the scene. Both heard what inevitably must have passed current among the officers

close to General Grant. General Porter's book says that Grant remained serene after the first fierce attack by General Lee in the Wilderness; General Wilson's book says that Grant threw himself upon his cot in a paroxysm of sobbing. General Wilson's account is apparently the one to be accepted. It shows that Grant's imperturbability was not proof against a new experience in warfare, unprepared for by a Western career of successes won over feebler opposition and with losses slight as compared with those of Meade at Gettysburg. It is plain that General Porter, writing long afterward, was simply repeating a version of the incident deemed expedient at the time of its occurrence.

General Grant's memoirs and General Sheridan's need to be checked by reference to General Humphreys' scientific narrative and by Colonel Carswell McClellan's analysis. As to the value of Carl Schurz's judgment in military matters, there is a significant correspondence between Generals Sherman, Thomas and others revealing an effort to find a place for Schurz behind the lines, where he could do no harm. Thomas wanted to be rid of him because if Schurz remained an abler general would have to go, and bluntly said he did not think Schurz was "much good". The dispatches of Charles A. Dana, Assistant Secretary of War, from City Point to Washington and his book of memoirs are in frequent conflict with the facts. Towards Dana's mission to City Point, higher officers of the Army of the Potomac maintained a degree of aloof contempt, and when his arrival became known talk was tempered with discretion by common consent. To this aloof attitude of responsible soldiers may be attributed the military insignificance of many of Dana's dispatches to Washington. He fell back on gossip, and got it, not from Meade, Hancock, Humphreys or Wright at the front, but from the members of Grant's staff, of whom Colonel Theodore Lyman, a shrewd and experienced observer, wrote that with few exceptions they were a commonplace group of men. If the officers who, for nearly four years, had been offering in behalf of the Union every sacrifice that duty called for, enduring long, dirty Summer marches and Winter camps in the desolation of Virginia mud, could have read Dana's dispatches they would have had plenty of justification for their caution. In the midsummer Gettysburg campaign, marching day or night from the Rappahannock to the Pennsylvania battle field and back again, the corps commander, General Sedgwick, did not have his clothes off in six weeks.

The battle of Antietam gave to Lincoln the opportune moment for the Emancipation Proclamation. If General Thomas had lost the battle of Nashville, the fortunes of Sherman, Grant and Lincoln would have been in jeopardy. If General Meade had lost Gettysburg, Lincoln would be remembered today as Hamlet is.

IV

In Illinois Lincoln had trained himself and developed on well defined lines further than any other American has ever gone, but not as a war leader or administrator. Horace Binney, in his day head of the American bar, who defeated Daniel Webster in the Girard will case because Webster did not know the law, in his old age accounted for the deterioration of the Philadelphia bar on the ground that the removal of the National Capitol had caused a disappearance of the large problems that produced great lawyers. At Springfield, Lincoln had no chance to master problems that could qualify him as a great administrator or as commander-in-chief of the army and navy in a great war. Nowhere in America at that time could such experience be had. Army and navy officers learned as the war went on, profiting by their failures. But these officers gave their whole time and thought to military matters. Lincoln had unending civil problems to exhaust his thought and energy. Political considerations influenced him in the appointment of war Democrats like Butler

and Sickles to military commands for which they were unfit. Similarly, Schurz, Sigel and Blencker owed their military positions to their German following, the Germans both in America and Germany giving sympathy to Lincoln's cause. A political, not a military reason was behind the refusal at Washington after the Gettysburg campaign of Meade's proposal to abandon the always threatened Orange and Alexandria line of communication. The removal of McClellan from command just after his great service in the Antietam campaign, when he had shown as marked an improvement as Lee displayed after his disjointed Peninsular Campaign of 1862, and the substitution of the incompetent Burnside are not to be explained on military grounds.

Army officers of high intelligence knew before Lincoln selected Pope, Burnside and Hooker to command the army covering Washington that those officers were unfitted for so difficult a military position. Either Lincoln did not know it or he shared to an unwarranted extent the American faith in miracles. In either case he was at fault. A succession of disasters under his chosen military leaders, culminating in the battle of Chancellorsville, at last forced him to seek intelligent military counsel, and in the emergency of Lee's invasion of Pennsylvania he found in Meade a general who, as Colonel Lyman wrote, could handle an army of 100,000 men and do it easily. But to the end Lincoln appeared less appreciative of greater military achievement than of the political effect of the comparatively easy victories of Sheridan in the Shenandoah Valley, won near the close of the Presidential campaign, and of more significance as an election day influence than as a feat of arms.

On the military side of Lincoln's record in the war which established his fame are his shortcomings; on the civil side his virtues and strength. With Washington and William of Orange, from whom was borrowed Washington's appellation, "The Father of his Country", Lincoln looms high among the few of earth's great ones who have exercised great power in a large way. Of the three Welshmen, Henry VIII, Cromwell and Lloyd George, most widely known of all men who have represented English dominion, Cromwell, like the Prince of Orange, Washington, Frederick the Great and Napoleon, won a twofold fame, military and civic, but Lincoln's place in history is in an especial manner due to the victorious army commanders at Vicksburg, Nashville and Gettysburg. Lincoln's Gettysburg address made accurate measure of the comparative importance of soldier and civilian in the war, but Americans find it easier to follow his sentiment than his sense. Lincoln has a distinction shared with Washington, but differing from that of the European leaders named in that he was ready to lay power aside. Few men have ever shown that they could use power with his self-restraint. Lincoln would have executed no rebels as England was of late executing the Irish. His wisdom was clearly greater than that of the present rulers of France. The Lincoln who viewed the prospect of Jefferson Davis' escape with relief, were he alive today, would be sending all war-time political prisoners home to their families.

Many monarchs have excelled Lincoln in the sphere of military leadership. He was fortunate in that his armed opponents were poorly equipped for what they undertook; fortunate even in escaping by death an inevitable contest in which he, who was without hate, would have run counter to passions, always more fierce with civilians than with soldiers, fired to a white heat by decades of debate and four years of war; fortunate that his stage was set in a period when the Presidency was still within the compass of one man; fortunate that the country's great industrial development through organization learned in war, and led in most parts of the country by former warriors, had not yet taken place. Emperors or kings have surpassed, too, Lincoln's measure of administrative faculty. In exhaustless energy, hourly industry, method, sense of order, classification of practical de-

tails, Washington was superior to the Lincoln who carried legal papers in his tall hat or tied them in a bundle bearing the inscription, "When you can't find it anywhere else, look here."

It was the work of William of Orange, soldier and statesman, to bind together jealous provinces reluctant to submit to a union, and of Lincoln, statesman alone, to hold within a union already formed jealous states seeking to withdraw from it. In the similarity of conditions which each dealt with there is warrant for coupling the two in the admiration accorded human greatness. In the Netherlands and in the United States of Lincoln's time there were marked independence of character and strong individualities. In the one country personal attributes were stamped upon the different provinces of the United Netherlands and in the other upon the different colonies which formed the United States. Internal rivalries, jealousies, cross purposes, centrifugal groups clustered about energetic leaders, all threatening a political maelstrom perilous to the ship of state. William of Orange and Abraham Lincoln met and allayed these menaces with similar patience and skill until death came to each at the hand of an assassin.

In time the Netherlands, which Benjamin Franklin said had been our great example, lost their position as the foremost country of the world through an excess of democracy. That example which served Americans when they threw off England's control and formed the Constitution of our Union may serve once more now as a warning. Centuries ago the Dutch wrote free verse and refused to support their navy, an opportunity promptly embraced by envious commercial rivals. The period of free verse and navy limitation has arrived in the United States.

With the World War the remaining vestiges of Lincoln's America passed away, not to return. His period may prove to have been the best of our national life, and he, whom Lowell called "the first American", the last great American.

FOUR POEMS

By THEODORE DREISER

I

THE LITTLE FLOWERS OF LOVE AND WONDER

THE little flowers of love and wonder
That grow in the dark places
And between the giant rocks of chance
And the coarse winds of space.

The little flowers of love and wonder
That raise their heads
Beneath the dread rains
And against the chill frosts;
That peep and dream
In flaws of light
And amid the still gray places
And stony ways.

The little flowers of love and wonder
That peep and dream,
And quickly die.

The little flowers of love and wonder.

II

PROTEUS

BIRDS flying in the air over a river
And children playing in a meadow beside it.
A stream that turns an ancient wheel
Under great trees,
And cattle in the water
Below the trees.
And sun, and shade,
And warmth, and grass.
And myself
Dreaming in the grass.

And I am the birds flying in the air over the river,
And the children playing in the meadow,
And the stream that turns the ancient wheel,
And the wheel,
And the turn of the wheel,
And the great trees that stir and whisper in the breeze,
And the cattle under them;
The sun, the shade,
The warmth, the grass,
And myself
And not myself,
Dreaming in the grass.

For it is spring
And youth is in my heart.
For I am youth
And spring is in my heart.

III

FOR A MOMENT THE WIND DIED

FOR a moment the wind died,
*   And then came the sense of quieting leaves;*
And then came the great stillness of the landscape;
And then the chorus of unheard insects;
And then the perfect sky, pouring a blaze
*   of light through mottled leaves.*
And then the wind sprang up again—
And there was coolness in the air,
And for the face,
And the tired heart.

IV

TAKE HANDS

TAKE hands
*   And tell sad tales,*
One to another.

Has it filched from you your strength?
Your youth?
It has?
Has it robbed you of imagination?

Thwarted your dreams?
Withheld the fruits of hope?
The fruits of wit?
Of toil?
Of strength?
Of pain?
Has it blasted all
And left you chill,
Afraid,
Alone,
Yet facing still
A darker path
That must be trod
Alone?

Take hands with all who live
To left,
To right,
Or,
Make a gloomy choice of few
And with them sit
In some lone, sheltered place
Asking of each his story.
Or, better yet,
Or, best,
In silence sit
Harking the hopeless beat
Of each one's lonely heart
And wait,
Or dream,
Trusting a common misery to make soft
Or dull
The gorgon story
Of the human soul.

STEPHEN CRANE

BY CARL VAN DOREN

MODERN American literature may be said, accurately enough, to have begun with Stephen Crane thirty years ago. Its beginnings were far from clamorous and were at first very little noted. The nation in 1893 had the tariff, the panic, and the Columbian Exposition to think about. Among men of letters the elder classics were all dead but Holmes, who was chirping his valedictories in Boston; Mark Twain, Howells, Henry James, past middle age, had established their reputations on safe ground; the monthly magazines set the prevailing tone in literature—picturesque, kindly, and discreet. It is true that the sardonic Adams brothers were already at their work, but they, like the sons of Noah, concerned themselves with ancestral peccadilloes. It is true, too, that the poems of Emily Dickinson, posthumously issued, glittered like fireflies in the poetic twilight, but they were to have no heirs except Crane's ironic verses in their own century. Crane, breaking sharply with current literary modes, took the most contemporary life for his material and made himself heard before the decade ended.

Though "Maggie: A Girl of the Streets," appeared almost surreptitiously and by the public was altogether overlooked, it proved to Howells, at least, that Crane was a writer who had sprung into life fully armed. He had indeed gone through no formal training either as writer or as reader. So far as he had a profession, it was reporting for the newspapers; so far as he had literary models, they were odd volumes of Tolstoy and Flaubert which he had picked up. What was at once original and mature in Crane was his habit of thinking.

He called himself a man of sense, and deserved his title. For him the orthodox, the respectable, or the classical did not exist, or at any rate had no binding authority. He imagined the world as a ship which some god had fashioned carefully and then had heedlessly allowed to escape his jurisdiction,

So that, forever rudderless, it went upon the seas
Going ridiculous voyages,
Making quaint progress,
Turning as with serious purpose
Before stupid winds.
And there were many in the sky
Who laughed at this thing.

The state of mankind in such a world could not seem to Crane entirely glorious. Its orthodoxies and respectabilities were, he felt, only so much cotton in which it liked to pack itself; and its classical—that is, traditional—ways of representing itself in art, often mere frozen gestures. Too unschooled and too impatient to look for the reality behind accepted forms of manners or of art, Crane was too honest to pretend that he saw it there. If he could not see life face to face, he did not particularly care to see it at all. He had, therefore, to study it below or above the conventional levels; in the slums, on the battle-field, along the routes of difficult adventure. Reality for him, to be reality at all, had to be immediate and intense.

Both "Maggie" and its companion novel "George's Mother" illustrate this attitude. In the one a girl of the old Bowery neighborhood, driven from home by the drunken brutality of her mother, seeks refuge with a lover, loses him to a more practised woman, and drowns herself. In the other a young workingman of the same neighborhood, the last of five sons, falls in with a gang of toughs, loses his job, and breaks his mother's heart. For either of these stories the earlier nineties could have furnished Crane a formula by which he might have exhibited Maggie's career as edifying and George's as sentimental, taming the narratives by genteel expurgation and rounding them out with moral disquisition. When Crane went into the slums he did not go slumming. He would not condescend to his material. He reproduced the speech of his characters as exactly as his ability and the regulations of the Postoffice permitted him. He did not in the least mind that the savagery of some of his incidents would be sure to shock some of his readers. His method was as direct as his attitude. Without any parade of structure, without any of the pedantry of the well-made novel, he arranged his episodes on the simplest thread. Detail by detail, he caught hold of actuality as firmly as he could, and set it forth without regard to any possible censure except that which his own conscience would bring against him if he were less than honest. Then he left the rest to the ironical perception of any man of sense who might chance upon his books.

By a paradox which is a rule of art, Crane thus achieved, in his way, the effects which he had appeared to be neglecting, and wrote novels which are, in their way, classics, though minor classics. Certainly the moral tendency is indisputable. No girl ever ran away from home as a result of reading "Maggie"; no son ever forgot his parents as a result of reading "George's Mother." The fact that it seems ridiculous to point out the moral tendency of such stories shows how far Crane lifted them, as he has helped teach later novelists to lift their stories, out of the low plane of domestic sentimentalism, with its emphasis on petty virtues and vices, to the plane of the classics, with their emphasis on the major vices of meanness and cruelty and the major virtues of justice and magnanimity. In something of the same fashion he lifted his stories from the plane of art on which the guide-post is important or

necessary to the plane on which wisdom is communicated immediately, by example not by precept, and the reader, having lived something and not merely learned it, is less likely to forget. To his contemporaries Crane seemed heartless when he plunged into forbidden depths and brought up dreadful things which he showed the world without apology or comment. A less conventional taste perceives that it would have been more heartless, as it would have been less artful, for him to intrude his doctrines into the presence of Maggie's or of George's mother's tragedy. Here are certain veritable happenings, the books insist. What is to be thought, the books tacitly inquire, about the world in which such horrors happen?

Crane's procedure was not essentially different with his masterpiece, "The Red Badge of Courage." Less by Tolstoy or by Zola, a recent biographer points out, than by something much more native, Crane was led to his handling of war. Ever since Appomattox there had of course been going on a literary attempt to make the Civil War out an epic conflict, with all the appurtenances of pomp and heroism, But side by side with that had run a popular memory of it, not enshrined in books, which former soldiers exchanged in the vernacular and repeated, no doubt often tediously, to any others who would listen. In this popular memory Crane found his material. For his protagonist he chose an ordinary recruit, fresh from an inland farm, and carried him through his first experience of actual fighting. As the recruit naturally has no notion of the general plan of battle, he has to obey commands that he does not understand, that he resents, that he hates. His excited senses color the occasion, even the landscape. He suffers agonies of fatigue and almost a catastrophe of fear before he becomes acclimated to his adventure. Perhaps he seems unusually imaginative, but he is presented without too much subtlety. He speaks a convincing boyish dialect. His sensations are limited to something like his spiritual capacity. Though he is a pawn of war, he is also a microcosm. When Crane later saw a battle he found that he had been accurate in his account, not because he had studied military strategy but because he had placed the centre of the affair where it belongs, in the experience of the individual soldier.

If "The Red Badge" afforded Crane a happy opportunity to bring his ideas to bear upon a matter which he thought had long been swaddled in heroic nonsense, so did it afford him a happy opportunity to exercise his art. The soldier is a lens through which a whole battle may be seen, a sensorium upon which all its details may be registered. But, being in the fear of death, he is not a mere transparent lens, a mere passive sensorium. The battle takes a kind of mad shape within his consciousness as the tangled items of it stream through him. Since the action of the narrative is all laid in his excited mind, it has no excuse for ever being perfunctory or languid. All is immediate, all is intense. This gives the excuse for an occasional heightening of the language nearly to the pitch of poetry, as here: "As he listened to the din from the hillside, to a deep pulsating thunder that came from afar to the left, and to the lesser clamors which came from many directions, it occurred to him that they were fighting, too, over there, and over there, and over there. Heretofore he had supposed that all the battle was directly under his nose. As he gazed around him the youth felt a flash of astonishment at the pure, blue sky and the sun gleaming on the trees and fields. It was surprising that Nature had gone tranquilly on with her golden process in the midst of so much devilment." And yet the thrill of the narrative does not arise from the language, so rarely and so delicately is it elevated. It arises from a certain air of integrity which the whole novel owes to the closeness with which the action is imagined and the candor with which it is represented. Once more Crane, disregarding the heroic and throwing the grand style overboard, had been justified, and had taken a long step in the direction

which American literature was to travel for a generation.

Not merely American literature. In England where, says H. G. Wells, "The Red Badge" came as "a record of an intensity beyond all precedent," Crane seemed "the first expression of the opening mind of a new period." By comparison Henry James looked a little tenuous, Kipling a little metallic, Stevenson a little soft. Joseph Conrad, significantly, was among Crane's particular admirations and admirers. Without Conrad's brooding vision and his ground swells of rhythm, the younger man had something of the same concentration upon vivid moments. But the influence of Crane in England, as in America, was toward brilliance, toward impressionism. After the success which "The Red Badge" brought him he flashed brightly across many scenes. He went as a journalist to the Southwest and to Mexico; he tried to go filibustering to Cuba. He who had never witnessed a battle was asked, on the strength of his book, to be a war correspondent, in Greece and in the Caribbean. He moved back and forth between New York and London, always in the cleverest company. Scandal endowed him with a legendary eminence in wild oats which he would have been too busy to sow even if he had been disposed. In these circumstances, he tended to have better fortune with short stories than with novels. By some queer turn of irony the author of "The Open Boat", "The Monster", "The Blue Hotel" has been left out of the canon which the queer experts in the short story have gradually evolved, but of late his mastery of the form is coming to be more and more admitted. He could, as in "The Open Boat", tell a straight story of adventure with breathless ferocity. He could, as in "The Monster", expose the stupidity of public opinion in a cramped province. He could, as in "The Blue Hotel", show fate working blindly and causelessly in the muddled lives of men. At other times he was full of comedy. And always he was spare, pungent, intense.

He had Melville's bold combination of largeness and humor, with a pungency of phrase which is Crane's alone. Thus, for example, he gives an episode of the perilous voyage in "The Open Boat": "Canton flannel gulls flew near and far. Sometimes they sat down on the sea, near patches of brown seaweed that rolled on the waves with a movement like carpets on a line in a gale. The birds sat comfortably in groups, and they were envied by some in the dingey, for the wrath of the sea was no more to them than it was to a covey of prairie chickens a thousand miles inland. Often they came very close and stared at the men with black bead-like eyes. At these times they were uncanny and sinister in their unblinking scrutiny, and the men hooted angrily at them, telling them to be gone. One came, and evidently decided to alight on the top of the captain's head. The bird flew parallel to the boat and did not circle, but made short sidelong jumps in the air in chicken-fashion. His black eyes were wistfully fixed upon the captain's head. 'Ugly brute', said the oiler to the bird, 'You look as if you were made with a jack-knife'. The cook and the correspondent swore darkly at the creature. The captain naturally wished to knock it away with the end of the heavy painter; but he did not dare do it because anything resembling an emphatic gesture would have capsized this freighted boat, and so with his open hand, the captain gently and carefully waved the gull away. After it had been discouraged from the pursuit the captain breathed easier on account of his hair." Without a touch of heroic language Crane here immensely heightens the scene by making it, though death crowds upon it, somehow droll. At such passages the drama grows breathless.

The demand for intensity in fiction, of course, goes in and out of fashion. Some other, calmer age may regard Crane as hectic. He occupies, however, a temperate position between the writers who seem flat and the writers who seem to have carried impressionism to a dizzy verge. Crane is never obscure. The first of the imagists, he never becomes jagged in his manner, nor sacrifices movement to the elaboration of striking detail. To call him a journalist of genius helps to define him, but there still remains the problem of his haunting charm. That charm springs, in large measure, from his free, courageous mind. Lucidity like his is poetry. Even when he is journalistically crude and incorrect, as he often is, he reveals an intelligence working acutely upon its observations. He has therefore the smallest possible burden of nonsense to carry with him. He does not worry himself with insoluble mysteries, such as the duties of the cosmic whole to the finite individual.

> A man said to the universe:
> "Sir, I exist!"
> "However," replied the universe,
> "The fact had not created in me
> A sense of obligation."

Thus jauntily Crane can dismiss the larger metaphysics. He works within a tangible area. And when his intelligence has brought him close to his material he feels for it the desire of a lover. That he sees life under the light of irony does not diminish his passion but increases it. Are these characters, these situations, these comic or tragic consequences, after all, only the brief concerns of fate? Doubtless. But they have importance for the ephemeral creatures who are involved in them. And they have pattern and color for the unduped yet affectionate spectator.

FOUR GENERATIONS

BY RUTH SUCKOW

"Move just a little closer together—the little girl more toward the centre—that's good. Now I think we'll get it."

The photographer dived once more under the black cloth.

"Stand back, ma," a husky voice said. "You'll be in the picture."

Aunt Em stepped hastily back with a panicky look. Mercy, she didn't want to show! She hadn't had time to get her dress changed yet, had come right out of the kitchen where she was baking pies to see the photograph taken. She was in her old dark blue kitchen dress and had her hair just wadded up until she could get time to comb it. It didn't give her much time for dressing up, having all this crowd to cook for.

The boys, and Uncle Chris, standing away back on the edges, grinned appreciatively. Fred whispered to Clarence, "Laugh if ma'd got in it." The way she had jumped back, and her unconsciousness of the ends sticking up from her little wad of hair delighted the boys. When they looked at each other, a little remembering glint came into their eyes.

There was quite a crowd of onlookers. Aunt Em. Uncle Chris in his good trousers, and his shirt sleeves, his sunburned face dark brown above the white collar that Aunt Em had made him put on because of Charlie's. Uncle Gus and Aunt Sophie Spfierschlage had come over to dinner, and stood back against the white house wall, Aunt Sophie mountainous in her checked gingham. The boys, of course, and Bernie Schuldt who was working for Chris; and another fellow who had come to look at

some hogs and who was standing there, conscious of his old overalls and torn straw hat, mumbling, "Well, didn't know I was gona find anything like this goin' on." . . . Charlie's wife, Ella, had been given a chair where she could have a good view of the proceedings. She tried to smile and wave her handkerchief when little Phyllis looked around at her. Then she put the handkerchief to her eyes, lifting up her glasses with their narrow light shell rims, still smiling a little painfully. She had to think from how far Katherine had come. . . .

Aunt Em and Aunt Sophie were whispering, "Aint it a shame Edna couldn't get over! They coulda took one of Chris and her and Marine and Merle, with Grandpa, too. . . . That little one looks awful cute, don't she? . . . Well, what takes him so long? Grandpa won't sit there much longer. I should think they coulda had it taken by this time a'ready."

They all watched the group on the lawn. They had decided that the snowball bushes would "make a nice background." The blossoms were gone, but the leaves were dark green, and thick. What a day for taking a picture! It would be so much better out here than in the house. Katherine had made them take it right after dinner, so that little Phyllis would not be late for her nap—nothing must ever interfere with that child's nap. It was the brightest, hottest time of day. The tall orange summer lilies seemed to open and shimmer in the heat. Things were so green—the country lawn with its thick grass, the heavy foliage of the maple trees against the blue summery sky of July. The thin varnished supports of the camera stand glittered yellow and

15

sticky. The black cloth of the lens looked thick, dense, hot. The photographer's shirt was dazzling white in the sun, and when he drew his head out from under the cloth his round face shone pink. His coat made a black splotch tossed on the grass.

"The little girl more toward the centre."

All three of the others tried anxiously to make little Phyllis more conspicuous. "Here, we've got to have you showing—my, my!—whether the rest of us do or not," Charlie said jovially. Grandpa's small aged frail hand moved a little as if he were going to draw the child in front of him—but, with a kind of delicacy, did not quite touch her little arm.

They had to wait while a little fleecy cloud crossed the sun, putting a brief strange cool shadow over the vivid lawn. In that moment the onlookers were aware of the waiting group. Four generations! Great-grandfather, grandfather, mother, daughter. It was all the more impressive when they thought of Katherine and Phyllis having come from so many miles away. The snowball bushes were densely green behind them—almost dusky in the heat. Grandpa's chair had been placed out there —a homemade chair of willow branches. To think that these four belonged together!

Grandpa, sitting in the chair, might have belonged to another world. Small, bent like a little old troll, foreign with his black cambric skull cap, his blue far-apart peasant eyes with their still gaze, his thin silvery beard. His hands, gnarled from years of farm work in a new country, clasped the homemade knotted stick that he held between his knees. His feet, in old felt slippers with little tufted wool flowers, were set flat on the ground. He wore the checked shirt of an old farmer. . . . It hardly seemed that Charlie was his son. Plump and soft, dressed in the easy garments, of good quality and yet a trifle careless, of middlewestern small town prosperity. His shaven face, paler now than it used to be and showing his age in the folds that had come about his chin; his glasses with shell rims and gold bows; the few strands of grayish hair brushed across his pale luminous skull. A small town banker. Now he looked both impressed and shamefaced at having the photograph taken. . . . And then Katherine, taking after no one knew whom. Slender, a little haggard and worn, still young, her pale delicate face and the cords in her long soft throat, her little collar bones, her dark intelligent weak eyes behind her thick black-rimmed glasses. Katherine had always been like that. Refined, "finicky," studious, thoughtful. Her hand, slender and a trifle sallow, lay on Phyllis' shoulder.

Phyllis . . . Her little yellow frock made her vivid as a canary bird against the dark green of the foliage. Yellow—the relatives did not know whether they liked that, bright yellow. Still, she did look sweet. They hadn't thought Katherine's girl would be so pretty. Of course the care that Katherine took of her—everything had to revolve around that child. There was something faintly exotic about her liquid brown eyes with their jet-black lashes, the shining straight gold-brown hair, the thick bangs that lay, parted a little and damp with the heat, on the pure white of her forehead. Her little precise "Eastern accent" . . . Grandpa looked wonderingly at the bare arms, round and soft and tiny, white and moist in the heat. Fragile blue veins made a flower-like tracery of indescribable purity on the white skin. Soft, tender, exquisite . . . ach, what a little girl was here, like a princess!

The cloud passed. Katherine's white and Phyllis' yellow shone out again from the green. The others stood back watching, a heavy stolid country group against the white wall of the farm house that showed bright against the farther green of the grove. Beyond lay the orchard and the rank green spreading corn fields where little silvery clouds of gnats went shimmering over the moist richness of the leaves.

"Watch—he's taking it now!"

In the breathless silence they could hear the long whirr and rush of a car on the brown country road beyond the grove.

II

Well, the picture was taken. Every one was glad to be released from the strain.

Grandpa's chair had been placed nearer the house, under some maple trees. Charlie stayed out there with him a while. It was his duty, he felt, to talk to the old man a while when he was here at the farm. He didn't get over very often—well, it was a hundred miles from Rock River, and the roads weren't very good up here in Sac township. His car stood out at the edge of the grove in the shade. The new closed car that he had lately bought, a "coach," opulent, shining, with its glass and upholstery and old-blue drapes, there against the background of the evergreen grove with its fallen branches and pieces of discarded farm machinery half visible in the deepest shade.

It wasn't really very hard to get away from Rock River and the bank. He and Ella took plenty of trips. He ought to come to see his father more than he did. But he seemed to have nothing to say to Grandpa. The old man had scarcely been off the place for years.

"Well, pa, you keep pretty well, do you?"

"Ja, pretty goot . . . ja, for so old as I am—"

"Oh now, you mustn't think of yourself as so old."

Charlie yawned, re-crossed his legs. He lighted a cigar.

"Chris's corn doing pretty well this season?"

"Ach, dot I know nuttings about. Dey don't tell me nuttings."

"Well, you've had your day at farming, pa."

"Ja . . . ja, ja . . ."

He fumbled in the pocket of his coat, drew out an ancient black pipe.

Charlie said cheerfully, "Have some tobacco?" He held out a can.

The old man peered into it, sniffed. "Ach, dot stuff? No, no, dot is shust like shavings. I smoke de real old tobacco."

"Like it strong, hey?"

They both puffed away.

Grandpa sat in the old willow chair. His blue eyes had a look half wistful, half resentful. Charlie was his oldest child. He would have liked to talk with Charlie. He was always wishing that Charlie would come, always planning how he would tell him things—about how the old ways were going and how the farmers did now, how none of them told him things—but when Charlie came, then that car was always standing there ready to take him right back home again, and there seemed nothing to be said. He always remembered Charlie as the young man, the little boy who used to work beside him in the field—and then when Charlie came, he was this stranger. Charlie was a town man now. He owned a bank! He had forgotten all about the country, and the old German ways. To think of Charlie, their son, being a rich banker, smoking cigars, riding around in a fine carriage with glass windows . . .

"Dot's a fine wagon you got dere."

Charlie laughed. "That's a coach, pa."

"So? Coach, is dot what you call it? Like de old kings, like de emperors, de Kaisers, rode around in. Ja, you can live in dot. Got windows and doors, curtains—is dere a table too, stove—no? Ja, dot's a little house on wheels."

He pursed out his lips comically. But ach, such a carriage! He could remember when he was glad enough to get to town in a lumber wagon. Grandma and the children used to sit in the back on the grain sacks. His old hands felt of the smooth knots of his stick. He went back, back, into revery. . . . He muttered just above his breath, "Ach, ja, ja, ja . . . dot was all so long ago. . . ."

Charlie was silent too. He looked at the car, half drew out his watch, put it back. . . . Katherine crossed the lawn. His eyes followed her. Bluish-gray, a little faded behind his modern glasses—there was resentment, bewilderment, wistfulness in them at the same time, and loneliness. He was thinking of how he used to bring

Kittie out here to the farm when she was a little girl, when Chris used to drive to Germantown and get them with a team and two-seated buggy. They had come oftener than now when they had the car . . . "Papa, *really* did you live out here— on this farm?" He had been both proud and a little jealous because she wasn't sun-burned and wiry, like Chris' children. A little slim, long-legged, soft-skinned, dark-eyed girl. "Finicky" about what she ate and what she did—he guessed he and Ella had encouraged her in that. Well, he hadn't had much when he was a child, and he'd wanted his little girl to have the things he'd missed. He'd wanted her to have more than his brothers' and sisters' children. He was Charlie, the one who lived in town, the successful one. Music lessons, drawing lessons, college . . . and here she had grown away from her father and mother. Chris' children lived close around him, but it sometimes seemed to him that he and Ella had lost Kittie. Liv-ing away off there in the East. And when she came home, although she was carefully kind and dutiful and affectionate, there was something aloof. He thought jealous-ly, maybe it would have been better if they hadn't given her all those things, had kept her right at home with them. . . . It had-n't been as much pleasure as he had antici-pated having his little grandchild there. There was her "schedule" that Kittie was so persnickerty about. He'd been proud to have people in Rock River see her beauty and perfection, but he hadn't been able to take her around and show her off as he'd hoped.

All day he had been seeing a little slim fastidious girl in a white dress and white hair ribbons and black patent leather slippers, clinging to his hand with little soft fingers when he took her out to see the cows and the pigs . . . "Well, Kittie, do you wish we lived out here instead of in town?" She shook her head, and her small under lip curled just a little . . .

He saw Chris and Gus off near the house. They could talk about how crops were

coming, and he could tell them, with a banker's authority, about business condi-tions. He stirred uneasily, got up, yawned, stretched up his arms, said with a little touch of shame:

"Well, pa, guess I'll go over and talk to Chris a while. I'll see you again before we leave."

"Ja—" The old man did not try to keep him. He watched Charlie's plump figure cross the grass. Ja, he had more to say to the young ones . . .

III

Aunt Em was through baking. She had gone into the bedroom to "get cleaned up." She had brought out chairs to the front porch. "Sit out here. Here's a chair, Ella—here, Katherine. Ach, Sophie, take a better chair than that." "Naw, this un'll do for me, Em."

"The womenfolks"—Katherine shud-dered away from that phrase. She had al-ways, ever since she was a little girl, de-spised sitting about this way with "the womenfolks." Planted squat in their chairs, rocking, yawning, telling over and over about births and deaths and funerals and sicknesses. There was a kind of feminine grossness about it that offended what had always been called her "finickiness."

Her mother enjoyed it. She was different from Aunt Em and Aunt Sophie, lived in a different way—a small plump elderly woman with waved grayish-silvery hair and a flowered voile dress with little fussy laces, feminine strapped slippers. But still there was something that she liked about sitting here in the drowsy heat and going over and over things with the other women. Sometimes, to Katherine's suffer-ing disgust, she would add items about the birth of Katherine herself—"Well, I thought sure Kittie was going to be a boy. She kicked so hard—" "Oh, *mother*, spare us!" Aunt Em would give a fat comfort-able laugh—"Don't look so rambunctious now, does she? Kittie, aint you ever gona get a little flesh on your bones? You study too hard. She oughta get out and ride the horses around like Edna does."

Aunt Sophie Spfierschlage—that was the way she sat rocking, her feet flat on the floor, her stomach comfortably billowing, beads of sweat on her heavy chin and lips and around the roots of her stiff dull hair. Well, thank goodness she was only Aunt Em's sister, she wasn't really related to the Kleins. Aunt Em was bad enough.

They used to laugh over her fastidious disgust, when she sat here, a delicate critical little girl who didn't want to get on one of the horses or jump from rafters into the hay. "Kittie thinks that's terrible. Well, Kittie, that's the way things happen." "Ach, she won't be so squeamish when she grows up and has three or four of her own." Now she sat beside them, delicate, still too thin to Aunt Em's amazement. "Aint you got them ribs covered up yet? What's the matter? Don't that man of your's give you enough to eat?"—her soft skin pale and her eyes dark from the heat, dressed with a kind of fastidious precision, an ultra-refinement. A fragile bar pin holding the soft white silk of her blouse, her fine dark hair drooping about her face. "Well, you aint changed much since you got married!" Aunt Em had said. They expected to admit her now to their freemasonry, to have *her* add interesting items about the birth of Phyllis.

Phyllis—her little darling! As if the exquisite miracle of Phyllis could have anything in common with these things! Katherine suffered just as she had always suffered from even small vulgarities. But she sat courteous and ladylike now, a slight dutiful smile on her lips.

"Where does she get them brown eyes? They aint the color of your's, are they? Turn around and let's have a look at you—no, I thought your's was kinda darker."

Aunt Em had come out now, had squatted down into another chair. "I guess her papa's got the brown eyes."

"Yes, I think she looks a little like Willis."

Ella said almost resentfully, "Well, I don't know whether she takes after Willis' folks or not, but I can't see that she looks one bit like Kittie or any of us."

"Well," Aunt Em said, "but look at Kittie. She don't look like you or Charlie neither. But I guess she's your's just the same, aint she, Ella? . . . Say, you remember that Will Fuchs? Ja, his girl's got one they say don't belong to who it ought to. Her and that young Bender from over south —"

Katherine did not listen. How long before they could leave? She had thought it right to bring Phyllis over here where her great-grandfather lived, as her father had wished. But it seemed worse to her than ever. She knew that Aunt Em wouldn't let them go without something more to eat, another of her great heavy meals with pie and cake and coffee. Her mother had always said, as if in extenuation of her visible enjoyment of the visit and the food, "Well, Aunt Em means well. Why don't you try and talk with her? She wants to talk with you." But Aunt Em and the Spfierschlages and the whole place seemed utterly alien and horrible to Katherine. For a moment, while they had been taking the photograph out on the lawn, she had felt touched with a sense of beauty. But she had never belonged here. She felt at home in Willis' quiet old frame house in New England, with his precise elderly New England parents—"refinement", "culture", Willis' father reading "the classics", taking the *Atlantic Monthly* ever since their marriage. She had always felt that those were the kind of people she ought to have had, the kind of home. Of course she loved father and mother and was loyal to them. They depended upon her as their only child.

This porch! It seemed to express the whole of her visits to the farm. It was old-fashioned now—a long narrow porch with a fancy railing, the posts trimmed with red. Her ancestral home! It was utterly alien to her.

They were talking to her again.

"Where's the girl—in taking her nap yet?"

"Yes, she's sleeping."

"Ach, you hadn't ought to make her sleep all the time when she's off visiting. I baked a little piece of pie crust for her. I thought I'd give it to her while it was nice and warm."

"Oh, better not try to give her pie crust," Ella said warningly.

"Ach, that aint gona hurt her—nice homemade pie. Mine always et that."

"Ja, mine did too."

Katherine's lips closed firmly. She couldn't hurry and hurt father and mother—but oh, to get Phyllis home! Father—he was always trying to give the child something she shouldn't have, he wanted to spoil her as he had tried to spoil Katherine herself . . . She shut her lips tight to steel herself against the pitifulness of the sudden vision of father—getting so much older these last few years—looking like a child bereft of his toy when she had firmly taken away the things with which he had come trotting happily home for his grandchild. He had gradually drawn farther and farther away. Once he had hurt her by saying significantly, when Phyllis had wanted a pink blotter in the bank—"You'll have to ask your mother. Maybe there's something in it to hurt you. *Grandpa* don't know." He had wanted to take Phyllis to a little cheap circus that had come to town, to show her off and exhibit her. Mother was more sympathetic, even a little proud of retailing to the other "ladies" how careful Katherine was in bringing up the child, what a "nice family" Willis had. But even she was plaintive and didn't understand. Both she and Father thought that Katherine and Willis were "carrying it too far" when they decided to have Willis teach the child until they could find the proper school for her.

She heard a little sleepy startled voice from within the house—"Moth-uh!"

"Uh—huh! There's somebody!" Aunt Em exclaimed delightedly.

Katherine hurried into the darkened bedroom where Phyllis lay on Aunt Em's best bed spread. The shades were down, but there was the feeling of the hot sunlight back of them. Phyllis' bare arms and legs were white and dewy. Her damp golden-brown bangs were pushed aside. Katherine knelt adoring. She began to whisper.

"Is mother's darling awake? . . . Shall we go home soon—see father? Sleep in her own little room?" . . . Her throat tightened with a homesick vision of the little room with the white bed and the yellow curtains . . .

IV

They had left Grandpa alone again. Charlie and the other men were standing out beside the car, bending down and examining it, feeling of the tires, trying the handles of the doors.

Grandpa had left his chair in the yard and gone to the old wooden rocker that stood just inside the door of his room. His room was part of the old house, the one that he and Grandma had had here on the farm. It opened out upon the back yard, with a little worn narrow plank out from the door. It looked out upon the mound of the old cyclone cellar, with its wooden door, where now Aunt Em kept her vegetables in sacks on the damp cool floor, with moist earthen jars of plum and apple butter on the shelf against the cobwebbed wall. The little triangular chicken houses were scattered about in the back yard, and beyond them was the orchard where now small apples were only a little lighter than the vivid summer green of the heavy foliage and where little dark shiny bubbles of aromatic sap had oozed out from the rough crusty bark.

The shadows in the orchard were drawing out long toward the East, and the aisles of sunlight too looked longer. The groups of people moved about more. Everything had the freshened look of late afternoon.

Grandpa rocked a little. He puffed on his pipe, took it out and held it between his fingers. It left his lower lip moistened and shining above the fringe of silvery beard. His blue eyes kept looking toward the orchard, in a still fathomless gaze. His lips moved at times.

"Ach, ja, ja, ja . . ." A kind of mild sighing groan. It had pleased him that they had wanted the photograph taken, with the little great-grandchild. But that was over now. They had left him alone. And again, with a movement of his head, "Ja, dot was all so long ago."

Beyond the orchard, beyond the dark green corn fields that lay behind it, beyond the river and the town . . . beyond all the wide western country, and the ocean . . . what were his fixed blue eyes, intent and inward and sad, visioning now?

The rocker was framed in the doorway of his room. Even the odor of the room was foreign. His bed with a patchwork quilt, a little dresser, a chest of drawers. The ancient wall paper had been torn off and the walls calcimined a sky-blue. Against the inner one hung his big silver watch, slowly ticking . . . His eyes blue, and his hair under the little black cap, his beard, were silvery . . . A German text with gaudy flowers hung on a woolen cord above the bed. "Der Herr ist mein Hirte."

He started. "Nun—who is dot?"

He did not know that little Phyllis had been watching him. Standing outside the door, in her bright canary yellow, her beautiful liquid brown eyes solemnly studying him. She was half afraid. She had never seen anything so old as "Great-grandfather". The late afternoon sunlight shimmered in the fine texture of his thin silvery beard. It brought out little frostings and marks and netted lines on his old face in which the eyes were so blue. One hand lay upon his knee. She stared wonderingly at the knots that the knuckles made, the brownish spots, the thick veins, the queer stretched shiny look of the skin between the bones. She looked at his black pipe, his funny little cap, his slippers with the tufted flowers . . .

"Ach, so? You t'ink Grandpa is a funny old

man den? You want to look at him? So?"

He spoke softly. A kind of pleased smiling look came upon his face. He stretched out his hand slowly and cautiously, as if it were a butterfly poised just outside his door. A sudden longing to get this small pretty thing nearer, an ingenuous delight, possessed him now that he was alone with her. He spoke as one speaks to a bird toward which one is carefully edging nearer, afraid that a sudden motion will startle its bright eyes and make it take wing.

"Is dis a little yellow bird? Can it sing a little song?"

A faint smile dawned on the serious parted lips. He nodded at her. She seemed to have come a little closer. He too looked in wonderment, as he had done before, at the shining hair, the fragile blue veins on the white temples, the moist pearly white of the little neck, marveling at her as he would have marveled at some beautiful strange bird that might have alighted a moment on his door step . . .

"Can't sing a little song? No? Den Grandpa will have to sing one to you."

He had been thinking of songs as he sat here, they had been murmuring somewhere in his mind. Old, old songs that he had known long ago in the old country . . . His little visitor stood quite still as his faint quavering voice sounded with a kind of dim sweetness in the sunshine. . . .

"Du, du, liegst mir im Herzen,
Du, du, liegst mir im Sinn,
Du, du, machst mir viel Schmerzen,
Weist nicht wie gut ich dir bin—
Ja, ja, ja, ja, weist nicht wie gut ich dir bin."

The gaze of her brown shining eyes never wavered, and a soft glow of fascinated interest grew in them as the sad wailing simplicity of the old tune quavered on the summer air. For a moment she was quite near, they understood each other.

"You like dot? Like Grandpa's song?"

She nodded. A tiny pleased smile curved her fresh lips. . . . Then suddenly, with a little delicate scared movement, as if after all she had discovered that the place was strange, she flitted away to her mother.

HUNEKER ON HUNEKER

To Dr. T. C. Williams.[1]

The Carrollton,
981 Madison Ave.,
New York, April 2, 1908.

DEAR TOM: I'm glad you read (or dipped into) "Visionaries", as duly reported by my spouse. The book contains the scrapings of my magazine articles for the past ten years. It does not hang together—but what volume of short stories does? I'm writing to Scribners to send you my "Chopin" and "Iconoclasts". Perhaps you may remark that the first—since translated into German and French—is a real book, not a compilation. It demanded for its execution years of concentrated effort. It is now the standard work for teachers, so I am assured. The study of Ibsen—O joyful whiskers!—was, up to the time of his death, the longest in the English tongue—168 pages. Both of these books will be of value to you in your practise, being warranted to cure, or alleviate, insomnia, varicose veins and the pip. I am going to write that novel, but two other books are on the bridge ahead of it—my Liszt life and a volume of literary essays, due in 1919.

Yours with brittle veins,

JIM.

II

To Edward Ziegler.[2]

Marienbad, August 26, 1909.

DEAR BILL: We work here like convicts. Get up at 6 with a chorale; go to bed at 8 with a hunger. *Bergsteigen* all day, six hours at a lick. Think of your fat papa walking up narrow paths at an angle of 45 degrees! But the results! I've lost 16 lbs. in 15 days

and have only begun. My doctor kicks, but as my nerves are good I sleep well, and he can't stop me. My clothes hang on my bony shoulders, my pretty jowls are gone, and my belly, O Bill, my fat belly has gone, vanished, disappeared! The waters are easy. Between you and me, it's all in the avoidance of liquids at meals—a thing I never found difficult. My gout has disappeared, my uric acid is diminished, and I am about to send to a tailor to have my clothes reefed in. Of course, I'll get 10 lbs. back on the voyage, but—no more beer or potatoes for this gentleman! I feel too spry ever to relapse into obesity again. My waist has shriveled from 45 to 38 and is still dwindling. What joy! I elbow Edward VII every morning and enjoy his huge coarse chuckle. He is a good fellow. So is the King of Greece. So is the Duc d'Orleans, and all the rest of the over-ripe gang down here flushing their insides. I read German every day—but my accent!

As ever,

JIM.

III

To John Quinn.[3]

Westminster Court,
1618 Beverly Road,
Brooklyn, June 4, 1914.

DEAR JOHN: I'm at work on magazine articles—various sorts. The one on Conrad reads fairly well in typescript, but you can't tell until it's in actual type. Have just finished for *Puck* a diatribe against Socialism and a review of the "best" fiction of the day—American. Dreiser leads in seriousness, but he writes clumsily. I think Rupert Hughes is a winner ("What Will People Say?"), and "The Salamander", by

[1] For many years Huneker's physician and friend.

[2] At the time of this letter, musical critic for the New York *Herald*.

[3] Lawyer, book collector and art connoisseur.

Owen Johnson, is a realistic study of a type known to us youths as teasers. But my favorite is Katharine Fullerton Gerould ("Vain Oblations"). She is the real thing —much art for a beginner, and more temperament, more red blood, than Edith Glacial Wharton.

As ever, yours,
JAMES HUNEKER.

IV

To Mme. Frida Ashforth.[4]
Brooklyn, August 11, 1918.

DEAR FRIDA: There is a possibility of our going to Philadelphia to end my days (I'll be 59 in January, 1919), as I have a fine offer from the *Press*. But it will be pulling teeth to leave New York; even Flatbush is nearer the Bowery than Philadelphia. And I've been here since 1886—left Philadelphia in 1878. Jozia[5] was born here. So we sorely contemplate the change—but what to do! The war has killed my business; newspapers and magazines want only war news or stories. I am not so spry as I was. Last season the Philadelphia job was comparatively easy—twice a week. However, "needs must when the devil drives." I'll take what I get and be glad of anything in these trying times. Four years of outgo, and no fixed income—phew! It has knocked my never corpulent bank-account into a skeleton. But I'm not a man easily beaten, and with health and a pen I'll pull through. Hard-luck stories are not interesting, so pardon this little wail of woe! Only—I don't like moving! I belong to one of the best clubs over in Philadelphia, my brother lives there, and I have many friends—still !?!?

Yours for cooler weather,
JIM.

V

To W. C. Brownell.[6]
Brooklyn, June 15, 1919.

MY DEAR MR. BROWNELL: Of course you are right, and if you had presented 1000

[4] The well-known singing teacher.
[5] Mrs. Huneker.
[6] Literary adviser to Charles Scribner's Sons.

more reasons against the inclusion of those Shaw letters in "Steeplejack" I couldn't say nay. But one thing is overlooked: the vital issue, which reduces to the futile the academic discussion of the matter, *i.e.*, will or will not the letters sell the book? All other considerations are naught to me. The London sales would be negligible—they always have been with my books—, but the American sales might not be. Even a *succès de scandale!* Anything but the collecting of dust on top shelves! I am through with such nonsense, as for example, non-ethical, lack of taste, etc. The two offending words occur in a quasi-scientific communication, and to speak of their exclusion makes me rub my eyes. Is this 1880 or 1920? However, these are minor splotches. The chief thing is: will Shaw consent? You think the tale of our quarrel stale and silly? *Soit!* But the book is composed of ancient and often silly memories. That's why I wrote it—*en souvenir*. I believe the letters will materially swell the sales here and in London. You do not. A difference of opinion, but a serious one to our bank accounts. What will you say to the Mary Garden book, with its *mélange* of essays and short stories, many of them morbid, even risky? As for my novel, now well under way, it will shock you, I'm sure, for the title page bears a motto from Walt Whitman's poem, "A Woman Waits For Me". In a word, the book is frankly erotic, though well within the law. I hardly think your house will print it. When Mr. Scribner wired and later wrote I was told that whatever I chose to print would be tolerated by him. Already you are balking. It was for this precise reason that I had considered the offers of another publisher—one who wanted the book because of the Shaw letters. He was willing to take the risks—of lawsuits, etc. You are not. Now, why shouldn't I write to G. B. S.? If he says no, then you will know how to act. I haven't given up hope yet. But one thing I insist on, even if it comes to a disagreement: my copy must go in as it appeared in the *Press*. All of it—not only the Shaw letters. I must not be hampered by any moral (so-called) reasons. I'm weary of the dusty primrose path. We are in for a puritanical suppression of individuality at all costs, so I'm taking time by the forelock. As a matter of fact, there is nothing in "Steeplejack" or "Mary Garden" (the book,[7] not the adorable girl!) that is vulgar, obscene, or, I hope, tasteless except those damnable Shaw letters, and they are so brim full of vitality and sparkling *aperçus* that I honestly believe I should be a public benefactor if, aided and abetted by Charles Scribner's Sons, I gave them to the world. (Of course, this is only self-mystification, but I enjoy it.) If G. B. S. consents, then the letters must be printed.

Sincerely as ever,
JAMES HUNEKER.

VI

To Maxwell E. Perkins.[8]

Brooklyn, June 25, 1919.

DEAR MR. PERKINS: A woman rang me up yesterday. She belongs to a little so-called art magazine. She told my wife—I was not at home—that Mr. Scribner had consented to the republication of one of my articles from "Promenades". Furthermore, she was so blithely impertinent as to say that I should call her up this morning, otherwise the article in question would be reprinted, as they were "pressed for time"! I don't know whether you know who gave this alleged permission without first consulting me, but do please make inquiries and tell whoever it may be not to give assent to any such swindling propositions. They are trying to get something for nothing, and to that game I vigorously object. If they would pay a sum, say $100, then it would be different; Mr. Brownell suggests that in that case a fair division could be made with Scribners. But this damn nervy way of phoning and informing you that, etc., etc.! God! It's absurd to get hotter on a hot day over such a little matter, but when Rodin died I had to call down

[7] The title was changed to "Bedouins" before publication.

[8] Of Chas. Scribner's Sons.

the *Evening Post*, sanctified ——, for printing about a page of my Rodin study in the "Promenades", and shortly afterward the *Tribune* for swiping without the ghost of an acknowledgment my Flaubert letter from "Egoists". Sorry to bother you. Life is so short and sweaty!

Cordially,
JAMES HUNEKER.

VII

To Maxwell E. Perkins.

DEAR MR. PERKINS: Here is the blurb for the "Steeplejack" cover. A rotten job. If I don't set forth the incomparable merits of this unique book, then the blurb no longer blurbs; if I told the truth you wouldn't print it; if I say nice, sweet, Dr. van Dyke phrases, then—that way egotism lies. So I did what most people do when they must face the music of facts: I dodged.

Sincerely,
JAMES HUNEKER.

VIII

To John Quinn.

MY DEAR JOHN: You missed a hell of a hot spell, July 2 to 5 or 6. Another is due. We are, neither of us, lively. I have no urge, as Walt W. says. No booze since April 27, and never miss it. Yet I believe alcohol is a driving force when taken moderately, as I took it, say 12 or 15 bottles of beer daily. I'm writing 10,000 words weekly for my new autumn book, 1920, with a pen. It's to be 100,000 words. Fiction. "Steeplejack" (October), two big volumes, is discharging proof. I'm busy. Then the weekly stunt in the *Times*. We must eat, even if we can't drink.

With love from Jozia and
JIM.

IX

To Thomas R. Smith.[9]

Brooklyn, November 28, 1919.

MY DEAR TOM: You will certainly see the story when Scribners get through with it next week. It can stand on its merits with-

[9] Of Boni & Liveright, publishers of "Painted Veils."

out humorous elements. Of obscenity, vulgarity or indecency there is not a trace—only extreme frankness, and the sex side dealt with as if by a medical expert. Might I say—gynecologist?

As ever,

Jim.

X

To John Quinn.

Brooklyn, December 30, 1919.

My dear John: My novel will likely appear in the same series as George Moore's "Storyteller's Holiday", "Avowals", etc. The next to appear is "Aphrodite"; then "Istar"—title not yet decided on: either "Istar" (daughter of sin: you recall the old Babylonian epic) or "Painted Veils". But the chief point is that the story thus far has laid the experts out cold. Scribners, who want to publish the book *expurgated*, told me—and I blush to repeat the words! —that not in this generation have they read a fiction so original, brilliant, *human*, or so well composed and written! The joke is, John, that I wrote the damned thing in 7 *weeks*, less 2 days, although I planned it for 2 months. I wrote it because I had a story to tell, because it is largely characterization, with plenty of action. It may be made into a play next summer. Now, if you should care to read it in clean, clear typescript I'll fetch you a copy. The chief thing is that I should like you to see the publisher's contract. The best of publishers will bear watching. I need money and I'm going to get it. First the unexpurgated copy; then, later, for the purer public, the bowdlerized edition—catch them coming and going!

As ever,

Jim.

XI

To Henry B. Fuller.[10]

Brooklyn, April 18, 1920.

My dear Old Friend Fuller: Suffering from intercostal neuralgia and diabetes—a bad case—I couldn't acknowledge your

gift. I do so now. I may go to London in June, but, frankly, I care less for travel than I did. *J'ai mes soixante ans!* I'm doing Henry James' letters for the May *Bookman;* also the hideous musical season for the July *Century*. But I'm ill for the first time in precisely 50 years.

Cordially,

James Huneker.

XII

To Horace B. Liveright.[11]

Brooklyn, September 2, 1920.

My dear Liveright: When the expurgated volume publicly appears I shall use my original title, "Istar, Daughter of Sin". But for this forthcoming private edition I don't like "The Seven Veils", for, apart from the fact that it is not new, being used everywhere from ballet to opera, from book titles to vaudeville, I think it flat, commonplace, and not sufficiently arresting. Nor is it pertinent to the contents of the book. "The Seven Gates" would be closer, but that, too, is not eye-catching. Let me propose something far more striking and dramatic, *i.e.*, "The Seven Deadly Sins" . . . The money can be paid in two instalments, but really I think you might bring out 1500 copies easily.

As ever,

James Huneker.

XIII

To Horace B. Liveright.

Brooklyn, November 23, 1920.

Dear Liveright: I hear indirectly from London that "Painted Veils" is soon to be published there. Is this true? If it be—and I hope it is—I wish to suggest three typographical changes in the sheets. Last line, page 186, a bad "p", not to be found in the corrected proof. On page 272, seventh line from bottom of page, there is "or" instead of "nor"—not much of an error, but it should be corrected. The most annoying break is on the last page of the book, second line from last. "Lamp" should read "map". This is all the more an eyesore be-

---

[10] The well-known novelist.

[11] Managing partner of Boni & Liveright.

cause it makes nonsense of the sentence and also because I must have passed it. Don't forget that I am to get 12 free copies—don't send me signed ones—and that, for my bother in signing the sheets, you promised to mail free for me a half dozen extra copies, to Arnold Bennett, Joseph Conrad, Havelock Ellis, George Moore and Edgar Saltus. And how about that check, for I presume the book has been over-subscribed? Can't you send the entire amount in one check? Then we could talk over another book I have in mind.

Cordially,
James Huneker.

XIV

To Mme. Frida Ashforth.

Brooklyn, September 22, 1920.

My dear Frida: Your letter found me at my desk correcting the final proofs of "Painted Veils", in which you figure as Frida Ash. Liveright, with whom I made a fairly good contract—I'm not giving away my books; I can't afford it—told me he recognized the portrait at once. You go straight through the story. Its merits, if any, are its frankness and character dissection. Naturally, you will get a complimentary copy from me. The book is expensive —at least $10. Later it will fetch bigger prices, but neither Liveright nor I will benefit; there are only 1200 numbered and signed copies; another *de luxe*. If you show the enclosed circular to any of your friends, as you so kindly suggested, tell them that the book is not to be advertised, nor, indeed, talked about. For you, unprejudiced and acquainted with good French and German literature, the story will not offend. It is not a smutty story. It's truthful. The New York, artistic and Bohemian, of 1895-1905, is the theme. The old Felix Hotel where I lived, in West Twenty-fifth street; your music-room in Eighteenth street— these old landmarks are described. But it is the characterization that will, I hope, interest you.

As ever,
Jim.

XV

To Horace B. Liveright.

Brooklyn, December 3, 1920.

Dear H. B.: Only this, Friday, morning I opened the "Painted Veils" package which came last night and saw the book. It is truly a stunning volume and I'm all het up at the thought of such a beautiful garb. Altogether the goose hangs high. I sent a circular to my old friend, Senator Henry Cabot Lodge, this morning. If he should subscribe, try to dig him up a volume some place: he is an epicure of literature.

Sincerely,
James Huneker.

XVI

To H. B. Fuller.

Brooklyn, December 19, 1920.

My dear Mr. Fuller: I can't help telling you that, after "The Chevalier", which was a marking-stone in my development, nothing you have written has so stirred me as "Bertram Cope's Year". I've read it three times, the last in London during a rainy spell last July. Its portraiture and psychological strokes fill me with envy and also joy. *Ça y est!* And Chicago! It is as desolate, your dissection, as a lunar landscape. We are like that, not like Whitman's camarados and his joyful junk. Why do you speak of your last book? You are only beginning, you implacable Stendhal of the lake! My first novel, written in my sixtieth year, is a fragment: if I had a copy I'd send it to you. But you won't like it. It's too bitter, and cynicism is always unreal. I had to get it off my chest. The book is privately printed at a prohibitive price and sold like the first oysters of the season. Its title is "Painted Veils".

In all friendship,
I am yours,
James Huneker.

EDITORIAL

THE AIM of THE AMERICAN MERCURY is precisely that of every other monthly review the world has ever seen: to ascertain and tell the truth. So far, nothing new. But the Editors cherish the hope that it may be possible, after all, to introduce some element of novelty into the execution of an enterprise so old, and upon that hope they found the magazine. It comes into being with at least one advantage over all its predecessors in the field of public affairs: it is entirely devoid of messianic passion. The Editors have heard no Voice from the burning bush. They will not cry up and offer for sale any sovereign balm, whether political, economic or aesthetic, for all the sorrows of the world. The fact is, indeed, that they doubt that any such sovereign balm exists, or that it will ever exist hereafter. The world, as they see it, is down with at least a score of painful diseases, all of them chronic and incurable; nevertheless, they cling to the notion that human existence remains predominantly charming. Especially is it charming in this unparalleled Republic of the West, where men are earnest and women are intelligent, and all the historic virtues of Christendom are now concentrated. The Editors propose, before jurisprudence develops to the point of prohibiting skepticism altogether, to give a realistic consideration to certain of these virtues, and to try to save what is exhilarating in them, even when all that is divine must be abandoned. They engage to undertake the business in a polished and aseptic manner, without indignation on the one hand and without too much regard for tender feelings on the other. They have no set program, either destructive or constructive. Sufficient unto each day will be the performance thereof.

As has been hinted, the Editors are not fond enough to believe in their own varieties of truth too violently, or to assume that the truth is ascertainable in all cases, or even in most cases. If they are convinced of anything beyond peradventure, it is, indeed, that many of the great problems of man, and particularly of man as a member of society, are intrinsically insoluble—that insolubility is as much a part of their essence as it is of the essence of squaring the circle. But demonstrating this insolubility thus takes on something of the quality of establishing a truth, and even merely arguing it gathers a sort of austere virtue. For human progress is achieved, it must be manifest, not by wasting effort upon hopeless and exhausting enigmas, but by concentrating effort upon inquiries that are within the poor talents of man. In the field of politics, for example, utopianism is not only useless; it is also dangerous, for it centers attention upon what ought to be at the expense of what might be. Yet in the United States politics remains mainly utopian—an inheritance, no doubt, from the gabby, gaudy days of the Revolution. The ideal realm imagined by an A. Mitchell Palmer, a King Kleagle of the Ku Klux Klan or a Grand Inquisitor of the Anti-Saloon League, with all human curiosity and enterprise brought down to a simple passion for the goose-step, is as idiotically utopian as the ideal of an Alcott, a Marx or a Bryan. THE AMERICAN MERCURY will devote itself pleasantly to exposing the nonsensicality of all such hallucinations, particularly when they show a certain apparent plausibility. Its own pet hallucination will take the form of an hypothesis that the progress of knowledge is less a matter of accumulating facts than a matter of destroying "facts". It will assume constantly that the more ignorant a man is the more he knows, positively and indignantly. Among the great leeches and barber-surgeons who profess to medicate the body politic, it will give its suffrage to those who admit frankly that all the basic diseases are beyond cure, and who consecrate themselves to making the patient as comfortable as possible.

In some of the preliminary notices of THE AMERICAN MERCURY, kindly published in the newspapers, apprehension has been expressed that the Editors are what is called Radicals, *i.e.*, that they harbor designs upon the Republic, and are bound by a secret oath to put down 100% Americanism. The notion is herewith denounced. Neither is a Radical, or the son of a Radical, or, indeed, the friend of any known Radical. Both view the capitalistic system, if not exactly amorously, then at all events politely. The Radical proposals to destroy it at one blow seem to them to be as full of folly as the Liberal proposals to denaturize it by arousing its better nature. They believe that it is destined to endure in the United States, perhaps long after it has broken up everywhere else, if only because the illusion that any bright boy can make himself a part of it remains a cardinal article of the American national religion— and no sentient man will ever confess himself doomed to life imprisonment in the proletariat so long as the slightest hope remains, in fact or in fancy, of getting out of it. Thus class consciousness is not one of our national diseases; we suffer, indeed, from its opposite—the delusion that class barriers are not real. That delusion reveals itself in many forms, some of them as beautiful as a glass eye. One is the Liberal doctrine that a prairie demagogue promoted to the United States Senate will instantly show all the sagacity of a Metternich and all the high rectitude of a Pierre Bayard. Another is the doctrine that a moron run through a university and decorated with a Ph.D. will cease thereby to be a moron. Another is the doctrine that J. P. Morgan's press-agents and dish-washers make competent Cabinet Ministers and Ambassadors. Yet another, a step further, is the doctrine that the interests of capital and labor are identical—which is to say, that the interests of landlord and tenant, hangman and condemned, cat and rat are identical. Such notions, alas, seem to permeate all American thinking, the shallowness of which has been frequently remarked by foreign observers, particularly in the Motherland. It will be an agreeable duty to track down some of the worst nonsense prevailing and to do execution upon it—not indignantly, of course, but nevertheless with a sufficient play of malice to give the business a Christian and philanthropic air.

II

That air, of course, will be largely deceptive, as it always is. For the second time the nobility and gentry are cautioned that they are here in the presence of no band of passionate altruists, consecrated to Service as, in the late Mr. Harding's poignant phrase, "the supreme commitment". The Editors are committed to nothing save this: to keep to common sense as fast as they can, to belabor sham as agreeably as possible, to give a civilized entertainment. The reader they have in their eye, whose prejudices they share and whose woes they hope to soothe, is what William Graham Sumner called the Forgotten Man—that is, the normal, educated, well-disposed, unfrenzied, enlightened citizen of the middle minority. This man, as everyone knows, is fast losing all the rights that he once had, at least in theory, under American law. On the one hand he is beset by a vast mass of oppressive legislation issuing from the nether rabble of cowherds, lodge-joiners and Methodists, with Prohibition as its typical masterpiece. And on the other hand he is beset by increasing invasions of his freedom of opinion, the product of craven nightmares among the usurers, exploiters and other rogues who own and try to run the Republic. If, desiring to entertain a guest in the manner universal among civilized men, he procures a bottle or two of harmless wine, he runs a risk of being dragged to jail by official blackmailers and fined and lectured by some political hack in the robes of a Federal judge. And if, disgusted by the sordid tyranny and dishonesty of the government he suffers under, he denounces it righteously and demands a return to the Bill of Rights, he runs a grave risk of being posted as a paid agent of the Bolsheviki.

This Forgotten Man, when he is recalled at all, is thus recalled only to be placarded as infamous. The normal agencies for relieving pyschic distress all pass him over. The Liberals have no comfort for him because he refuses to believe in their endless series of infallible elixirs; most of these very elixirs, in fact, only help to multiply his difficulties. And the Tories who perform in the great daily newspapers and in the Rotary Club weeklies and in the reviews of high tone—these prophets of normalcy can see in his discontent nothing save subversion and worse. There is no middle ground of consolation for men who believe neither in the Socialist fol-de-rol nor in the principal enemies of the Socialist fol-de-rol—and yet it must be obvious that such men constitute the most intelligent and valuable body of citizens that the nation can boast. The leading men of science and learning are in it. The best artists, in all the arts, are in it. Such men of business as have got any imagination are in it. It will be the design of THE AMERICAN MERCURY to bring, if not alleviation of their lot, then at least some solace to these outcasts of democracy. That they will ever actually escape from the morass in which they now wander so disconsolately is probably too much to hope. But at all events there is some chance of entertaining them to their taste while they flounder.

III

In the field of the fine arts THE AMERICAN MERCURY will pursue the course that the Editors have followed for fifteen years past in another place. They are asking various other critics to share their work and they will thus be able to cover a wider area than heretofore, but they will not deviate from their old program—to welcome sound and honest work, whatever its form or lack of form, and to carry on steady artillery practise against every variety of artistic pedant and mountebank. They belong to no coterie and have no aesthetic theory to propagate. They do not believe that a work of art has any purpose beyond that of being charming and stimulating, and they do not believe that there is much difficulty, taking one day with another, about distinguishing clearly between the good and the not good. It is only when theories begin to enter into the matter that counsels are corrupted—and between the transcendental, gibberishy theory of a Greenwich Village aesthete and the harsh, moral, patriotic theory of a university pedagogue there is not much to choose. Good work is always done in the middle ground, between the theories. That middle ground now lies wide open: the young American artist is quite as free as he needs to be. The Editors do not believe that he is helped by nursing and coddling him. If the obscure, inner necessity which moves him is not powerful enough to make him function unassisted, then it is not powerful enough to make a genuine artist of him. All he deserves to have is aid against the obscurantists who occasionally beset him—men whose interest in the fine arts, by some occult Freudian means, seems to be grounded upon an implacable hatred of everything that is free, and honest, and beautiful. It will be a pleasure to pursue such obscurantists to their fastnesses, and to work the *lex talionis* upon them. The business is amusing and now and then it may achieve some by-product of good.

The probable general contents of the magazine are indicated by this first number, but there will be no rigid formula, and a number of changes and improvements, indeed, are already in contemplation. In the department of *belles lettres* an effort will be made to publish one or two short stories in each issue, such occasional short plays as will merit print, some verse (but not much), and maybe a few other things, lying outside the categories. The essays and articles, it is hoped, will cover a wide range; no subject likely to be of interest to the sort of reader before described will be avoided, nor will there be any limitation upon the free play of opinion, so long as it is neither doctrinaire nor sentimental. To the departments already set up others may be added later on, but this is a matter that will have to determine itself. The Editors will welcome communications from readers, and those that seem to be of general interest will be printed, perhaps with editorial glosses. No effort will be made in the book reviews to cover all the multitude of books that come from the publishers every month. The reviews will deal only with such books as happen to attract the staff of reviewers, either by their virtues or by their defects. The dramatic reviews will, however, cover the entire range of the New York theatre.

In general THE AMERICAN MERCURY will live up to the adjective in its name. It will lay chief stress at all times upon American ideas, American problems and American personalities because it assumes that nine-tenths of its readers will be Americans and that they will be more interested in their own country than in any other. A number of excellent magazines are already devoted to making known the notions of the major and minor seers of Europe; at least half a dozen specialize in the ideas emanating from England alone. This leaves the United States rather neglected. It is, as the judicious have frequently observed, an immense country, and full of people. These people entertain themselves with a vast number of ideas and enterprises, many of them of an unprecedented and astounding nature. There are more political theories on tap in the Republic than anywhere else on earth, and more doctrines in aesthetics, and more religions, and more other schemes for regimenting, harrowing and saving human beings. Our annual production of messiahs is greater than that of all Asia. A single session of Congress produces more utopian legislation than Europe has seen since the first meeting of the English Witenagemot. To explore this great complex of inspirations, to isolate the individual prophets from the herd and examine their proposals, to follow the ponderous revolutions of the mass mind—in brief, to attempt a realistic presentation of the whole gaudy, gorgeous American scene—this will be the principal enterprise of THE AMERICAN MERCURY.

THE DROOL METHOD IN HISTORY

BY HARRY E. BARNES

THE GENERAL tendency of the human race to stampede when confronted by the truth is nowhere more evident than in its reaction to history. As it says in the preface to Anatole France's "Penguin Island," "if you have any new insight, any original idea, if you present men and affairs under an unwonted aspect, you will surprise the reader. And the reader does not want to be surprised. He seeks in a history only the stupidities with which he is familiar." In the recent and still continuing war of the accountants, plumbers, druggists, blacksmiths and lawyers who constitute our school committees upon feeble and helpless historians who have been making some faint beginnings in the way of telling some small fraction of the truth with respect to our national development, this attitude has been frankly avowed.

In a recent number of the *American Historical Review* Dr. J. F. Jameson introduces his readers to a "pure history law" passed in the most progressive State in the Union—Wisconsin—which thus encourages fearless candor on the part of textbook writers:

No history or other textbook shall be adopted for use or be used in any district school, city school, vocational school, or high school which falsifies the facts regarding the War of Independence, or the War of 1812, or defames our nation's founders or misrepresents the ideals and causes for which they struggled and sacrificed, or which contains propaganda favorable to any foreign government.

The law further provides that the State superintendent of education must hold a hearing when any five citizens complain that a book does not, for example, make it clear that the Irish volunteers won the Battle of Bunker Hill, or fails to emphasize properly that the Loyalists in the Revolution were a gang of degenerate drunkards and perverts, or mentions the smuggling proclivities or land piracy of the Fathers, or refers to the fraudulent sale of United States citizenship papers preceding the War of 1812, or suggests that there has ever been a civilized German. If, with an eye to his political future, the superintendent rules the book unfit for exhibition to the young morons whose parents have thus manifested their righteous indignation, it is to be withdrawn immediately from every school in the State under penalty of the forfeiture of all pecuniary aid to the offending district.

The Drool Method in history thus becomes official, and as State after State follows the example of Wisconsin it will become necessary for every professional historian to study and master its technique. What are its essentials? They may be stated briefly and certainly. First, every orthodox American history book must start off with Gobineau's dogma of the superiority of the Aryans, the sole builders of civilization, and then show how all able-bodied and 100% Americans are members of the noblest of all the Aryan tribes: the Anglo-Saxon sub-division of the great Nordic Blond people. The colonial period must then be expounded in such manner as to make plain the fact that a spiritual urge to complete religious and political liberty was the sole cause of our ancestor's embarking upon the wintry seas; no hint may be given of sordid economic motives, nor any suspicion aroused of any failure to set up and foster that liberty to the full. It

31

must not be said, directly or indirectly, that by 1787 more than half of the inhabitants of one of the most populous colonies were descended from redemptioners and indentured servants, or that there was a large admixture of criminals in all our Nordic ancestry. But it must be made clear that all the French and Indian wars in the colonial period were won solely by the colonists, with no help from England.

In treating the Revolution it must be interpreted as a determined effort of all Englishmen to back their German king in the effort to exterminate the liberty-loving Americans, who were united as a man in the disinterested effort to repel foreign tyranny and secure for the world at large the blessings of freedom. Drawing and quartering would be inadequate punishment for the historian who dared to utter the falsehood that New Englanders were addicted to smuggling, or the landlords and frontiersmen to envying and lusting after the land west of the Alleghenies. Only punishments not permissible to name in print will suffice for the pedagogue so depraved as to suggest that the Loyalists were about as numerous as the Patriots and really constituted the intellectual and social aristocracy of the colonial age—before whom the Patriot leaders had been only too willing to scuff and bow a few years earlier. Blasphemy laws may be appropriately invoked against those who have the shameless audacity to aver that George III was eager to conciliate the colonists and not to conquer them, and that his commander-in-chief in America was as appropriately appointed as though Mr. Wilson had selected the Great Commoner from Lincoln, or Eugene Debs, to lead our troops overseas in 1917.

Space does not permit bringing this syllabus of "proper" American history down to the present time, but many additional articles will suggest themselves to the judicious reader. For example, it will be apparent that no discreet historian will think for a moment of mentioning the gigantic land steals synchronous with the establishment of national independence and unity, of inquiring just how George Washington had millions thrust upon him in moments of absentmindedness, so that he died the richest man in the country, or of questioning the unswerving loyalty of Timothy Pickering, the calm analytical powers of Andrew Jackson, the dignified bearing and incorruptible character of Ben Butler, the aristocratic leanings and other worldly detachment of Abraham Lincoln, the wise and statesmanlike tolerance of Thad Stevens, or the political subtlety and acumen of General Grant. John Brown's distinguished achievements as a horse-thief may be adduced only as a proof of his need of ever swifter steeds to carry him forward in the Lord's work. And, of course, an attractive daily chant will have to be provided on the basic *motif* of Gladstone's revelation that the American Constitution "is the most wonderful work ever struck off at a given time by the brain and purpose of man."

As to the choice of subject matter, the Drool Method will recommend undivided concentration on the more gentlemanly and heroic activities—the diverse major and minor slaughters in our national history, the escapades and intrigues of diplomats, and the quadrennial political buffooneries by which one batch of grafters and incompetents is replaced by another. The achievements of "great" men will be described at length, but it must be borne in mind that true greatness is a quality possessed alone by generals, diplomats and politicians. Only a pensioner of George V will ever suggest that Franklin was greater as a scientist than as a diplomat; no one but a snivelling subaltern of Ludendorf will hold Eli Whitney to be more important in his country's history than General Gates, and no more certain proof of the receipt of a weekly check from Moscow will ever be found than a hint that Cyrus McCormick or William Kelly ought to rank higher in American annals than William H. Marcy or Winfield Scott. The history of ideas, opinions and institutions is especially to be eschewed, for the cultivation of this field may well lead to the conviction that the majority of our conventional views and custom-bound institutions are about as anachronistic as the spinning-wheel. Texts which introduce the student to such incendiary notions will be burned with formal ceremony. Above all, the historian must be impressed with his duty to prove the American race, language, culture and institutions superior to all other examples of God's creative ingenuity.

Those who thus follow piously the precepts of the Drool Method may not achieve success in certain university history departments, some of which are already honeycombed with anarchists, communists, renegades and traitors, but they will develop great popularity with the alumni and will be highly esteemed in the public school systems, approvingly decorated by superintendents, commended by state departments of education, invited to address the most diverse organizations on Washington's birthday and the Fourth of July, and given an opportunity to syndicate articles on cosmic philosophy, universal history and contemporary politics in the daily press.

II

In their palmiest days neither Kid Lavigne nor Tommy Ryan possessed any approximation to the shiftiness and elusiveness of truth as she is wooed by the historian. He begins his attempt at seduction with the handicap of two millstones about his neck. He is himself a frail product of clay, with his own complexes, restrictions, biasses and prejudices derived from his Baptist, Republican, Nordic, Confucian, single-tax, protective tariff, Pennsylvanian or Texan heritage, and his most painful effort to achieve impartiality can do little more than suspend momentarily and partially the operation of the more flagrant of them. Worse, even, than these personal defects is the fact he can rarely gather his data by direct observation, but has to rely for

them upon the accounts and interpretations of a yet more notorious group of liars and distorters than he is himself. Religious bias, for example, has been steadily debasing history from the days when the Assyrian monarchs praised God that He had made it possible for them to serve Him by assembling pyramids of the heads of their rivals. It is difficult for a youthful Protestant to comprehend that a Catholic playmate can actually be a member of the same biologic species, even though the young papist apparently can swear, swim and steal apples with almost Protestant zeal and efficiency. But even his parents, if they were pressed for their reasons for holding the Catholic inferior, would be hard put to it for anything beyond some vague innuendo concerning certain idolatrous Catholic practices and a disloyal acquiescence in papal suzerainty. But both Catholic and Protestant are willing to unite in a pogrom against the Jews, from whom they both received a vast majority of their religious practices and beliefs, bigotry and illusions. And Catholic, Protestant and Jew will, when occasion arises, lock arms in a savage onslaught on Mohammedans, Buddhists and free-thinkers.

Another prejudice distorting the vision of the historian is that growing out of the alleged racial monopoly of superior capacities. As a matter of truth, it can scarcely be shown that, even as between the three major races, there is any proof of comprehensive superiority. Racial superiority or inferiority is as yet as undemonstrable as hellfire or the immortality of the soul. The Chinese had a genial and urbane civilization of respectable antiquity when our Nordic ancestors were drinking the blood of their enemies out of human skulls, and the Negro exhibits a marked superiority over the white race in meeting the requirements of the environment in which he was differentiated and to which he is adjusted. But this is the least of our troubles with racial mythology; we are asked, by various chauvinists, to believe that only the Nordic, the Celt, the Slav or the Iberic type within the white race is capable of civilization. The most offensive nonsense that has been recently loosed in this field is that in Madison Grant's "Passing of a Great Race." This book, consciously or unconsciously but a literary rehash of Gobineau and Houston Stewart Chamberlain, is in its implications as flagrant a blast of *Deutschland über Alles* as ever was issued from Potsdam, and might have led to the deportation of its author if he had been an East Side Jewish Socialist instead of a rich New York lawyer. Progressively debased, this doctrine has been widely disseminated by Lothrop Stoddard, Clinton S. Burr, Charles W. Gould and others, until now we are asked by one Eckenrode to interpret the American Civil War as a struggle between the degenerate commercial Nordics of the North, and the haughty tropical Nordics south of Mason and Dixon's line. The preposterous absurdities of this racial doctrine ought to be apparent to anyone with no more historical knowledge than is normally possessed by the inspector of historical studies in a state education department. The plain facts of history are that the Nordics in relative purity have never built up a single high civilization, save in Scandinavia, in modern times,—and this civilization, singularly enough, Mr. Grant repudiates. They seem, in general, to have been gifted in war and physical prowess, but, whatever their innate intellectual and cultural capacity, they have thus far fallen short of the cultural achievements of the Celtic and Mediterranean types. All of the great historic civilizations down to those of western Europe in modern times were, without exception, non-Nordic in their physical basis.

The worthless nature of this Nordic garbage becomes even more apparent when one critically examines the attempt to expound national culture on the basis of race. Granting, for the sake of argument, that France, for example, has produced the highest civilization in the history of mankind, shall we interpret this as due to the Nordics of the Northeast, the Celts of the central plain and the Northwest, the Mediterraneans of the South, or the more numerous mongrels who are a mixture in varying degrees of all these types? The most regrettable aspect of this comedy of errors is that its absurdities have tended to obscure or discredit the real significance of biological factors in history. The important element is not the indeterminate, and perhaps non-existent, difference in capacity between separate races or sub-races, but the very real and demonstrable difference in capacity between members of the same race. If it cannot be shown that the evolution of culture has been due to Nordic impulses, it can at least be demonstrated that all civilization has been the product of the labors of an able minority. As Professor Thorndike has phrased it, "the ability of a hundred of its most gifted representatives often accounts more for a nation's or race's welfare than the ability of a million of its mediocrities." The biological key to history, then, is to be found along the path pointed out by Galton, Carr-Saunders, Schallmayer and Pearson rather than in the illusory labyrinth suggested by Gobineau, Edmond Demolins, Madison Grant and William McDougall.

Nationalism and patriotism are sentiments not less barbarous and uncivilized than racial egotism and arrogance, to which they are so closely, if fallaciously, allied. To be sure, if one defines patriotism as the sense of civic obligation, as was done by the philosophers of classical antiquity, and by German idealism, then we may frankly admit that it is one of the highest and noblest of human emotions. But we are not concerned with that here, for what passes for patriotism with the vast majority of the population of modern states is no such lofty sentiment, but that essentially savage type of attitude and behavior, the contemporary American manifestation of which is popularly known as hundred percentism. The tribal hunting-pack ferocity towards strangers endured but little diluted among the great masses of mankind down to the middle of the Eighteenth Century. The modern methods of swift communication were suddenly foisted upon these barbarians, and now a hundred millions who still retain almost unimpaired the psychological attitude of the Todas or Bantus are able simultaneously to open their daily papers and learn that the American consul in Timbuctoo has been foully slain by a native official, and to be moved with almost perfect synchronism to the demand that our country's honor be summarily avenged by the invasion of this dastardly land and the putting of all its inhabitants to the sword. To give complete cultural and pyschological harmony and symmetry to the breakfast table equipment of the average patriot of this variety we should add to his coffee, rolls, shredded-wheat and morning paper a tomahawk and a scalping knife.

The manner in which this mob influence affects historical writing is easy to understand. The most scholarly historian, like all of us, is something of a group-conditioned savage himself, even in times of peace, and may be entirely so in times of war, as was evidenced by the words and behavior of many American historians in 1917-19. As if his own weakness were not enough, the mob camps on his trail, seats itself resolutely on the library steps awaiting his exit, and clamors for his head if he has the courage and honesty to exhibit candor in his utilization of the sources of information at his disposal—which are themselves likely to be very largely the product of an earlier barbaric interpretation of the relations between states. While there are in some cases relatively good approximations, it may be safely said that there is not in existence a single complete and impartial history of the foreign relations of any modern state. But suppose there were? The lust of the herd would still be for what it desires to believe—what it likes to think is true.

This is exemplified by the ideas yet prevailing in the United States about the origins of the World War. Due to revo-

lutionary overturns in several of the major states which were at war, particularly Russia, Austria and Germany, the activities of the various politicians and diplomats from 1908 to 1914 have been revealed to their own generation—something hitherto unique in the history of war and diplomacy. These newly opened archives have not lessened our contempt for the Austrian and German militarists but they have completely upset all of the mythology upon which the Allies and Wilson built their high sounding appeals to the idealism of the world. Not only is this material available in great collections of documents, such as those by Pibram, Kautsky, Gooss, Siebert, Marchand and Baker, most of them translated into English, but it has been analyzed, sifted and clearly condensed by Mr. Nock and by Professors Pevet, Fay, Gooch and Beard. Nevertheless, it has not affected by an iota the thinking of the French, English and American people. Not only have all the criminals who brought on the war escaped the gallows, in spite of the fact of their perfectly demonstrable guilt, but Poincaré, probably the most culpable of the lot, has been allowed to do nearly as much injury to Europe in the last two years as was caused by the war itself.

III

Not less foolish, but also not less human and natural than these religious, racial and patriotic prejudices is the myopia due to partisan affiliations and obsessions. As is well stated in a paragraph cited by Professor Schlesinger from the London *Chronicle* of over a century and a half ago: "Party is a fever that robs the wretch under its influence of common sense, common decency, and sometimes of common honesty; it subjects reason to the caprice of fancy and misrepresents objects; . . . we blame and pity bigotry and enthusiasm in religion, . . . but are party principles less reprehensible, that, in a worse cause, are apt to intoxicate and disorder the brain, and pervert the understanding?'' Since classical days republican and imperial historian, supporter of pope and emperor, protagonist of Whig and Tory have slanderously assaulted the persons, deeds, motives and policies of their opponents and cried up their own brands of thievery and imbecility. Partisan zeal has corrupted the history of our own country from Colonial days. An almost Persian cosmic dualism appears in the strictures of John Church Hamilton on Jefferson and his party, while in Randall's apology Jefferson appears as in daily communion with the Almighty. The following comment of Theodore Dwight, an eminent publicist of the Jeffersonian period, upon the objects of the followers of the Sage of Monticello reminds one of some of the hysterics of the Lusk Report dealing with the fatal and dastardly menace of Bolshevism. The Jeffersonians, he contended, ''aim to destroy every trace of civilization in the world, and force mankind back into a savage state. . . . We have a country governed by blockheads and knaves; the ties of marriage with all its felicities are severed and destroyed; our wives are cast into the stews; our children are cast into the world from the breast and are forgotten . . . Can the imagination paint anything more dreadful this side of hell?'' Yet it was little more than a decade later when George Bancroft pronounced his eulogy upon Jeffersonian democracy and prepared the way for the egalitarian orgy of Jacksonianism by declaring that ''the popular voice is all powerful with us; this is our oracle; this, we acknowledge, is the voice of God.'' And again, ''true political science venerates the masses. Listen reverently to the voice of lowly humanity!'' This sort of burlesque and buffoonery has continued in the interpretation of American party history through the Abolitionist-Slavery controversy, the Civil War and Reconstruction, to Bryan and our own day.

It may, of course, be conceded that James Ford Rhodes and Professor Dunning long ago eliminated much of the diabolism and eschatology from the history of the Civil War and Reconstruction periods, and that Professor Hart has gathered a group of scholars who have told the whole story of American political life with reasonable freedom from partisan distortion, but the majority of American citizens still view their party opponents and their past in the temper of Dwight and of the editorials of the New York *Tribune* on Bryan and Cox. The writer remembers that as an exuberant youthful Republican he was perplexed by the possession of an unusually talented, urbane and genial relative who had, by the viscissitudes of conjugal mesalliance, been born under the astral auspices and party crest of the donkey. He impressed me as possessing most of the physical stigmata of *Homo sapiens*, but it was apparent by definition that he thereby presented but a biological illusion.

Scarcely less disconcerting than partisan travesty is the interpretation of history in terms of the alliance of God with a particular economic class. From the time of Cato and the Gracchi we have had interpretations of history representing all culture and civilized decency as the sole product of the landlords, the *bourgeoisie* or the laborers. The landlords held sway until the Seventeenth Century, when the *bourgeois* epic began to make its appearance; it culminated in the dithyrambic pæns of Macaulay, Guizot, James Mill, Bright, Say, Bastiat and John Fiske. Then, beginning with Owen and Marx, we discover the appearance of the proletarian apology and the critique of capitalism, though the panegyrics and prostrations to *bourgeois* benevolence and omniscience have not ceased, as is evidenced by the rantings of Chancellor Day, Walker, Hillis, Eddy and Francis. The honest and fair-minded historian will find much to accept and more to reject in all of these warped claims for the possession of a monopoly on divine aid and wisdom. He will freely admit the remarkable contributions to culture and civilization made by the landlord, merchant and manufacturer, and will also accept much of the proletarian claim that without the lowly laborer the efforts of agrarian and town classes would have been futile and immaterial.

It is difficult to understand how either a capitalist or a Socialist can feel like showing his face again publicly after having read Marx's works—the capitalist from shame over the waste and cruelties which his system has perpetrated, and the Socialist from mortification over the naïveté and simple-mindedness of the Marxian proposals for a substitute. One point is, however, worth making here, inasmuch as it is rarely called to the attention of the contemporary reader of history, namely, that whereas we are adequately warned against the biasses of the socialistically inclined historians, we are never cautioned against those of the infinitely greater number of professional historians who assume that the capitalistic system is as permanent and faultless as the wisdom of God. No honest and educated person can maintain that we need less to be put on our guard in reading the last two volumes of Rhodes's "History of the United States" than in preparing for the perusal of Gustavus Myers' "History of the Great American Fortunes."

Another source of bitter discouragement to the optimists who expect an interest in truth on the part of the human race is the tendency of the intellect to collapse when confronted with an antique exhibit from the museum of the past follies of mankind. We tend immediately to lose our critical spirit and to fall into a reverential and credulous mood whenever we are asked to contemplate ancient myths and institutions, and we almost identify good and evil with the old and the new respectively. This tendency is probably in part a vestige of the primitive myth-making proclivity, the worship of ancestors and subservience to ancient tabooes. In part it may also be a neurotic flight from reality, seeking compensation for the inadequacy of the present in the illusion of a former golden age. This particular variety of human mental frailty

leads to what may be described as the spontaneous generation of the historical epic. An institution or practice which was originally approved and adopted only after a bitter struggle, and which at the time was admitted by its most ardent protagonists to be but a working approximation to adequacy, becomes after several generations a colossal product of collaboration between God and supermen. Likewise an ordinary mortal who may have attained to some position of importance through a lucky combination of fortunate ancestry and accident, and who exhibited during his lifetime every symptom of human weakness will, after a few generations, be erected into a giant of unimpeachable virtue and unparalleled omniscience. It is this fact of the impotence of our cerebration in the presence of the antique which, more than anything else, vindicates the Sneer Method, with all its admitted defects, as an infinitely more salutary and healthy approach to history than the attitude fostered by the Drool Method.

IV

The above observations, I hope, will make it reasonably clear that mankind in general, and even a majority of the teachers of history, still have little regard for the majesty of truth. Even those who have been able to emancipate themselves from the more vulgar types of national and racial prejudice are rarely able to keep an open mind on all subjects. An historian, for example, who can preserve a nice balance of impartiality in regard to the question of Celt versus Teuton in the Middle Ages or of Democrat versus Whig in later times may develop a moral fervor surpassing that of Tacitus when confronted with a case of sex dereliction. The writer once remembers sending a Freudian analysis of the character of Abraham Lincoln to a distinguished historian who had triumphed over both partisan and sectional bias. His enthusiasm for this document, based wholly upon repugnance to the sex issue involved, was comparable to that which might be exhibited by a Southern Baptist King Kleagle for a plate of Irish stew.

But the immunity of society from the ravages of truth is further safe-guarded by the obstacles interposed in the path of the rare bird who has a real urge to disseminate it and possesses enough intelligence to acquire some slight modicum of his stock in trade. He will be viewed with suspicion by trustees of colleges, denounced in the columns of newspapers, (which will also send his books for review to notoriously unfavorable critics), excluded from respectable periodicals, railed against by ministers of the gospel, ostracised from the favor of school committees who select textbooks, persecuted privately and publicly by innumerable hundred per cent organizations, and regarded as queer and unstable by his closest neighbors and intimate circle of friends. He may even be driven from the academic field into the professions of life insurance agent or plumber—which may at least enable him to acquire a competence and enjoy an old age of contemplative leisure. The intimidation of secondary school teachers to induce them to refrain from any ogling, to say nothing of wooing, of truth is even more direct and effective. But though we may well bewail the fate of the exceptional historian who meets disaster as a result of his professional candor, we are in danger of unnecessary and misplaced grief concerning the alleged "repression" of a vast host of teachers who, we tend to assume, would carry the flaming torch of truth with ecstatic enthusiasm but for their fear of dismissal. As a matter of fact, the majority of history teachers swallow with infinite gusto the great collection of buncombe which constitutes the mental and cultural equipment of the man in the street, assimilate readily what is true to what is "prop-er", and approve heartily the martyrdom of their few intelligent and courageous colleagues. Mr. Pierce has drawn the following admirable picture of the mental content and attitude of the majority of secondary school teachers, which would probably apply equally well to most of the teachers in the general run of colleges:

Knowing nothing thoroughly, unable to take pride in his skill or to feel a sense of mastery, the high school teacher cannot be a real scholar. He cannot achieve a critical intelligence. He thinks, as he teaches, without depth. One need never fear, when he is invited to meet a group of his colleagues socially that he will have to exert himself mentally. Nowhere on Main Street is a critical discussion or a serious conversation more taboo than among high school teachers. The weather, the children, a show, a concert, school politics and a few empty platitudes comprise our subjects of conversation. . . . Indeed, for intellectual stimulation, the last place to go is to a group of teachers. Discussions about capital and labor, foreign events, local civic affairs or even important movements in education itself, are limited to the barest and most elementary observations. If one were to mention Bryan and evolution, or the Rev. Dr. Grant and Bishop Manning, or the higher criticism, our confrères would stand aghast and the subject of conversation would be hastily changed. . . . In his social life the high school teacher has not emancipated himself from the *mores* of the small town. . . . Physicians, lawyers and engineers do not permit the most conservative elements to dictate their social life. Teachers do. They tamely submit when an ignorant village parson raves at dancing and the sin of an occasional game of bridge.

In the midst of His early enthusiasm Christ is said not only to have believed in the possible attainment of truth, but also that it would emancipate man from his fetters of superstition and bondage. At the close of His ministry, when He could boast of more contact with human material, He had become so disillusioned in this respect that He declined to accept the invitation of the representative of the majesty of the Roman Empire to open a discussion of the matter. Most thoughtful and seasoned historians can make a valid claim to an *imitatio Christi* in this respect, if in no other.

Mr. MOORE AND Mr. CHEW

BY SAMUEL C. CHEW

DRAMATIS PERSONÆ:

GEORGE MOORE.

SAMUEL C. CHEW, *an American.*

A MAID-SERVANT.

SCENE: *The dining-room at 121, Ebury Street, London, S.W.*

THE MAID. Mr. Chew.

MOORE. Oh, my dear Mr. Chew. I am so happy that you received my message and could come. I rather reproached myself for not asking you to dinner, for a friend sent me some grouse from the country; but afterwards I was glad you were not here, for the birds were dreadfully tough and doubtless you had a better dinner at your hotel. Come, sit here by the fireside; it is more comfortable than upstairs in the drawing-room; and Molly shall bring you a glass of port. Or would you prefer coffee?

CHEW. Port, please.

MOORE. But why haven't you brought Mrs. Chew with you?

CHEW. She was so very tired. We've been at South Kensington all the afternoon, and nothing is more exhausting than a museum, if one tries to observe the collections intelligently.

MOORE. And still more exhausting if one observes them unintelligently. I am distressed that your wife isn't with you. I fear you keep her too constantly in the galleries and museums. She seemed a bit weary when I met you the other day at the Tate.

CHEW. Perhaps it was the sight of the forlorn portraits of yourself and Mr. Hardy that wearied her there.

MOORE. Perhaps. The artist has a very genuine feeling for color, but the likeness is poor. The portrait by Mark Fisher hanging over there by the side-board is a better likeness. I do not remember the picture of Hardy. But really this visit is not complete without Mrs. Chew. She is a charming woman.

CHEW. She will be pleased when I tell her you have said so.

MOORE. There is one advantage in her absence, however. I have been reading the Conversation, the dialogue between you and me, which you brought me the other day. She might be hurt by what I feel I must say about it.

CHEW. I don't think so, for the fact is she didn't like the Conversation herself. She thought the descriptions of you which I introduced were not in the best taste.

MOORE. Well, to tell the truth, I was somewhat puzzled by your comparison of me to somebody's picture of the White Knight; and I suppose no man would really relish the remark that he was "just a little pathetic, here in his prim little house by himself." But never mind the question of taste; I have not always spared the self-esteem of my own subjects. But in a Conversation it is better to leave out description altogether or else to put your descriptions in the form of dialogue.

CHEW. You departed from that strict form in the dialogue with Mr. Husband which you have just published.

MOORE. True; but I think I was wrong.

CHEW. I think my Conversation would be considerably less interesting if I omitted

39

the descriptions of how your "gently waving hand traces unelaborate patterns in the air" as you talk, and of how when silence falls here by your fireside your expression becomes languid and your eyes, which, when you are talking, are so full of wit, become for the moment dull and overcast. And I should hate to cancel the passage about "the pleasant turn and fall of the silken snow-white hair."

MOORE. Yes, of course your readers will like such impressions of me, and I do not advise you to omit them altogether. But I feel strongly that it would be better to work them into your dialogue.

CHEW. Perhaps it would be better; at any rate I can try.

MOORE. However, there are far graver faults with your Conversation than the mere introduction of descriptive passages. You do not distinguish between art and reality. In life we talk of a dozen different things, but in art we talk of one thing, especially in a Conversation. In other words, we choose a subject.

CHEW. The old problem of unity of action, unity of impression! My intention was that beneath the diversity of subjects, as the talk flitted from one theme to another, there should be a unity. You were to provide the unity, for the Conversation was a portrait in miniature of you.

MOORE. That is not the function of a literary Conversation, except incidentally. You must choose a theme and then develop it.

CHEW. But why? It seems to me that you are setting up *a priori* rules as strict as those of the old French drama. Why can't there be a variety of forms of the literary Conversation?

MOORE. Possibly there can be; but at all events that is how I have composed my Conversations.

CHEW. You wouldn't have me write mere pastiche?

MOORE. I don't know that you could do anything better, to begin with.

CHEW. But—

MOORE. If you will listen I'll try to show you what I have in mind. If you had chosen the art of painting as your subject, you would have done well to talk to me about my experiences in the French studios, why I gave up painting, if I ever dabbled in it still. Modern painting would lead up to modern sculpture, and I should tell you stories of Rodin and should explain why I consider sculpture so inferior to painting.

CHEW. But—

MOORE. After this we should pass—but I need not develop that train of thought further. Let us take another theme. If, for example, you wished to write a Conversation with me about literature, you would have done well to contrive some carefully selected remarks that would fill a couple of pages and lead up gracefully to—shall we say Balzac? And then we would proceed to contrast Balzac with the Russian novelists.

CHEW. But—

MOORE. And that would lead naturally to English novels, and I should tell you what I thought of my prose narratives, and we would contrast them with other books. We would speak of your article on "Héloïse", and I should tell you more about "The Brook Kerith", and so forth.

CHEW. But, Mr. Moore—

MOORE. Just a moment. If you had chosen my relation to painting as your subject, you would, of course, have had to leave out Balzac and the Russian novelists, "Héloïse" and all the rest; and if you had chosen literature, you would have had to leave out Siegfried Wagner and a half a dozen other matters that have no connection with the art of prose narrative.

CHEW. But why may not one follow actuality closely enough to branch off at least occasionally, as in real life, from the chosen topic? That incident of Siegfried Wagner recognizing the piece of music as by Grandpapa Liszt is certainly amusing.

MOORE. Amusing, yes; but out of keeping, unless indeed you had chosen as a theme the influence that music has had upon my life.

CHEW. I can't help thinking that your rules are more rigid than your own practice. Take, for instance, the long account of "Les Arcanes de l'Amour" in "Avowals". What on earth has a description of that disreputable book to do with a Conversation on the English novel?

MOORE. That is episodic.

CHEW. I intended some of my incidents to be episodic. But where, by the way, did you come across "Les Arcanes de l'Amour"? An extraordinary book!

MOORE. I did not come across it; I invented it myself. There is no such book. What fun I had composing the French verses! I thought of several of the lines while riding on top of omnibuses. I chuckled so loudly over some of them that my fellow-passengers were alarmed for my sanity. There are some very clever elisions in those verses, and the caesura is managed very nicely. And the best of the joke is that I selected Gosse as my auditor for them—the prudish Gosse! Some people affect to be shocked at the introduction of such anecdotes into a serious criticism of literature. Fudge, my dear Mr. Chew, fudge! They give a relish to a book. I have no objection to your introducing some such episode into your dialogue—that story I told you about the death of Watts-Dunton, for example. Why don't you bring that into the Conversation?

CHEW. I could hardly do that.

MOORE. Perhaps not. But to return to the dialogue you have written—

CHEW. It is good of you to take so much interest in it. Aren't you tired of talking of it?

MOORE. No; I am able to illustrate your faults by reference to my own successes. You will have to take your Conversation to pieces and do it again. You will have to rely upon your imagination for the dialogue, supplying me with words and yourself with words, and you'll have to develop your subjects. As it is, you do nothing, for example, with Mr. Hardy. You just make me shake my shoulders and say he is a very bad writer. There is nothing interesting in that. What I probably said was that Mr. Hardy's novels were merely melodramatic stories, ill-constructed and ill-written. But even if you had quoted my very words, they would have been insufficient; you would have had to develop the subject for yourself, and then develop an answer to it. You might make me outline to you the story of Lord Uplandtowers—an absurd name, an impossible name for a nobleman—in Hardy's "Group of Noble Dames". You remember: the husband defaces the bust of his wife's former lover so that it becomes the likeness of her lover after, instead of before, the accident that disfigured him for life. The wife finds the defaced portrait and shrieks and faints, and is a dutiful and loving wife to Lord Uplandtowers ever after. Sheer melodrama! And written in a style that is bog-water! Now, if you admire that story, which I hope you don't (though you have thought it worth your while to write a book about Mr. Hardy), you should put my outline into your Conversation and then, in reply, attempt to show me where I am wrong. When I was writing "Esther Waters" somebody told me that Hardy had just published a book on somewhat the same theme. I at once bought a copy of "Tess" and read it, and failed to find any reason why I should not continue my work on "Esther Waters". You might bring in that remark and develop a comparison between the two books. But I think it would be a mistake to devote much of the Conversation to Mr. Hardy. And remember: you must not rely too much upon your memory; you must create; memory plays us false. Let me cite a specific instance from the dialogue you gave me to read. Zola never said to me that he could tell by my eyes that I was a story-teller; there's no sense in such a remark. I was saying that I wrote with difficulty, and he said "Your eyes tell me that you write with difficulty". There's nothing in the remark; it isn't worth quoting; but if it has to be quoted it had better be quoted correctly.

CHEW. Well, evidently, as the caterpillar said, it's all wrong from beginning to end.

MOORE. I don't understand the reference to the caterpillar—but don't trouble to explain. Let me epitomize: you've not only not attempted to create, but you have not even selected; and as your very sincere friend I advise you to begin again, select a definite subject, and remain within it. To be still more frank: my own impression is that your talents lie in another direction. Why don't you write a book about your wanderings in Italy?

CHEW. There have been so many books written about wanderings in Italy. I could not hope to do anything that would compare with Symonds's "Sketches".

MOORE. Symonds—Oh yes, the consumptive literary critic. I do not know the "Sketches" you speak of.

CHEW. Well, you should read his essays on, say, Orvieto, or Girgenti.

MOORE. I have, as I've frequently remarked, lost the art of reading; and even if I had not, I do not think I should turn to Addington Symonds again. He is associated in my mind with despots and assassinations and Jesuits and Tasso; and what I remember of him struck me as being rather rococo in taste, like the plaster ceilings of some of his late Renaissance palaces.

CHEW. Then how about Vernon Lee? Certainly her "Genius Loci" is an extraordinary book—don't you think so? Its title is not empty of meaning nor a mere boast, for she conveys to her reader the very spirit of a place, its bygone traditions and bygone grandeur.

MOORE. I've really read very little of Vernon Lee. I've always understood that she was a sort of she-Pater of inferior taste and greatly reduced mentality.

CHEW. Em! A follower of Pater? You ought not to object to that.

MOORE. We cannot all follow Pater successfully.

CHEW. Then—to return to Italy—you think I have a free field? For I won't venture to ask your opinion of Grant Allen and Augustus Hare and Maurice Hewlett and Mr. Lucas.

MOORE. No, we need not speak of them. Yes, I think there is an opportunity to write about Italy.

CHEW. But would such a book meet with any success?

MOORE. You must not worry about that; if you are at all inclined to write about Italy you must go ahead and do so. Whether your book is successful or not is a very unimportant matter. Surely you have not been eight months in Italy without gathering impressions that you'd like to preserve. Were you ever there before?

CHEW. Yes, twice—long ago and again a few years before the War.

MOORE. Then you have an opportunity to compare the impressions received as a boy with those received as a young man and again with those of the last few months.

CHEW. But my memories of those earlier visits are very dim and vague.

MOORE. That is not a disadvantage, for memory should soften contours and blur outlines. The touch of sentiment is imparted by the very indistinctness, as in my—

CHEW. Then you would have me write a sort of new "Sentimental Journey" through Italy? Your remark about sentiment suggests an opening to me. What do you say to this opening?—"They order these things better in Italy, I thought, sipping Frascati as I sat in the *loggia* of the Cesare Restaurant and looked out towards the Palatine."

Moore. I don't say anything to it, Mr. Chew, for I do not understand. Your opening seems to be a sort of parody of Sterne.

Chew. So it is, and by "these things" I of course mean wines, and I should go on to compare those unfortunate fellow-countrymen of mine who stay at home and drink furtively the wretched substitutes that Prohibition has forced upon them with those other Americans who, like myself, are beyond the reach of the enforcement acts. There is no wine in the world more delicious than *Orvieto bianco* unless it be the divine *Mavrodaphne* one gets in Greece.

Moore. Let us talk of the comparative merits of Greek and Italian wines some other evening. I'd like to hear more about them, for I've always understood that the Greeks put resin in their wines.

Chew. Not in *Mavrodaphne*—

Moore. Never mind the Greek wines. We were talking of the opening of your book.

Chew. You don't approve of it?

Moore. No; it will not do to bring the question of Prohibition into your book. If the Americans find themselves mentioned on the first page they will expect to be discussed throughout the book and won't be content to read about Italy.

Chew. I had not thought of that. The idea of the opening sentence came to me on the spur of the moment.

Moore. It was obvious that you had not thought it out thoroughly. But you have not been married long. You must begin your book with the suggestion that you were tired of your old way of life, and marriage offered the opportunity for a change, and you said to your wife, "Come, let's see something of the world together." What a fortunate fellow you are to have a companion! Why, your travels in Italy and Greece have been a sort of honeymoon.

Chew. Pray don't call it a honeymoon! The word has disagreeable associations,

for only three days after we were married my wife fell desperately ill with influenza—it was in the winter of 1918—and nearly died. We had a dreadful time, for nurses were not to be had and doctors were terribly busy, and we were in a big New York hotel.

Moore. Why, my dear Mr. Chew, what better beginning could you possibly find? It's a far better one than I could invent for you. You simply must begin with that illness. Three days after marriage, you say? And you nearly lost her? That charming woman! To think you nearly lost her! What an admirable opening for a book!

Chew. It has possibilities for the literature of autobiographic reminiscence, hasn't it?

Moore. I'm afraid you are a little sly, Mr. Chew. But you are certainly lucky to have kept your delightful companion. Sometimes, when I go to visit friends out beyond the West End, where the air has a little of the freshness of the country, I almost come to think that I may have made a mistake, that marriage is best. I can even contemplate myself pushing a perambulator. No; I had no companion, and so I never visited Italy. To my mind Italy, companionless, would not be Italy.

Chew. But how strange, Mr. Moore—you who have ventured alone so much farther, all the way to Palestine!

Moore. Ah, but that was absolutely necessary in order that I might write "The Brook Kerith". I did not want to go; in fact I tried to write the book without going. But it simply would not do. I could not depend on other people's descriptions. People never describe the things one wants to know. In one chapter I found myself wondering whether a line of hills bounded the horizon when viewed from a certain point, and I could not discover if the hills were in sight from that point or no. Why, composition absolutely stopped. Again, I wanted to know the exact position of a particular well, and no book told me, and composition stopped. The whole thing was quite impossible. So I packed my bag and went to Palestine. No one was with me except my dragoman, and he was insufferable. I was horribly bored. But I attended strictly to business and made a quantity of notes and sketches, and came home. I hate travelling, especially by water. I am a good sailor, but I have had miserable experiences crossing the Channel. Oh, miserable experiences! Only last May I crossed in a terrible storm. I stayed on deck; below it was indescribable. All the stewards were busy, and a woman next to me was sick, Oh, very sick! I had to help her; in common decency I had to do what I could for her. The wind blew her skirts about, and she kept moaning "My legs! Cover my legs! Pull my dress down around my legs!" and I said "Never mind your legs, Madame; nobody is looking at your legs." It was a dreadful scene.

CHEW. It must have been.—But tell me: did you have as much anxiety about the background of "Héloïse and Abélard" as you did in the case of "The Brook Kerith"?

MOORE. No; for I know France, and I did not know Syria. The mere fact that I had to deal with the France of eight hundred years ago did not present any great difficulty, for the contours of a country remain from age to age the same, just as human nature does not change. Woodlands vanish, and the beauty of the countryside may be marred by modern buildings, and small holdings may take the place of the vast old common lands and great estates; but the essential features of undulating fields and winding rivers and enfolded hills do not change. Nor does human nature. It is with these essentials of character and environment that I have to do as a story-teller. Great harm was done to the art of prose narrative when writers began to concern themselves with what is called local color. I think it was Scott who first began to try to achieve what the critics call an "atmosphere" by delving into ancient documents and by inquiring into the mere ephemeral details of the past. You may expend infinite pains upon the exact pattern of a helmet or the precise fashion in which a lute was constructed, only to have some archaeologist confront you with documents proving that that particular kind of helmet had been discarded fifty years before your period, or that that sort of lute was not used till the following century. Human nature is such that the writer of the book flies into a rage and attempts to defend his antiquarian accuracy and his story is judged and pronounced a failure on quite other grounds than those on which it should be judged. Yes, Scott was much to blame.

CHEW. The quest of local color begins in France, I think, rather than England. Certainly it can be traced considerably farther back than Scott—to Fénelon, for example, or to the oriental tales which Galland's translation of "The Arabian Nights" brought into vogue, or to some of Voltaire's remarks about Shakespeare. As for Scott, his antiquarianism is neither very profound nor very accurate except when he depicts Scotland. There are glaring faults in "Ivanhoe", especially with regard to the relations between Normans and Saxons, a matter of great moment since the action of the story depends upon it. But "Quentin Durward" is an astonishing recreation of the past, for Scott had never visited the scenes which he describes and for the history and biography of the period was mainly dependent upon Philippe de Comines.

MOORE. Indeed! I had imagined that he delved very deeply into old records.

CHEW. Not so deeply as is often thought. But in any case the problem of local color came much to the fore about a century ago. You remember, no doubt, the wise remark of Stendhal on the subject.

MOORE. No, I do not. What is it?

CHEW. Let me see if I can quote it; let me see: "A serf's dress and brass collar"— yes: "L'habit et le collier de cuivre d'un serf du moyen age sont plus faciles à décrire que les mouvements d'un coeur humain."

MOORE. That is admirably said. It exactly sums up my own view of the matter.

CHEW. Nevertheless it was an achievement to describe such externalities so accurately and so vividly that they seemed to embody and symbolize the spirit of an epoch. Scott was especially successful in his descriptions of great edifices, and it was from him that Victor Hugo learned how to crystallize, as it were, an age in his picture of Notre Dame de Paris.

MOORE. Perhaps so. The inordinate emphasis upon local color was not reached till Flaubert.

CHEW. Yes; Flaubert certainly occupies a large chapter in the history of *couleur locale*.

MOORE. He read, I believe, two thousand books in preparation for "Salammbô". And the result—a stark magnificence, quite dead.

CHEW. Not quite. There are magnificent things in "Salammbô": the crucified lions and the Mercenaries starving in the valley and the scene on the Aqueduct.

MOORE. Such things count for very little. Flaubert was more interested in archaeological details than in human nature. He could describe a Carthaginian weapon, but he could not make Hamilcar and Salammbô live before us. You may remember that in "Avowals" (I think it is) I have said something about his inability to imagine conversation, an inability that grew more and more pronounced in his later years. It is specially evident in "Bouvard et Pécuchet". The ability to write natural dialogue is a test of the novelist. Jane Austen was as wonderful in this respect as in her knowledge of the heart. She had a complete mastery of patter. After

her I know of no such mastery until you come to my own books.

CHEW. How curious it is, Mr. Moore, that Flaubert should have prided himself upon the least essential part of his work. You remember, I suppose, the letters to Ste. Beuve and to some other critic whose name I have forgotten who had taken him to task about inaccuracies in his reconstruction of ancient Carthage —the water-supply, for example, and the ritual of Moloch. His letters triumphantly prove the accuracy of his knowledge.

MOORE. No, I do not remember the letters. Perhaps Flaubert would not have triumphed in a controversy which turned upon the truth of the characterization of his heroine. But I do not think I want to talk about Flaubert. Let us turn to other examples of the use of local color.

CHEW. I suppose you do not object to it in novelists of what is called the regionalist type—Miss Edgeworth, for instance, or John Galt, or Mrs. Gaskell.

MOORE. I have not looked into their books for years; Mrs. Gaskell is the most commonplace of writers.

CHEW. Well, how about Mr. Hardy? I know you do not admire his books; but surely you must admit the beauty of his Dorsetshire settings: the cidermakers and the heath-dwellers and the harvesters and the burning rick and shepherds returning at evening with—

MOORE. Yes; the shepherds returning at evening with crooks on their shoulders and their flocks following them and a full moon, three times too large, rising over their left shoulder! Barbizon school! A mere exaggeration of Troyon and Rousseau. That's a very good comparison; I must keep it in mind and make use of it in a Conversation some day.

CHEW. Really, you are scarcely fair to Mr. Hardy.

MOORE. Perhaps not. But I noticed that you yourself used the phrase "the beauty of his Dorsetshire settings". The explanation of Hardy's failures lies in that word "settings". He sets his stage. He is theatrical, melodramatic. And even if his local color be accurate, his pessimism is out of place in such surroundings. If we must have pessimism, let it be offered us in the golden vase of Ecclesiastes or Shakespeare, not served up in a pie-pot. An admirable phrase, that! I shall certainly introduce it into a Conversation on Mr. Hardy. Let me fix it in memory: If we must have pessimism, let it be offered us in the golden vase of Ecclesiastes or Shakespeare, not served up in a pie-pot.

CHEW. Surely you can't call "The Dynasts" a pie-pot!

MOORE. I have not read "The Dynasts". "Jude the Obscure" is certainly a pie-pot. Have I ever told you what Henry James said about that book? But I won't tell you now. I don't want to talk about Mr. Hardy. I want to point out to you that the little discovery I made in "The Brook Kerith" and in "Héloïse and Abélard" was anticipated by Shakespeare, who took it for granted that ancient stories were just as good as modern, as interesting in every way, on condition that the writer did not trouble the reader with archaeology, dress, furniture, and, above all, ancient modes of speech. But Shakespeare's admirable example was not followed and the lust for archaeology spoilt many good novels. I think I was the first since Shakespeare to discard archaeology, for in writing "Héloïse and Abélard" I thought only of a woman and a man, and became passionately interested in the story when I discovered that Abélard wrote songs in the popular idiom, was, in fact, a *trouvère*. This discovery provided me with a most entertaining means of escape from the tedium of theological controversy. If you ever expand your article on "Héloïse and Abélard", in order to include it in the volume of criticisms which I hope you are going to publish, I wish you would insist on this matter of archae-

ology. Pray wheedle my remarks into your text, if you care to do so.

CHEW. I shall certainly bear them in mind. What you have just been saying about the tedium of theological controversy suggests another phase of the interest aroused by "Héloïse and Abélard". You were concerned primarily with the love-story, and yet you have managed to give a vivid portrait of Abélard as a philosopher and theologian.

MOORE. True; but you must note how all that side of Abélard's character is pictured early in the book. I was keenly aware that when once the love-story was paramount it would be impossible to return to mere disputation. Even at the risk of wearying the reader I had to show Abélard in the lecture-room at once. Then that part of his character could be taken for granted later on, and when for long years he disappears from my story my readers would be able to picture to themselves his controversies with the church and his manner of conducting them.

CHEW. The parting of the lovers is of course the parting of the ways in your narrative. I have sometimes wondered how you faced the problem of conducting the latter part of your story. You could not return to the old clumsy method of Scott, telling a bit about Héloïse and then turning to her husband with a "Meanwhile Abélard was doing such and such a thing."

MOORE. No, I certainly could not. I had to choose between them. And the temptation was strong to place Héloïse in the convent at Argenteuil and leave her there while I followed the fortunes of Abélard. There were great allurements in the prospect of Abélard's adventurous life, his wanderings, his conflict with the church, culminating in a scene of terror and atrocity which presented a wonderful opportunity for a storyteller. But all the while that I meditated upon Abélard's years of separation from Héloïse the thought pressed in upon me that my tale was of Héloïse. You will recall that in one of my imaginary conversations with Gosse I spoke of Miss Austen's great achievement: that it was she who first introduced "the burning human heart" into English prose narrative. That was my theme in "Héloïse and Abélard," and though Abélard's wandering life in the pleasant French country offered so many attractions, I all the while knew that I must follow the woman into the convent, where the only adventures were those which the changing seasons brought and where she waited for her husband. All that it was possible to do with Abélard's life during these years was to have him recount it briefly to Héloïse when they met again.

CHEW. And the beautiful conclusion of your story—tell me whether it was always in your mind or whether the idea of it came suddenly.

MOORE. It came suddenly. My original intention was to carry the tale on to the death of Héloïse; but as I was composing the narrative of their last ride together, to the convent of the Paraclete, there came to me the thought: Here I must leave them, for the rest of their lives is known from the Letters; and what better place is there for me to break off than this?

CHEW. Certainly there was very genuine inspiration in that thought, Mr. Moore, for you could not have more movingly brought your story to a close. But it is late; I must be going.

MOORE. Don't go yet awhile, Mr. Chew. I never go to bed early. Sit for half an hour longer. You have led me astray from what I really wished to talk about —your book on Italy.

CHEW. "Héloïse and Abélard" is a better subject for conversation than a book on Italy which will probably never get written.

MOORE. Keep your book in mind nevertheless; and keep in mind what I said about the literary conversation. You must select; you must have a unified theme. Our pleasant chat to-night, for example, would not do for a literary conversation. It has ranged too widely; it lacks unity.

CHEW. Yes, it lacks unity; but I believe that if it were recorded it might give an impression of actuality and truth to life, and hence might be not uninteresting. But I must really be going. It is a long way to my hotel.

MOORE. I am selfish in keeping you from Mrs. Chew. Be sure to bring her with you the next time you come. But wait a moment; I'll get my hat and walk with you as far as Victoria.

AMERICANA

ALABAMA

FINAL triumph of Calvinism in Alabama, October 6, 1923:

Birmingham's exclusive clubs—and all other kinds—will be as blue hereafter as city and State laws can make them. Commissioner of Safety W. C. Bloe issued an order today that Sunday golf, billiards and *dominoes* be stopped, beginning tomorrow.

ARIZONA

FROM an harangue delivered to the Chamber of Commerce of Tucson by the Hon. H. B. TITCOMB:

The person who objects to the ringing of cracked bells from a church-tower I do not believe is a good citizen of any community.

CALIFORNIA

RENAISSANCE of a neglected art in the home of the movie, as reported by the Los Angeles *Times:*

In response to thousands of requests from the almost countless admirers of this famous American star, I take pride in announcing Mr. Guy Bates Post's return to the speaking stage. The consensus of many of America's foremost critics is—"His intensity disturbs and arrests. As the greatness of his genius governs the trend of thought, aroused in the genius that is—to a greater or lesser degree—the thing that governs —controls—dwarfs or magnifies—the actions— attitudes—good or bad qualities—that makes or unmakes man. By his genius compelling every auditor to feel they are parcel and part of the play—causing their pulses to throb with his, their hearts yearn—glow—ache and are glad with the beats of his heart, until actor and audience become welded as one—fused in the finesse of a single thought."
THE PLAY—"The Climax," a play filled with suspense that comes spontaneously from that soul, secreted in every normal person's breast of thinking age—interspersed with natural effervescing comedy that bubbles into chuckles and bursts into roars, causing tears to recede into the ducts from whence they came, at the critical moment when more sorrow would be anguish—more selfishness produce pain.
MELVILLE B. RAYMOND, Director of Tour.

CONNECTICUT

THEOLOGICAL news note from the free imperial city of Middletown, the seat of Wesleyan University, the Berkeley Divinity School and the Connecticut State Hospital for the Insane:

The Rev. Minard Le G. Porter, pastor of the Methodist Church at Long Hill, near Middletown, has won the Bible Marathon by reading the New Testament in thirteen hours. Commencing shortly before midnight, he kept reading without interruption save for a few minutes to take nourishment.

DISTRICT OF COLUMBIA

REPORT of a modern miracle in the shadow of the Capitol, from the Washington *Herald:*

The odor of perfume was wafted through Centennial Baptist Church, Seventh and I Streets, Northeast, last night, as the Rev. E. Hez Swem, emphasizing a vigorous sermon, waved a scented handkerchief at his congregation.
"Want to smell it?" he asked. "It's perfume, and it came from the Lord above."
Inspiration for a message had come to him when a feminine member of his flock gave him a bottle of perfume, the Rev. Mr. Swem said. He really wanted some perfume, and God knew he wanted it and gave it to him through this good woman, he said.

GEORGIA

MIRACULOUS work of the Holy Spirit at Arlington, Ga., as reported in a special dispatch to the Fort Worth (Texas) *Star-Telegram:*

The boll weevil hasn't touched the seven acres set aside here for the Lord.
Furthermore, the seven farmers who consecrated an acre each to the church are prospering in everything they have planted.
In contrast to their flourishing farms is the devastation that has been wrought everywhere in this section by the boll weevil. Cotton has been eaten up bodily and almost without exception the only farmers near Arlington who will make money this year are the seven who set aside an acre each for God's work.
At the opening of Spring, the Rev. H. M. Mel-

48

ton, pastor of the Bluffton Baptist Church, near here, asked each farmer in his church to stake off one acre and give the proceeds to the church.

Seven pledged themselves to do this and signed the following agreement: "We the undersigned farmer members of the Bluffton Baptist Church, do agree to stake off, plant, cultivate, and harvest one acre of our respective farms. The product of said acre, when in marketable condition, is to be turned over to a committee appointed by the church to receive and sell, and the proceeds of said acre to be used in the work of the Lord."

Through the acres devoted to the Lord, the church expects to raise money enough to pay its pastor's salary.

ILLINOIS

MAKING the bride an honest woman in Chicago, as described by the local newspapers:

The Chicago meat packing industry and the University of Chicago, long rival attractions shown to visitors as examples of the city's industrial and cultural activity, are to be united. Meat packing is to take its place in the curriculum of the university, along with Latin, economics, psychology, and the rest.

IOWA

COLLAPSE of the work of the Sulgrave Foundation in Iowa, as reported from Sioux City:

When Lady Eleanor Smith, daughter of Lord Birkenhead, former lord chancellor of England, smoked a cigarette on the campus of Morningside College here last Wednesday, and when Lord Birkenhead himself produced his own bottle of wine at a luncheon at which he was the guest of the Methodist college professors, they started something. Now the members of the Women's Christian Temperance Union of Sioux City want the world to know that they do not approve of the conduct of the distinguished guests. The women declare that in addition to the aforementioned acts, Lord Birkenhead, just before his lecture at Grace Methodist Church, attended a gathering of lawyer acquaintances in the basement of the church, where he opened for them a bottle of "the king's own". Resolutions adopted by the women declare that "the union wishes to go on record as being opposed to the earl's propaganda against the established laws of this country and the lack of propriety of his daughter."

KANSAS

LATEST triumph of the Higher Patriotism in Kansas, as reported by E. W. Howe in his interesting *Monthly:*

The attorney general of Kansas has ruled that if a child in school refuses to repeat the flag pledge, its parents may be arrested and fined. A good many children are tired of repeating the flag pledge every day, which is as follows: "I pledge allegiance to my flag and to the republic for which it stands, one nation indivisible, with liberty and justice for all." . . . The pledge was invented, and forced on the children, by an old maid engaged in welfare work.

MARYLAND

NEW zoölogical classification from the estimable Baltimore *Evening Sun:*

Two men were sentenced to jail for 30 days and a negro for six months in the Traffic Court today.

MISSOURI

CALLING out the *Landsturm* against the Devil in Kansas City, as reported by the United Press:

A world's record for Bible class attendance was set here yesterday by the men's class of the First Baptist Church, when 17,833 men jammed Convention Hall. The Baptist Church here is in a contest with a business men's class in Long Beach, Calif. The Long Beach class, according to messages received here, had 9,756 yesterday.

NEW YORK

FROM an interview with the Hon. John S. Sumner, Secretary of the Society for the Suppression of Vice, in the New York *World:*

The stage last season was the cleanest in years and this season it is the worst in history, according to John S. Sumner:

"It has touched a lower level than ever before," he declared, "both in the exploitation of salacious themes and in the exhibition of nudity. Complaints to the society have been very numerous. Many organizations have shown great interest in the matter."

He said the statement had been made to him *that the moral character of the scene shifters was being imperiled in one or two shows.*

OHIO

PHILOSOPHICAL conclusions of the massed realtors of Toledo, as given in the Toledo *Realtor*, the organ of the Toledo Real Estate Board:

1. Everyone should strive to give to the world a distinct personality as the one contribution above all others to make.

2. No personality will be marked with any particular individuality that has constantly been copied from others.

3. New ideas in human endeavor are scarce.

PENNSYLVANIA

FROM a list of "Educational Books For Home Study" sent out by a bookseller in Youngsville, Pa.:

> The Art of Making Love (2 vols.), $1.00.
> The Life of Harding (illustrated), $2.50.
> Salesmanship as a Fine Art, $2.00.
> How to Develop a Strong and Healthy Mind, $2.50.
> How to Make Shoes Waterproof, $.25.
> How to Tie Different Knots, $.35.
> 1000 Ways of Getting Rich, $.50.

SOUTH CAROLINA

FROM a call for 33,373 volunteers to teach the 33,373 white adult illiterates of the State how to write their names:

> Just a few days ago a man said in our presence that a strong, vigorous man had come to him very much exercised about his spiritual welfare. He was at once referred to certain passages in the Bible, which would unquestionably throw light upon his perplexity. This strong, vigorous man was forced to reply: "I am very sorry, but I cannot read."
> We wonder whether any other argument is really necessary to make the people of this State determine to remove adult illiteracy, thus putting it within the power of every white man and woman in this State of ours to search the Scriptures and thus learn of Him, whom to know aright is life everlasting.

Additional inducement:

> A revised copy of Aesop's Fables will be given by Mr. Ambrose E. Gonzalez to each pupil who learns to write his name.

TEXAS

SPECIMEN of literary criticism by Prof. Dr. Leonard Doughty, a favorite pedagogue of the republic of Texas, where the great open spaces breed a race of men with hair on their chests and red blood in their veins:

> It might have been thought of the Teuton that he had reached earth's nadir of stupid badness and graceless shame in Hauptmann and Sudermann and their frowzy compeers. But the race that could produce Sudermann and Hauptmann and their like knows no nadir of mental sordidness or moral perversion; there are depths below all other depths for them. The actual, original "scientific" writings of Krafft-Ebing are less vile and pervert than the current "literature" of the Germans today. The stain of that yellow, bastard blood is upon much of the "authorship" of the United States. It is only a matter of procuring a grade-school "education" under our free system and Americanizing an ungainly name. Except for these, the modern "authorship" that makes the "books" upon our stalls is of those dread middle races, Aryan, indeed, but interminable mixed and simmered in the devil's cauldron of middle Europe, and spewed out of Italy and France, and off the dismal Slavic frontiers, and out of that dismal and cankered East, that like a horde of chancre-laden rats are brought to swarm down the gang-planks of a thousand ships upon our shores. It is the spawn of the abysmal fecundity of this seething mass, which now, with the mental and moral deficiency of a thousand generations of defective parentage and low breeding behind and within them, emits these "volumes", as the insane emit shrieks or as a putrid corpse emits odor. After some inquiry I have learned to a confident surety that no one of the "writers" of all this unhappy array was in the service of the United States in the great war.

VIRGINIA

EXAMPLES of neo-Confederate English from examination papers submitted by Virginia schoolmarms attending the Summer School at the University of Virginia:

> He run down the street, but it was too late to cought him . . .
> I like James Witcomb Rily, because he is not dead, and writes poems in the paper that one can see all right . . .
> The flames shot into the sky a few foot above the house . . .

WASHINGTON

HURRYING on the Kingdom in the Chinook State, as reported by the *Editor and Publisher*:

> Newspaper advertising was the best invest-made in 1923 by the Garden Street Methodist Episcopal Church, Bellingham, Wash., according to the pastor, the Rev. Dr. J. C. Harrison, who added that $100 worth of advertising had brought in more than $1,700 in silver plate collections.

AESTHETE: MODEL 1924

BY ERNEST BOYD

H E IS a child of this Twentieth Century, for the Yellow Nineties had flickered out in the delirium of the Spanish-American War when his first gurgles rejoiced the ears of his expectant parents. If Musset were more than a name to him, a hazy recollection of French literature courses, he might adapt a line from the author of "La Confession d'un Enfant du Siècle" and declare: I came too soon into a world too old. But no such doubts trouble his spirit, for he believes that this century is his because he was born with it. He does not care who makes its laws, so long as he makes its literature. To this important task he has consecrated at least three whole years of his conscious—or rather self-conscious—existence, and nothing, as yet, has happened to shake his faith in his star. In fact, he finds the business rather easier than he had anticipated when, in the twilight sleep of the class-room, vague reports reached him of Milton's infinitesimal fee for "Paradise Lost", of Chatterton's death, of the harassed lives of Shelley and Keats, of the eternal struggle of the artist against the indifference of his age and the foul bludgeonings of fate.

The Aesthete's lot has been a happier one. His thirtieth birthday is still on the horizon, his literary baggage is small, or non-existent—but he is already famous; at least, so it seems to him when he gazes upon his own reflection in the eyes of his friends, and fingers aggressively the luxurious pages of the magazine of which he is Editor-in-Chief, Editor, Managing Editor, Associate Editor, Contributing Editor, Bibliographical Editor, or Source Material Editor. His relationship to the press must always be editorial, and to meet the changed conditions of the cosmos, a changed conception of the functions of an editor provides him with a vast selection of titles from which to choose. The essential fact is that he has an accredited mouthpiece, a letter-head conferring authority, a secure place from which to bestride the narrow world in which he is already a colossus. Thus he is saved from those sordid encounters with the harsh facts of literary commerce which his predecessors accepted as part of the discipline of life: Meredith reading manuscripts for Chapman & Hall, Gissing toiling in New Grub Street, Anatole France writing prefaces for Lemerre's classics, Dreiser polishing dime novels for Street & Smith.

It is natural that he should thus be overpowered by a mere sense of his own identity, for there is nothing, alas, in his actual achievements, past or present, to warrant his speaking prematurely with the voice of authority. That he does so unchallenged is a proof to him that he himself is his own excuse for being. In a very special sense he accepts the Cartesian formula: I think, therefore I am. When he went to Harvard —or was it Princeton or Yale?—in the early years of the Woodrovian epoch, he was just one of so many mute and inglorious Babbitts preparing to qualify as regular fellows. If some brachycephalic shadow lay across the Nordic blondness of his social pretensions, then, of course, the pilgrimage assumed something of the character of a great adventure into the Promised Land, the penetration to an Anglo-Saxon Lhasa. His immediate concern, in any case, was to resemble as closely as possible every man about him, to acquire at once the marks of what is known as the education of a gentleman, to wit, complete and absolute conformity to conventions, the suppression of even the faintest stirrings of eccentric personality. To this day he feels a little embarrassed when he calls on his father in Wall Street, carrying a walking-stick and wearing a light tweed suit, but he trusts that even the door-opener's scorn will be softened by the knowledge that here is an artist, whose personality must be untrammeled.

Those who knew the Aesthete during the period of his initiation will recall how he walked along the banks of his Yankee Isis, or lolled behind the bushes, discussing Life; how he stood at the Leif Ericson monument and became aware of the passage of time;—*Eheu fugaces, labunter anni*, he now would say, especially if he were writing a notice of the Music Box Review; how he went to the cemetery to contemplate the graves of William and Henry James, and noted in himself the incipient thrill of Harvard pride and acquired New Englandism. But these gentle pursuits did not mean so much to him at first as the more red-blooded diversions of week-ends in Boston, and such other fleshly sins as that decayed city might with impunity offer. More refined were the evening parties on the northern side of the town where, in a background of red plush curtains and chairs but recently robbed of their prudish antimacassars, whispers of romantic love might be heard from well-behaved young women, whose highest destiny, before lapsing legally into the arms of a professor, was to be remembered when, at a later stage, a sonnet evolved from a brain beginning to teem creatively. For the rest, football games and lectures, the former seriously, the latter intermittently, maintained in him the consciousness of the true purpose of a university education.

From the excellent Professors Copeland and Kittredge he distractedly and reluctantly acquired a knowledge of the elements of English composition and of the more virtuous facts of English literature. He read, that is to say, fragments of the classical authors and dutifully absorbed the opinions of academic commentators upon them. American literature was revealed to him as a pale and obedient provincial cousin, whose past contained occasional indiscretions, such as Poe and Whitman, about whom the less said the better. Latin and French were filtered through the same kind of sieve, but without so many precautions, for in neither case was it possible for the aspirant after knowledge to decipher easily the kind of author to whom the urge of adolescence would naturally drive him. The Loeb classics left the un-Christian passages in the original, while the estimable Bohn unkindly took refuge in Italian, the language of a "lust-ridden country", as Anthony Comstock points out in that charming book of his, "Traps for the Young". However, he still possesses enough Latin to be able to introduce into his written discourse appropriate tags from the Dictionary of Classical Quotations, though his quantities, I regret to say, are very weak. I have heard him stress the wrong syllable when speaking of Ouspensky's "Tertium Organum", although he will emend a corrupt passage in Petronius, and professes to have read all the obscurer authors in Gourmont's "Latin Mystique."

There came finally a subtle change in his outlook, from which one must date the actual birth of the Aesthete as such—*der Aesthetiker an sich*, so to speak. I suspect it was after one of those parties in the red plush drawing-rooms, when he returned to his rooms with what seemed like the authentic beginnings of a sonnet in his ears. From that moment he had a decided list in the direction of what he called "creative work". While the stadium shook with the hoarse shouts of the rabble at football games he might be observed going off with a companion to indulge in the subtle delights of intellectual conversation. His new friends were those whom he had at first dismissed as negligible owing to their avowed intention of not being he-men. The pulsation of new life within him prompted him to turn a more sympathetic eye upon this hitherto despised set, and they, in their turn, welcomed a new recruit, for the herd instinct is powerful even amongst the intellectual. Under this new guidance he came into contact with ideas undreamt of in the simple philosophy of the class-room. Strange names were bandied about, curious magazines, unwelcomed by the college library, were read, and he was only too glad to discover that all the literary past of which he was ignorant or strangely misinformed counted as nothing in the eyes of his newly emancipated friends. From the pages of the *Masses* he gathered that the Social Revolution was imminent, that Brieux was a dramatist of ideas; in the *Little Review* he was first to learn the enchantment of distance as he sat bemused by its specimens of French and pseudo-French literature. Thus the ballast of which he had to get rid in order to float in the rarefied atmosphere of Advanced Thought was negligible. He had merely to exchange one set of inaccurate ideas for another.

II

It was at this precise moment in his career that the Wilsonian storming of Valhalla began. With the call to arms tingling in his blood, the Aesthete laid aside the adornments of life for the stern realities of a military training camp. Ancestral voices murmured in his ears, transmitted by instruments of dubious dolichocephalism, it is true, but perhaps all the more effective on that account, for Deep calls unto Deep. I will not dwell upon the raptures of that martial period, for he himself has left us his retrospective and disillusioned record of it, which makes it impossible to recapture the original emotion. Harold Cabot Lilienthal—and, I suppose I should add, in deference to my subject, *hoc genus omne*—was apparently not capable of the strain of ingesting the official facts about the great moral crusade. It was government contract material and proved to be as shoddy and

unreliable as anything supplied by the dollar-a-year men to the War Department. By the time the uniformed Aesthete got to France he was a prey to grave misgivings, and as his subsequent prose and verse show, he was one of C. E. Montague's Disenchanted—he who had been a Fiery Particle. He bitterly regretted the collegiate patriotism responsible for his devotion to the lofty rhetoric of the *New Republic*. By luck or cunning, however, he succeeded in getting out of the actual trenches, and there, in the hectic backwash of war, he cultivated the tender seeds just beginning to germinate. He edited his first paper, the *Doughboys' Dreadnought*, or under the auspices of the propaganda and vaudeville department made his first contribution to literature, "Young America and Yougo-Slavia". Simultaneously with this plunge into arms and letters, he made his first venture into the refinements of sex, thereby extending his French vocabulary and gaining that deep insight into the intimate life of France which is still his proudest possession.

When militarism was finally overthrown, democracy made safe, and a permanent peace established by the victorious and united Allies, he was ready to stay on a little longer in Paris, and to participate in the joys of La Rotonde and Les Deux Magots. There for a brief spell he breathed the same air as the Dadaists, met Picasso and Philippe Soupault, and allowed Ezra Pound to convince him that the French nation was aware of the existence of Jean Cocteau, Paul Morand, Jean Giraudoux and Louis Aragon. From those who had nothing to say on the subject when Marcel Proust published "Du Côté de chez Swann" in 1914 he now learned what a great author the man was, and formed those friendships which caused him eventually to join in a tribute to Proust by a group of English admirers who would have stoned Oscar Wilde had they been old enough to do so when it was the right thing to do.

The time was now ripe for his repatriation, and so, with the same critical equipment in French as in English, but with a still imperfect control of the language as a complication, the now complete Aesthete returned to New York, and descended upon Greenwich Village. His poems of disenchantment were in the press, his war novel was nearly finished, and it was not long before he appeared as Editor-in-Chief, Editor, Managing Editor, Associate Editor, Contributing Editor, Assistant Editor, Bibliographical Editor or Source Material Editor of one of the little reviews making no compromise with the public (or any other) taste. Both his prose and verse were remarkable chiefly for typographical and syntactical eccentricities, and a high pressure of unidiomatic, misprinted French to the square inch. His further contributions (if any) to the art of prose narrative have consisted of a breathless phallic symbolism —a sex obsession which sees the curves of a woman's body in every object not actually flat, including, I need hardly say, the Earth, our great Mother.

But it is essentially as an appraiser of the arts, as editor and critic, that the young Aesthete demands attention. He writes a competent book review and awakes to find himself famous. The next number of the magazine contains a study of his aesthetic, preferably by the author whose work he has favorably reviewed. By the end of the year a publisher announces a biographical and critical study of our young friend, and his fame is secured. He can now discourse with impunity about anything, and he avails himself of the opportunity. He has evolved an ingenious style, florid, pedantic, technical, full of phrases so incomprehensible or so rhetorical that they almost persuade the reader that they must have a meaning. But the skeptical soon discover that this is an adjustable and protean vocabulary, that by a process of reshuffling the same phrases will serve for an artistic appreciation of Charlie Chaplin, an essay on Marcel Proust, or an article on Erik Satie. His other expedient is an arid and inconceivable learning, picked up at second hand. Let him discuss "The Waste Land" and his erudition will rival the ponderous

fatuity of T. S. Eliot himself. He will point out on Ptolemy's map the exact scene, quote the more obscure hymns of Hesiod, cite an appropriate passage from Strabo's geography, and conclude with a cryptic remark from the Fourth Ennead of Plotinus. Yet, one somehow suspects that even the parasangs of the first chapter of Xenophon's Anabasis would strain his Greek to the breaking-point.

Nevertheless, information is the one thing the Aesthete dreads. To be in the possession of solid knowledge and well-digested facts, to have definite standards, background and experience, is to place oneself outside the pale of true aestheticism. While foreign literature is his constant preoccupation, the Aesthete has no desire to make it known. What he wants to do is to lead a cult, to communicate a mystic faith in his idols, rather than to make them available for general appreciation. Articles on the subject are an important feature of his magazines, but they consist, as a rule, of esoteric witticisms and allusive gossip about fourth-rate people whom the writer happens to have met in a café. He will sweep aside the finest writers in French as lumber, launch into ecstasies over some Dadaist, and head the article with a French phrase which is grammatically incorrect, and entirely superfluous, since it expresses no idea that could not be correctly rendered in English. If one protest that the very title of a book which is a masterpiece of style has been mistranslated, that the first page has several gross errors, the Aesthete will blandly point out that in paragraph two there are four abstract nouns each with a different termination. It is useless to show him that there are no equivalent nouns in the text. Finally, one gives up arguing, for one remembers that Rimbaud once wrote a poem about the color of the vowels. Literary history must repeat itself.

The almost Swedenborgian mysticism of the Aesthete is implied in all his comments, for he is usually inarticulate and incomprehensible. He will ingenuously describe himself as being "with no more warning than our great imagination in the presence of a masterpiece". One reads on to discover the basis for this enthusiasm, but at the outset one is halted by the naïve admonition that "it isn't even important to know that I am right in my judgment. The significant and to me overwhelming thing was that the work was a masterpiece and altogether contemporary". In other words, this work, which the writer says "I shall make no effort to describe", may or may not be a masterpiece, nevertheless it is one . . . presumably because it is "altogether contemporary". It is on this point of view that the solemn service of the Younger Aestheticism depends. If a piece of sculpture is distorted and hideous, if the battered remains of a wrecked taxi are labeled, "La Ville tentaculaire", the correct attitude is one of delight. One should "make no effort to describe" what is visible, but clutch at the "altogether contemporaneous" element, indicating a masterpiece. In music one must not seek in the cacophonies of the current idols the gross, bourgeois emotion which one receives from Brahms and Beethoven. The Aesthete holds that a cliché, in French for preference, will dispose of any genius. One should make play with *le côté Puccini* and *le faux bon*.

The pastime is an amusing one, for it involves no more serious opposition than is to be found in the equally limited arsenal of the Philistines. What could be easier than to caper in front of the outraged mandarins waving volumes of eccentrically printed French poetry and conspuing the gods of the bourgeoisie? It is like mocking a blind man, who hears the insults but cannot see the gestures. The Aesthete tries to monopolize the field of contemporary foreign art and he is accustomed to respectful submission or the abuse and indifference of sheer ignorance. When he needs a more responsive victim he turns his attention to the arts adored by the crowd, the "lively arts," Mr. Seldes calls them, as if the Fifth Symphony were depressing. The esoteric reviews publish "stills" of Goldwyn pictures and discover strange beauties in follow-up letters and street-car advertisements. The knees of Ann Pennington, the clowning of Charlie Chaplin, the humors of Joe Cook and Fannie Brice must now be bathed in the vapors of aesthetic mysticism. But here there is a difference. The performances of the "lively" artist are familiar to every one above the age of ten; most of us have enjoyed them without feeling compelled to explain ourselves. A reference to Gaby Deslys finds its place as naturally in the works of Havelock Ellis as one to "Der Untergang des Abendlandes." But the Aesthete takes his lively arts uneasily. He is determined to demonstrate that he is just as other men. It is evidently not only in foreigners that one encounters that "certain condescension" of which the late Mr. Lowell complained.

III

In the last analysis the Aesthete may be diagnosed as the literary counterpart of the traditional American tourist in Paris. He is glamored by the gaudy spectacle of that most provincial of all great cities. French is the tube through which he is fed, and he has not yet discovered how feeble the nourishment is. When he turns to other countries, Germany, for instance, he betrays himself by an incongruous and belated enthusiasm for the novelties of the eighties and nineties. The contemporaries of Thomas Mann, Schnitzler and Hauptmann elsewhere are beneath his notice. Spain and Italy come onto his horizon only when Paris becomes aware of their existence. In a few years, however, his younger brother will go up to Cambridge, in his turn, and then we shall doubtless be enlightened concerning the significant form of Kasimir Edschmid, Walter von Molo and Carl Sternheim. One cannot be "altogether contemporary" all the time.

The signs, indeed, already point that way, for I notice that Hugo Stinnes is mentioned as a modern Marco Polo, and the American realtor is praised as a reincarnation of the creative will of Leonardo da Vinci. This new-found delight in publicity experts, election slogans, billboards and machinery may result in a pilgrimage across the Rhine where, in the dissolution of so many fine things, an aesthetic of Philistinism has emerged. The tone of democratic yearning which has begun to permeate German literature, recalling the dreams of Radical England in the days of Lord Morley's youth, may facilitate the understanding between two great democracies. But the fatal attraction of French, not to mention the difficulty of German, is a serious obstacle to any new orientation of the younger Aestheticism, and Paris, as usual, can provide what its customers demand. Thus the cult of the movies, with its profound meditations on "Motion Picture Dynamics", and all the vague echoes of Elie Faure's theory of "cineplastics", involves a condemnation of "The Cabinet of Dr. Caligari", a tactless Teuton effort to put some genuine fantasy into the cinema. Instead of that the faithful are called upon by a French expert to admire the films of William S. Hart and Jack Pickford, and some one carefully translates the poetic rhapsodies inspired in him by the contemplation of their masterpieces.

"Two souls", in the words of the German bard, "dwell in the breast" of the Aesthete, and his allegiance is torn between the salesmanager's desk, where, it appears, the Renaissance artist of to-day is to be found, and the esoteric editorial chair where experiments are made with stories which "discard the old binding of plot and narrative", the substitute being "the structural framework which appeals to us over and above the message of the line". Thus it becomes possible simultaneously to compare Gertrude Stein with Milton and to chant the glories of the machine age in America. This dualism, obviously, foreshadows the ultimate disintegration of the type, although for the moment the process is ingeniously disguised by such devices

as the printing of prose bearing all the outward marks of super-modern eccentricity but made up cunningly of a pattern woven from phrases culled from billboards and the advertising pages of the magazines; by reproducing the weirdest pictures together with business-like photographs of cash-registers and telephones. The household gods of Babbitt are being pressed into service, just as his innocent amusements are being intellectualized.

Here the Aesthete departs from the traditions of the species at his peril. Hitherto his technique has been perfect, for it has been his practice to confine his enthusiasm to works of art that are either as obscure or as inessential, or both, as his own critical comment. He realized that it was unsafe to trifle with subjects about which his public might be better informed than himself. Now his incantations lose their potency when applied to matters within the experience and comprehension of the plain people, and not one cubit is added to the stature of William S. Hart, so far as his devotees are concerned, by the knowledge that his name is pronounced with aesthetic reverence on the Left Bank of the Seine.

The process of change is at work, for the transitional youth is already in at least one editorial chair, frowning upon the frivolities of the Jazz Age, calling for brighter and better books, his dreams haunted by fears of Sodom and Gomorrah. The Aesthete, meanwhile, is retiring with an intellectual *Katzenjammer*, which produces in some cases a violent and unnatural nausea, a revulsion against the wild delights of his former debauches. In others the result is a return to the cosy hearth of the American family; his head aches a little but his hand is steady. He is refreshed by a journalistic bromo seltzer. There is pep in the swing of his fist upon the typewriter as he sits down to a regular and well-paid job, convincing others, as his employer has convinced him, that he really knows what the public wants.

THE TRAGIC HIRAM

BY JOHN W. OWENS

IT OUGHT to be possible to extract from some Christian eye, somewhere, somehow, a tear of pity for Hiram Johnson. Hordes of people are sorry for Borah because he is too reckless in minor crises, or because he is never reckless in major crises. Other hordes weep for La Follette because he lacks the will to start a new party, or because he possesses too much will to start schisms in the old party—for, with his talent for practical politics, he would be mighty within the old party if only he were regular. One horde or another, indeed, is sorry for nearly all the politicians who do not quite make the front rank. But here is Johnson, facing the probability that he has thrown away the Presidency which he craves beyond all things else, mortal or immortal, and one hears mainly mocking laughter. The excuse given is that he has probably thrown it away through mere selfishness—no paradox, but a fact. But ought selfishness, then, be set up as a bar to sympathy for a politician?

Observe the facts in this Johnson case, so sad, so full of lessons. Three years ago, when the Presidential fight was over, Hiram had the popular leadership of the Republican party within his grasp, and the popular leadership of the Republican party was equivalent to the popular leadership of the country. No one supposed, even at the height of poor Harding's brief triumph that he would be a popular leader; La Follette was still in disgrace; Borah appeared a prima donna with whom no section of public opinion was able to establish contact long enough to feel assured of him; Kenyon was too distinctly of Iowa, Iowan, to make a national appeal; Hoover obvi-

ously had no political sense. That left only Johnson. And Johnson had certain distinct assets of his own.

He had made good in the popular melodramatic rôle of a fighting Governor out in California, and thus his figure had far more clarity of outline than a Senator is usually able to achieve. His same record at home had fixed him in the public imagination as a good manager—and the masses instinctively call for a good manager when heroic deeds are to be done. He had been a leading actor in the primary campaign of 1920, and his downright stand on the League of Nations had made him seem important and alive to both the friends and the foes of the League at a time when most other Republican candidates were inclined to pussyfoot. Finally, he had touched the great heart of the common people with his ringing demand for freedom of speech and assemblage; his rivals were apparently unaware of the depth of public interest in such matters. Behind all was the fact that the country, despite the election of Harding, remained overwhelmingly hopeful and Progressive, as all the elections of the last two decades had shown—and Johnson could qualify as one of the original prophets of the Progressive revelation.

II

Such were his advantages when Harding was elected. What happened? Following the inauguration, the great masses of the plain people turned their minds expectantly to domestic affairs, and at once there was a call for Progressive leadership. Harding himself, of course, was wholly unfit for the task, and scarcely made any attempt upon it. Within six months of the beginning of his administration signs of trouble began to appear. Within a year they were innumerable, North, East, South and West—and soon afterward a staggering series of primary defeats mowed down his friends and left him dismayed and helpless. The Autumn elections completed the work; the way was open for Johnson. Imagine Roosevelt in such a situation—galloping toward the White House! Imagine Roosevelt nine months later, with Harding dead, his mortgage upon the nomination lapsed, and a thin, blank conformist in his shoes! But Johnson—well, Johnson simply railed at fate, and then alternately pined and hoped.

His trouble was this: In 1920 he wanted to be President so badly that when he was defeated he thought the world had come to an end. The injustice of depriving Hiram Johnson of that colossal prize assumed unthinkable proportions. Paradise was lost. The enemy of mankind ranged and devoured the Republic. Thus, when Congress convened after the November election, Johnson appeared as one sunk so far in the depths of horror and despair that not the faintest ray of sunshine could reach him. A black pall enshrouded him. The country, having decided the election by some 7,000,000 plurality, shook itself and remarked "That's settled; let's go!" but Johnson was so deep underground that he could not hear.

Unluckily for him, the other wounded were less flabbergasted. They continued to be seen and heard. Borah, for example, began yelling lustily for economy. He cried out against Federal commissions and bureaux, and against bureaucracy in general as a sponge that absorbed the people's substance. He cried out against proposals to spend millions upon millions on great armies and navies, and he sustained that cry in such penetrating tones that he became the most potent force in summoning the Disarmament Conference. He bolted his party in the tariff fight; he charged that the Fordney-McCumber tariff bill was a device for robbing the many to the profit of the few; he made a great stir.

La Follette, too, was in full function. Refusing in his old age to remain a pariah to his enemies and a martyr to his friends, he shared Borah's tariff fight, and resumed in full vigor his own ancient attack upon the Interests. Kenyon turned up again as the friend of the working man. He became the champion of the West Virginia miners, and the advocate of an industrial code designed to govern the relations between labor and capital in the great industries. Norris was at work in his accustomed way, specializing in the incurable ills of the farmer. All the other old Progressives were hard at it, uncovering atrocities, making hay. Progressivism was on the march again—not clear about where it was going, but moving.

But nobody could find the dashing hero, Johnson. Day after day he was returned *non est*. Not until Harding appointed David H. Blair, of North Carolina, to be Commissioner of Internal Revenue, was he heard of at all. Then he rushed forth suddenly as the defender of political morality. But it quickly appeared that Blair was simply one of the devils responsible for the crime at Chicago, when the doors of Paradise were slammed in Johnson's face. Blair had been largely to blame, the country was vehemently told, for the "disloyalty" of the North Carolina delegation. But the country was not interested, and Johnson subsided again. Occasionally thereafter he bobbed feebly to the surface, as in the contests over the Colombian treaty and the Four-Power pact. But that was all.

He was unheard of in the fight for the reduction of government expenses, in the big row over the unjust distribution of the burdens of taxation, in the forensic collisions caused by the woes of the workers, and in the battle royal over responsibility for the disaster that had overtaken the farmers. In the tariff fight his only concern was that California's interests be protected up to the hilt; in return, he was willing to protect other industries, located anywhere, up to the hilt. In the Newberry fight he played the sorriest part of any man in the Senate; he did not aid his Progressive colleagues when they held aloft the banner of political purity and neither did he stand boldly with the Old Guard when it shouted defiance. Very unfortunately, his train reached Washington too late for him to vote—a fact which led some skeptics to observe that after he unexpectedly carried Michigan in the 1920 primaries, the Newberry influence, unlike the Blair influence in North Carolina, was not disloyal and did not help slam the doors of Paradise.

For the rest, he was merely a pale fat man, moping in and out of the Senate. Often he came late and left early; often he disappeared from the floor. The debates in which he had once joined with such infinite relish now bored him unspeakably. A common sight was Johnson entering the main door and looking weariedly around, and Johnson leaving through the main door, his shoulders aslump. In conversation with other Senators or lesser politicians, his expression habitually was either listless or suspicious. Never was there a worse case of dyspepsia of the spirit. Convinced, apparently, that his chance of getting the Presidency was lost forevermore, he was also convinced that the world had gone to pot.

Not until after the 1922 elections did he lift his head. And even then he lacked the strength to keep it lifted; he could do no more than peer around. Those elections raised the question whether a man so easygoing and unambitious as Harding would insist that his mortgage on the 1924 nomination be honored. That, of course, carried a renewal of hope for Johnson. He did two things at this juncture. He looked over the organization of Progressives of both parties that La Follette had formed, and decided that joining it offered him more danger than benefit. And he began to flirt chastely with certain members of the Old Guard, notably the cheerful, sparkling

Tory from New Hampshire, Senator Moses Those Tories began to believe early in 1923 that Harding was doomed to defeat, and that the only way to save the Republican party was to offer a sop to the Progressives and the Radicals. Their thought was that Johnson was the sop that would cost the least. They believed that the plain people could be made to rally around him again; at the same time, the knowledge of him since 1920 which they had, and which they supposed the masses did not have, encouraged them to believe that he would not be troublesome to Right Thinking if installed in the White House.

But, as everybody knows, when the death of President Harding made Johnson a real candidate again, and gave him a chance that might have been converted into virtual assurance of the Presidency, all the Tories with whom he had been flirting —or, at least the most energetic of them, Senator Moses—ran away from him so fast that one might have supposed him a sudden victim of smallpox. Seeing a new deal all around, and a chance to win with one of the Tories' own, and a fellow New Englander besides, Moses showed speed in getting away from Johnson that was downright humorous. His vast celerity, indeed, offered one of the two genuine comedies of those lugubrious days. The fun of the other was also in speed—the speed with which Senator Borah hurried to the front from some place in the remote West with an endorsement of Coolidge. The obvious purpose was to check any possible stampede of the uninformed Progressives to Johnson in the first days of the new régime. Borah, of course, has nothing in common with Coolidge, but he knew that the moment his endorsement was printed, every man in the country who had looked upon him as Johnson's twin brother in 1920 would see a signal to stop, look and listen. So far as a diligent reading of the newspapers and close attention to the words of politicians disclose, no other outstanding Progressive has ever done anything to counteract the effect of Borah's *volte face*.

III

Johnson's chances at present rest on two fragile possibilities, uproarious though he be. The first is that Coolidge may energetically espouse the World Court, that the rank and file of the Republicans may revolt, and that Johnson may be able to capitalize the revolt. But it is greatly to be doubted that Coolidge ever will do anything that could conceivably cause a party rebellion. He may start one unwittingly by doing nothing; but a revolt due to deliberate and positive action against the popular will is something beyond the imagination of those having contact with the President. The second of Johnson's chances grows out of another thin possibility—that next summer the Old Guard, with the votes in hand to nominate Coolidge, may turn him down because nominating him would throw the election away. But even if Coolidge were jettisoned by the Old Guard, Johnson would have no assurance whatever of being chosen as the life-saving Progressive pilot. The Old Guard, it is fair to assume, would be keenly interested to know the views of La Follette in the selection of that pilot. And it also is fair to assume that La Follette would be likely to go into a rage at the suggestion of Johnson. The other Johnson—Magnus—on arriving in Washington a few days ago, told the La Follette story. "I used to be for Hiram", he said simply, "but he has backslid".

All this accounts for the enfeebled condition of the Johnson candidacy. It is the simple story of a man of personal rectitude and large talent for public affairs who has been thrown back on his haunches at the moment of brilliant opportunity for no other reason than that he was narrowly and unintelligently selfish, and that in his selfishness he guessed wrong—guessed absurdly that he had come upon a period in which it was useless to be athletic in the cause of the great plain people. But does this error justify the prevalent curved lip and glittering eye? As I asked in the beginning, Ought selfishness be set up as a bar

to sympathy for a politician? There is the consideration that if we make it a bar we shall have the devil's own time in finding political heroes in the future. More than that, there is the consideration that in point of fact selfishness has not been a bar in numerous instances in the past. Great hordes of people, in fact, are constantly weeping over politicians who have failed to reach the heights because their selfishness became apparent to the naked eye —at the wrong time. Why, therefore, the cold view of poor Johnson paying the price?

My own belief is that the almost universal weariness with him among those who have been in close contact with him in the past few years is not due to his selfishness as the term is ordinarily used; my notion is that their weariness is due to the peculiar form of his selfishness, a form that usually causes the man afflicted with it to be described as a short sport. Johnson might have come through such incidents as the tariff battle and the Newberry scandal— things commonly cited against him—with little loss of sympathy if his proceedings therein, or a few similar acts, had been all. The American people are accustomed to that sort of chicane, and discount it as the necessity of the best intentioned politician. Other Progressives capitulated on the tariff, and the return of political favors to men like Newberry is regarded by many people of all shades of political opinion as a part of what may be called the gang morality of politicians. But when Johnson paralleled those episodes with a three-year record of sulking while the balance of his old crowd had a dozen snickersnees in air all the time, he became a bore, and men who had been his ardent supporters in 1920 began to precede discussions of him with hollow laughs.

And they were not unfair to him thereby, for the childish sulking that began after his defeat for the 1920 nomination was not a strange disease in Johnson, to be overlooked as transient. It was, indeed, but one manifestation of a strain in the man's nature that is permanent and dominating.

Johnson, undoubtedly a man of considerable size, is nevertheless part baby. The baby in him does not rob him of courage in conflict; nobody takes and gives blows more willingly than he when the fight is on and going well. But the baby in him does make him run from bawling to sulking when the breaks are suddenly bad. Neither nature nor self-discipline has ever taught him to bury the hurt, to force a smile, to play the game so hard that the sheer exercise of effort obliterates all else. He simply cannot do it. Perhaps he realizes the weakness and struggles to overcome it. But he cannot overcome it. His career abounds in tiny but tremendously significant instances of his shortcoming.

IV

No one in Chicago, when the Old Guard threw the gaff into him, will ever forget his utter inability to take it sportingly. He was in a blind, Berserker rage and the hotel lobbies hummed with stories of his highly colored speeches and his bellicose messages to politicians who besought him to be reasonable. It was at that time that Borah, who had supported Johnson with a hearty generosity rarely seen in politics, remarked in a puzzled way: "Johnson's a funny fellow." And it was at that time that Johnson, offended by an article or two written by the correspondent of a Philadelphia newspaper, sent for the man, roundly abused him, and then, like a triumphant City Councilman, paraded forth with a stenographic copy of the proceedings to prove that he had out-damned the reporter! There he was, a man of high standing in a presumably dignified profession and a politician of brilliant record—and yet, when the hour of denial and chagrin struck him, no reserve of poise stood between him and the practices of downtown politics. He was wholly unable to see that no rational person in Chicago cared three whoops in a gale of wind what had been printed about

him in Philadelphia, or what he thought of the man who had printed it.

The same weakness has caused endless amusement at his expense in Washington. Somebody printed an article in which Borah was reported to have said that the difference between him and Johnson was that he cared for principles and Johnson cared for personalities. What was the effect? The story in Washington was that Johnson was thrown into a great temper and hurtled over to Borah's office to learn whether Borah had ever said such a terrible thing. "The Mirrors of Washington" appeared, impaling Johnson in company with a dozen or so other celebrities. All except Johnson did their wincing and grimacing in their private apartments. Johnson engaged in furious pursuit of the then anonymous author, and became involved in an acrimonious correspondence with a man whom he suspected, but who had no more to do with the authorship of the "Mirrors" than with the authorship of the Declaration of Independence.

So we have him today, a Progressive hero gone *déclassé* among those who know his course most intimately, and, worse than that, gone *déclassé* in the centre of a circle of hard, dry eyes. Some of the Californians tell a story of an exchange between Johnson, when he was in his heyday as Governor of their State, and Fremont Older, the San Francisco editor. Older, the story goes, had been a dinner guest at the Governor's mansion. The dinner had been excellent and the two men had moved out to the porch. Johnson, gently rubbing the portion of his periphery that an enthusiast gone mad once described lyrically as "the delicious curve of his little paunch", rolled out this sentiment: "Well, Fremont, it is a good old world after all." Older exploded: "It's a hell of a world!" and was called upon to offer proof. It may be suspected that for some time past Johnson has been in the mood to admit Older's case without argument.

TWO YEARS OF DISARMAMENT

BY MILES MARTINDALE

THERE IS but one way to estimate a treaty and that is by its results. Usually they are long in becoming manifest. Two years, however, have shown so many practical and important results of the Treaty on the Limitation of Naval Armaments, ratified by the Senate on March 29, 1922, that a balance sheet may even now be drawn with fair accuracy.

First, perhaps, in world-wide significance is the slowly growing realization that something new happened in diplomatic history when the treaty was signed. A treaty was negotiated in which there was no real contest between the signatories! It is now claimed by some that the United States won a victory; that is true. Others say that Japan won and yet others that it was Great Britain; these statements also are true. But when it is alleged that these "victories" were gained at the expense of some other signatory, the plain facts are disregarded. The victory was actually one of common sense over exaggerated fear, of logic over hysteria. The sober men of all countries won against the war-breeders of all countries. I do not say against the "militarists", for save for a few Germans, a few Frenchmen and a few Japanese, militarism does not exist anywhere in strength sufficient to cause alarm. Wars are not bred by soldiers any more, nor even by diplomats, but by the voters who hire both. Diplomats and legislators keep their ears to the ground, and act as the whispers or roars they hear direct them. Soldiers do as they are told. Neither can we blame the international bankers. Members of a team do not fight one another while the game is in progress; the bankers were the first to clutch at the impossible Article X of the so-called Peace Treaty. Two forces, swaying whole peoples, make wars: Intolerance and Fear. The Conference struck a telling blow at both.

This was the setting: three nations spending more than they could afford in preparation for a war that none of them wanted. Great Britain would have been a spectator in that war, but she would have been obliged to mobilize just the same. Hampered on one side by her alliance with Japan, and on the other side by the anti-Japanese sentiment of Canada, Australia, New Zealand and even India, she would have been forced to watch two of her best customers destroy each other's buying power. All three countries regarded war as inevitable; and when people think that war is inevitable, it is, unless something unusual happens. The Conference happened. Overlaid as its accomplishments were by the hosannas of the pacifists and sentimentalists, they were nevertheless real. The Conference has been called mushy. A great deal of the blather that accompanied it undoubtedly was so; but hard achievement was under the sentimentality.

II

When the Conference was called, the pound sterling was at its lowest point, and the British income tax was six shillings in the pound. With tight lips, the British were facing another period of naval expansion forced upon them by the building programs of the United States and Japan. Their debt to the United States hung over them like a pall. To delay and equivocate about payment did not suit the national financial temper; the most unbearable thing to the British mind is uncertainty. But when every penny paid to the United States meant crippling the British defense program and helping the building program of the United States, the dilemma was dire. No Britisher definitely desired a war with the United States, but a great many Britishers were brandishing anti-American torches in a very dangerous way. The resentment of the poor and desperately taxed against the United States was noticeable to all visiting Americans. We were accused of shirking our share in the war until we had collared all the real money in the world, and then using that money to build up a naval power sufficient to destroy British trade and with it Britain herself.

Peace has never been secure in modern times when any nation showed a desire to pass England in naval strength; and on paper we had already passed England. Holland was much more the friend and ally of England than we have ever been until she began to build excellent fighting ships. Charles II is usually blamed for the war that followed in 1672, but it must be admitted that seldom has a war been more popular. The trouble at Agadir in 1911 simmered down into loudly expressed regret in England, "There goes the last chance of thrashing Germany while she is still easy!" In 1920 we were rapidly assuming the position from which Germany, France, the Netherlands, Spain, even Denmark in the long-ago, had been toppled by an England which felt her life menaced by naval power. It was a long way in the future, perhaps, but it seemed fairly certain even to the English laborer, who knows his job depends upon foreign trade, that another war would be the only alternative to a ruined England and a disintegrated Empire.

Much was written in our newspapers of the visible delight of the British delegation at the end of the final sitting, with the conclusion that they had "put something over" on Mr. Hughes. They had put nothing over, but they had gained something of enormous value. Two years have shown plainly that as long as the work of the Conference endures there will be no Anglo-American war. We have made it clear that we have no desire to drive England from the seas and no willingness to be driven ourselves. We have security from attack, but no ability to take the offensive in a really dangerous way. The anti-American agitation in Great Britain has now practically vanished, and taxes have been reduced one shilling in the pound. The debt to the United States has been thoroughly discussed, and satisfactory arrangements for its payment have been made. The consequent clearing of the financial skies has already been of great benefit and steadying effect on both sides of the water. A deficit in the trade balance has become a surplus. The pound having risen, is now down again—but certainly not because, but in spite of the Conference.*

With her present superiority of two battle-cruisers and greater gun-elevation, (a superiority existing before the Conference, by the way, and not increased since,) Great Britain is in a position to repel attacks on her shores, but she has not the strength to attack across the ocean herself. This last is no drawback in British eyes, for anyone who holds that Great Britain would deliberately attack the United States has not gone very deeply into our merchant marine situation nor into foreign trade as a whole.

These benefits, already achieved, were plainly visible to the British delegation at the close of the Conference. They knew that for years to come, in spite of curtailed building, they would be secure from naval attack and could turn all their energy into a commercial revival. Why should they not be delighted?

III

Now for Japan. In the Spring of 1921, conditions in that country were extremely

*The German-French situation, of course, has been responsible for its recent fall.

disquieting. Unhampered by checks and balances, the Government had tried the old experiment of repealing the laws of economics by act of parliament, with the result that panic had hit Japan harder and was lasting longer than in any other country. Revolution, for years not too far under the surface, was thrusting up its head here and there; people were hungry. The war party, called Chosiu, was in power, principally because nearly every voter in the Empire had become firmly convinced that the United States was plotting war. In spite of terribly heavy taxes, Japan was rapidly building battleships, at least one of them by popular subscription. War with America was regarded as inevitable and Japan was making ready. The common man believed that we were preparing to attack. The Chosiu politicians, carrying out a program outlined in 1858, believed war the only alternative to bloody revolution.

Prior to 1854, Japan's whole history was a sequence of efforts to prove herself independent of China. The influx of foreigners, backed by fleets of war vessels, brought the added fear of partition and domination by white men. Seventy years ago the Elder Statesmen advised avoidance of all disputes until Japan grew strong enough to deal with one rival at a time. This advice underlies the amazing modernization of Japan, centuries of development being compressed into decades. In accordance with the program, China was humbled in 1894 and Russia in 1904. Germany's turn came in 1914, for to the peasant's mind, the opera bouffe campaign of Tsing Tao bulks as large as if the entire war power of Germany had been engaged. The years ending in "4" were thus fixed in the Japanese mind as years of invincibility. The Americans were plotting war on Japan? Then let them have it; but it will be when we choose, and that is in 1924!

Our lavish expenditure and great effort during the world war impressed even Chosiu with the difficulties of the program. The scheme of invasion through Mexico, once in favor, was abandoned, and the Japanese prepared for a swift blow without warning, like the naval attack with which they opened the war with Russia. Seizing the Philippines, and isolating Manila Bay if it did not fall easily and cheaply enough, they would sit tight with the advantage of defense and distance, waiting for our attempt to recapture the Islands. They counted two years as necessary for us to organize the required effort; expected a majority of our people to consider the Philippines not worth recovering; believed the war would be intensely unpopular in America and that we would ask for peace rather than undertake the pain and loss of fighting it out to the end. Whether their plan correctly appraised our psychology or not, it involved heavy losses on our part. To attack across several thousand miles of empty sea in a war involving land forces would require at least a 5-3 superiority in fighting ships, a million tons of auxiliaries and at least three million tons of transports.

The war was not desired by the Japanese for aggrandizement, nor to provide extra room for their people. Japan has not yet filled some of her own home islands, notably Hokkaido and Saghalien. The war was simply a part of the Chosiu program, considered necessary to preserve the divinity of the Emperor and the cohesion of the Empire. The Chosiu politicians were not over-optimistic, but they believed war the safest course. Like the occupation of Belgium, it was *planmässig*, and the plan had three times succeeded in the past.

The immediate effect of the Conference was to take the guiding power from Chosiu and give it to Satsuma. Satsuma is convinced that Japan cannot whip the world. The war with Russia taught the statesmen of this party that the modern victor gains little besides heavy debts and high taxes, together with the distrust of other nations. They admit the danger of revolution at home but believe that this danger is increased by every move tending to emphasize the divinity of the Emperor. They plan for a better-educated Japan, headed by a competent man-Emperor, prospering commercially through a widening circle of friends. The Conference convinced not only Satsuma, but the Elder Statesmen as well that America is planning no war in the Pacific.

The first real step forward was taken when Mr. Hughes limited the agenda to naval matters, thus assuring a Satsuma delegation, for Satsuma is traditionally charged with the Navy and the Foreign Office. The position of the Japanese at the Conference was difficult in the extreme. Their one ally, Great Britain, showed appalling alacrity in throwing the alliance overboard. In some quarters, they found their proposals receiving even less consideration than those of the Chinese. If by any chance Chosiu had been right in alleging that America wanted war, they must have left the Conference with a complete failure on their hands, and Japan would have been committed to heavier and yet heavier taxes for armament.

But it soon became apparent to them that Mr. Hughes meant what he said. America refused to listen to a naval ratio which would have made the defense of the Philippines impossible; but she agreed to one which made an attack on Japan foolhardy. Since eighteen years of war-scares had been insufficient to induce Congress to properly fortify Guam and Olongapo, Mr. Hughes knew that there was no chance for fort-building during a period of retrenchment. He therefore readily agreed to Japan's demand for the *status quo* in the fortification of the islands. He did not permit its extension to include Hawaii; but Hawaii is a long way from the weak link in Japan's chain, the Pescadores. It became plain that Japan would have no sympathy from the world in a war with America, and that America would fight hard if it came to fighting, but would infinitely rather not.

Satsuma therefore took back complete justification of her domestic policy and the Elder Statesmen made war-breeding Chosiu step down. The transition from war- to peace-psychology was gradual though rapid. A former premier was permitted to speak in the Diet in favor of a curtailed military program and the extension of the franchise, and the Elder Statesmen noted the approval of the solid, better-class commoners. As an experiment, when the Crown Prince toured Europe, inspired press notices had stressed his democratic behavior in walking the streets alone, shaking hands with common men and otherwise conducting himself like a human being. This news caused such a roar of popular applause that the Elder Statesmen listened with renewed attention to Satsuma's contention that the god-game was played out. I do not venture to deny that Yoshihito is really a sick man; but his illness and abdication were very opportune.

The Conference thus lightened Japan's burden and broke her will to war. Since the earthquake, not a single member of the war party sits in the Cabinet.

IV

In the United States the paramount necessity of 1921 was to keep income and expenditure balanced. The Budget Act gave the first real opportunity to compare the two in advance, and the outlook in the winter of 1920-1921 was not bright. More than our own recovery was at stake. Alone in the world, we were solvent. If we had then been obliged to over-spend, to depreciate our dollar by inflating our national credit, the financial *débâcle* of the whole world could not have been prevented. Our people were already paying taxes to the extent of one dollar in each six and were in no mood to pay more. It was imperative to reduce expenditures. Congressmen, listening to the voices of their districts, were hearing loud shouts of "No more war, nor war expenses!"

In spite of this, because of the building programs of Japan and Great Britain, our most conservative naval experts were pointing to the necessity of building far beyond the program already authorized. The fourteen capital ships projected were but the backbone. In some lesser classes we had approximately enough. In others, practically none.

Even in capital ships our position was not unassailable. The figures of Whitaker's Almanac, which made England nervous, were misleading, as such figures usually are. In 1920 they stood as follows:

	United States	Great Britain	Japan
Capital Ships	33	32	17
Displacement	1,117,850	808,200	543,140
Battle guns	340	284	164
Foot tons energy	28,597,176	19,080,000	13,415,400

This looks as if we were offering to give up a tremendous superiority in 1921. If naval battles were fought by appointment at close quarters, at ranges permitting the lesser guns to bear, that would have been true. But we all know that battles are not so conducted. Our *New York* and *Texas* and all ships previously built would have been hopelessly outranged and outmaneuvered by more than half the existing British tonnage. A good half of our "battle-guns" were 12-inch, and most of them were carried by ships which could not float after one or two direct 15-inch hits, with speeds from three to eight knots an hour less than those of the newer half of the British Fleet. The ships which the Conference permitted us to retain represented practically all really available for the first line that were then built or approximately complete. Similar elimination of the expensive unfit was applied to the British tonnage, and the Treaty provides that the slight tonnage discrepancy shown in the table below will disappear automatically with the passage of years:

United States	525,850
Great Britain	558,950
Japan	301,320

In gun-power there is little to choose between the two leading fleets. Our older guns are a little inferior, our newer guns are superior. Gun for gun, the greater elevation of the British guns gives them a slightly longer range; but our Navy is making hits at ranges above any used at Jutland or Dogger Bank.

It is frequently urged that the completion of the rest of the *Massachusetts* class and the four battle-cruisers would have given us a superiority even greater than that shown in Whitaker's table. That may be, though it is probable that the British program would have kept pace. As things stood, however, an increased number of capital ships would not have greatly increased our long-range striking power. During the World War we finally succeeded in sending across five battleships. They were not our newest and best. In 1917 the emergency seemed to call for more than five; but the fact remained that we could not support more capital ships overseas without curtailing our transport, minelayer and antisubmarine campaign. A battleship cannot support itself. Aside from provisions and fuel, our *New Mexico*, provided her guns held out, could in one day fire away ammunition weighing several times the total carrying capacity of the ship herself. This condition is not a new one. In 1907 we sent sixteen small battleships around the world, and they were supported by British and German auxiliaries. Had a European war broken out while that fleet was in Manila, it is estimated that with the available American merchant tonnage, five years would have been necessary to get the ships back home. Our wartime building of merchant ships has helped that situation; but it justifies a fleet of capital ships of half a million tons only, and that is what we kept under the Treaty. Great Britain, which could support more capital ships, has been cut down to our limit, not hers.

Beside, it was becoming increasingly apparent that our advertised capital ship program would not be carried out. If the Budget was to be balanced, that program could not be executed unless some other vital department of the Government was practically discontinued. Congress could not see the need of this. One prominent member of the House Appropriations Committee had already stated that he could find no justification for naval expenditure in any amount greater than that of 1913. It may be that he would have been overruled by the House itself, but completion of the program was by no means certain.

One thing *was*, however, quite certain: if the battleships were built, no other naval craft would be. Since the beginning of the white Squadron, the peace-time story has been the same, year after year. Congress has granted battleships with fair regularity, but has not allowed for minor craft in anything like adequate numbers. Small submarines were always easy to obtain, not because of a lobby, as has been alleged, but because they were considered cheap and efficient substitutes for the extra battleships demanded by the Navy General Board. Little notice was taken of other vessels until the war broke out. Cruisers had been so neglected that in figuring our effective scouting strength in 1921, the only cruisers counted on our side were the ten, not yet completed, authorized during the war. The table of cruisers, including some not yet launched, now stands:

	Tons
United States	75,000
Great Britain	252,000
Japan	176,400

This shows us to be 219,000 tons short of a 5-3 ratio with Japan, and gaining no ground. Without the Conference and a stoppage of battleship construction, the discrepancy would never have become visible to Congress or to the people.

We built destroyers during the war as a counter to the German submarines, so the tonnage table is in our favor here:

United States	334,917
Great Britain	247,546
Japan	104,960

However, only 126,360 tons of our destroyers are in commission, for we have no men to put on board them. There was no hope in 1921 of getting more men in the Navy, nor is there now. Destroyers out of commission deteriorate rapidly. A very short period without a crew on board will make them of doubtful value. Beside, we have none of the type called "flotilla leaders", developed in England during the war. One ranking naval officer testified during a recent inquiry that the presence of a flotilla leader might have prevented the loss of seven destroyers on the California coast. Here, again, our superiority is largely on paper.

Before the Conference, we had the old collier *Jupiter* being made over into the aircraft carrier *Langley*, and we had the small carrier *Wright* being made from a Shipping Board freighter. Neither is an efficient carrier when compared to some of the speedy ships developed abroad. No carriers were included in the building program authorized, and since the close of the war, Congress had twice refused to grant any. The table stood in 1921:

	Vessels	Tons
United States	1	12,700
Great Britain	6	82,550
Japan	3	29,900

Only the Conference persuaded Congress to allow vessels of this type, and then only because two of the doomed battle-cruisers were far enough along to make completion as carriers about as cheap as cancellation. The Conference then, presented us with two excellent carriers, otherwise unobtainable.

The same inadequacy shows in the submarine situation when analysed. Whitaker again takes the cheerful view of our power, giving the United States 107 built and 41 building, Great Britain 92 built and 8 building, Japan 24 built and 15 building. This seems to show America leading by a long margin; but here are the facts:

	Small submarines for coast or harbor use only, tons	Large submarines for use with the battle-fleet, tons
United States	66,695	9,693
Great Britain	40,253	19,960
Japan	42,714	32,655

In view of the above, it is apparent that the frequent plaint that "the Conference sank the finest Navy in the world" is totally unfounded. Our naval situation was bad; and the paper superiority in prospective battleships was blinding us to just how bad it was and how rapidly it was becoming worse. The Conference gave us the Irish gain of not losing as much as we might otherwise have done. More, it forced upon us the first real naval policy that we have ever had. In the past, all arguments over appropriations began with an agreement that Congress should maintain an "adequate" navy. Before the annual bill was large enough to make any real difference in the total expenditure, Congress listened to the naval experts and gave them more or less what they requested. But when the bill ran over one hundred millions they began to check the figures of the naval experts and to cut down every estimate regarding which they could not be convinced—and sometimes a conscientious Congressman, in times of piping peace, is not easily convinced. Until the Conference, the voters had no measure of an "adequate" navy. They considered all naval officers hipped on the subject and very naturally believed that Congress, weighing all the evidence, had provided the required adequacy. In short, we had no naval policy at all other than political and financial convenience in peace and fright in war.

That is now changed and we have a naval policy which is not hard for the layman to understand. It is expressed in the ratio 5-5-3; and that ratio applies to all useful types. It is beginning to be realized that the Treaty Navy is one much better balanced and more powerful than any we have ever possessed. As long as we had to build battleships at forty-odd million dollars apiece, there was no money to be had for other craft. Congress could not be brought to see the necessity of them and the people believed Congress. Since the Conference, true enough, no move has been made to supply our deficiencies, but the people are no longer hopelessly convinced that minor ships are not necessary. They now know what an adequate navy should be, and that is one which fulfills the 5-5-3 ratio. Battleships no longer overshadow other necessary types, for each type must run true to the ratio. The newspapers are all glad the battleship race is over; but with few exceptions they advocate lesser craft in the proportions laid down by the Navy General Board.

V

I do not claim that the Arms Conference has ended war. It has, however, removed all the causes for war that were showing their ugly heads in 1921. If war comes, there will have to be found a new *casus belli*. The Conference made all the old ones ridiculous. And if a new excuse for war *is* found, the Treaty Navy will make us safer than we have ever been,—provided we build it before hostilities begin!

SANTAYANA AT CAMBRIDGE

BY MARGARET MÜNSTERBERG

Ah, did you once see Shelley plain?
   And did he stop and speak to you,
And did you speak to him again?
   How strange it seems and new!

PERHAPS it is not quite appropriate to begin my reminiscences of George Santayana with a quotation from Browning, considering that when the philosopher was invited to address the ladies of the Boston Browning Society, he began by telling them that he really did not care for Browning at all.

Yet to have met him unawares at Cambridge street-corners on his way to a lecture, to have heard his laughter under my own roof, to have listened to his leisurely artless talk in the smoking-room of an ocean steamer—all this, now in retrospect, seems a privilege not so very unlike that of seeing Shelley plain. It must be said in frankness, however, that if I had not been touched by the magic of his books, the recollection of those casual meetings might not be endowed with any glamor. If Shelley had not already been the Shelley of "The Skylark", no matter how vivid his glance, I doubt if "seeing him plain" would ever have given his fellow-poet a thrill. But once acclaimed a master spirit, the man—the "human" man—becomes a visible symbol of the poet or the philosopher. His glance, his simple gestures, his careless words we instinctively reinterpret in the light cast by his later achievements. This instinct cannot be rooted out of the mind, and perhaps, after all, it is worth preserving.

To remember George Santayana as he appeared in the late nineties in academic Cambridge is to remember his glance when he recognized us on the street. In his dark Spanish eyes there was a sudden illumination, an extraordinary focusing of light-rays having the effect of a blaze of pure spirit. His face was handsome, delicate, pale against the black hair and small moustache; it seemed the face of a dreamer rather than of a scholarly thinker. But his eyes had sprites in them and a light from fairy-lands forlorn. Though we were but children at the time, whenever, on our way from school, we saw Santayana coming in his picturesque long cape, we felt the glow of a poet's approach. And then his laugh! He laughed not with his lips only, but with his whole face. His was a laugh to delight a child's heart, the laugh of Peter Pan, brimming over with pure merriment.

Santayana had a natural preference for solitude. Indeed, one did not expect to see him in a crowd, at a business meeting, in a hurry to catch a train for an appointment or otherwise going through the motions of a busy man in the whirl of the world's work. I remember leaning over the railing of an ocean liner anchored at Southampton and watching passengers from the English tender crowd up the gang-plank to the steamer: one only stood apart at the edge of the tender, with calm and amused detachment observed the haste and struggle of his fellow-travelers, and not till the deck had been cleared, followed himself.

"Who could it be but Santayana!" a voice said beside me, and we all felt the satisfaction of finding a character true to himself.

In an active, gregarious society, the man who stands aside and contemplates is naturally regarded with uneasiness. So there were some who could not quite swallow this apparent self-sufficiency, and, as about all men who are hard to understand, myths began to be woven around the Spanish philosopher. With a kind of awe-struck horror I learned, when still in my early teens, that Santayana was a Solipsist—a man who has the audacity to believe that he is the only soul alive! Many years later, on reading his "Soliloquies in England", I discovered the ground from which this news had sprung. It seems that Santayana had indeed indulged in Solipsism, either as play of fancy or as philosophical speculation: ". . . and later I liked to regard all systems as alternative illusions for the Solipsist."

But the aloofness to which men objected was really of the most inoffensive kind. Santayana was not a snob—he did not take either the world or himself seriously enough for that—and still less the traditional *zerstreute Professor*. He was simply a quiet spectator, a smiling philosopher. His was the modesty of one who has plenty of humor and few illusions. He was capable of taking a bird's eye view of society and, without dizziness, seeing his own small place on the map. For a trivial example—when he filled out the questionnaire on the Customs declaration, he called himself not university professor, but simply "teacher".

II

When the question arose at Harvard, in the year 1898, whether Santayana or another young aspirant should be promoted to a professorship, his colleagues James, Royce and Münsterberg strongly advocated his advancement. Extracts from a letter by Hugo Münsterberg to the President of Harvard may throw some light on the situation:

. . . I take it as my duty to do whatever I can in the interest of a most desirable promotion in our Philosophical Department, and as I understand that it is not unusual that members of the faculty bring such matters directly before you, I take the liberty of doing so.

My hope and desire is that Dr. G. Santayana will be promoted for the next year to an assistant professorship.

The reasons are firstly personal. Mr. Santayana has done by his teaching and by his writing through a series of years a work which cannot be appreciated highly enough and for which an early promotion seems a just and fair act of acknowledgment from the side of Harvard. His teaching has surpassed in every direction the usual routine work of philosophical instructors; it has been in every respect original and its influence on the more advanced students is a most important one, as it supplements in a characteristic way the methods and systems of the other Harvard philosophers. Especially the aesthetical tone which he has added to the philosophical chord obliges all of us.

But the promotion is not only necessary as an appreciation of Santayana's personal merits, it is secondly desirable in the interests of the whole Philosophical Department. It would emphasize in an impressive way before the academic public those ideas of specialized university work and productive scholarship for which we contend. We appear to deny these principles if we seem to ignore the difference between an average philosophy teacher and an original scholar like the author of "The Sense of Beauty". If the department clearly shows that we acknowledge and appreciate such a type of scholarly productive activity, we shall give by that a strong and suggestive impulse to many advanced students in that direction in which we try to go forward.

I feel the more obliged to express this belief as I know that a most interesting book on ethical problems will follow soon the mentioned volume, which is surely the best book ever written on aesthetics in America.

In another letter the same writer characterized his colleague as a "strong and healthy man" and "a good, gay, fresh companion."

This testimony was important in view of the prevailing Puritan and utilitarian attitude toward the meditative aesthete. The greatest American educator thus expressed his doubts and fears:

. . . The withdrawn, contemplative man who takes no part in the everyday work of the institution, or of the world, seems to me to be a person of very uncertain value. He does not dig ditches, or lay bricks, or write school-books; his product is not of the ordinary useful, though humble, kind. What will it be? It may be something of the highest utility; but, on the other hand, it may be something futile, or even harmful, because unnatural and untimely.

But all doubts were finally dispelled; and although President Eliot had said that he confessed to misgivings when he imagined Santayana a full professor at fifty years of age—yet the young Spaniard was received with open arms into the family of Harvard philosophers.

Given to solitary contemplation as he was, yet when Santayana did step out of his charmed solitude, he brought with him a gaiety that men often lose in the rub of too much human contact. Now and then there gleamed in him a Shakespearean grain. Strange as it is to remember, the most delicate of modern writers, in his artless conversation, put to flight all misgivings as to his "humanity" by revealing at times a humor unmistakably broad—for instance, when he submissively spoke of seasickness as "a good spring cleaning". This malady, of which he was a long-suffering victim, must have confirmed his belief in the hard reality of material fact. Yet he knew one infallible remedy, and that was a fragrant dish of arrow-root; a fellow-passenger who could supply him with that magic potion won his gratitude forever.

Santayana's gaiety may have been of the kind that prompted Spinoza to pause in his cosmic speculations and burst into laughter at the sight of a fly escaping the ruse of a spider; and yet it was not without a sense of cheer in human fellowship. Otherwise how could he have given us his altogether perfect interpretation of Dickens? Perhaps his humorous distaste for the pompous gesture and for taking one's self too seriously may have had something to do with his almost tender love for England and English manners. This merry side of Santayana was little known except to his friends. To others, who knew him only from a distance, he seemed, no doubt, an aloof and alien spirit.

III

George Santayana is a Spaniard by birth; but when he was nine years old his mother brought him with her to live in America, while his father remained in Spain. So young George spent his school-years in New England, but his summer vacations with his father in Spain. Thus it came about that he acquired an intimate knowledge of his native land and retained a true affection for it, while, on the other hand, though Spanish and English were both natural to him, English became the language of his studies and of his writings both in prose and verse. He was graduated from Harvard in 1886 and, although he studied also at German and English universities, it was at Harvard that he received his doctor's degree. Thereupon he was immediately appointed instructor, nine years later assistant professor and after another nine years full professor at Harvard.

Santayana's influence on his students was more than the influence of classroom and lecture platform. It was deep and direct. I have the word of one of them—and one, I believe, who was not of the chosen ones— that no man ever impressed him so profoundly. The young men who took draughts from that cool, sparkling, lucid fountain took them for life. There must have been very little of the didactic, very little condescension in Santayana's intercourse with his students. Before the common interests of the mind, the common passions of the spirit, barriers of age break down. For academic youth and the friendships of youth Santayana had and has the finest understanding. To one of his young pupils he was tenderly attached, and the young man's untimely death affected him like the death of a son. Among his sonnets are beautiful elegies to this youth, as to a second Lycidas.

Santayana seemed never to grow older. If he had not in the later years at Harvard grown a beard, there would have been no sign of advancing age; he would, like Ahasver, have remained the eternal youth. Perhaps his sympathy for young men was facilitated by the fact that his daily external life did not greatly differ from theirs. A portly *paterfamilias* soon gets removed from youth into the hemisphere of another generation; the gravity of business, of bread-winning for dependents, of domestic and social obligations, the more it renders him respectably Philistine, the more it alienates him from the companions of his sons. Santayana knew no such bondage. In student dormitories he made his abode. At first he lived in old Stoughton Hall in the Harvard Yard, and ate his meals at one of the private students' clubs. He also, at that time, belonged to a French club of young men who met at the members' rooms to read aloud, until the club was disbanded because they could no longer endure one another's French.

Later Santayana had rooms in a made-over private house in Brattle Street, and finally he was our near neighbor when he had his quarters in Prescott Hall, a modest dormitory only a block away from the philosophy building, Emerson Hall, where he gave his lectures. Near his abode was the Colonial Club, an old Cambridge house, frequented by professors, some of whom met there regularly at lunch time. At this old club Santayana had his meals—whether in company with his colleagues or content to watch them, I do not know.

The philosopher delighted in long walks, during which, no doubt, he spun his fine meditations. Three times a week regularly he walked the considerable distance from his Cambridge quarters to Brookline, to the house of his mother and sister. To them he was devoted, and through continual contact with them he must have kept constantly fresh the spring of his Spanish associations, which otherwise might have dried on Cambridge soil. To his Cambridge friends his Spanish family, who evidently lived in retirement, was wholly unknown.

"What do your mother and sister do all day?" someone asked him once.

"What Spanish ladies generally do," he answered. "In the morning they wait for the afternoon and in the afternoon they wait for the evening."

Yet I have the impression that Santayana has a profound respect for Spanish women —not only for those of his own kin, but for the whole tribe; and I know from his casual remarks that he admires their rather lazy and luxurious style of beauty.

A characteristic letter comes to my hand, one that he wrote to a colleague who had tried to find him at his mother's house:

75 Monmouth Street,
Brookline
Jan. 13

Dear Professor: Thank you very much for your kind letter, and the invitation for next Tuesday, at seven o'clock, which it will give me great pleasure to avail myself of.

I am sorry you should have taken the trouble to hunt for this house. Much as I should like to see you, I don't expect any of my friends to come so far. Don't think it necessary to stand on such formalities as returning visits. Thanking you again, I remain,

Yours very sincerely
G. *Santayana*.

P. S. I have not thanked you for "Also sprach Zarathustra", which arrived safely, and which I have read with pleasure. The title is also good, although I don't see that there is anything very new at bottom, or very philosophical, in the new ethics. Has it, for instance, any standard of value by which we can convince ourselves that the *Uebermensch* is a better being than ourselves? I should like some day to hear your own opinion of this ideal.

With his colleagues in the Harvard Philosophical Department — James, Royce, Palmer, Münsterberg—Santayana was on most friendly terms, even though the philosophical views of each one of them were thoroughly at variance with his own. But a genial hospitality of thought was characteristic of that five-starred Pleiade, and theoretical opposition in no way clouded the friendliness among the philosophers. As Santayana was not given to controversy, as he had a charitable inclination to leave others in peace if they would but leave him alone, as he was not, during the earlier half of his Harvard life, well known to the general public and did not figure in the newspapers, he had no outspoken enemies.

That, in the early years of his Harvard career, he should have been somewhat lionized and made the center of a Cambridge salon is not surprising when one considers that in that Puritanic community in the nineties aestheticism was still a novelty and the brilliant young Spaniard was alien but dazzling. Among some of the admiring Cambridge ladies there developed a veritable Santayana cult, suggesting a little the vogue of Schopenhauer among the ladies of Frankfurt-am-Main. That was in the days before poetry societies and magazines of free verse, and when Santayana, in the picturesque library of one of his colleagues, read his just completed theological drama "Lucifer" a congenial audience was held spellbound by the beauty of his lines and the visible harmony between the poet and his work.

When his first slender volume of sonnets appeared, a charming and vivacious Cambridge woman gave the little book a birthday party. The poet requited his hostess and the other guests with graceful little verses in their honor. Occasionally he even entertained them at tea in his bachelor rooms. Once he planned a dinner-party for a young New York girl who was visiting one of his favored hostesses, and promised to invite for her the richest, the handsomest and the nicest young man at Harvard; she was to guess which was which, and when the party was over, her guesses proved to be right.

Santayana has never married. He once said that he dreaded what he called "the eternal silence" that ensues when husband and wife sit opposite each other and have nothing more to say. But gossip will not leave an unusual man in peace, and in his Cambridge days it was rumored that there was some mysterious lady who commanded his heart and kindled his Muse. Who she was no one could say, or, indeed, if she ever really existed at all. The spirit of Dante and Petrarch breathes out of Santayana's love sonnets, but she who may have inspired them is destined to remain a Beatrice unknown.

IV

Persona grata though he was in hospitable Cambridge houses, idolized by an exquisite circle of admirers and by discriminating youth, Santayana never took firm root in New England soil. In the long summer vacations he generally migrated abroad— to his native Spain, where he had a married sister, to France, Germany and his beloved England. There always remained his desire for freedom, his love of solitude and his distaste for routine duties imposed from without. To take an active share in the practical work of the community had no charm for him; he did not even like to burden himself with the small irksome obligations of social life. Rather than be forced by chance circumstance to escort a strange unattended lady home after a Cambridge dinner party, he has been known suddenly to vanish.

He was a pilgrim with a staff. It is not surprising, then, that President Eliot's misgivings were justified when he said that he could not imagine Santayana a full professor at fifty. Before he had reached his half-century mark, the philosopher turned his back upon the class-room, and took up his pilgrim staff for good. His mother was dead; there was no hearth and home to bind him, and so it was painlessly, probably in response to a long-nursed nostalgia, that he followed the call of his skylark spirit. Of course the academic world was astonished. To leave Harvard in order to contemplate in Spain, in Paris, in Oxford and on the banks of the Cam was to cut off an enviable career for idle musing. Such a great refusal was shocking to the Puritan. Besides, after so much admiration had been lavished upon him, it seemed ungrateful to scatter the incense to the breeze. And, really, how could one leave Harvard and Boston by choice?

Though Santayana seems to prefer England to other lands—not, however, with any pronounced intention of becoming an Englishman—though English ways and customs have roused in him an almost romantic attachment, nevertheless it seems to me that he owes his peculiar genius, the distinguishing lucidity of his understanding as well as the finest inspiration of his poetry to his southern European heritage. In spite of his own philosophical detachment from the faith of his youth, he remains for me in the first place the Spanish Catholic. As small children we were sent with a returned book to his rooms and so had the privilege of seeing what they looked like. "I don't know if it is proper for me to invite you in", said the Spanish gentleman to the highly flattered little girls who, however, did not share his doubts. What impressed us most, as we looked round curiously, were the beautiful bright-colored Catholic pictures of saints and Paradise—vague now in my memory as regards detail, but an indelible sign of the philosopher's native inclination.

The southern heritage is two-fold: it has brought with it Hellenism and Catholicism. In the Græco-Roman world Santayana feels at home. Not only is he, of course, thoroughly familiar with Platonic philosophy, but he also has for Pre-Socratic cultured paganism a remarkably keen understanding, as appears in his summary of the ideals of that lost world in his interpretation of Lucretius. Santayana had the southern European's eye for sculpture and in the finite simplicity of Greek art he has a delight that Northerners rarely attain. The ideals, the sanity, the reason of Greek life appeal to him, and it was the best praise that he could bestow on his beloved England that he should compare its life with that of classic Greece. The god Hermes he has made the symbol for sweet reasonableness.

But Hermes is not the only winged patron of his heart; side by side with the Olympic messenger hovers the angel Gabriel. The Roman Catholic religion in which he was bred has both energized and disciplined his imagination, has strengthened his sympathy and given him not only a wealth of imagery for literary use, but a peculiarly keen insight into the meditations of the heart. His early poetry is full of Catholic inspiration. The significance of this influence on him I emphasize in the face of his recent statement that Catholicism is for him only a "vista for the imagination, never a conviction." For the poetry of his youth and early manhood seems to me a more eloquent and more convincing testimony of the true tone of his inner life

than any cool, self-analytical statement written in ironical middle age.

We can imagine the young Spanish Catholic, versed in the catechism and familiar from earliest childhood with the high ritual of the Church, meditating in King's College Chapel on the inner estrangement of the English youths from the pristine meaning of the "gorgeous windows" and "storied walls" that form the background of their devotions.

> The college gathers, and the courtly prayer
> Is answered still by hymn and organ-groan;
> The beauty and the mystery are there,
> The Virgin and Saint Nicholas are gone.
>
> No grain of incense thrown upon the embers
> Of their cold hearth, no lamp in witness hung
> Before their image. One alone remembers;
> Only the stranger knows their mother tongue.

Between Catholicism and Hellenism there is no dilemma: indeed, did not the Church absorb many vestiges of the Græco-Roman world, of classic form and discipline? Did not Virgil show the most Catholic poet the intricate way to beatitude? A dilemma far more profound confronted the Spanish poet-philosopher. In his poetry, and therefore in his heart—for poetry and religion are almost interchangeable concepts to his mind—Santayana is a Catholic; in his philosophy he is a hard materialist. The naturalistic philosopher and the devout poet stand gazing at each other across an abyss that cannot be bridged. In his sonnet, "Gabriel", he has revealed the very pathos of the dilemma.

If he were a Faust nature—which he not only is not, but for which he has not the slightest sympathy—he might exclaim: "*Zwei Seelen wohnen, ach, in meiner Brust!*" and find zest in the struggle for the mastery of one over the other. But the storm and stress gesture is not to Santayana's taste. A classicist, a lover of orderly reason, he prefers to leave to each of the two souls its own place.

CLINICAL NOTES

BY GEORGE JEAN NATHAN AND H. L. MENCKEN

Critical Note.—Of a piece with the absurd pedagogical demand for so-called constructive criticism is the doctrine that an iconoclast is a hollow and evil fellow unless he can prove his case. Why, indeed, should he prove it? Is he judge, jury, prosecuting officer, hangman? He proves enough, indeed, when he proves by his blasphemy that this or that idol is defectively convincing—that at least *one* visitor to the shrine is left full of doubts. The fact is enormously significant; it indicates that instinct has somehow risen superior to the shallowness of logic, the refuge of fools. The pedant and the priest have always been the most expert of logicians—and the most diligent dis minators of nonsense and worse. The liberation of the human mind has never been furthered by such learned dunderheads; it has been furthered by gay fellows who heaved dead cats into sanctuaries and then went roistering down the highways of the world, proving to all men that doubt, after all, was safe—that the god in the sanctuary was finite in his power, and hence a fraud. One horse-laugh is worth ten thousand syllogisms. It is not only more effective; it is also vastly more intelligent.

Confessional.—The older I grow, the more I am persuaded that hedonism is the only sound and practical doctrine of faith for the intelligent man. I doubt, indeed, if there ever has lived an intelligent man whose end in life was not the achievement of a large and selfish pleasure. This latter is often shrewdly swathed in the deceptive silks of altruism or what not, but brush the silks aside and the truth of self-gratification is visible in all its nudity. Mahomet's altruism was as completely hedonistic as Napoleon's frank hedonism. The greater the idealist, the greater the hedonist behind the whiskers.

Note En Passant.—The armies of England and America may fight shoulder to shoulder; the diplomats of England and America may stand side by side in their uplifting of the world; the two navies may salute each other with constant salvos of cannon; the two governments may be as Siamese twins—but it all does not and will not amount to a damn unless the average Englishman can soon train himself to be less patronizing to the average American when he shows him to his restaurant table or sells him a shirt.

Hint to Theologians.—The argument by design, once the bulwark of Christian apologetics, is so full of holes that it is no wonder that it has been abandoned. The more, indeed, the theologian seeks to prove the acumen and omnipotence of God by His works, the more he is dashed by evidences of divine incompetence and irresolution. The world is not actually well run; it is very badly run, and no Huxley was needed to point out the obvious fact. The human body, magnificently designed in some details, is a frightful botch in other details; every first-year student of anatomy sees a hundred ways to improve it. How are we to reconcile this mixture of infinite finesse and clumsy blundering with the concept of a single omnipotent Designer, to whom all problems are equally easy? If He could contrive so efficient and durable a machine as the human hand, then how did He come to make such dreadful

75

botches as the tonsils, the gall-bladder, the uterus and the prostate gland? If He could perfect the hip joint and the ear, then why did He boggle the teeth?

Having never encountered a satisfactory —or even a remotely plausible—answer to such questions, I have had to go to the labor of devising one myself. It is, at all events, quite simple, and in strict accord with all the known facts. In brief, it is this: that the theory that the universe is run by a single God must be abandoned, and that in place of it we must set up the theory that it is actually run by a board of gods, all of equal puissance and authority. Once this concept is grasped all the difficulties that have vexed theologians vanish. Human experience instantly lights up the whole dark scene. We observe in everyday life what happens when authority is divided, and great decisions are reached by consultation and compromise. We know that the effects, at times, particularly when one of the consultants runs away with the others, are very good, but we also know that they are usually extremely bad. Such a mixture of good and bad is on display in the cosmos. It presents a series of brilliant successes in the midst of an infinity of bungling failures.

I contend that my theory is the only one ever put forward that completely accounts for the clinical picture. Every other theory, facing such facts as sin, disease and disaster, is forced to admit the supposition that Omnipotence, after all, may not be omnipotent—a plain absurdity. I need toy with no such nonsense. I may assume that every god belonging to the council which rules the universe is infinitely wise and infinitely powerful, and yet not evade the plain fact that most of the acts of that council are ignorant and foolish. In truth, my assumption that a council exists is tantamount to an *a priori* assumption that its joint acts are ignorant and foolish, for no act of any conceivable council can be otherwise. Is the human hand perfect, or, at all events, practicable and praiseworthy? Then I account for it on the ground that it was de-

signed by some single member of the council—that the business was handed over to him by inadvertence or as a result of an irreconcilable difference of opinion. Had more than one member participated actively in its design it would have been measurably less meritorious than it is, for the sketch offered by the original designer would have been forced to run a gauntlet of criticisms and suggestions from all the other councillors, and human experience teaches us that most of these criticisms and suggestions would have been inferior to the original idea—that many of them, in fact, would have had nothing in them save a petty desire to maul and spoil the original idea.

But do I here accuse the high gods of harboring discreditable human weaknesses? If I do, then my excuse is that it is impossible to imagine them doing the work universally ascribed to them without admitting their possession of such weaknesses. One cannot imagine a god spending weeks and months, and maybe whole geological epochs, laboring er the design of the human kidney without assuming him to be moved by a powerful impulse to express himself vividly, to marshal and publish his ideas, to win public credit among his fellows—in brief, without assuming him to be egoistic. And one cannot assume him to be egoistic without assuming him to prefer the adoption of his own ideas to the adoption of any other god's. I defy anyone to make the contrary assumption without plunging instantly into clouds of mysticism. Ruling it out, one comes inevitably to the conclusion that the inept management of the universe must be ascribed to clashes of egos, *i.e.*, petty revenges and back-bitings among the gods, for any one of them alone, since we must assume him to be infinitely wise and infinitely powerful, could run it perfectly. We suffer from bad stomachs simply because the god who first proposed making a stomach aroused thereby the ill-nature of those who had not thought of it, and because they proceeded instantly to wreck that ill-nature upon him by improving, *i.e.*, botching, his work. Every right-thinking man admires his own heart, at least until it begins to break down; it seems an admirable machine. But think how much better it would be if the original design had not been butchered by a board of rival designers!

Outline of the History of a Man's Philosophical Knowledge From Early Youth to Old Age.— 1. I am wrong. 2. I am right. 3. I am wrong.

Idle Paradox.—If the combined aim and object of art lies in the stirring of the emotions, and is praiseworthy, why should the similar aim and object of the vices be regarded as meretricious? If the Madonnas of Raphael, Holbein, Murillo and Da Vinci are commendable in that they stir the imagination, why are not the whiskeys of Dewar, Macdonald, Haig and Macdougal commendable for the same reason? If a Bach fugue is praised for stimulating the mind, why not a Corona Corona? If the senses are commendably excited by Balzac and Zola, why shouldn't they be excited, and equally commendably, by means that may be described as being somewhat less literary?

Metaphysics of the Movies.—

I

From a signed story by Mary Miles Minter, published in the Los Angeles *Times:*

Over my mother's protest I went to William Desmond Taylor's apartments, but his body had been removed to an undertaker's establishment. I went to the undertaker's rooms, and the undertaker let me in all alone with him. I pulled back the sheet and looked at him. But he was not the same. His skin was waxen. I leaned down and put my arms about him, my cheek to his. His face was cold, so cold, but not as cold like ice.

"Do you love me, Desmond?" I asked.

He answered me; I could hear his voice.

"I love you, Mary, I shall love you always," he whispered.

II

From an interview with Ruby Miller, published recently in the same journal:

How do I get reality into an impassioned love scene? Well, that is easy enough on the stage when one has three or four weeks of rehearsal and gets to know the actor. But, on the screen! Oh boy!

I must have time to know my hero and always insist that my love scenes come last of all. Then I have time to study the actor. I talk to him of music, literature, art, etc., etc., and find out his hobbies and let him talk to me. I'm always a sympathetic listener.

He then begins to like me mentally and thinks me brilliant when I permit him to explain, by the hour, how he would have "holed" in two if only that d—— caddie had kept his eye on the ball. This is but one step to the physical attraction. Despite this "intimate" conversation, my very lack of familiarity in every way breathes a mysticism about me that is always certain to vanquish the male specie.

So the days pass. Then dawns the day of the big love scenes. I appear in a beautiful gown. By this time the hero is so crazy to kiss me that it requires no effort upon my part. His natural fervor awakening my own —and hence the perfect love scene.

I am told that my method is very dangerous and liable to wreck the homes of my heroes. My reply is, "I am first, last and all the time an artist—and if my love scenes are destined to thrill millions, why worry about wrecking a few thousand homes?"

Text for a Wall-Card.—It is lucky for a young woman to be just a bit homely. The fact helps her to get a good husband, and, what is harder, to keep him after she has got him. The flawless beauty has no durable joy in this life save looking in the glass, and even this departs as she oxidizes. Men, knowing her intolerable vanity, are afraid of her, and, if snared into marriage with her, always look for the worst.

From the Book of a Bachelor of Forty.—1. Toward men, ever an aristocrat; toward women, ever a commoner—that way lies success.

2. Among men, women admire most those who have all the attributes and qualities of the actor and yet are not actors by profession.

3. Love is always a tragedy for the woman. That tragedy she never succeeds entirely in escaping. It is sometimes the tragedy of a broken heart, sometimes the greater tragedy of fulfilment. A broken heart is a monument to a love that will never die; fulfilment is a monument to a love that is already on its deathbed.

On Critics.—There are critics whose taste is sound, but whose judgment is unsound: who like the right things, but for the wrong reasons. There are other critics whose judgment is sound, but whose taste is defective: these like the right things and for the correct reasons, but the absence of background of taste and depth of taste alienates their followers. There are still other critics who are forthright apostles of emotional reaction, who have but a small measure of taste and utterly no judgment: these are ever the most popular critics, since they deal in the only form of criticism that the majority of persons can quickly and most easily grasp.

Veritas Odium Parit.—Another old delusion is the one to the effect that truth has a mysterious medicinal power—that it makes the world better and man happier. The fact is that truth, in general, is extremely uncomfortable, and that the masses of men are thus wise to hold it in suspicion. The most rational religious ideas held in modern times are probably those of the Unitarians; the most nonsensical are those of the Christian Scientists. Yet it must be obvious to every observer that the average Unitarian, even when he is quite healthy, is a sour and discontented fellow, whereas the average Christian Scientist, even when he is down with gallstones, is full of an enviable peace. I have known, in my time, several eminent philosophers. The happiest of them, in his moments of greatest joy, used to entertain himself by drawing up wills leaving his body to a medical college.

Story Without a Moral.—A number of years ago, in my newspaper days, I received from what would now be called the Ku Klux Klan a circular violently denouncing the Catholic Church. This circular stated that the Church was engaged in a hellish conspiracy to seize the government of the United States and put an agent of the Pope into the White House, and that the leaders of the plot were certain Jesuits, all of them foreigners and violent enemies of the American Constitution. Only one such Jesuit was actually named: a certain Walter Drum, S.J. He was denounced with great bitterness, and every true American was besought to be on the watch for him. Something inspired me to turn to "Who's Who in America"; it lists all the principal emissaries of Rome in the Republic, even when they are not Americans. This is what I found:

Drum, Walter, S.J.; *b.* at Louisville, Ky., Sept. 21, 1870; *s.* Capt. John Drum, U.S.A., killed before Santiago.

I printed the circular of the *Ur*-Klansmen —and that eloquent sentence from "Who's Who". No more was heard against the foreigner Drum in that diocese. . . .

Eight or ten years later, having retired from journalism with a competence, I was the co-editor of a popular magazine. One day there reached me the manuscript of a short story by a young Princeton man, by name F. Scott Fitzgerald. It was a harmless and charming story about a young scholastic in a Jesuit seminary. A few months later it was printed in the magazine. Four days after the number was on the stands I received a letter from a Catholic priest, denouncing me as an enemy to the Church, belaboring the story as blasphemous and worse, and stating that the writer proposed to make a tour of all the Catholic women's clubs in the East, urging their members to blacklist and boycott the magazine. The name signed to the letter was "Walter Drum, S.J."

I offer the story, but append no moral. Perhaps its only use is to show how Christians of both wings have improved upon John XV, 12.

THE COMMUNIST HOAX

BY JAMES ONEAL

IN A RECENT volume of historical studies Sir Charles Oman considers the potency of rumor in war time. Despite the increased facilities for the transmission of information, rumor is then given a new and vigorous lease of life, and an exaggerated credulity persists as a survival after the conflict ends. He cites, among other instances, the familiar tale of the Mons Angels, a troop of shining figures which, so many credulous men and women believed, saved the left wing of the British Army during the Mons retreat. This curious story was traced back to a work of fiction published in an obscure magazine in September, 1914. Considering the psychology of war rumor, Sir Charles concludes "that we are the children of our fathers, that we should not jest too much at 'mediæval credulity,' and that we should recognize in the rumor-phenomena of our own day the legitimate descendants of those which used to puzzle and amaze our ancestors, whom we are too often prone to regard with the complacent superiority of the omniscient Twentieth Century. The Great War has taught us—among other things— a little psychology and a good deal of humility."

It is well to remember this statement, now that so many Americans seem to be under the spell of a fear complex regarding Communism in the United States. Of course, we have Communists, just as we had Jacobins in New York in the days of Robespierre, but this obvious and trivial fact has given rise to grotesque beliefs regarding the number of them, as well as ludicrous exaggerations of their influence upon the generality of organized work-men. Practically all the estimates that appear in the newspapers, usually sponsored by some public official or some functionary in a "tame" trades union, bear no more relation to reality than the belief in the Angels of Mons. Since the year 1919, when the first organized group of Communists was formed, I have collected their leaflets and books, manifestoes and propaganda papers, convention proceedings and other documents. I have followed their bitter controversies with each other. I have studied their beliefs and the origin, development and varying fortunes of each organized group. The materials gathered during the four years convince me that the estimates recently made that there are from 1,000,000 to 1,500,000 Communists in the United States are quite absurd.

Seventeen Communist organizations, practically all of them claiming to be of national scope, have been formed since 1919. This represents an average of four new ones each year. Stated thus, Communism appears to be a formidable force, but upon analysis it is shown to be extremely feeble. The numerous organizations reveal all sorts of weaknesses and dissensions. Most of them represent men and women resorting to new expedients, new programs and methods, precisely because of their failure to impress any considerable number of people with their old ones. One characteristic of every group has been its charge that all the others followed methods not adapted to winning converts. Another is that after trying its own methods it abandoned them and either formulated new policies or united with others. Yet each new program and each coalition of two or more groups has usually produced only fresh schisms and desertions. Due to these factors and contrary to the general belief, Communism reached its highest tide in 1919, while in 1924 it is probably at its lowest ebb.

II

A short survey of this movement and its various sects will make this evident. The parent Communist organization in the United States was the Left Wing, a faction within the Socialist party and representing an emotional reaction to the Russian revolution. Forced out of the Socialist organization by the executive committee of the latter in 1919, the Left Wing took with it 30,000 or 35,000 members. In New York it drafted a "Left Wing Manifesto" early in 1919 in which it severely denounced the Socialists for their alleged neglect of various party opportunities during the war. It outlined its own position in the following words:

The party must teach, propagate and agitate exclusively for the overthrow of capitalism, and the establishment of Socialism through a proletarian dictatorship.
The Socialist candidates elected to office shall adhere strictly to the above provisions.

This Left Wing established an organ, the *Revolutionary Age*, which carried on a bitter struggle to capture the Socialist organization and materially weakened the latter. It soon developed, however, that the Left Wing was developing factions of its own, which finally culminated in a split and the organization of the first two Communist parties.

The faction of extremists may be designated as the Left Wing of the Left Wing. It opposed organizing a rival to the Socialist party until after an appeal was made to the national convention of the Socialists, apparently in the hope that its expulsion would be reversed by the convention. It did carry its appeal to the convention of 1919, but, observing at once that its chances there were hopeless, its delegates

soon withdrew. Then the Left Wing of the Left Wing found that it had drifted too far from its own parent body to effect a reconciliation. The result was the organization of two Communist parties out of the membership of the two wings.

The parent Left Wing organized the Communist party in September, 1919. The dissenting faction was meeting in the same city, Chicago, at the same time and attempts were made to unite the two, but without success. The Communist party declared that industrial unionism "is a factor in the final mass action for the conquest of power, and it will constitute the basis for the industrial administration of the Communist Commonwealth." It urged that "councils of workers" be organized in shops and factories and declared that political action was "of secondary importance." The influence of the Russian revolution is evident in this program. Police raids a few months later drove the organization underground and it became a secret society. Two years of this existence finally convinced the leaders that its program was hopeless. Its organ, the *Communist*, in the issue for October, 1922, said: "It cannot be denied that the Communist party of America practically does not exist as a factor in the class struggle. . . . The crying need is an open political rallying centre." It finally abandoned its covert existence in 1923 and found a leading place in the Workers' party, to be considered later. Its membership cannot be estimated accurately. The quarrel between it and the other wing undoubtedly made for many desertions and a rough estimate would give it, at most, not more than 10,000 members.

The Left Wing of the Left Wing organized the Communist Labor party at the same time. The differences between the two parties were actually very slight. One claim of the Communist Labor party was that it had abandoned foreign language federations while its rival retained them. It also charged that "in the Communist party there are innumerable political deals between the incongruous elements which make it up," meaning that it contained factions that could not be reconciled. Each party claimed a majority of the members of the original Left Wing. It is probable that the two organizations had about the same number of members.

The Proletarian party was the third faction of this type organized in 1919. It was an offshoot of the Michigan section of the Socialist party. Its charter had been revoked by the Socialist executive committee in June, 1919, owing to its adoption of a program requiring its speakers to attack religion. It had little faith in the organization of trade unions and in ameliorative political measures. It was associated with the parent Left Wing in organizing the Communist party but it eventually resumed its independent existence, claiming that it was the genuine Communist organization. Recently advances have been made to it by the Workers' party for union and this has revived the old controversy as to which represents the true Communist faith in this country.

The Industrial Communists constituted the fourth organization formed in 1919. Organized in November of that year, this group did not have more than 25 members, yet it claimed a national existence and drafted a national program! It established a small monthly organ of four pages, the *Industrial Communist.* Denouncing all the other parties, it contended that "any one of them put into power could not establish industrial communism." It proposed to organize the workers in the six basic industries, agriculture, transportation, mining, manufacturing, construction and education, and so build the framework of a new society. It expired within a year.

The Rummager's League, organized in 1922, was the successor to the Industrial Communists. The new organization derived its name from the first sentence in the preamble to its constitution: "We rummage the field of history and science so as to develop the keenest intellect possible." This organization established a "Rummager's Institute" in Chicago with courses

in various subjects and proposed to establish study classes in all the States. The elaborate scheme of organizing the "six basic industries" was abandoned. The Rummagers paid no attention to political and economic organization and in this respect they present a marked variation from the usual Communist type. They dragged out a precarious existence till the end of the year and then disappeared.

The United Communist party appeared on the scene in 1920. This was a union of the Communist and Communist Labor parties. The union was effected in June, but when and where was not disclosed. The program of the new organization declared that "capitalism today faces complete collapse" and that "civil war between the classes now holds the world in its grip." Its program urged "parliamentary action only for the purpose of revolutionary propaganda" while at "appropriate times" it would boycott the elections. It looked forward to the time when a struggle between the classes would develop "into open conflict" which would end in a Communist dictatorship. A large section of the program was devoted to outlining the "Communist reconstruction of society." Some 34 delegates, however, refused to be united. They withdrew and declared that the new program "reeks with the bourgeois horror of the destruction of property and lives."

The year 1921 brought into existence five sects. A small group remaining in the Socialist party caught the infection and organized as the Committee of the Third International. It was dissatisfied because the Socialists refused to affiliate with the international organization of the Communists. It became the object of satirical criticism by other groups and was eventually swallowed by the next organization formed.

This proved to be The Workers' Council, organized in New York City in the Spring of 1921. It established a bi-weekly organ devoted to bitter criticism of the Socialists. It drew its inspiration from the work of the

Committee of the Third International just mentioned, which probably did not have more than 50 members. It believed that there was "a growing sentiment that stands behind the Third International and its principles. All that is needed is a force that will cement this unorganized sympathy and understanding and loose allegiance into a compact body." Like all other organizations of its kind, it proposed to unite all the communist factions. It wanted an "open party" as well. In December of this year it was one of a number of groups that founded the Workers' party.

The African Blood Brotherhood appeared simultaneously. It consisted of a handful of radical Negroes who organized in 1921 to carry the Communist message to their race. It assumed to be of national importance, but there is no evidence that it has ever added to its original small numbers or that it has made any impression upon the Negro people. One of its leading representatives states that its program provides for "racial unification for a free Africa," protection of Negro labor "from exploitation by capitalism," and welcomes "men of the race without attempting to dwarf them before one giant master mind." This is a reference to Marcus Garvey, leader of the Universal Negro Improvement Association, who was recently sent to prison.

The American Labor Alliance, also organized in 1921, was a coalition of numerous scattered groups. Its object was that of the other groups—a union of the forces that had so persistently refused to unite. When it finally merged with others in founding the Workers' party in December, 1921, its report of its membership showed that it was everything but an American alliance. The following sections, it appeared, were affiliated with it: Finnish, Hungarian, Irish, Greek, South Slavic, Spanish, Armenian, Esthonian, Italian, German, Jewish, Lithuanian, Russian and Ukranian. These all represented small groups profoundly impressed by the Russian revolution.

In the Autumn of the same year the Workers' League was founded in New York City. It at last united the Communist parties and most of the other groups. It nominated six candidates in the city election and adopted a platform denouncing the Socialists. While the program demanded "a Workers' Soviet Republic in the United States," it also proposed such moderate reforms as "legislation to combat and stop the reduction of wages," protection of labor organizations "against the open shop drive," and "relief for the unemployed." With its small but active forces devoted to campaign appeals, the candidates of the party polled about 3,000 votes. Despondent over this result, it began to take stock of its resources.

Within one month it reorganized as the Workers' party. The union of the groups in the new party was hailed as an "epoch-making event" and one leader of the old American Labor Alliance wrote that the leaders had displayed "proletarian strategy in fighting the enemy and winning the masses." Such statements, so frequently found in Communist publications, represent an unconscious translation into American experience of the military struggles of the Russian Communists against their invading enemies. But even this union failed to unite all the groups. What was called the Proletarian party maintained a separate existence, while another new organization was formed in bitter antagonism to the Workers' party in 1922. This was the United Toilers, organized in New York City in February of that year. Its organ, the *Workers' Challenge*, declared that all the other organizations betrayed a "total lack of understanding of the correct tactics to be pursued in the labor movement of the United States." It proposed to participate in "daily struggles of the workers," to foster unity of all elements, and to establish propaganda classes and publish literature. It represented a coalition of Ukranian, Lettish and Lithuanian organizations, a woman's organization, two Polish societies, and a number of labor unions independent of the American Federation of Labor. Its official publication reeked with the most offensive vituperation its editor could command in denunciation of all other Communists, especially those who had organized the Workers' party. Nevertheless, when the Communist International ordered the United Toilers to disband and join the Workers' party it complied with the order and abandoned its organ as well.

The Workers' party is the final product of all these Communist sects and its official publication proudly boasts of it. Only the small Proletarian party remains out of the fold. But this bringing together of a complex variety of discordant sects in a relatively simple coalition has been accomplished chiefly by a recantation of all the extremist doctrines of 1919 and 1920. In some respects the Workers' party has become more moderate than even the Socialists. The first period of 1919-20 was marked by a sharp drift to the left, but since then the march has been just as marked to the right. Today the greatest apparent ambition of the average Communist is to be a member of a genuinely national labor party. So pronounced is this drift that even the Workers' party could not resist the temptation that had beset all its predecessors—that of forming still another organization.

In New York City the Workers' party had reaped the same disappointment in the November election of 1922 which the Workers' League had realized the year before. It had not won the support of more than a tiny fraction of the voters of the city. The movement entered its fourth year in 1923, and, as we have seen, all the various groups and factions, except one or two, had merged into one organization. Despairing of its future, the Workers' party seized the opportunity offered by the Farmer-Labor party when it issued a call for a national conference in July. It sent delegates to this conference and captured it. This was accomplished by duplicating its representation over and over again—by sending delegates from singing societies,

benefit clubs, gymnastic clubs, educational associations and similar organizations. Through this *coup* it organized a Federated-Farmer-Labor party, now claiming 600,000 members. But this absurd estimate is based upon the padded reports of its own local organizations and the membership of many other organizations, most of which refuse to affiliate with it. Its program contains no Communism whatever. It represents a complete reversal of the extremist doctrines of a few years ago. Thus we have the remarkable spectacle of a movement of various sects competing for extreme positions for a number of years, and then finally uniting in a coalition which competes with more conservative organizations for the most moderate position.

III

Another organization, the I. W. W., remains to be considered. Popular opinion credits the I. W. W. with an intimate relationship with the Communist Internationale. There is no evidence whatever to sustain this theory save that William D. Haywood is associated with the Communist regime in Russia. But against it stands the important fact that Haywood has lost caste with the American organization. He is regarded by his former American associates as a deserter of their cause, precisely because he fled to Russia and accepted Communism.

Contrary to the general opinion, bitter war is waged between the I. W. W. and the Communists. An elementary knowledge of the theories of the two movements would lead one to expect this antagonism. The I. W. W. is opposed to political action and has an intense fear of the state, whether it be the present state of the capitalist countries or the Communist state of Russia. It favors the industrial organization of the wage workers and the extension of this type of organization until it has power enough to take over the industries of the nation, which are then to be owned by the industrial unions.

Political action by the masses would lead to ownership of the nation's industries by the state and in the view of the I. W. W. the state controlled by workingmen is no better than the state controlled by capitalists.

Here are opposing views that form the basis of a fundamental antagonism between the I. W. W. and Communism. The I. W. W. sent a delegate to the Third Congress of the Communist Internationale, held in Moscow in 1921, in the hope of effecting some working agreement or of modifying the conditions prescribed for affiliation. The mission proved to be a fruitless one. A writer in an official publication of the I. W. W. wrote in January, 1922, presenting the reasons why the organization could not affiliate with the Communist Internationale. The I. W. W. view, he explained, is that "it would be suicidal for any revolutionary syndicalist or industrialist labor organization to submit to the dictates of any political party." Another reason, he continued, is that Communists oppose the I. W. W. idea that the industrial union should constitute the "structure" of a new society and also serve as the "midwife" for ushering in this new society. These fundamental differences have made the two movements uncompromising enemies and their partisans engage in bitter controversy whenever they meet.

The Trade Union Educational League, represented by William Z. Foster, is not a political organization, but it boasts of fraternal relations with the Communist movement. It was originally intended for educational work in the trade unions, to make the latter more effective instruments for organized workmen. It came under Communist influence about a year ago, but it does not represent any increase in either numbers or of prestige for the Communists. It has merely provided another type of organization through which Communists may carry on their activities. It has a small membership and has only succeeded in winning for itself the distrust and bitter hostility of the organized workmen of the country.

This brings us to a consideration of the leading question in this survey. How many organized Communists are there in the United States? My own estimate is something less than 20,000, about one-half the number in 1919. This figure is confirmed by good Communist authority. The Russian Communists subsidize a weekly publication in Berlin, the *International Press Correspondence*, which carries news of Communist movements in all countries and of the internal affairs of Russia. It is an invaluable source of information if we make allowance for certain exaggerations. In the issue for April 19, 1923, a prominent American Communist places the membership of the Workers' party at 20,000. Of this number, he adds, only 1,500 are English-speaking. Communists are accustomed to exaggerate their numbers and power and there is reason for believing that the membership of this organization is even lower than that given. It is this little band of emotional men and women that has been magnified into millions by those unacquainted with the facts and that has inspired wild fears of a neat conspiracy against the Republic! It is the greatest hoax in history. It is an example of that nervous psychology of fear which produced the illusion of the Angels of Mons.

THE WEAVER'S TALE

BY JOHN McCLURE

Beneath a street lamp at an intersection of alleys, transfigured to a singular beauty by the yellowish glow, sat an Arabian beggar playing a curious instrument. The sound he was making was beyond question something from far away, a desert melody or a herdsman's song from the hills, and it echoed no less beautifully than strangely in the narrow alleys of Cairo, accustomed only to the barbarous rhythms of dance-halls. It would be inaccurate to term it a Jew's-harp, said Diodorus, yet it comes of a similar family.

"It is a Numidian lyre," said the person at his elbow. "He makes a large part of the music by clicking his teeth."

"That accompaniment could be dispensed with," said Diodorus, "to the advantage of the harmony. It is the metallic vibrations that produce the haunting refrain. You are a musician?"

"I am by profession a weaver," said the man at his elbow. "I know the words of 'The Alligator's Bride', and can play it on gongs or whistle it, as well as 'The Metropolitan Night's Delight', 'The Loving Weaver', and 'Whose Old Mare?' But I consider myself simply an amateur."

"I made a study of harmony in youth," said Diodorus, "but have neglected it lately. You find the market is stable, in weaving?"

"I have nothing to complain of," said the weaver.

"The summer is hard," said Diodorus. "You are in luck if you prosper."

"I have delivered a quilt to a customer since dinner," said the weaver. "I have received pay in advance for fabric for six pairs of pajamas. As a consequence, I boast a pocketful of money and am on my way to a dramshop."

"If you are going to the Fishes," said Diodorus Carnifex, "I will accompany you."

The Three Fishes was deserted, more or less, at this hour. Those who came to eat dinner had gone, and those who came to finish their evenings had not yet arrived. Diodorus and the weaver established themselves at a table in a corner. There were two or three men in the room who made a noise swallowing wine, but did not disturb them. The man on the floor was snoring, but the sound was inoffensive. From the bartender Diodorus and the weaver ordered two mugs of wine.

As they sampled it, there was a blare of horns and a rattle of drums from the street outside. Diodorus leaped from his bench.

"Anything warlike always upsets me," he explained hastily. "Is it the military?"

"It is the firemen's band," said the bartender. "They are carrying torches, and all dressed in yellow breeches. They have not looked so grand since the mayor was buried. They are on their way back from a euchre party that they gave for the benefit of the pension fund."

Diodorus seated himself. The weaver's mug by this time was empty.

"The best friend I had in the world was a fireman," the weaver said. "Nobody could fight fire any better than he could. He would go up a ladder like a squirrel. But he was hanged two years ago when they proved he set fire to a pothouse that refused to pay tribute. He had had the liveliest life of any fellow I know of. He admitted everything to me one night when he was liquored, and such a biography has not been invented since they published 'The Golden Ass'."

"I had always considered a fireman's life was drowsy except when something was burning," said Diodorus Carnifex.

"He became a firefighter only as a last resort," the weaver said, "and he did not, as I observed, keep the position long. He had been nearly everything, and he began in the cloth."

"That is unusual," said Diodorus.

"It is the fact," said the weaver. "He told me the story complete."

"I should like to make a note of it," said Diodorus Carnifex.

II

The weaver began:

"He was born in Cappadocia. As a child, will-o'-the-wisps played round his head while he was sleeping. This in his parents' opinion portended exceptional sanctity, and he was compelled to memorize texts which he recited with accuracy in the temple on feast days. He was much favored by the deacons before he was ten, and before he was twenty he had been selected chief of the choir.

"It was about this time he discovered he was pious enough to charge money for it. He entered the church at once, as an evangelist, always taking up a collection. He attracted great flocks, for he announced he had seen the statue of Apollo stir in its sleep and that he could prophesy things to come and had analysed hell-fire. He was popular wherever they booked him.

"But he got into delicious difficulties with eight or nine women at home and fell into grievous errors—including a weakness for raspberry punch—while on a visit to Byzantium, and on his return the elders unfrocked him before a great multitude.

"He did not delay in leaving the place. He announced he was a citizen of the world, and he returned to Byzantium with a good deal of money and lived like a person of fashion. He was a famous fellow: he distinguished himself as the best pingpong player on the Golden Horn and his supporters challenged all Turkey. He was a dog with the women. He would never go out without a nosegay. During that winter he caught the influenza standing at the exit of a show-house holding a posy. He became popular, and developed a streak of ambition. A charlatan who read fortunes from the configuration of the toes told him he would become a commissioner. And he was indeed on the highroad to glory, and all this might have come about, had he not suffered financial reverses.

"But his fall was sudden. He vouched for a traveling tinker at a pawnbroker's, and when the tinker defaulted the sheriff seized even his shirt. There were phrases in the bankruptcy laws of which my friend could have taken advantage, but he was put into prison fraudulently, he told me, by the prosecutor who duped the magistrate by citing a large portfolio. He remained in a cell for months.

"When he emerged, ragged and destitute, wearing a beard, and attempted to explain his absence by saying he had eaten of a magic cheese and been transported to Persia, nobody believed him. At the clubs they shut the door in his face. So he earned what money he could raking manure off the streets and peddling soap, and begged a bit from old friends when they would recognize him, for he had learned, what you and I know well enough, that victuals are more important than honor.

"Of course he conceived of himself as a victim, and his only comfort in those dark weeks, he told me, was the hope that he might become celebrated for his misfortunes. His appearance had become that of a complete ragamuffin. He always walked down an alley instead of a street when possible so as to avoid meeting any of the women he used to spend money on. As a result of this suspicious carriage he almost got hanged, for he was arrested by the secret police and accused of a puzzling series of murders. Fortunately for my friend, they were traced to an undertaker.

"After this, and partly because of it, he fell into a sort of a palsy. Nothing seemed to relieve him and he became worthless at any work whatsoever. A mendicant poet who had lost everything speculating on a volume of original odes, and was as penniless as himself, attempted to cure him by reciting hexameters. A rope-dancer at the Hippodrome told him to take tar-water for it. A dancing waitress at the cabaret where he was at the time washing dishes taught him an orison composed by a monk in Odessa which was a specific against swamp-fever, diabetes and small-pox, but it did him no good. They agreed he was fit only to die, and things came to such a pass that nobody would hire him.

"But his malady responded to silver as the pox to mercury, and when he inherited two thousand piastres he was as brisk as a fox. In no time the clubs had received him again, and he made a match with the handsomest woman in Byzantium. He was as fond of pomp as an Ethiopian, and she became enamored of him because of the way he was dressed. They lived magnificently, and rode a great deal in a carriage. His wife, worried about her complexion, would never go out without a silk parasol because she was afraid she would freckle.

"But this money, which he had inherited from a great uncle, did not vegetate like the true cross. It dwindled when he depleted it. And he was on the verge of bankruptcy again when, by good fortune, his wife turned blue, and, leaving Byzantium, he made an excellent living for two or three years taking her about in circuses.

"This arrangement was broken up by an acrobat, and my friend found himself single again, without resources entirely and in the heart of the provinces. However, as it was a rural district he soon obtained employment as secretary of a pig exchange. He did very well, but contact with farmers was not to his taste, and, under the stress of transactions in pork, his mind yearned for more intellectual pastimes. He read history and made a study of primroses, and in his spare hours invented a gimcrack with quicksilver in it that walked like a man.

"Then he became infatuated abruptly with the daughter of a planter for whom he sold pigs, and got himself into disrepute carving his love-songs on the walls of the market. The women in those days were wearing mirrors on their stomachs, and he told me he saw her first wearing a large one, looking more magnificent than anyone at the prayer-meeting.

"It developed into quite an affair, and one day they departed together, he with all the funds and commissions that had not yet been distributed in the pig exchange, going very fast toward Corinth. They lived pleasantly there for some time, and were not overtaken, when suddenly he discovered that his sweetheart was a pythoness. He had not imagined what spirit was in her, he told me, and, though he would not go so far as to say that it was a devil possessed her—for he had found it impossible to drive her out of the house by poking his fingers at her—it was a familiar, he said, that was most incompatible. So he left Corinth, traveling all by himself.

"It was soon after this that he came to Cairo, but not until after he had become a scandal in Thebes. I do not know what he did there, for he was very reticent about it, but it must have been shocking. I first encountered him here at several taverns, drinking very hard and trying to avoid his destiny. But he was a good fellow. We became friends over beer and he told me this story weeping.

"Here he soon got into an entanglement with a fat woman, married like one of the Graces to an incompetent fellow, whom I suspected with good reason of keeping his wallet supplied. He never discussed the subject and evaded it when it was possible. But I encountered him one evening emerging from the place in darkness and he blushed till he shone like sulphur.

"It was in attempting to extricate himself from this affair that he conceived the idea that a fortune could be accumulated by any ingenious fireman, especially by himself if he could get an appointment to the brigade. This end he accomplished in collusion with an alderman, and when he had once got employed they both made a great deal of money. He became a distinguished member of the ladder company and three times was decorated with ribbons.

"But, as I told you, there was a fire at the Bull of Isis pothouse which seemed to have been somewhat incendiary. A summary inquiry on the spot with six witnesses present, including the proprietor, established conclusively that my friend had demanded a love-offering of two hundred piastres, not in the form of a check, that the proprietor had refused this indignantly, and that my friend had been seen in the alley shortly before the fire with a bucket of grease. When my friend was informed of these revelations, he left the city with incredible speed.

"He was intercepted at Alexandria and returned to Cairo in handcuffs with a flat-iron on his ankle. He was tried at once for conspiratory arson. The alderman did what he could, but that official had lost his prestige during the testimony and feared for his neck. My friend, though he swore cleverly, was found guilty without the right of appeal and was sentenced to be hanged on the following Wednesday between seven and eight in the morning.

"I visited him after the verdict, taking him, with the jailor's permission, a vessel of beer. He was not complaining. The sentence was just, he said, according to law, and he simply had gambled and lost. But he wept when he remembered the fortune-teller who had told him he was to become a commissioner, and he spoke bitterly of how he had never in his life acquired any political distinction whatever, going now to his grave without having once boasted a wig or a uniform. I left him after an hour, and he was furious when I bade him god-speed, for this was on Tuesday and he was still expecting a pardon.

"On Wednesday he was informed there was nothing for it but to be hanged, and that any reasonable request would be granted. He then asked to be allowed to walk to the gallows in a suit with silver buttons, which was conceded, and he died proudly."

"Did he die without issue?" asked Diodorus.

"He would never attempt to count his children," the weaver said, "because he had traveled so much."

Architecture

THE NEW SKY-LINE

By C. Grant La Farge

SEVEN years ago New York City adopted a law limiting the heights of new buildings. This law was the outcome of the many evils attendant upon the assumption that economic balance was the only restriction needed, and that freedom consisted in letting everyone do as he liked, especially if he was making money. The city suddenly awoke to the fact that its property-owners were biting—or perhaps building—each other's noses off, and playing the very devil with real-estate values. When the pocket nerve began to ache pretty badly, the doctor got his show.

The basic purpose underlying the new height regulation is the preservation of a fixed angle of light. On whatever street you build, the vertical height of your front wall cannot go beyond a certain ratio to the street width; if you want to go higher than that, you must set back a given amount for each foot of added height. The effect of this, plus the rules as to the area that must be left open altogether, which increases with height, is that the upper part of your building tends to become a tower. How high you will carry the tower, once you have reached the point where its diminished floor area and increased cost of elevator service will no longer leave you a profit, will be determined by what you may consider its advertising value. This affords a true economic balance.

But it is not with the economic or social aspects of the law that I am here concerned, enormously important as they are; it is

*Under this heading THE AMERICAN MERCURY will print each month a variety of short articles by writers of authority.

with its aesthetic consequences, which could hardly have been foreseen, except dimly as conjectures, and with some moral considerations, entertaining to the humorist. Of the latter, perhaps the first is that, having restrained the orgy of individualism to which we were so devoted, we have opened the way for a display of individuality hitherto exceptional, but now rather strikingly evident. Another is that a law devised to cure a practical evil—a number of practical evils, indeed—should also work for beauty. This, paradoxically, though it happened accidentally, is hardly an accident. Many students of our municipal architectural problem, mindful of great European examples, had long felt the wish for some sort of regulation, some imposition of order, some check upon the riot. Their views probably tended mainly toward uniformity—toward the similarity of type and continuity of principal lines seen, say, in Paris. There is still reason for advocating those same views. Dignified repose is obviously worth more than uneasy restlessness; Fifth Avenue is capable of betterment; imagine what might be done with Riverside Drive!

But we haven't got anywhere near this direct control of design by legal enactment and it is probably alien to us, anyhow. The present law, however, may be expected to produce a great deal more group uniformity than we now suspect, when enough buildings have been erected under it with their main cornices of even height; while at the same time it opens the door to a variety of mass and sky-line in the larger buildings undreamt of before its advent. Thus beauty will be born of the merely practical; of halting speculative license; of putting some check upon intolerable congestion; of trying to stabilize values by guaranteeing permanency; of agreeing not to build out the other fellow's light and air. Nothing very improbable about that to the architect, who has been trained in the theory that his art is one pre-eminently of fitness, however far-fetched that may seem to the man in the street. Nothing strange, either, to those who have been preaching, largely to inattentive ears, the principles of city planning—the need of foresight, prevision, order, convenience, economy, as things necessary to and before embellishment, and who are commonly supposed to be impractical visionaries, full of aesthetic dreams.

The effects of the new law first proclaim themselves in large buildings—offices, hotels, high apartments; this was to be expected. How is it influencing design? Our skyscrapers hitherto have been, almost unvaryingly, rectangular boxes; their variation has been in height and width only. This variation, however, has been very great; we see everything from a building covering an entire block to one which is a mere slice of façade carried to an inordinate height. As the range of designing ability has been wide, and the utmost latitude in the use of design motives prevalent, we have achieved a singular effect of discordant, tormented monotony—monotony of fundamental scheme, the box; discord of scale and quality. The architect is not to be blamed for all this; a herculean task was thrust upon him. Almost over night came the steel frame and its fantastic possibilities. Aside from the vastly intricate mechanical problems involved, the economic demands to be met, was the truly appalling fact that nowhere in all the wide earth was there any precedent in design for the architect to cling to. And he *must* have precedent!

The box is not a bad type in itself; Italian palaces are boxes. But when the Italian palace is stretched to incredible altitudes and peppered with windows in a thin wall, it goes to pieces. All sorts of schemes have been tried to meet the problem; there is no space to review them here; moreover, they are all on exhibition for whosoever will take the trouble to look. The upper strata of talent has produced buildings of extraordinary competence and distinction, but they are lost in the general hodge-podge. Here and there a really fine building is seen across one of our far too few open spaces; here and there is a good tower, built just for "dog", but none the less welcome; here and there is a real roof, for which we give thanks when we can see it. But mostly there are stretches of canyon walls, to be inspected at embarrassing angles, if we really do look at them at all. And therein lies the difficulty—we *don't* look at them; it requires too great and conscious an effort.

The great majority of people who pass through city streets receive only a vague general impression; their attention is normally upon things near the ground; the human eye turns only to where it is led by some definite cause. The eye is not led to contemplate high unbroken walls along narrow streets—and almost any street is narrow if it has high enough buildings along it. What does attract the eye is interesting, striking silhouettes; great masses so composed that they make us look up at them; very especially, *light*. Now, the virtue of the new law is that it enables the designer to treat his building as a sort of tower. Whether or not that building starts as a solid rectangle at the ground, its required offsets as it rises lead to a grouping of diminishing masses. So it acquires perforce a profile of interest, and attracts the eye, and goes on detaching itself more and more against the sky. This is something very different from the hard line of a straight cornice, set at the greatest height possible, and it is something very much better.

From the new order of things, therefore, two results may reasonably be expected to flow. One is that our buildings will be more observed by the public, and that perhaps there will be more interest taken in them, more opinion about them. As it is, the absence of such opinion, the dismal lack of critical interest, the prevalent ignorance, are among the most discouraging things that confront the architect who regards his calling as an art. The other result lies in the hands of the architects. Hitherto, in the case of such structures as we are considering, they have been largely limited in their treatment of façades to the study of detail. Very comprehensive detail, it is true, but broadly speaking, it has been detail as against mass. Really exquisite refinement has been often conscientiously, skillfully displayed; a constantly greater appreciation of the value of simplicity, of the elimination of the extraneous, has been shown—all this, in no small degree, to be overwhelmed at once by the impact of size, number and discordance. Suppose you design a building of, say, twelve stories and moderate width; study your scale very faithfully; refine your detail charmingly. Then come, on either side of you, and across the street, some great whales, with coarse detail, of a scale utterly unrelated to yours. You are trampled out of existence! There are juxtapositions of size, height, and character of design in our principal thoroughfares that would make us howl with agony if we had any aesthetic nerves.

Now the architect's bulk material has become more plastic; he can handle big shapes, mould them into real compositions. This should free his hands in an entirely new way. It should make him far more independent of detail; make him concentrate upon the greater elements, not the lesser. Apparently, one of the most important effects of the change should be a stronger reliance upon simplicity; it's the whole shape of the building that will count as never before; hence, there will be less need for clever stunts in parts of it. The law, among its other peculiarities, puts a premium upon large lots—the commercial building on a small lot cannot be carried very high, because when it has been pared down by its offsets there isn't enough left to be of any use. Therefore, the tendency will be toward a far greater uniformity of size in any given region. The new law is thus an aesthetic portent.

Medicine

THE POTHER ABOUT GLANDS

By L. M. Hussey

STARTLING reports still come out of Vienna about the philoprogenitive exploits of aged rats, marvelously rescued from senility by the Steinach operation, that is to say, vasectomy. And not only rats. Testimony also pours out that a far more august mammal, *Homo sapiens*, is susceptible of a like rejuvenation by so simple a surgical procedure as the ligation of the *vas deferens*. The Germans have made a verb of the Professor's name and Dr. Zeissl entitles a paper in the *Wiener klinische Wochenschrift*, "Warum und wie ich ohne Erfolg *gesteinached* wurde". But here it will be observed that the Doctor was steinached "without result". This, alas, seems to happen only too often! Unprejudiced examination of the evidence, indeed shows that the new *elixir vitae*, like all of its predecessors, is largely a chimera.

For several decades the mysteries of the secretory glands have not only invited scientific investigation, but also inflamed the popular imagination. The wonders of adrenalin (epinephrin), a secretory product of the suprarenal capsules, although a bit stale, still resound in the press. Lately a Chicago Paracelsus is reported to have restored the life of a recently moribund patient by squirting epinephrin into the defunct heart. Here the sound and excellent work of Banting, Best, Scott, Fisher, Thalhimer, *et al* has served only to launch new popular fallacies concerning the endocrine system. With so many marvels already reported, and more probably to follow, it may be interesting to inquire what, briefly, is known about the endocrine glands and their mysterious secretions. Is it true that one of the favorite themes of the decadent writers of Greek and Roman comedy, the situation wherein a *pater-familias* contends with his son for the sprightly favors of young Lucretia, is about to become a common incident of every-day life? Has the *elixir vitae* been found at last? Will the dead, too impatient to await the millenium, arise at the command of a hypodermic needle and a drop of glandular secretion? What is the basis in fact for all these new necromancies?

Anticipating a great revelation, the earnest inquirer suffers quite a disappointment when he searches the pages of such a sober compend of endocrine knowledge as, let us say, Professor Biedl's exhaustive "Innere Sekretion". The mind athirst for a draught of assured wonders discovers but a mild and cautious beverage. In short, the investigation of the inner secretions has only just begun, and the properties of even the best-known glandular substances remain chiefly hypothetical.

Those most carefully studied to date are derived from the pituitary in the brain, the thyroid, the pancreas, the suprarenals and, to a less extent, the ovaries. The first product of glandular secretion to be isolated from an excised gland in a relatively pure state was epinephrin from the suprarenals, and that was done by J. J. Abel at the Johns Hopkins over twenty years ago. The startling effects of epinephrin on blood pressure led, in the beginning, to the facile conclusion that the maintenance of blood pressure was a direct function of suprarenal secretion. Later work, some of it done within the past year, has caused an abandonment of this too easy hypothesis. Epinephrin is no longer credited with the exclusive or even the most important rôle in maintaining blood pressure. After twenty years of intensive investigation it is still impossible to say, with any certainty, what definite part the suprarenals and their secretion play in the human animal.

Certain things that epinephrin will do are, of course, known. Even amateurs of physiology are aware that an animal heart may be kept beating by means of this drug after it is removed from the body. It is also true that a human heart *in situ*, which has, for a few seconds, given up the living rhythm of systole and diastole, may by a successful injection of epinephrin be made to beat again. But that the waiting angels are thrown into dismay by any such procedure I hesitate to argue. A man does not die at the precise moment when his heart ceases to beat. Death, to be sure, follows shortly after that event—by asphyxiation. But not instantly. Certain organs and tissues resist for relatively long periods. But once the brain and cord are asphyxiated, the candidate is ready for the hereafter. Epinephrin will not recall him then.

The only other pure secretory product isolated from an endocrine gland is thyroxin, which was separated from the thyroid gland scarcely more than a year ago. Its properties remain virtually unknown. When it was hailed, at first, as the essential, yes, the only, secretory substance of the thyroid, murmurs of doubt began to arise from the savants. Now it is known that thyroxin does not exhibit *all* the effects of thyroid substance—*i.e.*, there are probably other active substances in the gland. This gland, in spite of the prolonged attention paid to it, remains itself very mysterious. What is the purpose of its secretion, or secretions? Too much activity on the part of the thyroid produces, as nearly everyone knows, one form of goiter. Too little, another form. But goiter is a pathologic accident. What is the function of the normal gland, producing just enough of its secretory products? After an examination of much conflicting evidence, Professor Noël Paton, of Glasgow, sums up the available knowledge by saying: "The thyroid supplies to the organism an internal secretion which has a stimulating action on the course of metabolism, thus increasing the activity of development and of growth of the soma and gonads." In other words, the thyroid does an important something and nobody knows how or exactly what.

Setting aside, for a moment, the pancreas, the shadows of doubt that fall upon the functions of the suprarenals and thyroid become, in relation to the other glands, a stygian obscurity. What of the pituitary? The nature of its secretion is unknown. The active substance has never been isolated. When the gland is diseased singular physiological effects result. Giantism is one result of its over-growth. Bernard Shaw, seeking to demonstrate that there must be a definite pathological reason why any man should diverge from the morals of a Scotch Presbyterian, attributed an hypertrophied pituitary to Oscar Wilde and asserted him to be a victim of giantism. But the diagnosis was dubious. Of the function of the pituitary in health little is known. Like the thyroid, it is apparently associated with the development of sex characteristics.

But although these glands have long been known to exercise this influence over sexual development, they are not the endocrines chosen by the professors of rejuvenation for their experiments. Instead they have devoted themselves to the glands specifically and almost exclusively associated with sexual functioning. The stimulation of the quiescent gonads by such a procedure as the Steinach operation, or their replacement by grafts of young and exuberant glands are, briefly, the methods employed in all the current attempts at rejuvenescence. What hope is there for success? Can such glands be effectually stimulated to renewed activity? Professor Steinach answers affirmatively. Until lately he has devoted most of his work to the problem of male rejuvenation. What were formerly called Leydig's cells he re-names the "puberty gland" and to the activities of this gland he attributes all the legendary splendours of Don Juan. But, as a recent medical periodical points out, certain facts obtained at necropsies seem to shatter this theory completely. A certain splendidly bearded man, a fine basso-profundo in life,

was discovered to be wholly without the puberty gland when dissected by the pathologist. On the other hand, a young woman who had always been a very feminine creature was found to be abundantly provided with Leydig-cells. What is still more convincing is the melancholy testimony of such steinached individuals as Professor Zeissl. The truth leaks out that these partakers of the surgical elixir, as well as those who have submitted to glandular transplantations, still find it necessary to wear the laurel wreath.

But there is a vast difference between such gaudy endocrine promises as rejuvenation and such sober, admirable work as Dr. Bantling and his collaborators have contributed to our knowledge of the pancreas and the treatment of diabetes. Of course it has long been known that the pancreas is primarily a digestive gland. At the same time it has also been known that the pancreas has another function than simply to produce a digestive ferment. In certain diseases of the pancreas, and after removal of the gland, diabetes results. The most striking symptom of diabetes, as everyone knows, is the appearance of an excess of sugar (glucose) in the blood and its constant excretion. But this hyperglycemia is but a symptom and does not explain the fatal outcome of the disease. Diabetics, in fact, do not die of the excessive sugar in their blood, but of acidosis. They suffer from an incomplete combustion, or metabolism, of the carbohydrate and fatty substances taken in as food. The metabolism of the fats appears to be related to the proper combustion of glucose. And that combustion, or utilization, is largely controlled by a substance secreted in the pancreas.

Banting and his co-workers have finally isolated it and called it insulin, a name derived from the islets of Langerhans, its chief source in the gland. In the past, extracts of the pancreas showed little or no effect on the blood sugar, because, as it now appears, the insulin that might have been extracted was destroyed by antiferments. By Banting's method of extraction the insulin remains, but the antiferments are eliminated. What, then, does insulin do? When injected into a diabetic it causes a prompt reduction of his excess of blood-sugar. In fact, an excess of the drug itself can reduce the sugar below its necessary and normal limit, and serious symptoms may follow; glucose must then be administered to counteract the excess of insulin. But in every patient a proper dosage may be ascertained, and by thus providing the missing ferment all the symptoms of diabetes, while the treatment continues, disappear. This is an excellent discovery. It is one authentic thing that has been done with glands. But it is well to bear in mind that the insulin obtained by present methods is not a pure chemical substance. We know very little about its nature and properties. It partakes of the obscurity that shrouds the complete action of all glandular secretions.

One may sum up by saying that the system of endocrine glands is an apparently related mechanism of secretory tissues. That mechanism is in mysterious and delicate adjustment. Important isolations of active ferments and chemical substances, such as insulin or epinephrin, may be expected from other endocrines in the future. But the judicious, recalling the delicate balance or adjustment between the different glands of the system, and the related glands, should look with a sceptical eye upon transplantation schemes, and all other such crude interpolations of new cogs in a subtle machine.

Philology

THE TEST OF ENGLISH

By George Philip Krapp

No apple contains in itself a perfect and complete combination of all the characteristics that may appear in apples, yet a person eating an apple is never in doubt that any particular apple is an apple. So also, although no aspect of English is the absolute and essential language, nevertheless any individual manifestation of English is immediately recognizable as English. What, then, is the test, the touchstone, by which one determines that a particular form of speech is or is not a part of the English language?

Obviously it will not do to dispose of any debatable word or phrase which happens not to be in one's own dialect, or in the dialect that one approves, by saying, That isn't English. The touchstone for English must be one that will do more than draw to it, like a magnet, only speech of a single kind. What I approve or disapprove in speech may be an important matter in determining my chosen relations to my fellowmen, but my choices do not exhaust the possible choices of the language. Even ungrammatical and incorrect English is still English, and the person who chooses ungrammatical forms cannot be pushed completely beyond the circle that marks the limits of the language.

A more practicable touchstone for English may perhaps be sought in the term idiomatic English. English is said to be most genuinely English when it is idiomatic. Now, the terms idiom and idiomatic call for a moment's examination. A very common notion of idioms is that they are forms of the language which lie beyond grammatical explanation. The great body of the language, according to this conception, is grammatically explicable, but here and there peculiar phrases and constructions crop up, as unaccountable as the whims and fancies of our friends. And these idioms, being so individual, so racy of the life of the language, are the very parts of it that express most fully its essential nature, just as one may know one's friends best by their foibles and eccentricities.

But all this shows an imperfect and shallow understanding of the term idiom. For in the first place there are no forms of the language which are beyond interpretation in the sense that they are expressions of an uncontrolled, unregulated and irresponsible genius of the language. All forms of speech originated in the minds of individuals, and the mental processes which produced them can be analyzed and placed under grammatical categories, if the categories are only made wide and subtle enough. Nor can these seemingly irrational idioms be supposed to express the essential nature of the language better than the more regular parts of it. They are not primitive untamed survivals from the infancy of the speech, but are more likely to be late developments, resulting from some obscuring analogy or some partial dilapidation in the language. They are its eccentricities, not the central heart and core of it.

Much more inclusive than this grammatical conception of idiom is another which makes the term practically synonymous with the speech of a nation or a people. Thus the idiom of the English people is the language by the possession of which they are most readily recognized to be a people, that is, the English language. This speech is the peculiar language possession of the English people. It is their distinctive linguistic mark, just as French is the distinctive linguistic mark, the idiom of the French people.

Manifestly, however, this sense of the term idiom is of little avail in the attempt to discover some test by which one can establish grounds for the assurance one has that English is genuinely English. For if the English idiom is the peculiar speech of the English people, the term is obviously merely a synonym for the English language. Every nation, every race of people, has its peculiar idiom in this sense. The term is all-inclusive, embracing everything which gives to the nation or the race its sense of linguistic unity. But as it is merely the name for the whole group of the language experiences of the race, it provides no test by which the curious inquirer can determine that any particular fact of language is or is not properly idiomatic.

A different kind of test of the authenticity of any form of English under scrutiny would be one which examines it from the point of view of its authority. The question to be considered here is naturally the character of the authority it must enjoy before one can confidently affirm it to be English. What sanction must English speech receive before it can be included sympathetically within the circle of the English idiom?

One kind of authority might conceivably be that of usage. The English language by this test would be the language commonly accepted in the usage of the English people. But how general must this acceptance and this usage be in order to give it such power? Few uses, perhaps no uses, in the English language, are universal in their occurrence. Just how general must a form of English speech be to acquire the right to be called English idiom? And the more general a form of speech becomes, does it become thereby the more idiomatic? By this test ungrammatical English, since it is undoubtedly the speech of greater numbers of English persons than grammatical speech, would be more idiomatic than the conventionally correct language.

It is not true, however, that a form of speech must be widely or even familiarly used in order to be immediately recognizable and acceptable as English. This assertion can be verified by reading almost any English poet. In the lines of the poets will be found forms of expression never before heard in the language, often never again repeated in it. English poetry is full of compound words invented by the poets for immediate occasions and never used again. When Shakespere wrote in his sonnets of the "swart-complexioned night," or of "self-substantial fuel," it mattered little whether or not anyone had done the same before him. He wrote these words in an English context, with the expectation that they would be accepted as English words by his readers, and they became thereby, to the extent to which they have been read and understood, parts of the English language.

It is a pertinent question therefore to ask, when does a word become an English word? By a judicial decision in a court of law in the State of New York it was once decreed that a word shall be known as an English word by the fact that it is recorded in the reputable dictionaries of the language. This decision may have been practically convenient to the judge and the others concerned, but it was not linguistically sound. For the fact of inclusion in reputable dictionaries does not necessarily make a word English. The words *zeitgeist* and *hinterland* will be found in reputable dictionaries, but it is questionable whether many persons feel them to be English words. So also with *bonne, demi-monde, déjeuner, éclat*, and other French words. The dictionaries contain, moreover, hundreds of words of a scientific character never meant to be spoken by human lips and practically never heard by human ears. Are all these scientific monstrosities parts of the English idiom?

On the other hand, the fact that a word is not contained in reputable dictionaries is no proof that it does not occur as a living element in the language. It is true that in this day of competitive dictionary making few words current in the language are likely to escape the collector. The dictionary makers, indeed, are more inclined to err on the side of including words doubtfully English than on the side of omitting words genuinely English. But the dictionary makers still omit a number of widely-used but improper words—and they have not always been so industrious as they are now. The comprehensive, encyclopedic dictionary is of recent origin. Dr. Johnson's dictionary was small compared with the many volumed lexicons of our day. And before Dr. Johnson, in the beginnings of English lexicography, word treasuries of this sort were still smaller. But the language itself was not appreciably smaller. The dictionaries have increased enormously in size, but this growth does not mean a corresponding increase in the extent of the language. It merely means that many ele-

ments long present are more fully recorded. There was a time when no dictionaries at all existed, and still the English language was there. And if all the English dictionaries that have ever been made were completely wiped out of existence and recollection, the language would remain, and the words comprising it would have as much authority and justification for their existence as they have now. Dictionaries are, in short, merely records of language after the event. They do not make the facts of language, but at most can only faithfully describe them.

Every cultivated language of the modern world contains many words of foreign origin. In English these constitute no inconsiderable part of the vocabulary. Sometimes these foreign words retain the character of foreign elements, but often they become embodied in the language so completely that they cease altogether to be foreign and become simply English. For it scarcely need be said that the etymological origin of a word has nothing to do with determining the ultimate fate of it. In the English language are words from German, French, Dutch, Chinese, Japanese, Malay and a dozen other languages which have become as English as any of the words of purest Anglo-Saxon descent. Only the expert etymologist is aware of the fact that these foreign words have not always been accustomed to English surroundings. How have they become English, and what is the test by which we shall know that a foreign word is no longer foreign but has changed its nature?

One test often proposed is that a word shall be considered a foreign word as long as it retains the form and pronunciation that it had in the language from which it was derived, and that it shall be considered as having become an English word when it has become Anglicized in form and pronunciation. Thus *cadet* is an English word, because English pronounces the final *t*, whereas French does not. One might urge that a complete Anglicization of *cadet* would put the stress on the first syllable.

But if *cadet* becomes English only because the final *t* is pronounced, then *buffet* cannot be English, since the final *t* is not pronounced. Yet the common fact of experience is that countless numbers of people, in homes, hotels and on railway trains, use the word *buffet* without the slightest realization that it is anything but an English word.

A moment ago the words *zeitgeist* and *hinterland* were mentioned as doubtfully English, but if they are doubtful, it is not because they look and sound like German words. The word *kindergarten* is just as German as either of the two, and yet *kindergarten* may be successfully defended as a genuine English word—that is, English in the sense that it is a part of the idiom of the race. So we have many words like this in the language, foreign in form and as foreign in pronunciation as one language is likely to permit the pronunciation of the words of another language to be. Such words are *matinée, studio, soprano, alto, mirage, garage,* and other similar terms from French and Italian. Not a few English words are perfectly good Latin in sound and appearance, words like *bonus, onus, index, data, referendum, opera, vim, sculptor,* and many others with the ending *-or*. In the light of these illustrations, one must say therefore that the visual form of a foreign word and the aural form of it have little or nothing to do with determining whether or not it has become an English word. For a foreign word may remain unchanged in both and still by the test of experience be an English word.

If, then, etymological origins, grammatical analysis and extent of use prove to be unsatisfactory tests whereby English may justify itself, apparently one must appeal to a different kind of court. All these tests have the advantage of being definite and concrete, but they have the disadvantage of not explaining the facts. Etymology, grammar, usage,—all are factors in the practical experiences which together make up the English idiom, but there is something beyond any of these theoretical observations and of greater significance in determining our sense of the unity and the living character of our native speech.

What this something is only a psychologist should venture to set forth with full realization of its origins and its many subtle ramifications. But the thing itself is common enough in every man's experience; it is, in fact, a necessary part of his experience. It is so simple that pride of intellect may lead to the rejection of it as unworthy to serve as a source of linguistic light and leading. It is, in a word, the *feeling* for the mother tongue. What we *feel* to be English, we *know* to be English. If we do not feel a form of speech to be English, no amount of etymological learning, of refined grammatizing, of rational explanation of any kind can make it seem English to us. Only when we accept it and incorporate it into the living structure whereby we realize ourselves as having a native speech can a word or a phrase become a part of our idiomatic English. Reason is not needed as a guide to the recognition of a native speech. One does not recognize one's mother tongue by definition, but by the unassailable evidence and direct knowledge of feeling. The idiomatic life of the language is not something external, to be constructed by the accumulation of a number of demonstrable facts. It lies within us, a part of every person's living experience.

This feeling for the mother tongue is of slow and long growth. It has its beginnings in the earliest years of infancy, and it does not stop growing until speech, together with all other mental faculties, ceases forever. The elements which enter into the formation of it are incalculable in number, and in subtlety and variety they surpass any man's power to know them. They are elements arising not only from the experiences of the individual in his own inner personal world, but also from the experiences of the individual in his relations to all the other beings by whom he is surrounded. The feeling for the mother tongue is indeed an epitome of the whole personal and social experiences of the persons whose life it expresses.

If a feeling of this kind is our surest touchstone by which to know that English is English, then it becomes the most subjective of all tests. This, indeed, is necessary from the nature of language. English has no existence apart from the experience of individuals. It exists in no dictionary, in no man's grammatical description, however elaborate, of the language. It has being only as it is an active part of the mental and emotional life of men and women. But men and women in their use of language exhibit an infinite number of differing customs or dialects. No two can be absolutely the same in their use of language; no two can feel absolutely the same even with respect to what we call their common speech. It results therefore that what I feel to be English must be English—for me, and that what you feel to be English, must be English—for you. What is English to me cannot be English in precisely the same way to any other person. Certain forms of speech may seem English to other persons which seem to me not at all English. To some speakers even *zeitgeist* and *hinterland*, *bonne* and *déjeuner* may seem English. Everything depends upon feeling, upon the degree of assurance with which a word or other usage is drawn within the circle of sympathetic inclusion in the language. Even in the heart of the same person this feeling may not always be the same. At one moment a word may be used without the slightest shadow of doubt or hesitation as to its being authentic English. At another moment, and in other circumstances, we may reject the word altogether, or use it only with mental quotation marks around it.

What I feel to be English therefore may not and need not arouse a similar feeling in my neighbors. In all probability, however, it will, for the large sense of unity in the language comes from the fact that under like circumstances various persons will have approximately the same reactions. In the end, the sum of these approximate similars in the speech habits of the group may come to exert a far-reaching control over the linguistic actions of individuals through the establishment of a kind of moral tone for the use of the language. But the exercise of this control is subtle and diffused, and it is like speech itself, one of the general social possessions of the group.

The extraordinary vitality and variability of the language come home to us when we reflect on the millions of users of English, each with his own individual sense of the life of the native idiom, each sure of himself within his own circle, and yet each at the same time genuinely living only because his little circle is part of the great circle of the language. The life of the language thus has a double aspect, and like all life, it can be known only because it is experienced. But the unity of linguistic feeling by which one realizes the greater circle of the language does not necessarily imply approval of all within that circle. There are empires within the great empire. We may agree to call many uses idiomatic English which we do not commend or propose to put into practice. Approval and disapproval are minor aspects and moods of the all-embracing life of the language. When our native speech sits close to the hearts of the people, as all speech should, it is quick and manifold in its changes. It is a great ocean of speech, closed within its own shores, but never twice the same in the many forms which its moving waters are constantly taking.

SWEENEY'S GRAIL

BY LEONARD LANSON CLINE

By one definition, life is the careless visitation of little indignities, negligible doubtless in themselves but with a cumulative effect that may become tragic. Society is a conspiracy to heckle the halt, to drop nails in the blind man's tin cup and snicker at his unwitting benediction, to leave lighted cigarettes on the costly tapestries that our landlady spreads on our table. And it is because of this that there is such an appallingly high suicide rate among cops. Sneered at by the motorist, shot at by the impatient second-story man, jostled by the bootlegger, bricked by the strike-breaker, scratched by the feminist agitator, scorned by the absconding cashier, not a week goes by without some cop clutching destiny with a fist erstwhile so diligent with the espantoon. If a few of them were able to write, they might leave behind them messages that would give society a new understanding of the police. But no; they perish inarticulate as they lived, friendless and forlorn, the most persecuted of all earth's unfortunate.

If cops could only plead their own cause! For it is due to misunderstanding that we harass these wistful dreamers of the bludgeon. We hear them swearing at women and children, we see them engaged in light conversation with unemployed highwaymen and grifters, we mark the eupeptic contours of their paunches, the flat feet, the sloping brows. And, victims of our prejudices, we never stop to wonder if these men, even as Omar, even as Joel, do not sometimes pant with yearning to shatter this hodge-podge scheme of things and rebuild it nearer to the heart's desire.

We never fancy that Officer Sweeney, too, may seek a grail.

To the observant, of course, there are glimpses of the spirit in a thousand casual episodes of everyday life. There comes to mind now memory of a dimly lit and tapestried hall, on a night of wisdom, gaiety and love. At the small tables, beautiful women and distinguished men debated together the problems of this perplexing age, or laughed together over a shimmering play of wit. Waiters hurried noiselessly from table to table, bringing chromatic viands and synthetic gin. All elegance and refinement. And at one end of the room a cop began to pound vehemently on the bar with his club.

We might have yielded to a gathering sense of affront and ejected the noisy fellow. But presently he turned and addressed those of us who were near.

"Who in hell's gonna bring me some whisky?" he said, his lips quivering. "This is a hell of a way to treat me. Why, fer a quarter I'd pinch the place. They're a gang of robbers and they oughta be closed up. You drink this stuff and if they wasn't so much water in it a swallow of it'd kill you dead."

A hush fell over that place, just now so bright. In silence we watched while an apologetic zany put the bottle on the bar, and while the cop poured himself three stiff drinks. It had come upon us that this man too might be named in the secret roll of the great despisers, that something more than a tadpole soul welled in that shuffling carcass, that a hurt and disillusioned spirit squinted at the world through those little eyes. And hardly had our cop departed before, still taciturn, we got our coats and hats and hastened forth, each to his own chamber, to meditate alone upon this thing.

In the morning we read in the papers that our cop was no more. He had been shot down by a rascally taxi-driver who was trying to get away with the corpse without paying the fee.

II

Killed in the line of duty was our cop, and once in a while another is slain thus. But the astounding suicide rate is what most jeopardizes the force. And the manner in which vacancies are filled is a further testimonial to the qualities that make for the typical cop. It is not, as one might think, only the ditchdigger and the ambitious thug, the unsuccessful barber and the man who otherwise might have been a mail-carrier, that join the force. Spiritualists find it a desirable vocation. The department is full of them. One has but to follow the detective squad in its work on any baffling crime to see a striking demonstration of this. Before a month has passed seven or eight mediums will have been consulted, and two or three arrests will have been made on the testimony of the ouija board. Indeed, there is a retired lieutenant of detectives in New York who writes to the officials of other cities offering to put at their disposal his familiarity with spirits who, hovering on the astral Third avenue or Bowery, may have been actual eye-witnesses of the murder.

And not only spiritualists, but also doctors of so-called medicine, lawyers, botanists, army officers, masters of art clamor to be admitted to the force. It is one of the most inspiring phenomena of the age, this exodus from the professions into the *Polizei*. Newspapermen often come in contact with grave scholars trudging beats, and write stories about them. And we have evidence from no less a person than General Sir William Horwood, chief of Scotland Yard, who, at the last inter-national congress of police, told how the universities were pouring their best sons into his service. There are so many applicants for the club and the uniform of the London bobby, said Sir William, that he could reject 17 out of 20 and still keep ahead of the challenging, the unconscionable, the monstrous suicide rate.

It was at the congress that we got our first idea of what the ideal world for which the cop is striving would be like. And never will the memory of that assemblage leave us. Here, in one chamber together, were the great detectives of the age, the intrepid men of action that fling themselves so boldly into the murky rookeries of crime; the plotters, the arch-clairvoyants who, from the smudge of a thumb on a throat or a calling card carelessly left behind, track the desperado to his lair.

The great detectives of the world!

Luncheon was served one day, and after the ice-cream, during an interval for smoking, forty or fifty of the great detectives took their napkins from their collars and disappeared. A few minutes later we happened to pass through an upstairs corridor, and there we found them all. Some of them were standing along the wall, deep in thought, while others were going up and down peeking into doors. An air of hardly contained excitement pervaded the corridor, and we paused, realizing that these men were seeking something, and that by observing them we could learn a little of their subtle methods. Thrill in our heart, we too took our position against the wall, and waited.

It was a large oval man with black moustache from a Canadian city that first opened a door marked "President" and walked in. He emerged in a moment, mumbling thanks to somebody inside, looked about him, and then advanced to a door farther down the hall, marked "Private. Entrance at 416". Without a moment's hesitation the large man opened this. Again he emerged, followed by words of a rather uncordial nature. He looked at his watch, lit his cigar with fingers that trembled slightly, and leaned once more on the wall.

The man that followed him came from Kalamazoo, if we remember correctly. He went to the door marked "President", opened it, and stepped in. Then he too came out, gazed about him, marched to the door marked "Private, Entrance at 416", and entered. Again he came out, rather gingerly, followed by language that was touched with strain.

Over by the window was standing a swarthy, perfectly groomed man in spick khaki, with several handsome medals and a lot of chevrons; we knew him as the commissioner of public safety from, we believe now, Tegucigalpa or thereabouts. He had been frowning with thought, but now he strode briskly down the hall, as on a resolution adopted only after long and thorough debate, swung open the door marked "Private. Entrance at 416", and disappeared. In a jiffy he popped out again, just half a syllable ahead of a pack of words that included one or two mongrels. He pondered, but not for long. He turned impulsively, and dashed into the room labelled "President".

So we watched for five minutes, fascinated by this spectacle of the great detectives of the world solving some black and horrible mystery, wondering who had committed the crime and if it was quite horrible. Then, just after the door marked "President" had been energetically locked, one of the detectives approached us. "Say," he whispered, "where's th' lavatory?"

Well, we led him to the lavatory, just around the corner. A gonfaloniere from Tuscany was leaning against the door, which was marked "Gentlemen." We dislodged him, and led our companion in. When we returned to the corridor, the black-whiskered gentleman from the North plucked at our sleeve and whispered anxiously, "M'sieu, can he say, w'ere iss de lavatoree?" And now word of the discovery trickled through the corridor. In less than half an hour all of the great detectives had found their way to, meta-phorically, the scene of the crime. The room marked "President" and that marked "Private. Entrance at 416" were invaded no more. Cops cannot read, perhaps,—but they can learn!

Thus, we meditated, go all the notable exploits of police history. You cannot escape these men. They will not be deceived. They will not be put off. If the sign at the cross-roads says "To the right for Rome," they will go the left first, and when at last they find you in the Vatican they will have assured themselves that you are not hiding in Hong-Kong or Nome. And when at last they lay their hands upon you, they will know already that not one of the seven men they have hanged for the crime was guilty of it.

III

But to the point. Here also at this congress we learned much about those nostalgic yearnings for a better and more beautiful world that the cop cherishes in his lonely vigil.

It was the chief of the bureau of identification at Buenos Aires that proposed to finger-print the world. In Argentina, he said, they began a decade ago to finger-print the nation, and they are getting along with the thing very well now. Every person who leaves the country must carry with him a little book certifying that he has left his finger-prints at headquarters. If he cannot show this certificate to the inspectors on his return, he will not be admitted into the country. Children in Buenos Aires, on admission to the public schools, are finger-printed, and by this scheme, in two generations or so, there will be, in the bureau of identification, a graph of the thumb of every citizen.

Ugly rumors persisted on the floor of the congress, while the visitor from Argentina was explaining his institution. It was whispered that he was accepting money from a Brazilian firm that has already undertaken the manufacture of rubber thumbs, without which, in the future, no burglar's kit will be complete. It was pointed out that such use of the bureau of identification records may be made by the manufacturers, that the slayer may leave behind him in thumb prints indisputable evidence that Governor Smith himself shot Hearst. But none was bold enough either to argue against the scheme, or charge the commissioner from Buenos Aires with receiving bribes.

Another project toward that dim utopia on which the cops' vision fawns was broached by General Sir William himself; and his, too, is already in operation in his own bailiwick. One could hardly appreciate it without knowing something of the man himself. And to that end we suggest Kipling. Sir William fairly exudes Kipling. He is large, and would sit thick in the saddle. His countenance is round and ruddy. His frayed collars, we understand, he presents to orphan asylums for use as basket-ball baskets. He is a sturdy knight, but no less susceptible to that sort of sentiment immortalized by the great poet in "Mandalay" and "Gunga Din".

"I was brought up among men", said Sir William, husky with emotion. "I have lived with men, and fought with men, and commanded men, all my life. And when one has a body of 22,000 of the finest men in the world under one, one gets perhaps a little too fond of them."

Then Sir William handed out a large package of photographs to be distributed among the congress. We seized them eagerly, to view these heroic bobbies. But the pictures were not of men. They were of horses. The horses used by the mounted division.

While the photographs of Sir William's horses were passing from hand to hand, he proceeded to outline his project. Sometime ago Sir William combed over his force until he found a number of detectives who could read. Then he subscribed to a lot of magazines from all over the world, and gave them to his readers, with instructions to look for any paragraph that might be seditious, salacious or otherwise offensive.

All these were to be clipped and filed away under the name of the man who vented them. Thus, Sir William pointed out, eventually he will have a library of clippings containing the favorite lines of every radical in the world. When such a person presents himself at an English port, he can be confronted with all the things he has ever said, and sent back home.

Sir William begged Commissioner Enright to aid him in this work, by sending to him all information he could find about the American radicals. And he urged that every country adopt the same system.

Really, once this idea is taken up, it will help as nothing else could to bring about the cops' millenium, by barring every man, woman and child who lets fall a horrid word from every city in the world. And it will not undermine the principle of freedom of speech, as any police chief will explain to you; for liberty is one thing and license is quite another. It is time we came to understand that. Our fathers fought for liberty and shed their blood to win it, the liberty that should be guaranteed to all men to stand up fearlessly, on City Hall square as in their own chambers, and sing at the top of their voices "The Star Spangled Banner." But our fathers, and all other historic liberators and democrats, would never have tolerated license; and it is license to sing the "Internationale", or expound contraceptive measures to the alumnae of a lying-in hospital, or whisper that if Coolidge should get buried in a landslide it would sprout turnips.

Out of license, you see, comes revolution. To be sure, these United States were born out of one revolution, but that is no reason why people should talk of another. Besides, it is so unpleasant. Birth, one must remember, is a matter of biological necessity, and becomes aesthetic only when one appeals to the stork.

IV

Probably the most inspiring vision revealed and applauded at the congress emanated from Commissioner Enright of New York. He told how he took up with the authorities at one of the important American universities recently the advisability of instituting a department of police work. These shilpit educators blinked at him, it seems, and cupped their ears, and said "How?" He could get no satisfaction from them, and finally he returned to New York, disappointed but no whit discouraged, and founded a police school of his own.

It is to be hoped that another time he will have a more enlightened faculty to deal with. For Commissioner Enright's proposal is only in line with the development of modern pedagogy. The arts and the humanities that once were the province of colleges are seen now to be a mere waste of time. More and more there has come into being an austerely practical curriculum. It began of course with the bookkeeping courses, which have developed so rapidly during the past decade that nowadays hardly any clerk but boasts his Phi Beta Kappa key. In Europe educational methods have quite kept pace with ours, so that a rather inspiring exchange was made possible recently. A young man, graduate of one of our foremost Eastern universities, went to England to teach the manufacture of ice-cream, in which he had taken his degree. Meanwhile a young woman came to exercise her profession in America, after completing her studies at a prominent university in Scotland, where she majored in cheese-making. Needless to say, it is by such reciprocation of compliments that the two great nations can be brought more closely together.

But the one thing to which Americans can point with most pride is the newly established chair of hotel management at Cornell. An endowed institution, this was offered to several universities, and eight of them bid for it, including, we understand, Harvard and Pennsylvania. After due investigation it was awarded to Ithaca.

Finally, when one recalls that military training is now an accepted part of a university education, one must agree that it would be but a short step farther to ordain a department of practical bludgeonry. The espantoon shall be indeed mightier than the stick of chalk.

Little beams like these, though flickering palely in the heaving chaos of the future, do give one glimpses of that ideal to which the cops aspire. A world fingerprinted, documented, with all dissenting or froward voices doomed to a perpetual cruise beyond the three-mile limit. And, trudging through the quadrangles of our colleges, with club and grammar under their arms, the Sweeneys of the police force that is to come. Thus the cops dream, and we contemn them, never realizing that their reticence is of dignity and not of dullness, and their obscene outbursts those of spirits tormented rather than vulgar!

Ave, flatfoot Launfals of the street! Here at least is one that understands you.

THE NEW THOUGHT

BY WOODBRIDGE RILEY

THE NEW THOUGHT has a history in spite of its name. It began in Boston, the transcendental town, spread to Kansas City, the "Centre of Unity", and now focuses in Los Angeles, the "Home of Truth". Christian Science and the New Thought started at about the same time, but the former, in the early days, outgrew its rival. Its female founder worked all the tricks of the trade, under-selling her goods, vilifying her competitors, and suppressing those who would not knuckle down to her organization. Thus, the first edition of "Science and Health" was largely distributed gratis, the real inventor of the phrase "Christian Science" was called an old fool, and Mrs. Eddy's first formidable rival was dubbed an "adulteress" because she adulterated the "truth".

The New Thought was derived originally from the same well of wisdom as Eddyism. Old Dr. Quimby, the magnetic healer of Portland, Maine, was the source of both brands of "metaphysical" healing. Mrs. Eddy confessed as much when she published her famous testimonial in a Portland newspaper. Later she repudiated this confession, but meanwhile Quimby had gained other disciples who remained faithful to him. Such were the two Dressers, father and son, of whom the elder inherited the Quimby manuscripts, and the younger wrote the history of that system of mental "science" which later came to be known as the New Thought.

Unfortunately for the success of the New Thought movement the elder Dresser kept the original Quimby manuscripts in careful cold storage. If he had only published them at the time Mrs. Eddy proclaimed

herself the only original source of divine science he might have punctured her pretention and prevented her great success. But he did not do so, and so she got her start. "Christian Science" and the "Science of Health" were terms invented by Quimby. For interesting a religious and dyspeptic race these two phrases, both appropriated by Mrs. Eddy, were worth a fortune. But Evans, the Swedenborgian, who should have been the advertising agent of Quimby, thought he could write better stuff himself. So he put forth colorless titles, such as "Mental Medicine" and "Soul and Body", which meant nothing to the suffering public. Only after Mrs. Eddy published her "Science and Health with Key to the Scriptures" did Evans turn to the religious line and publish "The Divine Law of Cure".

The original New Thoughters, though they borrowed their ideas from precisely the same source, were unlike Mrs. Eddy in that they prided themselves on not seeking notoriety and not chasing the dollar. They held up to praise old Quimby as the "Pioneer Apostle of Christian Science" who taught without money and without price. A serious mistake. Even free dispensary patients are asked to pay for the bottles and thus preserve their pride. But gradually a change came over their technique. The esoteric Evans passed to a higher plane and those who remained below began to see that filthy lucre was not so filthy after all. So they started to imitate the Eddian sales department. They had no fixed fees for divine metaphysics, but those adherents who did not ante up with free will offerings soon disappeared from the organization. Magazines were started, such as the *Journal of Practical Metaphysics* and *Nautilus*. These were edited by wise men and wise women of the East. In the West arose *Universal Truth* in Chicago, *Unity* in bleeding Kansas, *Harmony* in San Francisco, and *Master Mind* in Los Angeles.

The secret of the eventual success of all these "metaphysical" publications was that they passed beyond the mere treatment of disease and began proclaiming the secrets of material success on this lowly earthly sphere. The *Nautilus* now advertises "greater success all along the line" and offers a long list of treatises, such as "The Life Power and How to Use It", "Use Your Forces", "Mother Power and How to Use It", "Marital Unrest", and "The Cause and Cure of Colds". Finally, the prospective purchaser is offered as a premium "How to Wake the Solar Plexus" and is thus taught how to become a perfect Dempsey in the dollar line. The *Unity* magazine of Kansas City carries on the same noble work in its Prosperity Column. A lady from Alabama writes: "After writing to you on the last named date, a wonderful consciousness of abundance came over me. I did not doubt Divine Supply, only I was curious as to how it would demonstrate. It became an interesting game to watch the checks and money flutter in out of thin air, one might say".

Thus the subsidiary companies are now becoming successful rivals to the original octopus. Christian Science is no longer the only pipe line to the springs of health. The *Nautilus* advertises "Practical Lessons in Self-Healing", and one patient says that since he started taking them he has lost his double chin and has reduced his weight thirty-five pounds. In contrast, a Fitchburg, Mass., man writes: "Have gained fourteen pounds in weight. All of the old doubts and fears and worries are gone". From Kansas City there goes forth daily at 9 P. M. (evidently Central Standard Time) a Healing Thought which has often reached "Australia, South Africa, and other far distant countries". Some aston-

ishing results flow from this Silent Unity Healing. By it a gentleman was cured of nervous prostration "brought on by riotous living in Boston, Mass." Then there was a young lady of Enterprise, Mississippi, whose "mind was deranged by the flu. The doctors had failed, the prayers of her church were of no avail, but after Kansas City was heard from in three days she was healed and home from the asylum".

If Missouri can do such things, obviously California can do more. A recent number of the *Master Mind* tells of one student who attended the University of Christ in Los Angeles and after five years of close application was cured of insanity and cancer. But to Kansas City should be given the prize for the most novel Prosperity Thought. This is included in the plan for a Unity Prosperity Bank. As the notice reads, "with the Prosperity lessons and prayers for success there is sent a Unity Bank in which the applicant deposits the subscription price of the magazine he sends to friends".

II

Such is New Thought today. It has become thoroughly commercialized. It advertises. It hires halls, theatres, and hotel ballrooms. It has successful magazines and its presses turn out carloads of metaphysics. Its latest enterprise is education in all its varied forms. In its early stages it was like a log-cabin school, with a single teacher and a few pupils. Now it has its University of Christ at Los Angeles, with field lecturers, correspondence courses, and a summer school, among whose teachers I notice a Mrs. Gott.

All this profitable practice must have some theory back of it. That theory is found in the early writings of such men as Quimby and Evans. Quimby began as a magnetic healer and ended with that "higher attenuation" of thought called "mental healing". Traces of his magnetic theory are to be found in his reference to vibrations, which are now modernized and prepared for the market by being hooked up with the argot of the wireless fan. Kansas City is the great broad-casting station and those who believe in its daily health and prosperity thoughts are called its receiving stations. The New Thoughters regard themselves as akin to Emerson and the other Transcendentalists, domestic and foreign; they are, indeed, very fond of appealing to the Sage of Concord. But Emerson certainly never tried to cure rheumatism by absent treatment, and when he was threatened with consumption he sought a Southern climate. The New Thoughters also appeal to the idealist Berkeley, not knowing apparently that he was no mental healer but pinned his faith to the healing virtues of tar water. In his system of immaterialism Berkeley went far, but he never would have been guilty of such an Irish bull as this: "There is no limit to this apparent effect of thought. If you are certain enough that you are dead, you are dead instantly".

When the real materials of New Thought are sought for they resolve themselves into a curious mixture of fetishism, occultism, and esoteric Buddhism. The fetishism is based on a belief in the magic power of words. Just as an Indian chief meditates on his tribal totem—the sacred beaver, or eagle, or what not—and yet never utters its name, so do the New Thoughters pick out some mysterious word or phrase and meditate upon it "in the silence". The thought for the day may be Health, or Wealth, or Happiness. Enter into the silence and meditate upon it! Then emerge out of the silence and you will be cured of cancer, receive a fat check, or be a social success. Says the editor of *Master Mind:* "The Word that marries the within and the without gives everyone what he or she wishes, and is the life of every party, the good time of the eternal years".

Beside the password to prosperity there is the opposite word or reversed formula. Mr. Henry Wood, for example, advises us to "erect a Mental Gymnasium and utilize every silent and unoccupied hour in swinging the dumb bells of concentration upon

high ideals", but in this daily dozen of mental gymnastics one must not let the dumb bells fall on one's feet. The magic formula reversed becomes a dangerous thing; there is dire power in an evil thought, or even in a single word. Mrs. Eddy once declared that the disease epizootic was never contracted by the horse until man's noble friend heard the fatal word from some ignorant horse-doctor. The New Thoughters carry on this same idea and offer hints on how microbes are made. "By thinking we manufacture microbes, whereas by impregnating the whole being with thoughts of love we exterminate disease germs". A similar passage in *Master Mind* reads as follows: "Resolved, That I will not unnecessarily describe accidents or plant a fear thought in my own mind or in that of another . . . Resolved, That I will not form the habit of warning others, especially little children, of danger, but will be a suggestion of faith to everyone."

All this sounds like an old melodrama in which the father's curse carries on from generation to generation until it is fulfilled at last in some dire calamity. The tragic side of the attempt to avoid disease by not thinking about it is that hundreds of innocent lives are probably sacrificed to neglect. Not long ago in California, the New Thoughters, the Christian Scientists and the whole tribe of drugless healers tried to prevent the medical examination of children in the public schools. The referendum on their prohibitory act was defeated, but I am told that the health laws are not carried out in many of the coast towns, where "metaphysics" flourish. A similar referendum will be brought before the voters of the State of Washington this year, and it remains to be seen whether the boards of health will be stronger than the masterminds of the immaterialists.

III

In addition to its debt to Quimby, the New Thought also probably owes much to

Troward's Edinburgh Lectures, which once had a great vogue in These States. The old divisional judge of the Punjab gave in its clearest form what is really at the bottom of the New Thought. His language is so eloquent that one hates to disturb the flow of his thought and seek flaws in his reasoning. Yet, for a valuable exercise in misapplied logic, nothing can beat his lectures on the "natural principles governing the relation between mental action and material conditions". Take, for example, his first grand assumption that, "spirit being independent of space and time, nothing can be remote from us in space and time", and see what follows. If space is nothing, then nothing is remote. Heaven is thus a mere suburb of Hoboken, and the New Thoughter can commute with the most distant stars with ease. But though he thus disparages time and space, he yet wants an infinity of each. His spirit would free itself of all human bonds only to soar in the space he denies and flit through eternity.

With a "universal here" even greater marvels may be achieved. It makes no difference where you live, there is the center of the universe. Here the New Thoughter surpasses the classical idealists and even the poets. The old geography is passing away; New Thought geography is taking its place. The child of the future (if I may make bold to speak of the future in the midst of an everlasting now) will be bothered no longer to bound the State of Maine, or to locate Montpelier. The new United States of Mind will not be bounded on the north at all, not even by the Aurora Borealis. Homes of Truth and Unity Centres will be the capitals of countless interlocking states of mind, all boundless, and the "Department of Whole World Realization" will be more of a reality than the League of Nations.

This obliteration of space and time is evidently an easy lesson in Einstein for the New Thoughter. But it only paves the way, we are told, for understanding the Unity of the Spirit. By this we are to understand that the whole of spirit must be present in every point of space at the same moment. "All spirit is concentrated at any point in space that we may choose to fix our thought upon". Let a mere mortal try to grasp this idea by an analogy. Suppose all the electric energy in the world were generated by the General Electric Company at Schenectady, and that it could be concentrated at any point in space that one fixed one's thoughts upon. I fix my thought, for example, on Poughkeepsie. Then all electrical energy is concentrated at Poughkeepsie. But this leaves Schenectady in the dark, its trolley cars stalled, its telephones dead, and the air filled with curses—while I, the egoist, concentrate my attention on my local habitat!

But there is more. Instead of having one mind, as the old-fashioned have long thought, the New Thought teaches that we have two, the objective and the subjective. The former is the ordinary, outer, logical part of the mental mechanism; the latter is the extraordinary, inner, intuitive part. It has marvelous powers. The subjective mind is "able to diagnose the character of a disease from which it is suffering". Again, it can build up a body in exact correspondence with the personality impressed upon it. A boy of twelve admires Charlie Chaplin. He sets his subjective mind to work that night, and wakes up in the morning with a fine little moustache.

So much for the human mind as such. Its relations to the absolute mind are now to be considered. There the original theories of Troward may be put in the form of syllogisms and the conclusions worked out by examples. The subjective mind is always subject to suggestion; the subjective mind is the universal intelligence; therefore, the universal intelligence is always subject to suggestion. By suggestion, evidently, mere man may thus do anything. Say to your crops, grow, and they will grow. Be a happy farmer by getting hold of this control. Then the boll weevil and corn blight will matter not, and the bulletins of the Department of Agriculture may be thrown into the waste-basket. Strangely enough, the New Thoughters do not actually apply their control of the absolute to agriculture. Mrs. Eddy, true enough, once did it when she performed one of her "floral trifles" and made a cherry tree blossom at Christmas time, but the New Thoughters are more modest. Your object, says Troward cautiously, is not to run the whole cosmos, but to draw particular benefits, physical, mental, moral or financial, to yourself. Chiefly, it would appear financial. The principle of concentration has worked like a charm in drawing in the dollars. "Financial Success through Creative Thought, or, The Science of Getting Rich" has attracted so many "little love offerings" that the editor of an eastern New Thought magazine gives an account of how, clad in her "steel beaded gray, red earrings and beads, and my new wisteria wrap", she ate a dinner of eight courses at the expensive Hotel Savoy, in London. A similar success visited the proprietor of a Pacific Coast magazine who had hardly a dollar to start with, but was last reported making a trip around the world with three students.

Obviously, New Thought ought also to be applied to politics. How convenient would be the use of the cosmic consciousness to party leaders! The chairman of the Republican steering committee concentrates on his legislative programme. In spite of Democratic opposition, that programme will be carried out—provided the chairman has been an early and powerful concentrator. But if, alas, some deserving Democrat is a better concentrator and can get the first hitch on the cosmic chariot, the Republican elephant will be stalled. The New Thoughters, indeed, do not make enough of their opportunities. Besides politics they should take up military science; a New Thought army would be irresistible. A suggestion towards this has already been made by the author of "How to Protect Our Soldiers." Instead of seeking cover they are advised to send out love thoughts to deflect the bullets of the enemy. Instead of using the language he now uses the New Thought top-sergeant will bawl to the awkward squad: "Meditate, you sons of guns, meditate!" Instead of ordering dough boys, dirty from the trenches, to enter the delousing station he will order them to enter the silence.

IV

Health thoughts and prosperity thoughts have been the standby of our new metaphysicians. By them they have accomplished results ranging from "bullet-proof soldiers" and "whole regiments saved" to "the realization of all the things that money can buy—automobiles, homes, clothes, gems, and facilities for travel". Still the wonder grows. Recently the New Thoughters have taken over a new field. The theatre is now to be regenerated by sending out thoughts of purity and uplift to the actors. The drama, so we are informed by Harriet Hale Rix, in a late number of *Master Mind*, is old, very old. The Garden of Eden saw the first melodrama. "At present," continues Miss Rix, "the two greatest amusement producing states are New York and California. At least one day a week should be dedicated this month to denying sensuality and materiality throughout these centres, finishing each denial with our noonday blessing." The new form of the theatre, the movie, is especially promising as an instrument of uplift. Therefore, let us uplift it in our

SUNRISE BLESSING FOR JANUARY
WE DECREE THAT THE TRUTH SHINES FORTH
IN EVERY
PLAY AND THROUGH EVERY PLAYER,
PURIFYING
EACH THOUGHT AND DEED, SO
THAT THE THEATRE GLORI-
FIES THE GREAT CREATOR

ON A SECOND-RATE WAR

BY X——

IN THE conflict which some still persist in calling the Great War, though it was great only in size, there was so much jumble and muddle and half-hearted experiment and so little visible military skill and ingenuity that a far-seeing and keen-thinking British colonel has declared that if the nations of the earth will only use their brains, the inevitable next war will show combat so transformed and reformed that the struggle of 1914-1918 will seem, by comparison, little more than a clash "between barbaric hordes, a saurian contest, not mediaeval but primeval, archaic, a turmoil." There were strokes of brilliancy, of course, but there was nothing to warrant the hero worship that is going on in Europe, where a person in mountainous Switzerland and an apologist in disturbed Germany devote their energies to debating which was the greater genius, Foch or Ludendorff. The answer is simple: neither was a genius at all. To many a soldier the feelings of today are well expressed by that gentleman with a fiery pen and a disenchanting manner, Mr. Montague, who writes:

Foch tells us what he thinks Napoleon might have said to the Allied commands if he could have risen in our slack times from the dead. "What cards you people have!" he would have said, "and how little you do with them! Look!" And then, Foch thinks, within a month or two he "would have rearranged everything, gone about it all in some new way, thrown out the enemy's plans and quite crushed him." That "new way" was not fated to come. The spark refused to fall, the divine accident would not happen. How could it? you ask with some reason. Had not trench warfare reached an impasse? Yes: but there is always an impasse before Genius shows a way through. Music on keyboards had reached an impasse before a person of genius thought of using his thumb as well as his fingers. Well, that was an obvious dodge, you may say, but in Flanders what way through could there have

been? The dodge found by genius is always an obvious dodge, afterwards. Till it is found it can as little be stated by us common people as can the words of the poems that Keats might have written if he had lived longer. You would have to become a Keats to do that, and a Napoleon to say how Napoleon would have got through to Bruges in the Autumn that seemed so autumnal to us. All that the army knew, as it decreased in the mud, was that no such uncovenanted mercy came to transmute its casualties into the swiftly and richly fruitful ones of a Napoleon, the incidental expenses of some miraculous draught of victory.

The fact is that in the World War all important results were accomplished by weight of numbers instead of by facility of thought. It has been said that Germany was the only country really prepared for the struggle; but even Germany was not properly prepared and trained, or at least did not act as though she were. True, she had guns, some of which she borrowed from Austria; true, she had available reserves; and true, she had learned forty-three years before how to use railways and telegraphs in war-time. But she started out to fight France as if she were still waging the war of 1870-1871. She saw a line of forts and swept around them to the North (very wise!), but she forgot that the needs in supplies, reserves, communications and transportation of her huge and cumbersome army were not the meagre needs of Prussia four decades before. That army, in truth, moved so fast that it became hopelessly disorganized. A German commander got sick and his forces went into confusion. And the "marvelous miracle" of the Marne was actually a withdrawal; the German order to retire was given *in advance* of the French order to attack! Down go two military idols!

Then came the race to the sea, as the historians call it, each opponent trying to apply time-worn principles of enveloping on a flank until both stretched their attenuated lines over more than four hundred miles of battle front. Instantly there was such a scattering of forces that ought to have been massed and such a confusion in the rear that neither army was able to hit—to concentrate, and hit, and disorganize its opponent. Instead both settled down to the brutal method of trying to wear each other down, starve each other out, exhaust each other's resources,—to snipe off individuals one by one from carefully concealed and adroitly camouflaged hiding places in shell-holes or ruined buildings—in brief, to practice assassination instead of war.

Both experimented tentatively with attacks, but discovered that machine guns wiped out their advancing lines. They invented from time to time "pill boxes" and "distribution in depth" and "leap frog attacks" and "filtering through" and I know not how many more childish devices. The French fiddled around with cavalry and tried to train horses to jump shell-holes and to extricate themselves from barbed wire; they even used mounted men on frontal attacks against trenches in the Champagne. The Germans tried gas, but only experimentally and in a very limited part of a very limited sector; clear thinking and sound foresight would have impelled them to conserve their surprise and use it on a wide front for an important strategic objective, not against single Indian or Canadian battalions. They discovered a new meaning in munitions, and multiplied production until they staged bombardments lasting week on week in an effort to smother and demolish all resistance, only to find that they had so torn up the ground in front of them that their own necessary transport and supplies could not go ahead, and so their troops could not go ahead either. Then came "assaults with limited objectives"—and another stalemate. The belligerents thought of tanks too late in the conflict, and used them improperly: and when they were used prop-

erly at Cambrai, other errors deprived the victors of the profits of their victory. They played about with airplanes, and of course accomplished some good with them. But the idea of individual use was predominant, and no one on either side had the vision to employ different types in combination, as a seaman employs different types of warships. The flying men even engaged in exhilarating man-to-man conflicts, wasting time and lives. If a fighting fleet of dreadnaughts is protected by destroyers, and meets far superior forces, it runs for home —if it can—, and the individual destroyer commander does not stop to indulge in a little duel with another individual destroyer commander. Yet "command of the air", we grew to believe, depended upon this or that "flying circus" instead of upon numerical strength and strategical manipulation, as "command of the sea" does in the navy.

II

Down in Mesopotamia, England sent inadequate forces to do a big job, and paid the penalty by the surrender of Kut and Townshend. Down in East Africa, a few Germans marshalled a motley collection of natives against the combined expeditions of England, Portugal and Belgium, and kept the field almost until Armistice Day. Down in Egypt, the British tried to protect the Suez Canal by sitting down safely and placidly on the western side of the waterway and watching the Turks float mines out to endanger passing ships, until someone in London woke up at last, and Allenby and Murray demonstrated that the best defense is an attack: a fact obvious in all the records of past wars. Down at the Dardanelles, the British Navy planned to lose a certain number of ships as the cost of conquest, lost almost that number, and then withdrew just at the moment the Turks were ready to quit and the government was fleeing with its national treasure from Constantinople into Anatolia. Then, having given warning, the British held back their landing forces just long enough to enable the waxing Crescent to mobilize sufficient troops to render Ian Hamilton impotent. In Serbia, the help came too late, and the force there assembled sat in idleness for two years, inadequately supported from home. The Italian *debacle* of 1917 was accomplished by sound but also perfectly obvious methods, all of which might have been foreseen, yet it happened. The Rumanian collapse was due to the Rumanians' over-eager desire to invade Hungary, and to a commonplace appreciation by German commanders of the shaky position into which they had thus put themselves. The French offensive into Alsace-Lorraine in the opening days of the war was a glorious gesture, but it was based upon political, not upon strategic motives, and it collapsed with colossal losses. The German submarine campaign and the German's persistent flouting of American interests and demands were political gambles, not military strategy. Indeed, most of the strategic errors of the war were caused by political motives. But no one has yet charged Napoleon with being regardless of politics and political effects. His strategy included a comprehension of such things in his time, and it would have included the same in the Twentieth Century.

There was much bravery in the World War, and much hardy endurance, but very little strategic genius. The Allies won, and deserve the credit for it, such as it is. But they won on man-power and not on brain-power. They experimented and muddled and fussed. The British started out with a volunteer army, but soon found that they would have to adopt conscription, yet they did so only after some of their best officer material had been wasted in battle. They thought they needed every man at the front, but after sending them there they discovered that the war was actually a war of manufactures. By this time, alas, multitudes of their most skilled mechanics had fallen in the field! The Americans had no army at the start and began by accepting volunteers. Then they adopted the draft—but still, for a long time, they continued taking volunteers, and so confused the two systems intolerably. If there was any consistency of plan in the war on either side or any continuous and broad appreciation of the struggle as a whole, military historians have so far failed to bring it out. If there was any Napoleon, he probably died at Mons, maybe even as a corporal in the ranks. Do not misunderstand these references to Napoleon. He startled the world by forced marches and surprises that were possible and effective in his day, but, as the Rheims attempt of the Germans showed, surprise maneuvers in the field have been practically prevented in our own day by aerial reconnaissance. The all-seeing aviator, the telephone and telegraph, and rapid motor and rail concentration of troops operate, in the Twentieth Century, to prevent surprises by rapid marching and solid massing. I am not saying, therefore, that the old Napoleon, had he arisen from the Invalides, could have repeated his historic tricks. Others, in fact, tried to do so by his formulae, and failed. I am merely saying that there was no *new* Napoleonic mind to meet the *new* conditions with something of the old divine spark. There was no "new way", as Mr. Montague has pointed out. The brains of the armies reached an impasse and settled down to a struggle of physical strength alone. The affair of the day was all engrossing, and troops were raised as they were needed, or not until after they were needed, and new implements and weapons were devised and tried as they also were needed, or after it was too late for them to be effective. Mentally and physically, the nations of the world were unprepared for a great war, although they did fight a big war. There is a difference between quantitative and qualitative measurement!

The war was won. Who won it? What won it? Listen to the words of General Maurice, of the British General Staff:

With greater experience the American infantry would have learned to overcome the German machine guns with less loss of life, and the services of supply would have worked more smoothly. . . . America placed the pick of her splendid manhood in the field, and that manhood went ahead at the job in front of it without counting the cost. By doing its job it gave us victory in 1918.

The pick of our manhood went over to fight, among the remnants of shattered European armies, against the war-weary Germans. The pick of our manhood, with only six months training on this side and only two months on the other side—on the average—went ahead at the job without counting the cost. In 1918 three leading commanders met, agreed, and signed a statement insisting that more men should be sent, as many more as possible and as promptly as possible, even though—these men said—they understood that many would have to be included who had not had sufficient training. The additional Yankees went over. American moral and physical strength was thrown into the balance, and the scales tipped. It was brute force that won the war.

Untrained troops, their casualties were unnecessarily large by 50%. In 1917 we knew nothing of war. In spite of the confusion among the volunteers "hastily assembled without organization or training" for the War of 1812, in spite of the lessons of the Mexican War, so strenuously taught by Taylor, in spite of Bull Run, and Chickamauga Park and Tampa, in spite of the glaring evils of the Mexican border mobilization in 1916—in spite of all, we had as a nation refused to learn anything about war or to adopt a sound military policy. Leaders might talk; a few enthusiasts might attend a Plattsburg camp; but the people thought of the forefathers who stalked redcoats along the Cambridge road in 1775 and believed that military training would descend as a sudden dispensation from heaven upon raw volunteers in a righteous cause. So we were unprepared. After Congress had passed its pretty resolutions, the Americans had to wait five months before they could even use their training camps. They had to wait a year before they staged an offensive action, and that a small and not satisfactory one. They had to waste billions on cost-plus contracts. They had to waste lives on the banks of the Marne, beside the hill city of St. Mihiel, and amid the tangles of the Argonne Forest. Surely it is to no one's credit to be able to boast like Falstaff: "I have lead my ragamuffins where they were well pepper'd. There's not three of my hundred and fifty left alive."

Of course there was much good work done. Soldier and subaltern went to work with a will and learned a great deal, although the first of their learning was, in many instances, with rifles whittled out of wood and cannon carved out of logs. Civilians cooperated and made sacrifices. All united in a fervent and feverish attempt to overcome the handicap of unpreparedness. Yet the fact remains that the United States, as usual, had to send men into battle insufficiently trained. With such troops as Winder had at Bladensburg, and many an American commander in France, or McDowell at Manassas, not Napoleon himself could have demonstrated a tangible gift of genius.

THE THEATRE

BY GEORGE JEAN NATHAN

IT is generally agreed that Eleonora Duse is the greatest of living actresses —very often by two sets of critics who peculiarly arrive at this estimate with arguments and reasons that are diametrically opposed. I privilege myself the suspicion that this is why Duse is called the "mystery woman". She is a mystery because she is the only actress of our time who is eulogized by half of the critics for one thing and by the other half for the exact opposite of that same thing. I have in mind specifically her performances of the mother in Gallarati-Scotti's pious claptrap, "Cosi Sia". In London last Spring, when she performed the rôle at the New Oxford, Duse played it in the spirit of a tigress who, suddenly 'wakened from sleep, snaps out a flaming snarl of defiance. This mood of defiance gave way in turn to an impassioned, nay almost a frenzied, faith, a sullen stubbornness, a burst of heart-rending appeal and, finally, a despairful agony of self-immolation. The London critics hailed the performance as the acme of intelligent and acute interpretation and Duse as the peerless actress of her day. In New York a month or so ago, when she performed the same rôle at the Century, Duse played it in the spirit of an imperturbable septuagenarian who accepts her mission coolly, calmly. This mood of resignation gave way in turn to a resigned, nay almost a melancholy, faith, a complacent sweetness, a passive acceptance of abuse and, finally, a welcome and highly comfortable surrender to fate. The New York critics hailed the performance as the acme of intelligent and acute interpretation and Duse as the peerless actress of her day.

Now surely, since "Cosi Sia" and the rôle no less are admitted, without dissenting voice, to be the veriest theatrical flapdoodle, and since, as in the instance of nobler drama and nobler rôles, two interpretations so violently, even absurdly, antagonistic are hardly to be reconciled—surely something must, to put it mildly, be a trifle odoriferous in Copenhagen. The truth is perhaps not far to seek. It is not that the eminence of the Italian actress is critically arrived at from two different and each in themselves possibly valid points of view; it is that her eminence—an eminence rightly won over a long period of years and with an incontrovertible talent—is today taken for granted even when her immediate performances are such as to give the more judicious very prolonged pause. I believe, with my colleagues, that Duse is the greatest of living actresses; I believe, further, that the performance of "Cosi Sia" which this greatest of living actresses gave in London was a superlatively fine performance; but I also believe that the performance of the same play which this greatest of living actresses gave in New York would have disgraced the rankest amateur. It was grotesquely out of key with the play—as grotesquely out of key as her London performance was in key; it was slipshod, careless; it was downright lazy and cheating. In a word, Duse loafed on the job. For in the audience at the Century Theatre there was no Maurice Baring to catch her napping, no Chaliapin or Walkley or Archer or any other fully experienced and understanding soul to catch on to her and give her away. And she seemed to know it. Just a lot of American boobs. Just a lot of poor, affected suckers. The night she opened at the Metropolitan, she took no

113

chances. Her Ellida Wangel was tremendous, as it was tremendous in London. Nor did she take any chances with her second audience, the audience, that is, at the second play in her repertoire. And here once again her Mrs. Alving had all the old greatness. But then—what was the use of spreading one's self for these Americans?—then came the bald let-down. The money was in; why bother? The greatest actress in the world—and she is greatest—deserved her little joke on these Americans and their—what do you call them?—critics. And the greatest actress in the world had it.

II

There has been, on the part of certain commentators whose linguistic gifts are confined to the English language, and who are proud of it, a disposition to wax ironical at such persons as have professed to comprehend, at least in a measure, and to be moved by, the performances in alien tongues of Duse, the Moscow Art Theatre company and, on a lower level, the Grand Guignol troupe and certain other dramatic immigrants. While, true enough, these commentators are not far wrong in their detection of a great deal of hypocrisy in the situation, it seems to me that they are less correct in their assumption that because they happen to know no language other than their own, therefore no one else does, and even less correct in their second assumption that thorough familiarity with an alien tongue is essential to an understanding of and to a sympathetic response to an acting performance in that tongue. Aside from the obvious fact that there is ample time for a critic to read in the English text the play in the alien tongue that he is about to see, and thus acquaint himself with it; aside from the even more obvious fact that if he is a professional critic he should already be thoroughly familiar with most of the standard works that these foreigners have presented and are presenting—surely, the critic who doesn't know "Ghosts", "The Lady from

the Sea", "An Enemy of the People", "Night Refuge", the plays of Tchekoff, etc., well enough by this time is pretty poorly equipped for his job—aside from these very obvious facts, a thorough knowledge of an alien tongue seems to me to be no more vitally essential to the grasping of an alien actor's performance than a knowledge of the deaf and dumb signal language is essential to a comprehension of pantomime. Let us imagine that Charlie Chaplin were a Greek and that his moving picture, "The Kid", were to be transfered from the screen to the stage and played in Greek. Would it be any the less intelligible, any the less moving? A somewhat ridiculous illustration, I appreciate, but not without its measure of convincing horse sense.

If drama consisted chiefly in words, if its effect were ever mainly conveyed through the spoken word, it might be otherwise; but drama is something different. The greatest moments of any drama are those moments that constitute the spaces of silence between the speaking of one character and the speaking of another. These silences between speech are the juices of drama. It is then that we get the effects for which the dramatist has paved the way with words. Every great play is a pantomime at bottom. Drama is pantomime adorned and embellished with literary graces. The dramatist, when first he imagines his play, imagines it not in terms of speech, but in terms of situation. He sees his theme, in his mind's eye, as a blue-print. The great drama of the world is not spoken by the characters so much as it is looked and, above all, felt by them. The play of the features and the joy and ache of the heart are as Esperanto: a universal language. One does not have to know Italian to understand a woman's tears, or Russian to understand a man's laughter. Drama is emotion. If we feel what a character, through its actor, feels, it is not entirely important that we should know what he thinks. All this, of course, would not hold water were these alien troupes on our shores to go in for the so-called intellectual drama—the most paradoxical and idiotic phrase in the English language —such plays, shall we say, as "Back to Methuselah" or one of the Granville Barker lectures. But their plays are far different, in the main the pure stuff of the emotions—save in the minds of such commentators as look on Ibsen as a great thinker first and a great dramatist second. Their plays are, with, so far as I can remember, the single possible exception of Tchekoff, emotional fabrics. The person who cannot grasp a play by D'Annunzio, and more particularly Duse's performance of the central rôle in such a play, without being an Italian scholar would be unable to grasp Wagner's Funeral March because he was not a corpse. He is the sort of dumbbell who would call one a posturer for pretending to enjoy and be moved by "Der Rosenkavalier" when one was not a professor of German, or for admiring Bach's "Bauern Cantate" when one was not a peasant. Show me the professional critic who says that he is not fit to criticize the Moscow Art Theatre company's performance of, say, Goldoni's "The Mistress of the Inn", because he is not thoroughly up on Russian, and I'll show you a critic who is not fit to criticize Zuloaga because he does not happen to be a Spaniard. . . . There are, let us incidentally not forget, fifty English-speaking people who understand the plays of Shakespeare for every English-speaking person who understands his language.

III

For the last two or three years, though my personal attendance upon his different acting performances has failed to convince me, I have been receiving on the average of once a week printed circulars from Mr. Walter Hampden telling me how good he is. It has been, I confess, a bit disturbing. I would go to the theatre, sit studiously through this and that performance of his, come away with an extremely dubious impression of his talents, and then the next morning wake up to find a circular in my mail assuring me that both Mr. Clayton Hamilton and the dramatic critic of Jenkintown, Pa., *News-Leader* regarded him, to say the least, as the equal of Salvini. Mr. Hampden has, I figure, spent fully thirty dollars on stamps, and fully one hundred dollars on half-tones and circulars, in an effort to persuade me to let himself and his admirers make up my mind for me in respect to his genius. Yet I have been, I fear, most stubborn and not a little objectionable in my impoliteness. It wasn't that I didn't try to be otherwise. After a particularly well-printed and beautiful circular arrived, I would time and again go back and have another look at the gentleman by way of trying to determine the reasons for my own apathy and, no doubt, ignorance. Surely, thought I, if many famous authorities like the critic for the Jenkintown, Pa., *News-Leader* and Mr. Towse, of the New York *Evening Post*, are firmly convinced that Mr. Hampden is an actor of the royal line, there must be something radically wrong with me if he seems to me to be a mere amalgam of forum reader and ham. But still I could not convince myself. I saw a Hamlet, a Macbeth and an Othello that were intelligent, but a Hamlet, a Macbeth and an Othello that were theatrically and dramatically as cold and unimpressive as so many college professors' essays on those characters. I saw a Petruchio that was essentially a Hamlet in a costume of gay hue—nothing more. I saw, before these, a Manson that was just a Methodist clergyman with rouge on his cheeks and with his eyelashes smeared with mascaro. I heard, again, Shakespeare read, and read well, but I did not see him acted.

And then came another expensive circular, followed by another and followed in turn by still another, announcing that Mr. Hampden was to do Cyrano. I may, under the circumstances, be forgiven for having pictured a Cyrano who would have all the poetic fire of a Sapolio rhyme, all the powerful sweep of a whisk-broom, all the

heroic magnificence and purple gesture of—
but enough of simile. Thus prejudiced—
but fortifying myself against too great
prejudice by another perusal of the encomiastic circulars—I went to the theatre.
And in that theatre I saw the Cyrano of all
our finest fancies, the Cyrano that Mansfield failed to convey even to the impressionable and easy young man that was I
at the time, a Cyrano stepped brilliantly,
dazzlingly, out of the heart and pages of
Rostand—a Cyrano, in short, that came
as close to the ideal Cyrano as closeness
well can come. Where was the college
grind, the stiff minuet body that vainly,
humorously, essayed to swing itself into
the waltz measures of great poetic dramatic literature, the forum reader in whose
mouth starlit verse became so much dia-
lectics—where was this Hampden of the
years before in this Hampden who, there
before us, was a truly gusty, a truly moving, a truly flashing, blazing and radiant
romantic actor? There was no sign of him,
not a trace. In his place was the Hampden
of all the Jenkintown, Hamilton and
Towse ecstasies and eulogies, the mythical
Hampden suddenly come to dramatic life.
The expensive circulars had found truth
at the end of the long road of their wholly
absurd, if honest and well-meant, exaggerations. Hampden was at last an actor. And
this Cyrano of his is one of the most completely meritorious performances that an
actor of his time and my own has contributed to the American theatre.

IV

The Theatre Guild is an organization not
the least of whose virtues is a successful
and praiseworthy cunning. This cunning
is on view whenever the Guild produces a
play by some new foreign dramatist about
whom the critical element in its public
is in the dark. On such occasions the
Guild's artifice is displayed to the full.
This artifice, embodied in its publicity
matter and program notes, is usually very
happy in accomplishing its end, as I have

noted, and we now once again engage an
instance of it in the case of the French
playwright, H. R. Lenormand, and the
production by the Guild of his drama,
"Les Ratés", translated as "The Failures".
In its preliminary press-agency of the play
and in its program notes, the Guild has
exercised the shrewdest care that Lenormand shall be presented to his American
audiences and critics as distinctly an art-
theatre playwright, the leader of the
Parisian group dramatically "in tune with
psychology and science", and the author
only of such dramatic work as goes in for
succès d'estime—"which", to quote the
program, "opened for him the doors of the
art theatre and inevitably closed those
of the commercial playhouses". There is,
further, elaborate mention of Gémier's
production of his "Poussière", of Pitoeff's
productions of his "Le Temps est un
Songe" and "Les Ratés", of his "La
Dent Rouge" at the Odéon,—of impressive
names on end by way of what our friends
the spiritualists call establishing the
proper mood. That the Guild has succeeded admirably in establishing this
mood so far as the local critics are concerned, and that through the establishment of this mood the latter have been
subtly thrown somewhat off the track of a
cool and sound appraisal of the Lenormand
drama which the Guild has presented and
have been blinded by the excellent hocus-
pocus to certain otherwise obvious and
not altogether auspicious secrets of its
genesis must be clearly apparent to anyone
who, without program notes, has followed
the career of Lenormand in France.

"The Failures" is a drama whose considerable poignancy and considerable theatrical effectiveness are due infinitely less
to its author's being "in tune with the
modern thought of today in psychology
and science" than to its author's long
antecedent practical acquaintance with
terse and effective commercial theatrical
writing gained from his association with
Max Maurey's Grand Guignol. "The
Failures" is in essence a series of typical

Grand Guignol one-acters. No less than eight of its fourteen episodes are completely in the Guignol key and manner. Echoes of such of Lenormand's Guignol pieces as, for example, "La Folie Blanche", "Vers La Lumière", "L'Esprit Souterrain" and "Terres Chaudes"—all carefully omitted by the Guild in its publicity matter—are clearly heard in scene after scene. The Guignol method is there, and unmistakably. The thrills and drama and comedy and technic are vastly less the thrills and drama and comedy and technic of the Théâtre des Arts than of the little box-office playhouse in the Rue Chaptal. "The Failures" is a thoroughly interesting drama of dissolution, decay and death not because Lenormand is the daring experimentalist, the revolutionary psychoanalyst and *succès d'estime* fanatic of the Guild's program notes, but because he is a hard, old-fashioned practical playwright schooled not in art theatres but in purely commercial theatres and because his psychological explorations into character are ever careful to be theatrically emotional instead of untheatrically cerebral. His "Les Ratés" is, first and foremost, a good show. If it does not make money, well then, neither does such a bad show as "A Mad Honeymoon". There is too much talk about art in the theatre.

The physical presentation of the play is in the best Guild tradition. I regret that I cannot say as much for all of the acting.

V

The "Queen Victoria" of David Carb and Walter Prichard Eaton is not so successful an experiment in dramatic biography as Guitry's "Pasteur", but it is very decidedly superior to Drinkwater's "Lincoln" and "Lee". The pompous wax-works quality that dominates the Drinkwater chronicle dramaturgy is completely absent from this "Victoria". There is life in it, and warmth; one is not merely regaled with the spectacle of a kaffeeklatsch at Madame Tussaud's. Victoria and her entourage are very real

persons, not simply mouthpieces for a highly self-conscious poet with a nice gift for ventriloquism. The play contrives adroitly and with engaging artlessness to give one a picture of the lovable woman who happened to be queen of England. The emphasis of the authors is upon the happened. It is the woman they have dramatized rather than the woman as queen. They have read Strachey, but they have also read Drinkwater and have thus learned what often not to do. They have dramatized not the making of history through a woman so much as the making of a woman through history. And they have thus written a real play rather than a tract with the proper names indented and misnamed a play. Their imagination, however, sometimes falls short and takes refuge in dramatic devices of the utmost essential banality as, for instance, in the setting off of Victoria's character by means of a series of violent contrasts and counterpoints. This is ever the easy trick of the confined playwright. Thus, while Victoria's nonchalant counting of the household silver in counterpoint to her summons to be empress of India, and her equally nonchalant counting of gray hairs in her husband's beard in counterpoint to the threat of war with Russia, to mention but two instances, may be valid theatre, they become by repetition weak means of limning character and even weaker drama. Yet these are minor defects in what is in the main a very good example of drama of its kind. The Victoria of the Messrs. Carb and Eaton is not merely a little fat actress cast for type and made to mouth a hundred or more familiar sayings laboriously culled from various works of reference: she is, if not the real Victoria, at least the Victoria that is real in our imaginations. And so, too, with the secondary characters. Albert of Coburg, the prince consort, superbly embodied by a newcomer to the Anglo-Saxon theatre, Ullrich Haupt, takes life and form from the imaginative shower of countless daguerreotypes and chronicles. And in a flash, in not more than three or four "sides", Wellington stands before us, and the Baroness Lehzen, and Gladstone, Palmerston and Stockmar. Disraeli is not merely a pair of bowlegs and a dozen epigrams that are called a Jew at appropriate intervals; he is Disraeli. Only Albert Edward, Prince of Wales, is made a mess of. The authors should study a bit more closely the speech and nature of the man at the time of the divorce scandal, and later. Miss Beryl Mercer looks Victoria, but is decidedly hansom-cab in much of her acting. The production by the Equity Players is highly commendable.

VI

Drinkwater's "Robert E. Lee", which I reviewed upon its London presentation, lost rather than gained force in its New York presentation. Drinkwater, as I observed when I first wrote of the play, has seen Lee, Stuart, Jackson and the rest as so many English actors dressed in gray uniforms and speaking American sentiments as they would be spoken by American actors in evening clothes playing in English drawing-room drama. This sounds flippant, but it gives the impression more quickly than I am able to convey it in as many words. In London, the effect of the play was accordingly greater than in New York, where our American actors found themselves conspicuously uncomfortable in rôles to which they were not, by virtue of their nationality, suited. Although Mr. Berton Churchill who played Lee here may, for all I know, be an Englishman by birth —as Sam Bernard is, one need not be surprised at anything—he is yet an American actor of such long service that the Lee of Drinkwater is as alien to him as it was dramatically native to Felix Aylmer who played the rôle at the Regent Theatre. And what is true of Churchill was true of many of the other actors in the American company.

Drinkwater's play is a chill and eminently second-rate attempt to woo the popular box office by presenting a great American gentleman and soldier as a posturing moving picture actor given to addressing titles and inserts to the first row of the balcony and to bequeathing an air of profundity to his most casual utterances by putting dashes after every word and letting his voice trail off at the end in the wistful paternal manner of the curés in French plays. Of the Lee that our superior generation knew at first hand and that we of the more immediate generation have gleaned from the various authentic chronicles, there is barely a trace, and that trace consists in those qualities of Lee which most closely approached the footlight self that was a part of him as often it is a part of the great of the earth. The rest of the Lee of Drinkwater is a bogus extended elaboration of this trace, and the Lee that results is, consequently, for the most part a footlight dummy, a creature in sock and buskin placed in a series of pretty melodramatic theatrical poses. The aides of Drinkwater's General Robert E. Lee are Colonel Theodore Kremer and Major Hal Reid, with Lieutenant-Major Lincoln J. Carter bringing up the reserves for the battle of Malvern Hill. Certain passages of the play are written with a touch of fine feeling; but the cinema Lee of John Drinkwater remains ever infinitely less the Virginia Lee than the Fort Lee.

VII

Zoë Akins' "A Royal Fandango" is a stage-struck short story. The short story has humor, wit, some ingenuity, literary grace and considerable originality, but it has a minimum of theatrical possibilities. This minimum, further, Arthur Hopkins promptly and expeditiously ousted by producing what was essentially a bubble as if it were a soap factory. What he had was thistle-down; what he produced was a cactus. Miss Akins' attempt was doubtless to fashion a play in the manner of her excellent "Papa". But where the latter, for all its deliberately mad lightness, finds a measure of theatrical weight in the skill with which that lightness, like a feather ball tossing atop a fountain's jet, is sustained, this later play collapses after its first act from its author's weakened fertility. It is a supper at which the caviar abruptly gives way to nothing but two pretentious champagne bottles filled with ice water.

Miss Akins writes better than any other woman now writing for the American stage, but unfortunately, despite her intention, she does not always write for the stage. I am surely not one of those profound dolts who believes that to write for the stage successfully one must write according to the strict rules laid down by Columbia University professors who have written for the stage unsuccessfully, but Miss Akins seems to me to go a trifle too far in the other direction. It is all very well to have contempt for the established forms, but contempt in such instances must be, for all its bravado, interesting. Miss Akins' contempt—a better word would be indifference—is this time not interesting enough. If anything in the theatre must have body, it is, as I have observed, such a bubble as her "Royal Fandango". The skeleton of a body is in the play, but the author has neglected sufficiently to cover the bones. Her comparative failure is, however, a dignified failure. It is a failure that is never common, never cheap, and that is always, even at its worst, a hundred cuts above the sort of thing that American playwrights usually give us. And, for all its disappointments, its author remains, as she has been from her "Papa" to her "Texas Nightingale", the first of the distaff talents in the native drama. Miss Ethel Barrymore's first act performance was in a delightfully relevant naughty-Barrie mood. Thereafter, save for such thoroughly effective instances as that at the conclusion of the second act wherein she momentarily poses an Anglo-Saxon Spanish picture on her way to Cadiz and her matador love, the necessary buoyancy and airiness were missing. The ideal casting of the rôle, were such a thing possible, would have been Miss Barrymore for Act I, Miss Billie Burke for Act II, and George Monroe for Act III. It is that kind of play.

VIII

Melchior Lengyel's "Sancho Panza" is a mild and agreeable little fantastic comedy that has been produced by Mr. Russell Janney as if it were the "Follies". With the production that Mr. Janney has uncovered in the Hudson Theatre the least that an audience expects is "Macbeth". And when, amidst all the elaborate, expensive scenery and costumes designed by Emilie Hapgood and Mr. Ziegfeld's James Reynolds, all the music and songs by Hugo Felix, the special curtain painted by Mr. John Murray Anderson's Reginald Marsh, the enlarged orchestra under the direction of Rupert Graves, and the general rainbow staging by Richard Boleslawsky of the Moscow Art Theatre—when amidst all this costly hula-hula the audience finds only a pleasant little comedy, the sensation is cousin to disappointment and consternation. It would take a great masterpiece to withstand Mr. Janney's production and to triumph over it. Lengyel's "Sancho Panza" is, alas, not such a masterpiece. It is merely a prettily imagined if sometimes confused bit of whimsy that would be tenfold more effective than it currently is if someone were to produce it in the Little Theatre for one-tenth the amount of money that the present entrepreneur has expended on it to its complete devastation. Mr. Otis Skinner's Sancho—the play is based on certain episodes from Cervantes—is a performance that in the matter of monotony reminds one of nothing quite so much as an articulate tom-tom.

THE LIBRARY

Russian Music

MY MUSICAL LIFE, by Nikolay Andreyevich Rimsky-Korsakoff, translated by Judah A. Joffe, with an introduction by Carl Van Vechten. New York: *Alfred A. Knopf.*

THIS is the full story—meticulous, humorless, full of expository passion—of the Immortal Five: Balakireff, Cui, Musorgski, Borodin and Rimsky-Korsakoff himself. The book is enormous, and details are piled on without the slightest regard for the reader's time and patience. One plows through exhaustive criticisms, often highly waspish, of concerts given fifty and sixty years ago; one attends to minute discussions of forgotten musical politics. Nevertheless, the general effect of the tome is surely not that of boredom. It somehow holds the attention as securely as Thayer's monumental "Beethoven" or the memoirs of William Hickey. And no wonder, for the world that the good Nikolay Andreyevich describes is a world that must always appear charming and more than half fabulous to western eyes—a world in which unfathomable causes constantly produced unimaginable effects—a world of occult motives, exotic emotions and bizarre personalities—in brief, the old Russia that went down to tragic ruin in 1917. Read about it in the memoirs of the late Count Witte, and one feels oneself magically set down—still with one's shoes shined, still neatly shaved with a Gillette!—at the court of Charlemagne, William the Conqueror, Genghis Khan. Read about it in Rimsky-Korsakoff's book, and one gets glimpses of Bagdad, Samarkand and points East.

The whole story of the Five, in fact, belongs to the grotesque and arabesque. Not one of them had more than the most superficial grasp of the complex and highly scientific art that they came so near to revolutionizing. Balakireff, the leader, was a mathematician turned religious mystic and musical iconoclast; he believed until middle age that writing a fugue was, in some incomprehensible manner, as discreditable an act as robbing a blind man. Cui was a military engineer who died a lieutenant general. Borodin was a chemist with a weakness for what is now called Service; he wasted half his life spoiling charming Russian girls by turning them into lady doctors. Musorgski was a Guards officer brought down by drink to a job in a railway freight-station. Rimsky-Korsakoff himself was a naval officer. All of them, he says, were as ignorant of the elements of music as so many union musicians. They didn't even know the names of the common chords. Of instrumentation they knew only what was in Berlioz's "Traité d'Instrumentation"—most of it archaic. When Rimsky-Korsakoff, on being appointed professor of composition in the St. Petersburg Conservatory —a typically Russian idea!—bought a *Harmonielehre* and began to experiment with canons, his fellow revolutionists repudiated him, and to the end of his life Balakireff despised him.

Nevertheless, these astounding ignoramuses actually made very lovely music, and if some of it, such as Musorgski's "Boris Godunoff", had to be translated into playable terms afterward, it at least had enough fundamental merit to make the translation feasible. Musorgski, in fact, though he was the most ignorant of them all, probably wrote the best music of them all. Until delirium tremens put an end to him, he believed fondly that successive fourths were just as good as successive thirds, that modulations required no preparation, and that no such thing as a French horn with keys existed. More, he regarded all hints to the contrary as gross insults. Rimsky-Korsakoff, alone among them, was genuinely hospitable to the orthodox enlightenment. He learned instrumentation by the primitive process of buying all the orchestral and band instruments, and blowing into them to find out what sort of sounds they would make. The German *Harmonielehre* filled him with a suspicion that Bach, after all, must have known something, and after a while it became a certainty. He then sat down and wrote fifty fugues in succession! Later he got tired of polyphony and devoted himself chiefly to instrumentation. He became, next to Richard Strauss, the most skillful master of that inordinately difficult art in Europe. Incidently, he and his friends taught Debussy and Schoenberg how to get rid of the diatonic scale, and so paved the way for all the cacophony that now delights advanced musical thinkers.

A curious tale, unfolded by Rimsky-Korsakoff with the greatest earnestness and even indignation. A clumsy writer, he yet writes brilliantly on occasion—for example, about the low-comedy household of the Borodins, with dinner at 11 P. M. and half a dozen strange guests always snoring on the sofas. Is there a lesson in the chronicle, say for American composers? I half suspect that there is. What ails these worthy men and makes their music, in general, so dreary is not that they are incompetent technicians, as is often alleged, but that they are far too competent. They are, in other words, so magnificently trained in the standard tricks, both orthodox and heterodox, that they can no longer leap and prance as true artists should. The stuff they write is correct, respectable, highly learned—but most of it remains *Kapellmeistermusik*, nay, only too often mere *Augenmusik*. Let them give hard study to this history of the five untutored Slavs who wrote full-length symphonies without ever having heard, as Rimsky-Korsakoff says, that the seventh tends to progress downward. Let them throw away their harmony-books, loose their collars, and proceed to write music.

H. L. MENCKEN

The New Freedom

RECENT CHANGES IN AMERICAN CONSTITU-TIONAL THEORY, by John W. Burgess, Ph.D., J.U.D., LL.D. New York: *Columbia University Press.*

THIS is a very small book, but it is packed with important matter. What it recounts, in brief, is the story of the decay of liberty in the United States since the end of the last century. The old Constitution, despite some alarming strains, held up very bravely until the time of the Spanish War. It survived the Alien and Sedition Acts of 1798, it survived the rise of *Homo boobiens* under Jackson, it survived the rough mauling that the sainted Lincoln gave it during the Civil War, and it even survived the Amendments that followed the Versailles-like peace of 1865. But at the hands of Roosevelt it began to buckle and give way, and at the hands of Wilson it went to pieces. Today the old constitutional guarantees have only an antiquarian interest, and the old scheme of checks and balances functions no more. Bit by bit, the Supreme Court has yielded to pressure, until now its very right to resist at all has begun to be threatened. The American citizen of 1924 who, menaced by bureaucratic tyranny, appealed to that decayed tribunal to save him would be laughed at in open court. For it has already decided against him (often unanimously) on almost all conceivable counts, and to make his chains doubly strong it has even begun to limit his right of mere remonstrance. The Draft Act, the Espionage Act, the Volstead Act, the various State Syndicalist Acts—these outrageous and obviously unconstitutional laws mark the successive stages of the Supreme Court's degradation. Having failed in its primary duty, it has failed in all its duties. What liberties remain to the citizen today remain by a sort of grace—perhaps, more accurately, a sort of oversight. Another Wilson, set upon the throne tomorrow by another fraud of 1916, might take them away from him with no more danger of challenge from the Supreme Court than from the American Legion or the Union League.

Dr. Burgess rehearses succinctly the fundamental principles of American constitutional theory before 1898, and shows how all of them have been subverted and abandoned. The most important of them was that which set up a sharp distinction between sovereignty and government, and rigidly limited the scope and powers of the latter. The Federal Government was not the United States; it was simply the agent of the United States, employed and authorized to perform certain clearly-defined functions and none other. Beyond the field of those functions it was as impotent as the individual office-holders composing it. That principle remained in force from the election of Thomas Jefferson in 1800 to the dawn of imperialism in 1898—roughly, a century. When it began to be conditioned, then the whole constitutional structure broke up. Today there is no clearly defined boundary between sovereignty and government. The President, in time of war, is indistinguishable from an oriental despot— and he is now quite free to make war whenever he pleases, with or without the consent of Congress. The raid against Russia, in 1918, was apparently, in the view of the Supreme Court, a perfectly legal war, though Congress had never authorized it, for persons who protested against it were sentenced to long terms of imprisonment under the Espionage Act, and the Court upheld the sentences. The invasions of the citizen's fundamental rights in time of peace are too numerous and notorious to need rehearsing. One will suffice. The Bill of Rights guarantees him an inviolable right to trial by jury; the Volstead Act takes it away from him; the Supreme Court has upheld the Volstead Act.

Dr. Burgess' exposition of the facts is temperate, learned and incontrovertible. The disease is accurately described. I wish I could add that the remedy he proposes promises a cure. But it actually seems to me to be hopeless. His plan, briefly, is to abandon the method of making constitutional amendments by the votes of the two houses of Congress and the State Legislatures, *i.e.*, by the votes of men professionally venal and dishonorable, and to return to the primary scheme of national constitutional conventions. Such conventions, he argues, would represent the people directly, would be chosen for the specific purpose of framing amendments, and would thus voice true sovereignty. He forgets two things. He forgets that their members would be elected precisely as members of Congress are now elected, and would probably be the same petty demagogues and scoundrels. And he forgets that there is no evidence that the people, given a free opportunity, would actually try to recover the rights that have been taken away from them. In point of fact, only a very small minority of Americans have any genuine respect or desire for liberty. The majority supported Wilson ecstatically, and, with him, Palmer, Burleson and all the rest of the cossacks. And when the majority is heard of today, it is not demanding a restoration of its old rights; it is tarring and feathering some fanatic who believes that they should, will and must be restored.

H. L. M.

The Uplift: Export Department

RACE AND NATIONAL SOLIDARITY, by Charles Conant Josey. New York: *Charles Scribner's Sons.*

FREDERICK THE GREAT, as everyone knows, had a friendly view of the utility of the learned. When he set out, in 1740, upon his first Silesian campaign, it was suggested to him by certain advisers that his claim to some of the territory he proposed to seize might be dubious in imperial law. "What of it?" he replied. "If I can only take the land the professors can be trusted to find me a title to it".

The modern Fredericks inhabit luxurious banking-houses in Wall street and thereabout, and their weapons are not the bones of Pomeranian grenadiers, but loans and consortiums. They have Silesias staked out in Santo Domingo, Haiti, Nicaragua and Cuba, and, like Frederick, they have a lost Bohemia in Mexico. Now, in Dr. Josey, of Dartmouth (already a familiar name to all law students), they have their professor foreordained. In his "Race and National Solidarity" Prof. Josey not only proves that the benign economic and political oversight of the darker peoples is the manifest destiny of Nordic man; he also proves, in 227 pages of very eloquent stuff, that it is a highly moral business, and unquestionably pleasing to God. "The way to please God", he says, "is to do good"—and "God helps those who help themselves". *Ergo*, helping one's self must be good.

Specifically, the professor argues at great length that it is a foolish and evil thing to take the boons of civilization to the backward races without making sure that they pay a good round price for what they get. But how is this payment to be exacted? First, by keeping the financing of the uplift (*i.e.*, the industrialization) of the poor heathen in our own hands, and taking such a share of the proceeds of their labor that they are never able to accumulate enough capital to finance themselves. Second, by keeping the technical management of industry a sort of national or race secret, so that they shall remain forever unable to run their own factories without our help. This will give us all the cream and leave them the skim milk. Even on this milk, of course, they may fatten; that is, they may increase in numbers so greatly as to offer us danger on the military side. To secure ourselves against this, we must keep their numbers down, first by "a general dissemination of knowledge of birth control", and then by prohibiting child-labor and so preventing "children

from becoming profitable". Thus virtue (but is birth control virtuous?) will go hand in hand with enlightened self-interest, and God will be pleased by good deeds.

Prof. Josey, as you may have guessed, is without much humor, and so his book is rather heavy going. But I have read every word of it attentively, and commend his Message to all who desire to become privy to the most advanced thought of this era of Service. However, it will not be necessary to read his actual book. The great bond houses issue weekly and monthly bulletins, free for the asking. Ask for them, and his ideas will be set before you, backed up by a great moral passion and probably in more lascivious English.

H. L. M.

Once More, the Immortals

FANTASTICA: BEING THE SMILE OF THE SPHINX AND OTHER TALES OF IMAGINATION, by Robert Nichols. New York: *The Macmillan Company*.

WHENEVER and so often as the choice is offered one to be born again, the wise will elect for revivification as a romantic myth. That is, I think, the perhaps not entirely premeditated moral of Mr. Robert Nichols' "Fantastica". . . .

I have enjoyed this book. I record at outset that sentence because it appears to me a triumphant and facile chef-d'oeuvre of understatement. This trio of stories, about such copious protagonists as Andromeda and the Sphinx and the Wandering Jew, have come, to me at least, as the most amiable literary surprise since Mr. Donn Byrne published "Messer Marco Polo". Here is beauty and irony and wisdom; here is fine craftsmanship; and here, above all, are competently reported the more recent events in the existence of favored persons whose vitality and whose adventuring each generation of mankind renews. I refer, of course, to such persons as Andromeda and the Sphinx and the Wandering Jew,—and to Prometheus and Pan and Judas and Queen Helen,—and to many others who were so lucky as to originate in a satisfy-ingly romantic myth, and who in consequence stay always real and always free of finding life monotonous.

Now, it is an ever-present reminder of our own impermanence to note that no human being stays real. In private annals a species of familiary canonization sets in with each fresh advent of the undertaker; no sooner, indeed, do our moribund lie abed than we begin even in our thoughts to lie like their epitaphs; and all of us by ordinary endure the pangs of burying ineffably more admirable kin than we ever possessed. Nor does much more of honesty go to the making of those national chronicles which Mr. Henry Ford, with a candor perhaps really incurable by anything short of four years in the White House, has described as "bunk". In history one finds everywhere an impatient desire to simplify the tortuous and complex human being into a sort of forthright shorthand. Alexander was ambitious, Machiavelli cunning, Henry the Eighth bloodthirsty, and George Washington congenitally incapable of prevarications. That is all there was to them, so far as they concern the average man; and thus does history imply its shapers with the most curt of symbols, somewhat as an astronomer jots down a four's first cousin to indicate the huge planet Jupiter and compresses the sun that nourishes him into a proof corrector's period. Always in this fashion does history work over its best rôles into allegories about the Lord Desire of Vain Glory and Mr. By-ends, about Giant Bloody-man and Mr. Truthful; and rubs away the humanness of each dead personage resistlessly, as if resolute to get rid in any event of most of him; and pares him of all traits except the one which men, whether through national pride or the moralist's large placid preference for lying, have elected to see here uncarnate.

Quite otherwise fare those luckier beings who began existence with the advantage of being incorporeal, and hence have not any dread of time's attrition. The longer that time handles them, the more does he enrich their experience and personalities. It was, for example, Euripides, they say, who first popularized this myth of Andromeda: and, for all that the dramas he wrote about her are long lost, it were time-wasting, of a dullness happily restricted to insane asylums and the assembly halls of democratic legislation, here to deliberate whether Andromeda or Euripides is to us the more important and vivid person, in a world wherein Euripides survives as a quadrisyllable and wherein Andromeda's living does, actually, go on. You have but, for that matter, to compare Andromeda with the overlords of the milieu in which her fame was born, with the thin shadows that in pedants' thinking, and in the even gloomier minds of schoolboys upon the eve of an "examination", troop wanly to prefigure Pericles and Cleon and Nicias, to see what a leg up toward immortality is the omission of any material existence. These estimable patriots endure at best as wraiths and nuisances, in a world wherein Andromeda's living does, actually, go on. It is not merely that she continues to beguile the poet and painter, but that each year she demonstrably does have quite fresh adventures. Only yesterday Mr. C. C. Martindale attested as much, in his engaging and far too little famous book, "The Goddess of Ghosts"; as now does Mr. Nichols in "Fantastica". . . . For it is, through whatever human illogic, yesterday's fictitious and most clamantly impossible characters who remain to us familiar and actual persons, the while that we remember yesterday's flesh-and-blood notables as bodiless traits.

So it comes about that only these intrepid men and flawless women and other monsters who were born cleanlily of imagination, instead of the normal messiness, and were born as personages in whom, rather frequently without knowing why, the artist perceives a satisfying large symbolism,—that these alone bid fair to live and thrive until the proverbial crack of doom. Their living does, actually, go on, because each generation of artists is irresistibly impelled to provide them with quite fresh adventures. . . . And I am sure I do not know why. I merely know that these favored romantic myths, to whom at outset I directed the stiletto glance of envy, remain the only persons existent who may with any firm confidence look forward to a colorful and always vary'ng future, the only persons who stay human in defiance of death and time and the even more dreadful theories of "new schools of poetry"; and who keep, too, undimmed the human trait of figuring with a difference in the eye of each beholder. For all the really fine romantic myths have this in common. As Mr. Nichols says, in approaching a continuation of the story of Prometheus one may behold in the Fire-Bringer, just as one's taste elects, a prefiguring of Satan or of Christ or of Mr. Thomas Alva Edison.

And this I guess to be—perhaps—the pith of such myths' durability, that the felt symbolism admits of no quite final interpreting. Each generation finds for Andromeda a different monster and another rescuer; continuously romance and irony contrive new riddles for the Sphinx; whereas the Wandering Jew—besides the *tour de force* of having enabled General Lew Wallace to write a book which voiced more fatuous blather than "Ben Hur"— has had put to his account, at various times, the embodying of such disparate pests as thunderstorms and gypsies and Asiatic cholera.

Well! here—just for one moment to recur to the volume I am supposed to be criticizing,—here is Mr. Nichols with remarkably contemporaneous parables about the Sphinx and her latest lover, about Andromeda and Perseus, about the Wandering Jew and Judas Iscariot. They are, to my finding, very wise and lovely tales, they are, I hope, the graduating theses of a maturing poet who has become sufficiently sophisticated to put aside the, after all, rather childish business of verse making. But the really important feature, in any event, is that he adds to the unending imbroglios of these actually vital persons, and

guides with competence and a fine spirit the immortal travellers. Nor is this any trivial praise when you recall that, earlier, they have been served by such efficient if slightly incongruous couriers as Charles Kingsley and Euripides and Eugène Sue, as Matthew of Paris and Flaubert and Nathaniel Hawthorne and the Reverend George Croly.

JAMES BRANCH CABELL

Brandes and Croce

MAIN CURRENTS IN NINETEENTH CENTURY LITERATURE, by Georg Brandes. New York: *Boni & Liveright*.

POESIA E NON POESIA, by Benedetto Croce. Bari: *Laterza*.

THIS latest addition to the canon of Croce's works, "Poetry and Non-Poetry", reached me just as I had been looking through the new edition of Brandes's "Main Currents in Nineteenth Century Literature". The title by no means suggested what the books turned out to be, namely, a fragment of a study which might have been an Italian counterpart to the great Danish work. In his preface Croce explains that he had intended to "re-examine the literature of the Nineteenth Century", in order to bring out "conclusions still implicit in the writings of those who have discussed it, or to demonstrate other conclusions more exactly, or to confute current prejudices, or to propose some new judgments, but especially to keep in mind pure literature which—in spite of the ease with which the fact is forgotten by those whose business is criticism—is the real concern of criticism and literary history". Apparently these essays are all we shall see of this projected work, for other studies have made the realization of Croce's original plan impossible. As it stands, however, the book consists of a series of provocative chapters on such figures as Alfieri, Schiller, Scott, Stendhal, Manzoni, Balzac, Heine, George Sand, Musset, Baudelaire, Ibsen, Flaubert and Maupassant. Brandes stopped his survey at the middle of the century, but within the limits where their work coincides both he and Croce necessarily discuss the same writers.

In the eyes of both their admirers and their detractors Brandes and Croce usually pass for the opposite extremes of critical method and attitude. The Italian stands for pure aestheticism; the Danish critic is accused of propaganda. Here in America, it is true, Croce is denounced as a subtle immoralist, but his crimes are more elusive than those with which the political radical, Georg Brandes, has been charged. "Main Currents in Nineteenth Century Literature" has been described by orthodox thinkers as an elaborate, prolonged and utterly ruthless indictment of all the ideals and conventions of bourgeois society. Croce is credited with being solely concerned about the intrinsic artistic qualities of the works he has studied.

At this stage, if life were not so short, one might begin again the eternal debate as to which of these two attitudes is right in a critic of literature. I prefer to point out the rather more interesting fact that, whatever the aesthetic theories of a critic may be, it is his practice that counts. In this case, as in most others, it would be difficult to show just wherein Croce's final estimate differs, in most cases, from that of Brandes, or wherein their judgments were actually governed by their politics. Just as some English and American novelists discourse airily and metaphysically about style, but produce works of their own remarkably similar to dozens of others, and quite unlike their theoretical ideal, so Messrs. Croce and Brandes agree in their judgments so often that I am left colder than ever by the disputes of the schools they are supposed to represent.

Their treatments of Walter Scott and George Sand supply two good examples of this similarity of judgment. Brandes is supposed to have belauded George because she was in revolt against the conventions of her sex. It is true, he gives a more or less sympathetic account of her

ideas on the subject of love and marriage, while Croce does not, but both critics see the artistic worthlessness of that part of her work and agree that the only books which deserve to survive are the simple idyllic studies of peasant life. So far as Scott is concerned, Brandes sums him up by saying that he is the kind of author whom "every adult has read and no grown-up person can read". Croce also describes his work as unreadable, but ends with an appeal for mercy, on the ground that a writer who delighted our parents and grandparents "does not deserve harsh treatment from their children and grand-children". Oh, aestheticism, where is thy sting? Oh, propaganda, where is thy victory? A critic must still be judged by his appreciation of specific works, and not by the theories which he evolves *in vacuo*. Whether in their treatment of the illustrious dead or of their contemporaries, neither Brandes nor Croce diverges from the all-too-human principle of personal taste and emotion, for that, in the last analysis, is the only basis of literary criticism. It then becomes a question of the quality of the mind employed, and this can never be disguised by aesthetic faith or propagandist good works.

ERNEST BOYD

Brazil from Within

PATRIA NOVA, by Mario Pinto Serva. S. Paulo: *Companhia Melhoramentos de S. Paulo.*

AND it comes to pass that after Brazil has been for one hundred years an independent nation, and for thirty-three years a republic, created in the image of its populace, Senhor Mario Pinto Serva looks upon it and finds it not good. Wherefore, in this "New Fatherland", he seeks to refashion a Patria nearer to his heart's desire, using his pen now as a pin to prick bubbles, and now as a sword to slash through shams. The President's in his chair and all's wrong with Brazil; the People, truly, does not yet exist; the Church is a perpetuator of illiteracy; the Intellectuals are lost in vaporous meditations; the one hope is the School, but where is it?

Senhor Pinto Serva is the modern man of action. "It's not," he says, "with the intellectualism of the Academy of Letters that we are going to build the Brazil of tomorrow. We need an intellectualism that shall intensify our potential energies, which today are absolutely rachetic." In the meantime, help must come from outside. There are the Germans, with their genius for scientific organization; there are the North Americans, "plethoric with capital and activity"; there are the English, eager to win foreign markets. Above all, for the vitalization of the thin national blood stream, there are the immigrants; for Brazil is destined, in the Twentieth Century, to be for Europe that melting-pot which the United States was in the Nineteenth. And yet, how ill-suited to the task! "The parliament is a vast caravansary, where the most curious types of prattler forgather from the different States, for the purpose of gossiping, putting deals through and boasting about the sprees they were on the night before. As for their speeches, even the stenographers to which they're dictated hardly lend ear." There is no free press; the cultured class is so small that the greatest literary success does not mean a sale of ten thousand copies; there is no political morality; there are really no parties; there are no political ideas.

For balm we must look to the State of Sao Paulo; here lies the sole guarantee of the future. Were it not for Sao Paulo, Brazil would never have been free in the first place; were it not for that State, the struggle today would be hopeless. The Paulist genius has been developed by accidents of history and of position; it has been nurtured by immigration, by a determined struggle with that hinterland which Euclydes da Cunha has so vividly described in his "Sertões",—one of the outstanding books in the nation's letters.

"Like the Atlas of ancient mythology, Sao Paulo bears upon its shoulders the burden of the nation."

If Sao Paulo is the symbol of that energy, that realistic facing of fact which Pinto Serva exalts as the salvation of Brazil, the national danger is incarnated in the Brazilian Academy of Letters in Rio de Janeiro. Too much poetry; not enough prose. Too much mooning; not enough roads and schools. From France come boatloads of novels that deal with the thousand and one varieties of adultery, awakening in youthful Latin bosoms precocious desires that lead to unmentionable consequences. Brazilian youth, the Brazilian "intellectuals", form a legion of poetasters and novelasters who have become incapacitated for a life of action; "in Brazil there are persons who, simply because they have learned grammar, and nothing else, consider themselves finished writers, preeminent intellectuals superior to the society in which they live." Worse still; behind a passionate cultivation of the art of expression lies an encyclopedic ignorance; the result is a verbal materialism, a mere business of manufacturing phrases, a gymnastics of the word. "This windy ignorance has its chief exponent in the numerous academies of letters. There is, in Rio, the Brazilian Academy of Letters, which represents the enthronement of gossiping vacuity, an exposition of empty loquacity, a cenacle of verbal uselessness, a curia of declamatory futility, a congress of frivolous dilletantism.... As such, the Brazilian Academy of Letters is the exact exponent of the Brazilian mentality, in which the superior function of thought and ratiocination has been replaced by mere tittle-tattle and logomachy.... The future greatness of Brazil will depend entirely upon a vast, complicated series of unremitting efforts; the Brazilian Academy is incapable of the most insignificant initiative for the good of the country."

ISAAC GOLDBERG

THE AMERICAN MERCURY AUTHORS

HARRY E. BARNES *is professor of historical sociology at Smith College and* ad interim *professor of economics and sociology at Amherst.*

ERNEST BOYD *is the well-known Irish critic, author of "The Irish Literary Renaissance" and other books. He came to America in 1914 and is now living in New York.*

SAMUEL C. CHEW, *author of the Conversation with George Moore, is a Ph.D. of the Johns Hopkins and Professor of English Literature at Bryn Mawr. He is the author of important studies of Byron and Thomas Hardy.*

LEONARD L. CLINE *is a member of the staff of the New York* World *and has done police reporting in many cities.*

L. M. HUSSEY *is a chemist and pharmacologist, and has had practical experience in the isolation of active physiological substances.*

GEORGE PHILIP KRAPP, Ph.D. (Johns Hopkins), *is professor of English in Columbia University. He is editor of the Oxford English Series and the author of half a dozen works on English.*

C. GRANT LA FARGE *is the well-known architect. His firm has designed many important buildings in New York and elsewhere.*

JOHN McCLURE *is the author of "Airs and Ballads", a book of poems. He is one of the editors of the* Double-Dealer *in New Orleans. He was born in Oklahoma.*

"MILES MARTINDALE" *is the* nom de plume *of a man who, because of his official position, cannot sign his article on the results of the Disarmament Treaty. He has devoted a lifetime to the study of the matters he discusses.*

MARGARET MÜNSTERBERG *is the daughter of the late Dr. Hugo Münsterberg and was brought up in the famous Harvard circle of which she writes in her paper on George Santayana.*

JAMES ONEAL ("The Communist Hoax") *is the author of "The Workers in American History" and was on the staff of the New York* Call.

JOHN W. OWENS *covers national politics for the Baltimore* Sun *and is a frequent contributor to the* New Republic.

ISAAC R. PENNYPACKER *has devoted many years to a study of the Civil War, and is a well-known authority upon its military history. He has written books upon the Valley and Gettysburg campaigns, and a life of General Meade.*

WOODBRIDGE RILEY, Ph.D. (Yale), *is professor of philosophy at Vassar. He has specialized in the history of American thought, and was the author of the suppressed chapter on Mormonism and Christian Science in the Cambridge History of American Literature.*

X—— *conceals the name of an American army officer.*

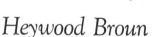

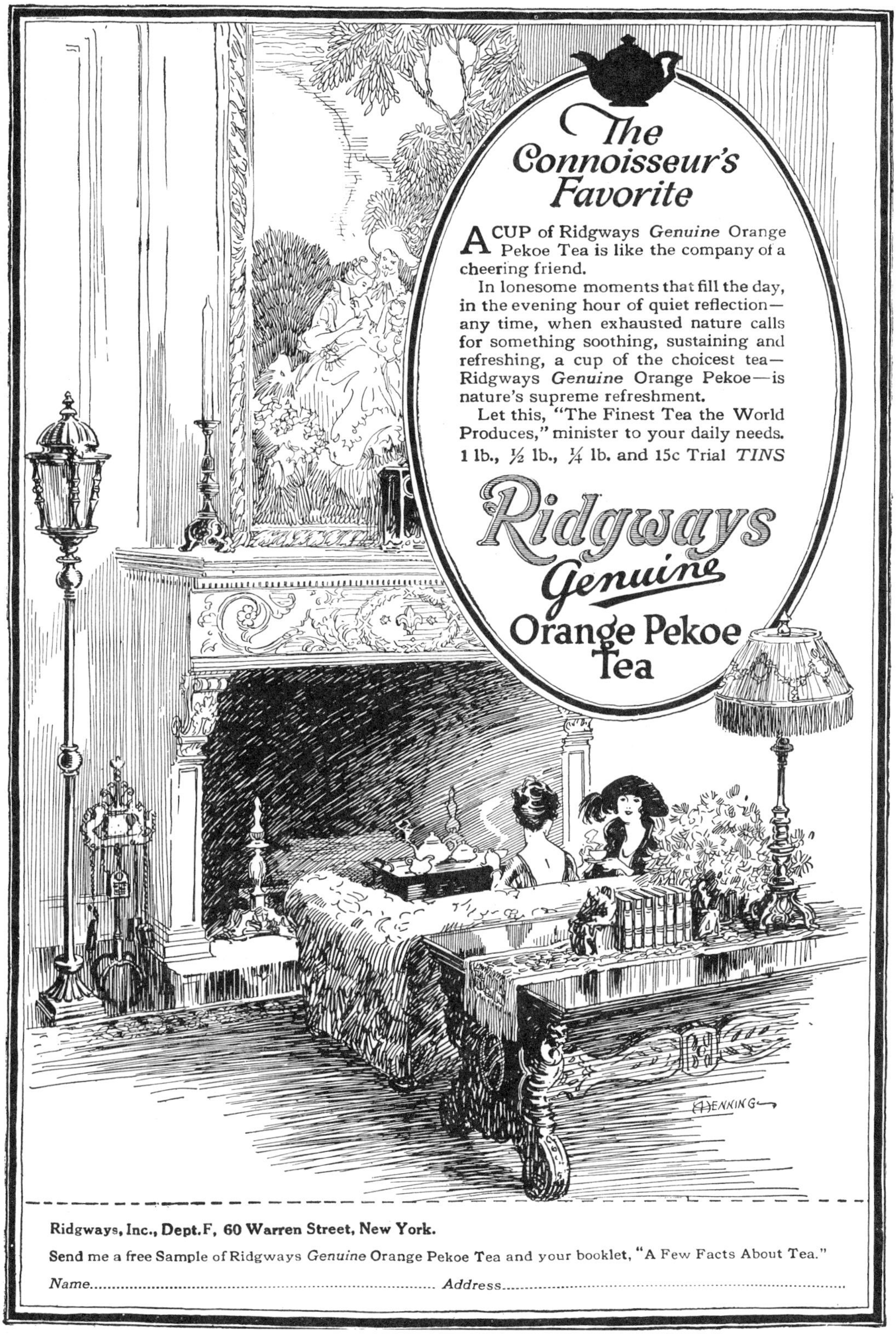
The Connoisseur's Favorite
A CUP of Ridgways *Genuine* Orange Pekoe Tea is like the company of a cheering friend.
In lonesome moments that fill the day, in the evening hour of quiet reflection—any time, when exhausted nature calls for something soothing, sustaining and refreshing, a cup of the choicest tea—Ridgways *Genuine* Orange Pekoe—is nature's supreme refreshment.
Let this, "The Finest Tea the World Produces," minister to your daily needs.
1 lb., ½ lb., ¼ lb. and 15c Trial *TINS*
Ridgways
Genuine
Orange Pekoe Tea
Ridgways, Inc., Dept. F, 60 Warren Street, New York.
Send me a free Sample of Ridgways *Genuine* Orange Pekoe Tea and your booklet, "A Few Facts About Tea."
Name.. *Address*..

The AMERICAN MERCURY

VOLUME I   February 1924   NUMBER 2

TABLE OF CONTENTS

ALL GOD'S CHILLUN GOT WINGS (*A Play*) . . Eugene O'Neill 129

THE GRAMMARIAN AND HIS LANGUAGE . . . Edward Sapir 149

THE PART-TIME MISSIONARY . . . . . Howell Sykes 156

EDITORIAL 161

CAUGHT (*A Story*) . . . . . . Sherwood Anderson 165

AMERICANA 177

PINCHOT . . . . Charles Willis Thompson 180

MORE LIGHT ON WHITMAN . . . . . Emory Holloway 183

OSTEOPATHY . . . . Morris Fishbein 190

AMERICAN PORTRAITS, I. THE LABOR LEADER . James M. Cain 196

CLINICAL NOTES . . H. L. Mencken and George Jean Nathan 201

THE KU-KLUXER . . . . Gerald W. Johnson 207

PANORAMA . . . . John McClure 212

THE ARTS AND SCIENCES:
    Alcohol and the Duration of Life . . . Raymond Pearl 213
    Modern First Editions . . . . . George H. Sargent 215
    The American Painter . . . . Guy Eglington 218

HEREDITY AND THE UPLIFT . . . . . . H. M. Parshley 221

CARRYING CIVILIZATION TO MEXICO . . . . Carleton Beals 227

THE COMIC PATRIOT . . . . Carl Van Doren 234

A NOTE ON SHAKESPEARE . . . . . . Leon Kellner 237

THE THEATRE . . . . George Jean Nathan 241

THE LIBRARY . . . . H. L. Mencken 248

ADDITIONAL BOOK REVIEWS:
    Origins of the Revolution . . . . . W. F. Robinson 254
    The Case of Luther . . . . John E. Lind 255

THE AMERICAN MERCURY AUTHORS 256

Unsolicited manuscripts not accompanied by stamped and addressed envelopes will not be returned and the Editors will not enter into correspondence about them. Manuscripts should be addressed to The Editors and not to individuals. All accepted contributions are paid for on acceptance, without reference to the date of publication. The whole contents of this magazine are protected by copyright and must not be reprinted without permission.

Published monthly at 50 cents a copy. Annual subscription, $5.00; Canadian subscription, $5.50; foreign subscription, $6.00. . . . The American Mercury, Inc., publishers. Publication office, Federal and 19th Streets, Camden, N. J. Editorial, advertising and subscription offices, 220 W. 42nd Street, New York. . . . Printed in the United States. Copyright, 1924, by The American Mercury, Inc. . . . Application for entry as second-class matter pending.

Alfred A. Knopf   George Jean Nathan } *Editors*
Publisher   H. L. Mencken

A Refreshing Bath Aid for Keen Out-of-Door Fellows

When you are sticky, hot and tired shift a little AMMO in the bath. In five minutes you'll feel as "fit as a fiddle."

AMMO gives water an added virtue and makes soap do double duty. Presto! Hard water is made as soft as rain water. With a little soap, AMMO creates a mountain of soft, creamy suds. Besides, it vanishes all odors.

Then too, AMMO in the water gives tired feet a new lease of life.

Refreshing—O'boy!

Enjoy this man's bath aid—unperfumed.

If your dealer cannot supply you, write us:
American Ammone Co., 1201 Times Bldg., New York.

AMMONIA IN POWDERED FORM

The American
MERCURY

February 1924

ALL GOD'S CHILLUN GOT WINGS

A PLAY IN TWO ACTS

BY EUGENE O'NEILL

CHARACTERS

JIM HARRIS
MRS. HARRIS, *his mother*
HATTIE, *his sister*
ELLA DOWNEY
SHORTY
JOE
MICKEY
Whites and Negroes

ACT ONE

SCENE ONE—*A corner in lower New York. Years ago. End of an afternoon in Spring.*
SCENE TWO—*The same. Nine years later. End of an evening in Spring.*
SCENE THREE—*The same. Five years later. A night in Spring.*
SCENE FOUR—*The street before a church in the same ward. A morning some weeks later.*

ACT TWO

SCENE ONE—*A flat in the same ward. A morning two years later.*
SCENE TWO—*The same. At twilight some months later.*
SCENE THREE—*The same. A night some months later.*

ACT I

Scene 1

A corner in lower New York, at the edge of a colored district. Three narrow streets converge. A triangular building in the rear, red brick, four-storied, its ground floor a grocery. Four-story tenements stretch away down the skyline of the two streets. The fire escapes are crowded with people. In the street leading left, the faces are all white; in the street leading right, all black. It is hot Spring. On the sidewalk are eight children, four boys and four girls. Two of each sex are white, two black. They are playing marbles. One of the black boys is JIM HARRIS. *The little blonde girl, her complexion rose and white, who sits behind his elbow and holds his marbles is* ELLA DOWNEY. *She is eight. They play the game with concentrated attention for a while. People pass, black and white, the Negroes frankly participants in the spirit of Spring, the whites laughing constrainedly, awkward in natural emotion. Their words are lost. One only hears their laughter. It expresses the difference in race. There are street noises—the clattering roar of the Elevated, the puff of its locomotives, the ruminative lazy sound of a horse-car, the hooves of its team clacking on the cobbles. From the street of the whites a high-pitched, nasal tenor sings the chorus of "Only a Bird in a Gilded Cage." On the street of the blacks a Negro strikes up the chorus of: "I Guess I'll Have to Telegraph My Baby." As this singing ends, there is laughter, distinctive in quality, from both streets. Then silence. The light in the street begins to grow brilliant with the glow of the setting sun. The game of marbles goes on.*

WHITE GIRL—[*Tugging at the elbow of her brother*] Come on, Mickey!

HER BROTHER—[*Roughly*]   Aw, gwan, youse!

WHITE GIRL—Aw right, den. You kin git a lickin' if you wanter. [*Gets up to move off.*]

HER BROTHER—Aw, git off de eart!

WHITE GIRL—De old woman'll be madder'n hell!

HER BROTHER—[*Worried now*] I'm comin', ain't I? Hold your horses.

BLACK GIRL—[*To a black boy*] Come on, you Joe. We gwine git frailed too, you don't hurry.

JOE—Go long!

MICKEY—Bust up de game, huh? I gotta run! [*Jumps to his feet.*]

OTHER WHITE BOY—Me, too! [*Jumps up.*]

OTHER BLACK GIRL—Lawdy, it's late!

JOE—Me for grub!

MICKEY—[*To* JIM HARRIS] You's de winner, Jim Crow. Yeh gotta play tomorrer.

JIM—[*Readily*] Sure ting, Mick. Come one, come all! [*He laughs.*]

OTHER WHITE BOY—Me too! I gotta git back at yuh.

JIM—Aw right, Shorty.

LITTLE GIRLS—Hurry! Come on, come on! [*The six start off together. Then they notice that* JIM *and* ELLA *are hesitating, standing awkwardly and shyly together. They turn to mock.*]

JOE—Look at dat Jim Crow! Land sakes, he got a gal! [*He laughs. They all laugh.*]

JIM—[*Ashamed*] Ne'er mind, you Chocolate!

MICKEY—Look at de two softies, will yeh! Mush! Mush! [*He and the two other boys take this up.*]

LITTLE GIRLS—[*Pointing their fingers at Ella*] Shame! Shame! Everybody knows your name! Painty Face! Painty Face!

ELLA—[*Hanging her head*] Shut up!

LITTLE WHITE GIRL—He's been carrying her books!

COLORED GIRL—Can't you find nuffin better'n him, Ella? Look at de big feet he got! [*She laughs. They all laugh.* JIM *puts one foot on top of the other, looking at* ELLA.]

ELLA—Mind yer own business, see! [*She strides toward them angrily. They jump up*

and dance in an ecstasy, screaming and laughing.]

ALL—Found yeh out! Found yeh out!

MICKEY—Mush-head! Jim Crow de Sissy! Stuck on Painty Face!

JOE—Will Painty Face let you hold her doll, boy?

SHORTY—Cissy! Softy! [ELLA *suddenly begins to cry. At this they all howl.*]

ALL—Cry-baby! Cry-baby! Look at her! Painty Face!

JIM—[*Suddenly rushing at them, with clenched fists, furiously*] Shut yo' moufs! I kin lick de hull of you! [*They all run away, laughing, shouting, and jeering, quite triumphant now that they have made him, too, loose his temper. He comes back to* ELLA, *and stands beside her sheepishly, stepping on one foot after the other. Suddenly he blurts out:*] Don't bawl no more. I done chased 'em.

ELLA—[*Comforted, politely*] T'anks.

JIM—[*Swelling out*] It was a cinch. I kin wipe up de street wid any one of dem. [*He stretches out his arms, trying to bulge out his biceps*] Feel dat muscle!

ELLA—[*Does so gingerly—then with admiration*] My!

JIM—[*Protectingly*] You mustn't never be scared when I'm hanging round, Painty Face.

ELLA—Don't call me that, Jim—please!

JIM—[*Contritely*] I didn't mean nuffin'. I didn't know you'd mind.

ELLA—I do—more'n anything.

JIM—You oughtn't to mind. Dey's jealous, dat's what.

ELLA—Jealous? Of what?

JIM—[*Pointing to her face*] Of dat. Red 'n' white. It's purty.

ELLA—I hate it!

JIM—It's purty. Yes, it's—it's purty. It's—outa sight!

ELLA—I hate it. I wish I was black like you.

JIM—[*Sort of shrinking*] No you don't. Dey'd call you Crow, den—or Chocolate—or Smoke.

ELLA—I wouldn't mind.

JIM—[*Somberly*] Dey'd call you nigger sometimes, too.

ELLA—I wouldn't mind.

JIM—[*Humbly*] You wouldn't mind?

ELLA—No, I wouldn't mind. [*An awkward pause.*]

JIM—[*Suddenly*] You know what, Ella? Since I been tuckin' yo' books to school and back, I been drinkin' lots o' chalk 'n' water tree times a day. Dat Tom, de barber, he tole me dat make me white, if I drink enough. [*Pleadingly*] Does I look whiter?

ELLA—[*Comfortingly*] Yes—maybe—a little bit—

JIM—[*Trying a careless tone*] Reckon dat Tom's a liar, an' de joke's on me! Dat chalk only makes me feel kinder sick inside.

ELLA—[*Wonderingly*] Why do you want to be white?

JIM—Because—just because—I lak dat better.

ELLA—I wouldn't. I like black. Let's you and me swap. I'd like to be black. [*Clapping her hands*] Gee, that'd be fun, if we only could!

JIM—[*Hesitatingly*] Yes—maybe—

ELLA—Then they'd call me Crow, and you'd be Painty Face!

JIM—They wouldn't never dast call you nigger, you bet! I'd kill 'em! [*A long pause. Finally she takes his hand shyly. They both keep looking as far away from each other as possible.*]

ELLA—I like you.

JIM—I like you.

ELLA—Do you want to be my feller?

JIM—Yes.

ELLA—Then I'm your girl.

JIM—Yes. [*Then grandly*] You kin bet none o' de gang gwine call you Painty Face from dis out! I lam' em' good! [*The sun has set. Twilight has fallen on the street. An organ grinder comes up to the corner and plays "Annie Rooney." They stand hand-in-hand and listen. He goes away. It is growing dark.*]

ELLA—[*Suddenly*] Golly, it's late! I'll git a lickin'!

JIM—Me, too.

ELLA—I won't mind it much.

JIM—Me nuther.

ELLA—See you going to school tomorrow.

JIM—Sure.

ELLA—I gotta skip now.

JIM—Me, too.

ELLA—I like you, Jim.

JIM—I like you.

ELLA—Don't forget.

JIM—Don't you.

ELLA—Good-by.

JIM—So long. [*They run away from each other—then stop abruptly, and turn as at a signal.*]

ELLA—Don't forget.

JIM—I won't, you bet!

ELLA—Here! [*She kisses her hand at him, then runs off in frantic embarrassment.*]

JIM—[*Overcome*] Gee! [*Then he turns and darts away, as*

THE CURTAIN FALLS

Scene 2

The same corner. Nine years have passed. It is again late Spring at a time in the evening which immediately follows the hour of Scene 1. Nothing has changed much. One street is still all white, the other all black. The fire escapes are laden with drooping human beings. The grocery-store is still at the corner. The street noises are now more rhythmically mechanical, electricity having taken the place of horse and steam. People pass, white and black. They laugh as in Scene 1. From the street of the whites the high-pitched nasal tenor sings: "Gee, I Wish That I Had a Girl," and the Negro replies with "All I Got Was Sympathy." The singing is followed again by laughter from both streets. Then silence. The dusk grows darker. With a spluttering flare the arc-lamp at the corner is lit and sheds a pale glare over the street. Two young roughs slouch up to the corner, as tough in manner as they can make themselves. One is the SHORTY *of Scene 1; the other the Negro,* JOE. *They stand loafing. A boy of seventeen or so passes by, escorting a girl of about the same age. Both are dressed in their best, the boy in black with stiff collar, the girl in white.*

SHORTY—[*Scornfully*] Hully cripes! Pipe who's here! [*To the girl, sneeringly*] Wha's matter, Liz? Don't yer recernize yer old fr'ens?

GIRL—[*Frightenedly*] Hello, Shorty.

SHORTY—Why de glad rags? Goin' to graduation? [*He tries to obstruct their way but, edging away from him, they turn and run.*]

JOE—Har-har! Look at dem scoot, will you! [SHORTY *grins with satisfaction.*]

SHORTY—[*Looking down other street*] Here comes Mickey.

JOE—He won de semi-final last night easy?

SHORTY—Knocked de bloke out in de thoid.

JOE—Dat boy's suah a-comin'! He'll be de champeen yit.

SHORTY—[*Judicially*] Got a good chanct—if he leaves de broads alone. Dat's where he's wide open. [*Mickey comes in from the left. He is dressed loudly, a straw hat with a gaudy band cocked over one cauliflower ear. He has acquired a typical "pug's" face, with the added viciousness of a natural bully. One of his eyes is puffed, almost closed, as a result of his battle the night before. He swaggers up.*]

BOTH—Hello, Mickey.

MICKEY—Hello.

JOE—Hear you knocked him col'.

MICKEY—Sure. I knocked his block off. [*Changing the subject*] Say. Seen 'em goin' past to de graduation racket?

SHORTY—[*With a wink*] Why? You int'-rested?

JOE—[*Chuckling*] Mickey's gwine roun' git a good conduct medal.

MICKEY—Sure. Dey kin pin it on de seat o' me pants. [*They laugh*] Listen. Seen Ella Downey goin'?

SHORTY—Painty Face? No, she ain't been along.

MICKEY—[*With authority*] Can dat name, see! Want a bunch o' fives in yer kisser? Den nix! She's me goil, understan'?

JOE—[*Venturing to joke*] Which one? Yo' number ten?

MICKEY—[*Flattered*] Sure. De real K.O. one.

SHORTY—[*Pointing right—sneeringly*] Gee! Pipe Jim Crow all dolled up for de racket.

JOE—[*With disgusted resentment*] You mean tell me dat nigger's graduatin'?

SHORTY—Ask him. [JIM HARRIS *comes in. He is dressed in black, stiff white collar, etc. —a quiet-mannered Negro boy with a queerly-baffled, sensitive face.*]

JIM—[*Pleasantly*] Hello, fellows. [*They grunt in reply, looking over him scornfully.*]

JOE—[*Staring resentfully*] Is you graduatin' tonight?

JIM—Yes.

JOE—[*Spitting disgustedly*] Fo' Gawd's sake! You *is* gittin' high-falutin'!

JIM—[*Smiling deprecatingly*] This is my second try. I didn't pass last year.

JOE—What de hell does it git you, huh? Whatever is you gwine do wid it now you gits it? Live lazy on yo' ol' woman?

JIM—[*Assertively*] I'm going to study and become a lawyer.

JOE—[*With a snort*] Fo' Chris' sake, nigger!

JIM—[*Fiercely*] Don't you call me that—not before them!

JOE—[*Pugnaciously*] Does you deny you's a nigger? I shows you—

MICKEY—[*Gives them both a push—truculently*] Cut it out, see! I'm runnin' dis corner. [*Turning to* JIM *insultingly*] Say, you! Painty Face's gittin' her ticket tonight, ain't she?

JIM—You mean Ella—

MICKEY—Painty Face Downey, dat's who I mean! I don't have to be perlite wit' her. She's me goil!

JIM—[*Glumly*] Yes, she's graduating.

SHORTY—[*Winks at Mickey*] Smart, huh?

MICKEY—[*Winks back—meaningly*] Willin' to loin, take it from me! [JIM *stands tensely as if a struggle were going on in him.*]

JIM—[*Finally blurts out*] I want to speak to you, Mickey—alone.

MICKEY—[*Surprised—insultingly*] Aw, what de hell—!

JIM—[*Excitedly*] It's important, I tell you!

MICKEY—Huh? [*Stares at him inquisitively—then motions the others back carelessly and follows* JIM *down front.*]

SHORTY—Some noive!

JOE—[*Vengefully*] I gits dat Jim alone, you wait!

MICKEY—Well, spill de big news. I ain't got all night. I got a date.

JIM—With—Ella?

MICKEY—What's dat to you?

JIM—[*The words tumbling out*] What—I wanted to say! I know—I've heard—all the stories—what you've been doing around the ward—with other girls—it's none of my business, with them—but she—Ella—it's different—she's not that kind—

MICKEY—[*Insultingly*] Who told yuh so, huh?

JIM—[*Draws back his fist threateningly*] Don't you dare—! [MICKEY *is so paralyzed by this effrontery that he actually steps back.*]

MICKEY—Say, cut de comedy! [*Beginning to feel insulted*] Listen, you Jim Crow! Ain't you wise I could give yuh one poke dat'd knock yuh into next week?

JIM—I'm only asking you to act square, Mickey.

MICKEY—What's it to yuh? Why, yuh lousy goat, she wouldn't spit on yuh even! She hates de sight of a coon.

JIM—[*In agony*] I—I know—but once she didn't mind—we were kids together—

MICKEY—Aw, ferget dat! Dis is *now*!

JIM—And I'm still her friend always—even if she don't like colored people—

MICKEY—*Coons*, why don't yuh say it right! De trouble wit' you is yuh're gittin' stuck up, dat's what! Stay where yeh belong, see! Yer old man made coin at de truckin' game and yuh're tryin' to buy yerself white—graduatin' and law, fer Hell's sake! Yuh're gittin' yerself in Dutch wit' everyone in de ward—and it ain't cause yer a coon neider. Don't de gang all train wit' Joe dere and lots of others? But yuh're tryin' to buy white and it won't git yuh no place, see!

JIM—[*Trembling*] Some day—I'll show you—

MICKEY—[*Turning away*] Aw, gwan!

JIM—D'you think I'd change—be you—your dirty white—!

MICKEY—[*Whirling about*] What's dat?

JIM—[*With hysterical vehemence*] You act square with her—or I'll show you up—I'll report you—I'll write to the papers—

the sporting writers—I'll let them know how white you are!

MICKEY—[*Infuriated*] Yuh damn nigger, I'll bust yer jaw in! [*Assuming his ring pose he weaves toward* JIM, *his face set in a cruel scowl.* JIM *waits helplessly but with a certain dignity.*]

SHORTY—Cheese it! A couple bulls! And here's de Downey skoit comin', too.

MICKEY—I'll get yuh de next time! [ELLA DOWNEY *enters from the right. She is seventeen, still has the same rose and white complexion, is pretty but with a rather repelling bold air about her.*]

ELLA—[*Smiles with pleasure when she sees* MICKEY] Hello, Mick. Am I late? Say, I'm so glad you won last night. [*She glances from one to the other as she feels something in the air*] Hello! What's up?

MICKEY—Dis boob. [*He indicates* JIM *scornfully.*]

JIM—[*Diffidently*] Hello, Ella.

ELLA—[*Shortly, turning away*] Hello. [*Then to* MICKEY] Come on, Mick. Walk down with me. I got to hurry.

JIM—[*Blurts out*] Wait—just a second. [*Painfully*] Ella, do you hate—colored people?

MICKEY—Aw, shut up!

JIM—Please answer.

ELLA—[*Forcing a laugh*] Say! What is this—another exam?

JIM—[*Doggedly*] Please answer.

ELLA—[*Irritably*] Of course I don't! Haven't I been brought up alongside—Why, some of my oldest—the girls I've been to public school the longest with—

JIM—Do you hate me, Ella?

ELLA—[*Confusedly and more irritably*] Say, is he drunk? Why should I? I don't hate anyone.

JIM—Then why haven't you ever hardly spoken to me—for years?

ELLA—[*Resentfully*] What would I speak about? You and me've got nothing in common any more.

JIM—[*Desperately*] Maybe not any more—but—right on this corner—do you remember once—?

ELLA—I don't remember nothing! [*Angri-*

ly] Say! What's got into you to be butting into my business all of a sudden like this? Because you finally managed to graduate, has it gone to your head?

JIM—No, I—only want to help you, Ella.

ELLA—Of all the nerve! You're certainly forgetting your place! Who's asking you for help, I'd like to know? Shut up and stop bothering me!

JIM—[*Insistently*] If you ever need a friend— a true friend—

ELLA—I've got lots of friends among my own—kind, I can tell you. [*Exasperatedly*] You make me sick! Go to—hell! [*She flounces off. The three men laugh.* MICKEY *follows her.* JIM *is stricken. He goes and sinks down limply on a box in front of the grocery-store.*]

SHORTY—I'm going to shoot a drink. Come on, Joe, and I'll blow yuh.

JOE—[*Who has never ceased to follow every move of* JIM'S *with angry, resentful eyes*] Go long. I'se gwine stay here a secon'. I got a lil' argyment. [*He points to* JIM.]

SHORTY—Suit yerself. Do a good job. See yuh later. [*He goes, whistling.*]

JOE—[*Stands for a while glaring at* JIM, *his fierce little eyes peering out of his black face. Then he spits on his hands aggressively and strides up to the oblivious* JIM. *He stands in front of him, gradually working himself into a fury at the other's seeming indifference to his words*] Listen to me, nigger: I got a heap to whisper in yo' ear! Who is you, anyhow? Who does you think you is? Don't yo' old man and mine work on de docks togidder befo' yo' old man gits his own truckin' business? Yo' ol' man swallers his nickels, my ol' man buys him beer wid dem and swallers dat—dat's de on'y diff'rence. Don't you'n'me drag up togidder?

JIM—[*Dully*] I'm your friend, Joe.

JOE—No, you isn't! I ain't no fren o' yourn! I don't even know who you is! What's all dis schoolin' you doin'? What's all dis dressin' up and graduatin' an' sayin' you gwine study be a lawyer? What's all dis fakin' an' pretendin' and swellin' out grand an' talkin' soft and perlite? What's all dis denyin' you's a nigger—an' wid

de white boys listenin' to you say it! Is you aimin' to buy white wid yo' ol' man's dough like Mickey say? What is you? [*In a rage at the other's silence*] You don't talk? Den I takes it out o' yo' hide! [*He grabs* JIM *by the throat with one hand and draws the other fist back*] Tell me befo' I wrecks yo' face in! Is you a nigger or isn't you? [*Shaking him*] Is you a nigger, Nigger? Nigger, is you a nigger?

JIM—[*Looking into his eyes—quietly*] Yes. I'm a nigger. We're both niggers. [*They look at each other for a moment.* JOE'S *rage vanishes. He slumps onto a box beside* JIM'S. *He offers him a cigarette.* JIM *takes it.* JOE *scratches a match and lights both their cigarettes.*]

JOE—[*After a puff, with full satisfaction*] Man, why didn't you 'splain dat in de fust place?

JIM—We're both niggers. [*The same hand-organ man of Scene 1 comes to the corner. He plays the chorus of "Bon Bon Buddie, the Chocolate Drop." They both stare straight ahead listening. Then the organ man goes away. A silence.* JOE *gets to his feet.*]

JOE—I'll go get me a cold beer. [*He starts to move off—then turns*] Time you was graduatin', ain't it? [*He goes.* JIM *remains sitting on his box staring straight before him as*

THE CURTAIN FALLS

Scene 3

The same corner five years later. Nothing has changed much. It is a night in Spring. The arc-lamp discovers faces with a favorless cruelty. The street noises are the same but more intermittent and dulled with a quality of fatigue. Two people pass, one black and one white. They are tired. They both yawn, but neither laughs. There is no laughter from the two streets. From the street of the whites the tenor, more nasal than ever and a bit drunken, wails in high barber-shop falsetto the last half of the chorus of "When I Lost You." The Negro voice, a bit maudlin in turn, replies with the last half of "Waitin' for the Robert E. Lee." Silence. SHORTY *enters. He looks tougher than ever, the typical gangster. He stands waiting, singing a bit drunkenly, peering down the street.*

SHORTY—[*Indignantly*] Yuh bum! Ain't yuh ever comin'? [*He begins to sing: "And sewed up in her yeller kimona, She had a blue-barrelled forty-five gun, For to get her man Who'd done her wrong." Then he comments scornfully*] Not her, dough! No gat for her. She ain't got de noive. A little sugar. Dat'll fix her. [ELLA *enters. She is dressed poorly, her face is pale and hollow-eyed, her voice cold and tired.*]

SHORTY—Yuh got de message?

ELLA—Here I am.

SHORTY—How yuh been?

ELLA—All right. [*A pause. He looks at her puzzledly.*]

SHORTY—[*A bit embarrassedly*] Well, I s'pose yuh'd like me to give yuh some dope on Mickey, huh?

ELLA—No.

SHORTY—Mean to say yuh don't wanter know where he is or what he's doin'?

ELLA—No.

SHORTY—Since when?

ELLA—A long time.

SHORTY—[*After a pause—with a rat-like viciousness*] Between you'n me, kid, you'll get even soon—you'n all de odder dames he's tossed. I'm on de inside. I've watched him trainin'. His next scrap, watch it! He'll go! It won't be de odder guy. It'll be all youse dames he's kidded—and de ones what's kidded him. Youse'll all be in de odder guy's corner. He won't need no odder seconds. Youse'll trow water on him, and sponge his face, and take de kinks out of his socker—and Mickey'll catch it on de button—and he won't be able to take it no more—'cause all your weight—you and de odders—'ll be behind dat punch. Ha ha! [*He laughs an evil laugh*] And Mickey'll go—down to his knees first—[*He sinks to his knees in the attitude of a groggy boxer.*]

ELLA—I'd like to see him on his knees!

SHORTY—And den—flat on his pan—dead to de world—de boidies singin' in de trees—ten—out! [*He suits his action to the words, sinking flat on the pavement, then rises and laughs the same evil laugh.*]

ELLA—He's been out—for me—a long time.

[*A pause*] Why did you send for me?

SHORTY—He sent me.

ELLA—Why?

SHORTY—To slip you dis wad o' dough. [*He reluctantly takes a roll of bills from his pocket and holds it out to her.*]

ELLA—[*Looks at the money indifferently*] What for?

SHORTY—For you.

ELLA—No.

SHORTY—For de kid den.

ELLA—The kid's dead. He took diptheria.

SHORTY—Hell yuh say! When?

ELLA—A long time.

SHORTY—Why didn't you write Mickey—?

ELLA—Why should I? He'd only be glad.

SHORTY—[*After a pause*] Well—it's better.

ELLA—Yes.

SHORTY—You made up wit yer family?

ELLA—No chance.

SHORTY—Livin' alone?

ELLA—In Brooklyn.

SHORTY—Workin'?

ELLA—In a factory.

SHORTY—You're a sucker. There's lots of softer snaps fer you, kid—

ELLA—I know what you mean. No.

SHORTY—Don't yuh wanter step out no more—have fun—live?

ELLA—I'm through.

SHORTY—[*Mockingly*] Jump in de river, huh? T'ink it over, baby. I kin start yuh right in my stable. No one'll bodder yuh den. I got influence.

ELLA—[*Without emphasis*] You're a dirty dog. Why doesn't someone kill you?

SHORTY—Is dat so! What're you? They say you been travelin' round with Jim Crow.

ELLA—He's been my only friend.

SHORTY—A nigger!

ELLA—The only white man in the world! Kind and white. You're all black—black to the heart!

SHORTY—Nigger-lover! [*He throws the money in her face. It falls to the street*] Listen, you! Mickey says he's off of yuh for keeps. Dis is de finish! Dat's what he sent me to tell you. [*Glances at her searchingly—a pause*] Yuh won't make no trouble?

ELLA—Why should I? He's free. The kid's dead. I'm free. No hard feelings—only—I'll be there in spirit at his next fight, tell him! I'll take your tip—the other corner—second the punch—nine—ten—out! He's free! That's all. [*She grins horribly at Shorty*] Go away, Shorty.

SHORTY—[*Looking at her and shaking his head—maudlinly*] Groggy! Groggy! We're all groggy! Gluttons for punishment! Me for a drink. So long. [*He goes. A Salvation Army band comes toward the corner. They are playing and singing "Till We Meet at Jesus' Feet." They reach the end as they enter and stop before ELLA. The CAPTAIN steps forward.*]

CAPTAIN—Sister—

ELLA—[*Picks up the money and drops it in his hat—mockingly*] Here. Go save yourself. Leave me alone.

A WOMAN SALVATIONIST—Sister—

ELLA—Never mind that. I'm not in your line—yet. [*As they hesitate, wonderingly*] I want to be alone. [*To the thud of the big drum they march off. ELLA sits down on a box, her hands hanging at her sides. Presently JIM HARRIS comes in. He has grown into a quietly-dressed, studious-looking Negro with an intelligent yet queerly-baffled face.*]

JIM—[*With a joyous but bewildered cry*] Ella! I just saw Shorty—

ELLA—[*Smiling at him with frank affection*] He had a message from Mickey.

JIM—[*Sadly*] Ah!

ELLA—[*Pointing to the box behind her*] Sit down. [*He does so. A pause—then she says indifferently*] It's finished. I'm free, Jim.

JIM—[*wearily*] We're never free—except to do what we have to.

ELLA—What are you getting gloomy about all of a sudden?

JIM—I've got the report from the school. I've flunked again.

ELLA—Poor Jim.

JIM—Don't pity me. I'd like to kick myself all over the block. Five years—and I'm still plugging away where I ought to have been at the end of two.

ELLA—Why don't you give it up?

JIM—No!

ELLA—After all, what's being a lawyer?

JIM—A lot—to me—what it means. [*Intensely*] Why, if I was a Member of the Bar right now, Ella, I believe I'd almost have the courage to—

ELLA—What?

JIM—Nothing. [*After a pause—gropingly*] I can't explain—just—but it hurts like fire. It brands me in my pride. I swear I know more'n any member of my class. I ought to, I study harder. I work like the devil. It's all in my head—all fine and correct to a T. Then when I'm called on—I stand up—all the white faces looking at me—and I can feel their eyes—I hear my own voice sounding funny, trembling—and all of a sudden it's all gone in my head—there's nothing remembered—and I hear myself stuttering — and give up — sit down—They don't laugh, hardly ever. They're kind. They're good people. [*In a frenzy*] They're considerate, damn them! But I feel branded!

ELLA—Poor Jim!

JIM—[*Going on painfully*] And it's the same thing in the written exams. For weeks before I study all night. I can't sleep anyway. I learn it all, I see it, I understand it. Then they give me the paper in the exam room. I look it over, I know each answer—perfectly. I take up my pen. On all sides are white men starting to write. They're so sure—even the ones that I know know nothing. But I know it all—but I can't remember any more—it fades—it goes—it's gone. There's a blank in my head—stupidity—I sit like a fool fighting to remember a little bit here, a little bit there — not enough to pass—not enough for anything—when I know it all!

ELLA—[*Compassionately*] Jim. It isn't worth it. You don't need to—

JIM—I need it more than anyone ever needed anything. I need it to live.

ELLA—What'll it prove?

JIM—Nothing at all much—but everything to me.

ELLA—You're so much better than they are in every other way.

JIM—[*Looking up at her*] Then—you understand?

ELLA—Of course. [*Affectionately*] Don't I know how fine you've been to me! You've been the only one in the world who's stood by me—the only understanding person—and all after the rotten way I used to treat you.

JIM—But before that—way back so high— you treated me good. [*He smiles.*]

ELLA—You've been white to me, Jim. [*She takes his hand.*]

JIM—White—to you!

ELLA—Yes.

JIM—All love is white. I've always loved you. [*This with the deepest humility.*]

ELLA—Even now—after all that's happened!

JIM—Always.

ELLA—I like you, Jim—better than anyone else in the world.

JIM—That's more than enough, more than I ever hoped for. [*The organ grinder comes to the corner. He plays the chorus of "Annie Laurie." They sit listening, hand in hand.*]

JIM—Would you ever want to marry me, Ella?

ELLA—Yes, Jim.

JIM—[*As if this quick consent alarmed him*] No, no, don't answer now. Wait! Turn it over in your mind! Think what it means to you! Consider it—over and over again! I'm in no hurry, Ella. I can wait months—years—

ELLA—I'm alone. I've got to be helped. I've got to help someone—or it's the end—one end or another.

JIM—[*Eagerly*] Oh, I'll help—I know I can help—I'll give my life to help you— that's what I've been living for—

ELLA—But can I help you? Can I help you?

JIM—Yes! Yes! We'll go abroad where a man is a man—where it don't make that difference—where people are kind and wise to see the soul under skins. I don't ask you to love me—I don't dare to hope nothing like that! I don't want nothing—only to wait—to know you

like me—to be near you—to keep harm away—to make up for the past—to never let you suffer any more—to serve you—to lie at your feet like a dog that loves you—to kneel by your bed like a nurse that watches over you sleeping— to preserve and protect and shield you from evil and sorrow—to give my life and my blood and all the strength that's in me to give you peace and joy—to become your slave!—yes, be your slave! —your black slave that adores you as sacred! [*He has sunk to his knees. In a frenzy of self-abnegation, as he says the last words he beats his head on the flagstones.*]

ELLA—[*Overcome and alarmed*] Jim! Jim! You're crazy! I want to help you, Jim— I want to help—

CURTAIN

Scene 4

Some weeks or so later. A street in the same ward in front of an old brick church. The church sets back from the sidewalk in a yard enclosed by a rusty iron railing with a gate at center. On each side of this yard are tenements. The buildings have a stern, forbidding look. All the shades on the windows are drawn down, giving an effect of staring, brutal eyes that pry callously at human beings without acknowledging them. Even the two tall, narrow church windows on either side of the arched door are blanked with dull green shades. It is a bright, sunny morning. The district is unusually still, as if it were waiting, holding its breath.

From the street of the blacks to the right a Negro tenor sings in a voice of shadowy richness—the first stanza with a contented, childlike melancholy—

Sometimes I feel like a mourning dove,
Sometimes I feel like a mourning dove,
I feel like a mourning dove.

The second with a dreamy, boyish exultance—

Sometimes I feel like an eagle in the air,
Sometimes I feel like an eagle in the air,
I feel like an eagle in the air.

The third with a brooding, earthbound sorrow—

Sometimes I wish that I'd never been born,
Sometimes I wish that I'd never been born,
I wish that I'd never been born.

As the music dies down there is a pause of waiting stillness. This is broken by one startling, metallic clang of the church-bell. As if it were a signal, people—men, women, children—pour from the two tenements, whites from the tenement to the left, blacks from the one to the right. They hurry to form into two racial lines on each side of the gate, rigid and unyielding, staring across at each other with bitter hostile eyes. The halves of the big church door swing open and JIM *and* ELLA *step out from the darkness within into the sunlight. The doors slam behind them like wooden lips of an idol that has spat them out.* JIM *is dressed in black,* ELLA *in white, both with extreme plainness. They stand in the sunlight, shrinking and confused. All the hostile eyes are now concentrated on them. They become aware of the two lines through which they must pass; they hesitate and tremble; then stand there staring back at the people as fixed and immovable as they are. The organ grinder comes in from the right. He plays the chorus of "Old Black Joe." As he finishes the bell of the church clangs one more single stroke, insistently dismissing.*

JIM—[*As if the sound had awakened him from a trance, reaches out and takes her hand*] Come. Time we got to the steamer. Time we sailed away over the sea. Come, Honey! [*She tries to answer but her lips tremble; she cannot take her eyes off the eyes of the people; she is unable to move. He sees this and, keeping the same tone of profound, affectionate kindness, he points upward in the sky, and gradually persuades her eyes to look up*] Look up, Honey! See the sun! Feel his warm eye lookin' down! Feel how kind he looks! Feel his blessing deep in your heart, your bones! Look up, Honey! [*Her eyes are fixed on the sky now. Her face is calm. She tries to smile bravely back at the sun. Now he pulls her by the hand, urging her gently to walk with him down through the yard and gate, through the lines of people. He is maintaining an attitude to support them through the ordeal only by a terrible effort, which manifests itself in the hysteric quality of ecstasy which breaks into his voice.*] And look at the sky! Ain't it kind and

blue! Blue for hope! Don't they say blue's for hope? Hope! That's for us, Honey. All those blessings in the sky! What's it the Bible says? Falls on just and unjust alike? No, that's the sweet rain. Pshaw, what am I saying? All mixed up. There's no unjust about it. We're all the same—equally just— under the sky—under the sun—under God—sailing over the sea—to the other side of the world—the side where Christ was born—the kind side that takes count of the soul—over the sea—the sea's blue, too—. Let's not be late—let's get that steamer! [*They have reached the curb now, passed the lines of people. She is looking up to the sky with an expression of trancelike calm and peace. He is on the verge of collapse, his face twitching, his eyes staring. He calls hoarsely:*] Taxi! Where is he? Taxi!

CURTAIN

ACT II

Scene 1

Two years later. A flat of the better sort in the Negro district near the corner of Act 1. This is the parlor. Its furniture is a queer clash. The old pieces are cheaply ornate, naïvely, childishly gaudy—the new pieces give evidence of a taste that is diametrically opposed, severe to the point of somberness. On one wall, in a heavy gold frame, is a colored photograph—the portrait of an elderly Negro with an able, shrewd face but dressed in outlandish lodge regalia, a get-up adorned with medals, sashes, a cocked hat with frills—the whole effect as absurd to contemplate as one of Napoleon's Marshals in full uniform. In the left corner, where a window lights it effectively, is a Negro primitive mask from the Congo— a grotesque face, inspiring obscure, dim connotations in one's mind, but beautifully done, conceived in a true religious spirit. In this room, however, the mask acquires an arbitrary accentuation. It dominates by a diabolical quality that contrast imposes upon it.

There are two windows on the left looking out in the street. In the rear, a door to the hall of the building. In the right, a doorway with red and gold portières leading into the bedroom and the rest of the flat. Everything is cleaned and polished. The dark brown wall paper is new, the brilliantly figured carpet also. There is a round mahogany table at center. In a rocking chair by the table Mrs. Harris *is sitting. She is a mild-looking, gray-haired Negress of sixty-five, dressed in an old-fashioned Sunday-best dress. Walking about the room nervously is* Hattie, *her daughter,* Jim's *sister, a woman of about thirty with a high-strung, defiant face—an intelligent head showing both power and courage. She is dressed severely, mannishly.*

It is a fine morning in Spring. Sunshine comes through the windows at the left.

Mrs. Harris—Time dey was here, ain't it?

Hattie—[*Impatiently*] Yes.

Mrs. H.—[*Worriedly*] You ain't gwine ter kick up a fuss, is you—like you done wid' Jim befo' de weddin'?

Hattie—No. What's done is done.

Mrs. H.—We mustn't let her see we hold it agin her—de bad dat happened to her wid dat no-count fighter.

Hattie—I certainly never give that a thought. It's what she's done to Jim—making him run away and give up his fight—!

Mrs. H.—Jim loves her a powerful lot, must be.

Hattie—[*After a pause—bitterly*] I wonder if she loves Jim!

Mrs. H.—She must, too. Yes, she must, too. Don't you forget dat it was hard for her—mighty, mighty hard—harder for de white dan for de black!

Hattie—[*Indignantly*] Why should it be?

Mrs. H.—[*Shaking her head*] I ain't talkin' of shoulds. It's too late for shoulds. Dey's o'ny one should. [*Solemnly*] De white and de black shouldn't mix dat close. Dere's one road where de white goes on alone; dere's anudder road where de black goes on alone—

Hattie—Yes if they'd only leave us alone!

Mrs. H.—Dey leaves your Pa alone. He comes to de top till he's got his own business, lots o' money in de bank, he

owns a building even befo' he die. [*She looks up proudly at the picture.* Hattie *sighs impatiently—then her mother goes on*] Dey leaves me alone. I bears four children into dis worl', two dies, two lives, I helps you two grow up fine an' healthy and eddicated wid schoolin' and money fo' yo' comfort—

Hattie—[*Impatiently*] Ma!

Mrs. H.—I does de duty God set for me in dis worl'. Dey leaves me alone. [Hattie *goes to the window to hide her exasperation. The mother broods for a minute—then goes on*] The worl' done change. Dey ain't no satisfaction wid nuffin' no more.

Hattie—Oh! [*Then after a pause*] They'll be here any minute now.

Mrs. H.—Why didn't you go meet 'em at de dock like I axed you?

Hattie—I couldn't. My face and Jim's among those hundreds of white faces— [*With a harsh laugh*] It would give her too much advantage!

Mrs. H.—[*Impatiently*] Don't talk dat way! What makes you so proud? [*Then after a pause—sadly*] Hattie.

Hattie—[*Turning*] Yes, Ma.

Mrs. H.—I want to see Jim again—my only boy—but—all de same I'd ruther he stayed away. He say in his letter he's happy, she's happy, dey likes it dere, de folks don't think nuffin' but what's natural at seeing 'em married. Why don't dey stay?

Hattie—[*Vehemently*] No! They were cowards to run away. If they believe in what they've done, then let them face it out, live it out here, be strong enough to conquer all prejudice!

Mrs. H.—Strong? Dey ain't many strong. Dey ain't many happy neider. Dey was happy ovah yondah.

Hattie—We don't deserve happiness till we've fought the fight of our race and won it! [*In the pause that follows there is a ring from back in the flat*] It's the door bell! You go, Ma. I—I—I'd rather not. [*Her mother looks at her rebukingly and goes out agitatedly through the portières.* Hattie *waits, nervously walking about, trying to compose herself. There is a long pause. Finally the portières are parted and* JIM *enters. He looks much older, graver, worried.*]

JIM—Hattie!

HATTIE—Jim! [*They embrace with great affection.*]

JIM—It's great to see you again! You're looking fine.

HATTIE—[*Looking at him searchingly*] You look well, too—thinner maybe—and tired. [*Then as she sees him frowning*] But where's Ella?

JIM—With Ma. [*Apologetically*] She sort of —broke down—when we came in. The trip wore her out.

HATTIE—[*Coldly*] I see.

JIM—Oh, it's nothing serious. Nerves. She needs a rest.

HATTIE—Wasn't living in France restful?

JIM—Yes, but—too lonely—especially for her.

HATTIE—[*Resentfully*] Why? Didn't the people there want to associate—?

JIM—[*Quickly*] Oh, no indeedy, they didn't think anything of that. [*After a pause*] But—she did. For the first year it was all right. Ella liked everything a lot. She went out with French folks and got so she could talk it a little—and I learned it—a little. We were having a right nice time. I never thought then we'd ever want to come back here.

HATTIE—[*Frowning*] But—what happened to change you?

JIM—[*After a pause—haltingly*] Well—you see—the first year—she and I were living around—like friends—like a brother and sister—like you and I might.

HATTIE—[*Her face becoming more and more drawn and tense*] You mean—then—? [*She shudders—then after a pause*] She loves you, Jim?

JIM—If I didn't know that I'd have to jump in the river.

HATTIE—Are you sure she loves you?

JIM—Isn't that why she's suffering?

HATTIE—[*Letting her breath escape through her clenched teeth*] Ah!

JIM—[*Suddenly springs up and shouts almost hysterically*] Why d'you ask me all those damn questions? Are you trying to make trouble between us?

HATTIE—[*Controlling herself—quietly*] No, Jim.

JIM—[*After a pause—contritely*] I'm sorry, Hattie. I'm kind of on edge today. [*He sinks down on his chair—then goes on as if something forced him to speak*] After that we got to living housed in. Ella didn't want to see nobody, she said just the two of us was enough. I was happy then—and I really guess she was happy too—in a way—for a while. [*Again a pause*] But she never did get to wanting to go out any place again. She got to saying she felt she'd be sure to run into someone she knew—from over here. So I moved us out to the country where no tourist ever comes—but it didn't make any difference to her. She got to avoiding the French folks the same as if they were Americans and I couldn't get it out of her mind. She lived in the house and got paler and paler, and more and more nervous and scarey, always imagining things—until I got to imagining things, too. I got to feeling blue. Got to sneering at myself that I wasn't any better than a quitter because I sneaked away right after getting married, didn't face nothing, gave up trying to become a Member of the Bar—and I got to suspecting Ella must feel that way about me too—that I wasn't a *real man!*

HATTIE—[*Indignantly*] She couldn't!

JIM—[*With hostility*] You don't need to tell me! All this was only in my own mind. We never quarreled a single bit. We never said a harsh word. We were as close to each other as could be. We were all there was in the world to each other. We were alone together! [*A pause*] Well, one day I got so I couldn't stand it. I could see she couldn't stand it. So I just up and said: Ella, we've got to have a plain talk, look everything straight in the face, hide nothing, come out with the exact truth of the way we feel.

HATTIE—And you decided to come back!

JIM—Yes. We decided the reason we felt sort of ashamed was we'd acted like cowards. We'd run away from the thing —and taken it with us. We decided to come back and face it and live it down in ourselves, and prove to ourselves we were strong in our love—and then, and that way only, by being brave we'd free ourselves, and gain confidence, and be really free inside and able then to go anywhere and live in peace and equality with ourselves and the world without any guilty uncomfortable feeling coming up to rile us. [*He has talked himself now into a state of happy confidence.*]

HATTIE—[*Bending over and kissing him*] Good for you! I admire you so much, Jim! I admire both of you! And are you going to begin studying right away and get admitted to the Bar?

JIM—You bet I am!

HATTIE—You must, Jim! Our race needs men like you to come to the front and help— [*As voices are heard approaching she stops, stiffens, and her face grows cold.*]

JIM—[*Noticing this—warningly*] Remember Ella's been sick! [*Losing control—threateningly*] You be nice to her, you hear! [MRS. HARRIS *enters, showing* ELLA *the way. The colored woman is plainly worried and perplexed.* ELLA *is pale, with a strange, haunted expression in her eyes. She runs to* JIM *as to a refuge, clutching his hands in both of hers, looking from* MRS. HARRIS *to* HATTIE *with a frightened defiance.*]

MRS. H.—Dere he is, child, big's life! She was afraid we'd done kidnapped you away, Jim.

JIM—[*Patting her hand*] This place ought to be familiar, Ella. Don't you remember playing here with us sometimes as a kid?

ELLA—[*Queerly—with a frown of effort*] I remember playing marbles one night— but that was on the street.

JIM—Don't you remember Hattie?

HATTIE—[*Coming forward with a forced smile*] It was a long time ago—but I remember Ella. [*She holds out her hand.*]

ELLA—[*Taking it—looking at* HATTIE *with the same queer defiance*] I remember. But you've changed so much.

HATTIE—[*Stirred to hostility by* ELLA'S *manner —condescendingly*] Yes, I've grown older, naturally. [*Then in a tone which, as if in spite of herself, becomes bragging*] I've worked so hard. First I went away to college, you know—then I took up postgraduate study—when suddenly I decided I'd accomplish more good if I gave up learning and took up teaching. [*She suddenly checks herself, ashamed, and stung by* ELLA'S *indifference*] But this sounds like stupid boasting. I don't mean that. I was only explaining—

ELLA—[*Indifferently*] I didn't know you'd been to school so long. [*A pause*] Where are you teaching? In a colored school, I suppose. [*There is an indifferent superiority in her words that is maddening to* HATTIE.]

HATTIE—[*Controlling herself*] Yes. A private school endowed by some wealthy members of our race.

ELLA—[*Suddenly—even eagerly*] Then you must have taken lots of examinations and managed to pass them, didn't you?

HATTIE—[*Biting her lips*] I always passed with honors!

ELLA—Yes, we both graduated from the same High School, didn't we? That was dead easy for me. Why I hardly even looked at a book. But Jim says it was awfully hard for him. He failed one year, remember? [*She turns and smiles at* JIM—*a tolerant, superior smile but one full of genuine love.* HATTIE *is outraged, but* JIM *smiles.*]

JIM—Yes, it was hard for me, Honey.

ELLA—And the law school examinations Jim hardly ever could pass at all. Could you? [*She laughs lovingly.*]

HATTIE—[*Harshly*] Yes, he could! He can! He'll pass them now—if you'll give him a chance!

JIM—[*Angrily*] Hattie!

MRS. HARRIS—Hold yo' fool tongue!

HATTIE—[*Sullenly*] I'm sorry. [ELLA *has shrunk back against* JIM. *She regards* HATTIE *with a sort of wondering hatred. Then she looks away about the room. Sud-*

denly her eyes fasten on the primitive mask and she gives a stifled scream.]

JIM—What's the matter, Honey?

ELLA—[*Pointing*] That! For God's sake, what is it?

HATTIE—[*Scornfully*] It's a Congo mask. [*She goes and picks it up*] I'll take it away if you wish. I thought you'd like it. It was my wedding present to Jim.

ELLA—What is it?

HATTIE—It's a mask which used to be worn in religious ceremonies by my people in Africa. But, aside from that, it's beautifully made, a work of Art by a real artist—as real in his way as your Michael Angelo. [*Forces* ELLA *to take it*] Here. Just notice the workmanship.

ELLA—[*Defiantly*] I'm not scared of it if you're not. [*Looking at it with disgust*] Beautiful? Well, some people certainly have queer notions! It looks ugly to me and stupid—like a kid's game—making faces! [*She slaps it contemptuously*] Pooh! You needn't look hard at me. I'll give you the laugh. [*She goes to put it back on the stand.*]

JIM—Maybe, if it disturbs you, we better put it in some other room.

ELLA—[*Defiantly aggressive*] No. I want it here where I can give it the laugh! [*She sets it there again—then turns suddenly on* HATTIE *with aggressive determination*] Jim's not going to take any more examinations! I won't let him!

HATTIE—[*Bursting forth*] Jim! Do you hear that? There's white justice!—their fear for their superiority!—

ELLA—[*With a terrified pleading*] Make her go away, Jim!

JIM—[*Losing control—furiously to his sister*] Either you leave here—or we will!

MRS. H.—[*Weeping—throws her arms around* HATTIE] Let's go, chile! Let's go!

HATTIE—[*Calmly now*] Yes, Ma. All right. [*They go through the portières. As soon as they are gone,* JIM *suddenly collapses into a chair and hides his head in his hands.* ELLA *stands beside him for a moment. She stares distractedly about her, at the portrait, at the mask, at the furniture, at* JIM. *She seems*

fighting to escape from some weight on her mind. She throws this off and, completely her old self for the moment, kneels by JIM *and pats his shoulder.*]

ELLA—[*With kindness and love*] Don't, Jim! Don't cry, please! You don't suppose I really meant that about the examinations, do you? Why, of course, I didn't mean a word! I couldn't mean it! I want you to take the examinations! I want you to pass! I want you to be a lawyer! I want you to be the best lawyer in the country! I want you to show 'em—all the dirty sneaking, gossiping liars that talk behind our backs—what a man I married. I want the whole world to know you're the whitest of the white! I want you to climb and climb—and step on 'em, stamp right on their mean faces! I love you, Jim. You know that!

JIM—[*Calm again—happily*] I hope so, Honey—and I'll make myself worthy.

HATTIE—[*Appears in the doorway—quietly*] We're going now, Jim.

ELLA—No. Don't go.

HATTIE—We were going to anyway. This is your house—Mother's gift to you, Jim.

JIM—[*Astonished*] But I can't accept— Where are you going?

HATTIE—We've got a nice flat in the Bronx—[*With bitter pride*] in the heart of the Black Belt—the Congo—among our own people!

JIM—[*Angrily*] You're crazy—I'll see Ma— [*He goes out.* HATTIE *and* ELLA *stare at each other with scorn and hatred for a moment, then* HATTIE *goes.* ELLA *remains kneeling for a moment by the chair, her eyes dazed and strange as she looks about her. Then she gets to her feet and stands before the portrait of* JIM's *father—with a sneer.*]

ELLA—It's his Old Man—all dolled up like a circus horse! Well, they can't help it. It's in the blood, I suppose. They're ignorant, that's all there is to it. [*She moves to the mask—forcing a mocking tone*] Hello, sport! Who d'you think you're scaring. Not me! I'll give you the laugh. He won't pass, you wait and see. Not in a thousand years! [*She goes to the window and looks down at the street and mutters*] All black! Every one of them! [*Then with sudden excitement*] No, there's one. Why, it's Shorty! [*She throws the window open and calls*] Shorty! Shorty! Hello, Shorty! [*She leans out and waves—then stops, remains there for a moment looking down, then comes back into the room suddenly as if she wanted to hide—her whole face in an anguish*] Say! Say! I wonder?—No, he didn't hear you. Yes, he did too! He must have! I yelled so loud you could hear me in Jersey! No, what are you talking about? How would he hear with all kids yelling down there? He never heard a word, I tell you! He did too! He didn't want to hear you! He didn't want to let anyone know he knew you! Why don't you acknowledge it? What are you lying about? I'm not! Why shouldn't he? Where does he come in to—For God's sake, who is Shorty anyway? A pimp! Yes, and a dope-peddler, too! D'you mean to say he'd have the nerve to hear me call him and then deliberately—? Yes, I mean to say it! I do say it! And it's true, and you know it, and you might as well be honest for a change and admit it! He heard you but he didn't want to hear you! He doesn't want to know you any more. No, not even him! He's afraid it'd get him in wrong with the old gang. Why? You know well enough! Because you married a—a—a—well, I won't say it, but you know without my mentioning names! [ELLA *springs to her feet in horror and shakes off her obsession with a frantic effort*] Stop! [*Then whimpering like a frightened child*] Jim! Jim! Jim! Where are you? I want you, Jim! [*She runs out of the room as*

THE CURTAIN FALLS

Scene 2

The same. Six months later. It is evening. The walls of the room appear shrunken in, the ceiling lowered, so that the furniture, the portrait, the mask look unnaturally large and domineering. JIM *is seated at the table studying, law books piled by his elbows. He is keeping his*

attention concentrated only by a driving physical effort which gives his face the expression of a runner's near the tape. His forehead shines with perspiration. He mutters one sentence from Blackstone over and over again, tapping his forehead with his fist in time to the rhythm he gives the stale words. But, in spite of himself, his attention wanders, his eyes have an uneasy, hunted look, he starts at every sound in the house or from the street. Finally, he remains rigid, Blackstone forgotten, his eyes fixed on the portières with tense grief. Then he groans, slams the book shut, goes to the window and throws it open and sinks down beside it, his arms on the sill, his head resting wearily on his arms, staring out into the night, the pale glare from the arc-lamp on the corner throwing his face into relief. The portières on the right are parted and HATTIE *comes in.*

HATTIE—[*Not seeing him at the table*] Jim! [*Dicovering him*] Oh, there you are. What're you doing?

JIM—[*Turning to her*] Resting. Cooling my head. [*Forcing a smile*] These law books certainly are a sweating proposition! [*Then, anxiously*] How is she?

HATTIE—She's asleep now. I felt it was safe to leave her for a minute. [*After a pause*] What did the doctor tell you, Jim?

JIM—The same old thing. She must have rest, he says, her mind needs rest— [*Bitterly*] But he can't tell me any prescription for that rest—leastways not any that'd work.

HATTIE—[*After a pause*] I think you ought to leave her, Jim—or let her leave you— for a while, anyway.

JIM—[*Angrily*] You're like the doctor. Everything's so simple and easy. Do this and that happens. Only it don't. Life isn't simple like that—not in this case, anyway—no, it isn't simple a bit. [*After a pause*] I can't leave her. She can't leave me. And there's a million little reasons combining to make one big reason why we can't. [*A pause*] For her sake—if it'd do her good—I'd go—I'd leave—I'd do anything—because I love her. I'd kill myself even—jump out of this window this second—I've thought it over, too—

but that'd only make matters worse for her. I'm all she's got in the world! Yes, that isn't bragging or fooling myself. I know that for a fact! Don't you know that's true? [*There is a pleading for the certainty he claims.*]

HATTIE—[*Yes*, I know she loves you, Jim. I know that now.

JIM—[*Simply*] Then we've got to stick together to the end, haven't we, whatever comes—and hope and pray for the best. [*A pause—then hopefully*] I think maybe this is the crisis in her mind. Once she settles this in herself, she's won to the other side. And me—once I become a Member of the Bar—then I win, too! We're both free—by our own fighting down our own weakness! We're both really, truly free! Then we can be happy with ourselves here or anywhere. She'll be proud then! Yes, she's told me again and again, she says she'll be actually proud!

HATTIE—[*Turning away to conceal her emotion*] Yes, I'm sure—but you mustn't study too hard, Jim! You mustn't study too awfully hard!

JIM—[*Gets up and goes to the table and sits down wearily*] Yes, I know. Oh, I'll pass easily. I haven't got any scarey feeling about that any more. And I'm doing two years' work in one here alone. That's better than schools, eh?

HATTIE—[*Doubtfully*] It's wonderful, Jim.

JIM—[*His spirit evaporating*] If I can only hold out! It's hard! I'm worn out. I don't sleep. I get to thinking and thinking. My head aches and burns like fire with thinking. Round and round my thoughts go chasing like crazy chickens hopping and flapping before the wind. It gets me crazy mad—'cause I can't stop!

HATTIE—[*Watching him for a while and seeming to force herself to speak*] The doctor didn't tell you all, Jim.

JIM—[*Dully*] What's that?

HATTIE—He told me you're liable to break down too, if you don't take care of yourself.

JIM—[*Abjectly weary*] Let 'er come! I don't care what happens to me. Maybe if I

get sick she'll get well. There's only so much bad luck allowed to one family, maybe. [*He forces a wan smile.*]

HATTIE—[*Hastily*] Don't give in to that idea, for the Lord's sake!

JIM—I'm tired—and blue—that's all.

HATTIE—[*After another long pause*] I've got to tell you something else, Jim.

JIM—[*Dully*] What?

HATTIE—The doctor said Ella's liable to be sick like this a very long time.

JIM—He told me that too—that it'd be a long time before she got back her normal strength. Well, I suppose that's got to be expected.

HATTIE—[*Slowly*] He didn't mean convalescing—what he told me. [*A long pause.*]

JIM—[*Evasively*] I'm going to get other doctors in to see Ella—specialists. This one's a damn fool.

HATTIE—Be sensible, Jim. You'll have to face the truth—sooner or later.

JIM—[*Irritably*] I know the truth about Ella better'n any doctor.

HATTIE—[*Persuasively*] She'd get better so much sooner if you'd send her away to some nice sanitarium—

JIM—No! She'd die of shame there!

HATTIE—At least until after you've taken your examinations—

JIM—To hell with me!

HATTIE—Six months. That wouldn't be long to be parted.

JIM—What are you trying to do—separate us? [*He gets to his feet—furiously*] Go on out! Go on out!

HATTIE—[*Calmly*] No, I won't. [*Sharply*] There's something that's got to be said to you and I'm the only one with the courage— [*Intensely*] Tell me, Jim, have you heard her raving when she's out of her mind?

JIM—[*With a shudder*] No!

HATTIE—You're lying, Jim. You must have—if you don't stop your ears—and the doctor says she may develop a violent mania, dangerous for you—get worse and worse until—Jim, you'll go crazy too—living this way. Today she raved on about "Black! Black!" and cried because she said her skin was turning black—that you had poisoned her—

JIM—[*In anguish*] That's only when she's out of her mind.

HATTIE—And then she suddenly called me a dirty nigger.

JIM—No! She never said that ever! She never would!

HATTIE—She did—and kept on and on! [*A tense pause*] She'll be saying that to you soon.

JIM—[*Torturedly*] She don't mean it! She isn't responsible for what she's saying!

HATTIE—I know she isn't—yet she is just the same. It's deep down in her or it wouldn't come out.

JIM—Deep down in her people—not deep in her.

HATTIE—I can't make such distinctions. The race in me, deep in me, can't stand it. I can't play nurse to her any more, Jim,—not even for your sake. I'm afraid —afraid of myself—afraid sometime I'll kill her dead to set you free! [*She loses control and begins to cry.*]

JIM—[*After a long pause—somberly*] Yes, I guess you'd better stay away from here. Good-by.

HATTIE—Who'll you get to nurse her, Jim, —a white woman?

JIM—Ella'd die of shame. No, I'll nurse her myself.

HATTIE—And give up your studies?

JIM—I can do both.

HATTIE—You can't! You'll get sick yourself! Why, you look terrible even as it is—and it's only beginning!

JIM—I can do anything for her! I'm all she's got in the world! I've got to prove I can be all to her! I've got to prove worthy! I've got to prove she can be proud of me! I've got to prove I'm the whitest of the white!

HATTIE—[*Stung by this last—with rebellious bitterness*] Is that the ambition she's given you? Oh, you soft, weak-minded fool, you traitor to your race! And the thanks you'll get—to be called a dirty nigger—to hear her cursing you because

she can never have a child because it'll be born black—!

JIM—[*In a frenzy*] Stop!

HATTIE—I'll say what must be said even though you kill me, Jim. Send her to an asylum before you both have to be sent to one together.

JIM—[*With a sudden wild laugh*] Do you think you're threatening me with something dreadful now? Why, I'd like that. Sure, I'd like that! Maybe she'd like it better, too. Maybe we'd both find it all simple then—like you think it is now. Yes. [*He laughs again.*]

HATTIE—[*Frightenedly*] Jim!

JIM—Together! You can't scare me even with hell fire if you say she and I go together. It's heaven then for me! [*With sudden savagery*] You go out of here! All you've ever been aiming to do is to separate us so we can't be together!

HATTIE—I've done what I did for your own good.

JIM—I have no own good. I only got a good together with her. I'm all she's got in the world! Let her call me nigger! Let her call me the whitest of the white! I'm all she's got in the world, ain't I? She's all I've got! You with your fool talk of the black race and the white race! Where does the human race get a chance to come in? I suppose that's simple for you. You lock it up in asylums and throw away the key! [*With fresh violence*] Go along! There isn't going to be no more people coming in here to separate—excepting the doctor. I'm going to lock the door and it's going to stay locked, you hear? Go along, now!

HATTIE—[*Confusedly*] Jim!

JIM—[*Pushes her out gently and slams the door after her—vaguely*] Go along! I got to study. I got to nurse Ella, too. Oh, I can do it! I can do anything for her! [*He sits down at the table and, opening the book, begins again to recite the line from Blackstone in a meaningless rhythm, tapping his forehead with his fist. ELLA enters noiselessly through the portières. She wears a red dress-*

ing-gown over her night-dress but is in her bare feet. She has a carving-knife in her right hand. Her eyes fasten on JIM *with a murderous mania. She creeps up behind him. Suddenly he senses something and turns. As he sees her he gives a cry, jumping up and catching her wrist. She stands fixed, her eyes growing bewildered and frightened.*]

JIM—[*Aghast*] Ella! For God's sake! Do you want to murder me? [*She does not answer. He shakes her.*]

ELLA—[*Whimperingly*] They kept calling me names as I was walking along—I can't tell you what, Jim—and then I grabbed a knife—

JIM—Yes! See! This! [*She looks at it frightenedly.*]

ELLA—Where did I—? I was having a nightmare—Where did they go—I mean, how did I get here? [*With sudden terrified pleading—like a little girl*] O Jim—don't ever leave me alone! I have such terrible dreams, Jim—promise you'll never go away!

JIM—I promise, Honey.

ELLA—[*Her manner becoming more and more childishly silly*] I'll be a little girl—and you'll be old Uncle Jim who's been with us for years and years—Will you play that?

JIM—Yes, Honey. Now you better go back to bed.

ELLA—[*Like a child*] Yes, Uncle Jim. [*She turns to go. He pretends to be occupied by his book. She looks at him for a second—then suddenly asks in her natural woman's voice*] Are you studying hard, Jim?

JIM—Yes, Honey. Go to bed now. You need to rest, you know.

ELLA—[*Stands looking at him, fighting with herself. A startling transformation comes over her face. It grows mean, vicious, full of jealous hatred. She cannot contain herself but breaks out harshly with a cruel, venomous grin*] You dirty nigger!

JIM—[*Starting as if he'd been shot*] Ella! For the good Lord's sake!

ELLA—[*Coming out of her insane mood for a moment, aware of something terrible, frightened*] Jim! Jim! Why are you looking at me like that?

JIM—What did you say to me just then?

ELLA—[*Gropingly*] Why, I—I said—I remember saying, are you studying hard, Jim? Why? You're not mad at that, are you?

JIM—No, Honey. What made you think I was mad? Go to bed now.

ELLA—[*Obediently*] Yes, Jim. [*She passes behind the portières.* JIM *stares before him. Suddenly her head is thrust out at the side of the portières. Her face is again that of a vindictive maniac*] Nigger! [*The face disappears—she can be heard running away, laughing with cruel satisfaction.* JIM *bows his head on his outstretched arms but he is too stricken for tears.*]

CURTAIN

Scene 3

The same, six months later. The sun has just gone down. The Spring twilight sheds a vague, gray light about the room, picking out the Congo mask on the stand by the window. The walls have shrunken in still more, the ceiling now barely clears the people's heads, the furniture and the characters appear enormously magnified. Law books are stacked in two great piles on each side of the table. ELLA *comes in from the right, the carving-knife in her hand. She is pitifully thin, her face is wasted, but her eyes glow with a mad energy, her movements are abrupt and spring-like. She looks stealthily about the room, then advances and stands before the mask, her arms akimbo, her attitude one of crazy mockery, fear and bravado. She is dressed in the red dressing-gown, grown dirty and ragged now, and is in her bare feet.*

ELLA—I'll give you the laugh, wait and see! [*Then in a confidential tone*] He thought I was asleep! He called, Ella, Ella—but I kept my eyes shut, I pretended to snore. I fooled him good. [*She gives a little hoarse laugh*] This is the first time he's dared to leave me alone for months and months. I've been wanting to talk to you every day but this is the only chance— [*With sudden violence—flourishing her knife*] What're you grinning about, you dirty nigger, you? How dare you grin at me?

I guess you forget what you are! That's always the way. Be kind to you, treat you decent, and in a second you've got a swelled head, you think you're somebody, you're all over the place putting on airs, why, it's got so I can't even walk down the street without seeing niggers, niggers everywhere. Hanging around, grinning, grinning—going to school—pretending they're white—taking examinations—[*She stops, arrested by the word, then suddenly*] That's where he's gone—down to the mail-box—to see if there's a letter from the Board—telling him—But why is he so long? [*She calls pitifully*] Jim! [*Then in a terrified whimper*] Maybe he's passed! Maybe he's passed! [*In a frenzy*] No! No! He can't! I'd kill him! I'd kill myself! [*Threatening the Congo mask*] It's you who're to blame for this! Yes, you! Oh, I'm on to you! [*Then appealingly*] But why d'you want to do this to us? What have I ever done wrong to you? What have you got against me? I married you, didn't I? Why don't you let Jim alone? Why don't you let him be happy as he is—with me? Why don't you let me be happy? He's white, isn't he— the whitest man that ever lived? Where do you come in to interfere? Black! Black! Black as dirt! You've poisoned me! I can't wash myself clean! Oh, I hate you! I hate you! Why don't you let Jim and I be happy? [*She sinks down in his chair, her arms outstretched on the table. The door from the hall is slowly opened and* JIM *appears. His bloodshot, sleepless eyes stare from deep hollows. His expression is one of crushed numbness. He holds an open letter in his hand.*]

JIM—[*Seeing* ELLA—*in an absolutely dead voice*] Honey—I thought you were asleep.

ELLA—[*Starts and wheels about in her chair*] What's that? You got—you got a letter—?

JIM—[*Turning to close the door after him*] From the Board of Examiners for admission to the Bar, State of New York— God's country! [*He finishes up with a chuckle of ironic self-pity so spent as to be barely audible.*]

ELLA—[*Writhing out of her chair like some fierce animal, the knife held behind her— with fear and hatred*] You didn't—you didn't—you didn't pass, did you?

JIM—[*Looking at her wildly*] Pass? Pass? [*He begins to chuckle and laugh between sentences and phrases, rich, Negro laughter, but heartbreaking in its mocking grief*] Good Lord, child, how come you can ever imagine such a crazy idea? Pass? Me? Jim Crow Harris? Nigger Jim Harris—become a full-fledged Member of the Bar! Why the mere notion of it is enough to kill you with laughing! It'd be against all natural laws, all human right and justice. It'd be miraculous, there'd be earthquakes and catastrophes, the seven Plagues'd come again and locusts'd devour all the money in the banks, the second Flood'd come roaring and Noah'd fall overboard, the sun'd drop out of the sky like a ripe fig, and the Devil'd perform miracles, and God'd be tipped head first right out of the Judgment seat! [*He laughs, maudlinly uproarious.*]

ELLA—[*Her face beginning to relax, to light up*] Then you—you didn't pass?

JIM—[*Spent—giggling and gasping idiotically*] Well, I should say not! I should certainly say not!

ELLA—[*With a cry of joy, pushes all the lawbooks crashing to the floor—then with childish happiness she grabs* JIM *by both hands and dances up and down*] Oh Jim, I knew it! I knew you couldn't! Oh, I'm so glad, Jim! I'm so happy! You're still my old Jim—and I'm so glad! [*He looks at her dazedly, a fierce rage slowly gathering on his face. She dances away from him. His eyes follow her. His hands clench. She stands in front of the mask—triumphantly*] There! What did I tell you? I told you I'd give you the laugh! [*She begins to laugh with wild unrestraint, grabs the mask from its place, sets it in the middle of the table and plunging the knife down through it pins it to the table*] There! Who's got the laugh now?

JIM—[*His eyes bulging—hoarsely*] You devil! You white devil woman! [*In a terrible roar, raising his fists above her head*] You devil!

ELLA—[*Looking up at him with a bewildered cry of terror*] Jim! [*Her appeal recalls him to himself. He lets his arms slowly drop to his sides, bowing his head.* ELLA *points tremblingly to the mask*] It's all right, Jim! It's dead. The devil's dead. See! It couldn't live—unless you passed. If you'd passed it would have lived in you. Then I'd have had to kill you, Jim, don't you see —or it would have killed me. But now I've killed it. [*She pats his hand*] So you needn't ever be afraid any more, Jim.

JIM—[*Dully*] I've got to sit down, Honey. I'm tired. I haven't had much chance for sleep in so long—[*He slumps down in the chair by the table.*]

ELLA—[*Sits down on the floor beside him and holds his hand. Her face is gradually regaining an expression that is happy, childlike and pretty*] I know, Jim! That was my fault. I wouldn't let you sleep. I couldn't let you. I kept thinking if he sleeps good then he'll be sure to study good and then he'll pass—and the devil'll win!

JIM—[*With a groan*] Don't, Honey!

ELLA—[*With a childish grin*] That was why I carried that knife around—[*She frowns —puzzled*]—one reason—to keep you from studying and sleeping by scaring you.

JIM—I wasn't scared of being killed. I was scared of what they'd do to you after.

ELLA—[*After a pause—like a child*] Will God forgive me, Jim?

JIM—Maybe He can forgive what you've done to me; and maybe He can forgive what I've done to you; but I don't see how He's going to forgive—Himself.

ELLA—I prayed and prayed. When you were away taking the examinations and I was alone with the nurse, I closed my eyes and pretended to be asleep but I was praying with all my might: O, God, don't let Jim pass!

JIM—[*With a sob*] Don't, Honey, don't! For the good Lord's sake! You're hurting me!

ELLA—[*Frightenedly*] How, Jim? Where? [*Then after a pause—suddenly*] I'm sick, Jim. I don't think I'll live long.

JIM—[*Simply*] Then I won't either. Somewhere yonder maybe — together — our luck'll change. But I wanted—here and now—before you—we—I wanted to prove to you—to myself—to become a full-fledged Member—so you could be proud— [*He stops. Words fail and he is beyond tears.*]

ELLA—[*Brightly*] Well, it's all over, Jim. Everything'll be all right now. [*Chattering along*] I'll be just your little girl, Jim—and you'll be my little boy—just as we used to be, remember, when we were beaux; and I'll put shoe blacking on my face and pretend I'm black and you can put chalk on your face and pretend you're white just as we used to do— and we can play marbles—Only you mustn't all the time be a boy. Sometimes you must be my old kind Uncle Jim who's been with us for years and years. Will you, Jim?

JIM—[*With utter resignation*] Yes, Honey.

ELLA—And you'll never, never, never, never leave me, Jim?

JIM—Never, Honey.

ELLA—'Cause you're all I've got in the world—and I love you, Jim. [*She kisses his hand as a child might, tenderly and gratefully.*]

JIM—[*Suddenly throws himself on his knees and raises his shining eyes, his transfigured face*] Forgive me, God—and make me worthy! Now I see Your Light again! Now I hear Your Voice! [*He begins to weep in an ecstasy of religious humility*] Forgive me, God, for blaspheming You! Let this fire of burning suffering purify me of selfishness and make me worthy of the child You send me for the woman You take away!

ELLA—[*Jumping to her feet—excitedly*] Don't cry, Jim! You mustn't cry! I've got only a little time left and I want to play. Don't be old Uncle Jim now. Be my little boy Jim. Pretend you're Painty Face and I'm Jim Crow. Come and play!

JIM—[*Still deeply exalted*] Honey, Honey, I'll play right up to the gates of Heaven with you! [*She tugs at one of his hands, laughingly trying to pull him up from his knees as*

THE CURTAIN FALLS

THE GRAMMARIAN AND HIS LANGUAGE

BY EDWARD SAPIR

THE normal man of intelligence has something of a contempt for linguistic studies, convinced as he is that nothing can well be more useless. Such minor usefulness as he concedes to them is of a purely instrumental nature. French is worth studying because there are French books that are worth reading. Greek is worth studying—if it is—because a few plays and a few passages of verse, written in that curious and extinct vernacular, have still the power to disturb our hearts—if indeed they have. For the rest, there are excellent translations.

Now, it is a notorious fact that the linguist is not necessarily very deeply interested in the abiding things that language has done for us. He handles languages very much as the zoölogist handles dogs. The zoölogist examines the dog carefully, then he dissects him in order to examine him still more carefully, and finally, noting resemblances between him and his cousins, the wolf and the fox, and differences between him and his more distant relations, the cat and the bear, he assigns him his place in the evolutionary scheme of animated nature, and has done. Only as a polite visitor, not as a zoölogist, is he even mildly interested in Towzer's sweet parlor tricks, however fully he may recognize the fact that these tricks could never have evolved unless the dog had evolved first. To return to the philologist and the layman by whom he is judged, it is a precisely parallel indifference to the beauty wrought by the instrument which nettles the judge. And yet the cases are not altogether parallel. When Towzer has performed his tricks and when Ponto has saved the drowning man's life, they relapse, it is true, into the status of mere dog—but even the zoölogist's dog is of interest to all of us. But when Achilles has bewailed the death of his beloved Patroclus and Clytæmnestra has done her worst, what are we to do with the Greek aorists that are left on our hands? There is a traditional mode of procedure which arranges them into patterns. It is called grammar. The man who is in charge of grammar and is called a grammarian is regarded by all plain men as a frigid and dehumanized pedant.

It is not difficult to understand the very pallid status of linguistics in America. The purely instrumental usefulness of language study is recognized, of course, but there is not and cannot be in this country that daily concern with foreign modes of expression that is so natural on the continent of Europe, where a number of languages jostle each other in every-day life. In the absence of a strong practical motive for linguistic pursuits the remoter, more theoretical, motives are hardly given the opportunity to flower. But it would be a profound mistake to ascribe our current indifference to philological matters entirely to the fact that English alone serves us well enough for all practical purposes. There is something about language itself, or rather about linguistic differences, that offends the American spirit. That spirit is rationalistic to the very marrow of its bone. Consciously, if not unconsciously, we are inclined to impatience with any object or idea or system of things which cannot give a four-square reckoning of itself in terms of reason and purpose. We see this spirit pervading our whole scientific outlook. If psychology and sociology are popular sciences in America today, that is mainly due to the prevailing feeling that they are convertible into the cash values of effective education, effective advertising, and social betterment. Even here, there is, to the American, something immoral about a psychological truth which will not do pedagogical duty, something wasteful about a sociological item which can be neither applied nor condemned. If we apply this rationalistic test to language, it is found singularly wanting. After all, language is merely a lever to get thoughts "across." Our business instinct tells us that the multiplication of levers, all busy on the same job, is poor economy. Thus, one way of "spitting it out" becomes as good as another. If other nationalities find themselves using other levers, that is their affair. The fact of language, in other words, is an unavoidable irrelevance, not a problem to intrigue the inquiring mind.

II

There are two ways, it seems, to give linguistics its requisite dignity as a science. It may be treated as history or it may be studied descriptively and comparatively as form. Neither point of view augurs well for the arousing of American interest. History has always to be something else before it is taken seriously. Otherwise it is "mere" history. If we could show that certain general linguistic changes are correlated with stages of cultural evolution, we would come appreciably nearer securing linguistics a hearing, but the slow modifications that eat into the substance and the form of speech, and that gradually remold it entirely do not seem to run parallel to any scheme of cultural evolution yet proposed. Since "biological" or evolutionary history is the only kind of history for which we have a genuine respect, the history of language is left out in the cold as another one of those unnecessary sequences of events which German erudition is in the habit of worrying about.

But before pinning our faith to linguistics as an exploration into form, we might cast an appealing glance at the psychologist, for he is likely to prove a useful ally. He has himself looked into the subject of language, which he finds to be a kind of "behavior," a rather specialized type of functional adaptation, yet not so specialized but that it may be declared to be a series of laryngeal habits. We may go even further, if we select the right kind of psychologist to help us, and have thought itself put in its place as a merely "subvocal laryngeating." If these psychological contributions to the study of the nature of speech do not altogether explain the Greek aorists bequeathed to us by classical poets, they are at any rate very flattering to philology. Unfortunately the philologist cannot linger long with the psychologist's rough and ready mechanisms. They may make shift for an introduction to his science, but his real problems are such as few psychologists have clearly envisaged, though it is not unlikely that psychology may have much to say about them when it has gained strength and delicacy. The psychological problem which most interests the linguist is that of the inner structure of language, in terms of unconscious psychic processes, not that of the individual's adaptation to this traditionally conserved structure. It goes without saying, however, that the two problems are not independent of each other.

To say in so many words that the noblest task of linguistics is to understand language as form rather than as function or as historical process is not to say that it can be understood as form alone. The formal configuration of speech at any particular time and place is the result of a long and complex historical development, which, in turn, is unintelligible without constant reference to functional factors. Form is even more liable to be stigmatized as "mere" than the historical process which shapes it. For our characteristically pragmatic American attitude, forms in themselves seem to have little or no reality, and it is for this reason that we so often fail to divine them or to realize into what new patterns ideas and institutions are balancing themselves or tending to do so. Now, it is very probable that the poise which goes with culture is largely due to the habitual appreciation of the formal outlines and formal intricacies of experience. Where life is tentative and experimental, where ideas and sentiments are constantly protruding gaunt elbows out of an inherited stock of meagre, inflexible patterns, instead of graciously bending them to their own uses, form is necessarily felt as a burden and a tyranny instead of the gentle embrace it should be. Perhaps it is not too much to say that the lack of culture in America is in some way responsible for the unpopularity of linguistic studies, for these demand at one and the same time an intense appreciation of a given form of expression and a readiness to accept a great variety of possible forms.

The outstanding fact about any language is its formal completeness. This is as true of a primitive language, like Eskimo or Hottentot, as it is of the carefully recorded and standardized languages of our great cultures. By "formal completeness" I mean a profoundly significant peculiarity which is easily overlooked. Each language has a well defined and exclusive phonetic system with which it carries on its work and, more than that, all of its expressions, from the most habitual to the merely potential, are fitted into a deft tracery of prepared forms from which there is no escape. These forms establish a definite relational feeling or attitude towards all possible contents of expression and, through them, towards all possible contents of experience, in so far, of course, as experience is capable of expression in linguistic terms. To put this matter of the formal completeness of speech in somewhat different words, we may say that a language is so constructed that no matter what any speaker of it may desire to communicate, no matter how original or bizarre his idea or his fancy, the language is prepared to do his work. He will never need to create new forms or to force

upon his language a new formal orientation—unless, poor man, he is haunted by the form-feeling of another language and is subtly driven to the unconscious distortion of the one speech-system on the analogy of the other.

The world of linguistic forms, held within the framework of a given language, is a complete system of reference, very much as a number system is a complete system of quantitative reference or as a set of geometrical axes of coördinates is a complete system of reference to all points of a given space. The mathematical analogy is by no means as fanciful as it appears to be. To pass from one language to another is psychologically parallel to passing from one geometrical system of reference to another. The environing world which is referred to is the same for either language; the world of points is the same in either frame of reference. But the formal method of approach to the expressed item of experience, as to the given point of space, is so different that the resulting feeling of orientation can be the same neither in the two languages nor in the two frames of reference. Entirely distinct, or at least measurably distinct, formal adjustments have to be made and these differences have their psychological correlates.

Formal completeness has nothing to do with the richness or the poverty of the vocabulary. It is sometimes convenient or, for practical reasons, necessary for the speakers of a language to borrow words from foreign sources as the range of their experience widens. They may extend the meanings of words which they already possess, create new words out of native resources on the analogy of existing terms, or take over from another people terms to apply to the new conceptions which they are introducing. None of these processes affects the form of the language, any more than the enriching of a certain portion of space by the introduction of new objects affects the geometrical form of that region as defined by an accepted mode of reference. It would be absurd to say that Kant's

"Critique of Pure Reason" could be rendered forthwith into the unfamiliar accents of Eskimo or Hottentot, and yet it would be absurd in but a secondary degree. What is really meant is that the culture of these primitive folk has not advanced to the point where it is of interest to them to form abstract conceptions of a philosophical order. But it is not absurd to say that there is nothing in the formal peculiarities of Hottentot or of Eskimo which would obscure the clarity or hide the depth of Kant's thought—indeed, it may be suspected that the highly synthetic and periodic structure of Eskimo would more easily bear the weight of Kant's terminology than his native German. Further, to move to a more positive vantage point, it is not absurd to say that both Hottentot and Eskimo possess all the formal apparatus that is required to serve as matrix for the expression of Kant's thought. If these languages have not the requisite Kantian vocabulary, it is not the languages that are to be blamed but the Eskimos and Hottentots themselves. The languages as such are quite hospitable to the addition of a philosophic load to their lexical stock-in-trade.

The unsophisticated natives, having no occasion to speculate on the nature of causation, have probably no word that adequately translates our philosophic term *causation*, but this shortcoming is purely and simply a matter of vocabulary and of no interest whatever from the standpoint of linguistic form. From this standpoint the term *causation* is merely one out of an indefinite number of examples illustrating a certain pattern of expression. Linguistically—in other words, as regards form-feeling—*causation* is merely a particular way of expressing the notion of "act of causing," the idea of a certain type of action conceived of as a thing, an entity. Now the form-feeling of such a word as *causation* is perfectly familiar to Eskimo and to hundreds of other primitive languages. They have no difficulty in expressing the idea of a certain activity, say "laugh" or "speak" or "run," in terms of

an entity, say *laughter* or *speech* or *running*. If the particular language under consideration cannot readily adapt itself to this type of expression, what it can do is to resolve all contexts in which such forms are used in other languages into other formal patterns that eventually do the same work. Hence, "laughter is pleasurable," "it is pleasant to laugh," "one laughs with pleasure," and so on *ad infinitum*, are functionally equivalent expressions, but they canalize into entirely distinct form-feelings. All languages are set to do all the symbolic and expressive work that language is good for, either actually or potentially. The formal technique of this work is the secret of each language.

It is very important to get some notion of the nature of this form-feeling, which is implicit in all language, however bewilderingly at variance its actual manifestations may be in different types of speech. There are many knotty problems here—and curiously elusive ones—that it will require the combined resources of the linguist, the logician, the psychologist, and the critical philosopher to clear up for us. There is one important matter that we must now dispose of. If the Eskimo and the Hottentot have no adequate notion of what we mean by causation, does it follow that their languages are incapable of expressing the causative relation? Certainly not. In English, in German, and in Greek we have certain formal linguistic devices for passing from the primary act or state to its causative correspondent, *e.g.* English *to fall, to fell*, "to cause to fall"; *wide, to widen;* German *hangen*, "to hang, be suspended"; *hängen*, "to hang, cause to be suspended"; Greek *phero*, "to carry"; *phoreo*, "to cause to carry." Now this ability to feel and express the causative relation is by no manner of means dependent on the ability to conceive of causality as such. The latter ability is conscious and intellectual in character; it is laborious, like most conscious processes, and it is late in developing. The former ability is unconscious and non-intellectual in character, exercises itself with great rapidity and with the utmost ease, and develops early in the life of the race and of the individual. We have therefore no theoretical difficulty in finding that conceptions and relations which primitive folk are quite unable to master on the conscious plane are being unconsciously expressed in their languages—and, frequently, with the utmost nicety. As a matter of fact, the causative relation, which is expressed only fragmentarily in our modern European languages, is in many primitive languages rendered with an absolutely philosophic relentlessness. In Nootka, an Indian language of Vancouver Island, there is no verb or verb form which has not its precise causative counterpart.

Needless to say, I have chosen the concept of causality solely for the sake of illustration, not because I attach an especial linguistic importance to it. Every language, we may conclude, possesses a complete and psychologically satisfying formal orientation, but this orientation is only felt in the unconscious of its speakers—is not actually, that is, consciously, known by them.

III

Our current psychology does not seem altogether adequate to explain the formation and transmission of such submerged formal systems as are disclosed to us in the languages of the world. It is usual to say that isolated linguistic responses are learned early in life and that, as these harden into fixed habits, formally analogous responses are made, when the need arises, in a purely mechanical manner, specific precedents pointing the way to new responses. We are sometimes told that these analogous responses are largely the result of reflection on the utility of the earlier ones, directly learned from the social environment. Such methods of approach see nothing in the problem of linguistic form beyond what is involved in the more and more accurate control of a certain set of muscles towards a desired end, say the hammering of a nail. I can only believe that explanations of

this type are seriously incomplete and that they fail to do justice to a certain innate striving for formal elaboration and expression and to an unconscious patterning of sets of related elements of experience.

The kind of mental processes that I am now referring to are, of course, of that compelling and little understood sort for which the name "intuition" has been suggested. Here is a field which psychology has barely touched but which it cannot ignore indefinitely. It is precisely because psychologists have not greatly ventured into these difficult reaches that they have so little of interest to offer in explanation of all those types of mental activity which lead to the problem of form, such as language, music, and mathematics. We have every reason to surmise that languages are the cultural deposits, as it were, of a vast and self-completing network of psychic processes which still remain to be clearly defined for us. Probably most linguists are convinced that the language-learning process, particularly the acquisition of a feeling for the formal set of the language, is very largely unconscious and involves mechanisms that are quite distinct in character from either sensation or reflection. There is doubtless something deeper about our feeling for form than even the majority of art theorists have divined, and it is not unreasonable to suppose that, as psychological analysis becomes more refined, one of the greatest values of linguistic study will be in the unexpected light it may throw on the psychology of intuition, this "intuition" being perhaps nothing more nor less than the "feeling" for relations.

There is no doubt that the critical study of language may also be of the most curious and unexpected helpfulness to philosophy. Few philosophers have deigned to look into the morphologies of primitive languages nor have they given the structural peculiarities of their own speech more than a passing and perfunctory attention. When one has the riddle of the universe on one's hands, such pursuits seem trivial enough, yet when it begins to be suspected that at least *some* solutions of the great riddle are elaborately round-about applications of the rules of Latin or German or English grammar, the triviality of linguistic analysis becomes less certain. To a far greater extent than the philosopher has realized, he is likely to become the dupe of his speech-forms, which is equivalent to saying that the mould of his thought, which is typically a linguistic mould, is apt to be projected into his conception of the world. Thus innocent linguistic categories may take on the formidable appearance of cosmic absolutes. If only, therefore, to save himself from philosophic verbalism, it would be well for the philosopher to look critically to the linguistic foundations and limitations of his thought. He would then be spared the humiliating discovery that many new ideas, many apparently brilliant philosophic conceptions, are little more than rearrangements of familiar words in formally satisfying patterns. In their recently published work on "The Meaning of Meaning" Messrs. Ogden and Richards have done philosophy a signal service in indicating how readily the most hard-headed thinkers have allowed themselves to be cajoled by the formal slant of their habitual mode of expression. Perhaps the best way to get behind our thought processes and to eliminate from them all the accidents or irrelevances due to their linguistic garb is to plunge into the study of exotic modes of expression. At any rate, I know of no better way to kill spurious "entities."

This brings us to the nature of language as a symbolic system, a method of referring to all possible types of experience. The natural or, at any rate, the naïve thing is to assume that when we wish to communicate a certain idea or impression, we make something like a rough and rapid inventory of the objective elements and relations involved in it, that such an inventory or analysis is quite inevitable, and that our linguistic task consists merely of the finding of the particular words and groupings of words that correspond to the terms of the objective analysis. Thus, when we observe an object of the type that we call a "stone" moving through space towards the earth, we involuntarily analyze the phenomenon into two concrete notions, that of a stone and that of an act of falling, and, relating these two notions to each other by certain formal methods proper to English, we declare that "the stone falls." We assume, naïvely enough, that this is about the only analysis that can properly be made. And yet, if we look into the way that other languages take to express this very simple kind of impression, we soon realize how much may be added to, subtracted from, or rearranged in our own form of expression without materially altering our report of the physical fact.

In German and in French we are compelled to assign "stone" to a gender category—perhaps the Freudians can tell us why this object is masculine in the one language, feminine in the other—; in Chippewa we cannot express ourselves without bringing in the apparently irrelevant fact that a stone is an inanimate object. If we find gender beside the point, the Russians may wonder why we consider it necessary to specify in every case whether a stone, or any other object, for that matter, is conceived in a definite or an indefinite manner, why the difference between "the stone" and "a stone" matters. "Stone falls" is good enough for Lenin, as it was good enough for Cicero. And if we find barbarous the neglect of the distinction as to definiteness, the Kwakiutl Indian of British Columbia may sympathize with us but wonder why we do not go a step further and indicate in some way whether the stone is visible or invisible to the speaker at the moment of speaking and whether it is nearest to the speaker, the person addressed, or some third party. "That would no doubt sound fine in Kwakiutl, but we are too busy!" And yet we insist on expressing the singularity of the falling object, where the Kwakiutl Indian, differing from the Chippewa, can generalize and make a statement which would apply equally well to one or several stones. Moreover, he need not specify the time of the fall. The Chinese get on with a minimum of explicit formal statement and content themselves with a frugal "stone fall."

These differences of analysis, one may object, are merely formal; they do not invalidate the necessity of the fundamental concrete analysis of the situation into "stone" and what the stone does, which in this case is "fall." But this necessity, which we feel so strongly, is an illusion. In the Nootka language the combined impression of a stone falling is quite differently analyzed. The stone need not be specifically referred to, but a single word, a verb form, may be used which is in practice not essentially more ambiguous than our English sentence. This verb form consists of two main elements, the first indicating general movement or position of a stone or stone-like object, while the second refers to downward direction. We can get some hint of the feeling of the Nootka word if we assume the existence of an intransitive verb "to stone," referring to the position or movement of a stone-like object. Then our sentence, "the stone falls," may be reassembled into something like "it stones down." In this type of expression the thing-quality of the stone is implied in the generalized verbal element "to stone," while the specific kind of motion which is given us in experience when a stone falls is conceived as separable into a generalized notion of the movement of a class of objects and a more specific one of direction. In other words, while Nootka has no difficulty whatever in describing the fall of a stone, it has no verb that truly corresponds to our *fall*.

It would be possible to go on indefinitely with such examples of incommensurable analyses of experience in different languages. The upshot of it all would be to make very real to us a kind of relativity that is generally hidden from us by our naïve acceptance of fixed habits of speech as guides to an objective understanding of the nature of experience. This is the relativity of concepts or, as it might be called, the relativity of the form of thought. It is not so difficult to grasp as the physical relativity of Einstein nor is it as disturbing to our sense of security as the psychological relativity of Jung, which is barely beginning to be understood, but it is perhaps more readily evaded than these. For its understanding the comparative data of linguistics are a *sine qua non*. It is the appreciation of the relativity of the form of thought which results from linguistic study that is perhaps the most liberalizing thing about it. What fetters the mind and benumbs the spirit is ever the dogged acceptance of absolutes.

To a certain type of mind linguistics has also that profoundly serene and satisfying quality which inheres in mathematics and in music and which may be described as the creation out of simple elements of a self-contained universe of forms. Linguistics has neither the sweep nor the instrumental power of mathematics, nor has it the universal æsthetic appeal of music. But under its crabbed, technical, appearance there lies hidden the same classical spirit, the same freedom in restraint, which animates mathematics and music at their purest. This spirit is antagonistic to the romanticism which is rampant in America today and which debauches so much of our science with its frenetic desire.

THE PART-TIME MISSIONARY

BY HOWELL SYKES

WHAT is a part-time missionary? A part-time missionary is a man of God, financed and sent to China by the churches of the Western world, who spends part of his time saving the immortal souls of the yellow heathen, and the rest buying from these same heathen their jewelry, mandarin coats, mah jong sets and other such trifles, and shipping them home to sell at a profit. No mission board, of course, knowingly sends part-time missionaries to the foreign field, but China is far away, and mission boards are quite generally made up of pious and ignorant old maids, male and female. Less pious, perhaps, but even more ignorant are the faithful, lay and clerical, who provide the funds. The picture painted by the pastor of the Main Street church when he begs contributions for the foreign missions box is drawn from inspiration alone. Knowledge, in such high matters, is held to be unnecessary; God will give him light and power. Perhaps so, but God so far has given him distressingly little geography, and even less understanding of the missionary.

The word China, to the business man sitting next the aisle in the fifth pew, brings up a vague, shadowy picture. In the foreground is a rolling yellow river; on the bank stands a little group of mud huts, small and dark within. It is late afternoon. Suddenly a shout goes up from a watcher by the river. A figure on a toiling donkey comes slowly up through the middle distance, and halts by the squalid huts. It is a missionary, with collar reversed and pie hat at a pious angle, all true to stage and movie tradition. More shouts follow. A crowd gathers around the bringer of light;

156

he draws from a pocket of his long-tailed black coat the magic Book; in a deep solemn voice he reads the Word. The pig-tailed listeners huddle around him like sheep about a shepherd. The voice stops; the hands are raised in benediction; the heathen heads bow low to a new and mightier power. As the round tones of the voice raised in prayer mingle with the murmur of the mighty river, a golden-throated bell rings in a Chinese temple nearby, as though ringing out its last call to heathen worshippers—a call unanswered by the little group kneeling about the bringer of light. The sun sets, shedding a warm red glow over a hazy background in which assorted Fujiyamas, as seen in Japanese prints, are the predominant feature. It is a restful picture. The business man is content to drop his quarter or dollar into the box. From that time on he feels that he is a part of a mighty and good work.

It is a pretty picture, but far from true. There are, of course, some missionaries living back in the hills of China under conditions that are rightly described as primitive, but for every one of them there are twenty city dwellers, and it is among the latter that the part-timers flourish. These city missionaries live under conditions far more pleasant than those confronting most of their brethren in the home churches. Life in the seaboard cities of China, indeed, is often more comfortable and amusing than in even our largest cities at home. Good servants are to be had by the month for the equivalent of five American dollars, and the food of each servant comes out of his pay. Practically all missionary compounds and private homes have electric lights, and a large number have hot and cold running water. Aided by the low exchange of the current Mexican dollars, by the lower prices, and by the amazing cheapness of labor, a missionary who at home would be nightly helping his wife with the dishes and putting little Teddy to bed is able to have three or four servants, a Chinese nurse-maid for his heir, and a modern and well-equipped home to house his staff, his supply of tracts and Bibles, and his family.

I do not say that this is wrong. It is, indeed, only right that the ambassadors of God should have all the comforts of home, and more. I do say, however, that the facts should be known by those who provide the money for these comforts, and that the drivel emanating from the pulpit whenever a foreign mission fund is to be raised should be stopped. It is not fair to take comforts from the widow and the workingwoman at home by means of an untrue appeal,—a fanciful picture on a false canvas—, and give them to missionaries living in luxury beyond the dreams of the donors.

II

So much for the privations that the brave missionary suffers. What about the dangers? They are always good for a moving paragraph in a begging sermon. As a matter of sober fact, the American missionary holds the safest job in the Far East. He is, by treaty and understanding, a piece of the sacred soil of the Republic. Hands off! The Legation is bound to protect him wherever he goes, and extricate him from whatever troubles his zeal may bring upon him. Not so the business man, the tourist, and the explorer and scientist in search of knowledge. These are always turned away from bandit-suspected districts. "At your own risk!" is the password for them. "The Legation will take no official responsibility." But the missionary goes everywhere, preaching his gospel of peace with security in his heart, knowing that the bayonets of his country are backing him, that the Chris-

tian world will demand swift revenge if he be harmed. China has paid out too much good silver in harsh indemnities to make a practice of harming missionaries; she has lost too much valuable land through the rash and thoughtless acts of heathen Buddhists and damned followers of Confucius. Christians, the Chinese have learned by bitter experience, preach turn the other cheek, but practice a tooth for a tooth.

But the missionaries have many other advantages. They are sent out for long periods at the home churches' expense; they are provided with funds while learning the language,—an accomplishment which takes one or two years' time—; they are subsidized while they familiarize themselves with the country and its people. This period of study and observation is essential if they are to do their saving of the heathen efficiently—but it is also valuable to anyone who wishes to do business with the Chinese. The undisguised business man pays for a like training from his own pocket, looking upon the loss of time and money as a means to a future gain. Under the circumstances, have the missionaries any right to use their special advantages for their own benefit? The business people in China say no. But the missionaries see no reason why they should not pick up a little profit for themselves in a business way, so long as it does not interfere with their religious work. Thus there is a distinct line between the missionaries in China and the Americans representing business. It is a sharp line, and it breeds suspicion and dislike.

Can you imagine a Methodist minister in Iowa, after finishing his Sunday sermon, and taking a bowl of jelly to a sick parishioner, doffing his clerical attire and donning a butcher's apron behind the counter of his neat little butcher shop? Would you dare accuse him of short weight, no matter how dwarfed the steak? The part-time missionary in China is just such a consecrated and protected trader. He can go to places the business man cannot go to; he can drive bargains in the native tongue. Because of his preaching he gains the confidence of the Chinese; because of the Legation protection he has access to remote and cheap sources of supply; because he has the language he is able to drive sharp bargains. Therefore, he gets the cream of the business in Chinese silks, jewels, jades and curios. The business man knows this, and it irks him exceedingly. He pays an income tax at home, and he carries the regular overhead expenses of a legitimate business, —and yet he must compete with the missionary, whose expenses are nil. The missionary can pay a higher price for an article and yet make more profit on it than his business rival. Do you wonder at the latter's lack of cordiality and good fellowship?

III

The part-time missionary is a product, not of original sin, but of his environment. I am sure that nearly every young man who goes to China to do religious work is actuated, at least at the start, by the highest motives and filled with holy zeal. He is prepared to sacrifice all—comforts, health, life itself, if need be—on the foreign field of battle beneath the standard of the Cross. The trouble comes when he finds that all this ardor is wasted. He expects to live in a mud hut, and gets a home as comfortable as the one he has forsaken for the great cause, and several servants to boot. He expects privations and dangers, but meets with none, save maybe an occasional train holdup, and then he is the first to be rescued. He expects to find on the faces of brother missionaries the lean and hungry look of martyrdom; he finds instead men grown fat on easy living, men full of practicable ideas for spending church money, men with their heads filled with schemes. He is taken aback at first, but he is human. Soon he adjusts himself, gets on to the ropes. Eventually he belongs.

I had a friend go to China three years ago, a very fine friend, with ideals higher than mine, with a purpose that I respected but could not grasp. He went as a mis-sionary, supported by missionary funds, with the avowed purpose of studying the Chinese, their language and character. After his three years were over he intended to return to a theological seminary in New York, there to prepare for the ministry. Next on his program was his triumphant return to China, rich both in theology and in knowledge of China's needs. A worthy program! Alas for it!

His first year he earnestly sought to stand by his convictions. Around him were fellow missionaries openly engaged in buying goods to send home for friends to sell. He disapproved of their actions. He told them so. They said that in that case it wouldn't be right for him to do it, and he went on with his studies. But at the beginning of his second year he was sending home things for his mother to sell to his friends. Nothing in a business way, you understand, just a little money-saving for his friends at home. He took no profit. At the end of the second year the volume of his trade had grown too large for his mother to handle, and through her he got some home town friends to handle it. These friends, of course, wanted a little slice for their trouble. He gave it to them, and then began to take a little slice for himself.

The story has a sad ending. The third year he was too busy to keep up with all his Chinese-English Bible classes, so he gave half of them to a fellow worker fresh from home, who needed the experience anyway. He arranged his mission classes so that they would all come in the morning, or, in other words, he rearranged his missionarying to suit his business. He left for home a few months ago, after making arrangements with a fellow Christian to ship to him on order. They are using Bentley's Code, I think. The last shipment was valued at $800 gold. So endeth a prospective propagator of the faith. He now plans to go formally into the import-export business. He will be back in China next year, after he has established connections in the States, but not as a holy clerk.

Now, I do not say that all the American missionaries in all the big cities of China carry on this sort of business. There are always some real missionaries among them. However, I do know that in Canton, Shanghai, Hankow, Tientsin, Nanking and Peking there are enough engaged in exporting Chinese goods, either in large or small quantities, to give the Chinese the impression that doing it is the general rule. A conversation that I lately had with a Chinese scholar,—a product of the old régime, and a former officer under imperial rule,—revealed the fact that he and other men of his class looked upon the missionaries from the West as simply business agents in disguise. The conversation was in Chinese, and his descriptions were most picturesque and forceful. First, he said, the missionary arrives in China in the form of a chrysalis, wrapped in folds of dogma, webs of creed, dull black, dead to the bright world of colors—and dollars. Next comes the slow awakening—a few awkward bargains, a mandarin coat here, a mah jong set there. A weary wait of four months,—doubts, prickings of conscience. Then a letter comes. The mandarin coat and mah jong set were received in good condition, and sold for three times their cost. The bread cast upon the waters has returned, and with it a thick golden crust. The missionary stirs in his cocoon. Next the swift unfolding of financial wings, the shedding of the now encumbering, once nurturing chrysalis, and then the quick upward flight into the gay world of finance, where every American dollar equals two Chinese.

My Chinese friend named several of the prominent foreign business men of the city. Some were engaged in trade, others in real estate or insurance. All that he named were formerly either missionaries or Y. M. C. A. secretaries. One of them, who now owns a good deal of valuable land in the city, is still a sort of advisory missionary when pressure of business permits. The Chinese dislike all this. They want to deal with business people when they have business, and with religious people when they feel the itch for soul-saving. They cannot understand the combination that is found in the modern American missionary. Many years ago they arrived at the famous conclusion found in the missionaries' Good Book: "Ye cannot serve two masters." This "God-loves-you-How-much-for-the-mah-chong-set?" dualism does not impress them as being a working combination. They are wondering what we want to do most—give them the Lord God Jehovah or get the mah jong set.

The Chinese knows how to deal with business men. If he is bested in a deal he takes it as part of the game and resolves to get the better of somebody else to make up for the loss. He is, in brief, quite like the Western business man. That is why the missionary in business puzzles and distresses him. If he puts over a clever deal and makes a little money at the expense of a missionary he is immediately assailed as being ungrateful to those who have left home and loved ones to come and save him from damnation. He is held up as having bitten the hand that feeds him. So he is growing very cynical.

IV

In Peking even the wives of the missionaries have gone in for the export business. They have a *gung chong*, or work shop, in which more than a hundred Chinese girls work daily. The wages and conditions, it must be said, are a little better than in the secular *gung chongs*. The products of the establishment—tea-sets, napkins, doilies, etc.—are shipped home in large lots to be sold to department stores. The missionary women defend themselves thus: "We provide work for girls who might not otherwise have work; we pay well, better than (with a sniff) business *gung chongs;* we have a religious atmosphere in the place."

Let us examine this defence. They *do* provide work; that is true. But it is only skilled work, and if the mere desire to give work were their motive, it would be much more sensible to give unskilled work to men with dependent families. They pay well; that is true also—a little more, maybe, than other places,—and thereby they get the best workers. They can do this because the women running the shops are the wives of missionaries, and their husbands are paid from home. Therefore they, the wives, can work for much less and still make more money than secular entrepreneurs. Finally, "we have a religious atmosphere." This consists, in one shop I visited, of a fifteen minute Bible reading every noon, while the sewing girls are eating their lunch.

Where does the money earned by this *gung chong* go? It all comes back, you are told, and into the fund for further helping the poor. But some skeptics are not so sure. A good deal of the stuff is sold on the ground to missionaries at cost prices, and the buyers ship it home as individuals. That profit, I fear, does not come back. However, where it actually goes is not the main point. No matter where it goes, you will never convince a Chinaman that it goes into further philanthropic work for the Chinese. And, after all, it is what the Chinese think that counts. Even assuming that these missionary wives have the best intentions in the world—and I, for one, am willing to grant them—the fact remains that they are doing the cause of Christianity a great harm so long as the Chinese will not credit them with those intentions. Meanwhile, they are in the disfavor of all other interests in China because they use the advantages provided them by their religious position to further themselves in business dealings. As a result of these advantages they can do business on a cheaper basis, and so the secular export merchant thinks they offer him unfair competition. What they do, he argues, is unfair to him in China, to the legitimate importer at home, and more important still, to the little old lady who drops her dime in the foreign mission box as she leaves the church every Wednesday night. She does not put in that dime thinking to pay for Chinese lessons for a person who will later use his knowledge to bargain for jade necklaces and send them home at a fat profit. She drops it there thinking that she is saving some poor Chinaman from hell. Is it too much to ask that she be told plainly what her mite actually does?

EDITORIAL

Perhaps the chief victims of Prohibition, in the long run, will turn out to be the Federal judges. I do not argue here, of course, that drinking bootleg liquors will kill them bodily; I merely suggest that enforcing the unjust and insane provisions of the Volstead Act will rob them of all their old dignity. A dozen years ago, or even half a dozen years ago, a Federal judge was perhaps the most dignified and respected official yet flourishing under our democracy. The plain people, many years before, had lost all respect for lawmakers, whether Federal, State or municipal, and, save for the President himself, they had very little respect left for the gentlemen of the executive arm, high or low. More, they had begun to view the State judiciary very biliously, and showed no sign of surprise when a member of it was taken in judicial adultery. But for the Federal judges they still continued to have a high veneration, and for plain reasons. *Imprimis*, the Federal judges sat for life, and thus did not have to climb down from their benches at intervals and clamor obscenely for votes. Secondly, the laws that they were told off to enforce, and especially the criminal laws, were few in number, simple in character, and thoroughly in accord with almost universal ideas of right and wrong. No citizen in his right mind had much sympathy for the felons who were shipped to Atlanta each morning by the marshals of the Federal courts—chiefly counterfeiters, fraudulent bankrupts, adulterators of food and drugs, get-rich-quick swindlers, thieving letter-carriers, crooked army officers, and so on. Public sentiment was almost unanimously behind the punishment of such rogues, and it rejoiced that that punishment was in the hands of men who carried on the business in an austere manner, without fear or favor.

I describe a Golden Age, now lamentably closed. The Uplift in its various lovely forms has completely changed the character of the work done by a Federal judge. Once the dispenser of varieties of law that only scoundrels questioned, he is now the harassed and ludicrous dispenser of varieties of law that only idiots approve. It was the Espionage Act, I suppose, that first brought him to this new and dreadful office, but it is Prohibition—whether of wine-bibbing, of drug-taking, of interstate week-ending, or of what not—that has carried him beyond the bounds of what, to most normal men, is common decency. His typical job today, as a majority of the plain people see it, especially in the big cities, is simply to punish men who have refused or been unable to pay the bribes demanded by Prohibition enforcement officers. In other words, he is now chiefly apprehended by the public, not as a scourge of rascals, but as an agent of rascals and a scourge of peaceable men. He gets a great deal more publicity than he used to get in his palmy days, but it is publicity of a sort that rapidly undermines his dignity. Unfortunately for him, but perhaps very fortunately for what remains of civilized government among us, the plain people have never been able to grasp the difference between law and justice. To them the two things are one—or ought to be. So the fact that the judge is bound by law to enforce all the intolerable provisions of the Volstead Act, including even its implicit provision that men wearing its badges shall get a fair percentage upon every transaction in bootlegging—this fact does not relieve the judge himself of responsibility for the ensuing oppressions. The only thing that

161

the vulgar observe is that justice has departed from his court room.

If this were all, of course, it might be possible to dismiss the whole matter on the ground that the public is an ass. That men of the highest worth are not always respected, even when they wear official robes, is a commonplace. But in the present case there is more to it than merely that. Not a few of the Federal judges have begun to show signs that the noisome work that has been forced upon them has begun to achieve its inevitable subjective effects; in other words, not a few begin to attack their sneaking sense of its lack of dignity and good repute by bedizening it with moral indignation. The judicial servant of the Anti-Saloon League thus takes on some of the neo-Christian character of the League's own dervishes and sorcerers. He is not content to send some poor yokel to jail for an artificial crime that, in the view of at least 80 per cent of all Americans, is no crime at all; he must also denounce the culprit from the bench in terms fit for a man accused of arson or mayhem. Here the Freudians, perhaps, would have something to say; the great masses of the innocent and sinful, knowing nothing of Freud, observe only that the learned jurist is silly as well as unjust. There issues from that observation a generally bilious view of his office and his person. He slides slowly down a fatal chute. His day of arctic and envied eminence passes.

II

The truth is, indeed, that the decline in dignity from which the Federal judges now suffer is not wholly due to the external fact of Prohibition; it is due quite as much to their own growing pliancy and lack of professional self-respect. All that Prohibition does to them is to make brilliantly plain, even to the meanest understanding, their lamentable departure from that high integrity of purpose, that assiduous concern for justice, that jealous watchfulness over the rights of man which simple men, at all times and everywhere, like to find in the judges set over them, and which the simple men of the United States, not so long ago, saw or thought they saw in the learned ornaments of the Federal bench. Before ever Volstead emerged from the Christian Endeavor belt with his preposterous Act, confidence had begun to shake. The country had seen Federal judges who were unmistakably mountebanks; it had seen some who were, to the naked eye, indistinguishable from rascals. It had seen one step down from the highest court in the land to engage in an undignified stumping-tour, soliciting the votes of the rabble. It had seen another diligently insinuate himself into the headlines of the yellow press, in competition with Jack Dempsey and Babe Ruth. It had seen others abuse their powers of equity in the frank interest of capital, and deny the commonest justice to poor men in their clutches. And during the war it had grown accustomed to seeing the Federal bench converted into a sort of rival to the rostrum of Liberty Loan orators, with judges hurling pious objurgations at citizens accused of nothing worse than speaking their minds freely, and all pretense to fair hearings and just punishments abandoned.

True enough, a majority of the Federal judges, high and low, stood quite clear of all such buffooneries. Even in the midst of the worst hysteria of the war there were plenty who refused to be run amok by Palmer, Burleson and company. I need cite only Hand, J., and Rose, J., as admirable examples of a large number of judges who preserved their dignity 'mid the rockets' red glare. But the headlines in the newspapers had nothing to say about such judges; their blackest ink was reserved for the other kind, as it was more recently reserved for Mayer, J. That other kind gradually established a view of the Federal bench that still persists, and that is growing more and more fixed as the farce of Prohibition enforcement unrolls. It is a view which, in brief, holds that the Federal bench is no longer the most exalted and faithful protector of the liberties of the citizen, but the most relentless and inordinate foe of them—that its main purpose is not to dispense justice at all, but to get men into jail, guilty or not guilty, by fair means or foul—that to this end it is willing to lend itself to the execution of any law, however extravagant, and to support that execution with a variety of casuistry that is flatly against every ordinary conception of common sense and common decency. The Espionage Act cases, the labor injunction cases, the deportation cases, the Postal Act cases, the Mann Act cases, and now the Prohibition cases—all of these, impinging in rapid succession upon a people brought up to regard the Bill of Rights as a reality and liberty as a precious thing, have bred suspicion of the Federal courts, including especially the Supreme Court, and, on the heels of that suspicion, a positive and apparently ineradicable distrust. I doubt that the Radical fanatics who dodge about the land have ever converted any substantial body of Americans to their crazy doctrines; certainly there is not the slightest sign today of the Revolution that they were predicting for last year, and the year before. But when they have denounced the Federal courts and produced the overwhelming evidence, their shots have gone home.

III

Now and then a judge has argued, defending himself against some manifestation of popular discontent, that he is helpless—that he is the agent, not of justice, but of law. Even in the hey-dey of the Espionage Act a few were moved to make that apology from the bench, including, if I remember rightly, the judge who sentenced Debs. The distinction thus set up is one that seems clear to lawyers, but, as I have said, it seldom gets a hospitable hearing from plain men. If the latter believe anything at all it is that law without justice is an evil thing; that such law, indeed, leads inevitably to a contradiction in terms; that the highest duty of the judiciary is not to enforce it pedantically, but to evade it, vitiate it, and, if possible, destroy it. The plain man sees plenty of other sorts of law destroyed by the courts; he can't help wondering why the process is so seldom applied to statutes that violate, not merely legal apothegms, but the baldest of common sense. Thus when he beholds a Federal judge fining a man, under a constitutional amendment prohibiting the sale of intoxicating beverages, for selling a beverage that is admittedly not intoxicating, or jailing another man who has got into the dock, as everyone knows, not because he ran a still but because he refused to pay the bribe demanded by the Prohibition enforcement officer, or issuing against a third an injunction whose sole and undisguised purpose is to deprive him, by a legal swindle, of his constitutional right to a trial by a jury of his peers—when he observes such monkey-shines going on in the name of the law, is it any wonder that he concludes dismally that the law is an ass, and its agent another? In ordinary life men cannot engage in such lunatic oppressions of their fellow men without paying a penalty for it; even a police captain must be measurably more plausible and discreet. If a judge is bound by his oath to engage in them, then so much the worse for the judge. He can no more hope to be respected than a hangman can hope to be respected.

But is a judge actually so bound? I am no lawyer, but I nevertheless presume to doubt it. There were judges in 1918 who did not think themselves bound to sacrifice the Bill of Rights to the Espionage Act, and who resolutely refused to do so, and yet, so far as I know, nothing happened to them; at least one of them, to my knowledge, has been since promoted to a circuit. Why should any judge today enforce the injunction clause of the Volstead Act, which is not only not authorized by anything in the Eighteenth Amendment, but is flatly and unquestionably subversive of the Fourth, Fifth and Sixth Amendments? Its enforcement is surely not an automatic act; it involves deliberation and decision by the judge; he may refuse his injunction without offering any explanation to anyone. What would follow if he arose one day in his high pulpit, and announced simply that his court was purged of all such oblique and dishonest enactments henceforth— that he had resolved to refuse to lend himself to the schemes of blackmailers with badges, or to harass and punish free citizens in violation of their fundamental constitutional rights and their plain dignity as human beings, or, in brief, to engage in any other enterprise as a judge that he would shrink from engaging in as a good citizen and a man of honor? Would the result be impeachment? I should like to meet a Congressman insane enough to move the impeachment of such a judge! Would it be a storm of public indignation? . . . Or would it be a vociferous yell of delight?

It seems to me, indeed, that the first judge who rises to such a rebellion will be the first judge ever to become a popular hero in the Republic—that he will be elevated to the Supreme Court by a sort of acclamation, even if it is necessary to get rid of one of the sitting justices by setting fire to his gown. But, it may be said, even imagining him so elevated, the remaining eight justices will still function, and all of us know what they think of the Bill of Rights. Wouldn't such a rebel judge succumb to the system of which it was a discreet particle? Couldn't the other eight judges nullify and make a mock of his late heroic defiance? Could they, indeed? Then how? If a judge, high or low, actually called in justice to rescue a citizen from the law, what precisely could the Supreme Court do about it? I know of no appeal for the District Attorney in Federal cases, once the prisoner has been put into jeopardy; I know only of impeachment for judges who forget the lines of the farce to which they are sworn. But try to imagine the impeachment of a judge charged with punching a hole in the Volstead Act, and letting in some common justice and common decency!

So far, no such rambunctious and unprec-

edented judge has been heard of, nor do I specifically predict his advent. He may come, but probably he won't. The law is a curse to all of us, but it is a curse of special virulence to lawyers. It becomes for them a sort of discreditable vice, a stealthy and degrading superstition. It robs them of all balance, of all capacity for clear thought, of all imagination. Judges tend to show this decay of the faculties in an exaggerated form; they become mere automata, bound by arbitrary rules, precedents, the accumulated imbecilities of generations; to their primary lack of sense as lawyers they add the awful manner of bureaucrats. It is thus too much to hope for a judge showing any originality or courage; one Holmes in an era of Hardings and Coolidges is probably more than a fair allotment. But while the judges of the District Courts go on driving wild teams of jackasses through the Bill of Rights, and the rev. seniors of the Supreme Court give their approval to the business in solemn form,—sometimes, but not always, with Holmes, J., and Brandeis, J., dissenting— while all this is going on, there are black clouds rolling up from the hinterland, where the Constitution is still taught in the schools and even Methodists are bred to reverence Patrick Henry. The files of Congress already show the way the wind is blowing—constitutional amendments to drag down and denaturize the Supreme Court, simple acts to the same end, other acts providing for the election of Federal judges, yet others even more revolutionary. I know of no such proposal that has any apparent merit. Even the best of them, hamstringing the courts, would only augment the power of a Congress that is ten times worse. But so long as judges pursue fatuously the evil business of converting every citizen into a subject, demagogues will come forward with their dubious remedies, and, soon or late, unless the bench pulls up, some of these demagogues will get themselves heard.   H. L. M.

CAUGHT

BY SHERWOOD ANDERSON

IT SEEMS but yesterday, although a year has passed since that afternoon when Edward and I sat talking in a restaurant. I was staying at a small hotel in a side street in the city of New York. It had been an uncertain day with us, such days as come in any relationship. One asks something of a friend and finds him empty-handed or something is asked and a vacant look comes into one's own eyes. Two men, or a man and woman, were but yesterday very close and now they are far apart.

Edward came to lunch with me and we went to a restaurant in the neighborhood. It was of the cheap, hurried, highly-sanitary sort, shiny and white. After eating we sat on and on, looking at each other, trying to say to each other something for which we could find no words. In a day or two I would be going away to the South. Each of us felt the need of something from the other, an expression of regard perhaps. We were both engaged in the practice of the same craft—story-tellers both of us. And what fumblers! Each man fumbling often and often in materials not well enough understood—that is to say, in the lives and the drama in the lives of the people about whom the tales were told.

We sat looking at each other and, as it was now nearly three o'clock in the afternoon, we were the only people in the restaurant. Then a third man came in and sat as far away from us as possible. For some time the women waiters in the place had been looking at Edward and myself somewhat belligerently. It may have been they were employed only for the noon rush and now wanted to go home. A somewhat large woman, with her arms crossed, stood glaring at us.

As for the third man in the place, the fellow who had just come in, he had been in prison for some crime he had committed, and had but recently been let out. I do not mean to suggest that he came to Edward and myself and told his story. Indeed, he was afraid of us, and when he saw us loitering there, went to sit as far away as possible. He watched us furtively with frightened eyes. Then he ordered some food and, after eating hurriedly, went away, leaving the flavor of himself behind. He had been trying to get a job but on all sides had been defeated by his own timidity. Now, like ourselves, he wanted some place to rest, to sit with a friend, to talk, and by an odd chance I, and Edward as well, knew the fellow's thoughts while he was in the room. The devil!—he was tired and discouraged and had thought he would go into the restaurant, eat slowly, gather himself together. Perhaps Edward and myself—and the waitress with her arms crossed who wanted to get our tip and cut out to some movie show—perhaps all of us had chilled the heart of the man from prison. "Well, things are so and so. One's own heart has been chilled. You are going away to the South, eh? Well, good-by; I must be getting along."

II

I was walking in the streets of the city, that evening of November. There was snow on the roofs of buildings, but it had all been scraped off the roadways. There is a thing happens to American men. It is

165

pitiful. One walks along, going slowly along in the streets, and when one looks sharply at one's fellows something dreadful comes into the mind. There is a thing happens to the backs of the necks of American men. There is this sense of something drying, getting old without having ripened. The skin does something. One becomes conscious of the back of one's own neck and is worried. "Might not all our lives ripen like fruit—drop at the end, full-skinned and rich with color, from the tree of life, eh?" When one is in the country one looks at a tree. "Can a tree be a dead dried-up thing while it is still young? Can a tree be a neurotic?" one asks.

I had worked myself into a state of mind, as so often happens with me, and so I went out of the streets, out of the presence of all the American people hurrying along; the warmly dressed, unnecessarily weary, hurrying, hustling, half-frightened city people.

In my room I sat reading a book of the tales of Balzac. Then I had got up to prepare for dinner when there came a knock at the door and in answer to my call a man entered.

He was a fellow of perhaps forty-five, a short strongly-built broad-shouldered man with graying hair. There was in his face something of the rugged simplicity of a European peasant, perhaps. One felt he might live a long time, do hard work, and keep to the end the vigor of that body of his.

For some time I had been expecting the man to come to see me and was curious concerning him. He was an American writer, like Edward and myself, and two or three weeks before he had gone to Edward pleading. . . . Well, he had wanted to see and talk with me. Another fellow with a soul, eh?

And now, there the man stood, with his queer old boyish face. He stood in the doorway, smiling anxiously. "Were you going out? Will I be disturbing you?" I had been standing before a glass adjusting a necktie. "Come on in," I said, perhaps a little

pompously. Before sensitive people I am likely to become a bit bovine. I do not wag my tail like a dog. What I do is to moo like a cow. "Come into the warm stall and eat hay with me," I seem to myself to be saying at such times. I would really like to be a jolly friendly sort of a cuss . . . you will understand . . . "It's always fair weather, when good fellows get together" . . . that is the sort of thing I mean.

That is what I want and I can't achieve it, nor can I achieve a kind of quiet dignity that I often envy in others.

I stood with my hands fingering my tie and looked at the man in the doorway. I had thrown the book I had been reading on a small table by the bed. "The devil!—he is one of our everlastingly distraught Americans. He is too much like myself." I was tired and wanted to talk of my craft to some man who was sure of himself. Queer disconnected ideas are always popping into one's mind. Perhaps they are not so disconnected. At that moment—as I stood looking at the man in the doorway—the figure of another man came sharply to my mind. The man was a carpenter who for a time lived next door to my father's house when I was a boy in an Ohio town. He was a workman of the old sort, one who would build a house out of timber—just as it is cut into boards by a sawmill. He could make the door frames and the window frames, knew how to cut cunningly all the various joints necessary to building a house tightly in a wet, cold country.

And on Summer evenings the carpenter used to come sometimes and stand by the door of our house and talk with mother, as she was doing an ironing. He had a flair for mother, I fancy, and was always coming when father was not at home—but he never came into the house. He stood at the door speaking of his work. He always talked of his work. If he had a flair for mother and she had one for him it was kept hidden away, but one fancied that, when we children were not about, mother spoke to him of us. Our own father was not one with whom one spoke of children. Children existed but vaguely for him.

As for the carpenter, what I remembered of him on the evening in the hotel in the city of New York was just a kind of quiet assurance in his figure, remembered from boyhood. The old workman had spoken to mother of young workmen in his employ. "They aren't learning their trade properly," he said. "Everything is cut in the factories now and the young fellows get no chance. They can stand looking at a tree and they do not know what can be done with it . . . while I . . . well, I hope it don't sound like bragging too much . . . I know my trade."

III

You see what a confusion! Something was happening to me that is always happening. Try as much as I may, I cannot become a man of culture. At my door stood a man, waiting to be admitted, and there stood I —thinking of a carpenter in a town of my boyhood. I was making the man at the door feel embarrassed by my silent scrutiny of him, and that I did not want. He was in a nervous, distraught condition and I was making him every moment more distraught. His fingers played with his hat nervously.

And then he broke the silence by plunging into an apology. "I've been very anxious to see you. There are things I have been wanting to ask you about. There is something important to me—perhaps you can tell me. Well, you see, I thought— sometime, when you are not very busy, when you are unoccupied. . . . I dare say you are a very busy man. To tell the truth now, I did not hope to find you unoccupied when I came in thus, at this hour. You may be going out to dine. You are fixing your tie. It's a nice tie. . . . I like it. What I thought was that I could perhaps be so fortunate as to make an appointment with you. Oh, I know well enough you must be a busy man."

The deuce! I did not like all this fussi-ness. I wanted to shout at the man standing at my door and say . . . "the deuce with you!" You see, I wanted to be more rude than I had already been—leaving him standing there in that way. He was nervous and distraught and already he had made me nervous and distraught.

"Do come in. Sit there on the edge of the bed. It's the most comfortable place. You see I have but one chair," I said, making a motion with my hand. As a matter of fact there were other chairs in the room but they were covered with clothing. I had taken off one suit and put on another.

We began at once to talk, or rather he talked, sitting on the edge of the bed and facing me. How nervous he was! His fingers twitched.

"Well now, I really did not expect I would find you unoccupied when I came in here at this hour. I am living, for the time being, in this very hotel—on the floor below. What I thought was that I would try to make an appointment with you. 'We'll have a talk'—that's what I thought."

I stood looking at him and then, like a flash, the figure of the man seen that afternoon in the restaurant came into my mind—the furtive fellow who had been a thief, had been sent to prison, and who, after he was freed, did not know what to do with himself.

What I mean is that my mind again did a thing it is always doing. It leaped away from the man sitting before me, confused him with the figures of other men. After I had left Edward I had walked about thinking my own thoughts. Shall I be able to explain what happened at that moment? In one instant I was thinking of the man now sitting before me and who had wanted to pay me this visit, of the ex-thief seen in the restaurant, of myself and my friend Edward, and of the old workman who used to come and stand at the kitchen door to talk with mother, when I was a boy.

Thoughts went through my mind like voices talking.

"Something within a man is betrayed.

There is but the shell of a man walking about. What a man wants is to be able to justify himself to himself. What I, as a man, want is to be able, some time in my life, to do something well—to do some piece of work finely just for the sake of doing it—to know the feel of a thing growing into a life of its own under my fingers, eh?"

IV

What I am trying to convey to you, the reader, is a sense of the man in the bedroom, and myself, looking at each other and thinking each his own thoughts, and that these thoughts were a compound of our own and other people's thoughts too. In the restaurant Edward and myself, while wanting to do so very much, had yet been unable to come close to each other. The man from prison, wanting us also, had been frightened by our presence, and now here was this new man, a writer like myself and Edward, trying to thrust himself into the circle of my consciousness.

We continued looking at each other. The man was a popular American short story writer. He wrote each year ten, twelve, fifteen magazine stories which sold for from five hundred to fifteen hundred dollars each.

Was he tired of writing his stories? What did he want of me? I began to grow more and more belligerent in my attitude toward him. It is, with me, a common effect of feeling my own limitations. When I feel inadequate I look about at once for someone with whom I may become irritated.

The book I had been reading a half hour before, the book of "The Tales of Balzac," lay on a table near where the man sat and his fingers now reached out and took hold of it. It was bound in soft brown leather. One who loves me and who knew of my love for the book had taken it from my room in a house in Chicago and had carried it off to an old workman who had put it in this new suit of soft brown leather.

The fingers of the man on the bed were playing with the pages of the book. One got the notion that the fingers wanted to begin tearing pages from the book.

I had been trying to reassure him. "Do stay, I have nothing to do," I had said and he smiled at my words as a child might smile. "I am such an egotist," he explained. "You see, I want to talk of myself. I write stories, you see, but they aren't any good. Really they aren't any good at all, but they do bring me in money. I'm in a tight hole, I tell you. I own an automobile and I live on a certain scale that is fixed—that's what I mean—that's what's the trouble with me. I am no longer young, as you'll see if you look at my hair. It's getting gray. I'm married and now I have a daughter in college. She goes to Vassar. Her name is Elsie. Things are fixed with me. I live on a certain scale—that's what I mean—that's what's the trouble with me."

It was apparent the man had something of importance to himself he wanted to say and that he did not know how to begin.

I tried to help. My friend Edward had told me a little of his story. (For the sake of convenience and really to better conceal his identity we will call him Arthur Hobson—although that is not his name.) Although he was born in America he is of Italian descent, and there is in his nature, no doubt, something of the Italian spirit of violence, strangely mingled, as it so often is in the Latins, with gentleness and subtlety.

However, he was like myself in one thing. He was an American and was trying to understand himself—not as an Italian but as an American.

And so there was this Hobson—born in America of an Italian father—a father who had changed his name after coming to America and had prospered here. He, the father, had come to America to make money and had been successful. Then he had sent his son to an American college, wanting to make a real American of him.

The son had been ambitious to become a well-known football player and to have, during his college days, the joy of seeing his name and picture in the newspapers. As it turned out however, he could not become one of the great players, and to the end of his college career remained what is called a substitute—getting into but one or two comparatively unimportant games to win his college letter.

He did not have it in him to be a great football player and so, in a world created in his fancy, he did what he could not do in life. He wrote a story concerning a man who, like himself, was of Italian descent and who also remained, through most of his college career, a substitute on a football team—but in the story the man did have, just at the end of his days in college, an opportunity of which he took brilliant advantage.

There was this Hobson in his room writing, on an afternoon of the late Fall. It was the birth of a story-teller. He moved restlessly about the room, sat a long time writing and then got up and moved about again.

In the story he wrote that day in his room long ago he did what he could not do in the flesh. The hero of his story was a rather small, square-shouldered man like himself and there was an important game on, the most important of the year. All the other players were Anglo-Saxons and they could not win the game. They held their opponents even but could make no progress toward scoring.

And now came the last ten minutes of play and the team began to weaken a little and that heartened the other side. "Hold 'em! . . . hold 'em! . . . hold 'em!" shouted the crowd. At last, at the very last, the young Italian boy was given his chance. "Let the Wop go in! We are going to lose anyway. Let the Wop go in!"

Who has not read such stories? There are infinite variations of the theme. There he was, the little dark-skinned Italian-American, and who ever thought he could do anything special! Such games as football are for the nations of the North. "Well, it will have to be done. One of the halfbacks has injured himself. Go in there, you Wop!"

So in he goes, and the story football game, the most important one of the year for his school, is won. It is almost lost, but he saves the day. Aha, the other side has the ball and fumbles, just as they are nearing the goal line. Forward springs the little alert dark figure. Now he has the ball and has darted away. He stumbles and almost falls but . . . see . . . he has made a little twisting movement with his body, just as that big fellow, the fullback of the opposing team, is about to pounce upon him. "See him run!" When he stumbles something happens to his leg. His ankle is sprained but still he runs like a streak. Now every step brings pain but he runs on and on. The game is won for the old school. "The little Wop did it! Hurrah! Hurrah!"

The devil and all! These Italian fellows have a cruel streak in them, even in their dreams. The young Italian-American writer, writing his first story, had left his hero with a slight limp that went with him all through life, and had justified it by the notion that the limp was in some way a badge of honor, a kind of proof of his thorough-going Americanism.

Anyway, he wrote the story and sent it to one of our American magazines and it was paid for and published. He did, after all, achieve a kind of distinction during his days in college. In an American college a football star is something but an author is something, too. "Look! There goes Hobson. He's an author! He had a story in the *National Whiz* and got three hundred and fifty dollars for it. A smart fellow, I tell you! He'll make his way in the world. All the fraternities are after the fellow."

And so there was Hobson and his father was proud of him and his college was proud of him and his future was assured. He wrote another football story and another and another. Things began to come his way and by the time he left college he was engaged to be married to one of the most popular girls of his class. She wasn't very enthusiastic about his people, but one did not need to live in the same city with them. An author can live where he pleases. The young couple came from the Middle-West and went to live in New England, in a town facing the sea. It was a good place for him. In New England there are many colleges and Hobson could go to football games all Fall and get new ideas for stories—without traveling too far.

The Italian-American has become what he is, an American artist. He has a daughter in college now and owns an automobile. He is a success. He writes football stories.

V

He sat in my room in the hotel in New York, fingering the book he had picked up from the table. The deuce! Did he want to tear the leaves? The fellow who came into the restaurant where Edward and I sat was in my mind perhaps—that is to say, the man who had been in prison. I kept thinking of the story writer as a man trying to tear away the bars of a prison. "Before he leaves this room my treasured book will be destroyed," a corner of my brain was whispering to me.

He wanted to talk about writing. That was his purpose. As with Edward and myself, there was now something between Hobson and myself that wanted saying. We were both story-tellers, fumbling about in materials we too often did not understand.

"You see now," he urged upon me, leaning forward and now actually tearing a page of my book, "You see now, I write of youth . . . youth out in the sun and wind, eh? I am supposed to represent young America, healthy young America. You wouldn't believe how many times people have spoken to me saying that my stories are always clean and healthy, and the editors of magazines are always saying it too. 'Keep on the track,' they say. 'Don't fly off the handle! We want lots of just such clean healthy stuff.'"

He had grown too nervous to sit still and getting up began to walk back and forth in the narrow space before the bed,

still clinging to my book. He tried to give me a pic ure of his life.

He lived, he said, during most of the year, in a Connecticut village, by the sea, and for a large part of the year did not try to write at all. The writing of football stories was a special thing. One had always to get hold of the subject from a new angle and so, in the Fall, one went to many games and took notes. Little things happened on the field that could be built up and elaborated. Above all, one must get punch into the stories. There must be a little unexpected turn of events. "You understand. You are a writer yourself."

My visitor's mind slipped off into a new channel and he told me the story of his life in the New England town during the long months of the Spring, Summer and early Fall, when, as I understood the matter, he did no writing.

Well, he played golf, he went to swim in the sea, he ran his automobile. In the New England town he owned a large white frame house where he lived with his wife, with his daughter when she was at home from school, and with two or three servants. He told me of his life there, of his working through the Summer months in a garden, of his going sometimes in the afternoons for long walks about the town and out along the country roads. He grew quieter, and, putting my book back on the tab'e, sat down again on the edge of the bed.

"It's odd," he said, "You see, I have lived in that one town now for a good many years. There are people there I would like to know better. I would like really to know them, I mean. Men and women go along the road past my place. There is a man of about my own age whose wife has left him. He lives alone in a little house and cooks his own food. Sometimes he also goes for a walk and comes past my place and we are supposed to be friends. Something of the kind is in the wind. He stops sometimes by my garden and stands looking over and we talk but do not say much to each other. The devil, that's the way it goes, you see—there he is by the fence and there am I with a hoe in my hand. I walk to where he stands and also lean on the fence. We speak of the vegetables growing in my garden. Would you believe it, we never speak of anything but the vegetables or the flowers perhaps? It's a fact. There he stands. Did I tell you his wife has left him? He wants to speak of that—I'm sure of it. To tell the truth, when he set out from his own house, he was quite determined to come up to my place and tell me all about everything, how he feels, why his wife has left him and all about it. The man who went away with his wife was his best friend. It's quite a story, you see. Everyone in our town knows about it but they do not know how the man himself feels as he sits up there in his house all alone.

"That's what he has made up his mind to talk to me about but he can't do it, you see. All he does is to stand by my fence and speak of growing vegetables. 'Your lettuce is doing very well. The weeds do grow like the deuce, don't they though? That's a nice bed of flowers you have over there near the house.'"

The writer of the football stories threw up his hands in disgust. It was evident he also felt something I had often felt. One learns to write a little and then comes this temptation to do tricks with words. The people who should catch us at our tricks are of no avail. Bill Hart, the two-gun man of the movies, who goes creeping through forests, riding pell-mell down hillsides, shooting his guns bang-bang, would be arrested and put out of the way if he did that at Billings, Montana, but do you suppose the people of Billings laugh at his pranks? Not at all. Eagerly they go to see him. Cowboys from distant towns ride to where they may see his pictures. For the cowboy also the past has become a flaming thing. Forgotten are the long dull days of following foolish cows across an empty desert place. Aha, the cowboy also wants to believe. Do you not suppose Bill Hart also wants to believe?

The deuce of it all is that, wanting to believe the lie, one shuts out the truth, too. The man by the fence, looking at the New England garden, could not become brother to the writer of football stories. *"They tell themselves so many little lies, my beloved."*

VI

I was sidling across the room now, thinking of the man whose wife had run away with his friend. I was thinking of him and of something else at the same time. I wanted to save my Balzac if I could. Already the football-story man had torn a page of the book. Were he to get excited again he might tear out more pages. When he had first come into my room I had been discourteous, standing and staring at him and now I did not want to speak of the book, to warn him. I wanted to pick it up casually, when he wasn't looking. "I'll walk across the room with it and put it out of his reach," I thought, but just as I was about to put out my hand he put out his hand and took it again.

And now, as he fingered the book nervously, his mind jumped off in a new direction. He told me that during the Summer before he had got hold of a book of verses by an American poet, Carl Sandburg.

"There's a fellow," he cried, waving my Balzac about. "He feels common things as I would like to be able to feel them and sometimes as I work in my garden I think of him. As I walk about in my town or go swimming or fishing in the Summer afternoons I think of him." He quoted:

"Such a beautiful pail of fish, such a beautiful peck of apples, I cannot bring you now. It is too early and I am not footloose yet."

It was pretty evident the man's mind was jerking about, flying from place to place. Now he had forgotten the man who on Summer days came to lean over his fence and was speaking of other people of his New England town.

On Summer mornings he sometimes went to loiter about on the main street of the town of his adoption, and there were things always going on that caught his fancy, as flies are caught in molasses.

Life bestirred itself in the bright sunlight in the streets. First there was a surface life and then another and more subtle life going on below the surface, and the football-story writer felt both very keenly —he was one made to feel all life keenly— but all the time he kept trying to think only of the outside of things. That would be better for him, he thought. A story writer, who had written football stories for ten or fifteen years, might very well get himself into a bad way by letting his fancy play too much over the life immediately about him. It was just possible—well, you see it might turn out that he would come in the end to hate a football game more than anything else in the world—he might come to hate a football game as that furtive fellow I had seen in the restaurant that afternoon no doubt hated a prison. There were his wife and child and his automobile to be thought about. He did not drive the automobile much himself—in fact, driving it made him nervous—but his wife and the daughter from Vassar loved driving it.

And so, there he was in the town—on the main street of the town. It was, let us say, a bright early Fall morning and the sun was shining and the air filled with the tang of the sea. Why did he find it so difficult to speak with anyone regarding the half-formed thoughts and feelings inside himself? He had always found it difficult to speak of such things, he explained, and that was the reason he had come to see me. I was a fellow writer and, no doubt, I also was often caught in the same trap. "I thought I would speak to you about it. I thought maybe you and I could talk it over," he said.

He went, on such a morning as I have described, into the town's main street and for a time stood about before the post-office. Then he went to stand before the door of a cigar store.

A favorite trick of his was to get his shoes shined.

"You see," he exclaimed, eagerly leaning forward on the bed and fingering my Balzac, "you see there is a small fish stand right near the shoe-shining stand, and across the street there is a grocery where they set baskets of fruit out on the sidewalk. There are baskets of apples, baskets of peaches, baskets of pears, a bunch of yellow bananas hanging up. The fellow who runs the grocery is a Greek and the man who shines my shoes is an Italian. Lord, he's a Wop like myself.

"As for the man who sells fish, he's a Yank.

"How nice the fish look in the morning sun!"

The story-teller's hand caressed the back of my book and there was something sensual in the touch of his fingers as he tried to describe something to me, a sense he had got of an inner life growing up between the men of such oddly assorted nationalities, selling their merchandise on the streets of a New England town.

Before coming to that, however, he spoke at length of the fish, lying amid cracked ice in a little box-like stand the fish merchant had built. One might have fancied my visitor also dreamed of some day becoming a fish merchant. The fish, he explained, were brought in from the sea in the evening by fishermen and the fish merchant came at daybreak to arrange his stock, and all morning, whenever he sold a fish, he re-arranged the stock, bringing more fish from a deep box at the back of his little coop. Sometimes he stood back of his sales counter, but when there were no customers about he came out and walked up and down the sidewalk and looked with pride at the fish lying amid the pieces of cracked ice.

The Italian shoe-shiner and the Greek grocer stood on the sidewalk laughing at their neighbor. He was never satisfied with the display made by his wares but was always at work changing it, trying to improve it.

On the shoe-shining stand sat the writer of football stories and when another customer did not come to take his place at once he lingered a moment. There was a soft smile on his lips.

Sometimes when the story writer was there, sitting quietly on the shoe-shining stand, something happened at the fish-stand of which he tried to tell me. The fat old Yankee fish merchant did something—he allowed himself to be humiliated in a way that made the Greek and the Italian furious—although they never said anything about the matter.

"It is like this," the story writer began, smiling shyly at me. "You see, now—well, you see the fish merchant has a daughter. She is his daughter but the American, the Yank, does not have a daughter in the same way as a Greek or an Italian. I am an American myself, but I have enough memory of life in my father's house to know that.

"In the house of an Italian or a Greek the father is king. He says—'do this or that,' and this or that is done. There may be grumbling behind the door. All right, let it pass! There is no grumbling in his presence. I'm talking now of the lower classes, the peasants. That's the kind of blood I have in my veins. Oh, I admit there is a kind of brutality in it all, but there is kindness and good sense in it, too. Well, the father goes out of his house to his work in the morning and for the woman in the house there is work too. She has her kids to look after. And the father,—he works hard all day—he makes the living for all—he buys the food and clothes.

"Does he want to come home and hear talk of the rights of women and children, all that sort of bosh? Does he want to find an American or an English feminist perhaps, enshrined in his house?

"Ha!" The story writer jumped off the bed and began again walking restlessly back and forth.

"The devil!" he cried. "I am neither the one thing or the other. And I also am bullied by my wife—not openly but in secret. It is all done in the name of keeping up appearances. Oh, it is all done very quietly and gently. I should have been an artist but I have become, you see, a man of business. It is my business to write football stories—eh! Among my people, the Italians, there have been artists. If they have money—very well, and if they have no money—very well. Let us suppose one of them living poorly, eating his crust of bread. Aha! With his hands he does what he pleases. With his hands he works in stone—he works in colors, eh! Within himself he feels certain things and then, with his hands, he makes what he feels. He goes about laughing, puts his hat on the side of his head. Does he worry about running an automobile? 'Go to the devil,' he says. Does he lie awake nights thinking of how to maintain a large house and a daughter in college? The devil! Is there talk of keeping up appearances for the sake of the woman? For an artist, you see,—well, what he has to say to his fellows is in his work. If he is an Italian his woman is a woman or out she goes. My Italians know how to be men."

"*Such a beautiful pail of fish, such a beautiful peck of apples, I cannot bring you now. It is too early and I am not footloose yet.*"

VII

The story writer again sat down on the edge of the bed. There was something feverish in his eyes. Again he smiled softly but his fingers continued to play nervously with the pages of my book and now he tore several of the pages. Again he spoke of the three men of his New England town.

The fish seller, it seemed, was not like the Yank of the comic papers. He was fat and in the comic papers a Yank is long and thin.

"He is short and fat," my visitor said, "and he smokes a corncob pipe. What hands he has! His hands are like fish. They are covered with fish scales and the backs are white like the bellies of fish.

"And the Italian shoe-shiner is a fat man too. He has a mustache. When he is shining my shoes—sometimes—well, sometimes, he looks up from his job and laughs and then he calls the fat Yankee fish-seller—what do you think?—a mermaid."

In the life of the Yankee there was something that exasperated my visitor, as it did the Greek grocer and the Italian who shined shoes and as he told the story my treasured book, still held in h s hand, suffered more and more. I kept going toward him, intending to take the book from his hand (he was quite unconscious of the damage he was doing) but each time as I reached out I lost courage. The name Balzac was stamped in gold on the back and the name seemed to be grinning at me.

My visitor grinned at me, too, in an excited nervous way. The seller of fish, the old fat man with the fish scales on his hands, had a daughter who was ashamed of her father and of his occupation in life. The daughter, an only child, lived, during most of the year in Boston, where she was a student at the Boston Conservatory of Music. She was ambitious to become a pianist and had begun to take on the airs of a lady—had a little mincing step and a little mincing voice and wore mincing clothes too, my visitor said.

And in the Summer, like the writer's daughter, she came home to live in her father's house and, like the writer h mself, sometimes went to walk about.

To the New England town, during the Summer months, there came a great many city people—from Boston and New York—and the pianist did not want them to know she was the daughter of the seller of fish. Sometimes she came to her father's booth, to get money from him or to speak with him concerning some affair of the family, and it was understood between them that —when there were city visitors about—the father would not recognize his daughter as being in any way connected with himself. When they stood talking together and when one of the city visitors came along the street the daughter became a customer intent upon buying fish. "Are your fish fresh?" she asked, assuming a casual lady-like air.

The Greek, standing at the door of his store across the street, and the Italian shoe-shiner were both furious and took the humiliation of their fellow merchant as in some way a reflection on themselves, an assault upon their own dignity, and the story writer having his shoes shined felt the same way. All three men scowled and avoided looking at each other. The shoe-shiner rubbed furiously at the writer's shoes and the Greek merchant began swearing at a boy employed in his store.

As for the fish merchant, he played his part to perfection. Picking up one of the fish he held it before his daughter's eyes. "It's perfectly fresh and a beauty, Madam," he said. He avoided looking at his fellow merchants and did not speak to them for a long time after his daughter had gone.

But when she had gone, and the life that went on between the three men was resumed, the fish merchant courted his neighbors. "Don't blame me. It's got to be done," he seemed to be saying. He came out of his little booth and walked up and down, arranging and rearranging his stock, and when he glanced at the others there was a pleading look in his eyes. "Well, you don't understand. You haven't been in America long enough to understand. You see, it's like this —" his eyes seemed to say, "—we Americans can't live for ourselves. We must live and work for our wives, our sons and our daughters. We can't all of us get up in the world, so we must give them their chance." It was something of the sort he always seemed to be wanting to say.

It was a story. When one wrote football stories one thought out a plot, as a football coach thought out a new formation that would advance the ball.

But life in the streets of the New England village wasn't like that. No short stories with clever endings—as in O. Henry—happened in the street of the town at all. Life went on and on and little illuminating human things happened. There was drama in the street and in the lives of the people in the street, but it sprang directly out of the stuff of life itself. Could one understand that?

The young Italian tried but something got in his way. The fact that he was a successful writer of magazine short stories got in his way. The large white house near the sea, the automobile and the daughter at Vassar—all these things had got in his way.

One had to keep to the point, and after a time it had happened that the man could not write his stories in the town. In the Fall he went to many football games, took notes, thought out plots, and then went off to the city, where he rented a room in a small hotel in a side street.

In the room he sat all day writing football stories. He wrote furiously hour after hour and then went to walk in the city streets. One had to keep giving things a new twist—to get new ideas constantly. The deuce, it was like having to write advertisements. One continually advertised a kind of life that did not exist.

In the city streets, as one walked restlessly about, the actuality of life became as a ghost that haunted the house of one's fancy. A child was crying in a stairway, a fat old woman with great breasts was leaning out at a window, a man came running along a street, dodged into an alleyway, crawled over a high board fence, crept through a passageway between two apartment buildings and then continued running and running in another street.

Such things happened and the man walking and trying to think only of football games stood listening. In the distance he could hear the sounds of the running feet. They sounded quite sharply for a long moment and then were lost in the din of the street cars and motor trucks. Where was the running man going and what had he done? The old Harry! Now the sound of the running feet would go on and on forever in the imaginative life of the writer and, at night, in the room in the hotel in the city, the room to which he had come to write football stories, he would awaken out of sleep to hear the sound of running

feet. There was terror and drama in the sound. The running man had a white face. There was a look of terror on his face and for a moment a kind of terror would creep over the body of the writer, lying in his bed.

That feeling would come and with it would come vague floating dreams, thoughts, impulses—that had nothing to do with the formation of plots for football stories. The fat Yankee fish-seller in the New England town had surrendered his manhood in the presence of other men for the sake of a daughter who wished to pass herself off as a lady and the New England town where he lived was full of people doing strange unaccountable things. The writer was himself always doing strange unaccountable things.

"What's the matter with me?" he asked sharply, walking up and down before me in the room in the New York hotel and tearing the pages of my book. "Well, you see," he explained, "when I wrote my first football story it was fun. I was a boy wanting to be a football hero and, as I could not become one in fact, I became one in fancy. It was a boy's fancy, but now I'm a man and want to grow up. Something inside me wants to grow up.

"They won't let me," he cried, holding his hands out before him. He had dropped my book on the floor. "Look," he said earnestly, "my hands are the hands of a middle-aged man, and the skin on the back of my neck is wrinkled like an old man's." Must my hands go on forever, painting the fancies of children?"

VIII

The writer of football stories had gone out of my room. He is an American artist. No doubt he is, at this moment, sitting somewhere in a hotel room, writing football stories. As I now sit writing of him my own mind is filled with fragmentary glimpses of life caught and held from our talk. The little fragments caught in the field of my fancy are like flies caught in molasses—they cannot escape. They will not go out of the house of my fancy and I am wondering, as no doubt you, the reader, will be wondering, what became of the daughter of the seller of fish who wanted to be a lady. Did she become a famous pianist or did she in the end run away with a man from New York City who was spending his vacation in the New England town, only to find, after she got to the city with him, that he already had a wife? I am wondering about her—about the man whose wife ran away with his friend, and about the running man in the city streets. He stays in my fancy the most sharply of all. What happened to him? He had evidently committed a crime. Did he escape, or did he, after he had got out into the adjoining street, run into the arms of a waiting policeman?

Like that of the writer of football stories, my own fancy is haunted. Today is just such a day as the one on which he came to see me. It is evening now and he came in the evening. In fancy again I see him, going about on Spring, Summer and early Fall days, on the streets of his New England town. Being an author, he is somewhat timid and hesitates about speaking with people he meets. Well, he is lonely. By this time his daughter has no doubt graduated from Vassar. Perhaps she is married to a writer of stories. It may be that she has married a writer of cowboy stories who lives in the New England town and works in a garden. I am told that our American two-gun man, Bill Hart of the movies, is a native New Englander.

Perhaps, at this very moment, the man who has written so many stories of football games is writing another. In fancy I can hear the click of his typewriting machine. He is fighting, it seems, to maintain a certain position in life, a house by the sea, an automobile, and he blames that fact on his wife, and on his daughter who wanted to go to Vassar.

He is fighting to maintain his position in life, and at the same time, there is another fight going on. On that day in the hotel in the city of New York, he told me, with tears in his eyes, that he wanted to grow up, to let his fanciful life keep pace with his physical life, but that the magazine editors would not let him. He blamed the editors of magazines—he blamed his wife and daughter—as I remember our conversation, he did not blame himself.

Perhaps he did not dare let his fanciful life mature to keep pace with his physical life. He lives in America, where as yet to mature in one's fanciful life is thought of as something like a crime.

In any event there he is, haunting my fancy. As the man running in the streets will always stay in his fancy, disturbing him when he wants to be thinking out new plots for football stories, so he will always stay in my fancy—unless, well, unless I can unload him into the fanciful lives of you readers.

As the matter stands, I see him now, as I saw him on that Winter evening long ago. He is standing at the door of my room with the strained look in his eyes and is bewailing the fact that after our talk he will have to go back to his own room and begin writing another football story.

He speaks of that as one might speak of going to prison, and then the door of my room closes and he is gone. I hear his footsteps in the hallway.

My own hands are trembling a little. "Perhaps his fate is also my own," I am telling myself. I hear his human footsteps in the hallway of the hotel and then through my mind go the words of the poet Sandburg he has quoted to me:

"*Such a beautiful pail of fish, such a beautiful peck of apples, I cannot bring you now. It is too early and I am not footloose yet.*"

The words of the American poet rattle in my head and then I turn my eyes to the floor where my destroyed Balzac is lying. The soft brown leather back is uninjured and now again, in fancy, the name of the author is staring at me. The name is stamped on the back of the book in letters of gold.

From the floor of my room the name Balzac is grinning ironically up into my own American face.

AMERICANA

ARIZONA

EXTENSION of bibliomania to the great open spaces, where red-blooded he-men still roam the primeval lava, as reported by the Tucson *Star:*

Harold Bell Wright is personally autographing every copy of *The Mine with the Iron Door* that is sold by the Wyatt book store. Mr. Wright also has had an extra page inserted in these books containing a picture of himself and the entrance gate leading into the patio of his home.

CALIFORNIA

ETHICAL effects of excessive theological passion in the capital of the New Thought and the movies:

The business men's Bible class of Long Beach, which yesterday reported an attendance of 31,034 in the final session of its attendance contest with a similar organization of Kansas City, today was accused flatly of cheating by J. W. Lingenfelter, representative of the Kansas City organization.

He asserted he checked yesterday's attendance at Long Beach with the aid of a score of private detectives armed with counting machines and that the actual attendance in the Municipal Park where the gathering was held was 13,930, or 17,104 less than the total announced.

OFFICIAL view of the aims and usufructs of the late war in San Francisco, as stated in a sermon by the Rev. James L. Gordon, pastor of the First Congregational Church:

The great war was humanity's battle for humanity. That human liberty might be preserved! That universal freedom might be perpetuated! That democracy of the world might be safeguarded! That Christianity might survive! That the world's last and best civilization should not break down!

CONNECTICUT

APPEAL to the music-lovers of Yale University in an advertisement in the *Yale Daily News:*

BESSIE SMITH
Bessie Smith, the Babe Ruth of all blues singers, comes to bat now with "Nobody in Town Can •

Bake a Sweet Jelly Roll Like Mine." She's blued about her troubles, she's blued about her men, she's blued about her baby, and now she blues again. If she bakes a jelly roll as well as she sings about it—no wonder everybody wants to cut himself a piece of cake!

Roll that record over. What's this Bessie says? Oh, yes, "If You Don't, I Know Who Will." Well, Bessie, after hearing this we will. Released at
WHITLOCK'S
Today.

DISTRICT OF COLUMBIA

FROM a public bull by the Hon. James John Davis, director-general of the Loyal Order of Moose and Secretary of Labor in the Cabinet of Mr. Coolidge:

There should be a fourth R added to the modern school course. With reading, 'riting and 'rithmetic you should put religion, for if you are going to make a success of life in the American way you must have the fourth R.

DECAY of the Higher Morality in the House of Representatives, as reported by the *Congressional Record:*

Mr. CLARK of Florida. Mr. Speaker, I desire to ask unanimous consent that I may proceed for one minute on a matter of great interest to the House.

The SPEAKER. The gentleman from Florida asks unanimous consent to proceed for one minute. Is there objection?

There was no objection.

Mr. CLARK of Florida. Mr. Speaker, while this House seems to be in the way of liberalization, I want to suggest that for a long time—and I am not so old, either—there has been a rule, as I understand, which forbids Members of Congress having a couch or lounge or something on which they might rest for a few minutes in their offices if they desire to do so. That I regard as a reflection on the integrity and the honor of the membership of the House, and I wanted to raise this question now, Mr. Speaker, in order that the commission having charge of that building might take into consideration the question of allowing the Members who desired it the privilege of having some convenience there if they desire to rest for a few moments some time during the day. (*Applause.*)

GEORGIA

THE gay life in the capital of the Invisible Empire, as described by the Society Editor of the Atlanta *Journal:*

One of the most unique, as well as one of the most enjoyable events ever given in Atlanta was the dinner Friday evening at the Piedmont Driving Club at which Mr. Wilmer Moore, chairman of the board of deacons of the North Avenue Presbyterian Church, entertained in honor of the Rev. Richard Orme Flinn, pastor of the church.

Invited to meet the pastor were the elders and deacons of the church and in especial compliment to these guests the table was arranged with many little groups of Biblical figures.

Adam and Eve, made of gum drops, were seen seated under a tiny apple tree, the bright red apples being represented by cranberries, and the old serpent, made of raisins, was seen very near them.

Moses was shown, made of peanuts, in a grapefruit rind basket placed in the bulrushes, with Pharaoh's daughter, a lollipop.

At the places of the pastor and the elders were tiny Bibles, made of candy, with a quotation in the tiniest of letters, and the bookmarks were sprays of rosebuds.

HAWAII

PROGRESS of the tone-art in Honolulu, as reported by the weekly paper of the Honolulu Ad Club, the chief organization of up-and-coming go-getters in the archipelago:

C. W. Stetson, secretary of the Army and Navy "Y" at Pearl Harbor, played "Träumerei" and "The Rosary" on drinking goblets filled with varying depths of water. He says it took three years to collect those goblets. To many in the audience it was a new trick and brought forth a storm of applause. But Stetson had another up his sleeve. He brought forth an old handsaw and a fiddle-bow, and introduced 98 per cent of the audience to real backwoods music for the first time. More saw-mill harmony was produced with a flock of circular saws which Stetson had trained to tinkle out "Old Black Joe" and "Mother McChree." A good time was had by all.

ILLINOIS

FROM an editorial in the *Kiwanis Magazine* by the Hon. Roe Fulkerson:

Kiwanis is no longer a child. Kiwanis is full grown and a club of consequence and standing in every community. This standing and social prominence it gives to these wonderful wives and daughters of ours throw on us a responsibility to live up to them—*LOOK* like what we are.

If this means anything it means an end of affairs in Kiwanis which are marked "Informal."

It means that our club, our women folks, our standing, are all as good as any set of men ever had and if so, we must live up to them.

Appearances count. Evening clothes count. Our ladies, our social standing and our organization are entitled to evening clothes.

KANSAS

EFFECTS of the Volstead Act in moral Kansas, as reported by E. W. Howe:

Talk about liquor drinking in the city! You ought to see it in the country! In the old days when a town man was a drunkard they sent him out into the pure, open spaces to reform, but now it's the farmers' sons that are getting to be drunkards and they send them to town to straighten up. You go out to the country sales around Atchison and you see so much bootleg liquor drinking it's disgraceful. I know fellows in Atchison who have as much as two barrels of bootleg in their cellars.

MARYLAND

FROM a tract by Dr. Howard A. Kelly, emeritus professor in the Johns Hopkins Medical School:

I look with equanimity upon evolution, or any other theory, nor do I care (relatively speaking) whether it is true or false, but I do care a great deal to drive men back to God's Word, the fountain of living waters, and *that they shall hold it to be true from Genesis i to Revelation xxii.*

MICHIGAN

FOSTERING the Higher Learning at the University of Michigan:

The University of Michigan Club of Detroit is responsible for entering about twelve athletes in the University this Fall. This required hard work, as positions had to be secured for the Summer and also for the school year. Michigan was sold to these boys, even though they had received attractive offers from other schools.

FROM a hortatory article in the *Kiwanis Magazine* by the Hon. Verner W. Main, president of the Kiwanis Club of Battle Creek, 1919-1921, and of the Chamber of Commerce, 1922:

The only fair attitude of any member of a community toward his Chamber of Commerce is that of an honest search after, and a willingness to promote, such activities in the Chamber of Commerce as will best serve to make his Chamber of Commerce the kind of Chamber of Commerce he would like.

MISSOURI

BRAVE attempt of St. Louis to make the country forget the shutting down of the breweries, as reported by the estimable *Globe-Democrat:*

> St. Louis district now produces more commercial horseradish roots than the combined acres of all other sections of the United States. With favorable weather and marketing conditions, 500 carloads of roots are shipped during a season.

HUMAN progress under the Nineteenth Amendment in St. Louis, as described by a dispatch in the estimable New York *Times:*

> Her thirteenth divorce was granted to Mrs. Cora Yates in the City Court today. Witnesses testified that her husband, Alexander Yates, had been unfaithful. In the same court, on December 11 last, Mrs. Yates obtained a divorce from Albert Lilley, to whom she had been married three times. He was found guilty of extreme and repeated cruelty. Before her first marriage to Lilley the woman had been wedded to nine different men, and in the course of her marital career she has answered to the names of Walker, Truxler, Joyce, Barnes, Butcher, Crow, Whitney, Lilley, Porter, Swanson and Yates.

NEW YORK

LITERARY note from the learned *Bookman:*

> President Harding's death deeply grieved us. He was, it seems to us, the most thoroughly *trusted* by the people at large of any President of our time. Every citizen has felt a great personal loss.

EXTRACT from a review of Carl Van Vechten's "The Blind Bow Boy" in the same issue:

> If it does not offend you at the start, it may possibly amuse you, and if you are really a nice person, you will not understand a great deal of it, thank Heaven!

NORTH CAROLINA

A LATE flowering of Christian doctrine among the Fundamentalists, as reported by the Charlotte *Observer:*

> Vividly bringing out the similarity between John the Baptist and Billy Sunday, the Rev. Joseph A. Gaines, pastor of St. John's Baptist Church, preached at the evening service Sunday at St. John's Church a powerful sermon on "There Came a Man."
> Billy Sunday is the same type of man as John the Baptist and as time goes on the world is coming to place upon him an estimate similar to the one that John the Evangelist placed upon John the Baptist, declared Mr. Gaines.

OREGON

EFFECTS of the cheap dispersion of human knowledge in Oregon, as reported in a dispatch from Medford in that State:

> John M. Eisenhour, 23 years old, died last night at Sacred Heart Hospital as the result of a 35-day fast. Suffering from ill health and reading in a physical culture magazine that fasting would cure him, he forsook food. When the case was reported to the local Red Cross Tuesday he was removed to the hospital, but the food and care administered there came too late.

PENNSYLVANIA

PATRIOTIC jocosities along the Delaware river, as reported by the Philadelphia *Evening Bulletin:*

> Several members of the Chester Rotary Club left the meeting last night after a speaker had made several bitter attacks on the United States, and had praised the I. W. W. At the end of his speech he removed a set of false whiskers and revealed himself as C. E. Swayze, chairman of the educational committee of the American Legion. He then addressed the Rotarians on the perils of Socialism, and told what the American Legion was doing to protect the government from its enemies. He was brought to the hall by Chief of Police Vance, and was supposedly an arrested prisoner.

TEXAS

FROM an harangue to the Kiwanis Club of San Antonio by Major William G. Morgan, U. S. A.:

> The ignorance of the American people as regards their own ignorance is a most remarkable thing.

PINCHOT

BY CHARLES WILLIS THOMPSON

WHEN Theodore Roosevelt, speaking of some vagaries of certain Progressives, said that every reform was bound to have a lunatic fringe, the context hinted that he had in mind Amos Pinchot and John A. H. Hopkins. So might Luther have spoken of the Anabaptists, or Peter and Paul of Simon Magnus. It was Amos and John, you will remember, who surprised by themselves, as Count Smorltork would say, the party of the Forty-Eighters in 1920. True, the party of the Forty-Eight ditched them, but that was not because the Forty-Eighters were more lunatic; nay, it was because the Forty-Eighters knew exactly what they wanted.

Now Gifford, the brother of Amos, is on no lunatic fringe. He stops the required step short of it, which is why Roosevelt never had occasion to rule him out of his inner council. Amos had much money, and it was a bitter thing to let him go; Theodore, indeed, did it so gently that probably Amos does not know to this day that he was let out. But Gifford, also with money, had consorted with politicians and built himself up on Theodore, and so he stayed. In fact, he had got so far as to acquire a mooncalf sort of perception of Theodore's methods, which must have amused that great politician immensely. Every act of Gifford's since Roosevelt died shows his half-way perception of the Rooseveltian tactics. He captured the gubernatorial nomination in Pennsylvania by one of the chief tricks of it—the charge-bayonets against a machine too strongly intrenched to be attacked otherwise, with the bayonets commanded by money made to appear more than it really was.

Yet he is only a pinchbeck Roosevelt. Take, for instance, his attempt to steal from President Coolidge the Congress of Governors and the leadership of the drys. There can be no question that the manœuvre was a close imitation of Roosevelt's mere manner. If the man upon whom Pinchot founded his system of gestures, if Roosevelt himself had had this thing to do, he would have done it in just that way. Harding had summoned the Governors with the idea of assuming the leadership of the drys, and Coolidge intended to do the same thing. But whereas Harding would have made an elaborate thing of it, Coolidge meant merely to take the centre of the stage, lay down the law, and dismiss the Governors to their several homes. Now if Roosevelt, desiring to be a candidate for President, had been one of those Governors, would he have waited to let the President fire into the mess and dismiss it? You can see Pinchot debating that question with himself, with his finger implanted in the middle of his forehead. "Why, no," is Pinchot's answer to himself; "he wouldn't let Coolidge get away with it for a minute. He would fire off the first gun before Coolidge got a chance to open his mouth. Therefore, that is what I, Pinchot, should do, for I am Roosevelt the second. It is perfectly true that I have made myself a laughing-stock in my own State by my enforcement of Prohibition, but, as the late David B. Hill sagely said, 'I care not who writes the news of a story if I can write the headlines'; and beside, the drys never reason anyhow. With what an ill-concealed grin of satisfaction did William H. Anderson answer his indictment by saying that he had the churches with him yet! Anyhow, it's the Rooseveltian method and I'll try it."

"A substitute shines brightly as a king, until the king be by," wrote Shakespeare, who certainly did write at least that much of "Titus Andronicus." Pinchot gave an imitation of Roosevelt, but it was a bad one. If Roosevelt had wanted to assume the dry leadership against Coolidge he would have kept his own record clear, or at least defensible, and he would not have begun his attack nine or ten months before the Convention, thereby giving the Coolidge scouts every opportunity to find the black spots, nay, the wellsprings, as Carlyle would have put it, in that record. Also Roosevelt, who was very particular about such things, and never left a bush in his rear, would have seen to it that his State organization would at least keep quiet after he had fired his volley. Instead, the Pennsylvania State organization, stirred to uneasy wrath by Pinchot's voluntary contribution to a campaign six months off, hastily announced that if he expected to get the Pennsylvania delegation he would have to take it away from Senator Reed, Senator Pepper, Boss Leslie, Boss Grundy, and, in short, every local boss in the State. True enough, Boss Vare, of Philadelphia, kept quiet, but everybody knows that Pinchot can't get the Philadelphia delegation. Now, these are little things—but Roosevelt wouldn't have left his rear open to bushwhackers while charging valiantly on an immovable front.

II

Immovable? Let's see. Maybe Coolidge can't enforce the Volstead Act. But he can say he is *trying* to, and that is all that Pinchot can do. It's all the tongueful Governor Neff of Texas can do; it's all the Governors of Kansas and Maine can do. Pennsylvania is the wettest State in the Union. In New York, held up as a wet State by the Prohibitionists from mere force of habit, you can travel down such aforetime abodes

of dampness as Eighth Avenue and see the closed saloon. But in Philadelphia there is the old-time brass rail and spittoon, with Mike and his bottles behind it. From the back room still rings the merry laughter of girls and sailors. The cop still collects his schooner at the ladies' entrance. Mike will sell you, stranger though you are, a good glass of whisky for twenty-five or thirty cents—good as Volstead whisky goes— and a sounding six percent beer for ten or fifteen. Philadelphia is not open to the reproach so freely made elsewhere that the Volstead Act deprives the poor man of his liquor while giving it to the rich. Rich and poor stand or stagger on an even footing. The enforcement officers let Mike know twenty-four hours before they pull off a raid, and Mike never has more than a bottle on the premises to treat the enemy with.

But Philadelphia is a big city, the third in the Union. How about the smaller towns? Of course, we must except Pittsburgh because that is a big town too, and as wet as the Atlantic Ocean. But take any of them: Allentown, Scranton, Wilkes-Barre, any place you like, with the exception of a few where the sentiment of the people has always been dry. From the point where the Delaware comes down from New York State to the point where it slips through Philadelphia down to tide water, Pennsylvania is the wettest State in the Union, much wetter than Coolidge's own State, in spite of the attempts to fix the championship on Massachusetts. Beside, Coolidge hasn't been Governor of Massachusetts since 1920, and Pinchot has been Governor of Pennsylvania since 1922. It is true that he asked the Legislature to pass an enforcement bill, and that it did. Pinchot says it's a splendid measure. But the law-makers didn't appropriate a cent to enforce it. Why, they innocently asked, should Governor Pinchot need money to enforce it when he had the State constabulary at hand? So the chiefs of the State constabulary told their young men to go into saloons, drink whisky, and then arrest the proprietors. The local courts, however, quickly formed a habit of dismissing such complaints, telling the young soldiers that their superiors ought to be ashamed of themselves, and asking what their mothers would think if they formed the liquor habit. So Pennsylvania is in a devil of a mess, and the saloonkeepers continue to sell as before. In such circumstances, can you imagine Roosevelt attracting public attention to himself nine or ten months before the Convention?

Pinchot is not a real reformer, or only enough of a reformer to keep in with Brother Amos of the Forty-Eight and John A. H. Hopkins. He learned politics from T. R., who took care to explain to everybody from the housetops that you couldn't succeed as a reformer unless you played politics too. Roosevelt said that over and over again, and was privately much disgusted that the lunatic fringe wouldn't take him at his word. Pinchot, by dint of long listening and admiring attention, got the idea, though Brother Amos was one of those who wouldn't listen. There was, however, no more moderation in Gifford than in Amos. Amos wouldn't believe that there was any politics in reform; Gifford got to the point where he couldn't believe that there was anything in it *but* politics. Since Roosevelt died he has been getting worse and worse, until now he is a machine politician in disguise and nothing else. Roosevelt wouldn't have approved of that.

When Pinchot became Governor of Pennsylvania he issued a high-sounding statement to the effect that an office-holder who did his duty had nothing to fear from him. This eased the minds of the office-holders, all of whom held their tenures from one of the numerous local machines scattered through Pennsylvania or from the great central machine. Pennsylvania, as is often the case with machine-governed States, is very well administered; so the office-holders went on doing their duties until five o'clock and supporting their bosses after hours. Pinchot saw that they hadn't understood him, and so he is-

sued another pronunciamento. This one was to the effect that doing their duty meant deserting their own bosses, supporting him, and in general going out for Pinchot delegates to the next Republican National Convention, and that anybody who betrayed any slackness in this matter would be regarded as not performing his duty to the State. At first the office-holders could not believe that the good Mr. Pinchot meant it. They knew something of reformers; they knew that the good Mayor Moore and the good Mayor Blankenburg had never gone quite as far as that. So some of them went on obeying Boss Leslie and Boss Grundy and the other bosses. As fast as their names were brought to Pinchot he imitated Colley Cibber and said "Off with their heads!" All through eastern and western Pennsylvania office-holders have been summarily fired, not because they didn't do their work well but because they refused to join the Pinchot machine.

Pinchot is a pleasant fellow personally, somewhat as Bryan is. Bryan's geniality would not prevent him from sacrificing his best friend on the altar of his own political ambitions, if you can call it an altar; nor would Pinchot's. Republican newspapers, in denouncing Bryan for his theories, generally give him credit for being sincere. He is not. Neither is Pinchot. The exception should be made that they are both sincere, frantically sincere, in anything that affects their political fortunes. Both are continually on the lookout for a winning issue. Roosevelt was miles and miles above them, and not only risked but ruined his political career at least twice—oftener, I think—by disregarding the rule of taking care of Number One first. But he was no parlor reformer, and was willing to play with Quay and Hanna and even make a pretense of playing with Platt. He did this to gain his ends, which in general were the public's ends. Pinchot observed this without studying out the reason, and undertook to imitate it. He has succeeded in imitating the skin of Roosevelt, but not the hard muscles.

MORE LIGHT ON WHITMAN

BY EMORY HOLLOWAY

A TRUE biography of Walt Whitman must have relief; it must show his growth, his coming to himself. But such a biography cannot be written until we know his youth as he himself never gave it to us. With this in mind, I began, ten years ago, a search for materials for such a study. Partly as a result of that research, light has been thrown in recent years on a number of very obscure periods of the poet's life. But concerning the five years before he began to write for the Brooklyn *Eagle* almost nothing has been known hitherto except the names of the newspapers with which he was connected and a limited number of magazine articles, sketches and poems. The purpose of the present paper is to present what has recently been learned concerning his writings for the Brooklyn *Evening Star* in 1845-6, the only editorial work identified as his between the ages of twenty-one and twenty-seven.

The *Star* was the oldest and one of the less sensational daily papers in Brooklyn, then a city of forty thousand inhabitants. That it was a Whig organ, whereas Whitman was a Democrat, need surprise no one who is acquainted with his journalistic career. With another Whig paper, the Brooklyn *Advertizer*, he was to have an anonymous connection in 1850. And in 1848, although he disapproved of slavery, he was willing to write for the New Orleans *Daily Crescent*, which carried slave-auction announcements. He was a Union man throughout the Civil War, but we have no record of anything from his pen published to advance the cause during the first year of the conflict; instead there is only a series of antiquarian sketches. In the present instance it is probable that Whitman was offered a position with the *Star* for personal rather than political reasons. As a twelve-year-old boy he had set type for the paper, then edited by Colonel Aldin Spooner, whom he always admired. When Whitman came up from the country in 1841 to seek his fortune in the city and to try his hand at party politics, the *Star*, now edited by Colonel Spooner's son, made light of his political prospects and advised him to return to his newspaper apprenticeship. This he did, though doubtless for other reasons than that the *Star* had patronizingly advised it. It was the *Star*, again, which found space for his long memorial to the City Council in 1854 on the subject of certain recent blue-law ordinances. His regular connection with the paper extended from August, 1845, or before, to March, 1846. Since it announced a policy of publishing unsigned editorials, with collective responsibility, there is a possibility that more of the *Star's* editorials were written by Whitman than can be identified. Correspondents, however, used their initials or pen names; and Whitman, who was both editor and correspondent, used both. His *nom de plume* was "O. P. Q."

II

Some idea of what Whitman thought of the *Star* may be had from an editorial he published shortly after taking charge of its Democratic rival, the *Eagle*. E. B. Spooner, in the former, had been twitting him upon his editorial deficiencies. He wrote:

Wouldst thou behold a newspaper which is the incarnation of nervelessness? the mere dry bones of a paper, with all the marrow long withered up?—Behold that paper in our venerable contemporary of the *Evening Star*. Conducted for years by one of the worthiest, best-hearted, most respected, and now of the most venerable citizens—we mean that veteran editor and excellent man, Colonel Spooner—the *Star* was an interesting weekly budget of news, well digested, and making a readable family companion. But heaven bless us! it is fallen now into the sere and yellow leaf, (for a new era in the press has long since passed) and it must soon die of inanimation. It is of the olden time—respectable enough perhaps;—but, great powers! for a paper like that to talk of "weakness." Why, one little drop more of "weakness" in its already too full cup of that article, and it would have to get somebody's assistance before it could even lean against the wall and die!

Additional light is thrown upon Whitman's position on the *Star*, and also on his rupture with the *Eagle* two years later, by an editorial tilt between his successor as editor of the latter journal, S. G. Arnold, and Henry A. Lees, editor of the *Advertizer*. Lees was seldom friendly toward Whitman, but he was quick to take political advantage of the split in the Democratic ranks. On July 19, 1849, he wrote, concerning that friction:

The true secret of Whitman's rupture with the *Eagle* consisted in two facts. One was that he was determined that the paper, while he edited it, should not be the organ of old hunkerism;—and the other was, that on one occasion, when personally insulted by a certain prominent politician, Mr. Whitman kicked that individual down the editorial stairs.— These two solemn facts were the head and front of his "incompetency."

The *Eagle* lost no time in replying to the *Advertizer* and in dealing Whitman a blow into the bargain:

Mr. W. came here from the *Star* office where he was getting four or five dollars a week; he was connected with the *Eagle* for about two years and we think we had a pretty fair opportunity to understand him. Slow, indolent, heavy, discourteous and without steady principles, he was a clog upon our success, and, reluctant as we were to make changes, we still found it absolutely necessary to do so . . . Mr. W. has no political principles, nor, for that matter, principles of any sort; and all that the *Advertizer* says in the above paragraph is totally and unequivocally untrue. Whoever knows him will laugh at the idea of his *kicking any body*, much less a prominent politician. He is too indolent to kick a musketo [*sic*].

This is obviously *ex parte*, perhaps written by the publisher himself, Isaac Van Anden, and so overshoots the mark. But it reveals something of the picture Whitman presented to those of his fellow journalists who had reasons for viewing him unsympathetically. It accounts in part for his frequent changes from paper to paper. It suggests that the "rows with the boss and the party" of which Whitman speaks were violent enough at least to start a rumor that there was a spark of fight in his big and indolent-seeming body, that the worm turned at least once. The quotation also establishes the fact that Whitman had regular if not constant employment in the office of the *Star* for which his pay was by no means munificent. But in August, 1845, the poet's father moved back to Brooklyn from Dix Hills, L. I., and took up his residence first in Gold Street and then at 71 Prince Street; so that Whitman was probably at less expense for board than he had been when living as a freelance writer in New York.

There was less than a page of reading matter in the *Evening Star* in 1845, and it does not appear that Whitman's writings always appeared on the same page as the editorials. He was probably more nearly a modern reporter than an editor (though the distinction belongs by right to a later day), but he did not find the impersonal, anonymous reporting to his liking. He therefore commonly wrote in the first person—in the "Postscript Letters" sent from New York over the signature "O. P. Q." it was usually the first person singular— and indulged as freely in comment, reminiscence, prediction and exhortation as one might in a modern "column."

III

One of the things he reported was the theatre. He was a great student of Shakespeare and was familiar with the work of the best actors of his day; yet he seldom wrote so enthusiastically of the theatre as he did of the opera. Brooklyn had, and has, always been backward in the erection of theatres; yet Whitman, in recommending the construction of a place of public entertainment, takes pains to specify that it should not be a theatre—chiefly, it would appear, because the theatre in 1845 was not good enough for a still idyllic Brooklyn. The acting of the next two years caused him to modify his attitude a little, but in October, 1845, he was disgusted enough. He then wrote:

Would we have a theatre? With all due respect to the dramatic art—with all honor and glory to those immortal geniuses who have enlightened humanity and shone before the world in plays—we answer, *no*. As at present conducted, no man or woman of purified taste can care much for theatres, or wish one in Brooklyn. Of course, our readers will give us the credit of knowing too much to think that a playhouse *must* be bad, *per se*. We have a real love of the drama. Good principles and good manners can be taught through its means—and agreeably taught, too, which is no small advantage. But, until some great reform takes place in plays, acting and actors, nothing can be done in this country with the theatre, to make it deserve well at the hands of good men. It has worn the tinselled threadbare robes of foreign fashion long enough. It must be regenerated, refashioned, and "born again." It must be made fresher, more natural, more fitted to modern tastes—and, and above all, it must be Americanised, ere we say, put up more theatres. For what person of judgment, that has ever spent one hour in the Chatham or Bowery theatres in New York, but has been completely nauseated with the stuff presented there? And though the Park claims higher rank, yet even the Park is but a respectably stupid imitator or eld—a bringer-out of English plays imbued with anti-republican incident and feeling—an usherer before us of second-rate foreign performers, and the castings-off of London and Liverpool.

Give us no theatre in Brooklyn until the drama is pulled down and built all over again.[1]

If the best that the New York theatre had to offer thus impressed Whitman as "sad blotches," what must have been the effect of amateur theatricals! Once he attended an amateur production of Shakespeare. Of course he expected nothing of it, declaring in advance,

The worst of the thing in such cases is, that the unhappy prince is not only murdered by his usurping uncle, but by himself—which makes it bad. I shall attend and give you a specific account of it to-morrow, for the amusement of your readers. Hamlet! Oh soul-cracked gentleman!—so often represented by head-cracked simplemen, if thy daddy's ghost had wrongs enough to make *him* re-visit "the glimpses of the

moon," how mights [*sic*] *thou*, for "murder most foul," done over again and still again—revenge thyself in like manner, and with more cause, upon *thy* numerous assassins.

This promise was kept, and on December 13 appeared his caustic review, captioned "Hark! the Murder's Doing!" The following excerpts will reveal the character of the whole, as well as give evidence of a sense of humor which critics have sometimes denied Whitman:

"The rose and expectancy of the State"was a long-necked, shambling fellow, with a walk such as never before was seen in Christian, Jew or Pagan. Principally, his eyes were turned up, like a duck's in a storm, and his mouth occasionally would relax into a fearfully hideous grin, which put one in mind of mad dogs. He introduced several new ways into the piece: for instance, when saying "The world is out of joint," he illustrated the text by twisting himself round two or three times without stopping—a feat which did very well for M. Sylvain, in a double *pas* with Fanny Ellsler, but which we never before saw attempted by Denmark's "glass of fashion." Then such monstrous spasms as passed over his face, at times—the token whereof was certainly never seen except in a cholera hospital! . . .

Then the character of the King must certainly have been a wag—or else a profound republican, who wished to make monarchy ridiculous—or else tipsy—or else foolish—which latter perhaps is nighest the truth. At the conclusion of the mock play, he skipped out of his seat, and with such a flippant dance step as people use to "cross over" in the first figure of a quadrille, took himself off the stage, leaving the spectators in agonies of laughter. His richest joke was reserved for the last. "Hold on!" said he, interrupting the combat between his nephew and Laertes—"Hold on! let's take a drink!"

As to the ghost, if the dark hereafter changes ordinary mortal men into *such* men, death is indeed a dreadful contingency. The part, however, has one thing to be said in its favor—it was totally unlike any *living* thing we ever saw, and therefore may possibly be a very good representation of a ghost(!). And in passing, never before, we venture to affirm, were the members of the Court of Denmark so studious of their *caps*—which puzzled us a while, until we discovered that, concealed in the crowns thereof, were books of the play, from which they read their parts.

The most ridiculous character, (if we may use such a phrase where there was hardly anything but a monotony of the ridiculous) seemed, by general consent, to be awarded to Polonius. It was lucky for us that he died in the third act—for we felt ourself rapidly giving way under his most superlatively comical violations of time, harmony, text, and common judgment.

Foregoing all reference to the women actors as either ungallant or untrue, Whitman addressed himself, in conclusion, to the men:

We beseech them, and all others like them, never to attempt any thing of this sort in a similar way again.

[1]Compare the title of a Whitman essay published the following month in the *American Magazine*, "Tear Down and Build Over Again." But the identification of Whitman's hand in the excerpts from the *Star* on which this article is based does not depend upon evidence of that sort. Aside from the statement of the *Eagle* already quoted, we have the republication by Whitman in the *Eagle*, almost verbatim, of one of the musical reviews he printed in the *Star*, signed "O. P. Q."

And the audacious presumption of seizing "Hamlet,"
of all plays in the world!—a piece whose divine, and
almost unfathomable, beauty raises it far beyond even
the art of accomplished genius to enact thoroughly;
—and *they* to attempt it! They should be lashed well
for it.

IV

But if Whitman was disappointed in the
theatre, he felt his time to be better repaid
at the concert and the opera. Only in his
poems, such as "The Mystic Trumpeter"
and "Proud Music of the Storm," was he
able fully to express what music meant to
him. But he often tried, in the days when
he was slowly coming to himself. The
oratorio of "St. Paul" left him exalted,
but inarticulate:

It is utterly impossible to describe in words the effects produced by this fine composition—for music,
more subtle than words, laughs to scorn the lame attempts of an every day medium . . . Who shall define
the cabalistic signets of the undying soul? Who shall
sound the depths of that hidden sea, and tell its extent from a few dim and dull reverberations aneath its
surface? Who shall tell the how and the why of the
singular passion caused by melodious vibrations?
Nor is all this transcendental. We know that many
will idly read, and understand not. But there are
many, too, who have had similar experiences to what
we describe, and may not unlikely be able to parallel
their own feelings with those which moved us while
hearing that Oratorio.

Not always, however, was it the mystical and ineffable harmony of music in its
grander forms that caught the ear of the
growing young poet. He could enjoy concerts of the simplest sort as well. Indeed,
if he might have naturalness of execution,
he was willing to sacrifice something of
range and technique. On November 5 he
wrote:

For the first time we, on Monday night, heard something in the way of American music, which overpowered us with delightful amazement.—We allude
to the performances of the Cheney family at Niblo's
Saloon.

Not content with announcing this "discovery" in the press, he sat down and
wrote a short essay, "Art-Music and
Heart-Music,' which Poe published in the
Broadway Journal for November 29. The
sentiments expressed in the article were
personally endorsed by Poe in a footnote,
and the little essay was the occasion of the
only meeting of the two poets through

whom American poetry chiefly claims
recognition abroad today. It was earlier in
this year, by the way, that Poe had found
himself famous through the publication
and republication of "The Raven." The
Broadway Journal piece Whitman republished later in the *Eagle*, and he frequently
commended the Cheneys. When we remember how closely his own poetry is bound
up with his sense of rhythm and when we
recall how his whole intellectual bent was
in line with the strident and self-conscious
nativism of the time, it is easy to see how
such music as this advanced him by a great
stride toward the creation of "Leaves of
Grass," to be begun in 1847.

V

It was natural that so sensitive a person
should have been by temperament a pacifist. One might equally well say that he was
a pacifist by inheritance, for pacifism has
from the first been a deep-rooted American
tradition, whether one consider its expression most characteristic in Washington's "Farewell Address" or in the first
series of "The Biglow Papers." But Whitman had a peculiar sort of imaginative
sympathy which caused him to share
the pain he beheld and a feeling of sentimental democracy which made it impossible for him to close his eyes to the
world's suffering. War with England was
being played up, in 1845, by some of the
New York papers over the Oregon boundary dispute. Bryant, editing the *Evening
Post*, was for firmness as a matter of justice,
but hoped that this would avert rather
than precipitate war. Whitman was chiefly
concerned with combating the influence
of jingo journalists on both sides of the
water, who, he feared, might rush the
country into needless bloodshed. He wrote:

Here are two countries, with hardly a decent pretext between them for sharp words,—and some dozens
of obscure journalists on both sides of the ocean are
working hard for the future death and mangling of
ten thousand fellow citizens. more or less!—National
honor (?) Bah! For *such* to espouse it, were like perfumes showered in the baskets of the street-scavengers!
I have hardly any patience with the people for allow-

ing demagogues of this sort to go unwhipped of public opinion.

But just as he was congratulating the country on the fact that the storm-cloud seemed to be blowing over, his favorite *Democratic Review* published an article whose untimeliness Whitman thought likely to breed war; and in indignation he sat down to compose "Some Calm Hints on an Important Contingency:"

We believe in a high and glorious destiny for this republic!—We believe she is to outcap all the nations whose names and deeds are now recorded in historic annals. Not Tyre, or Hundred-Gated Thebes—not imperial Rome—not even England, greater as she is than all the rest—can bring us the mote of the mighty greatness assuredly to be achieved by our nest of eagle-empires! We drew the sword once—but it was for life and liberty. We drew it again, but it was to defend our plundered ships, and our citizens insolently taken from under our very flag. But what crying outrage have we now to avenge? In what respect are our liberties or our goods jeopardised? What one of our citizens has been seized and what cent's worth of property has been unlawfully wrested from its owner? If our proud destiny were to be achieved through blood and rapine —if our fame and honor could come in no other path except the path of the cannon balls, and if our advance is to be signalized by the smoke of cannon and the groans of dying men—we could turn our face aside and almost say, let us never be a great nation! If we teach mankind nothing better than the old lesson of wars, recriminations and hatred—if we cannot march forward to our mission with bloodless hands, and treading not upon the slain—the life and essential glory of our high example is dissolved utterly away. Our policy is peace; our system of government recommends itself to the world in the strength of its own gentle benefits, not by the enforcement of physical strength; and we have nothing to gain by any war, except one for repelling invasion, or supporting our own dearest inherent rights, when attacked. Let but such occasions arise as we speak of, and the nation will unite with enthusiasm in support of the strong arm—which would be bad enough even then.

We have no mawkish horror of physical suffering, when we remind our readers of the terrible fruits of war. But we can soberly realize that it is an awful contingency, from the loss of life alone. . . . Strange is the inconsistency of the rational soul! we can deliberately and even eagerly advise the prosecution of steps which will result in horrors compared to which those of the surgeon's table are as a key-hole draft of air to the hurricane in its hottest fury!

Despite Whitman's disavowal of any "mawkish horror of physical suffering," and notwithstanding his brave facing of such suffering in the hospitals of the Civil War, there was in his soft-fleshed, femininely sensitive body a woman's shrinking from causing physical pain, and in his soul a notion that to handle the body

roughly was to commit the supreme indignity. One evening he attended an address on education by Horace Mann. In reporting the speech, he elaborated, on his own account, certain passages in praise of moral suasion as a substitute for the whip in schools. A Brooklyn teacher thereupon sent to the *Star* a spirited but courteous rejoinder over the signature "Mastix." Within a few days Whitman brought up his big guns of sentiment and satire, of appeal and ridicule, and silenced his antagonist with more than a column of what may serve as the best specimen of his style at that period:

None of that puerile folly do we possess which is willing that the youthful mind, with all its whims, its undirected aims, its hot impatience, and the thousand distortions it early acquires from custom, should be left to run riot either in the school or at the parental home. Neither, if a child be indolent or averse to study, is ours the voice that would cry content. A disorderly way of conduct he must not have, and learning he must have. The orthodox teacher and parent would whip him out of the one and into the other. According to them, whether he says "damn" or breaks a glass—whether he insults his mother or tears his trowsers—whether, tempted by God's beautiful sunshine and air, he plays "hookey," or prompted by hunger, eats the forbidden pound-cake, kept for "company" only—whether he invents a falsehood or loses his pocket handkerchief—the *whip*, the quick and sharp infliction of physical pain, is the great cure-all and punish-all. The sting of the whip is supposed capable of making him know that the puzzling five or ten should be added, not subtracted. The whip will place him on good terms with his Maker, whose name he has taken in vain. The whip is to crush and tame the mettlesome, soothe the feverish and nervous, reduce the spirits where they are too high, and transform impertinence and obstinacy to mildness and soft obedience. But oh, wondrous universality! the same precious agent can also spur on the sluggard, put clearness and sharpness in the dull brain, encourage the timid, inspire the bashful, make the foolish discreet, and the vacant mind teem with life and substance. Macbeth's physician assured his master of nothing that could "minister to a mind diseased." But thou, O potent whip! art that great desideratum, and much more beside.—Thou curest faults of memory, and flaws of temper, thou mendest the morals, and repairest the breaches of sin; thou coverest over bad deeds with a thicker cloak than charity's; thou art not only the "Schoolmaster's Assistant" and the "Parents' Guide," but the true "Young Man's Best Companion," and the choicest "Teacher's Gift." Thou art indeed a miserable instrument of a miserable ambition—thou emblem of authority more dreaded than that which monarchs' sceptres wield! How many brutal wretches have, with thee, succeeded in hardening for their children or pupils both cuticle and soul! How many dark streaks made by thee upon the flesh, have deepened into darker streaks within! What spite, and hypocrisy, and fierce malignance, hast thou awakened, in breasts where error haply sometimes found entrance—but would have been routed so much quicker and more easily by love.

The birch had been for Irving a subject of jest; Whitman made it a matter of reform. Teachers today are tempted at times to think that Whitman succeeded rather too well. But it is interesting to note that the same feeling really lies back of his whole conception of government. "The results of severity and frequent physical pain as applied in schools are not unlike the result of tyranny in nations." Naturally he sided with Aldin Spooner and Greeley and Bryant in attacking capital punishment. The *Star* copied, in two long instalments, his skilful Socratic "Dialogue" on the subject from the *Democratic Review*, and published many reports of anti-capital punishment meetings. There is a touch of Swift's bitter and grim irony in some of Whitman's satire, as I have shown at length elsewhere.[1] Answering the argument that hanging is necessary as a deterrent from crime, and by the same token should be public, Whitman seized upon a news item for a *reductio ad absurdum*. He noted that five or six persons were under sentence of death in the State, and suggested that, for the greater moral effect, they all be publicly hanged together.

VI

I have quoted from the *Star* representative Whitman deliverances for the purpose, in part, of showing the manner in which he "absorbed" his country in the middle of the Nineteenth Century. His thinking was original, and his feeling was sincere, in that both thought and feeling were his own, for which he had paid and was willing to pay a price; but they were conventional in that they were shared by others of his day. One might say of many of his ideas, indeed, that they were in the air. The excerpts that follow, dealing with local and more trivial matters, emphasize still more the fact that the originality of

[1] *Studies in Philology,* July, 1923.

"Leaves of Grass" rested upon a very broad base of conventionality. His series of homilies to Brooklyn apprentices— "Hints to the Young"—are so trite as to make it difficult for us to believe that they are from the same pen that ten years later was to compose what Emerson called "the most extraordinary piece of wit and wisdom that America has yet contributed." He who was to remove the stigma from philosophic idleness with a line,

I loaf and invite my soul,

once lectured after this fashion the young man starting in business:

Industry is the thing, if you would thrive.—Let "Loaf not!" be to you an eleventh commandment . . . Indeed, idleness is never commendable at any time . . . Not that we would have you a mere muck-worm—a plodder on in the monotonous track of wealth, without enjoying the beauty of the earth, and the pleasant capacities of young life . . . Life was made for activity. Long as it may be stretched out, it is far too short for the purposes of an ambitious spirit.

In dress he enjoined as great simplicity as he was himself soon to display:

A poor youth has no business to wear elegant clothes. Neatness, cleanliness, and careful taste should preside over his wardrobe; but let him forbear to imitate the prevailing custom of superfine apparel, which is lately much more in vogue with shop-boys, apprentices, black-legs, and waiters, than among those of real rank and wealth.

Books of etiquette being less ubiquitous then than now, Whitman undertook to supply their want by exhortations such as this:

Swear not! smoke not! and rough-and-tumble not! These laws in society . . . must not be forgotten by all who seek to be agreeable. And they are much needed too—for most youths think they do great things in learning to chew or smoke a weed which the very pigs refuse to touch—to fill their mouths with something still more offensive in the way of blasphemous language—or showing their self-possession by loud talking or coarse conduct in company. Believe us, young man, the quieter and more modest you are the better.

And in order to avoid the vices we have been mentioning, you must avoid them altogether, in society or out of it. Manners cannot be put on like a suit of clothes.

Had the present article been published before his death, I wonder whether the Sage of Camden would have been forced to smile, as we are, at the picture of himself, a young journalist of twenty-six, earning his daily bread by communicating to the benighted province of Brooklyn fashion news from the distant metropolis across the East River:

No "calls" were made by the ladies yesterday [New Year's], the weather being so extremely bad. I am informed, however, that if the skies are clearer, it is quite as proper to make them to-day.—These little matters of etiquette are very important to some folks; and therefore it is that I have jotted them down for your readers' information.

Regardless of the weather, New Year's was wet in those days:

I don't remember to have seen more general hilarity. It was rather a damper, however, on the pleasure of the scene, that towards evening quite a large number of groups and individuals grew rather uproarious, and made night noisy, under the influence of something more potent than coffee or tea.

One judges that the calls were made, at least by the men. Though Whitman had published his temperance novel, "Franklin Evans," three years before and was to republish it in disguised form the following year, he seems not always to have insisted upon total abstinence. But he did enjoin temperance. Thus:

The holidays are here—which of course is no news. But we may, in passing, give a hint to those who, on such occasions, "go it with a rush." Take things moderately, gentlemen, young and old. Do not overload your stomachs with eatables and drinkables, which it may take weeks afterward to obviate! Enjoy the roast turkeys, and the rich cake, and even a glass or two of wine, (no more,) but in all things remember temperance. True enjoyment is averse to extremes—which generally lead to the opposite extreme. Among the various means of fun—and do not forget the boys and girls—allow us to suggest a visit—(you and a lot of your children, young brothers and sisters, or other young friends) to the equestrian performances at Tryon's Bowery Circus. We were there, having in charge some of our young fry, a night or two since ...

In 1845 Mrs. Mowatt's "Fashion" had been produced in New York, a broad satire against the prevailing mode of aping European manners and morals. But to Whitman the introduction of Parisian manners came as a wholesome and natural release from that stiffness into which an age of conventional sentiment always falls. In November, he wrote:

The coming season promises to be one of considerable stir in the fashionable world ... Parties, concerts, balls, and lectures are announced at a great rate.—The Polka increases in popularity. As for manners, we are assimilating to the Parisian, more and more—and I must confess I like it so. Stiffness and reserve are banished—dignified silence laughed at—all kinds of keeping one's state, sent to Coventry. A dash of familiarity even with the strangers, (either sex to either sex) you meet at parties, &c., is good breeding now; and the man or woman ("lady" and "gentleman" is counterjumperish) who should play haughty as a general thing, would be quizzed most mortally. We are now speaking of the *true* fashion—the heart of hearts—of New York society.

Whitman attending the parties of New York society, even as a representative of the press, is a trifle difficult to imagine. But it is easier to follow him when he sends to his paper a very brief contribution, ending it with:

The pleasant air and soft sunshine dispose me to a saunter. I will "trail" up Broadway, and give you the result of my walk tomorrow.

As often happened, he failed to keep his promise to his readers; but perhaps he gave the result of his walk and of countless other trailings up Broadway in "Manhattan's Streets I Saunter'd, Pondering," "Faces," and "Give Me the Splendid Silent Sun." He admired the crowds—if only they would not push and hurry so. He has been to the Fair at Niblo's:

What a silly propensity it is in people to go there, to push and squeeze as if life depended on their getting along so very quickly!—And, by the by, how some women *can* push! There was a pretty little creature, in whose track we had the fortune to get, with an utter impossibility of advancing or receding: and the way her elbows and bustle "gave it" to us was quite a caution!

On February 26, 1846, the Brooklyn *Eagle* lost its popular editor, William B. Marsh, by death. On March 3 Whitman published over his initials an appeal for aid to Marsh's destitute family. Within a week he was editor of the *Eagle*, happy in the best and longest editorship of his life. And here the student is on familiar ground again.

OSTEOPATHY

BY MORRIS FISHBEIN

Despite our remarkable advance of knowledge, nonsense is ever becoming bolder and more rampant: it is pre-eminently a time of fads and crazes, and the question as to how people are to be brought to their senses grows urgent.—*W. Duncan McKim.*

For centuries deductions based upon hypotheses have served as the basis upon which the thought and conduct of the human individual have been interpreted.—*Stewart Paton.*

I

"ON JUNE 22d, 1874," says Andrew Still, in his autobiography, "I flung to the breeze the banner of osteopathy." Before flinging it Still had been a free-lance doctor among the Shawnee Indians in Kansas. "I soon learned to speak their tongue," he says, "and gave them such drugs as white men used, cured most of the cases that I met, and was well received by the Shawnees." After the Civil War, the founder and promulgator of this extraordinary doctrine of human disease became interested in some bones dug up in an Indian graveyard. From his subtle cogitations on these remnants, he became convinced that the bones are the most important elements in the functioning of the human body, and that the backbone is the bone of all bones in the control of disease. On this point, in fact, he felt himself the recipient of a divine revelation, as he emphasizes repeatedly in his story of his life. "Have faith in God as an architect and the final triumph of truth, and all will end well," he says; and again: "Osteopathy is the greatest scientific gift of God to man." This belief in private and confidential communion with the Deity seems to be an inevitable part of the credo of every healing cult that has interfered with the progress of scientific medicine. It is perhaps a necessary ingredient: it lights an inward flame which gives the founder and prophet the power to attract his great hordes of fanatical followers.

The original divine revelation to Still was that the primary cause of every disease is some interference with the blood supply or nerve function, always caused by a dislocation of one of the small bones which make up the spinal column. This dislocation, he argued, brings about a change in the size of the little openings between the bones, through which the nerves and blood vessels pass. The result, according to Still, is pressure on the nerves and blood vessels, and disease at whatever distant point in the body the nerve or blood vessel may lead to. But this primeval osteopathy, handed down from heaven almost fifty years ago, was a somewhat different osteopathy from that which exists today. The gradual departure from the original tenets by his followers was a disappointment to the inspired founder. In numerous lectures delivered during 1894 and 1895 he remonstrated with them for their growing heterodoxy, and in the *Ladies' Home Journal* in 1908 he was still "believing . . . that the mechanical displacement of the bony vertebrae constitutes most of the lesions causing disease." But even in his own school in Kirksville, Missouri, students were soon being taught to take care of a disturbance affecting the liver by adjusting the spinal column first, then waiting a week, and then adjusting the liver itself. Still was against all this. The arterial supply to the organ was solely responsible for its health, he claimed, and adjustment of

190

the bones to release the arterial supply would cure whatever disease beset it.

The modern osteopath, while still clinging warily to these spinal adjustments, reaches out to embrace all that he can of modern medicine. He attempts electrical treatment, water treatment, massage, anesthesia, even surgery; and when the Harrison and Volstead acts were passed he made desperate efforts to secure the privilege of prescribing narcotics and liquor. The simon pure theory of Still denies flatly that drugs may have any favorable effect on the course of disease, but the modern osteopath is apparently convinced that chloroform and ether will induce unconsciousness, that morphine and cocaine will relieve or deaden pain, and that the fermented juice of the grape has certain agreeable effects when administered in proper dosage, at proper times and to good ends. All this must be taken as evidence that the osteopathy of today is essentially an attempt to enter the practice of medicine by the back door.

II

There was a time when the standard of medical education in the United States was a matter for despair. Half educated plowboys and section hands attended a few sessions of medical lectures and burst forth in the regalia of the physician. The medical schools were shambles. Scientific medicine makes no secret of this; it glories, however, in the fact that it did its own house-cleaning. More than twenty years ago the *Journal* of the American Medical Association, under the editorship of Dr. George H. Simmons, began to publish the appalling facts regarding American medical education. That publication was like the finger of the housewife who writes her name in the dust on the mantelpiece to show the maid where to wipe. The organized medical profession promptly appointed a special committee to investigate the medical schools, to establish standards, and to hold the schools up to those standards, once they were established. The weapon used to

achieve all this was publicity. School after school, searched out and exposed, either met the standard or passed into limbo. The number in the country dwindled from almost two hundred to less than ninety. The proprietary medical school, conducted for the pecuniary profit of the professors, gave way to the endowed institution which spends on the student far more than his fees. No longer was it possible for those who could hardly read and write to emerge in two years with a medical degree. The American M.D. of today has had a high school education, two to four years of college preparation, four years among the laboratories, lecture rooms and clinics of a well-equipped medical school, and one or two years enforced attendance as an interne in a standardized hospital. Before he can minister to the sick in private practice he must also pass a State examination. The route is a long and difficult one. It is costly. That is one of the chief reasons why there are now osteopaths and other such nondescript healers.

But there are, of course, other reasons. With the advance of medical research, the naïve belief in pills and philtres with which the medical profession of the past was afflicted met a crucial test. There came a nearer and nearer approach to an actual science of medicine. Again the physicians did their own house-cleaning. They created a Council on Pharmacy and Chemistry to examine the claims made for all drugs, new and old, and to determine their actual virtues. If what was offered could not pass the test, it was put into an Index Expurgatorius and the facts were published. The public, catching this spirit from the medical profession, began to waver in its allegiance to powders and pills. It thus became psychologically receptive to the claim of the drugless healer that his "system" was superior to drugging. Many such healers went even further. Still, for example, claimed that drugs were not only of no value in the treatment of disease, but even that they were *responsible* for most disease.

III

Let us pause here a moment to consider this matter of "systems." If there is anything the normal American loves it is a "system." Consider the immense number offered to him month in and month out in the advertising pages of his favorite magazines: systems of mind training, house decorating, salesmanship, motor repairing, mushroom growing, health building, muscle building, eyesight training—systems for everything. If you would see the preposterous lengths to which the business may be carried in the pursuit of health, study the pages of the popular physical culture magazines. Now, scientific medicine offers no such system. It aims, by the utilization of *all* available knowledge, to determine the cause of disease, and then, by the use of *all* intelligent methods, to benefit and heal the disease. It does not promulgate any theory or principle to the exclusion of established facts. It does not say, for example, that "all disease arises in the spine and all diseases can be healed by manipulating the spine." Neither does it say that all disease arises in the mind and can be removed by manipulating the mind. No doubt the acceptance of such systems by what are said to be intelligent persons is based on the fact that while they are wholly fallacious they are essentially simple. Even a moron knows that when you remove the brake on a motor car the wheels can go round. And when you tell him that there are brakes in the spinal column which keep the blood from flowing freely, or the nerves from functioning properly, he thinks of the brake on the car, and is sure that the idea is right. Imagine that same type of mind trying to understand how a tubercle bacillus, which he has never seen and of which he cannot conceive, makes a cavity within a human lung! As for such matters as the way in which insulin acts to metabolize sugar in diabetes, or the way in which salvarsan controls the insidious spirochaeta pallida—to explain these things to him would be as hopeless as explaining the theory of the well-advertised Professor Einstein. Scientific medicine admits that there are diseases of the mind and diseases of the spine, and its practitioners treat the former by mind-healing methods and frequently the latter by braces and supports and other manipulative measures. But scientific medicine does not treat an abscess of the liver by adjusting the back, nor a broken leg by attacking the mind. The great fallacy of all the "systems" of disease and their healing lies in this "all or nothing" policy. When that policy runs counter to demonstrable facts the result is invariably disaster.

IV

It was the pride of Andrew Still that a number of States had legally empowered the graduates of his school to practice osteopathy. It is our thesis that osteopathy as it is practiced today is essentially an attempt to get into the practice of medicine by the back door. In 1917, for example, the Supreme Court of Washington convicted a licensed osteopath of practicing medicine without a license because he had treated diseased tonsils by administering an anesthetic, placing a snare around the tonsils and cutting them out with a knife, after which he administered stypticin to stop bleeding. The court said:

A perusal of the successive catalogues of the schools of osteopathy will show that their teachings are gradually being expanded and that the more modern of them now teach in some degree much that is taught in the older schools of medicine. The parent school has been more marked in this respect than perhaps any of them. It now teaches that in childbirth lacerations, in certain types of congenital deformities, in certain kinds of tumors, etc., surgery must step in, and that surgery must be resorted to for the removal of tissues so badly diseased or degenerated that regeneration is impossible by the process of adjustment. *But this advance is modern. In 1909, the time of the enactment of the medical act, it was not in vogue.*

In fact, the laws of the various States which have attempted to regulate osteopathy have had a hard time of it to keep pace with the shifts of the osteopath in his attempt to break into the practice of medicine. The Supreme Court of California, for example, told an osteopath who wanted to practice optometry that he was not licensed to fit glasses. He argued that his license to practice osteopathy under the medical practice act made him a physician and that the optometry law excepted duly licensed physicians. The Court ruled that the law permitted him to practice osteopathy and nothing more.

We have forty-nine States in the Republic and we have forty-nine different medical practice acts. The Federal Government encountered great difficulty in regulating the administration of narcotics because of this lack of uniformity. In some States osteopathy is, by legal enactment, the practice of medicine; in many others it is not. The Treasury Department, facing this conflict, became confused, and finally attempted to solve the problem by issuing the following order: "Osteopaths should be permitted to register and pay special tax under the provisions of the act of December 17, 1914, provided they are registered as physicians or practitioners under the laws of the State and affidavit to that effect is made in the application for registration. . . ." But this decision made the confusion worse than before. The word "practitioners" might include clairvoyants, Christian Scientists, seventh sons of seventh sons, and all the motley crew that prey on the weak and ailing. It might— and often did—include osteopaths.

The evolution of osteopathic practice, as shown by these and many other court decisions and departmental regulations into something resembling the practice of actual medicine is probably the reason for the relatively slow development of the cult in the matter of numbers and for the outgrowth from it of the malignant tumor, chiropractic, which is apparently about to engulf the mother organism. Osteopathy, growing complex and "scientific," ceases to meet the demand for simplicity. Chiropractic falls into no such error. It appears to be essentially a reversion to the original hypothesis of Andrew Still, so simple that even farm-hands can grasp it; indeed, an

osteopath, viewing with alarm the inroads of the new cult, has said that "chiropractic is the first three weeks of osteopathy."

In 1908 the adherents of osteopathy claimed that the mother school had graduated 2,765 students, that schools merged with it had shed upon the community another 1,181, and that there was a total of 3,946 osteopaths. According to the United States Census, there were in the United States, in 1920, about 5,030 osteopaths. There were at the same time, according to the same figures, 144,977 graduate physicians and surgeons, and 14,774 nondescript healers. Now, for a population of about 105,000,000 persons, that is certainly not a tremendous number of osteopaths. Apparently the public is finding it possible to stagger along fairly well with the attentions of the medical profession, which has been steadily raising its standards of education. It is, indeed, a confession of failure on the part of the cult that it should have departed from its original hypothesis and gradually embraced the adjustment of parts other than the spine, not to mention the use of water, heat and electricity, and of anesthetics, antiseptics and narcotics. In fact, a considerable number of its practitioners have even adopted the extraordinary hocus-pocus of Albert Abrams as a part of their diagnostic and therapeutic armamentarium. Imagine what anathema would have been hurled upon the latter group by Andrew Still! How he would have ridiculed this apotheosis of buncombe! At least there is something real about a jolt applied with the thumb and finger to the back or directly to the seat of a throbbing, inflamed organ. But think of what Still would have said, in his peculiarly exalted language, about the diagnosis of disease by hitching up a drop of blood on a piece of blotting paper to a crude and confused mass of electric wiring, connecting this inanimate, impossible electric jumble to a strange subject, and then percussing areas of dulness on this subject, and from them diagnosing disease!

It was, indeed, a weakness of osteopathy that it had ambitions to be a science. When its schools increased their entrance requirements to demand a high-school education —usually on the insistence by legislators in the form of stringent practice laws—and when they extended their hours of study, the blacksmiths, barbers, motormen and beauty specialists who sought an easy road to healing turned by the thousand to the chiropractic schools, which demanded no preliminary education for matriculation and guaranteed a diploma to any aspirant who could pay their fees.

V

Scientific medicine possesses today adequate records of its schools and its practitioners. In the offices of the American Medical Association in Chicago are all the pertinent facts about the medical colleges of the United States—the subjects taught, the hours, the teachers, the pupils. There is a card for every physician in America, and on it is recorded all that is known concerning his qualifications. As one Southern practitioner said on seeing the card devoted to his own record: "Doctor, they've got things on that card that even my wife don't know, and I've been a married man goin' on forty years." Regularly all the medical schools are submitted to a rigid inspection. But nobody knows anything for certain about most of the osteopathic schools or osteopathic practitioners. Even granting that the facts presented by the schools themselves are reliable, hours of study do not necessarily mean hours of training. Truth and scientific fact are not guaranteed by the time spent in instruction but by the reliability of the subject matter taught. And what of the training of the teachers in the colleges of osteopathy: is it perhaps a case of the blind leading the blind? The truth of the osteopathic theory as to the causation of disease has never, of course, been established. If diphtheria bacilli are placed on the membranes of the throat of animal or man, the result is diphtheria. In their ab-

sence, no possible dislocation or distortion of bones, muscles, ligaments, blood vessels or nerves will bring about that result.

VI

Here are two quotations from a report written by the editor of an osteopathic magazine; they refer to the death of his own son:

Billie had diphtheria four days before we knew what he had . . . I had never seen a case of diphtheria before; never even thought of looking at his throat . . . Dr.—— was called the fourth day and diagnosed the trouble at once. He is an M.D.; has had wide experience; has had the training so many of us have not had.

And then later:

I don't understand antitoxin; I can't understand how a poison can cure disease or neutralize poisons. Yet when the death rate is cut from 50 per cent. to 10 per cent., isn't it best to be a physician first, and an osteopath second?

Osteopathy, chiropractic, Couéism, Christian Science, every system of healing without regard to established facts, comes a cropper when confronted with the established proof of the diagnosis and treatment of infectious diseases. The case of Billie is an exposure of the fallacy that an individual may be safely permitted to practice a single branch of medicine without first undergoing complete instruction in all the fundamentals of medical science. But when the incompetent undergoes such a complete course of instruction, there is revealed to him, alas, the underlying lack of truth in the "system" or cult to which he has been addicted!

Physicians see almost daily in their practice the results of patients peddling their ailments among the variegated assortment of peculiar practitioners. Perhaps none of the cases which might be cited is more striking than the one described by a well-known eastern neurologist:

Recently I examined a boy, aged 17, lying in bed, very weak, extremely emaciated, totally blind, barely able to swallow. The ophthalmoscope [the instrument which the physician uses to look into the back of the eye] revealed double optic atrophy [destruction of the optic nerves]. The history of the case is briefly: failing vision over nine months, terminating in blindness last August; for several months in the spring and summer of 1920, very severe headaches and frequent attacks of vomiting, often when there was no food in the stomach, and repeated convulsive seizures limited to the right leg without loss of consciousness. It was easy to make a diagnosis of brain tumor; but the condition of the patient was such that surgical interference was out of the question. The diagnosis, which seemed perfectly clear, might easily have been made many months ago. The condition of the patient for many months was certainly grave and alarming, and might have suggested to anyone that it needed thorough investigation. During all these months, while the vision was fading and blindness coming on, what did the boy receive? Treatment by an osteopath and then a chiropractor and then treatment by another peculiar practitioner and still another chiropractor, and so on, but never an ophthalmoscopic examination.

VII

Well, why do people go to osteopaths anyway? Don't they ever help anybody? People go to osteopaths because they have been directly approached through advertising, in which reputable physicians do not indulge. They go because some friend who has been aided by an osteopath, or thinks he has, has urged them to go. They go when physicians have failed them. Ah! yes. I grant you freely that physicians fail. There are diseases in which science can be of but little service, and if the doctor is honest he will tell you so. I know a woman who has been suffering three years or more with a gradually progressing case of paralysis agitans or shaking palsy. Three eminent neurologists told her that her condition was incurable; they prescribed a simple regime of life and told her to save her money for the invalidism of her remaining years. But during three and one half years she has spent every cent of her income on massage, on electric treatment, on nature cures, and on osteopathy, and she is undoubtedly worse. And I am willing to admit that among those who treated her was a physician who should have known better. The incompetent or unprincipled physician, licensed to practice medicine by a too complaisant State, is the greatest menace to scientific medicine—as

great a menace as all the cultists put together.

Osteopathic or any other kind of manipulation undoubtedly produces, at times, temporary benefit, or the feeling of benefit. The old-time physician used to put his hands on the patient; he used to work him up a bit, while at the same time he encouraged him mentally. There are many who feel that the modern physician might practice a little more of this laying on of hands. But it does not require an extraordinary mentality to see how serious it is to practice merely the laying on of hands and the conferring of a temporary feeling of benefit when a child is beginning to strangle with the accumulated debris of a diphtheritic membrane, or when the life of a woman is being slowly sapped by an internal, malignant tumor, or when some previously uncautious man is beginning to show the first signs of paralysis and the delusions of grandeur associated with an early encounter with the spirochaeta pallida of syphilis. These are surely no times for the laying on of hands; these are times for accurate diagnosis, and the speedy administration of the life-saving diphtheria antitoxin, the merciful surgical knife, and the destroyers of spirochetes: mercury and salvarsan.

In 1875, when Andrew Still went from Kansas to Kirksville, he found a letter addressed to his brother Edward from another brother, the Rev. James M. Still of Eudora, Kansas, "stating that I was crazy, had lost my mind and supply of truth-loving manhood." Still's comment on this letter, taken from his autobiography, offers a remarkable sidelight on the motives of the founder of osteopathy. "I read it," says Still, "and thought, 'As the eagle stirreth up her nest, so stir away, Jim, till your head lets down some of the milk of reason into some of the starved lobes of your brain.' I believed Jim's brain would ripen in time, so I let him pray, until at the end of eighteen years he said: 'Hallelujah, Drew, you are right; *there is money in it*, and I want to study Osteopathy'!"

The italics are mine.

AMERICAN PORTRAITS

I. The Labor Leader

BY JAMES M. CAIN

HE is recruited from people of the sort that nice ladies call common. Such people are mostly out of sight in the cities. The streets they inhabit are remote from the boulevards; their doings are too sordid and trivial for newspaper notice, save when the police are called in. In the small towns they are more openly on view, to the horror of the old families. Big city or small town, they are all alike. They are of the sort that mop up the plate with bread. That have 6 x 8 porches on their homes, and wash flapping on the clotheslines. That take a bath every Saturday night, and slosh blue, soapy water down the gutters. That own a $25 phonograph and these four records: "In the Shade of the Old Apple Tree," "Barney Google," "Walking with Jesus" (Orpheus Quartet), and "Cohen on the Telephone." That join the Heptasophs, the Junior Order, and (if getting up in the world), the Odd Fellows. Whose women-folk grow fat and rock on the porches wearing blue check dresses. Whose men-folk are laid up with elusive ailments related to the stummick. Whose female children know gross names for the anatomical parts and harass other children by yelling:

> I dare you like a dare dog,
> I treat you like a hound;
> I sell you to the rag man,
> Two cents a pound!

And whose male children sing:

> There she goes, sweet as a rose,
> All dressed up in her best Sunday clo'es!

Who say Mom and Pap, I'll Thank You for the Beans, Ain't No Use to Hisself, Yes'm, See You Later, Lick That Kid, Make Him Shut Up. . . .

196

Cockney or yokel, that is where he starts. He is of the same clay as this grotesque company, and sees nothing queer about it. The village blacksmith, who whispers to a lot of boys about the bank president's daughter, he considers a very sharp and well-informed man. He believes the plumber's wife who swears she saw a ghost in the graveyard, and hunches close to her while she jibbers. . . . The boy who follered 'em and seen 'em; women muttering over backyard fences; the Grand Exalted Keeper of Records and Seals, dusting off the regalia; the party that went to the morgue to see the razor-slashed body of the woman in the big mystery murder; the wife who says the Mister ain't home when his growlings are plainly audible; the man who knowed the feller didn't kill hisself; the man who says there are some funny things a-going on, I'm a-telling you; the preacher who says Prepare to Meet Thy God, the End of the World is at Hand. . . . All these sisters and brothers he accepts without question. Doesn't he see ghosts himself, sometimes? Wasn't he thinking about that very suicide case? Didn't he go to the morgue himself and hold that kid's perspiring hand while she gasped? What is out of the way in all this? What else would you? Suspicion, credulity, secrecy, hog meat, cabbage, fat: all perfectly natural, all part of the zest of life.

II

Given sufficient numbers of them and a *casus belli*, it is very easy to organize such people into labor unions. Why they organize has been explained by labor economists from Karl Marx down, with many abstruse theories involving algebra, the Sermon on the Mount, and the law of diminishing returns; but it is commonly overlooked that it is part of their nature to pack into a hall and hearken to a speaker from state headquarters, to cheer a resolution "that a committee be appointed to notify McCabe that we want a straight 40 cents an hour or they needn't blow the whistle Monday morning," and then to forget to take a vote. For the lady recording secretary to bounce up from her notebooks and announce that all she wants to say is there's two spies in the hall and everybody knows who they are and they can go back and tell everything they seen and heard and make it twice as strong if they want to. For a gentleman to say there's another thing he wants to know, and that is why do they pay them truck drivers $15 a day when they wouldn't give their own men the 55 cents an hour they asked for, which it was only fair and reasonable, and besides no more'n they was promised the first of the year. For a gentleman in the rear to shout "How about McCabe?"—and for the rest to hiss. For the temporary chairman to say, "Well, the way I git it is we ain't going to work Monday unless we git 40 cents an hour straight, and if ever'body is agreeable, we'll adjourn until Sunday afternoon— oh, there's one more thing, I got to name that there committee. . . . Now, remember, Sunday afternoon, and ever'body come."

Organization usually takes one afternoon, with constitution and by-laws to be mailed down from state headquarters, charter to follow. There is a temporary chairman who does not count. After preliminary details, the chief business of the local is the election of permanent officers. Automatically every member becomes a candidate for office—openly or secretly, mostly openly, as follows:

For President: Every man, woman, and child in the local.

For Vice-President: The incumbent temporary chairman.

For Recording Secretary: Every female, with active members of the Rebekah Lodge to the fore.

For Corresponding Secretary: Every female, with active members of the Rebekah Lodge to the fore.

For Treasurer: Every man, woman, and child in the local.

For members of the Executive Committee: The woman who bawled out the foreman that time he got fresh, together with nine crafty males who hope to impress the management with their cleverness, and thereby get company jobs.

If it is a new local, and particularly a local in a weakling union, like the textile workers', electioneering will be heated but not serious. Most of the candidates will go around saying it seems to them the main thing is to get a good president, a union ain't no good unless them that runs it has some git up and git; that they had ought to be careful about the man they pick for treasurer, and make him put up a bond; that this here committee is an important thing, now, and they had better git some fellers that know what they are doing and not none of this no-account element that is trying all the time to run things to suit theirself and don't know what they want, nohow. . . . But if it is a well-established local with a fat treasury, and particularly if it is a local in a big national union, with good jobs farther up the line, then electioneering is fast, furious, and to the death. Down in West Virginia, for example, where there are 80,000 miners, an election by the United Mineworkers of America causes more excitement than the election of a governor, and is fraught, I believe, with greater public consequences. There are numerous fat jobs—president, vice-president, and secretary-treasurer of districts and subdistricts; all sorts of committeemen who draw $10 *per diem* and traveling expenses, beside offices in local unions. The candidates scurry about in their flivvers, handing out cards bearing their likenesses and their qualifications for office, and buttonholing everybody. The election is held under strict rules and every effort is made to get out a big vote. There are watchers, judges, challengers, now and then a recount, good lusty fights.

All this is pretty much like a county election, and it has similar results. That is, the fellow who gets elected proves that he is adept at vote-getting, but otherwise is as much like those who elected him as a member of the State Assembly is like those who elected *him*. But there are differences. The county vote-getter has mainly to possess craftiness and a talent for petty intrigue. The union vote-getter must possess these too, but even more he must possess youth, physical courage, and heavy-hitting fists. When a gentleman in the rear arises and demands to know of the president of the local what became of that money that was voted for strike relief over in Croxton yards and never a nickel of it was spent there, as he knows from a fellow that was over there the whole time the strike was on; and when the president of the local replies that anybody who puts out a report that there was anything wrong with the way that money was spent is a dirty liar and he can prove it,—when this situation arises, and it is, so to speak, a standard, conventional situation, why the one that wins the fight is going to be the next president of the local. If the president can hold his spurs, all right; if not, he steps down. The fight settles the minor issue of the money, and the winner is elected by acclamation. These people are all for the fellow who is on top, who can prove himself Some Man. Particularly the women, if it is a mixed local, are for the brawny lads, with loud voices and a good front.

III

So, as a result of many such situations, the American labor leader begins to emerge as a type. He is a youngish, big, powerful man, with thick red neck and a suit wrinkled at elbow and knee by bulging muscles; a man with wary, catlike physical poise; a man with a head shaped a little like a prize fighter's. He presides at local meetings, pounds his gavel, and announces that it has been moved and seconded. He lays the charge of dirty liar and proves it. He goes through a strike or two, and finds out that a strike has its compensations. There are fine whisperings and plottings, unaccustomed and elevating intimacy with the women. He goes to state conventions, expenses paid, and maybe to a national convention. After two or three years, if he is an exceptionally good slugger and even ordinarily crafty, he becomes a state committeeman, a national committeeman, finally, International Representative. By now his cup is full. A good salary, traveling expenses (and plenty of travel), hardly any work, a lot of authority, all conferred by the constitution, page 17, article 5.

Now he maintains an office. A labor headquarters is a curious place. Usually it is tucked away up some dark stairway, and the doors, dimly visible, bear all sorts of long-winded legends: International Seamen's Union of America; International Brotherhood of Locomotive Engineers; International Association of Longshoremen; United Mineworkers of America; International Brotherhood of Railway and Steamship Clerks, Freight Handlers, and Station Employes. Two thirds of the doors bear the additional legend, Keep Out. Inside, these offices carry unmistakably the flavor of the old front stoop. The furniture is expensive enough, but the wrong color. There is no rug, only bare boards. The mural decoration usually consists of the American Federation of Labor chart calendar, setting a goal of 4,000,000 members by January 1 next. Spittoons, typewriters, one or two filing cases. But the invariable and inevitable piece of furniture is a great black safe. . . . The lady employes suggest somehow the laundry and shirt factory, although two-thirds of them are pretty, for your labor leader has a sporty taste in women. They are hostile and mysterious. They can't give out any information on that; you'll have to see the International Representative. No, he isn't in today. They don't know when he'll be in. You may think I exaggerate. Once out of curiosity I made a round of one of the floors of the American Federation of Labor Building in Washington. Half the doors were locked, although it was not a holiday. In the rest of the offices every legislative representative was out, and not a single stenographer could tell where one of them was or when he would be in. . . . Eventually, after you go out and call the International Representative over the telephone, you find out that he was in all the time. He informs you, when you finally get to him, that if he had known it was you it would have been all right, but they've been watching him so close here lately he has to be careful as the devil.

They've been watching us! This is the ever-recurrent *motif* in the whole American labor turmoil. Probably no strike has ever been called that this note was not sounded in it. In the mines, building trades, print shops, clothing factories, railroads, everywhere; let a strike be called, and "they're watching us." But they don't catch us asleep, not by a long shot! We're watching them, too. We got information out there in that safe that's going to wake this old town up one of these days, all this stuff they've been pulling. We ain't quite ready with it yet, but when our people send in some more confidential reports it'll be something tremenjous. You wouldn't hardly believe it, sitting right there in that chair, if I was to tell you, but it's a fact, and we can prove it, that he didn't kill hisself, and she did have a nigger baby last summer. . . . The Blow from Behind, or, The Mystery of the Stolen Papers, by Old Sleuth.

IV

After you finally get into his office, you perceive that certain changes have come over the International Representative. He is still boorish: he doesn't rise when you enter; he has his feet on the desk; he keeps his hat on. But he has developed a bit since the time he slugged his way into the presidency of the local. For one thing, he slings the English language in a more free and easy fashion. As the American business man has come to the point where everything, from the advent of his first born to the death of his best beloved, is a Proposition, so the International Representative has come to the point where everything is a Matter. "This Matter you speak of, now, I don't want to be quoted in it, see? but if there's anything going in I want it to go in like it is, the truth about it, I mean, and not no pack of dam lies like the papers generally prints. What I say, now, don't put it in like it come from me, because I don't know nothing about it, except what I read in the papers, not being notified in no official way, see? Besides, it's a matter which you might say is going to have a question of jurisdiction to it, and I don't want to have nobody make no charges against me for interference in no matter which it ain't strickly a point where I got authority. But I can give you a idea about it and you can fix it up so's them that reads the paper can figger out their own conclusion on how we stand in the matter."

He is also getting up in a wordly way. He has a car now and a tin garage back of his home. The porch has a canvas swing in it. The old $25 phonograph is gone, and in its place is a nice $350 machine, with Japanese birds on the door, and these records: "In the Shade of the Old Apple Tree," "Calvary" (Homer Rodeheaver), "Barney Google," "Yes, We Have No Bananas," "Rock of Ages" (Shannon Quartet), "Walking with Jesus" (Orpheus Quartet), "Cohen on the Telephone," and "Mose Brown's Suicide" (Comedy Monologue). The old chromos that once adorned the walls are gone also, and in their place are prints like "Love's Coronation," in nifty gilt frames. His wife wears bungalow aprons and the favorite toy of his child—his kid—is a cap pistol. He doesn't take his wife and kid to conventions, however. Nix; convention ain't no place for a woman! "Say, you look like you know how to keep something to yourself: tell you something funny happened up to our last convention. Believe me, that was some gang there, too. Them guys had money every color there was, and all on the table, too. I seen $3,000 in one pot in one game there. . . . Well, anyhow, was a feller there from Indianapolis had his wife with him. Said it was his wife. I don't know, I reckon it was. Anyhow she was some cute baby. I seen her in the lobby one night and she give me a smile, so I says to myself, 'Me for you, kid.' So I gets the guy and takes him to a near-beer s'loon and we gets soused, see? Anyhow, he gets soused and I takes ginger ale. Then they give him the bum's rush and I has to take him back up to his room at the hotel. She is there waiting for him, like I figgered, and her and me puts him to bed and he passes out. Then her and me goes down and has some real likker. . . . Some baby, believe me!"

So this is he who, according to the newspapers, takes matters under advisement, studies questions, delivers ultimatums, directs strike activities, makes counter proposals, signs tentative agreements. He who, according to the Liberal weeklies, is a burning idealist, with lofty brow and glistering eye, panting to deliver the Oppressed, abolish the Sweatshop, and realize the Brotherhood of Man; something between a ritualist revolutionary, a jail poet, and a mountain preacher. The newspaper picture puzzles him a little, for he doesn't understand all the words, and he is suspicious of newspapers, anyhow: he associates them with police courts and injunctions. The Liberal picture doesn't bother him a whit, for he never sees it. Most of the Liberal weeklies he has never heard of; those he has heard of he usually confuses with something else (as witness the recent excoriation of the *Nation* by Sam Gompers). . . . The picture he has of himself is of a powerful, crafty fellow, a fellow of infinite brawn and terrifying jaw, a fellow of big shoulders and unfoolable shrewdness; in short, a sort of combination of Jack Dempsey and William John Burns.

V

Well, all good men come to an end some time. So with the International Representative. Sooner or later somebody with a louder voice and harder fist will push him out.

"What will you do then?" I once asked a miners' official.

"Who, me?" he replied. "Why, man, I can go back to the mines any time. I haven't forgot my trade."

I looked at the big blue Stutz, the sporty clothes, the pretty wife, and smiled. He laughed.

"Well, hell," he said, "I can always sell out to the operators. They got a good job waiting for me whenever this blows up."

CLINICAL NOTES

BY H. L. MENCKEN AND GEORGE JEAN NATHAN

The End of an Imperfect Day.—The beautiful day, the day of blue and gold and sunshine, is God's gift to the plain people; the bad day, the day of gloom and gray and rain, He has reserved for the exclusive pleasure of the aristocracy. The artist, the connoisseur of emotions, the philosopher —these have no use for the fair day: it distracts them, summons them from their introspection and solitude, calls them into the open. On such a day, work and those pleasures dear to men with a taste for the sequestered are impossible: the outdoors beckons too persuasively and too disconcertingly. But when the world is full of wet and fog and the monotony of rain, then the artist, the connoisseur of quiet, the philosopher and all their brothers are happy. It is on such days, while the yokelry is eating dill pickles and cheese sandwiches on the roadsides, or riding in Fords through the Jersey swamps, or chasing small white balls across the grass with a répertoire of clubs, that men of soul and sadness revel in the happiness that only God's elect can comprehend.

Portrait of an Ideal World.—That ethyl alcohol in dilute aqueous solution, when taken into the human organism, acts as a depressant, not as a stimulant, is now so much a commonplace of knowledge that even the more advanced varieties of physiologists are beginning to be aware of it. The intelligent layman no longer resorts to the jug when he has important business before him, whether intellectual or manual; he resorts to it after his business is done, and he desires to release his taut nerves and reduce the boiler-pressure in his spleen. Alcohol, so to speak, unwinds us. It raises the threshold of sensation and makes us less sensitive to external stimuli, and particularly to those that are unpleasant. It reduces and simplifies the emotions. Putting a brake upon all the qualities which enable us to get on in the world and shine before our fellows—for example, combativeness, shrewdness, diligence, ambition—, it releases the qualities which mellow us and make our fellows love us—for example, amiability, generosity, toleration, humor, sympathy. A man who has taken aboard two or three cocktails is less competent than he was before to steer a battleship down the Ambrose Channel, or to cut off a leg, or to draw up a deed of trust, or to conduct Bach's B minor mass, but he is immensely more competent to entertain a dinner party, or to admire a pretty girl, or to subscribe to the Near East Relief, or to *hear* Bach's B minor mass. The harsh, useful things of the world, from pulling teeth to digging potatoes, are best done by men who are as starkly sober as so many convicts in the death-house, but the lovely and useless things, the charming and exhilarating things, are best done by men with, as the phrase is, a few sheets in the wind. *Pithecanthropus erectus* was a teetotaler, but the angels, you may be sure, know what is proper at 5 P. M.

All this is so obvious that I marvel that no utopian has ever proposed to get rid of all the sorrows of the world by the simple device of getting and keeping the whole human race gently stewed. I do not say drunk, remember; I say simply gently stewed—and apologize, as in duty bound, for not knowing how to describe the state in a more seemly phrase. The man who is in it is a man who has put all of his best qualities into his showcase. He is not only immensely more amiable than the cold sober man; he is also immeasurably more decent. He reacts to all situations in an expansive, generous and humane manner. He has become more liberal, more tolerant, more kind. He is a better citizen, husband, father, friend. The enterprises that make human life on this earth uncomfortable and unsafe are never launched by such men. They are not makers of wars; they do not rob and oppress anyone; they invent no such swineries as high tariffs, 100 per cent Americanism, Methodism and Prohibition. All the great villainies of history, from the murder of Abel to the Treaty of Versailles, have been perpetrated by sober men, and chiefly by teetotalers. But all the charming and beautiful things, from the Song of Songs to terrapin à la Maryland, and from the nine Beethoven symphonies to the Martini cocktail, have been given to humanity by men who, when the hour came, turned from well water to something with color to it, and more in it than mere oxygen and hydrogen.

I am well aware, of course, that getting the whole human race stewed and keeping it stewed, year in and year out, would present formidable technical difficulties. It would be hard to make the daily dose of each individual conform exactly to his private needs, and hard to get it to him at precisely the right time. On the one hand there would be the constant danger that large minorities might occasionally become cold sober, and so start wars, theological disputes, moral reforms, and other such unpleasantness. On the other hand, there would be danger that other minorities might proceed to actual intoxication, and so annoy us all with their fatuous bawling or maudlin tears. But such technical obstacles, of course, are by no means insurmountable. Perhaps they might be got around by abandoning the administration of alcohol *per ora* and distributing it instead by impregnating the air with it. I throw out the suggestion, and pass on. Such questions are for men skilled in thera-

peutics, government and business efficiency. They exist today and their enterprises often show a high ingenuity, but, being chiefly sober, they devote too much of their time to harassing the rest of us. Half-stewed, they would be ten times as humane, and perhaps at least half as efficient. Thousands of them, relieved of their present anti-social duties, would be idle, and eager for occupation. I trust to them in this small matter. If they didn't succeed completely, they would at least succeed partially.

The objection remains that even small doses of alcohol, if each followed upon the heels of its predecessor before the effects of the latter had worn off, would have a deleterious effect upon the physical health of the race—that the death-rate would increase, and whole categories of human beings would be exterminated. The answer here is that what I propose is not lengthening the span of life, but augmenting its joys. Suppose we assume that its duration is reduced 20 per cent. My reply is that its delights will be increased at least 100 per cent. Misled by statisticians, we fall only too often into the error of worshipping mere figures. To say that A will live to be 80 and B will die at 40 is certainly not to argue plausibly that A is more to be envied than B. A, in point of fact, may have to spend all of his 80 years in Kansas or Arkansas, with nothing to eat save corn and hog-meat and nothing to drink save polluted river water, whereas B may put in his 29 years of discretion upon the Côte d'Azure, *wie Gott im Frankreich*. It is my contention that the world I picture, even assuming the average duration of human life to be cut down 50 per cent, would be an infinitely happier and more charming world than that we live in today—that no intelligent human being, having once tasted its peace and joy, would go back voluntarily to the harsh brutalities and stupidities which we now suffer, and so idiotically strive to prolong. If intelligent Americans, in these depressing days, still cling to life and try to stretch it out longer and longer, it is surely not logically, but only atavistically. It is the primeval brute in them that hangs on, not the man. The man knows only too well that ten years in a genuinely civilized and happy country would be infinitely better than a geological epoch under the curses he must face and endure every hour today.

Moreover, there is no need to admit that the moderate alcoholization of the whole race would materially reduce the duration of life. A great many of us are moderately alcoholized already, and yet manage to survive quite as long as the blue-noses. As for the blue-noses themselves, who would repine if breathing alcohol-laden air brought them down with delirium tremens and so sterilized and exterminated them? The advantage to the race in general would be obvious and incalculable. All the worst strains—which now not only persist, but even prosper—would be stamped out in a few generations, and so the average human being would move appreciably away from, say, the norm of a Baptist clergyman in Georgia and toward the norm of Shakespeare, Mozart and Goethe. It would take aeons, of course, to go all the way, but there would be progress with every generation, slow but sure. Today, it must be manifest, we make no progress at all; instead we slip steadily backward. That the average American of today is greatly inferior to the average American of two or three generations ago is too plain to need arguing. He has less enterprise and courage; he is less resourceful and intelligent; he is more like a rabbit and less like a lion. Harsh oppressions have made him what he is. He is the victim of tyrants. . . . Well, no man with two or three cocktails in him is a tyrant. He may be foolish, but he is not cruel. He may be noisy, but he is genial, tolerant, generous and kind. My proposal would restore Christianity to the world. It would rescue mankind from moralists, pedants and brutes.

More Reflections at Forty.—1. The letter of a woman is always more honest and more sincere than the letter of a man. A woman writes what she thinks and feels at the moment; a man, what he thinks he may think and feel tomorrow in terms of what he thought and felt yesterday.

2. Politics is the refuge of scoundrels—from other scoundrels.

3. A man's wife is his compromise with the illusion of his first sweetheart.

4. One notices that those Englishmen who are most contemptuous of the American's regard for money are all over here lecturing their heads off.

5. A fool is one who is intelligent at the wrong time.

6. Perfect democracy is possible only in a royal household.

7. One of the greatest of all bores is the precisionist in the use of words, the kind of person who in conversation is meticulously concerned with the exact use of the English language. Scrupulous English is the murderer of interesting colloquy. Conversation under such circumstances becomes less verbal intercourse between two human beings than a contest between two etymologists and grammarians.

8. I have yet to attend a great social affair in England or America at which all the most eligible bachelors present were not trying to break away to keep a date with some Cinderella.

9. The worth-while man generally has a streak of laziness in him. It is the essentially snide fellow who is ever on the alert, ever up-and-doing, ever the consistent go-getter.

Homo Sapiens.—That the great majority of men are quite incapable of rational thought is a fact to which the *illuminati* have been made privy of late by the babbling of eminent psychologists. Granted. But let us not rashly assume that, above the level where genuine thinking begins, it goes on, level by level, to greater and greater heights of clarity and acumen. Nothing of the sort. The curve goes upward for a while, but then it flattens, and finally it dips sharply. Thinking, indeed, is so recent an accomplishment phylogenetically that man is capable of it only in a narrow area. To one side lie the almost instinctive cerebral tropisms and peristaltic motions of the simple; to the other side lie the complex but wholly irrational speculations of metaphysicians. Between a speech by a Grand Goblin of the Rotary Club and a philosophical treatise by an American Neo-Realist there is no more to choose than between the puling of an infant and the puling of a veteran of the Mexican War. Both show the cerebrum overloaded; both, strictly speaking, are idiotic.

Critics on Themselves.—The esteemed *Nation* has been publishing a series of articles written by various critics wherein the latter seek to analyze themselves that their followers may know what manner of men they are and the nature of the fonts of viewpoint and prejudice from which their judgments spring. An excellent editorial idea, but of little actual soundness or value, and this despite the various critics' unquestionable honesty in setting down the personal facts and deductions requested of them. It is next to impossible for any critic thoroughly to analyze himself fairly and squarely, that is, for any critic of the first grade. The first-rate critic may know himself in a vague way, and may be able to record that vagueness in terms of a deceptive literality and plausibility, but most of the qualities that go to make him the first-rate critic that he is inevitably elude his plumbing, for all its sincerity. One observes that in every one of the self-exposés that the *Nation* has thus far printed, the critic under his own microscope attempts to view himself through the eye not of a critic but through the eye of his lay reader, which is a very different thing. He presents the picture of himself not in terms of himself so much as in terms of that part of himself that is the normal, average man. He apologizes for those qualities in him that differentiate him from the normal, average man. Which constitutes a document approximately as valuable as a treatise by a normal, average man

outlining those qualities and prejudices and points of view of his own that differ from those of the first-rate critic.

Usually when a critic essays self-analysis, he misses the real point of himself for the simple reason that neither he, nor anyone else, knows what it is. It is as impossible accurately to define the quality that makes the first-rate critic as it is to define the quality that makes the first-rate musician, or painter, or sculptor. It is easy to speak of intelligence, culture, background, experience, sympathy, sensitiveness, originality and so on, but these are merely rubber-stamps, merely words. There have been critics possessed of all these qualities who have been second-rate critics. There have been critics who have possessed few of these qualities who have been first-rate critics. Great criticism is the product of a species of sleight-of-mind that tricks the most seeing eye and is to no little degree inexplicable. The critic of the Hoboken *Ünkblatt* may be able to lay bare the secrets of his personal craft and of his immortal soul, but Coleridge would be unable to if he tried a thousand years. The great critic no more knows why he is great than a seven-year-old chess prodigy knows why he is the expert that he happens to be. It is only the critics of the lower level who know why they are on that level. It is easier for men to know why they fail than for men to know why they succeed. Genius is ever a complete stranger to itself. It is reserved for mere talent alone to comprehend fully its loves and its hates.

Three British Playwrights.—While Mr. A. A. Milne is spending one-third of his time writing weakly humorous dialogue and the remaining two-thirds composing feuilletons indignantly denouncing nine-tenths of the British and American dramatic critics for not laughing themselves to death over it, one of his young English colleagues is concerning himself solely, and perhaps a trifle more relevantly, with fashioning as witty dialogue as the Anglo-American theatre has heard in the round of several seasons. If this second young Englishman were as apt in his fabrication of plays as he is in the manufacture of droll colloquy, one would be disposed to view him as a likely saviour of that London stage from which the spirit of finished light comedy seems lately to have evaporated. But the plays of Frederick Lonsdale show so much less invention and imagination than his verbal embroideries of those plays that one remembers them as one ever remembers a pleasant dinner party, recalling only the amiable conversation and not exactly remembering whether one had anything to eat or not. This, doubtless, is not at all bad: it may be Lonsdale's deliberate dodge agreeably to talk one out of thinking of his plays. It may be his stratagem to take a time-worn theme and by handling it with a circumspect obviousness throw his dialogue, through sheer contrast, into doubly high relief. (I surely need not name a certain great dramatic genius who indulged in the same practice.) But whether it is or is not his stratagem, Lonsdale's dialogic talent remains unmistakable. It is sophisticated without sophistication's usual brashness; it is polished without the air of that type of polish which suggests only the painted canvas drawing-room of the London actor-manager stage; it is at times as witty as Wilde and as acutely observant in a plain, everyday way as our own Kin Hubbard. At times. At other times—of such we have a sample in "Spring Cleaning" when the woman of the streets prattles wistfully of babies—he descends to the lowest depths of boobismus. To these depths, Lonsdale's more experienced and somewhat older compatriot and fellow wit, Maugham, never descends. The latter, further, is a more skilful playwright than the former. Yet, peculiarly enough, he is a playwright who has never quite realized himself. He has all the qualities that should make him the first polite comedy writer of the present day English theatre; he has salt and erudition, taste and dexterity, invention and viewpoint; yet an apparently inborn British conventionality contrives too often to reduce his high talents to the level of that conventionality. His themes are now and again brave, as in the instance of "Our Betters"; the writer himself is brave; but the British conventionality is there at bottom all the same despite the deceptive frosting of swagger and impudence. Maugham is as cosmopolitan a writer as England knows today, yet his cosmopolitanism ever flies the Union Jack at its masthead.

The Moral Kaleidoscope.—The bluer the nose, the greener the mind, the grayer the sense of beauty, the yellower the honor, the redder the indignation, and the more lavender the sex.

The Autobiography.—There is no such thing as an absolutely truthful autobiography. Every such work, though it may truthfully set down the discreditable facts, concerns itself ultimately with converting such discreditable facts into a compositely creditable picture of its author. There was never a writer of an autobiography who did not see to it that he emerged from that autobiography a picturesque and, for all his deficiencies, an appealing fellow.

A Mensa et Thoro.—From discussions by various eminent authorities, usually indignant, of the high divorce rate prevailing in the United States I dredge up the following theories as to the cause of the rapid decay of Christian monogamy among us:

1. That the movies, with their lascivious suggestions, are to blame.
2. That the cause lies in the decline of belief in the literal authority of the Holy Scriptures.
3. That the multiplication of delicatessen shops has destroyed home cooking, and so made for unbearable unhappiness at the domestic hearth.
4. That no woman ever truly loves her husband until she has had eight children.
5. That shyster lawyers are to blame.
6. That the steady fall in the price of Fords has enormously facilitated adultery.
7. That jazz is responsible.
8. That the judges in our courts are not Christians, or, if Christians, not honest and passionate ones.
9. That there would be no divorces if there were no yellow journals.
10. That it is too easy for women to get good jobs.
11. That the cheap sex magazines have done it.

12. That God is punishing the Republic for not joining the League of Nations.

13. That the education of women has caused them to take marriage lightly.

14. That the Republic is in decay, like Rome, and that the high divorce rate is but one symptom of it, others being bootlegging, the Ku Klux Klan, cheek-to-cheek dancing, mah jong, birth control and cocaine sniffing.

I could extend the list, of course, to a hundred articles, some of them highly ingenious, and a few not printable in a family paper. Unluckily, it is my impression, after long and hard study, that all of them are nonsensical. The high divorce rate in the United States, it seems to me, is chiefly if not wholly due to one single and simple cause—one so simple, indeed, that I marvel that all the legal and ecclesiastical bigwigs who labor the subject have so diligently overlooked it. That cause is the American custom of marrying for love. In countries where marriages are made by prudent third parties the divorce rate is negligible. In countries where, though romance is countenanced, it is never permitted to outweigh common sense, the divorce rate is still within bounds. But in countries where it is regarded as somehow discreditable to marry for anything but love—in such romantic and idealistic countries divorce is a pestilence. Of the countries of the third category the largest and most conspicuous is the American Republic, and it is precisely in the American Republic, as everyone knows, that divorce is resorted to most scandalously often.

The immovable objection to marriage for love alone is that it founds what is theoretically the most solid and permanent of relationships upon, not a conviction, but an emotion—and even professors of psychology must be aware by this time that the chief characteristic of an emotion is that it cannot last. True enough, it is apt to be followed, at least in those of emotional habit, by a series of other emotions, but there is not the slightest assurance that any of the series will resemble it in its effects upon practical conduct. It may happen, and it often does happen, that a woman, on ceasing to love her husband, begins to regard him with the genial fondness with which she regards her lap-dog, her pastor or her gossip, but it happens just as often that her love is followed by the quite foreign emotion of disgust, or even by that of hate. Then the marriage dies, and either the corpse remains in the house or there is a disorderly funeral in the divorce court.

In those countries where marriage is founded, not upon an emotion, but upon a conviction, or, at all events, upon a mixture of emotion and conviction, there is vastly less risk of disaster. For the considerations upon which the conviction is based may be demonstrated logically, and when they exist today it is pretty certain that they will also exist tomorrow. They are mainly, in practice, considerations of money, of family, of education, of position, of worldly prospects. These things, to be sure, may change in time, but it must be obvious that they are very much more apt to remain *un*changed. Family is a fact that is virtually immovable; so is social position; so is education. Even money is more secure than any emotion ever heard of; it is enormously more secure than the fragile emotion of love, which is founded, at best, upon illusion far more than upon reality. A man in love is simply one who believes that his inamorata is more charming than she is in fact. To deceive him equally about her family, her education, her social traditions, her worldly means—in brief, about any of the durable qualities that lie outside her mere physical charm—would be as difficult as to deceive him about her color. If he kept his mind on these things, he would seldom make a mistake. But looking only at the gal, he is often led into a disaster which wrecks his happiness, dissipates his estate, and makes him a public laughing-stock.

THE KU-KLUXER

BY GERALD W. JOHNSON

I THINK that my friend Chill Burton is an Exalted Cyclops, although he may be only a Fury, or a lesser Titan, for my knowledge of the nomenclature of the Ku Klux Klan is far from exact. At any rate, he is an important personage among klansmen in our town, but rather insignificant in the State organization. He may therefore be classified as a klansman ranking slightly above the average, but not far enough above it to be in any way identified with the Atlanta potentates, who are a breed different altogether from the ordinary members. So if one might determine what made Chill Burton a member of this curious organization, I believe that the secret of its rapid growth would be made plain; for an argument that would convince him would unquestionably convince millions of other obscure and worthy Americanos.

In the first place, the lurid imaginings of many writers on the Klan, particularly in the North, may be dismissed at once. It was not the prospect of participating in the celebration of some revolting Witches' Sabbath that fetched Chill, for he isn't that sort of man. He is fifty years old, a pillar of the church, an exemplary husband and the father of six head of healthy children. He believes in the verbal inspiration and literal interpretation of the Scriptures, and accepts the Athanasian Creed and the Democratic Platform with unquestioning faith. You might entrust your purse or your daughter to Chill with quite as much confidence as you might entrust either to the right reverend ordinary of the diocese, or to the pastor of the First Baptist Church. He will *not* take a drink, and he

will pay his debts. In brief, if Pope was right, Chill is one of the noblest works of God.

But he is incurably romantic. Doubtless that is an inheritance. His name indicates as much, for he was christened Achilles, which, considering the abbreviation as a guide to the pronunciation prevailing in the House of Burton, certainly indicates a disposition on the part of his immediate forebears to reach out for the undiscovered. His occupation proves it, too, for he has been on the road for thirty years representing a tobacco company, and a man who can sell snuff and plug tobacco for thirty years without even attempting suicide is obviously endowed with the romanticist's ability to create around himself a world of dreams to mask or replace reality. Again, his conversation demonstrates it, for he is perpetually discovering mare's nests of the most awful nature—conspiracies among municipal officials to loot the city treasury, conspiracies among Negro school-teachers to incite the pickaninnies to pillage, rapine and massacre, and daily new proofs that someone—formerly German spies, later I. W. W.'s, and later still Russian Bolshevists, with Mr. J. Pierpont Morgan playing in the interludes—spread the cotton boll-weevil through the South by casting the insect from moving trains.

Chill goes through life surrounded by the machinations of occult and Machiavellian intelligences. He walks briskly, planting his square-toed shoes with decision. He is sturdy, the least bit stooped, decently garbed in clothing of inconspicuous cut and neutral tint, and his iron-gray hair is growing thin on the top of his head. Occasionally his eyes light up with a pale blue flame, and his mouth tightens into a grim slit; but otherwise he gives no outward indication of the fact that his soul is tormented by tremendous and ghastly visions and his mind appalled by the perils that threaten the very existence of true religion and unpolluted Anglo-Saxon blood.

II

These visions and perils, and nothing base, were the considerations that made of Chill what is colloquially known in North Carolina as a "klucker." He certainly does not thirst for the heart's blood of Mary Amanda Emmeline Seymour Pleasure Belle Caroline Kearns, who presides in his kitchen. He is on perfectly friendly, if not intimate, terms with J. Leroy Goldstein, the pawnbroker, and Chris Skalchunes, who keeps the fruit stand, and he treats the Rev. Father Paul O'Keefe with faultless, frosty courtesy. Chill would sincerely deplore the lynching of any of these individuals; most emphatically would he refuse to have anything to do with their molestation, even in as mild a form as a cow-hiding, or a coat of tar and feathers. Yet from the bottom of his soul he believes that the dominance of the Anglo-Saxon is hourly imperilled by the Negro; that if the Nordic strain is polluted by infusion of any other blood, American civilization will collapse and disappear; that if the Protocols of Zion were fraudulent, then something worse exists still unrevealed; and that secret agents of the Pope, infiltrating the Bureau of Engraving and Printing, strove treacherously to convert America to Catholicism by introducing crosses, snakes and pictures of His Holiness among the decorations on the dollar bill of 1917. Therefore, when less scrupulous brother knights of the Invisible Empire commit outrages under cover of darkness, Chill's attitude is that while lawlessness is always to be regretted, it is better that a few individuals should suffer

injustice than that our civilization, our religion and our very race should be exposed to the secret assaults of foes without scruples and of superhuman cunning.

Nor is his belief a proof of insanity any more than it is a proof of insanity for his small son to believe that Caesar overcame the Nervii. The boy has no legal evidence that either Caesar or the Nervii ever existed in fact; the schoolmaster has simply taught him that the battle occurred, and that settles it for him. Equally oracular authorities, the pastor and the politician, had filled Chill with fear and distrust of Negroes, foreigners, Jews and Catholics long before William Joseph Simmons, of Atlanta, began to dream of a throne. The explanation is absurdly simple. Devil-drubbing is always easier and safer if the particular devil selected for chastisement is feeble, or far away. In the South, where the Ku Klux Klan originated, foreigners, Jews and Catholics are relatively few and far between, and Negroes are politically and socially impotent. Therefore every Southern demagogue, sacred or profane, has for generations covered his significant silence on industrial slavery, on race hatred, on baronial estates supported by legalized peonage, and on election frauds by thundering denunciations of the carpet-bagger, St. Peter, Judas Iscariot and Lenine, none of whom was then and there present or likely to demand embarrassing explanation.

The Cause was furthered in the South by other circumstances. It happens that the South actually was under Negro domination once, and after half a century the memory of that experience still keeps its racial sensibilities abnormally acute. A Northern observer recently pointed out that the Negro is all that it has to worry about, so it has made up for the lack of other major troubles by worrying itself into a pathological condition about the race problem. Thus, in view of the diligent tillage that had been going on for many decades, it is no marvel that the Invisible Empire reaped a rich and instantaneous harvest in the Southern field.

Yet it is commonly reported now that the banner Ku Klux State is not Georgia, but Indiana. It is evident, therefore, that the strongest appeal of the Klan is not to prejudice against the Negro—an assumption borne out by the significant fact that only in rare instances in the South have men wearing the regalia of the Klan attacked a Negro. Nor have Catholics, Jews and foreigners furnished the majority of the victims, except at such times as they have offered themselves as candidates and been politically massacred at the polls. The whippings, the tar and feathers, and similar attentions have usually been administered to known or suspected criminals or social outcasts. To this sort of work the klucker of a grade slightly lower than that of my friend Chill goes forth joyously, sublimely confident that he thereby serves the larger cause of white, Gentile, Protestant supremacy, just as the county chairman stuffs the precinct boxes with the county ticket only, thoroughly convinced that he is thereby helping God and the national committee to save the country.

The necromancy by which the guardian of the sacred fires of civilization, race and religion is transformed into a whipper of prostitutes and a lyncher of bootleggers is no mystery. It is no more than the familiar psychological phenomenon of "taking it out on somebody." Chill is profoundly convinced that the Nordic Protestant is in imminent danger; what could be more natural, then, than for him to regard with tolerance, if not with approval, the extra-legal chastisement of anyone who violates Nordic Protestant standards in whatever particular? No doubt some Gray Eminence is the man higher up; but he is not within reach, or even identified as yet. In the meantime, this strumpet also violates our Protestant Nordic standards. Go to, let us deal with her now, and catch His Eminence when we can!

But who impressed Chill with the notion that his duty to obey the law is less than his duty to defend racial, social and religious purity? Who but those who set up the great American fetish of equality, not merely before the law, but in every respect? Chill has been assured from childhood that in the United States of America every man is a king in his own right and so naturally he assumes royal prerogatives. The energy of a monarch in cutting legal red-tape in the cause of justice may very well be a virtue; but it is a virtue that cannot be democratized without disaster. To have a rigid and exacting standard of manners and morals set by an aristocracy may be of great benefit to a nation; but when the proletariat undertakes to confer that benefit—well, we have the result before us in America.

The Ku Klux Klan has swept beyond the racial boundaries of the Negro and flourishes now in the Middle West because it is a perfect expression of the American idea that the voice of the people is the voice of God. The belief that the average klansman is consciously affected by an appeal to his baser self is altogether erroneous. In the voice of the organizer he hears a clarion call to knightly and selfless service. It strikes him as in no wise strange that he should be so summoned; is he not, as an American citizen, of the nobility? Politics has been democratized. Social usage has been democratized. Religion has been most astoundingly democratized. Why, then, not democratize chivalry?

The klansman has already been made, in his own estimation, politically a monarch, socially a peer of the realm, spiritually a high priest. Now the Ku Klux Klan calls him to step up and for the trifling consideration of ten dollars he is made a Roland, a Lancelot, a knight-errant vowed to the succor of the oppressed, the destruction of ogres and magicians, the defense of the faith. Bursting with noble ideals and lofty aspirations, he accepts the nomination. The trouble is that this incantation doesn't work, as none of the others has worked, except in his imagination. King, aristocrat, high priest as he believes himself to be, he is neither royal, noble, nor holy. So, under his white robe and pointed hood he becomes not a Chevalier Bayard but a thug.

III

The shocked surprise of many prominent publicists and educators in the presence of the phenomenon of the Klan is the crowning absurdity of the farce. These men have spent years and gained great renown making just this thing possible. They have stuffed millions of youths, and filled miles of bookshelves with twaddle about the glory of the masses. By dint of herculean labor they have at length deprived the adjective "common" of its legitimate connotation when it is used to modify the noun "people." To do them justice, they seem to have produced an *un*common people, a people incapable of perceiving any essential difference between St. George and a butcher, a people unwilling to admit that spearing a dragon is a feat requiring mental and spiritual qualities not necessarily possessed by a pig-sticker.

Chill is no more to blame for his delusions than the Knight of the Rueful Countenance was for his. The romances are to blame. Chill, indeed, has an excuse that Quixote could not plead, for Chill's romances were offered and accepted as sober narrations of fact, as histories, as lectures, as sermons. They were offered by and accepted from authorities whom Chill respected too much to question; and whom it is not profitable in any case, and not safe in many cases, for anyone else to question.

Thus they are not merely woven into the fabric of his thinking—they are the very warp and woof thereof. The *chansons de geste* of the Republic are as real to him as were the details of the combat in Roncesvaux to a French peasant of the Fourteenth Century. He is no more firmly convinced that the sun rises in the east than he is that Washington, not Rochambeau, won the Revolutionary War, or that the War of 1812 was bravely waged and gloriously won by the patriots of America, or that the struggle of the sixties was notable among all wars for the brilliant strategy of the officers and the magnificent discipline of the troops on both sides, or that the battle of San Juan Hill was a terrible fight, or that Sir John Pershing's helpful hints were what enabled Foch to turn the trick. He has been taught such things from his youth up, so of course he believes that to doubt them would be to reduce his percentage of Americanism away below par. He has been taught romance in the name of history to the end that, glorying in the proud record of American arms, he might present an unfaltering front to any foe when his every instinct commanded him to go away from there. But instead of making a patriot of him, it has served merely to convince him that as an American he is "a mighty tur'ble man," one born to command, and disobedience to whom partakes of the nature of mutiny in the ranks.

The cult of the Nordic he accepts with the same sublime faith. It is not merely that he is totally unfamiliar with the arguments that may be advanced in favor of, say, Slavic, or Latin, or Semitic culture. He does not believe that any such arguments are possible. It simply never has occurred to him that there can be anything to say on the other side. This romance under the label of ethnology has been foisted upon him partly by fantastic imbeciles who believe it themselves, but largely by the economic overlords of the country, who are desperately afraid of what might happen if the nimble-witted economic soothsayers that the Slavs and Latins and Semites are producing in hordes ever began to inject their theories into the stolid Nordic brain. The idea was to make of the American proletarian an economic, as well as a political patriot. The result has been to make him a racial bully.

As for the impressions that Chill has received from his spiritual instructors, they are so nearly incredible that it is hard to believe that they were implanted with any sane object in view. I hesitate to attempt to outline his beliefs, but some conception of them may be conveyed by certain matters of fact. I have seen garbled extracts from the curse of Ernulphus, as quoted in "Tristram Shandy," circulated in pamphlet form with the information that they were part of an oath sworn by every Catholic priest at the time of his ordination. The "Protocols of the Elders of Zion" are still read with avidity by klansmen, and the exposure of their fraudulency is quite honestly believed to be Jewish propaganda. As for Protestant solidarity, I have known of a special prayer-meeting called for the purpose of offering supplications for the conversion to the Baptist faith of a merchant who was, in the literal sense of the word, a damned Methodist. This appalling travesty of Christianity must, it seems at first, have been inspired by no less malignant a genius than Satan himself; it is unquestionably the strongest evidence ever offered to prove the existence of a personal devil. But it is only the inevitable result of the labors of pious romancers who, with the sanctified object of inducing Chill to "put on the whole armour of God," have not hesitated to embellish the truth by assuring him that there is only one style of equipment that is regulation stuff, only one issue creed, only one genuine, o. d. church. The intention was to make a well-drilled soldier of Armageddon; the result seems to have been to produce a spiritual bushwhacker, with no stomach for fighting the common enemy, but delighting in every opportunity to raid the dugouts of the allies.

To inculcate patriotism, to immunize against foreign radical ideas and to strengthen the bulwarks of true religion are certainly prominent among the aims of the current program of Americanization, which is absorbing enormous quantities of money and time and the energy of innumerable massive brains. I submit that the magical rise of the Invisible Empire, Knights of the Ku Klux Klan, is one outstanding proof of the tremendous effect of that program. No romance that apparently tended to strengthen respect for the flag and the faith has been rejected by the Americanizers on the ground that it was blatantly false. But outraged truth has an uncomfortable habit of avenging itself. Spurious history, spurious ethnology, spurious religion have produced a spurious patriot, none the less existent because unexpected and undesired. The fact that nobody foresaw that Chill would blossom into a klansman does not alter the fact that the klansman is one of the flowers of our democracy.

But there is nothing spurious about the tragedy of my friend Chill Burton. That is as authentic as fear. The fact that he is the target of objurgations of the most violent sort is a trifle. What is important is that the man walks through a cloud of unseen presences, terrible and repulsive. The Negro Dominant is a *poltergeist* not unfamiliar to most Southern whites, but he is only one of Chill's invisible attendants. Salathiel creeps ever at his heels; the non-Nordic skips nimbly about, varying his hues chameleon-like, from swarthy white through yellow and brown to black; the Bolshevist, draped with bombs and attended by hordes of nationalized women, hovers near; and above them all looms Antichrist, just now equipped with mitre and crozier but capable, I suspect, of assuming at need the form of any sect other than Chill's own. It is a serious thing to be warrior, priest and king all rolled into one. It entails responsibilities. Democracy has armed, anointed and crowned Chill, but it has also sent him abroad attended by this ghastly train.

On the whole, I think that it would have been kinder to him and safer for the country if America had told him no lies to begin with.

PANORAMA

BY JOHN McCLURE

A COOL raw wind in his face for an instant. Like an apparition in dreams the flicker of light in a strange new town. A cloak over him suddenly. "The night air—he will sicken." A small boy on his father's shoulder, swaddled in darkness.

II

A thunderhead sprawling heaven-high over the world: the churning black bulk of cloud assuming contour and form, body and outline—suddenly with a trunk like an elephant's. A small boy watching all this from a window.

III

Grim swarthy gypsy-men with a schooner wagon, horses and women a-weary, a colt and a calf hobbling along behind, pots and pans in the wagon. Grim swarthy gypsy-men caravaning out of mystery. . . . And a small boy on a broomstick, prancing soberly beside them.

IV

A tree with candles, apples of silver, pomegranates and golden stars: a ruddy and whiskered deity in boots and ermine, proffering apples of silver, trumpets and butternuts. Suddenly a flash of fire and sizzle of ermine. As suddenly, the janitor in his undershirt. . . . A small boy dazed and resentful at the collapse of gods.

V

A crisp night in autumn with a million stars: a white moon hanging in the midst of them like a globe of marble; crickets and katydids. . . . And a small boy filling a coal-skuttle in the back yard, suddenly aware of immensity.

212

VI

Sunset on the prairie with trailing plumes of color and fire. . . . And a small boy watching it, suddenly aware of a little beauty.

VII

A thunder and whistle of steam. Flares of smoke and flame. A chugging of engines. Lanterns swinging in circles before and behind, a thousand miles from home. . . . And a boy there suddenly aware of a little adventure.

VIII

A girl out of glamorie, wistful on a rainswept night when the trees were shaking. . . . And a boy there, suddenly aware of immensity and of beauty and of mystery and of adventure and of romance.

IX

A woman completely desired in her new-world beauty, making a spectre of the moon because she was not to be had. A woman desired, unattainable. . . . And a young man suddenly aware of a little humor.

X

A woman completely desired in her old-world beauty, completely attainable and completely attained. . . . And a young man suddenly aware of a little irony.

XI

Sunsets with plumes of color and fire, crisp nights with a million stars, girls out of glamorie, women desired and lost, women desired and found—a vision of poor devils in graves who will never know these anymore. . . . And a young man who has lost patience with death and the dreamers of death.

Biology

ALCOHOL AND THE DURATION OF LIFE

By Raymond Pearl

WHILE Swift was perhaps right in depicting the abject horror with which the Struldbrugs contemplated their guaranteed earthly immortality, it is still a fact that the average human being is vastly interested in prolonging his life and in keeping young. To be sure, he has to be well past forty before he will make any considerable sacrifice of the immediate pleasures of the senses to achieve the business, but this paradoxical behavior, which has often been ironically commented upon by writers upon longevity, doubtless rests in some part upon the substantial body of human experience that a biological bird in the hand is worth at least two in the bush. The trouble is that in the present stage of development of biological wisdom there is a good deal of uncertainty on two points: first, whether these somewhat mythical birds in the bush can be caught later on when wanted, and, second, whether they will in fact be as plump and toothsome when captured as they are reputed in advance to be.

In consequence, to come forthwith to the point, the average man in these sad times takes a drink whenever he can get it. This does not necessarily mean that he is lacking in either sense or prudence. It merely indicates that his contact with alcoholic beverages has been, on the whole, pleasant, and that his general experience with the world and his fellow men has not substantiated the horrendous tales about the devastating consequences, in disease and early death, of any indulgence in alcohol which have been dinned into his ears from earliest childhood. He has seen people drink themselves to death, to be sure; but he has observed that a vastly larger number of persons have used alcohol with freedom, but not in excess, all their lives, and ultimately died of no different diseases and at no different ages than other people, so far as he can judge. Furthermore he notes that while in some countries and times a great deal more alcohol is consumed than in others, there are no striking, or even evident, corresponding changes in either general well-being or rates of mortality.

In spite of this general experience, most men do not feel quite easy about the matter, because of the teaching as to the direful effects of alcohol to which they were subjected in their youth. In a number of States it is a legal requirement that all elementary-school physiology and hygiene shall include the teaching that alcohol is harmful. Naturally, no real evidence can be presented, and probably it is fair to say that real evidence is the last thing that those responsible for the placing of this legislation on the statute books would have desired. School boys and girls, however, are apt to believe what teacher and text book tell them. So what would otherwise be the unquestioned conclusion from adult experience is in some degree clouded and shaken by the relics of childhood teaching.

Another thing which gives the common citizen pause in accepting whole-heartedly the idea that the moderate and judicious drinking of alcohol is not seriously harmful, is that he has been told that the experience of life insurance companies has proved that the use of even the smallest amount definitely shortens life. The deductions of

213

the actuary have a great reputation for deadly precision and finality among persons who know nothing about their basis. This reputation is probably somewhat higher, in general, than the real merits of the case would warrant. Certainly in the matter of present interest, what the insurance companies actually know about the effects of alcohol upon mortality can by no possibility be held to justify the conclusions which the public, sternly guided by the Anti-Saloon League and the W. C. T. U., have drawn. The insurance "evidence" on alcohol suffers from two fundamental defects. They are:

I. There is no definite knowledge of the alcoholic habits of the individual over any significant portion of his life. The only knowledge an insurance company has of an individual comes from (*a*) the statements of the individual himself when he applies for a policy; (*b*) the continuance of his life, as evidenced by the payment of premiums, and (*c*) his death, as evidenced by a claim under the policy contract. Now, granting that every applicant told the truth when he applied, the picture of his alcoholic habits then set down is, and can be, only of that time and the immediate past. But nothing is more certain than that the drinking habits of many individuals change from what they are at the comparatively early age at which insurance is applied for. These habits may and do change in both directions. Some persons become heavier drinkers, other less heavy, than when they applied for insurance. So then, in fact, it may be taken to be the case that in the non-abstainer section of insurance experience there is a mixture, in wholly unknown proportions, of (*a*) persons who, for the major portions of their lives, have been total abstainers; (*b*) moderate drinkers; (*c*) excessive drinkers. There will also be the same three classes, again in quite unknown proportions, represented in the abstainers' class in the experience of all companies except a very few which require an annual statement from the policy-holder as to his continued abstention.

II. Since most insurance companies are known to discriminate against persons using alcohol as a beverage in more than a certain (to the applicant unknown) amount or degree, an incentive is at once created for the applicant to understate the amount of his alcoholic indulgence. The discrimination may take the form of a refusal to accept the risk, or of a demand for an increased premium rate, or of a reduced participation in so-called bonuses or dividends. But in any case there is a powerful incentive for the applicant to make out as favorable a case as possible for himself.

I can best put the insurance case in this way: Suppose an experimenter wished to determine the effect of the typhoid bacillus upon longevity, and to that end fed a varying and unknown amount of a broth culture containing varying and unknown numbers of bacilli to a number of animals of varying and unknown hereditary constitutions and innate degrees of resistance to typhoid; then shut them up in a room with free and unlimited access to cultures of typhoid germs; *and made no further observation upon them whatever, except of the time of their death.* What possible deductions could be made from such an experiment? Yet it would furnish data which in every essential would be precisely of the same character and value as the experience of life insurance companies regarding alcohol and the duration of life.

Can we do no better than this? The question is an important one. What is needed is critical *ad hoc* data, in which the alcoholic habits of the individual throughout life are accurately known and recorded. Such evidence does not exist either in official or in insurance statistics. The data must be collected at first hand, with due regard to all the biological and statistical pitfalls along the way. A respectable body of such material I have recently been able to get through the activity of a group of trained eugenic field workers. It has been analyzed in detail in a recent book "The Action of Alcohol on Man," with results which can be only briefly summarized here.

The data included 1259 men and 788 women. They fell into three groups as to drinking habits: total abstainers, moderate and occasional drinkers, and heavy and steady drinkers. Appropriate mathematical analysis of the data showed that the average total duration of life of those entering the experience at the age of 20 was as follows:

	Males	
Total abstainers	60.05 years	
Moderate and occasional	61.04 "	
Heavy and steady	55.37 "	
	Females	
Total abstainers	58.49 years	
Moderate and occasional	61.70 "	
Heavy and steady	47.50 "	

For white urban dwellers the official United States life tables show an average total duration of life of males entering the experience at the age of 20 of 60.51 years, and of females of 63.51 years. These figures demonstrate that our material for the study of the alcohol problem is normal from an actuarial standpoint.

The conclusion which is reached from an elaborate and critical mathematical, biological, and sociological analysis of this material is that while heavy drinking distinctly shortens life, moderate drinking, on the other hand, is associated with no different duration of life than is total abstention. Actually, the moderate drinkers show a superior average of duration of life as compared with the abstainers, amounting to .99 of a year in the case of males and 3.21 years in the case of females, both groups entering the experience at the age of 20. No stress, however, is to be laid on these small differences.

In spite of the critical care with which these data have been collected, and the objectivity of their analysis, the plain conclusion to which they lead will be violently opposed by those who devote themselves to Prohibition propaganda. About this nothing, so far as I can see, can possibly be done. Propaganda of all sorts, in the very essence of its nature, can have no necessary relation to truth. Equally it is bound to be actively opposed to any truth which does not fit into and accord with the particular ends toward which it may at any given moment be working.

Book-Collecting

MODERN FIRST EDITIONS

By George H. Sargent

I HEAR much talk among my book-collecting friends about the craze for modern first editions. Some of these collectors, mostly elderly men, seem to be made unhappy because they can go into a second-hand bookstore in New York and for $2.50 take their choice between a first edition of Howells's "Their Wedding Journey," 1872, and Sherwood Anderson's "Many Marriages," 1923—because for $7.50 they may have either the first issue of the first edition of Holmes's "Autocrat of the Breakfast Table," 1858, with the rubricated title page, or Theodore Dreiser's "Jennie Gerhardt," 1911—because for $15 they may purchase either James Russell Lowell's "Fable for Critics" in the first issue of the first edition, 1848, or James Branch Cabell's "Gallantry," 1907. And so on.

Why, they ask, should the work of a modern author, untried by time, be sold in the market-place on even terms with a book that has helped to bring fame to one of the men recognized as in the front rank of American literature? What has created the demand for the work of contemporaneous writers, to the apparent neglect by collectors of the leading American authors of the Victorian period? Is the change which has come in collecting due to a lack of appreciation of the old or to an over-appreciation of the new?

Pertinent questions, these, but not easily answered, for many factors enter into the problem. But let us see first if there really is any "craze for modern first editions." The recent sale at the Anderson Galleries in New York of the library of first editions formed by John Quinn was illuminating on the point. The manuscripts of Joseph Conrad's writings, which went at such high prices, were in a class by themselves. Conrad is so firmly established as a writer that even an incomplete manuscript written by him is sure to bring a big sum. Moreover, every manuscript, of course, is unique. But did the "craze" extend to the generality of first editions offered at the Quinn sale? In this first part, A to C, only a few modern American authors were represented. The Bliss Carman collection was a large one, and the items showed an appreciation in prices, but Bliss Carman has been bibliographied and the rare first editions of his works have been the subject of magazine articles. Otherwise the one-page broadsheet, "Olaf Hjörward," 1891, might not have brought $23, when the first edition of his "Winter Holiday," 1899, containing one of his most exquisite poems, went for only $5. Sherwood Anderson's "Winesburg, Ohio" and Stephen V. Benét's "Five Men and Pompey" brought $4.50 each, which certainly does not indicate that dealers and collectors were scrambling over the seats to get their bids to the auctioneer. Willa Cather's "Youth and the Bright Medusa" fetched $5—an advance over the published price of three years ago, to be sure, but hardly indicating a "craze." The Princess Bibesco's "I Have Only Myself to Blame" and James B. Connolly's "Out of Gloucester" and many others brought only a dollar apiece, less than the published price. In fact, so far as this first sale of the first editions of modern American authors is concerned, there was nothing outside of the Conrad session which bordered on the sensational, and even many of the Conrad first editions went at lower prices than those at which they have been generally held in dealers' catalogues.

Ultimately, the law of demand and supply operates to govern the prices of books. The Quinn sale demonstrated what other sales of first editions have shown in the past—that the rare item, irrespective of its place in literature, will always bring a good price. It is a truism of the auction-room that a really unique item needs no watching—it will always take care of itself. Stevenson's doggerel verses "To the Thompson Class Club" brings more than the price of a first edition of "An Inland Voyage" or "Treasure Island." The pirated Toronto edition of Carman's "Low Tide on Grand Pré," most of which was destroyed by fire, fetched $57.50 in the Quinn sale, while one of the fifty large paper copies of the authorized edition, signed by the author, went for but $7.50, and the first English edition went for fifty cents. Precisely as is the case with the books of the older authors, the modern author's work is judged in the auction-room only by its rarity.

The collecting of first editions of contemporary authors is a comparatively new thing. Hawthorne was not bothered by collectors who came to him with copies of his works, fresh from the press, to be inscribed by the author. Thoreau remaindered his own first edition of the "Week." The collectors of books in those days were not concerned about getting the first editions of their contemporaries. They were collecting Americana, old plays, large paper editions, early editions of the classics, incunabula, Dibdin's dreary bibliographical rhapsodies and library editions of the standard authors. A few discerning ones, perhaps, were buying and preserving certain first issues of authors who were rising into fame, not, however, because these were the first editions, but because they represented what the collectors believed to be enduring literature. The collector who saved the separate parts, with wrappers and advertisements, of Dickens's "Posthumous Papers of the Pickwick Club" as they were issued, did so, not because he expected the work to reach its present prices in the auction-room—he could not have imagined these prices, even in his wildest dreams—, but because he believed that in Pickwick Dickens had created an immortal character. Rossetti, finding Fitzgerald's Omar in Quaritch's twopenny box, showed it to Swinburne as real poetry, and they looted the *cache*. Now and then a collector may have sought a first edition of one of his contemporaries merely because it was rare—for instance, Hawthorne's "Fanshawe" or Poe's "Tamerlane"—but it was probably without a thought that the latter would be one day holding the record as the highest-priced American first edition, with the Halsey copy bringing $11,600. Collecting was then limited to a few. Toward the end of the Victorian era, when the number of collectors increased, interest was directed toward the "elegant" and "sumptuously illustrated" edition, rather than toward the first, of contemporary writers.

In the middle eighties Leon & Brother, of New York, issued the first catalogue of first editions of American writers. Most of the works of Emerson, Lowell, Holmes, Longfellow, Whittier and Whitman were still in print, and many of these writers, with such newer lights as Clemens, Harte, Howells, Burroughs, Fiske and Stedman, were still producing. The publication of this list gave an impetus to first edition collecting, but the first editions of most of the works upon which the fame of Longfellow, Holmes, Whittier, Lowell and Hawthorne was established can still be picked up in second-hand stores at prices not much above those at which they were published. There are two reasons for this: they were published in large editions, and they are already in the principal public libraries and in all the great private collections of American authors. Let a new collector enter this field and for a time he will go on splendidly. Even when he gets to the common rarities, as they have come to be called, his difficulties will not be insurmountable. Take the case of Lowell, for instance. Most of the first editions of his works may be picked up for small sums, and it does not require a long purse to buy even the rarer items, such as "The Pioneer." The Birmingham address "On De-

mocracy" I find listed in a recent dealer's catalogue at $15. But when the collector comes to the "Commemoration Ode" and finds that the last copy sold brought $1,400—nearly twice the previous record price—and looks about for another copy of the "Memorial. R. G. S." like that which brought $320 at the Norton sale last May, and then learns that the only known copy of Lowell's "A Christmas Carol," 1866, is in the Aldis collection of the Yale University Library, he is apt to become discouraged and turn his attention to other fields, where finality seems possible.

The young collector may reason that he will surely get everything his favorite author has written if he buys that author's books as they come from the press. But even here he will meet difficulties. Few authors have leaped into fame with their first published work. The collector of Dreiser, for instance, will not easily find a copy of his "Studies in Contemporary Celebrities" published the year before "Sister Carrie," and long since suppressed. A few discerning ones several years ago believed that the ecstatic writings of Arthur Machen were deserving of preservation, and by buying first editions they laid the foundations of collections now recognized as valuable, as did those rare early collectors who sensed the future fame of Tennyson from his prize poem, "Timbuctoo."

Do not think that the collector of modern first editions poses necessarily as an appraiser of literary values—that he always believes that Dreiser is a greater novelist than Hawthorne, Robinson a greater poet than Whitman, or Cabell the superior of Edgar Allan Poe. Most of the men who are buying modern first editions —in fact a large proportion of book collectors anyway—do not attempt to estimate the literary quality of their purchases. They may buy the first editions of Huneker simply because they knew and liked Huneker himself. They may collect Amy Lowell because she writes free verse, of which they have no adequate conception save that it seems to be in fashion. Then there are those who buy modern first editions as they learn to play mah jong, because their friends collect modern first editions and play mah jong. It seems to them as necessary to be a book collector as it did to other folks a quarter of a century ago to be seen at the Horse Show. Fortunately, such collectors generally do not get much farther than Madame Du Barry, with her thousand volumes of elegantly bound "remainders" to match the example of the clever Pompadour. But while they remain in the field they are fair game for the dealer and help raise prices in the auction-room.

A few men, of unlimited wealth are gathering up the first editions, as they appear, of a large number of American and English writers of the present day, with the idea of ultimately weeding out those which do not stand the test of time. A collector may be sure, in this way, of getting the most desirable editions of that minority of authors who will maintain or increase their prestige. But this method of collecting is not one that commends itself to those of limited means. Moreover, it is

almost sure to result in mere speculation—book buying on the chance of financial gain. We all know collections which have been made for the sole purpose of putting them into the auction-room when conditions seemed favorable. That is not book collecting. The dealer who pays a large sum for a first edition in the hope of selling it again at a profit is working within his province. That is his business, and in it we wish him success; the literary merit of a work is of little consideration to him, and properly so. But the private collector should have a more substantial motive for collecting than the hope of profit. Too many men are buying the first editions of modern authors on the theory that when Jones is dead and produces no more first editions the works of the popular Mr. Jones will be scarce, and it will then be a good time to put his collection into the auction-room. The theory is sound—if Jones's popularity holds out. But Joneses come and go, and the fame of this one may prove as unsubstantial as that of Martin Farquhar Tupper, once the drawing-room favorite, whose works are now found under "Miscellaneous, 200 vols."

Painting

THE AMERICAN PAINTER

By Guy Eglington

"AMERICAN ART," says Mr. Royal Cortissoz, in the preface to his new book, "flows not from tradition but, in a specially marked sense, from the individuality of the artist". And he proceeds in a few words to propound the accepted theory that while most American artists receive their training in Europe, they apply it in a manner so fresh and personal that their art achieves nationality. Unfortunately, he leaves the matter there, as have all his predecessors, with the result that we have no opportunity of judging just how much water the theory will hold. The observer is faced with something like a paradox. On the one hand, there is the indubitable

national strain running through our finest (and they are finer than we yet know) productions. On the other, there is the no less undoubted domination of foreign schools.

On the face of it, it seems obvious that American painting has been subjected to successive waves of foreign influence, though the existence at every point of figures who remained outside any school makes the word domination inexact. The English gave place to the Dutch, the Dutch to the Barbizon, the Barbizon to the Impressionist. And now come the Post Impressionists, fighting with the Russians for mastery. The first questions, therefore, which the future historian of American art will have to answer are: At what point does Stuart cease to be an English portrait painter? What precisely distinguishes In-ness from the Barbizons? Is Childe Hassam something more than a French Impression-ist? Before he answers these questions he will do well to examine the manner in which American painting has responded to these invasions.

America is, I think, at the same time the most conservative and the most radical country in the world. Its conservatism is shown by its almost instantaneous and unanimous rejection of any new idea that is brought it; its radicalism by the almost equally unanimous acceptance and whole-sale application of that same idea, the moment its novelty has worn off. It is not the idea itself which repels at the start; it is simply the *insanity* (how familiar the word has become!) of proposing a new and subversive criterion. In other words, it is the image which they have made of the new thing that they fight. One remembers the howl that arose over the first Gauguins exhibited here. "Duffer" was good enough for Cézanne, but Gauguin . . . ! Well, not so long after, I had the pleasure of showing a particularly fine example,—the "Mater-nité," which Mr. Lewisohn now owns,—to a friend who abominated these "mod-erns." "Ah," said he, "but he doesn't belong with that crowd." Nor does he. Gauguin was fortunate enough to die be-fore the "crowd" was invented.

But the matter does not stay here. Slowly, imperceptibly, the tide changes, until one morning we wake up to find that the same epithets are being hurled at other names, other tendencies. The insane of yesterday are set in judgment on the out-laws of today. One by one the great Post Impressionists, and with them all the mediocrities who make up the "move-ment," are being hoisted to pedestals. In a few years the Academy will be full of their followers. Nothing more fatal to our own development could be devised. Every im-pulse in art has its periods of growth, fruition and decay, and of these only the first can be life-giving. For that is the period of research, when men instinctively

turn back to what they are sure is firm ground, discarding the overgrowth of previous generations. In its earlier stages a movement is nothing more than an impulse to fresh thinking along a certain series of lines roughly parallel. Only later, when genius has set its stamp upon it, does it tend, so to speak, to look like itself. Then follows the period of decay, when fundamentals are buried under a mass of sophistication.

It is our misfortune that, by virtue of our position and our peculiar nature, we never become aware of a new impulse until it has long passed its zenith and started on its downward path. For us, therefore, it appears as nothing but a formula which we try to apply with more or less success. As an example one may take Impression-ism, which, in France, culminated in figures as widely divergent as Monet, Pissarro and Seurat, to say nothing of Manet and Degas. In America, if we except Twachtman, who is too big to be claimed by any school, Im-pressionism has but one face; it is hardly more than a receipt for sunlight.

Now, if there is ever to be any helpful coöperation between Europe and America in matters of art, it must first be laid down as an axiom that a movement that is gen-uinely alive cannot be built on the rem-nants of a foreign movement that has lost its motive power. There might have been hope for an Impressionist movement among us, could we have breathed the air with Pissarro at Pontoise. There might still be hope for our Post Impressionists, could they have worked with Gauguin in Brittany, with Van Gogh and Cézanne at Auvers. These things might have been. But they were not.

No; I incline more and more to the be-lief, which for the moment I must pro-pound only as a belief, a possible hypoth-esis, that the vital impulse in American art has been and will be primitive in its manifestations. I believe that the Amer-ican man, artists included, is not only by nature and if left to himself, simple, but of a very childlike, primitive simplicity. The trouble is that he never is left to himself. He lives in perpetual terror lest the child in him be found out. Watch the same man who yelled himself hoarse at yesterday's ball-game, in a Fifth Avenue Gallery, best at one of those amazing parties where the "art lover" imbibes punch and an "artistic atmosphere." All the frank boyishness of his nature is crushed out of him. The pictures seem to be exercising a morbid fascination over him. He hates them, yet he dares not run away. His eyes stare at them as though trying to bore holes in the canvas. He is enchanted by the magic letters A-R-T.

And if the man in the street is enchanted, so too is the collector. In nine cases out of ten he buys, not for any pleasure he will get out of living with his pictures, but for a thousand other reasons, above all, that he may leave abiding proof that he *was* of the élite, loving art and knowing it. Nor does the hoodoo stop short at the collector. I hear its chuckle at the Academy; it stands beside me at the New Society. Do you believe that Mr. Glackens or Mr. Kenneth Hays Miller really *saw* everything that they painted into those magnificent pictures of theirs? I doubt it. But Renoir told them they were there, and *they didn't dare to leave them out.* You can take a train right across America and meet hardly a man who will dare to paint what he sees, just that and nothing more. Here it is Renoir, there Gauguin, elsewhere Cézanne, Sisley, Monet, back as far as Daubigny; everywhere you will find the hoodoo standing at the painter's easel, telling him what he shall paint.

But there are signs that the reign of the hoodoo is passing—faint signs, but reassuring. I believe that the growing passion for primitives, a particularly American passion, is one of them. Few, not so long back, would have dared to show enthusiasm for a hooked rug, a piece of Pennsylvania Dutch sgraffito ware, a Scandinavian peasant's table, decorated with his own naïve phantasy. On the surface there is still, of course, ineffable

twaddle about æsthetic values, but back of it all, I am sure, is a sincere pleasure. Child responds to child.

Among painters, too, there are signs of a return to fundamentals. Not among the big names, to be sure, but here and there, in dark corners, in the vast waste paper basket that is called the Independents, one finds men who respect the limitations of their vision, striving to effect a mastery over the things they actually see. Understand me, I am not saying that America has nothing to learn from Europe. The point is that she *cannot* learn much. A young man cannot and must not learn from an old philosopher who has been through it all and has attained to that wisdom which knows the futility of everything. He must go on, making mistake after mistake, until he learns for himself. For the most elementary truth does not become actual to a man, does not become a vital part of his knowledge, until he has discovered it for himself.

Europe, as I see it, is in a period of temporary decline. The summit of the Post Impressionist impulse, the most vital in modern times, was reached over twenty years ago. There are thousands of Post Impressionists today, but their work is no longer constructive. What began as a great structural idea has become no more than a decorative pattern. The ball which the Post Impressionists threw up with so magnificent a gesture is dropping to earth. It is nothing short of pitiful to see the energy of good artists wasted in a futile attempt to catch it and fling it up a second time. Let them have faith in themselves and build on their own foundations. Let the rest of us encourage the painter to do his own seeing. Let it be forbidden to praise a picture in such terms as: "It is as fine as Monet," or, "Corot never painted better." Let us rather say: This is *seen*, this is *actual*. Above all, let us not demand of the artist a complete vision of the world. The American's vision of life is bound to be partial. But it has been, and I think will be, very intense.

HEREDITY AND THE UPLIFT

BY H. M. PARSHLEY

In the most primitive human society and in the associations of animals and plants in a state of nature Darwin's struggle for existence is real and unmitigated; food and safety are won for the individual by a superiority that is demonstrated by the shouldering out and destruction of the weak, the incompetent, the unfit. This austere and beneficent process, acting through millions of years, has brought about a gradual advance toward perfect adaptation to mundane conditions in those species which possessed at the start the requisite potentialities, and at the same time it has destroyed ruthlessly all such as lacked any essential quality. Let it be clearly understood here that the successful types were *not* produced from inferior stocks through improvements imposed from *without*. There were no vice-crusaders among the apparently unpromising archaic mammals of the Mesozoic Age and compulsory education was unknown to the little five-toed horse of the Eocene, yet these benighted creatures were able to found the lines leading down through geologic time to the noblest animals of today. Thus evolution took its course, with the survival of the fit and the elimination of the feeble and botched, until man, developing with the other creatures, attained to his present stage of civilized social life—which, if it offers the spectacle of Bryan, the Fundamentalists, and the University of Tennessee as evidence for the prosecution, nevertheless presents in rebuttal Galton, the geneticists, and the Carnegie Institution at Washington.

But civilized humanity, grown soft with ease, now finds it impossible to view with equanimity the painful struggles and hopeless sufferings of the unfit in free competition with their betters; the immemorial struggle for existence affords too disagreeable and disquieting a spectacle to be tolerated in the public gaze. Hence charity, philanthropy, the Uplift. Begun and long carried on in the laudable spirit of Holy Writ, charity has now become a necessary part of our complex social organization; its purpose is to heal or hide the sore spots and so make it possible for the fortunate minority to enjoy life unharrowed by the sight of the sanguinary struggles and pitiful tragedies characteristic of feral existence. From it, however, has developed a monstrous growth, the Uplift, perhaps the most threatening enemy that civilization has to face today. Of the many counts against the Uplift that might be readily submitted to the intelligent reader, let us consider but one: namely, the utterly false hopes for the race which it bases upon measures that are, at best, nothing but temporary means of relief for the individual. It is here that the biologist and the social reformer come into irreconcilable conflict.

Since Darwin's day the greatest advances in biological knowledge have been made in connection with the experimental study of heredity—that is, of the transmission of inborn traits as opposed to the handing down of customs, property, and environmental materials in general. As a result of this study, it is now clear that the basic characteristics of every individual depend primarily, not upon any training that he has received or is capable of receiving in this life, but upon the protoplasmic units received in egg and spermatozoon from his parents, arranged in accordance with the simple, mathematical laws of Mendel. He may or may not succeed in fully developing these inherent capacities, but he certainly cannot go beyond them. Aside from rare and unpredictable mutations—sudden changes in racial characteristics, so far not accounted for—the essential quality of individuals and hence of social classes is thus fixed by inheritance, and by inheritance alone, and no program of reform which ignores this plain fact can be other than superficial and foredoomed to failure. Nevertheless, the circumstances in which an individual is placed undoubtedly *do* have a considerable influence upon his concrete acts and his fate—not upon his primary character and abilities, perhaps, but surely upon the way in which they are developed and manifested. To what extent, under civilization, is the first influence practically felt? To what extent the second? How much does what a man is, actually and potentially, depend upon his inborn qualities, and how much upon the habits born of his education and environment?

The philanthropist, the social worker, too often the sociologist, and always the uplifter have held, to state their views most extremely, that the individual is wholly the product of his circumstances. The child is "plastic." Placed in Fagin's clutches he becomes a criminal; but for the curfew she becomes a streetwalker. Surrounded, on the other hand, with swaddling care and subjected to edifying precept and example, with occasional touches of the bastinado, the same lumps of indifferent wax take on in time the form of stock-brokers and captains of industry, Chautauqua orators and senators, bishops and college presidents. This is the old environmentalist philosophy, which, though largely discredited and discarded by science, still feeds the flames of hope and envy in the breasts of the have-nots and remains the underlying principle of the Uplift. The modern biologist maintains the contrary view, which, in its most extreme form,

holds the child to be a rigid complex of inherited proclivities. He reminds us that we do not gather figs from thistles nor fashion silken purses from sows' ears, and he may even bid us to cherish the blood of the Nordic race as the *fons et origo* of all that is good, true and beautiful in modern civilization. Few serious students on either side, it may be, would now feel wholly at ease in either of these extreme positions, stated baldly as an article of faith, but if we enquire regarding some definite proposition—ask the social worker about universal education, working conditions, Prohibition; interview the anthropologist on inherent racial qualities; examine the biological psychologist on the results of the army tests and the relation of mental levels to democracy and socialism—if we put such concrete questions we are sure to catch a glimpse of the cloven hoof. The answer will, likely enough, reveal a virtual adherence to one or the other of the uncompromising views just set forth.

II

The basis for the environmentalist's attitude is, in the last analysis, something in the nature of a sentimental wish-fulfillment, fortified by common knowledge of the effects, often very noticeable, produced on individual development by beneficial or injurious surroundings. In what sort of evidence, then, does the scientific observer place his trust? To illustrate at once the related workings of hereditary and environmental influences, as well as the methods of modern genetics, let us consider briefly the extraordinary career of *Drosophila melanogaster*, the tiny fly which swarms about fermenting fruit.

In the year 1900, when the importance of Mendel's early experiments was suddenly appreciated, biologists, in the search for suitable organisms to use in experimental breeding, soon found that the fruit-fly would breed very rapidly in captivity, and was otherwise ideally fitted for the laboratory. Before long an individual was noticed which had white eyes, instead of the usual red, and from this peculiar specimen a white-eyed race was easily developed—the first of more than two hundred such true-breeding races to come to light. Some of these strains are marked by very striking characters, reminding us of the highly diversified breeds of domesticated animals, to which, in fact, they correspond essentially. In one the wings are reduced to useless vestiges, in others the body color may be black, brown, or yellow instead of gray, the eyes diminished or absent, the eye color vermilion, purple, or cream, the hairs of the body modified in various ways, and so on. These new and genetically stable types are called mutations; their mode of origin is unknown, but it is clear that their appearance is not correlated with any corresponding feature of the environment. Once in existence they breed true, and it is likely that they afford the basis for evolutionary progress, since in primitive stocks the odds would certainly not be prohibitive against any given modification being advantageous to the species. Let it be noted again that each of these strains, or any combination of them, constitutes an undeviating race, which, like the races of man, reproduces by inbreeding only its own kind, but is capable, nevertheless, of crossing with any of the others and bringing forth fertile hybrids as offspring. A fly of the normal pale type mated to a black one is just as sure to have young of dubious hue as is a white woman joined in wedlock to a Negro.

By prolonged and ingenious study of the hereditary behavior of these races of *Drosophila*, in connection with the results of similar experimentation on many other species of plants and animals, the riddle of heredity has been largely solved, the mechanism of the process exposed, and not only prediction of results but also purposive manipulation of characteristics—the production of synthetic races to order—has been made possible. Now, in contrast with such fixed hereditary units as eye color or wing size, which change only

by mutation, certain traits are found to be modified or even caused to appear and disappear by environmental influences. If the culture bottle, for example, contains poor food the flies will be small. But it remains true that if their offspring are provided with good nourishment growth to the hereditary limits will again take place. Thus the secondary nature of such phenomena stands clearly revealed, and the position of modern science becomes this: Heredity determines with overwhelming influence the presence or absence and the general nature of most of the characteristics of the individual; environment may sometimes, but not always, modify the degree of their development.

Even a Socialist may readily grant all this as demonstrated truth in so far as fruit-flies and waltzing mice are concerned, but he will demand with some heat to know what bearing, if any, it may have on the human problem. Can it be shown, for instance, that a given moron has derived his feeble intellect from his ancestors, or is his deficiency due merely to the fact that at an early age he failed to appreciate the value of his grammar-school studies and obstinately insisted upon going to work for the corner grocer? The consideration of a single phenomenon—that of sex-linked inheritance—is enough to show beyond question that the workings of the hereditary processes are precisely alike in *Drosophila* and in man, and hence that the findings of genetic research have a direct bearing upon human affairs.

If a male fly having red eyes is mated to a female having white eyes, the males among their offspring will have white eyes (like the mother) and the females will have red eyes (like the father). If a man with normal vision marries a color-blind woman their sons will be color-blind (like the mother) and their daughters will have normal eyes (like the father). This type of inheritance, which has equally peculiar and quite consistent results when the sexes are reversed, has long been recognized in man. That it occurs in the fruit-fly in precisely similar form is not due to coincidence; the correspondence is fundamental, as investigation of its chromosomal basis clearly indicates.

In *Drosophila* the sex of an individual is determined at fertilization by the arrangement of two special chromosomes, called sex-chromosomes and denominated X and Y. If the normal fertilized egg contains two X's the embryo will grow up to be a female; if one X and one Y, a male. Since the behavior of the character "white eye" in hybridization, as just described, follows exactly the distribution of the X-chromosome, the conclusion is obvious that the genetic factor or "gene" causing "white eye" must reside in this particular chromosome; hence the term "sex-linked inheritance." The occurrence in man of several hereditary traits behaving in the same peculiar manner, led to the prediction that the human chromosome group would prove to be like that of the fruit-fly in regard to the X and Y elements. This theory has been brilliantly confirmed during the past year by microscopic study of the human germ cells. The X and Y chromosomes are there, as was foretold, and man's oneness with the fly, at least so far as his hereditary mechanism is concerned, is fully established.

There is no longer room for doubt, then, that a man's physical traits are determined largely by genetic factors passed on to him by his ancestors; and research in eugenics is continually reducing the sphere of environmental influence in such matters as susceptibility to disease and to the effects of alcohol, as well as in the case of simpler manifestations like bodily form and strength. But can as much be said of psychological qualities? Is intelligence also an inherited attribute? There is no doubt that under civilization mental ability is the most important characteristic of the individual, and it is clear that this question must be answered as a preliminary step to the solution of many of the problems of modern life. Intelligence, talent, genius are not simple Mendelian unit characters; far from it. They imply the harmonious working of many diverse qualities and demand a good deal in the way of favorable surroundings for their full development. But mental power is after all dependent on the physical structure of the brain and *a priori* we should expect heredity to manifest itself here as elsewhere. Beyond this logical inference, however, there is abundant direct evidence, which we may briefly examine.

Psychic traits in animals are markedly hereditary, as is well known to every practical breeder. Certain strains of cattle are gentle, others savage. If the ordinary wild rat, which is of ferocious temper, is mated with the gentle white variety the offspring display all the savagery of the father, even when suckled and reared by the tame mother. Having in mind the fact, mentioned above, that the processes of inheritance are identical in man and t' e lower animals, we are quite prepared .or the result invariably obtained in investigations of the inheritance of human mentality. Feebleminded parents have never been known to produce offspring capable of a grammar-school education—and such offspring often are reared in an extremely favorable environment, especially planned for their care! Identical twins, having the same heredity, never diverge much, though their lives are lived far apart, while ordinary twins, differing somewhat in their inherited traits, always exhibit considerable divergencies in character and achievement, even though the circumstances of their upbringing are identical. The relatives of men of eminence are a thousand times as likely to be eminent as are individuals picked at random from the masses of the plain people. Studies of European royalty have shown that outstanding ability runs in a few families only, where there is obviously equal opportunity and the best of training for all. Finally, mental testing of school children and soldiers leads to the same conclusion. Mulattoes in the army made a better showing than Negroes, though they had enjoyed the same environment, and unschooled officers proved superior to common soldiers who had been educated.

III

Thus we reach the conclusion that the extreme view which we have attributed to the biologist comes much nearer to the truth than that of the humanitarian. In a word, the Uplift is powerless to raise any individual or class above the level of the hereditary constitution with which he or it is endowed by nature, and any program of social reform which fails to take this truth into account is bound to do more harm than good in the end. The practical implications of this conclusion are many and far reaching, and since they bear directly upon the most pressing problems of the day, we must attempt to formulate some of the most striking of them.

The vast and gaudy scheme of universal popular education is based on the sound biological principle that an optimum environment, a favorable opportunity, should be provided for individual development. But something is clearly wrong here. At this moment in the larger cities thousands of children have to be denied the equal opportunity supposedly inherent in the free citizenship of their parents; and in every town and hamlet of the country the expense of the public schools is becoming an intolerable burden, where adequate accommodations are still maintained. The difficulty is in reality very simple. The truth is that not one child in ten has the inherent qualities which will enable him to profit by an extended book education: no purpose of God or man is furthered by beating algebra and Latin into the head of a youth who can never comprehend any art beyond that of the curry-comb or the trowel. And not only are pupils scarcely if at all above the grade of moron dragged bodily through the high school, but they are permitted to infest the state universities, undeterred by entrance examinations, where they learn enough to become fifth rate dentists, shyster lawyers, free verse poets, labor leaders, and other pests of the body politic. The remedy is clear. Let the chief work of the first three primary grades be the careful testing of all pupils and the rigorous elimination of the mentally deficient, as soon as they have learned the little that their limited capacities permit of. Thus the problem of numbers will be solved; the condition of teachers ameliorated; taxes lowered enormously; the ranks of unskilled labor and the trades recruited; and the upper reaches of society made safe for the intelligent.

The problem of immigration is likewise at bottom a biological matter. The army tests proved conclusively that recent immigrants from southern and eastern Europe have been of extremely low mentality, for the most part scarcely above the Negro. It is beside the point to maintain that these fugitive newcomers are not representative of their native stocks. They constitute at any rate the national delegates to America and their assimilation can result only in lowering our already pitiful average of intelligence. Here again the solution is plain. Let admission to our shores depend primarily on success in passing appropriate mental tests, to which should probably be added a modest property qualification. Such measures, if severely applied, will materially reduce the numbers of a dangerous type to which the attention of the reader is invited in conclusion.

Modern civilized society in its infinite complexity affords varied and priceless satisfactions to the intellectual and artistic desires of first-rate men; but it is largely incomprehensible and hence a source of distrust, dissatisfaction, and hate to those of primitive, atavistic endowments. Now, the proletariat consists almost entirely of such elementary beings; hence the prime fallacy underlying socialism, communism, and radical schemes in general stands boldly forth. If the advantages of modern life are to be preserved for those capable of enjoying them it is clearly the first duty of the state to take measures, first, for the contentment and repression of the underman, and second, for the wise control of his misguided leaders. To the biologist it is obvious that all these considerations are closely related to the eugenic movement, but this is another story. Immediate action must precede and accompany the conscious direction of slow, natural processes.

The Uplift, considered from the viewpoint of the superior man, is clearly worthless as an agency of social betterment, since it is based upon hollow and fallacious premises; and whatever satisfaction sentimentalists may derive from coddling the meek and lowly, the weak and pitiable, there is no manner of doubt that the means at the command of society might be better employed in providing optimum conditions for the development of worth-while talents. There are indications that at last even those in charge of the public schools begin to see the obvious importance of giving the major share of the teacher's attention to the most promising pupils, not to the dullest—an ideal which, in fact, has always been steadfastly maintained in the musician's studio—and similarly in society at large the resources and privileges of civilization must be made more readily available for those fitted by nature to do the most with them. The teaching of modern biology is thus diametrically opposed to the abolition of free competition, as implied, for instance, in giving undue assistance to the weak at the expense of the strong or in maintaining uniform wages for variable workmen; and it not only reaffirms the soundness of Darwin's principles but urges even that society should further by every means available the sifting process implicit in the struggle for existence. *To him that hath shall be given!* This is indeed the very antithesis of all that the uplifter holds dear, but it expresses in a perfect phrase the scientific concept fundamental to any real progress in civilized living.

CARRYING CIVILIZATION TO MEXICO

BY CARLETON BEALS

"IN FIFTY years you people'll be wearing feathers!" An American farm-machinery agent was badgering a Mexican official who handles foreigners displeased with Mexico's agrarian laws. The Mexican is a quiet, cultured man, educated in Paris and Berlin.

The American thumbed his arm-pits; from his vest protruded three cigars. "You people blare around about your revolution and progress—just one bunch of thieves after another, looting the treasury and keeping honest producers from working. In fifty years you'll be wearing feathers!"

"At least," smiled the Mexican official, "feathers are not ugly."

II

Nowhere else in the world is one so ashamed of one's countrymen as in Mexico. In Europe, despite the comic papers, one sometimes encounters a relatively cultured type; in Mexico, one sees only the adventurer and the business man, with a few technicians in a dismal minority. One cannot help applying to them the cutting words of Lord Chesterfield in his letter to his son in Italy:

You are not sent abroad to converse with your countrymen; among them, in general, you will find little knowledge, and, I am sure, no manners. I desire that you will form no connections, nor (what they impudently call) friendships with these people; which are in truth, only conspiracies against good morals and manners.

It is, indeed, a great pity that the American eagle is so often carried to foreign countries by the get-rich-quick business-gambler and the noodle-shaped female missionary who can't find a husband at home. Spain sent her priests to Mexico and they added the beautiful Spanish ritual to Aztec splendors; she sent, too, her painters, sculptors and builders, and in spite of the gold-grabbing of the greedy creole, they sowed the seeds of a fine culture. But the Americans in the Mexican oil-fields, once the oil is exhausted, will leave behind them no culture and no monuments, but only a desert. Nor do the missionaries and school teachers, herded together in their narrow sectarian and national institutions, bring any new impulse to native art and handicrafts, as did the Spanish *padres* before them; their spirit is too cramped. They are only concerned with their petty jobs; they hate the "dirty greasers," and this inner war against their outward pretence of love makes their temperaments only the more rasping. Always their contempt crops to the surface. In a Presbyterian missionary school that I know a distinction is sharply drawn between the American and the Mexican teachers. The students who pay little, but come as converts, are obliged to scrub floors and do other menial work. One of the claims of this institution is that the children are required to speak English at all times; but the poorer children and the Mexican teachers are most Christianly relegated to a cheap dining-room where they eat coarse food and speak no English.

The majority of the Americans in Mexico are Southerners. Class-pride, race-hatred, and provincial backwardness mark their narrow minds. They despise the Mexican and his ways of living. They dwell stubbornly apart in their handsome homes in the Colonia Roma and San Angel.

From their motor-car pedestal, they repeat glib phrases about race superiority, the moral debasement of the Mexicans, their unfitness to govern themselves, their dirtiness, their dishonesty, their propensity to lie. With unwavering dreariness, the conversation of the best American society in the capital, over tea-cups and bridge-tables and in club-rooms, revolves around clothes, servants, and the baseness of the Mexicans. "Yellow bellies" is the decentest epithet applied to them.

III

At Mrs. Simpson's weekly bridge-party. Mrs. Noddle has just won a tea-set worth two hundred pesos. She is in an expansive mood.

MRS. N. You know, dear Mrs. Simpson, I tried your Mex. dressmaker, Señorita González, but she is so stupid. I paid her four pesos a day and her meals; I mean, of course, she ate with the other servants. But I shall never employ her again. Such bizarre taste—

MRS. S. Why pay her four pesos? Her price is three seventy five. And you know, my dear, I have her make only simple house things—aprons, underclothing, that sort of thing. I never suggested she was capable of making a frock.

MRS. N. I know. But she insisted she was an expert dressmaker. She just ruined that nice georgette. These Mex. are hopeless!

MRS. S. Yes, they will never learn. I've finally gotten a new servant for the upstairs rooms. I'm paying her fifteen pesos a month, which is good, very good, especially as she has no washing to do. But oh, she's worse than the others. Yesterday, when Mr. S. was shaving, she told someone over the 'phone that he was out. He came running out with soap on his face and gave her a good lacing. The stupid thing cried, said she'd never answered 'phones before. Of course, I had told her previously that Mr. S. was not to be disturbed, but a 'phone-call—! Of course, I'll have to let her

go. These Mex. will never amount to anything. They've no get-up, none at all!

IV

Many of the good women indulge in charity work; this gives them an endless opportunity to point to their own generosity and the ungratefulness of the natives. One woman told me, at great length, how she had fed starving Mexicans during the last revolution.

"And did they appreciate it? No! They left their old rags all over the front steps. I had to have a servant clean up after each meal. You'd think they'd have enough gratitude to keep things clean. Common decency—"

Another woman, during the same period, fed some twenty-five Mexicans with beans and *tortillas*, but she was so incensed when they had the impudence to request her to make some changes in their diet that she refused to feed them at all, evidently thinking that starvation—for that was what it meant in those days—was a suitable punishment for their temerity. I thought of the futility of trying to point out to her how these same Mexicans must have felt at beholding a wealthy foreigner living on the fat of the land, while they, its sons, had to beg at her door.

The American who breezes down to Mexico with his loud nasal voice, his brag, his money-grabbing instincts, is the worst sort to thrust upon a race with historical sensibilities and a matured, long-cherished courtesy—doubly bad because the Mexican will forgive almost anything except discourtesy.

The vulgarity begins on every southbound train: "Hell of a country! . . . These damn' greasers!"

In the Pullman sleeper. A bellowing American voice: "Why the Lord made Mexicans and mosquitos is more than I can see!"

Riding up from Vera Cruz. An American doctor from Cordoba, so profoundly convinced of his own superiority that he has been insulted by being ordered to take out a proper license to practice. He has pulled down his ornate shingle in order to punish the ungrateful Cordobans by depriving them of his services. His regretful comment: "Inside a couple of years, if they'd 've let me alone, I'd 've cleaned up half a million pesos in that rotten burg."

In general, the American business-man in Mexico considers himself born of a godlike superior race, above every law, and is willing to stoop to any chicanery, fraud, or evasion in his dealings with the natives, relying, if caught, upon bluster and his nationality to exonerate him.

A prominent officer of the American Club bursts into the American Drug Store and shouts: "You got any chewing gum? Shake a leg, will you! I gotta catch the next San Angel train." A Mexican just ahead of him, whom he shoulders out of the way, has just said to the clerk: "Good-afternoon, sir. Would you be so kind as to show me some hair-brushes?"

The luxurious Hotel Regis lobby. The "best" Americans. American newspaper correspondents lolling about half-stewed, hatching up readable lies. A commercial delegate from California:

"God, what a dead place!" He stretches himself in his plush chair and pulls his hat low over his eyes. "These people give me a belly-ache. Aren't worth a hang. Nothing here to do, nothing to see. Wouldn't invest a penny in this land on a bet."

"Have you been to the National Museum?"

"What the cuss, Bill, just a bunch of old rocks!"

"Have you been out to Amecameca? A fine view of Ixtaxihuatl and Popocatepetl from there."

"Fine view of what!"

"The volcanoes."

"Boy, we've got mountains right in my home state, I'm telling you; and a live bronco-busting volcano. What do I want to go out to some dirty Mex. town for?"

"You ought at least go out to San Juan de Teotihuacán to see the pyramid of Quetzlacoatl."

"Who 'n 'ell is Quetz—what you call him?"

"Quetzalcoatl was a snake-sheathed god who—"

"I guess I can see enough snakes right here." He jerks his thumb in the direction of the bar-room. "The only live place in the whole stinking land. Have a drink?"

V

Shortly before Carranza was overthrown, I visited an *hacienda* in the state of Campeche in company with the American owner, who hadn't been on the place for seven years. This man long held the reputation of being the worst *peón*-lasher in all Díaz Mexico; and more than one story is told of a *peón* shot or beaten to death at his hands. Now he lives in the capital, circulates in the "best circles," buys rose-water at the American Drug Store and gives his daughters the finest education money can buy. He confidently told me on the train: "Mexico won't be worth a damn until it gets back to the good old Díaz days. You've got to run these beasts—stick a bit in their mouths. Give 'em iron. They're mud . . . mud!"

The first day on the *hacienda*, he stalked out through the canefields with a Colt and a black-snake whip. "I'll show you," he promised me, "how these people have to be handled."

His son, who had been running the *hacienda* during the troublous times, tried to dissuade him.

But father snorted and stalked on. A *peón*, mending an irrigation-lock, looked up and nodded pleasantly. The neck-muscles of my companion bunched.

"Stand up, you ——!" and breaking into a string of oaths, he ripped out his black-snake. "Don't you know enough to stand up and take off your hat to a white-man, you dirty skunk of a nigger?"

The *peón* stood up, crossed his arms, and said quietly: "*Jefe*, don't be a fool. The times have changed. Go ahead, but before sundown you'll be dead or in prison."

The discourtesy, vulgarity, and shoddiness that begin on the railroad trains, the streets, the *fincas*, are carried up into so-called cultured circles. While attending a lecture by Doctor Antonio Caso, one of the most dignified and learned gentlemen I have met in any country, I was shamed by three teachers, fellow-countrymen, who, though they could understand no word of Spanish, sat in the front row of seats, giggling and making deprecatory remarks through an entire hour because the speaker's gestures struck them as funny. Why should they be polite to a Mexican?

When the American residents wished to honor visiting American students at a summer-session with a *thé-dansant*, they put on their posters, "only Anglo-Saxon students invited," and even had the effrontery to ask the university rector to post these on the bulletin boards!

VI

The lady descended upon me after my lecture like a locomotive spurting steam. I edged back from the spray of her words.

"So, *you* are the man who wrote that nasty article about Americans in Mexico! I don't see why Americans who come down here have to throw mud at their fellow-countrymen. Don't you know that Americans are doing things for the Mexicans? Take the Society for the Prevention of Cruelty to Animals—a most needed work."

"Assuredly," I replied, "if you exclude burros from your efforts. A burro is a hardy animal that thrives on beatings. Even so, I saw one of the poor beasts turn up his hoofs with a holy expression of despair, just like a medieval saint, when one of your kind-hearted ladies attempted to protect him. The approach of a ruddy northern goddess—"

The lady went on. "And the Americans here have a playground association. We have established playgrounds in a number of villages. But the ungrateful children prefer to go out and play in the hills with their dirty old goats."

"But my dear lady, surely, you, who advocate kindness to animals, would not wish to deprive the goats of their jolly associates."

"And the Rotary Club—the work of the Rotary Club—"

"I confess my ignorance. I only recall the resolution of the Mexican Confederation of Labor when the Rotary Clubs were invited to hold a convention in Mexico City: 'We protest against the president of Mexico inviting these silk-hatted, frock-coated North American Fascisti to Mexico. It is like inviting a swarm of locusts to a freshly-planted cornfield.'"

But my good informant was persistent. "And we are introducing phonographs. We expect to make the phonograph an integral part of the life of all the mountaineers—"

I collapsed from the sultriness of the atmosphere. I had a dream. And in that dream I recalled the numerous trips I had made through the mountains of Mexico, the gracious hospitality I had received from the Mexicans, of how, up in a mountain town of Durango called Tepehuanes, I had sat in the plaza and been asked by the kindly *vecinos* where I was going, whence I had come, how long I was sticking around; and how all these inquiries were accompanied by the proffer of a flower, a cigarette, an orange, an invitation to dinner— because I was a stranger in their midst. And once more I heard the lovely strains of "Borrachita" and "La Paloma Blanca" from the guitars in that same moon-lit plaza, with the great black Sierras shouldering behind. I recalled the songs and the folk-lore and the fiestas at a hundred ranches on a hundred trails from one end to the other of Mexico. I remembered long chill nights when I had sat out under the low *ramadas* beside blazing fires with the white stars close overhead, shining as they only do in the southland. . . . Then I jerked to my senses, hearing the raucous jazz of "Yes, We Have No Bananas."

My charming steam-engine was still hissing. "And these people are stupid. For two years I've been trying to drive English into the heads of my pupils but they simply won't learn. [She hardly speaks Spanish herself.] Before I came to Mexico I was a radical, yes sir, a radical. But these degenerate, vile people need an iron hand. I no longer believe in liberty. I'm going back to the United States."

VII

Most of the Americans in Mexico speak the language poorly, in glaring contrast to all other foreigners, who soon speak fluently and correctly. A teacher of a missionary school which I recently visited, a woman of seventeen years' residence, asked a Mexican friend and me to sit down, in the past subjunctive mood—a most exhilaratingly painful achievement. A relative of the directress "died next week." Americans with ten, fifteen, even twenty years of residence often scarcely know what is said to them and can use only the barest conventional phrases. They are ignorant, too, of Spanish history and literature, of Latin-American history, of Mexican history. They know little of the real social, and political antecedents of the Mexican or of his age-long struggle for survival and freedom. Engaged in exploitation only, they have not the culture, the time, or the inclination to become acquainted with the fundamental forces that move the people among whom they reside. Their life is a projection of Main Street, and as circumscribed as in Gopher Prairie.

The antecedents, the habits, the ignorance of the resident Americans, combine to make them hopeless reactionaries. They are out of touch with world-currents; they are even out of touch with their own country. They conceive of the United States as it was in Podunk, Texas, or Hinky Dink, Arkansas, when they left. They forget that even Podunk and Hinky Dink may have changed since twenty years ago. Their ideas are derived from the

Weekly Dauntless or the *Baptist Ladies' Friend*. They are still in the mental jungles of Fourth of July patriotism.

Naturally, their vision is blurred with regard to Mexican politics. Most of them talk longingly of the good old Díaz days. "How clean the city was under Díaz! . . . How safe to travel! . . . The *peóns* knew their place in the days of good old Don Porfirio; they wouldn't *dare* sit in the parks or walk along fashionable Francisco I. Madero Street!" If you finally force the reluctant admission that Mexico could not have continued to live under feudalism in a capitalistic age, they will turn to the superstrong men of the revolution, General Reyes, Felíz Díaz, and above all to Huerta the bloody. "If only Wilson had recognized Huerta! Huerta knew how to govern these greasers with iron. They'll never learn to govern themselves."

VIII

We are such a numerous and puissant people that it is hard to convince us that a race lacking the symbols of power and conquest may have qualities superior to our own. But the Mexicans have traits which we of the great nations lack, which we talk about as the ideals of life, to which we give lip service but no real service. I do not speak of the small Mexican middle-class, which is building up a more sentimental set of shabby respectabilities than even that of the American middle-class; I do not speak of the military upstarts who are shameless plunderers; I do not speak of the Mexican labor-leaders; I do not speak of the clergy whose power is waning; I speak of the upper social class and the great mass of *peóns*, the Indian-Mexicans, the real Mexicans.

The cultured and artistic circles of Mexico are not endowed with the psychology of the parvenu, the beef-maker, the shoe-manufacturer; they are endowed with the graces of the best European society, which means refinement, understanding of the world, and civilized sensibilities. The educated Mexican is acquainted with two great European cultures, the Spanish and the French. He knows his Baudelaire, his Gourmont, his Molière, just as he knows his Cervantes, his Calderon, his Benavente. And he can talk intelligently, too, about the politics and literature of the United States and England. He is among the most brilliant conversationalists in the world—informed, imaginative, keen, ruthlessly sarcastic.

But the real roots of Mexican culture are deep in the lower classes—which can be said for few other countries. The Nahuas were a race of princely men, and centuries of oppression have but intensified their good manners, love of beauty, and refinement. Even the Indians crowded into the cities, starving, dispossessed, retain a love for beauty; a glow of color and poetry plays over their sordid lives. This native nobility of spirit is especially demonstrated in the treatment of strangers. Go to any small town in Mexico. You are not despised. You are privileged and welcomed. You are promptly spied on the outskirts of the town by some kindly native; you are escorted wherever you care to go. You are greeted in the plaza; you are proffered hospitality, food, tokens of friendship. Like as not, the *alcálde* will come out to greet you; he may wear sandals and pajamas, but he is clever, graceful, courteous, proud. This has happened to me in a dozen towns: Topia, Tepehaunes, Tpotzlán, Arroyo Verde . . . how the names linger; even in such large places as Durango, Culiacán, Celaya.

The Mexican will give you his all if he discovers you *simpatico;* he will give you his bed and sleep on the floor; he will divide his scanty ration of *tortíllas* and *frijóles*. When you leave his hat sweeps his knees and his *"Vaya Ud. con Diós!"* rings after you, a leave-taking of genuine affection. I have traveled a thousand miles in Mexico without spending a cent. Make a Mexican friend and he is your friend for life; his loyalty is boundless until you show yourself utterly unworthy. Affection has no material restrictions. Your friend's house, his pocket-book, his time, his all is at your disposal. He will deny you nothing. Nor will he imagine that there is any obligation on your part to repay him unless he should be in need.

The Mexican's possessive instincts are not strongly developed. Property is not his god. In Europe there is no generosity; money is hoarded; the Frenchman counts his *sous*, the Italian his *centessimi*. The American is generous because he has a superabundance. But the Mexican is generous because he is used to little, because he can accommodate his needs to almost any contingency; he is not gagged and bound by an inflexible standard, nor is he envious of his betters. In the villages what one *cecino* has, the other shares. The Mexican is still close to the great communal traditions. Instead of material comfort, he cherishes personality, individuality, independence.

In Mexico the spoken word does not carry conviction; the poetry of life resides in action. But that which Americans often mistake for untruthfulness is merely etiquette or imagination. Among themselves the Mexicans understand just what to believe and what to doubt. The American business man, having no manners and less imagination, is promptly "disillusioned." The Mexican knows well the sensitiveness of his kind. He invents a complicated, imaginative, yet obviously untruthful excuse for some minor breach of duty. But his hearer is pleased, for this is the etiquette of the proceedings: an attempt has been made to avoid hurting his feelings. The Mexican synthesizes the Orient and the Occident. On the one hand, he does not lose himself in the clouds of otherworldliness, and on the other, he is not interested in efficiency, in mechanistic processes, in means rather than ends. He is always realistic, cognizant that life is the one end, that living is the only art.

IX

In the plaza of Culiacán. A tall handsome Mexican, wrapped in a blazing *serape*, black eyes and aristocratic features shaded into mysticism by his huge sombrero, big as a baobab tree.

"What do you do for a living?" I ask.

"Nothing." A humorous glint of teeth.

"Nothing?"

"Nothing, Señor." . . .

A similar specimen informed me that he was an election judge!

The Alameda in Mexico City. A ragged bootblack. He tells me that he prefers poverty to a nose-ringed job, that the middle-class is really miserable, eternally worrying about rent, clothes, petty appearances. "Blame rich or blame poor," is his motto. And he goes off singing a love-song: "*Si Adelita se casa conmigo.* . . ."

This attitude is not a mere rationalization of laziness. The poorest Mexican is mystic; he has emotional depths, and he respects this side of his nature. He does not wall off his hours into arbitrary compartments. To work is to play; to play is to work. He will not ruin life by hurrying it.

X

Racially, socially, psychologically, Mexico is far more alien to us than Europe. The United States is a projection of Europe, a new graft on the old trunk; Mexico is only superficially European. In spite of recognition, reparations commissions, and visiting Chambers of Commerce, Mexico and the United States are drifting apart. Mexico, more than at any other time in its history, is asserting its individuality.

It is one of the marvels of history that a handful of Spanish cavaliers and priests were able to impress their language and institutions upon a continent and a half; it is even more remarkable that the despised Indian, veneered with this glittering Latin culture, has been able to persist in a world of relentless imperialism and universal conflict. Eighty-five per cent of the people of Mexico are Indian or mixed, with Indian habits predominating. Take an interurban train out of Mexico City, walk for a few miles out to Contreras, to San Jerónimo; run down to Cuernevaca, to Cuatla, and you are upon the frontier again. The Caucasian has almost disappeared; little of his blood flows in the veins of these taciturn, mystical people.

The Spanish churches crumble, but the Aztec temples and the pre-Aztec pyramids are massive, rooted. The snake-sheathed Quetzalcoatl is still fanged and waiting. The aboriginal traditions keep the Mexican conscious of his group unity, his racial integrity. Mexican institutions, Mexican habits, Mexican etiquette, Mexican artistic perceptions, Mexican social psychology run back to civilizations that were great when Caesar was harrying the barbarians of Gaul. Today Mexico is in the throes of a vast revolution that has scarcely begun; it is seething with the re-emergence of unknown, aboriginal Mexico.

THE COMIC PATRIOT

BY CARL VAN DOREN

THERE might be, I suppose, a more precise term for my friend John Thane than the one he applies to himself when he says that he is a Comic Patriot; but he has not discovered the better term, and he seems to be well enough satisfied with the one he uses. He does not mean that it is comical to be a patriot or that he is a patriot in any comical way. He means rather, so far as I can gather from his definition, that he feels toward his native land and its inhabitants much as a comic poet or dramatist feels toward the race of men at large, without the elevation, and the occasional confusion and short-sightedness, which enter into epic or tragedy.

"A country," he once said to me, "is a comedy. It has its high hours, its noble gestures, its superb decisions. It has also, however, its doldrums, its shoddy episodes, its craven irresponsibilities. After all, a country is nothing but a body of human beings. As such, it drifts into imbecilities at least as often as it rises into admirable deeds. What right have we to expect anything else? If we do, we must expect sooner or later to be either disappointed or deluded. The disappointed patriots are those who have set their hearts on some national goal which is beyond the national reach or inclination. The deluded patriots are those who will not admit that their special goal has been missed. Between them, what sighs and howls, what songs and tragedies rise into the troubled air!

"Now, the Comic Patriot is rarely disappointed and never deluded. When his country fails to do what he had looked for it to do at some moment of its career, he merely sees that it was not the country he

234

thought it was, and revises his opinion. He does not break his heart with grief, nor pester the gods with questions. If he is cynical, he saves his skin among the ruins. If he is serious, he does what he can to change his compatriots. In no case does he go on fooling himself, compelling faith to undertake tasks it was never meant to undertake. He draws as long a breath as he needs and begins again with what is left."

"It strikes me," I told John Thane, "that your Comic Patriot is a light-hearted fellow."

"Not necessarily. He can be blue enough, but he trusts to his brains to pull him out. He has the sense to notice that things are never as simple in national affairs as most patriots imagine. Take the American Revolution, for instance, which, at one time and another, has drawn more ink than it ever drew blood. Seen through the spectacles of the grand style, the Revolution is a drama with a single plot. Virtuous men, according to those spectacles, rose against the oppressors who had long driven them, threw off the unendurable yoke, and assumed a separate and equal station among the powers of the earth. But to be dramatic such an action must be simple and passionate. And to be simple and passionate it must leave out of account a hundred or a thousand facts, such as that in certain sections of the country the Revolution was a civil war, that it dragged along with immense and shabby tedium, that it was partly won for the colonists by the opposition to the ministry in England, that it was followed by turmoil at home, that it took its eventual shape in the American memory only when poets and orators had laid hands upon the very raw materials which the thing itself presented. Try to go behind the accepted version and you stir up all the deluded patriots who have founded their piety upon what they call a rock, though it is only rubble tolerably well cemented by time. Being a Comic Patriot, I merely wonder at them.

"Or take the question of the frontier, which has lately been raked by a very sharp fire of criticism. Was it wholly peopled by lion-hearted venturers who had the weight of a national destiny on their backs? Hardly. It had, like all communities, plenty of crooks and blockheads, loafers and nuisances, men and women who fitted it only because they fitted no other region. Its average of energy was on the whole higher than its average of intelligence. But the romancers could not leave it alone. They had to turn it into something epic to make it fit for patriotic digestions. Thus it came to be regarded as the scene of the march of heroes against sullen nature and violent aborigines, the breeding ground of independent spirits, the nursery of empire. Sooner or later there was bound to come the discovery that the frontier had never been very congenial to the graces or to the arts. After that discovery, controversy and broken heads. The deluded patriots hold to the tradition, against no matter what evidence. The disappointed moan that such things could ever be. But the Comic Patriot, since he was never taken in, cannot be taken aback.

"As for the Civil War, when the Comic Patriot thinks of that he exercises every muscle in his mind. He hears one set of patriots declare that the conflict was merely the end of a long crusade against the evils of slavery; then he passes on. He hears another set of patriots declare that it was the defeated resistance of a courageous minority who did not want to be absorbed into the industrial mechanism of the changing nation; then he passes on. He recalls the important item that the North forced the tariff upon the South to help make Northern manufacturers rich.

He recalls the important item that the South forced the war with Mexico upon the North to help extend the territory in which slaves might be owned. He comes to the conclusion that it would be difficult to decide, without partisanship, whether the Abolitionists or the Bourbons cut the handsomer or the sorrier figure in the history of the time. With the spirits of comedy and pity both stirring in him, he marvels that the common man in the North could have given so much to free slaves he had never seen or to preserve a Union which was in the main a metaphysical or a mystical conception; or that the common man in the South could have given so much to defend the slaves of the more prosperous men who, by using slave labor, made the economic life of the community a burden for those who were neither slaves nor slave-owners. The Comic Patriot would marvel more, however, if he did not find in the records abundant testimony that the common man of both North and South was less ardent than has customarily been made out, and in fact often dodged the draft, which filled the armies, expertly and pertinaciously. The Civil War a simple and passionate conflict! It was as muddled as a street brawl.

"I can say more," John Thane added. "It was as muddled as the World War!"

"You talk a great deal about wars," I said. "I should think a Comic Patriot might regard them as tragic subjects."

"The true Comic Patriot is never blind to national tragedies, though he does not let them overpower his judgment. I am talking about wars just now because they are simpler than almost anything else in the life of a country, and I want the simplest cases I can find for the sake of my definition. What interests the Comic Patriot about the World War is the question why the United States should have got into it at all. Was it because one righteous nation must come to the aid of other righteous nations when they are in danger? Was it because the most unconcerned bystander feels obliged to take sides in a fight if it lasts long enough? Was it because a neutral in war-time has interests which must be regarded even at the price of ceasing to be neutral? Was it because the Allies, being nearer to American ears, had the advantage in propaganda? No one of these explanations will quite do for the Comic Patriot. He considers them all, as well as many others, and avoids hasty verdicts."

"But where are his moral sympathies"?

"His fault, perhaps, is that he is too moral. He cannot take sides with the facility of the ordinary patriot. He may be touched by the unselfish zeal with which the general run of Americans set out to free Cuba from Spanish misrule, but he still remembers that those same Americans were enduring within their own borders a misrule as gross—that of the Negroes by their white landlords and employers and terrorizers. Moreover, this spasm of unselfish zeal ended in as cool a piece of land-grabbing as any nation ever perpetrated. The Comic Patriot is such a moralist that he has to stand outside these dramas. Having a sense of humor, he does not expect his nation never to go wrong; but having a sense of humor, he also does not feel impelled to join in its wild oats. However cheerfully he may pay his taxes, he holds that no nation has the right to ask him to pay the extravagant price of indulgence in all its stupidities. What most marks him off from other patriots is his refusal to take a mystic's attitude toward his country, which is for him simply a portion of the surface of the earth whereon a portion of mankind, made more or less alike by the accident of association, lead a more or less uniform kind of life. When he feels the pull of mystical emotions, the expansion of the spirit which comes from the sense of being in the society of a mass of men all working together for a reasonably common goal, whatever it may be, he draws back. In that direction, the Comic Patriot knows, lie woolly notions about the souls of peoples, about the destinies of nations, about the existence of states which, conceived as something higher and more authoritative than the sum of the individuals who make

them up, may lawfully do what individual morality would not think of justifying."

"Admit at least," I said, "that your Comic Patriot, by his detachment, must seem inhuman."

"On the contrary, he is all humanity. He looks forever behind the nation, which is a kind of general idea, to the human beings who are the concrete details upon which the idea is established. These beings move him by their virtues, tickle him by their follies, distress him by their vices, enrage him by their obstinacy and cruelty, exalt him by their heroisms. It is they, he understands, who existed before the nation took its special shape; it is they who will outlast it. He is like a wise man at a play, who surrenders himself for the hour to the illusion of the scene but who knows that the action there represented is but a moment chosen out of a stream of life which never stops. At the same time, the Comic Patriot never loses himself in a vague universal philanthropy. Being a moralist, in his fashion, does not keep him from being a neighbor. He delights in the national memories which he shares with his countrymen. He savors the common tongue, with its familiar allusions and its hearty coloring. He responds to the laughter, recognizes the prejudices, participates in the fears, thrills to the songs, looks forward toward the hopes of his fellows. These things are familiar and so are dear to him, because he loves the feel of life when it comes close. To be a lucid critic of the show and to laugh at it as much as he must are, he considers, among his rights as a citizen as clearly as to look to the courts for justice. He fulfills his duties as a citizen none the less because he insists that he owes them to his neighbors and not to a metaphysical state, with a special soul and a particular destiny. He has learned, in short, how to combine affection with intelligence, the last lesson in the school of wisdom."

"It would be much easier," I said, "to be a Tragic Patriot and follow the passions."

"More men succeed at that," John Thane admitted.

A NOTE ON SHAKESPEARE

BY LEON KELLNER

EVERY reader of Shakespeare in one of the English or American standard editions is sure to be on terms of familiarity (not of friendship!) with the tiny marginal hieroglyphic resembling and therefore called a dagger (Greek: *obelus*), thus, †. This dagger is intended to act as a caveat to the unwary. "Don't run on," it warns, "with the idea that you have made sense out of this passage, because you haven't. And take care not to try and cudgel your brain in order to understand it, because you won't. It must not be tampered with in any way. It is taboo. The most eminent scholars have tortured their anointed heads about it and have given it up as 'corrupt' beyond the possibility of conjecture."

I have had a quarrel with this dagger for many years and I will now speak out. First, there is its arrogance in setting up, as it were by ecclesiastical authority, a canon of conjectures. Up to now, it seems to say everybody was free to suggest the true reading of this line, but henceforth the chapter is closed forever. Trying to get some sense into an absurd line by guessing at the proper reading was lawful, meritorious, a work of philological piety in the blessed time of the editors; today such efforts are of the devil.

Bad as this presumption is I could have put up with it. Clerical arrogance is proverbial. But the dagger is worse than that. By putting it against, say, forty passages in the whole of Shakespeare's work the editors state by implication that they understand everything else, and, consequently, that every reader who does not is an ass. Well, all I can say is that there re-main hundreds of passages in Shakespeare which I cannot make head or tail of, and I am gored by the cruel horns of this dilemma: either the dagger is a liar, or I am an ass. Naturally I cannot be expected to take this verdict lying down. It hurts. I must justify myself somehow, and that is why I now appeal to all fair-minded readers of Shakespeare. Judge, I pray you, O inhabitants of England, and men of America, betwixt me and the dagger!

Take down your Shakespeare, open the volume—say the Globe Edition, if you have got it—and I shall lay before you my difficulties as we go along. In "The Tempest," Act III, Scene 2, beginning with line 96, Caliban unfolds his plan for getting rid of Prospero:

Why, as I told thee, 'tis a custom with him,
I' th' afternoon to sleep: there thou mayst *brain* him,
Having first seized his books, or with a log
Batter his skull, or paunch him with a stake,
Or cut his weasand with a knife.

How is that? *Brain*, as a verb, means to kill by beating out the brains. What alternative is this: "to brain him or to batter his skull"?

There is no dagger against the passage. The editors evidently found it perfectly correct. Do you?

In the same play, III, 3, 79, I read:

Thee of thy son, Alonso,
They [*i. e.* the powers] have bereft; and do pronounce by me
Lingering perdition, worse than any death
Can be at once, shall step by step attend
You and *your ways*.

Can you imagine "lingering perdition" dogging somebody's "ways"? And if, by an effort, you can, do you think Shakespeare capable of writing a vacuous thing like that?

Again, in V, 155, Prospero, addressing his defeated enemies, says:

> I perceive, these lords
> At this encounter do so much admire
> That they *devour* their reason and scarce think
> Their eyes do offices of truth.

Need I expatiate on this as an impossible reading? I think not.

In the very first scene of "The Merry Wives of Windsor" I feel insulted by the absence of the dagger:

> EVANS. The dozen white louses do become an old coat well; it agrees well, passant; it is a familiar beast to man, and signifies love.
> SHALLOW. The luce is the fresh fish; *the salt fish is an old coat.*

If this is not sheer nonsense I do not know what is, and yet the editors will have us believe it to be sense!

"Measure for Measure" fairly bristles with difficulties for poor me, though the ingenious editors see none. Take, for example, Claudio's pathetic horror of death:

> Ay, but to die, and go we know not where;
> To lie in cold obstruction, and to rot;
> This sensible warm motion to become
> A *kneaded* clod . . .

By what stretch of imagination can you wrest sense from this? What possible connection is there between a dead body and dough?

Again, look up III, 1, 266, in the same play. The disguised Duke is trying to impress on the shrinking Isabel how important it is for her to lend herself to the suggested pious fraud:

> . . . and here, by this is your brother saved, your honor untainted, the poor Mariana advantaged, and the corrupt deputy *scaled.*

The word *scaled* is generally explained to mean "weighed in the balance," "tested," "found wanting." But it shows scant respect to the literary powers of the greatest master of English to saddle him with such a weak word, such a ludicrous anticlimax when we expect the strongest possible synonym of *exposed*.

The first scene of "The Comedy of Errors" concludes with what to all sensible readers and even to commentators has always been a vexing riddle. Old Aegeon,

when condemned to death, is told by the Duke that the sentence may be commuted by ransom. But the old man is a stranger in a strange land; how is he to find the generous soul to pay his ransom? So, when he goes on his bootless errand he says—

> Hopeless and helpless doth Aegeon wend,
> But to procrastinate his *lifeless* end.

Now, what reader outside the charmed circle of conscientious editors will accept this nonsense as having come from Shakespeare's pen?

Another passage in "The Comedy of Errors" (II, 2, 137) is a beautiful instance of what a liar the dagger can be when it is absent. Adriana, in her complaint about that neglectful husband of hers, says:

> Sister, you know he promised me a chain;
> Would that *alone, alone* he would detain,
> So he would keep fair quarter with his bed.

Why should such particular stress be laid on *alone?* Shakespeare, as a rule, is chary of emphatic repetitions. But there it is in the Globe Edition, and we are asked to make the best of it. Fancy my indignation when I found that the original reading, that of the First Folio, has nothing of the kind, and that the editors had gratuitously tampered with the text, and without the slightest improvement of the sense! The Folio has,

> Would that *alone a love* he would detain.

If the dagger is called for anywhere it ought to have been put here against the original text.

And what in the name of commonsense do the editors make of the following passage in the same play (II, 2, 137)?—

> How dearly would it touch thee to the quick,
> Shouldst thou but hear I was licentious
> And that this body, consecrate to thee,
> By ruffian lust should be contaminate!
> Wouldst thou not spit at me and spurn at me
> And hurl the name of *husband* in my face
> And tear the stain'd skin off my harlot brow . . . ?

II

I hope I need not go on with my list; as a matter of fact, I am afraid it is too long as it is. Have I been too severe in calling the obelus arrogant, untruthful and insincere? Surely not. Even with these grave charges the case against it is not complete. By its presence and still more by its absence it has, for fully fifty years, led serious lovers of Shakespeare away from scrutinizing the text. In other words, textual criticism, started by Theobald two hundred years ago and zealously and most successfully pursued by such ingenious men as Hanmer, Johnson, Malone, Singer, Dyce, Collier, and Walker, suddenly came to a standstill fifty years ago, just at the time when the fatal dagger was introduced into the standard editions. The work of the Shakespearean Massorah was done.

But was it? No more than that of the Old Testament Massorah was done two thousand years ago. The other day I happened to hit on seven stately volumes, "Marginal Notes on the Old Testament Text," by the late American scholar, Arnold B. Ehrlich. The illuminating suggestions of the book attracted me powerfully; I found that English, American, French and German scholars had emended the Old Testament text out of all recognition during the past fifty years—the very years when the text of Shakespeare's plays was resigned to the despair of amateurs. Why? Apparently because some bigwig had declared that, with the exception of some thirty to forty passages, Shakespeare had been made perfectly intelligible. The lying dagger says so.

But what is the truth? Focus your attention on the text when reading Shakespeare, and you will be surprised at the prodigious phenomena you meet with. A lover is transformed by his passion into an "orthography" ("Much Ado About Nothing"); courtiers are "mere fathers of their garments" and "wear themselves in the cap of the time" ("All's Well That Ends Well"); Coriolanus suggests that the "parasite," silk, should be made an "overture for the war" ("Coriolanus"); the Roman mob is a "bosom multiplied" and consists of "woolen vassals"; "gyves" are converted into "graces," and peace is

standing "as a comma" between two realms ("Hamlet"); Falstaff has no other "injuries" in his pocket than tavern reckonings and like things ("Henry IV"); Holofernes, the schoolmaster, enlarges our knowledge by telling us that "the hound imitates his master, the ape his keeper, the horse his rider" ("Love's Labor Lost"); Desdemona elopes at an "odd-even" hour of the night, and, in her married life, turns out to be an "unhandsome" warrior ("Othello").

The stringing together of these absurdities looks, I feel, like a piece of irreverence, but nothing short of burlesque will do if the reader is to be impressed with the fact that hundreds of passages in the current standard texts of Shakespeare's plays present a mixture of the sublime and ludicrous such as is unparalleled in the world's literature. Is it not as if some lines had been written by an inspired genius, and the next by a drivelling idiot? If we could take it for granted that Shakespeare wrote all of them we should be face to face with a mental marvel compared with which the weirdest wonders of mesmerism and thought transference would shrink to nothing.

Did Shakespeare actually write these lines as they stand? Most decidedly not. Shakespeare's writings have not escaped the unhallowed hands of ignorant copyists and compositors any more than the works of Greek and Latin authors, than the Bible itself. But while Sophocles and Plato, Plautus and Cicero have been subjected to methodical scrutiny, to textual criticism which in the hands of masters has become a fine art, and so purged of the stupidities of ignorance and sloth, the grossest mistakes due to the copyists and printers of Shakespeare's plays are taboo and must not be touched, for, say the experts, all the purging that is necessary was completed fifty years ago.

III

I fancy I hear the impatient reader exclaim: "You have told us quite enough about the sense lost; suppose you now tell us something about the sense regained?" I think that, in all modesty, I could do that. I cannot possibly develop the method by which my emendations have been arrived at within the space allowed me, but the proof of the pudding is in the eating; so let me give you my corrected versions of some of the passages quoted above, and you may judge for yourself.

The passage in "The Tempest," III, 2, 96, I read—

> there thou mayst *brave* him
> Having first seized his books. Or with a log
> Batter his skull, or paunch him with a stake,
> Or cut his weasand with a knife.

It was anything but difficult to arrive at this conjecture. Anybody conversant with Sixteenth Century handwriting knows that a *v* cannot be distinguished from an *n*; hence the very common confusion of these two letters.

In III, 3, 79, of the same play I read—

> Lingering perdition—
> shall step by step attend
> You and your *mates*.

Just as *v* was mistaken for *n* and vice versa, *w* was misread for *m* and *m* for *w*; *ways*, in Elizabethan spelling, was *waies*, and *i*, which was as often written without the dot as with it, closely resembled a medial *t*.

In V, 155, I read, as a matter of course, "*denounce* their reason," *i. e.*, slander. Again the original *n* misread for a *v*.

In "Measure for Measure" III, 1, 266, the emendation is obvious. Compare the substantive *stale* in "The Taming of the Shrew," I, 1, 58:

> KATHERINE. I pray you sir, is it your will
> To make a *stale* of me among these
> mates?

The letters *c* and *t*, owing to their similarity when in a medial position, were constantly misread for each other. The passage thus becomes:

> . . . and here, by this is your brother saved, your honor untainted, the poor Mariana advantaged, and the corrupt deputy *staled*—

id est, (in Elizabethan English) made a laughing stock, exposed to derision.

IV

Shall I go on with my emendations? I think not. I am absolutely certain that in "The Comedy of Errors" Shakespeare wrote, not "lifeless end," but "timeless end," *i. e.*, untimely or violent, for this meaning of the word was quite common at the time. But I am at a loss to account for the printer's error without launching into more palaeographical and grammatical arguments. And I am certain that no reader will accept the other emendations which I have up my sleeve unless I am given much more space than I have here. But I shall be perfectly satisfied, if in this short note, I have succeeded in raising suspicions against the dagger—and what it stands for.

THE THEATRE

BY GEORGE JEAN NATHAN

IT IS the ingratitude of criticism that it can never forgive established genius for being anything less than complete genius. Like a sharp-shooter, it hides behind a rock on the upward trail waiting, and not without an occasional smirk, for genius to slip on a stray pebble and descend ever so slightly from the heights. Genius is the one thing in the world that can never afford to be even itself; it must ever progressively be more than itself. The artist who has painted a great picture or chiseled out a great statue or composed a great symphony or written a great play must next paint a greater picture or chisel out a greater statue or compose a greater symphony or write a greater play. If he does not, criticism will wag its head in doubt, and speculate on its earlier high estimate of him, and even now and again, base ingrate!, laugh derisively. This modicum of derisive laughter is now heard once more in certain quarters in the instance of George Bernard Shaw and his latest work, "Saint Joan," and in these certain quarters and among these deplorable and ignominious scoffers I regret to report that I find myself. For though the genius who has given us the greatest modern English ironic historical drama and one of the greatest of modern English comedies and the best of all modern English satirical farces and the most intelligent of modern English dialectic fantasies has gradually slipping down, down the golden trail in the last decade and with his comparatively feeble one act plays like "The Inca of Perusalem" and ten act plays like "Heartbreak House" and two hundred and seventy-five act plays like "Back to Methusaleh" has gathered behind the mountainside rock an increasing number of skeptical *francs-tireurs*, there have been, and are still, those of us who look to him stubbornly and steadfastly to duplicate and even augment the dramatic gifts that these years ago were so dazzlingly his. But each new year with its new manuscript brings a new disappointment, and the treasures that the man of genius has given us in the past are with an ignoble thanklessness forgotten in the light of his more recent failures. I say failures, although of course such a man never fails as meaner men fail. There are streaks of diamond dust in even his shoddy. Yet one expects—has the right of expectation that the man himself has given us—that these streaks shall be not mere streaks. The cobra eyes of criticism ever fasten their deadly glare upon the artist who has already realized himself.

Thus, Shaw's "Saint Joan," though it is a work far above the general, fails to satisfy us. From a lesser genius, it might pass muster—at least to a degree. From the hand of Shaw, it comes as an *affaire flambée*. We have had the Drinkwater chronicle play, and now we have a Vegetarian one. It is relatively undernourished; it cries for Old Tawny and red meat. It is as literal as the inscription on an envelope; the incidents of history with which it concerns itself are sieved through an indubitable imagination whose holes in this instance are so large that the incidents remain much as they were before. One looks for brilliant illumination and one finds but pretty, unsatisfying candle light.

This "Saint Joan" seems to me to be for the major portion as affectation on Shaw's part to prove late in his career to a doubting world that he has, after all, a heart. Why Shaw should want to convince the world that he has a sympathetic heart baffles me quite as much as if Darwin or Huxley or Einstein had wished or would wish similarly to convince the world of the fact in their own cases. But age ever grows sentimental, and Shaw, whose genius lay in tonic cynicism and disillusion, has grown comfortably sweet. Relatively so, true enough, but the genius of incredulity and dissent cannot compromise with the angels and survive. Yet one cannot convince one's self that this late compromise on Shaw's part is not very largely another instance of his sagacious showmanship, or in other words, conscious hokum. Shaw is undoubtedly just selling his soulfulness to the box-office devil. The sentiment of his rare Cleopatra was wise, and not without its leaven of irony, and very truly beautiful. The sentiment of his Joan of Arc is the bald sentiment of a wartime soapbox plea for money to buy milk for French babies. It is effective in an open and shut way, but its artistic integrity is suspect. Now and again in the course of his play, Shaw, with the ghost of the Shaw of fifteen years ago mocking him, becomes for a moment himself again, and we get a flash of the old-time quick mind playing its smiling skepticism in counterpoint to the Rubinstein "Melody in F" dramatic motif. But splendid though these isolated moments are—the speeches of the Archbishop of Rheims in the second episode and of the bench of the Inquisition in the episode before the last are Shaw at his best—they yet paradoxically, because of the confusion of the sentimental and rational keys, weaken considerably the texture of the drama as a whole. The greatest love scene in all the drama of all the world, a scene of tenderness and passion and glory all compact, would fall promptly to pieces were the heroine to hiccough or the hero, embarrassingly finding an alien particle in his mouth, to spit. Shaw's hiccoughing is amusing and his expectorations are corrective and prophylactic, but they do not jibe with the story of Joan as he has set

out to tell it and as actually he has told it. The story of Joan is perhaps not a story for the theatre of Shaw, after all. It is a fairy tale pure and simple, or it is nothing—an inspiring and lovely fairy tale for the drunken old philosophers who are the children of the world. It vanishes before the clear and searching light of the mind as a fairy vanishes before the clear and searching light of dawn and day. It is a tale for the night of the imagination, and such a tale is not for the pen of a Shaw. It is a tale for a Rostand, or a Barrie at his best, or maybe for some Molnar. If irony creeps into it, that irony should be an irony that springs not from the mind but from the heart.

Speaking of Shaw's "Joan" from the purely theatrical rather than from the library point of view, I cannot persuade myself that such an essentially inferior—very, very inferior—play as Moreau's on the same subject does not constitute a much more persuasive and convincing spectacle. It takes all for granted, and it accordingly sweeps the necessary theatrical emotions up into its arms. It may be a very poor play, but it never falters in its grim, artistically pitiable, passion. Shaw, to the contrary, has sung his dramatic "Marseillaise" with a trace of British accent. The melody is there, still vibrant and still thrilling, but with too many disturbing suggestions of Piccadilly. It moves, yet we do not move. It thinks when we would feel; it is literal when we would soar into the clouds of fancy; it is humorous, with a Krausmeyer's Alley species of humor—as in the handling of the episode of the eggs in the first act—when we do not wish to be humorous. The old Shaw jokes on the dunderheadedness and insularity of the English somehow do not seem to belong here; the George V. Hobart dream allegory of the epilogue is the old derisory Shaw making an obviously desperate last jump for the step of the rearmost car as the train is quickly pulling out and away from him; the episode of Joan kneeling, sword aloft, head bathed by the spotlight man, before proceeding on her way to lift the siege of Orleans is the stained-glass stuff of the old Stair and Havlin circuit. When Shaw is literal, his literality lacks vital simplicity; when he is fanciful, as in the epilogue, his fancy is more literal still.

The Theatre Guild's presentation of the play is a poor one. The groupings are amateurishly contrived; the direction is frequently so lopsided, what with the characters quartered either wholly on the left or right side of the stage, that the stage itself seems imminently about to be resolved into a see-saw; movement is lacking; the manuscript is made static. Several of the actors are excellent, notably Mr. Albert Bruning as the Archbishop, Mr. A. H. Van Buren as the Earl of Warwick and Mr. Henry Travers and Ian Maclaren as the Chaplain of Stogumber and Bishop of Beauvais respectively. Miss Winifred Lenihan, however, is so unequal to the heroic demands of the rôle of Joan that the rest of the cast is plainly concerned with laboriously playing down to her. She may convince the Theatre Guild management that she could save the armies of France but not for a moment does she convince the actors who play the leaders of that army or, more important still, the folks out front. Her fire is a small blaze at Sargent's Dramatic School; her voice—"a hearty, coaxing voice, very confident, very appealing, very hard to resist," thus Shaw describes it—is dry, and coaxing and appealing only with the mechanical formality of a player-piano. Several of the minor moments she manages nicely; in scenes calling for cold directness and chill reserve she is competent; but otherwise she lacks, and lacks entirely, the warm spark that must set aflame such a rôle as this one.

II

To that branch of the native dramatic literature dealing with the American negro, which already includes such meritorious work as Ridgely Torrence's "Granny Maumee," Eugene O'Neill's "Emperor Jones" together with the play that leads the present number of the *American Mercury*, and Ernest Howard Culbertson's "Goat Alley," there has been added recently the "Roseanne" of Nan Bagby Stephens. This last play, while not up to the high level of the others named, is none the less a creditable and interesting contribution, with much honest observation in it, a considerable penetration of darky character, and several specimens of forceful dramatic writing. The weakness of the play lies in the author's attempt to over-elaborate what was originally a manuscript in one act. This attempt has been instrumental in spreading out the materials until they become very thin, notably in the instance of the last act which runs about half an hour and which is at best a five minute episode playing desperately against time. But much of the rest of the exhibit is excellent, particularly that portion which depicts a negro revival meeting. This has been admirably staged, simply, unpretentiously, yet vitally, and mounts to a stirring act-end. The fable concerns a black man of God who, glorying in the power his newly acquired position gives him in the community, uses that position to further each one of his own ends, whether of the pocket or the flesh. His detection and undoing constitute the body of the play.

Up to eight or nine years ago, it is doubtful if, in the entire range of the American drama, there was to be found a single authentic negro character. The negro of drama was then either of the white wool wig and kidney pain species, given to excessive hobbling, many a "Yas, yas, massa, I'se a-comin'," and a comic line on his every exit, or of the species that was essentially a mere blacked-up Caucasian minstrel end man in a cutaway coat three sizes too large for him and a snowy toupée who was rather dubiously transformed into a dramatic character by giving him one scene in which he taught little Frieda and Otto how to say their prayers and another in which he apologetically shuffled into his master's library when the mortgage on the latter's old Southern estate was about to be foreclosed by the Northern villain and, with tears in his eyes and a quaver in his voice, informed him that, come what might, he would stick to him until he was daid. It is further doubtful if up to eight or nine years ago there was on the American stage a single negro character under fifty years of age. In the dramatic credo of the antecedent epoch it was an invariable doctrine that no negro existed who did not have white hair and the misery in his back, and who had not been in the employ of the same family since boyhood. Those stage Ethiops were a peculiar lot, as far removed from the American negro of actuality as the raisonneurs of Galsworthy are removed from the raisonneurs of Viennese musical comedy. Now and again a playwright would come along and try to break from the established tradition, but the best he seemed to be able to negotiate was, as in Edward Sheldon's case, a partly blacked-up Sardou, or, in Thomas Dixon's, a melodramatic lay figure who served as the pursued animal in a fox hunt by the Ku Klux Klan. The effort to look under the old superficial burnt cork is a very recent one. Miss Stephens' is another such effort, and one contrived with much accuracy and competence. Miss Mary H. Kirkpatrick is the entrepreneur. She and her associates in the production have managed with great success the difficult business of instructing white actors in the manners and idiosyncrasies of the blacks.

III

The genius of Maurice Maeterlinck is a product of the talented imagination of second-rate critics. In all the civilized countries of the world there has been but one critic of the first rank who has succumbed to the Belgian Percy MacKaye, and James Huneker, for all his other high analytical gifts, was admittedly a poor

critic of the theatre and drama. At that, I single out the late Lord Jim somewhat unfairly, for, though he wrote of Maeterlinck in terms sweet and ecstatic, he was given—when his right foot rested upon a brass rail and his mind took on that rare noonday clarity of his—to a skeptical snickering at his own judgment. Those persons who have seen in Maeterlinck an artist of pure facet have been betrayed into that estimate by his posturing of genius rather than by any actual genius. An extraordinarily shrewd showman with a fine feeling for the poetry that lies ever at the breast of beauty but with a relatively small aptitude for imprisoning that feeling in words, he has succeeded—in the past, if not in more recent years—in persuading the susceptibles that the task he set himself was a task accomplished. Yet though his field was strewn with flowers and though his aim was at the heart of beauty, his arrow almost uniformly found its home in the rear of an earthly cow. And the reason therefore is at hand. The man himself is essentially less the spiritual artist that he would have us believe than a materialist in a Belasco getup, with the two qualities constantly warring with each other and with the latter, by virtue of its greater bulk, ever the confounding vanquisher of the former. Maeterlinck is like nothing so much as the nun in Reinhardt's production of "The Miracle": the performer of a pious rôle who, in order properly to impress the paying public, keeps to himself in his hotel room and permits himself seldom to be seen off the stage, and then only with eyes cast down and face made ascetic with a liberal smear of holy talcum powder. As his particular hotel room, Maeterlinck has affected a remote ruined castle, but for the rest he has conducted himself more or less faithfully after the instructions of whoever it is who would be Morris Gest's press-agent if Morris Gest lived and operated in Belgium. But the job of living up to his self-made legend was a difficult one, and thus it came about presently that the good Maeterlinck's foot slipped, as Halvard Solness' foot slipped before him, and that the good Maeterlinck found his circus pretentions crushed in the quarry whereinto he fell. He could, poor fellow, keep up the bluff no longer. Twenty years is a long time. There is a Boulevard des Italiens as well as a path of brambles and thorns that winds behind a Belgian retreat. There are rich movie lots in Hollywood as well as virgin meadows in Herenthals. There are Hilda Wangels in the world as well as bees. "And who are you?" *He pulls off his whiskers.* "I am Hawkshaw, the detective!"

Thus did the Belgian Shakespeare (how they must laugh who erst invented the phrase!), mayhap not wholly consciously, remove his spiritual plumage and reveal to his astonished eulogists the charlatan underneath. This charlatan, this pretender, has ever been there behind the venerable mystic whiskers, for as a man doeth so is he in his heart, and it has been this spirit of charlatanism and pretence in Maeterlinck that has conveyed itself to almost everything that he has written. For one touch of uncorrupted beauty, there have been a dozen touches of affectation and sham: like W. C. Fields' fly-paper, they have stuck irremovably to Maeterlinck's fingers for all his efforts to shake them off. For one honest flight of free imagination, there have been two dozen flights of mincing self-consciousness. The horses that the Stratford Shakespeare held in check outside the Globe Theatre turned into Pegasuses; the Pegasuses that the Belgian Shakespeare tried to hold in check for Tintagiles, Aglavaine, Sélysette, Joyzelle, Pelleas, Melisande and many such another promptly and disconcertingly turned back into so many everyday nags. Genius dramatizes itself. All that Maeterlinck has dramatized is the vague symbol of genius.

Although, true enough, "Pelleas and Melisande" came into being early in his career, it is a typical example of his generally defective artistry. While the play has some of the inevitable appeal that inheres in any story of romantic love, whether that story be told by the Shakespeare of "Romeo and Juliet" or the Richard Harding Davis of "Soldiers of Fortune," it otherwise misses in every detail the heightened appeal that comes from an imaginative orchestration of such a story's emotions and from a felicitous verbal embroidery of such a story's little fancies. Striving for the simplicity that the play must have or in the not having perish, Maeterlinck succeeds only in achieving the kind of simplicity that is achieved by a rich dowager dressed up as a country maid at a fancy dress ball. Striving again for drama at the play's numerous curtain falls, he contrives only such banalities as long, tense, silent gazes, bald announcements of peril imminently to descend, sudden streams of radiance from bunchlights turned on in the wings, and —if not quite all of Mr. Gene Buck's hokum trinity: Mother, the Baby and the Flag—at least Mother and the Baby. His verse or poetic prose has an occasional starlit glimmer—I say occasional very generously, as I can recall only two such instances in the entire play, and they are minor ones—but in the mass it is the stuff of an imagination chained to a linotype machine. It is uninspired; it is pompous, peacocky, snobbishly simple—royal raiment worn for rags' sake. Miss Jane Cowl's Melisande is a delicately shaded and noteworthy performance, one that, with her admirable Juliet, lifts her high in the sound esteem of the American theatre. Mr. Rollo Peters' Pelleas, however, tries so assiduously to capture the wistful romantic note that it becomes before long as unintentionally humorous as the lugubrious playing of "Träumerei" on a saw.

IV

Actresses usually keep scrapbooks of all the plays they have acted in. Occasionally one of them goes so far as to dramatize her scrapbook in the form of a synthetic vessel for her own particular stage use. Such a compound is "Hurricane," by Madame Olga Petrova. Not only has Madame Petrova put into it all the materials out of her past plays that were dearest to her actress heart, but also a lot out of several dozens of other plays of her sister stars, to say nothing of a few tasty touches of the Broadway hokum, currently believed to be so profitable, for good measure. The exhibit is a post-graduate study in the star actress play of commerce. In it the star vouchsafes to herself the opportunity to reveal herself to her audience at the outset as a poor, abused, bedraggled and illiterate young woman and, at the finish, as a regally accoutred creature with the mien of a queen, the wit of a Madame de Staël, and yet, with it all, the same heart of gold that was hers in the humbler day. We see again the sordid surroundings of eight-thirty and the gilt magnificence of eleven. We hear the heroine gradually being persuaded to say "he taught me" instead of "he learned me." We hear the lesson in French, with the comic byplay. We see the brave little crippled sister and give ear to her thus: "Oh, doctor, do you really think I'll be able to walk again like other girls and be able to feel the green grass under my feet—and maybe be able to dance and sing? Wouldn't it be wonderful—too wonderful! If I pray to God, dear doctor, do you think He'll let you cure me?" (Yes, little girl, never fear; you will be miraculously cured at exactly 10:45 P. M., when with a cry you will fling aside your crutch and braces and shout aloud: "Look! Look! It's true; it's true! I can walk—*I can walk!*") We see the love scene in the moonlight; we hear the heroine's confession of past sin; we hear the manly hero's asseveration that all that means naught to him—"It is not what you were; it is what you are today, darling. Through the murk of the past I can see the virgin purity of your untarnished soul." We hear the naughty epithet duly hurled at the heroine by the villain by way of dredging up the necessary box-office blush

out front. And we get, seriatim, all the stencils such as "If God wants poor people to have so many babies, why doesn't He look out for them after they're born and not let so many of them die?" and "Take me; I am yours, body and soul; do with me as you will; only—only—I cannot marry you; I cannot be your wife. Think of your name, your career, what your friends would say! I love you too much to let you sacrifice yourself! I love you, Michel, I love you . . ." Madame Petrova finds no difficulty in juggling these rubber-stamps into an effective performance. Miss Camilla Dalberg is extremely good in the small rôle of a Polish peasant woman given to excessive child-bearing. But the dramatic evening knows no trace of quality.

V

When a Frenchman turns coy and tries to write a chaste comedy, what follows is often as unfortunate as when an American paints his blue nose red and tries to write a risqué comedy. The Frenchman's comedy in such circumstance is generally so strainfully virtuous that it is deadly, as the American's is so laboriously smutty that it is deadly no less. The most recent brace of Frenchmen to attempt the sweetly sentimental are those erstwhile consistently naughty fellows, Maurice Hennequin and Romain Coolus; their product is "La Sonnette d'Alarme" ("The Alarm Clock") done into English by Avery Hopwood. While it is true that the original is not without a trace of blush bacteria, that trace is so small as to be negligible, and being so small gives to the comedy as a whole the aspect of a reformed roué holding hands with Mrs. Mary Baker Eddy. Entertaining clean sentimental comedy seems to be as far from the talents of the generality of French playwrights as entertaining risqué comedy is from the talents of the generality of American. For that matter, the American Harry Wagstaff Gribble in "March Hares," meeting the Frenchmen on their own ground, has written a better risqué comedy than any Parisian has turned out in the last half dozen years, while not a single Frenchman, meeting the American playwright on *his* own ground, has succeeded in composing an immaculate comedy of any sound merit whatsoever. Hennequin and Coolus are witty and engaging comic artists of the popular theatre; some of their risqué exhibits are gorgeously funny; but their "Sonnette d'Alarme" is as dull a sentimental comedy as an attempt at French naughtiness by an American like Wilson Collison. This original dulness has not been diminished in Mr. Hopwood's transposition of the text. The latter has cluttered up that text with obvious vaudeville jokes, allusions to Flo Ziegfeld and Greenwich Village, and wheezes on Prohibition, jazz and ladies' undergarments, and has otherwise vulgarized a manuscript whose only small virtue lies in its comparative abstention from such barbarisms. The comedy is further damaged by the staging of Mr. David Burton who, in an attempt to inject life and speed into the text, has caused the actors to run around, shout, and rattle off their lines as if the piece were a farce. Bruce McRae is the plausible and ingratiating actor that ever he is, and Miss Marion Coakley brings considerable charm and distinction to a rôle that is essentially as banal as one of Edward Childs Carpenter's little orphan heroines.

VI

Although I am not acquainted with the Edouard Bourdet comedy which George Middleton has adapted into "The Other Rose," I feel that it is a reasonably safe assumption, knowing pretty well some of the other work of the sprightly author of "The Rubicon," that the American has deleted from the original the one thing that made it perhaps entertaining in the French. Unless my guess is a bad one, the French original dealt with the humorous conflict in an idiotically impressionable young man of what Molnar has called heavenly and profane love, the pull of romantic feminine purity against romantic feminine sex. From the local version, the sex has been carefully pruned, the result being that what minimum of conflict remains is the hackneyed collision in the young man's Martha Washington heart between two sumnerized and sentimental women rivals. This hybrid has been produced by Mr. Belasco with his customary uncommon finish, and it is admirably played in its two leading rôles by Miss Fay Bainter and Henry Hull; but it is all a waste of good effort.

VII

Leon Cunningham's "Neighbors," produced by the Equity Players, is a swollen vaudeville sketch that seeks to extract humor from the bitter feud that springs up between two families as the result of a trivial occurrence. The author has managed certain minor technical details adroitly, but his play, for all its effort to capture the homely and authentic humors of such a comedy as "The First Year," seldom gets underneath the greasepaint on the faces of its actors. The dramatizing of a triviality into a pervading catastrophe calls for an exceptional imagination and talent, and in these the present craftsman is deficient. His sortie into the field of kindly irrision misses success by virtue of his inability to distinguish between the situation that breeds humor and humor that breeds a situation. His situations and his humor are visibly joined together with gutta percha; there is an air of humorous calculation that prejudices the reactions of the auditor; there is no natural flow to the dramatic events. Attempting to capture various lower middle-class, small town American characters, he has succeeded only in dressing up so many vaudeville comedians in overalls, suspenders and calico.

THE LIBRARY

How We Are Governed

THE GREAT GAME OF POLITICS, by Frank R. Kent. Garden City, N. Y.: *Doubleday, Page & Company.*

ASTONISHINGLY enough, this is the first book ever written in America which describes realistically and in detail the way in which the mountebanks and scoundrels who govern 110,000,000 free and brave people obtain and hold their power. There are, of course, multitudes of texts on the political institutions of the nation, and a great many solemn treatises on the ways in which those institutions might be improved, but nearly all such tomes have been written by pedagogues rather than by practical men, and so they are generally long on theory and short on fact. Dr. Woodrow Wilson's "Congressional Government" offers a good example, if only because it is probably the best of the lot. Considering that it was written by a young scholar, still a year short of his Ph.D., it is, in truth, a genuinely distinguished performance. But how different and how much better a volume upon the same subject the learned author might write today, with fifteen years of hard political experience behind him! Not even the title, I venture, would remain, for congressional government, as the thing was understood in 1885, is now as extinct as the Bill of Rights. Dr. Wilson helped to murder both. His story of either butchery would make a book, indeed!

Mr. Kent is no pale young man in the grove of Pallas, but a political reporter of twenty-five years unbroken service—a man whose knowledge of practical politics sweeps upward from the elementary devices whereby drivers of garbage-carts are selected from the great mass of 100 per cent

Americans to the far more intricate and subtle artifices whereby a Hiram Johnson's heart is broken and a Harding is set upon the throne. Add to this vast experience an unmistakable passion for the sinister craft and mystery that he discusses—he views politics, indeed, with something of the lyrical fervor that gets into a bibliophile's view of first editions—and there issues an equipment that is almost perfect. His book radiates authority from end to end. When he describes the inner machinery of a primary election he describes something that he obviously knows completely. And when he details the tricks and dodges whereby Corrupt Practices Acts are evaded, he doesn't have to give names and dates, for he is no more to be doubted than "Robinson Crusoe" is to be doubted.

It goes without saying that a man so crammed with facts is not greatly inflamed by Vision. Nowhere in his book does he offer a new sure cure for all the corruptions of our politics; nowhere, in truth, does he show much confidence in any of the sure cures already proposed. All that he has to say of a hortatory and moral nature is crowded into three and a half pages of fine type at the end. And that all is simply this: that political machines are absolutely essential to the functioning of democracy, and that getting rid of them is thus quite as hopeless as getting rid of rain or frost. If they were abolished by a miracle tomorrow, the result would not be Utopia, but chaos. *Some*one must divide up the money looted from the plain people and distribute the easy jobs; politicians are simply persons with a special appetite and capacity for that subtle art. But it is not necessary, says Mr. Kent, that they should all be alike—that is, that they

248

should all be unmitigated rascals. The plain people not only have a God-given right to substitute measurably decent ones for those who are beyond redemption; they have, in every American State, a means already at hand. This is the means of voting in the primaries. Not one honest burgher out of ten does it—but all politicians, high and low, do it. In the primary, says Mr. Kent, lies the boss's strength, and also his Achilles heel. He may lose general election after general election and still hold his power, but let him come to grief in a couple of primaries and he is done for. For it is on victory in the primary that control of the party depends, and a politician who cannot control his own party, within the limits of his bailiwick, is no longer a politician, but only an ex-politician. The woods and wailing-places are full of them, nearly all done to political death by other politicians. But the plain people, if they only had the resolution, could achieve the same end, and if they did it sufficiently often the whole race of politicians would greatly improve.

Here, perhaps, I devote far too much space to what is, after all, merely a footnote to the book. Of its 322 pages, 319 are devoted illuminatingly, not to what might be or ought to be, but to what is. The facts are set forth clearly, accurately and often amusingly. It is an odd and highly instructive book.

H. L. MENCKEN

One of the Immortals

REMEMBERED YESTERDAYS, by Robert Underwood Johnson. Boston: *Little, Brown & Company.*

THE literary conquest of the East by the Middle West was made in two waves of attack, and the first was very faltering. The earliest invaders, indeed, did not come to conquer; they came to apply humbly for entrance and countenance, hat in hand. Of such sort were Howells, Clemens, Hamlin Garland and John Hay. The sad story of the dephlogistication of Clemens by the blue-noses has been told affect-

ingly by Van Wyck Brooks; how Howells and Garland were polished, pomaded and embalmed has been told by themselves; of Hay it is sufficient to say that he arrived in the East an Antinomian and died a fop. All this was in the seventies and eighties of the last century, when Parnassus was a *papier-mâché* mountain on rollers, slowly lurching along the Boston Post-Road toward New York. The second rush of longhorns, set off by the Chicago World's Fair of 1893, was far less timorous and *pianissimo*. This time they came, not to woo the decrepit dons of tidewater, but to flout and rout them. Some Berserker blades were in that company—for example, Dreiser and Frank Norris, and, in the reserve, Masters, Sandburg, Lindsay, Anderson *et al*—and they made rough and effective practice. Today, as a result of that practice, the New England tradition survives only historically, and the New York tradition, never very vigorous, has taken refuge in the abandoned stables of Greenwich Village. The dominant voice in the American letters of today is obviously that of the Middle West. Even Cabell, who is so typically Eastern that he is almost wholly European, had to wait for fame until the West discovered him.

Robert Underwood Johnson *de l'Académie Américaine*, B.S., A.M., Ph.D., L.H.D. and all the rest of it, is an archaic and somewhat bewildered survivor of the first brigade of invading Westerners—that is, of the brigade that came on velvet foot, eager to be patronized. Brought up in a remote march of Indiana, where the Bible and Ayer's Almanac were the only books generally read, he arrived in New York in the seventies, got himself a job on *Scribner's Monthly* (later the *Century*), and instantly fell under the spell of its editor, Dr. J. G. Holland, author of "Letters to Young People" and "Plain Talks on Familiar Subjects," the Dr. Frank Crane of that era. The things that Dr. Holland admired were elegance, restraint, what he called good taste; the things that Dr. Johnson admires today are elegance, restraint, what he calls good taste. This good taste, it appears, takes the form of a rancorous hostility to every idea hatched since 1885. It would be amusing but somewhat cruel to list all the bad authors of whom the good doctor speaks with respect, beginning with the aforesaid Holland and ending with Frank R. Stockton; it would be even more amusing to list all the good ones he shows no sign of being aware of. Here is a book of 624 pages by a man who helped to edit one of the principal American magazines for forty years, and yet there is absolutely no mention in the index of Stephen Crane, Jack London, Edith Wharton, Theodore Dreiser, George Ade, Frank Norris, Willa Cather or James Branch Cabell—nor, indeed, of Joseph Conrad, Gerhart Hauptmann or Anatole France! But there is a long and lyrical chapter on the American Academy of Arts and Letters, in which it appears that one of the *literati* most active in organizing the underlying Institute was F. Marion Crawford, and that among the first members of the Academy were such brilliant lights as Crawford, Hamilton Wright Mabie, Donald G. Mitchell, Bronson Howard and Johnson himself! Surely a curious company of immortals! Dr. Johnson, at that time, was an assistant editor of the *Century* and had printed three trivial books of verse—chiefly dull set pieces in the college commencement manner of 1875. How Richard Harding Davis came to be left out it is hard to imagine.

Dr. Johnson says that he retired from the editorship of the *Century*, in 1913, because of a difference with the trustees over the policy of the magazine. Such forgotten successes of that day as *Everybody's*, *Munsey's* and *McClure's* were cutting into its circulation. The trustees favored popularizing it,—which is to say, I surmise, restoring to it the enterprise and timeliness that it had shown in the early eighties. Dr. Johnson, on the contrary, favored keeping it "unimpaired in tone and character," and proposed setting up an independent "cheap, illustrated, all-story periodical," clubbing it with the *Century*, and "thus utilizing the capital of our name." This difference is rather hard to understand. If the trustees actually planned to degrade the magazine, as Dr. Johnson hints, then they changed their minds after his retirement, for it continued very dignified, and remains so today. The chances are that the combat was not actually between dignity and cheapness, but between Dr. Johnson's notion of dignity and some other notion. The year he succeeded Richard Watson Gilder as chief editor of the *Century* Ellery Sedgwick became editor of the *Atlantic Monthly*. Without sacrificing dignity in the slightest, Sedgwick pumped the *Atlantic* full of new life, and by 1913 it was already an assured success, notwithstanding the competition of Munsey, McClure and the rest of the barbarians.

Despite the fact that Dr. Johnson is an Academician, a Ph.D., an L.H.D., a commander of the Order of the Crown of Italy, an officer of the Order of Leopold II of Belgium, a commander of the Order of St. Sava of Serbia, a grand cordon of the Order of SS. Maurice and Lazarus of Italy and a personal friend of King Victor Emanuel III, some curious slips are to be found in his book. For example, he seems to believe that the *one-he* combination is good English. Again, he speaks of the walls of a hospital being "discolored by pyaemia," which is much like saying that the windows were broken by headache. Yet again, he praises the following doggerel as "touching lines" in a "beautiful lyric":

the rain would come full often
Out of those tender eyes which evermore did soften:
He never *could* look cold until we saw him in his coffin.

The italics are from the text. I should add that this lovely fragment of the J. G. Holland school is not from the *Century*, but from the *Atlantic*. But Sedgwick is blameless: it was printed eleven years before he was born.

H. L. M.

Pseudo-Science

REJUVENATION AND THE PROLONGATION OF HUMAN EFFICIENCY, by Dr. Paul Kammerer. New York: *Boni & Liveright.*

REJUVENATION: HOW STEINACH MAKES PEOPLE YOUNG, by George F. Corners. New York: *Thomas Seltzer.*

THE RE-CREATING OF THE INDIVIDUAL, by Beatrice M. Hinkle, M.D. New York: *Harcourt, Brace & Company.*

A PLEA FOR MONOGAMY, by Wilfrid Lay, Ph.D. New York: *Boni & Liveright.*

THE PHILOSOPHY OF CIVILIZATION, by R. H. Towner. Two volumes. New York: *G. P. Putnam's Sons.*

CONTRACEPTION: THEORY, HISTORY AND PRACTICE, by Marie Carmichael Stopes. London: *John Bale, Sons & Danielsson.*

SIX books—all of them highly profound and scientific in manner, all of them addressed to the layman, and all of them concerned chiefly with the phenomena of sex! There is a moral in the fact, I have no doubt, but if so you must deduce it for yourself. As for me, I content myself with reporting that all six seem to me to be very unconvincing, and that five of them are also dreadfully dull. The worst of them is Dr. Hinkle's huge volume, for she takes 450 large pages to explain earnestly what psychoanalysis has revealed about the division of humanity into psychological types, and succeeds only in repeating in a pseudo-scientific jargon what all the more intelligent phrenologists were saying a century ago. Dr. Lay is less obvious, but still more garrulous: in the whole course of his long, laborious and often indignant treatise upon the physiology and pathology of holy matrimony he says so little that is new that a competent writer might have got it upon a postcard. Corners and Kammerer both cover the same ground, the one somewhat journalistically and the other with a great show of scientific solemnity. Both leave doubts behind them. Kammerer, I believe, is a highly romantic fellow: he has been announcing of late that he has discovered proofs of the inheritance of acquired characters. In his account of the Steinach operation, its theory, its technic and its effects, he constantly shows a great deal more evangelical enthusiasm than critical acumen. Whenever, in order to support Steinach, he has to embrace an absurdity, he embraces it boldly and without qualms. For example, on page 132, where he finds himself forced to argue that sexual continence is "strength-preserving." This is sheer nonsense. So is it nonsense to argue that "the very worst that could happen to the patient in consequence of the ligation of the spermatic duct would be that nothing whatever would happen." And so is it nonsense to argue obliquely that vasectomy can work improvement in a case of cancer.

Mr. Towner's two volumes are given over in large part to maintaining a quite novel thesis, to wit, that so-called cold women make the best mothers for the race—that their children tend to be measurably superior to the children of passionate mothers. All I can see in this is a truly stupendous example of the *post hoc, ergo propter hoc* fallacy. Mr. Towner first proves what everyone already knows, *i.e.*, that the women of the upper classes tend to be less loose and amiable than the women of the slums and barnyards, and then proceeds glibly to the conclusion that the superiority of their children is due to their relative sexual reserve. But isn't their sexual reserve itself a mere symptom of their general superiority, or, perhaps more accurately, a secondary and not invariable accompaniment? Certainly, not *all* of them shrink from motherhood. Well, what evidence is there that the children of those who do not shrink are inferior to the children of those who do? I can find none in Mr. Towner's book, and I can find none anywhere else. His accumulation of materials is gigantic, and much of it is very interesting, but it falls very far short of proving his case. When, in his second volume, he undertakes to show that the use of wine is beneficial to a race he is on far safer ground, but it was covered years ago by Sir Archdall Reid.

Dr. Stopes' tome on contraception is bellicose, bombastic and extremely unscientific. Whenever she sets up shop as an authority on physiology—as, for example, on page 117 and on page 76—she quickly becomes absurd. And whenever she discusses the theories of rival birth controllers she descends instantly to the raucous, waspish manner of all earnest propagandists and uplifters, at all times and everywhere. As for the contraceptive device that she advocates herself, I suggest that the opponents of birth control print 10,000,000 leaflets describing it, and distribute them from end to end of the Republic. The result, if I do not err, will be a doubling of the birth-rate within one calendar year—and the adoption of the name of Stopes for scaring children.

H. L. M.

Three Volumes of Fiction

HORSES AND MEN, by Sherwood Anderson. New York: *B. W. Huebsch.*
THE ROVER, by Joseph Conrad. Garden City: *Double-day, Page & Company.*
A LOST LADY, by Willa Cather. New York: *A. A. Knopf.*

SHERWOOD ANDERSON dedicates his new book of short stories to Theodore Dreiser and prints a short but eloquent hymn to the elder novelist as a sort of preface. A graceful acknowledgment of a debt that must be obvious to every reader of current American fiction. What Dreiser chiefly contributed to the American novel, next after his courageous destruction of its old taboos, was a sense of the tragedy that may play itself out among the lowly. The lowly, of course, had been familiar figures in our fiction for many years; the most popular of all American novels of the middle period, indeed, had had a hero who was an actual slave. But even the authors of text-books of literature for undergraduates must be aware by this time that Mrs. Stowe never actually saw into the soul of Tom—that she simply dressed up a dummy and then somewhat heavily patronized it. The same patronage continued unbroken until Dreiser wrote "Sister Carrie." In that book, for the first time, a girl of the Chandala suddenly became real. Dreiser did not patronize her in the slightest. In-

stead, he tried to see her exactly as she was, to understand her secret soul, to *feel* with her. It was a new kind of novel among us, and after the Comstocks, the college tutors and other such imbeciles had tried in vain to dispose of it, it began to have an influence. Today that influence is visible in stories as widely different otherwise as Miss Cather's "My Antonía" and Anderson's "Many Marriages," Tarkington's "Alice Adams" and Elliot H. Paul's "Impromptu."

"Horses and Men," indeed, is largely a set of variations on Dreiserian themes, though mere imitation, of course, is nowhere visible. The book represents a sort of reaction from the elaborate and often nonsensical psychologizing of "Many Marriages." In other words, Anderson here returns to earth—specifically, to the rural Ohio that he knows so well, and to the odd, pathetic peasants whose aspirations he sees into so clearly. I put the first story in the volume, "I Am a Fool," beside the most esteemed confections of the day, and call confidently for judgment. If it is not enormously better than anything ever done by Katherine Mansfield, Arthur Machen or any other such transient favorite of the women's clubs, then I am prepared to confess freely that I am a Chinaman. There is a vast shrewdness in it; there is sound design; there is understanding; above all, there is feeling. Anderson does not merely tell a story; he evokes an emotion, and it is not maudlin. So in "An Ohio Pagan," a story scarcely less adept and charming—the tale of a simple youth to whom going to school is a tragedy almost as poignant as the nationalization of men would be to an archbishop. And so, too, in "The Sad Horn Blowers," in "Unused," and in "The Man's Story." These are short stories of the very first rank. They are simple, moving, and brilliantly vivid. Another such volume and all of us will begin to forget the Wisconsin washing-machine manufacturer and his occult posturing in the altogether.

Mr. Conrad's "The Rover" contains indications that he has profited by the adverse criticism which began to rise against him in England two or three years ago. For a long while he had been accepted as a sort of overwhelming natural phenomenon or act of God, above and beyond ordinary criticism. Then a few anarchists began complaining that he was, after all, a bit too careless of design—that his great romances would be even greater if only he could be induced to articulate them more deftly. In "The Rover" there is an unmistakable improvement in this department. The story has a beginning, a middle and an end; it moves smoothly and logically; it is nowhere discursive or obscure; in truth, it is almost well-made. Personally, I was quite content with the garrulous, wandering, absent-minded Conrad of "Nostromo" and "Chance"—it seemed to me, indeed, to be foolhardy to risk alarming him by challenging him, as it was foolhardy to alarm Beethoven by suggesting that he change his shirt—, but now that the business has been dared and its effects are visible, I believe that there will be a measurable increase in Conradistas. There is nothing in "The Rover" to daunt the most naïve novel-reader. It is a simple story, very simply told. It has a good plot, plenty of suspense, and what the idiots who presume to teach short-story writing call rapid action. In brief, a capital tale, done by a great master. Scene: the south coast of France. Time: the year before Trafalgar. Hero: a retired French pirate who dies magnificently in an enterprise against *perfide Albion*.

Miss Cather's "A Lost Lady" has the air of a first sketch for a longer story. There are episodes that are described without being accounted for; there is at least one place where a salient character is depicted in the simple outlines of a melodrama villain. But this vagueness, I suspect, is mainly deliberate. Miss Cather is not trying to explain her cryptic and sensational Mrs. Forrester in the customary omniscient way of a novelist; she is trying, rather, to show us the effects of the For-

rester apparition upon a group of simple folk, and particularly upon the romantic boy, Niel Herbert. How is that business achieved? It is achieved, it seems to me, very beautifully. The story has an arch and lyrical air; there is more genuine romance in it than in half a dozen romances in the grand manner. One gets the effect of a scarlet tanager invading a nest of sparrows—an effect not incomparable to that managed by Hergesheimer in "Java Head." But to say that "A Lost Lady" is as sound and important a work as "My Antonía"—as has been done, in fact, more than once in the public prints—is to say something quite absurd. It is excellent stuff, but it remains a bit light. It presents a situation, not a history.

H. L. M.

The Chicago Outfit

MIDWEST PORTRAITS, by Harry Hansen. New York: *Harcourt, Brace & Company.*

THE appearance of this very serious tome probably marks the passing of the movement with which it deals. The center of literary gravity in the United States has hovered over Chicago since the Columbian Exposition of 1893, which taught the natives not only table manners but also connoisseurship. But now that most elusive mathematical point seems to be preparing to wander again, and just which way it will go no man can say. It may come eastward, to the New York that held it between the downfall of Boston and the rise of Chicago. It may move further West, though never, I am sure, as far as the Coast, where Methodism now makes all the fine arts impossible. It may even go southward. But that it will remain where it is seems highly improbable. For Chicago, running out of ideas, has begun of late to take refuge in postures, and so it tends to repel the young artist and to attract the young mountebank. The literary circle that Mr. Hansen describes is already almost indistinguishable from that of Greenwich Village. It has its Great Men, many of them bogus; it has its whips and arbiters; it is extremely self-conscious and it is beginning to be ridiculous.

What ails it, as I hint, is that it has run out of ideas. The older men in it, *e.g.*, Masters, Sandburg and Ben Hecht, either repeat what they have already said or descend to platitudes and worse. Masters, having written the most honest, the most eloquent and altogether the most important long poem ever done in America, now devotes himself to indignant and unconvincing novels. Sandburg, a true primitive, having got the harsh, sweaty drama of the prairie and the packing-house into lines as bold and musical as those of a Negro spiritual, now writes fairy tales that decline steadily in charm, entertains the hinds in fresh-water colleges with banjo-music, and heads tragically into the National Institute of Arts and Letters. Hecht, having marked out the American Philistine for his victim, now writes blood-tub melodramas to divert that Philistine on Sunday afternoons. As for the youngsters, who are they and what have they done? They have talked a great deal,* but they have written nothing. Anderson I pass over as one who has escaped, as Dreiser escaped before him. Greenwich Village, I believe, has done him some damage, but had he remained in Chicago he would have suffered damage far worse.

What a change in a few short years! Once a battleground; now a parade of literary Elks! I find on page 84 of Mr. Hansen's programme of the show a very ironical indication of the extent to which even the Middle West has begun to fall away from the Concord on the lake. He is describing a visit to Sandburg, and Sandburg is showing some of the letters received from his customers. "This," he says, "is from a chap in Grinnell College— on the faculty there, and let me tell you, *they are up and coming there*." Some time ago an American magazine printed a novelette obviously dealing with Grinnell College, called "A Part of the Institution." The author was Ruth Suckow, of Iowa, but

most assuredly not of Chicago. Read it, and you will find out just how up and just how coming Grinnell really is.

H. L. M.

Origins of the Revolution

REVOLUTIONARY NEW ENGLAND, 1681-1776, by James Truslow Adams. Boston: *The Atlantic Monthly Press.*

This is the second volume of a work that should constitute, when it is completed, a contribution to American history of the very first consideration. For the first time a serious and painstaking effort is made to disentangle the whole history of the New England colonies from the mass of sentimental legends that has surrounded it, and to present it objectively and with some approach to scientific accuracy. The result, of course, is an almost complete recasting of the familiar story; the record of the causes which brought on the Revolution becomes itself revolutionary. The tyrant king and the brave and altruistic patriots both depart. In place of them we have two sets of antagonists, and neither, alas, of the highest virtue. On the one hand, there is the battle between English traders and American traders—each seeking advantages, fair or foul; each eager to profit at the cost of the other. On the other hand, there is the battle between the rich men among the colonists—chiefly traders, but sometimes landowners—and the great masses of the dispossessed. How the two struggles eventually merged into one— how the rich colonists, by playing upon the credulities and sentimentalities of their propertyless brothers, finally managed to present a united and formidable front to the City of London and the British *raj*—this is the story that Mr. Adams tells.

It is told simply, clearly, without much rhetorical ornament, and yet always with a great deal of charm. Despite the immense mass of material digested, there is never any obscurity. Effects follow causes in logical chains. There is always room in the closely-packed narrative for touches of the picturesque, small sketches of character, even some sly humor. The book, no doubt, will strike more than one reader as pro-English—almost, at times, as a piece of special pleading for Parliament and the Lords of Trade. But it is actually nothing of the kind. It is simply history with the varnish knocked off—and inasmuch as most of the varnish was on the heroes of the school-books, the net effect is inevitably that of whitewashing some of the villains.

That such works should be appearing in the United States in the face of a formidable Fundamentalist movement in history, with laws getting upon the statute-books making the most absurd legends official and impeccable—this is surely something to cheer the despairing heart. One hopes only that, as the historians of the new school finish with the Revolution and come closer and closer to current times, they will not collide with the New Patriotism, and so find themselves in jail. The years 1860-1875, done as realistically as Mr. Adams has done 1681-1776, would make a chronicle at least twice as startling as the present one, and the years 1914-1923—but here, perhaps, we approach the limits of the lawfully thinkable!

W. F. ROBINSON

The Case of Luther

LUTHER NICHOLS, by Mary S. Watts. New York: *The Macmillan Company.*

UNPERTURBED by the ballyhooing at other and more pretentious booths, Mrs. Watts continues to do business at the old stand. Her goods are of the reliable variety—nothing flashy, you understand, but free from shoddy, and guaranteed to wear well.

In "Luther Nichols" she deals once more with the Hinterland. Luther is a country lout, poorly educated but good-looking, who, coming to a mid-western town in search of his fortune, drifts into the employ of a garage, as he might have become a hostler twenty years earlier. Then comes the war, and his friend, Roy McArdle, an inarticulate bumpkin, is drafted and leaves his gum-chewing fiancée in the care of Luther. She hankers after the good-looking chauffeur, but is restrained by the chastity of her class. Then Luther himself is drafted, and ordered to the front. The night before he leaves he and Roy's fiancée get married as a pleasant way to spend the evening, and the next morning wake up to the noise of the Armistice. So they settle down to an unexciting conjugality.

The second part of the book deals with the vamping of Luther by the blonde daughter of a *nouveau riche* family, whose chauffeur he becomes. At last she corners him in a roadhouse, but her stodgy brother conveniently blunders in. Luther is discharged, and the story really ends with him slinking away from the great house. But the author has tacked on a chapter. There is a scene at a club, a crash outside, and the bridge-players, running out, find a rum-running automobile smashed. Luther is unhurt, but his friend Roy is killed. So we have a happy ending after all. Luther, we hear, has rehabilitated himself. With his good looks and his luck (shown by his escape in the accident), he must go on inevitably to social and economic success. We leave him feeling that all will be well.

Unluckily, Mrs. Watts has set the stage for a comedy of manners which doesn't quite come off. The amorous young lady dallies with Luther in a lonely country lane—and her brother walks around the corner. She sits in his lap before a dying fire in a deserted library late at night—and we hear the brother's latch-key. Worse, Mrs. Watts has yielded to the temptation to moralize. Not quite at her ease in this, she speaks through the mouths of her characters, themselves apologizing. Just what moral she wishes to point is a trifle vague even at the end. Apparently, that things are different since the war, and that the classes show a regrettable tendency to mingle. This is bad; one must keep the servants below stairs.

JOHN E. LIND

THE AMERICAN MERCURY AUTHORS

CARLETON BEALS, A.M. (Columbia), *went to Mexico in 1918, and save for two years in Italy, has lived there ever since. He has published books on Mexico and on the Fascisti movement in Italy. His latest work is "Mexico: an Interpretation."*

JAMES M. CAIN, *author of the clinical study of the American labor leader, is now a professor in the University of Maryland, but he has spent most of his life in newspaper work, specializing in labor news.*

GUY EGLINGTON *is an American who has passed much time in Europe, chiefly engaged in the study of painting.*

MORRIS FISHBEIN, M.D., *is associate editor of the* Journal of the American Medical Association. *He teaches the history of medicine in Rush Medical College, and is the joint author, with Dr. Oliver T. Osborne, of a standard handbook of therapy.*

EMORY HOLLOWAY *is the author of the chapter on Whitman in the Cambridge History of American Literature. He has been engaged upon the early work of Whitman for the past eight years, and has already published two volumes upon the subject.*

GERALD W. JOHNSON *is associate editor of the* Daily News *at Greensboro, N. C.*

DR. LEON KELLNER *is a professor at the University of Vienna. His short history of American literature, published in translation*

in 1915, is the best ever printed. He is a frequent contributor to English philological journals.

DR. JOHN E. LIND *is a neurologist at St. Elizabeth's Hospital in Washington, and is a frequent contributor to medical and psychological literature.*

H. M. PARSHLEY, Sc.D. (Harvard), *is associate professor of zoölogy in Smith College, and a specialist in the* Hemiptera.

DR. RAYMOND PEARL *is head of the Department of Biometry and Vital Statistics in the Johns Hopkins School of Hygiene and Public Health, and an international authority upon biometrics. He is a member of many learned societies, American and foreign.*

EDWARD SAPIR, Ph.D. (Columbia), *is chief of the Canadian Division of Anthropology at Ottawa. He has been investigating American Indian languages for years, and is the author of a standard work on Language.*

GEORGE H. SARGENT *is a well-known bibliographer and a member of the American and English Bibliographical Societies.*

HOWELL SYKES *is an American who has lived in China for a long while. It should be added, in view of the complaint voiced in his article on the missionaries there, that he is not a business man.*

CHARLES WILLIS THOMPSON *has been a political writer for nearly thirty years, and has represented the New York* World *and* Times *at Washington.*

The Plimpton Press
NORWOOD · MASSACHUSETTS · U. S. A.

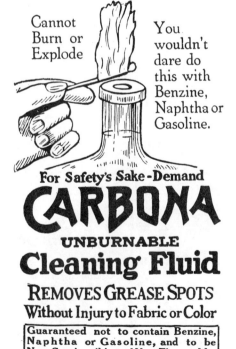

ALFRED A. KNOPF
PUBLISHER

BORZOI BOOKS

220 WEST 42d ST.
NEW YORK

The works of

WILLA CATHER

(Pulitzer Prize Winner of 1922)

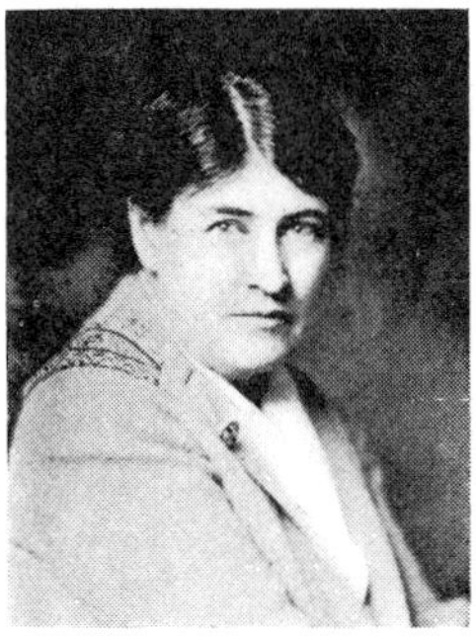

"The passion of the artist, the heroism of the pioneer—these are the human qualities that Miss Cather knows best."—*Carl Van Doren.*

Willa Cather, universally recognized as America's greatest woman novelist, was awarded The Pulitzer Prize for *One of Ours* in 1922. This prize served as a confirmation of her power and ability revealed in her earlier works, *The Song of the Lark*, *O Pioneers*, *My Antonia*, and *Youth and the Bright Medusa.* Sinclair Lewis, H. L. Mencken, Rebecca West, Henry Seidel Canby, Gamaliel Bradford, Carl Van Doren, Heywood Broun are just a few of the many critics who have united in her praise. In the poll of literary critics conducted by The Literary Digest, Miss Cather was the only woman included in the list of five leading American authors.

Miss Cather has just returned from Europe. While there, a fund was raised by the women of Omaha, her home state, to have a picture of Miss Cather painted by Leon Bakst. It is only fitting and proper that the memory of this great author should live in form as well as in her literary works.

A LOST LADY

"The best novel of its kind done by a woman writing in English in this generation. She is a towering writer."—*Rebecca West.* $1.75 net

ONE OF OURS

"As rugged and real a picture of a farm boy who grew to manhood as ever has been painted by an American. A passionate story of an aspiring youth who found manhood in service."—*William Allen White.* $2.50 net

APRIL TWILIGHTS AND OTHER POEMS

In reviewing *One of Ours* for The Atlantic Monthly Gamaliel Bradford said: "The sense of mystery and the sense of beauty make the charm of this book as they made the charm of the lovely *April Twilights*. . . . Verses which have sung so long in my memory." $2.00 net

YOUTH AND THE BRIGHT MEDUSA

"These stories have the radiance of perfect cleanliness, like the radiance of burnished glass. . . . One of the truest as well as, in a sober and earnest sense, one of the most poetical interpretations of American life that we possess."—*The Nation.* $2.50 net

IN CANADA FROM THE MACMILLAN CO. OF CANADA, LTD.
ST. MARTIN'S HOUSE, TORONTO

A Who's Who of WILLA CATHER

Willa Sibert Cather, born in Winchester, Va., December 7, 1875. Left Va. at age of nine as a pioneer to the West. Settled on a ranch in Nebraska. Her preliminary schooling was that of contact with the raw life of a newly settled and cultivated land. Went to High School at Red Cloud, Nebraska. Entered University of Nebraska, graduated at nineteen, and immediately went to Pittsburgh and worked in The Pittsburgh Leader. She was telegraph editor and dramatic critic for several years, then took the place of the Head of the English Dept. in the Alleghany High School. Published her first books. Went to New York to take a position on McClure's Magazine, of which she later became Managing Editor. Left McClure's and has spent the greater part of her time writing in New York.

THE
AMERICAN MERCURY

under the editorship of George Jean Nathan and H. L. Mencken will undoubtedly be the most discussed magazine of 1924. In covering the whole national scene—from politics to belles-lettres and from public hygiene to theology, it will publish much that you cannot well afford to miss.

If you are not a subscriber to THE AMERICAN MERCURY, fill out the coupon below, enclosing check or money order for five dollars ($5.00) and avoid the possibility of failing to secure the number which you most want to read. If you are already a subscriber you doubtless have several friends who would appreciate greatly a year's subscription to the magazine.

(Canadian postage fifty cents, foreign postage one dollar additional.)

- -

THE AMERICAN MERCURY, *220 West 42nd Street, New York*

Please send me THE AMERICAN MERCURY for one year, starting with the..........
issue. I enclose $...... (check or money order).

Name...............................Address...................................
Please send to the following names THE AMERICAN MERCURY for one year, starting

with the....:......issue. I enclose $...... (check or money order).

Name...............................Address...................................

Name ....Address...................................

Name...............................Address...................................

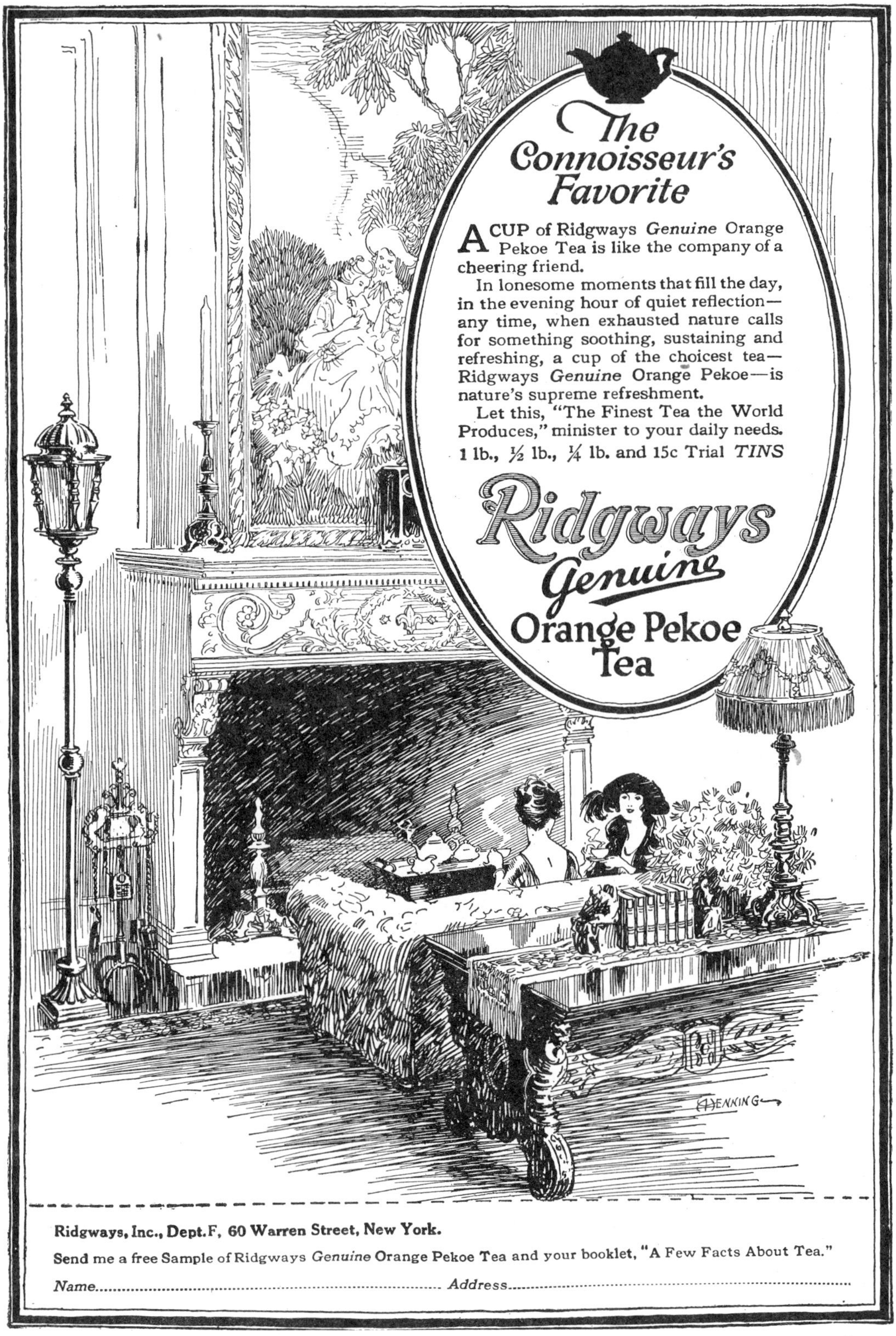
The Connoisseur's Favorite
A CUP of Ridgways *Genuine* Orange Pekoe Tea is like the company of a cheering friend.
In lonesome moments that fill the day, in the evening hour of quiet reflection—any time, when exhausted nature calls for something soothing, sustaining and refreshing, a cup of the choicest tea—Ridgways *Genuine* Orange Pekoe—is nature's supreme refreshment.
Let this, "The Finest Tea the World Produces," minister to your daily needs.
1 lb., ½ lb., ¼ lb. and 15c Trial *TINS*
Ridgways
Genuine
Orange Pekoe Tea
HENNING
Ridgways, Inc., Dept. F, 60 Warren Street, New York.
Send me a free Sample of Ridgways *Genuine* Orange Pekoe Tea and your booklet, "A Few Facts About Tea."
Name............ *Address*............

The AMERICAN MERCURY

VOLUME I March 1924 NUMBER 3

TABLE OF CONTENTS

CRETHEUS AND THE LIONS (*A Story*) . Stephen French Whitman 257

THE JOHN BROWN MYTH . . . . Leland H. Jenks 267

CHAUTAUQUA: ITS TECHNIC . . . . Gregory Mason 274

REFLECTIONS OF A BIBLE-READER . . . Arthur Davison Ficke 281

SIX ORCHESTRAL CONDUCTORS . . . . D. W. Sinclair 285

EDITORIAL 292

JOHN MAROUFAZ AND HIS SONS (*A Story*) . . . W. L. George 297

AMERICANA 306

EVERY SCIENCE AN EXACT SCIENCE . . Vilhjalmur Stefansson 309

THE TWO TAFTS . . . . Charles Willis Thompson 315

MANSFIELD PARK AND AMERICA . . . Arthur Bingham Walkley 320

CLINICAL NOTES . . . George Jean Nathan and H. L. Mencken 323

PORTRAIT OF AN OLD MOTHER (*A Poem*) . . Alice Mary Kimball 332

BYRON IN AMERICA . . . . Samuel C. Chew 335

AMERICAN PORTRAITS, II. THE WASHINGTON JOB-HOLDER
Harvey Fergusson 345

THE SIRE OF KIWANIS . . . . William Feather 351

SPANISH NIGHTS' ENTERTAINMENT . . . . . . C. E. Bechhofer 357

THE AMERICAN VIEW OF POLITICS . . . . Johan J. Smertenko 363

THE THEATRE . . . . George Jean Nathan 369

THE LIBRARY . . . . H. L. Mencken 376

REVIEWS BY OTHER HANDS:
The Popularization of Science . . . . . . H. M. Parshley 381

Walter von Molo . . . . Friedrich Schönemann 383

THE AMERICAN MERCURY AUTHORS 384

Published monthly at 50 cents a copy. Annual subscription, $5.00; Canadian subscription, $5.50; foreign subscription $6.00. . . . The American Mercury, Inc., publishers. Publication office, Federal and 19th Streets, Camden, N. J. Editorial, advertising and subscription offices, 730 Fifth Avenue, New York. . . . Printed in the United States. Copyright, 1924, by The American Mercury, Inc. . . . Application for entry as second-class matter pending. . . . Four weeks advance notice required for change of subscribers' addresses.

Alfred A. Knopf
Publisher

George Jean Nathan } *Editors*
H. L. Mencken

"Unquestionably better and more complete than any other Life of R. L. S." says Clayton Hamilton, author of "On the Trail of Stevenson," of

THE LIFE OF ROBERT LOUIS STEVENSON

By ROSALINE MASSON

Author of "I Can Remember Robert Louis Stevenson"

A remarkably vivid, distinctly readable biography whose interest is by no means confined to lovers of R. L. S. Miss Masson has had unusual opportunity to get at the mass of new material brought to light since the Sir Graham Balfour work of more than twenty years ago and has produced a full and authentic record of Stevenson's life. *Illustrated. $3.00*

CONTEMPORARY BRITISH DRAMATISTS

"Coming upon this group of British plays can be compared to coming upon a bright, bubbling stream in the midst of a burning desert," says the *Chicago Evening Post* of the first four volumes in this new series of plays by living British dramatists. The volumes ready are: "Exodus" by H. F. Rubinstein and Halcott Glover; "The Conquering Hero" by Allan Monkhouse; "Midsummer Madness" by Clifford Bax, and "What's Wrong with the Drama?" by H. F. Rubinstein. *Each, $1.50*

THE CONFESSIONS OF A PRIMA DONNA

Who can she be—this American prima donna who so frankly narrates her life-story? From a pathetic child in a Southern town, she emerged in Italy a triumphant prima donna, young, beautiful, singing in all the capitals of Europe. This is the whole story of the crowded experiences in the life of a successful opera singer, a tale that is amazingly interesting from first page to last. *$2.50*

MAKING BUSINESS ADVANCEMENT SURE

By WILLIAM M. JACKSON

A welcome relief from the usual smug advice to young workers exhorting them to forget the clock and cling to long hours, these fifty vigorous talks by the personnel manager of a metropolitan newspaper contain clear-cut suggestions as to how ambitious workers can get the most from their present jobs and make advancement to bigger ones sure. A questionnaire after each chapter enables the reader to check up on what each section has given him. *$1.50*

THE MYSTERY WOMAN

By Alice MacGowan & Perry Newberry

Authors of "The Million-Dollar Suitcase," etc.

A detective story that holds its suspense to the very last page and whose plot, disclosed by one exciting discovery after another, leads into San Francisco's highest and lowest circles. "The Mystery Woman" complicates things almost to the point of distraction, for she is very beautiful. *$1.75*

EIGHT PANES OF GLASS

By ROBERT SIMPSON

Author of "The Gray Charteris," etc.

A heart-warming romance of the Scottish Highlands. People who affectionately remember "The Stickit Minister" and "Beside the Bonnie Briar Bush" will enjoy this modern, truly dramatic romance of everyday life, with a deal of Scotch canniness and humor. *$2.00*

A Real Man's Book

Women, too, may like it —you never can tell!

THE OWLS' HOUSE

By CROSBIE GARSTIN

Here are adventure, romance, excitement:

Smuggling Wrecking
Horse-trading with Gypsies
Pirating Off the Barbary Coast
Fighting Lovemaking

"Something freshly new to delight lovers of robust fiction."

$2.00. —N. Y. Herald

443 Fourth Ave. FREDERICK A. STOKES COMPANY New York

THE DIARY OF SAMUEL PEPYS

Edited by
Henry B. Wheatley

Complete edition in 3 vols. on India paper

$15.00

A THEORY OF SOCIAL ECONOMY

By Gustav Cassel

A complete analysis and restatement of economic principles by the famous Professor of the University of Stockholm.

$5.00

THE MANCROFT ESSAYS

By Arthur Michael Samuel

Literary, archaeological, and historical essays which recapture the style and charm of Lamb, Hazlitt, and Sainte-Beuve. $3.00

TRAVELS IN EAST ANGLIA

By Frank V. Morley

A book of genial wandering through the tranquil English countryside.
Illustrated $3.00

Harcourt, Brace & Company

383 MADISON AVENUE :: NEW YORK

H. W. Nevinson's
CHANGES AND CHANCES

Nevinson's autobiography brings the reader into contact with a great company of distinguished writers and men of action. "The best book of any sort we have read in a long time."
—F. P. A. $4.50

CRITICISM IN AMERICA
ITS FUNCTION AND STATUS

A discussion of the nature of criticism in American literature.

Essays by Irving Babbitt, Van Wyck Brooks, W. C. Brownell, Ernest Boyd, T. S. Eliot, H. L. Mencken, Stuart P. Sherman, J. E. Spingarn, and George E. Woodberry. $2.50

John Maynard Keynes'
MONETARY REFORM

A book that should be read by every banker, businessman, statesman or philosopher. $2.50

LORD SHAFTESBURY
By J. L. & Barbara Hammond

"A clear picture of the melancholy, self-introspective, but courageous and humane man who lived close to his severe religious professions and in whose character there were elements of real moral grandeur."—*Daily News* (London). $3.50

Violet Bell's
BLINDNESS OF HEART

"A picture of romantic, youthful love, as fresh and charming, as spontaneous and passionate as Meredith gave us in 'Richard Feverel'."—*Philadelphia Ledger*.
"A finely conceived novel."—*N. Y. Times*. $2.00

Maxwell Bodenheim's
CRAZY MAN

The realistic story of a shop girl and a New York sinner who attempts to live according to an altruistic creed. $2.00

The American
MERCURY

March 1924

CRETHEUS AND THE LIONS

BY STEPHEN FRENCH WHITMAN

On a fragrant night of June, a great change reached its climax in the heart of Cretheus, and he determined to renounce the world. Having donned a robe belonging to one of his slaves, he walked for the last time through his great and splendid house, in order to bid a contemptuous farewell to all its beauties. The door-porter inquired at what hour the master would return. "Never," Cretheus answered, and went down through his gardens into the wicked city.

Around him in the soft night he observed the people sauntering to their follies. The torches in the theatre cast a nimbus against the sky. Symbolic lamps illuminated the Temple of Aphrodite. From under the plane-trees there issued the shouts of gamblers, the laughter of women, the music of the flute-players, the cries of the venders of sweetened snow from the mountain. And all about the town given up to its licentiousness, on the dark hillsides blotched with the flowering of magnolias and oleanders, twinkled the lights in the palaces of the rich, from whose colonnades and groves descended a faint clatter of revelry.

"Hapless people!" Cretheus groaned. "In your blindness you are preparing yourselves to be delivered, bound hand and foot, at the door of hell itself!"

Passing out through the city gate, he shook from his feet the dust of the place where he had been powerful, wealthy, reckless, drunken, and steeped in terrestrial love. Cretheus journeyed for three days and three nights, and arrived in the midst of the desert.

The huge undulations of gold and amethystine sand extended to the horizon, behind which the sun was setting in a glory of gold and ashes of rose. Before the traveler there emerged from the sand a little hill of rock. In the face of the rock was the cave that God had prepared in the beginning for the habitation of Cretheus.

But Cretheus found reclining in the cave a lioness and two lions.

He was filled with the delicious calmness that he had earned by his days and nights of solitude. "Fear nothing of me, little lions," he besought them, although they were not little—that was merely a diminutive of tenderness. "We are all in fact God's children. Let us then try to prove ourselves to be so, by loving one another."

The two lions and the lioness, crouching with their bellies against the floor of the cave, regarded Cretheus in terror; for they perceived that he had no fear of them. And when, on second thought, they bared their teeth at him, and attempted rattling barks of intimidation, he laid his hands upon their heads, and stroked their ears.

One lion, very old, was black-maned; the other was yellow-maned and young. The lioness also was young, and beautiful. Finally, assured that they were in no immediate danger, they seated themselves before him, and the lioness rolled on her back coquettishly at his feet, with her dainty paws in the air.

So Cretheus and the lions began to live together in the cave of the desert.

From the foot of the rocky hill a little spring of cold water gushed out into the sand; and there a wild date-palm bore its stony and providential fruit for Cretheus' nourishment. He rose at dawn, and, fasting, meditated on the true natures of God and man. At evening, when the lions and the lioness would have gone out to seek their prey, he preached them sermons, in which he pointed out to them the naughtiness of slaying their fellow-creatures, and promised that, if they trusted in God, they would be provided for in some more seemly way. He also sought to inculcate in the beautiful lioness the virtue of chastity. The three beasts, cowed by the words of Cretheus, slunk back into the recesses of the cave. But it is not unlikely that when Cretheus was asleep they slipped out into the desert for their meat. For sometimes in the morning, they seemed lethargic and bloated, their breath when he caressed them was fetid, and they avoided his affectionate gaze with a look as if of shame in their amber eyes.

II

After Cretheus had lived in the cave of the desert for a year, he was greatly emaciated; his hair and beard were very long; his skin was as dark as the skin of a Libyan; and his robe had become a few tatters bound about his loins. Moreover, his face was changed; for he had spent all his time in separating in his mind the world of good (*Animus Dei*) from the world of evil (*Anima Mundi*). And he had tried patiently every day to impart his thoughts to the lions.

In consequence of his many sermons and great viligance, the lions had grown, as it appeared, quite meek, and even seemed smaller than at first. But sometimes, when Cretheus was not looking at them, they regarded him subtly. Then, hiding their faces with their paws, they flicked their long tasseled tails from side to side, as if a prey to secret and dangerous thoughts. But the fair lioness, with the more exquisite duplicity of her sex, rubbed her fine coat against the knees of Cretheus, and purred as she looked at him with the loving attention of a woman who is plotting the humiliation of her lord and master.

"How gentle they are!" said Cretheus, with happy tears in his eyes. "Where the spirit of God is received into the heart Heaven exists."

Then one night he awoke to perceive that the old black-maned lion was not in the cave. At the same time he heard a clashing in the desert. It was Laomedon, a great general and an old acquaintance of his, approaching in the cool of the night to visit him.

Laomedon appeared at the mouth of the cave in a blaze of flames and of armer. Stooping his massive head, which was encased in brass and crested with vermilion horse-hair, he entered, bidding his officers remain outside. They obeyed, forming on the stony platform a bright wall of breastplates embossed with the deeds of Herakles and the Heroes, before which dripped down the sparks from the fat torches. Vibrations of carnal dignity and force filled the cave. Laomedon, seating himself upon a block of stone, shook his head disparagingly.

"So you have come to this, my poor Cretheus," he rumbled. "Are you, then, insane?"

"No, Laomedon," answered Cretheus, "I am happy."

What have you found here?" the general demanded. "Is there an ancient treasure in the depths of this cave, and are you guarding it till you can escape with it? Is it a place of magic, from which you hope to send forth spells, and gain a world? Or have you found somewhere a woman on whose account you feel so terrible a jealousy that you must hide her here?"

"No," said Cretheus serenely, "I have found God."

Laomedon's hard old face expressed commiseration. He mused regretfully:

"I am a soldier, a politician, and a practical man, and cannot discuss religious matters with you. I do for myself, and ask nothing of any god. Yet I am great, healthy, and rich; and I inspire fear. In fact, I myself am a god to innumerable people, creating or destroying their happiness, giving or taking their lives. When, having captured a city, I stand upon the walls, the groans of the dying, the screams of ravished women, rise up to me amid the smoke and the flames like incense, offered to my power. It is said that Zeus casts thunderbolts. I cast the lightning of my army against my enemies. In strange lands people feel a greater dread of me than of their most vindictive deities. I have seen tyrants faint from terror when brought into my presence; but nobody faints before the altars of the gods. For they are far off, while I am here. I exist—perhaps they do not. Perhaps they live merely in the minds of men. As for me, I have never felt weakness nor fear; so I have never had need of them. Of what were you afraid, my Cretheus, that you felt the need of a god?"

Cretheus, rising, walked to and fro. The young lion and the young lioness regarded him anxiously from the recesses of the cavern. He stood still before the general, who resembled, indeed, some sort of divinity, huge, square, implacable of attitude and dense of visage, surrounded by rays of light that struck in, through the entrance of the cave, upon his armor and helmet.

Cretheus, extending his wasted arms, spoke as follows:

"What should one fear, Laomedon, but one's conscience? All my life I was a wastrel and a profligate. The sweat of my agricultural slaves provided a strange jewel for some flighty girl, or perhaps the years of toil that broke them down sufficed to buy an erotic medallion in chrysophrase or jasper. At dawn I often lay on my dining-couch overcome with wine and snorting like a pig, while my people were being driven into the fields with blows. One night a servant let fall a drop of sauce on the robe of Limnanthis, the Milesian, who reclined beside me; and because she was angry I let him be beaten to death. I did many other things which I need not confess. At last a light providentially broke forth before my eyes; and I perceived by that light what I had been doing to others and to myself."

Laomedon protested:

"The sweat of slaves, the tears of silly women, the deaths of sundry men— whether killed for a whim or to advance one's fortunes—what does that amount to? How can one live like a gentleman without using the labor of others, or shedding a little blood from time to time? It is unseemly to disgrace one's caste by such actions as these. Conscience, remorse, brotherly love, and religion are for the lower classes, they themselves, no doubt, having invented such soporifics in order to make their lives seem easier."

Cretheus made a gesture of compassion.

"Laomedon," he asked mildly, "are you trying to destroy my new-born soul? Never mind: I do not regard you as an enemy, but pity and love you."

Sighing, Laomedon responded:

"Some angry woman who knows the abodes of the witches must have given you a philtre, to produce this effect. And I came here because I, in return, love you, as I might have loved my son if he had lived. When I heard that you had forsaken the wine-cups and wreaths, I told myself that you were preparing, in solitude, to live a different life, perhaps of energy and genius, grandeur and victory, in the service of the State. In my vain imagination I saw myself instructing you in all the arts of triumph. One day or another even I must die; but if you listened to me, and then received my sword, I should live on in you."

Cretheus inquired:

"What is it, dear Laomedon, that you have to offer me?"

The yellow-maned lion and the lioness raised their heads high again.

"I offer you the exaltation of predestined victories," Laomedon declared. "I offer the thrill of planting the heel upon the necks of nations. You shall walk amid fields of corpses and say, 'I have sown this seed.' Night shall be like day for you, in the light of burning cities. Returning home, with kings yoked to your chariot-pole, you shall see your gilded statue already erected, and receive the Father-land into your keeping."

Cretheus explained:

"But I am satisfied to be the conqueror of that man which I have been."

The young lion and the lioness let their heads sink down upon the floor of the cave. Laomedon departed.

III

Standing on the platform of rock before the cave, Cretheus watched the departing cortège of Laomedon. They had extinguished their torches; but the full moon had now risen; and one could see the general, his officers, and the escorting squadron rapidly riding over the silvery billows of sand, like a cavalcade of little images made of silver. At last they were lost in the glitter of stars that extended to the horizon. And a sensation of loneliness and futility descended into the soul of Cretheus.

He had unavoidably pictured himself as a general in flashing armor and vermilion crest, riding toward victories that could never be forgotten.

At dawn the old black-maned lion returned to the cave, avoiding the eyes of Cretheus with a look of guilt.

"Oh, what have you been doing, little brother!" cried Cretheus.

But the old black-maned lion made no response.

Cretheus became more assiduous than ever in pious meditation. Sometimes he remained in one attitude, oblivious of everything physical. Then, for a week, neither eating nor drinking, he contemplated—or so it seemed to him—the ultimate truth of existence, while all around him there appeared as it were a glow of heavenly fire.

"Now," he thought blissfully, "I am indeed with God."

Two months were gone since the visit of Laomedon. On a night of orange moonlight, in the height of the canicular heat, when the beautiful lioness had slipped out into the desert, a gust of perfume filled the cave. Helopsychria, the lovely hetaira, appeared before Cretheus, wearing many emeralds, sheer jonquil-yellow robes, and grass-green sandals.

IV

When she had entered the cave with her well-known, slow, undulating step, Helopsychria smiled sadly. She pronounced, in a voice like a threnody of Phrygian pipes: "So you have indeed lost everything, Cretheus? Do not be downcast any longer on that account. The Tender Goddess has sent you a treasure, myself, for whom tyrants and satraps would eagerly exchange their hoards of gold, their marbles, their gems, and the trophies of their ancestors."

A little blind slave-girl entered behind Helopsychria, bearing an ivory box inlaid, in mother-of-pearl, with the amours of Zeus. Sinking down, the child placed the box before her on the floor.

On the sands of the desert, two Ethiopian camelmen made the two camels kneel, as if they expected to wait there patiently for a long while.

Cretheus wondered why Helopsychria was not afraid of the two lions, who stood attentive in the shadows behind him. Then he remembered that she had never been afraid of beast or man, or of anything whatever except time. She stood with her neck slightly bent, leaning her weight on one foot, the outline of her incomparable figure revealed through the folds of her robe, against the moonlight. The splendor of her green eyes, and of her broad emerald necklace, pervaded the cavern. Her yellow hair, dressed in the triple rows of curls, was so tightly bound that her head seemed negligible, her body all-important. Yet Cretheus knew that in that little head was stored an immensity of guile, a profound talent for temptation, an amorous fatality that could be escaped by no man who was at any point unfortified by God.

He began to pray.

"But my dear, it is unnecessary to pray," Helopsychria remarked, "for I am already present."

"Helopsychria," said Cretheus firmly, "I am not he whom you knew in those other days."

Her ripe lips trembled. And Cretheus understood that he was more desirable to this woman than before, because of the novelty bestowed on him by his new, saintly face.

"I warn you," Cretheus announced, "that the world of pleasures and crimes, from which you come as an emissary and example, has no longer any power over me. In fact, it has ceased to exist, melting away before that heavenly reality amid which I have come to live. Go, beautiful phantom! Dissolve into the nothingness of which you are typical! Leave me with God, whose ineffable universe is the true and only one."

"But I, too, exist," Helopsychria protested more melodiously than ever. "My pulse beats. A warmth stirs even now in my body. I feel an ecstasy growing in my brain. Lay your hand beneath my breast, Cretheus; feel my quick heart; and then, if you can, say that I do not live."

The two lions, fawning round her feet in admiration, licked her little pink toes, which appeared between the grass-green thongs of her sandals, and which were so rouged that they shone like carnelians.

But Helopsychria had eyes for Cretheus alone. She continued:

"I am not unacquainted, my dear, with the idea of holiness. All those who enter the Orphic Mysteries do so with a sense of what they call evil, and with an imaginary need of purification. Nor are you the first man whom I have known to shrink from the beneficence of my goddess. I have been told before that love has its bitterness. But may there not be a greater bitterness in the absence of love?"

"The end of sin is death," Cretheus retorted in an awful voice.

"Is not the end of piety also death? I have heard that all the Initiators and Mystagogs teach a future life: but what superior power would dream of perpetuating us? In my opinion, one is sure of this hour only, and ought to fill it with joy."

"The goddess you serve," he returned bitterly, "is Aphrodite, in all her names, manifestations, attributes, and habits. But my God is not attained by kisses; the perfect peace at his disposal is not predicated on satiety, unless on that satiety which is disgust at everything unlike him. No, Helopsychria, you have made this journey for nothing. I no longer understand the words uttered by your tongue."

The little blind slave-girl wiped some tears from her eyes with the back of her hand. The lions, making themselves as flat upon the pavement as if they were rugs of skins, hid their unhappy faces under the hem of Helopsychria's robes. She cast around her a long, humid, yearning glance.

"I should have liked to regain your affection in this cave. I am so weary of my house with its marbles, its pillars garlanded with flowers, its garden in which butterflies kiss the lips of my statue of Eros. There, on all sides, I see nothing but luxurious objects. This is different. I could remain here happily for seven days and nights. On one of my camels are cages containing doves, sacred to my dear Mistress. We could suspend those cages here and there, and all day long an amorous cooing would be redoubled and enlarged by echoes. And then I have brought with me carpets, vases, perfumes, pillows, fans, wine, luxurious foods, and lutes—but nowadays perhaps you scorn such things. No matter: I should be able to devise a thousand tricks for transfiguring this place with simple and touching beauties. And even if there were no cooing of doves, even if you forbade the carpets and the perfumes, love would be here."

Cretheus turned his back on her.

"O God," he thought, "thou knowest that this woman is not actual, but merely some involuntary guilty thought of mine. I mean to say, Thou dost not know it; for Thou hast never contemplated evil. Nevertheless, save me!"

Her voice stole forth to him like a caress.

"Cretheus, it is not as hard as you imagine to yield to love. You have only to think about it, to determine not to think about it, to peep at it askance, to flee, while drawing nearer to it, to picture its realization, while denying that it can ever again have reality for you. Thought is always the creator. Think, Cretheus. Or better still, remember."

She spoke softly in another language to the small blind slave. The child produced from the ivory box, among other things, a double flute. Faint music began. With his mind's eye, Cretheus perceived some scenes of childhood, full of innocent happiness, and a little girl, now dead, whose cheek he had kissed one day in Spring, under the almond-blossoms. Despite him, the thin wedge of love, pointed with that lost chastity and adolescent joy, entered Cretheus' breast.

"Look at me," breathed Helopsychria.

She appeared a different person. Her robe was of white wool. Her hair was dressed like the hair of a girl. Her countenance was young, pure, and arch. Her jewels and her grass-green sandals had disappeared. One no longer smelled her perfume. She threw over her head a bridal veil, and blushed.

"Am I not she—immaculate of mind, constant, devoted for a lifetime—whose image all men bear in the most secret depths of their minds?"

He gave a cry of grief.

"How could you suppose, my Cretheus," she continued in reproachful tones, "that I was offering you anything but this? You shall find in me the bride and wife and mother, the dear and meek helpmate, the companion of your maturity and the comforter of your old age. When you come home you shall see me carding wool, or teaching your little sons to honor you. I will lift up my gaze to yours, and a wave of calm affection shall pass from me to you. All our conversation, as well as our thoughts, shall be noble and frank. We will stand with our arms 'round each other's necks, looking at the stars, and thanking fate that amid all the multitude of beings we have found each other. One of us must die first; and, if it be you, I will close your eyes so softly, and die quickly in my turn, and hasten out there to find you. For there will not exist for me in this world of men any other man; and to have lost you will be to have had my beating heart removed from my bosom, and carried away from me, into the shades."

Cretheus perceived large tears rolling down her cheeks. It seemed to him that he must inevitably clasp her in his arms, and lose himself in the fragrance that enveloped her. He could almost have knelt before her; he could almost have cried out, "Oh, it is you at last!"

Some influence stronger than Cretheus, and stronger even than Helopsychria, kept him motionless. Perhaps the God of Cretheus had been somehow able, despite His absolute goodness, to perceive Helopsychria not as she appeared at this moment, but as she really was. That, however, would be a question for the sophists.

"Cretheus! Cretheus! Cretheus!" she cried imploringly, and stretched out her exquisite arms, which presently fell to her sides. "I have done what I could," she muttered.

She tore off her white wool and her veil, which she threw to the blind child. The latter placed them in the ivory box, together with the flute, meanwhile shedding tears upon them. Helopsychria resumed her emeralds, her grass-green sandals, and her jonquil-yellow robes. She moved proudly, as fair women often do in their defeats, toward the mouth of the cave. There she turned, to have the last word.

"Good-by, Cretheus. I leave you my perfume."

In a flare of temper, she smashed a vial of scent upon the rock; and instantly its highly disturbing sweetness drenched the cave. Even the lions, which had followed her regretfully to the entrance, were spattered all over with it; but they seemed to like it.

Cretheus answered in a hollow voice:

"May you find God, my sister, if indeed you exist."

"Donkey!" Helopsychria spat at him.

She and the little slave-girl, going down to the sand, mounted the two camels, which the two Ethiopians led away into the orange moonlight.

The beautiful lioness returned to the cave at dawn.

V

For a long while the cave was polluted by Helopsychria's perfume. Cretheus, making with great pains a bucket out of palm leaves, brought up spring water and sand, and scrubbed the interior of his abode, using his hands as brushes. In consequence, some of the perfume was transferred to him, so that, awaking in the night with his hands across his nose, he had for a moment a dreadful delusion that Helopsychria had returned and was standing before him in her emeralds. As for the lions, their coats retained the aroma of Helopsychria the longest of all. When Cretheus tried to drag them down to the spring to be washed, they evaded him and bounded about like lambkins.

He redoubled his prayer and fasting. In the course of weeks he thought perhaps no more than a dozen times a day of the milky arms of Helopsychria, her long eyelashes, and little polished toenails. Then he thought of these things only half a dozen times a day, then only once or twice a day, then not at all. While waiting for the spirit of God to fill the emptiness left in his heart by his forgetting Helopsychria, he composed grateful songs, which he sang to the lions. Their paws extended, they looked at him with an air of sheepishness and boredom, now and then yawning so as to show their black and pink mottled gums, their pink tongues, and their strong back-teeth. Or else, they suddenly ignored him to search for a flea.

One night, three months after Helopsychria's apparition, while the young yellow-maned lion was absent, Thersander, formerly the bosom-friend of Cretheus, sauntered into the cave.

VI

Thersander, freshly shaven, had his hair arranged in waves, and wore a lavender himation, with over this a Tyrian chlamys fastened at the neck by an amethyst brooch. He even had 'round his head a wreath of small pink roses, as though he were coming from an evening party. His litter, embellished with gold, rested below on the sand, beneath a myriad blue stars, surrounded by stalwart Cappadocians, and mules bearing jars of snow to cool the brow and mouth of the elegant Thersander.

He was much amused by the appearance of Cretheus.

"What secret wager are you paying by this performance?" he inquired, laughing. "Now I cannot blame Helopsychria for saying that she came to offer her love to a man, but found, instead, an ass. Yet she must have remained here longer than to take one look at you; for some of her perfume still seems to cling to this den."

"Does it still cling, Thersander?" protested Cretheus woefully. "Ah, when will it evaporate from my lions?"

"What lions are you talking about?"

Thersander asked him in an innocent way, although at that moment the old black-maned lion and the lioness were standing one on each side of him, examining him with every evidence of approbation. "Was Laomedon right? Are you a trifle mad?"

Sitting down upon a stone, he sniffed a small bunch of violets. His plump fingers were covered with rings, the intaglios of which depicted satyrs being pursued by nymphs, Zeus summoning the rivers to Olympus, shepherds enamored of hamadryads, Zagreus being torn to pieces, and lynxes caressing mænads.

Thersander turned grave, and demanded: "When will you return to your natural life?"

"This is my natural life, now and henceforth forever, but ever more so."

"Alas!" Thersander lamented, "and what of that ideal of existence that you and I planned together? That sublime life—the creation of beauty in living—far above the ignobility of ordinary lives, in a noble and radiant spaciousness that merges with the loveliness of sunshine, mountains, sea, air, and sky! It is true that this ideal may be seized and maintained by an heroic effort only. But I thought that for the sake of beautiful living you would be heroic."

"God and the innumerable parts of him alone are beautiful," said Cretheus in trembling accents.

"You have become so primitive here that I suspect you are speaking of some Olympian," Thersander rejoined sarcastically. "Or have you been converted to mysticism at Eleusis? But I thought you and I had already rarified all divinities, and all mystical interpretations of a god, into a rational and scientific cause. It would not be absurd to admire Nature; but it would be absurd to worship it. As for seeking union with it, that we already have inevitably. But the whole genius of our race is expressed by activity in Nature, not by such passivity as this. Here you are creating nothing, except a very long beard. Moreover, your beard is not beautiful.

Such ugliness and squalor are a crime against the gift of life."

Involuntarily Cretheus wrung his hands, and returned:

"I was becoming happy again. Then you appeared."

"How can that be so?" Thersander objected. "Common sense should have told you that there is no happiness in fruitless introspection."

"There is happiness in the saving of one's soul."

"Your soul," smiled Thersander, in commiseration, "is a fragment of the soul of Nature, which you cannot escape. Your soul will be saved, as you call it, by your acting naturally. You are now acting artificially; and from your aspect I judge that Nature will presently grow overweary of you, as it invariably does of artificial things. It will find some other use for the atoms that compose you. As you now are, it were better for the beauty of life if you were to fertilize a flower or a melon."

Cretheus was greatly shaken; for he saw in his visitor, as it might be, an exact reflection of his own former self. Since there may be a pathos in the image of one's old likeness—as, for example, when one was ardent, defiant, attractive in the impudence of youth—the soul of Cretheus wept. He saw again the academic groves, and himself walking arm in arm with young men whose world this was, all its manifestations to be joyously accepted, or circumvented, or shaped anew, but never renounced. Theirs had been the aspiration to evolve, from nothing but the materials at hand, a life of richness and fastidiousness and intellectual pride, high above the herd, in a glamour of marble and foliage, to a pessimism ennobled by a determination to be happy, despite all the chances of life and death and fortune.

Cretheus, closing his eyes, prayed:

"O God, be present! For I know that logic was not thy logic, that beauty not thy beauty."

Then suddenly the genius of his God pervaded Cretheus; and he preached to Thersander, and to the old lion and the lioness, with these words:

"Parmenides tells us that logic makes it necessary for us to see the universe as an unchangeable unity. But our senses appear to show us a world of change. This is the world of opinion; but the opinion is false. Leucippus and Democritus point out that taste, smell, sound, color, do not yield us a true knowledge of things, but merely tell us how they affect us. In other words, no man can ever be sure of receiving an exact impression of his surroundings; and therefore the philosophies which are deduced from our surroundings must also be inexact. What, then, is this material phenomenon which we seem, in our blindness, to see, touch, hear, smell and taste? 'Matter,' as Plotinus says, 'has neither form, quality, unity, or power. It is absolute impotence and privation. It is the principle of evil. It is farthest removed from God; there is no trace of God in it. It is darkness.' Let us then seek the light."

Raising one arm above his head, Cretheus proceeded with his argument in ringing tones:

"Plotinus has shown us further that God is perfect—yet how imperfect, Thersander, is this world in which you invite me to rejoice! Did a perfect God create it? But how is that conceivable? The same philosopher has explained to us that the farther we are from the sunshine of God, the nearer we are to that darkness which is matter. But God, being light, cannot know darkness; and therefore he cannot know us as we exist in this darkness. Let us then turn our faces upward, and strive to regain his presence. But how is that to be done? Simply by not forgetting that this world, which surrounds us, is unknown to God in his perfection, and that it is to be ignored, if we are to regain Him. In short, we are like little frightened children, who in some mysterious way have lost their Father and gone far astray, and are suffering every hour from that loss. When we regain him, we shall indeed be his beloved children again, and suffer no more forever and ever and ever."

The old black-maned lion and the beautiful young lioness, cowering against the gilded sandals of Thersander, were shedding tears.

Cretheus seemed prodigious. The hair on his head arose and surrounded his face like the turban of an Asiatic magus.

"Repent, Thersander, if you are indeed Thersander!" he shouted. "All that you think and do is false and fatal. The loves that you seek are but a grotesque and horrible counterfeit of love. The dainty nourishment that you take is a sickening parody of that nourishment which God offers you. Your pride of mind is deadly to your salvation, whereas humility would still rescue you from hell. Your defiance will end in impotent weeping. But God, who is unacquainted with revenge, will not do it to you. You will have done it to yourself."

Thersander rose, tossed away the violets, wrapped his Tyrian chlamys round him, and responded:

"Farewell. I return to a garden where the garden god extends his sceptre of earthly fertility over the yellow roses, and where Helopsychria will sing to me, in her melting voice, Sappho's ode to Aphrodite. If you listen carefully, you may be able to hear our happy laughter."

He departed, and was carried back in his litter to the wicked city.

VII

For a while Cretheus, who should have been happy, was depressed. Also it worried him to think that, after all the pains he had taken with them, his lions had rejoiced in Laomedon, Helopsychria and Thersander. So he resolved to purify their hearts, no matter at what cost.

He began by forbidding them, once more, to leave the cave at night.

As he knew that they had been deceiving him in this, Cretheus now made his bed every night in the mouth of the cavern, in order to bar their way out. He no longer slept at all. At first, the lions and the lioness would come creeping toward him very stealthily to see if he was asleep; but in the darkness the green glare of their eyes invariably betrayed them. Then Cretheus would sit up, and talk to them reasonably.

The lions and the lioness retreated backward, with groans of misery. In their sorrow, they licked one another's ears, and huddled close together, meditating, no doubt, on the deliciousness of warm blood and quivering flesh. They grew thinner and thinner. Their hair fell out in patches; the vertebrae of their tails resembled a succession of knots. They lay all day in a stupor.

But Cretheus suffered with them. The weaker the lions became, the weaker he became; and he could gauge their sufferings by his own. Now and then there passed over him a flood of despair, as if, in depriving them of their former activities, he were depriving himself. However, he maintained his determination to purify the lions of their lusts.

One morning, the old black-maned lion, which was now little more than a skeleton, quietly lay over on his side, and gave up his life. At noon, the young, yellow-maned lion, which formerly had been so strong and frisky, also died. The beautiful lioness did not die till evening. While she was passing, Cretheus held her poor, lean head on his lap. With her last breath of life, she bit him feebly on the hand. Then her flat body, which had been so lithe and fair, slowly stiffened forever.

The following day Cretheus buried them. He himself was now so weak that he could hardly drag their diminished bodies down to the desert. It took him many hours under the hot sun to dig their graves with his hands. As he covered each one with sand, it seemed to him that he was covering forever a dear part of himself. Very feeble, he returned to the empty cave.

"My lions are gone," he sobbed.

He believed he could hear the rumor of his city—the cymbals clashing in the temples, the roar of the audience in the theatre, the rattle of chariots, the sighing of cypresses in the garden of his palace, the voice of Helopsychria singing to Thersander.

Indeed, for a moment the whole activity of the world that he was leaving seemed audible to Cretheus—the clangor everywhere accompanying the progress of conquerors; the vocal diapason raised to the gods that manifested all the impulses of nature; the rippling gaiety of waves, and branches, and young human throats distended by laughter; the universal murmur hovering above the multitude of lovers whose lips had been united, above the flowers that were receiving the wandering pollen, and the crystals of the rocks that were clinging to each other in a subtle fruition.

Then, as he lay expiring in the mouth of the cavern, before him, on the stony platform, there stood three apparitions, as it were, of Ares, Aphrodite, and Dionysus, taller than mortals, blinding in beauty, superbly pensive. It seemed to Cretheus that they spoke to one another.

"What is this strange idea that has come into our world?"

"A tiny point of corruption."

"And if it should infect all life?"

"But observe that this creature, in order truly to avoid us, has to die."

In fact, at that moment, Cretheus triumphantly breathed his last.

THE JOHN BROWN MYTH

BY LELAND H. JENKS

JOHN BROWN is one of the many characters in our history whose renown bulks vastly larger than his accomplishment. The deeds by which he achieved immortality were actually very few, and often far from creditable. He was the leader of a Kansas robber band which called out five pro-slavery neighbors in the middle of the night of May 23, 1856, murdered them and made off with their horses. A few days later, having traded the horses for others, faster and less incriminatory, Brown turned on a posse of pursuers, defeated them, and held them prisoners until overpowered by a detachment of United States cavalry. Two or three months later he and his followers, overhauled by a force of Missouri "border ruffians" who sought revenge for the murders, lost the fruits of their Summer's altruistic labor for Free Soil—a large string of horses, two hundred and fifty head of cattle and much miscellaneous merchandise. Two years later Brown led a raid from Kansas into Missouri, stole eleven Negro slaves from several plantations, and seized ten head of horses, three yoke of oxen, eleven mules, bedding, clothing, provisions, "in short, all the loot available and portable." He took the Negroes to Canada, where they were put to work, and sold the swag to pay the expenses of the trip.

On October 16, 1859, with about twenty men, Brown took possession of Harper's Ferry, a government arsenal at the junction of the Potomac and Shenandoah rivers, and held it for thirty-six hours. He declared that his intention was to arouse a general insurrection of Negro slaves, with arson and rapine to follow throughout the South. The property of slave owners was to be confiscated for the benefit of the insurrectionists and their leaders. For arming the untrained Negroes he had provided, with characteristic sagacity, a thousand pikes. But he had neglected to make the slaves aware of his purpose; the pikes were not in their possession; they did not rally to his standard. After a sharp struggle, his party surrendered to Colonel Robert E. Lee of the United States Army and its members were indicted for high treason against the State of Virginia. Brown and six associates were found guilty and hanged.

Such, in brief is the story of John Brown. As a horse-thief, it must be confessed, his operations were not extensive; they did not attract much attention in eastern Kansas. Even as a murderer he was far from industrious, as industry went in those days; he did not shoot at sight all the pro-slavery men that he met, though he had sworn eternal war upon them. As a leader of citizen volunteers, he was always far from the scene when his services were desired. And as the hero of a servile insurrection, the last of his occupations in the public eye, he does not merit the remotest comparison with Spartacus, Jack Cade and Toussaint l'Ouverture.

Yet, like many other Americans of mediocre talent, Brown has come to enjoy a posthumous fame that is grossly disproportionate to his actual acts, and often at variance with them. So wide, indeed, is the disparity between what he did and what he is venerated for that it may be fairly argued that the Brown of American

267

legend is not the real Brown at all, but merely the hypostasis of an idea, the personification of that remote ideal which the Nineteenth Century called Liberty. Liberty had a great deal to do with public events in mid-century Europe and America. Whether they were hard-swearing, property-loving Americans who thought they had it, or desperate Continental revolutionaries who were out to get it, most men prized it highly. And about their cult there grew a myth-epic which told of the adventures of their hero-goddess—the metamorphoses by which Liberty became incarnate in the flesh and as hero activated history, real and imaginary.

The John Brown of legend developed as the American projection of this myth. We shall not soon forget its glamour in our childhood. Liberty, become manifest as Brown, wrestled with the dragons of slavery, slew many, and finally went to the gallows. Who shall say the American lacks creative imagination? A folk-mind which can evolve such a myth has the genuine gift. But there is no point today in concealing the real Brown from a generation so talented that it believes Liberty has come to life again in the garb of a revenue officer. And fortunately the Emersons and Stearnses and Higginsons and Sanborns in whose imaginations John Brown took on the proportions of a demigod—fortunately, these myth-makers diligently accumulated documents from which the real Brown may be disinterred.

II

The Brown of the legend was a man of austere character, abstemious habits, ascetic mode of life. The asceticism of the real Brown did not interrupt his begetting of twenty children by two wives. Nor did his austerity prevent him breeding horses for the track and racing for money. Nor did his abstemiousness compel him to shun the best hotels upon his travels, or to abhor good mutton. He manufactured wine and consumed it. The sole basis for the notion of his frugality seems to be the fact that he had a sensitive digestion, to which butter and cheese were repugnant.

Imagination, seizing Mr. Oswald Garrison Villard, portrays Brown as a "self-denying Roundhead, . . . an armored searcher for the Grail. . . . He killed not to kill, but to free. . . . His motives were wholly unselfish. . . . His aims were none other than the freeing of a race." Fact, through George B. Gill, an intimate of Brown who had nothing to gain from belittling him, admonishes us that "he was very human . . ., very superstitious, very selfish, and very intolerant, with great self-esteem; . . . essentially vindictive in nature." Brown, in truth, was a Roundhead with doubts about the Bible, who was not clear whether the Providence which guided his hand was his Maker or the devil. His company of devout crusaders, sons included, were mostly hearty agnostics.

The mythical Brown was a man of inflexible determination, who early formed a purpose from which he never swerved and to whose accomplishment he marched straightforwardly. The Brown of fact had a good deal of temperament in his make-up. He changed his mind as frequently as he did his occupation and place of residence. He was farmer, tanner, surveyor, canal contractor, stock raiser, wool merchant, horse thief and professional mendicant. During most of his life, like most men with whom he did business, he was critical of slavery. Nevertheless, after his first bankruptcy in 1841, he laid plans to operate a plantation in Virginia.

The legendary Brown was a man of ruthless methods, ready to seize every advantage, override every law, that he might achieve his lofty ends. The historical Brown showed a remarkable sensitivity to opinion. As a business man he was careless of money but full of scruples. His firm and the wool growers he represented at Springfield, Massachusetts, in the forties were sacrificed to his inability or unwillingness to beat the manufacturers in the game of price-fixing. Brown himself ascribed his failure at Harper's Ferry to his weakness and irresolution.

The Brown of the legend was a stern realist in a world of political unrealities; he was the man of action in a movement of ineffectual dreamers; he stood in intimate contact with facts which public men of his day were seeking to shun or overlook. But the true John Brown, fancier of horse-flesh, had very little acquaintance with facts. He strove by every means to gloss them over. He deliberately accepted his legendary self as real, and foisted the imposition upon credulous Boston. He lied to his wife. He lied to his sons. He lied to the court in that speech in his own defense which eulogists have likened to Socrates' apology. The documents cannot be distorted. One doubts, indeed, that Brown knew fact from fiction, truth from falsehood, actuality from hallucination. Legend tells of an heroic fanatic, martyred in the cause of freedom; history recalls an unsuccessful business man of middle age turned adventurer.

III

The Brown of legend entered a Kansas which was the battleground of the forces favoring and opposing the extension of slavery. The latter, in the main, were pacific, and disposed to pursue their object by conciliation and compromise. They were on the verge of being overcome by their pro-slavery Missouri neighbors. The mythical Brown came upon this scene at a critical moment. His arrival, full of bellicosity, brought him at once to the leadership of the Free Soil forces, and his execution of pro-slavery men on the Pottawatomie struck terror into the border raiders. Thanks chiefly to his vigilance and that of his sons, the cause of Free Soil was triumphant, and Kansas was saved. This is the Brown whose effigy a grateful Legislature has caused to be shrined in the Hall of Atrocities at Washington as one of the two greatest Kansans.

The real Brown came to Kansas in the Autumn of 1855, a stock-raiser and wool-dealer landed, by successive failures, upon the rocks; a man aged fifty-five whose wife and family were dependent upon the patronage of Gerrit Smith, a wealthy New York Abolitionist. Leaving his family upon a portion of the Smith estate in the Adirondacks which was being turned into a Negro farm colony, Brown came to Kansas "to see if something would not turn up to his advantage." He financed the journey by taking up collections "for the cause of Kansas." He arrive in Osawatomie with sixty cents in his pocket, and got employment helping one of his sons, who had preceded him, to build a house. Two months later he led a small band to the defense of Lawrence, which was threatened by a Missouri "army." Upon this occasion a Free Soil victory was won by diplomacy and rum, and Brown did not contribute to the decision. The Winter was hard. Brown was obliged to sell his horse and wagon to buy food. He disbanded his company of "Liberty Rifles," and made plans to gain a living by stealing horses under the pretence of pursuing free-lance activities in the Free Soil cause. An ordinary horse sold for more than a month's earnings at day labor.

An incursion of the Missourians in May, 1856, gave this real Brown the opportunity to commence business. He began by robbing his neighbors at Dutch Henry's Crossing on Pottawatomie Creek; he then had them murdered to distract attention from the more vulgar crime. The assassinations did not frighten the champions of slavery; they provoked retaliation. They brought border raids and atrocities for the first time into a section of Kansas which had previously been spared. In the consequent confusion Brown found a good many things turning up to his advantage. His biographers draw a friendly veil over his activities during this most critical period in the Kansas war. While battles were lost and won Brown's new profession engaged his time, and to his considerable profit. By August he was able to send his sons, a half dozen of them, sick and faint-hearted and tired of the business, back to the Adirondacks. And he had a four-mule team and money in his pocket.

Here is a sample of Brown's work which is well-attested by documents. Arriving in Osawatomie with the team toward the end of August, within four days he collected, equipped and mounted upon stolen horses a company of ten men, including himself. In two days more he effected a consolidation with two other companies of "jayhawkers," as they termed themselves, and within three more he had gathered two hundred and fifty head of cattle, beside horses and other plunder, and assembled the whole for rendezvous at Osawatomie. There he was caught by a pro-slavery raid in force. Brown gave battle, and fame labels him John Brown of Osawatomie in consequence. But neither here nor upon any other occasion did he strike any "blow for freedom" which actually helped the Free Soil party. Brown, in those days, fought only when it was to his professional interest to do so— only when there was something in it for Brown.

Nevertheless there grew up a Brown saga along the border, which gradually spread to the East. James Redpath, a newspaper correspondent eager for copy, who had come to Kansas confessedly to foment civil war, found Brown in hiding on Ottawa creek soon after he commenced his marauding career. It was no strain on the imagination of a good reporter to turn the outlaw into a David hiding from Saul, a Wallace eluding Edward I. Redpath saw or affected to see in Brown's activities the correct and laudable alternative to the pusillanimous policy of the Free Soil politicians and land speculators. And so his facile pen diligently drew for the delectation of the East the picture of Old Brown, Brown the hero, Brown the indomitable warden of the Kansas marches, Brown the avenger, Brown who had

visions from Almighty God and marched to the execution of divine decrees!

Over the border General Atchison and the pro-slavery journalists soon began embroidering the legend. It is written that Satan, who certainly should have known better, "believed—and trembled." Southern publicists began to believe profoundly in Old Brown, though at first they did not tremble. They strove resolutely to impose upon their constituents and upon national opinion the identity of the Brown myth with the rising Republican party. Atrocities were multiplied from one end of the border to the other and laid at the door of a half-imaginary Brown and his omnipresent band of nigger-loving cutthroats. This was the sort of thing, voters were assured, which might be expected upon a large scale should the Republicans win the national election.

The Republicans won Congress, but not the Presidency. A new governor appeared in Kansas who quickly patched up peace in the border war. Control of their political affairs seemed assured for the time to the majority of Free Soil settlers, and opportunity for plausible jayhawking was at an end. Forced to find a fresh source of income for his numerous family, Brown now decided to capitalize the Brown legend and to sell stock to gullible New England. Committees all over the East had been raising funds to assist emigrants to Kansas, giving them supplies, relieving their destitution. Brown proposed to solicit funds from these committees upon his own account as the arch-hero of the Kansas war. Thus he became committed to the perpetuation of Old Brown.

IV

In lectures delivered after the raid on Harper's Ferry, Ralph Waldo Emerson thus recorded his impressions of a person he had once met at the house of Thoreau, the eminent anarchist:

Brown is so transparent that all men see him through. He is a man to make friends wherever on earth courage and integrity are esteemed—the rarest of heroes, a pure idealist, with no by-ends of his own. Many of us have seen him, and every one who has heard him speak has been impressed alike by his simple, artless goodness and his sublime courage....

He grew up a religious and manly person, in severe poverty; a fair specimen of the best stock of New England, having the force of thought and that sense of right which are the warp and woof of greatness....Thus was formed a romantic character, absolutely without any vulgar trait; living to ideal ends, without any mixture of self-indulgence or compromise...abstemious, refusing luxuries... quiet and gentle as a child in the house.

It is clear that Emerson was not talking about John Brown, the bankrupt wool-dealer and horse-thief. He had simply encountered a Politics Myth. If pressed, the transcendental radical would probably have admitted that no man was ever actually like that outside the pages of Walter Scott. But he was not alone in confusing Brown with a day-dream. A large circle of men in Boston and Concord found in the personality which they accredited to Brown a lodestone for their seditious yearnings, an idol to which they could dedicate their political passion. The "best people" of Concord listened to his words, wrote Alcott. "Emerson, Thoreau, Judge Hoar, my wife, and some of them contribute something in aid of his plans without asking particulars, such confidence does he inspire in his integrities and abilities." Thomas Wentworth Higginson, Samuel Howe, who invented the sewing-machine, the sweat-shop and philanthropy, and Theodore Parker, a pulpit orator with an obsession for blood, were among the amateurs of *haute politique* whom Brown met. And these men, with George Luther Stearns, a successful lead-pipe manufacturer, F. B. Sanborn, a young school-master fresh from Harvard, and Gerrit Smith, already Brown's patron, became a sort of board of directors to back his enterprises, as yet unrevealed. Radical Abolitionists all, imbued with Garrison's anarchism though not with his inclination toward non-resistance, they found that Brown's hypothetical career fitted precisely into their notion of what the career of a master politician should be.

It matters not the medium who evoked the ectoplasmic Brown, whether Brown himself or accessories. The seance was one of true believers. The credulity which he plays upon is enough, soon or late, to shake the sanity of any charlatan. The priests of Delphi, in the end, heeded the oracle. John Brown very easily came to believe that he was a hero. But he did not forget that his family on the Adirondack farm needed a frequent draft.

V

Brown's biographers compute his takings from the first New England campaign at twenty-three thousand dollars. Of this amount thirteen thousand came in the form of military supplies, rifles, revolvers, clothing, ammunition, mostly the property of the Massachusetts Kansas Committee deposited in Iowa and placed at Brown's disposal for use in Kansas. Seven thousand dollars were in the form of a letter of credit upon G. L. Stearns, to be used in equipping a company in Kansas. One thousand Brown wormed out of his patrons directly to buy a farm for his family in the Adirondacks. Thus it appears that the funds which he procured for immediate expenditure were not very large. In those days Yankee money-bags were not handed about recklessly, even to a Vision. The believers wanted action. They wanted Brown to go back to Kansas to stiffen the settlers' backbones. Reluctantly he departed to undertake the job. He was expected to raise a company at once, and do something dramatic to rescue bleeding Kansas from the harlot of slavery.

The harlot was actually frustrated—but Brown was not there. His rifles, his funds and his noble character did not contribute to the solution of the Kansas question in 1857. There are letters extant from the commander of the volunteer Free Soil forces begging Brown to bring on his weapons, but his unquenchable hatred of slavery did not stir him from his snug boarding-house in Tabor, Iowa, even when $150 cash was forwarded to him by the struggling Kansans. Brown the jayhawker, Brown the dauntless, Brown who acknowledged no master on earth, Brown who had a drawing account of seven thousand dollars, complained that he could not pay his board bill. Was this Brown a scoundrel or was he only a fool?

At any rate, it was while he was at Tabor that his correspondence began to give the first definite suggestion of the Virginia adventure. Its genesis and early development cannot be traced; it is possible that it originated while he was still in Boston, from some chance speculation of the fertile Parker. His friends, when they got the first news of the project, gathered the impression that Brown intended to raid the Southern plantations and run off with as many slaves as possible, to make slave property seem precarious. But this sort of enterprise required a zone of lawlessness from which to operate. Disorder alone could make it possible, not to speak of making it profitable to the promoters. Brown had a family to think of. And so, without revealing to anyone, possibly without fully realizing himself, all the implications of his venture, he planned his servile insurrection.

It is unnecessary to rehearse all his misadventures during the two years which separated the inception of the project and its performance. May, 1858, was the time first set for the raid. Brown's men, by this time, were enthusiastic. A convention at Chatham, Canada, enveloped the scheme in that curious ritualistic atmosphere which Americans love to wrap about their politics. The directors had held a special session with Gerrit Smith in the chair, and the financial arrangements were complete. Stearns had foreclosed a mortgage upon the rifles for Kansas, and they were now available for use where Brown wanted them. But then one of the Brown lieutenants gave the thing away, seeking blackmail, and the terrified directors ordered a postponement.

Brown now took his disappointed followers to Kansas for a season, assumed a new name, found a section of the border which was just far enough from being pacified to shelter him, and resumed his horse-stealing. This employment kept them all in funds until an opportunity for a renewal of the Virginia project made it possible to call upon the Boston backers for more working capital.

VI

The raid upon Harper's Ferry may be set down as the most considerable failure of a man whose career had exhibited little else. If any rudiment of caution or foresight might have been exercised, Brown gave no sign that he knew of it, although he puttered around in the vicinity of the Ferry an entire Summer getting the business in order. When the time came to move he left books, papers, documents intact at his rendezvous, where they easily fell into the hands of the law. He moved upon a position from which there was no retreat, and in which, when it was taken, no defense could be offered, even by a considerable force. And the point upon which the success of the whole enterprise depended, the rising of the slaves, Brown left wholly to chance.

Yet he was not crazy. The raid was no sudden aberration of a fanatic. More than a hundred people had been acquainted for months with one or another aspect of the undertaking, and had countenanced it. It was just such an act as heroes of political myths perform and in success or failure vindicate their heroism. It represented the dramatic moment that a man who becomes legend must achieve. Lincoln was shot. Roosevelt went to Africa. Wilson collapsed. Brown's enterprise was one for which he had every resource but one—capacity. His imagination could conceive the plan. His judgment could recognize the practicability and advantages of it if ably executed. But his talents were simply not up to the job.

A month in Charleston jail and the sight of the gallows brought him such efficiency as a provider for his family as he had never shown before. Loving hands have preserved the letters in which he set forth to the sympathetic the sad fate of his destitute wife and children. His board of directors were in flight pell mell to Canada or sighing their relief in Europe. They needed only a correspondence in an heroic vein, a suggestion of martyred fortitude, to reassure them that Brown was indeed the hero of their imaginings, and so their terrified purse-strings were opened with a great generosity. The letters from prison breathed piety and devotion. Overcoming his old doubts, Brown indited long justifications of the divine inspiration of the Scriptures. In compensation for his mundane failure, the inevitable triumph of the supernatural moral order became increasingly clear to his eyes. Recalling his sins, he grew more and more convinced of the merciful goodness of God. And recovering from the confusion in which he had blurted out the truth about his plans at Harper's Ferry, he delivered a speech declaring that he had intended only to free the slaves. "I never did intend to incite murder, or treason, or the destruction of property, or to excite or incite the slaves to rebellion, or to make insurrection." Brown was fast slipping into myth even in his own consciousness. And when he came to write his will, he forgot his debts entirely.

Emerson composed a lecture. Numbers of Miltons in Boston and vicinity, inglorious but unfortunately not mute, composed what they termed poems. Pulpit orators, as they returned from flight, delivered eulogies. And soon a hundred thousand men were singing

And his soul goes marching on!

But it was not the soul of any John Brown that really ever lived.

CHAUTAUQUA: ITS TECHNIC

BY GREGORY MASON

"WHAT will you have?" asked the tall, sallow waitress in the Fundamentalist "eating place."

"Is your service *à la carte* or *table d' hôte?*" I asked cheerfully.

The waitress looked puzzled, then hurt.

"We serve a regular dinner for forty cents," she said sharply, and patted the masses of hair which hid her ears.

The thin young man across the table chuckled.

"Gwendolyn don't get your French," he observed, smiling at her with the restrained condescension of one who knows his own superiority but tries hard to hide it.

"You shet up, Perfesser," retorted Gwendolyn. "You never got no nearer to French culchooer yourself than last night at the Chautauqua when you heard the band play the Mayonnaise."

The Perfesser roared, and winked at me. Gwendolyn moved off majestically to get the "regular dinner." She was immensely pleased with having put the Perfesser in his place.

A moment later that gentleman confided to me that he was the local Superintendent of Schools. He ate here occasionally, he said, as a relief from the monotony of his boarding-house. Between large bites of canned pork and beans he discussed the insoluble problems of the day. War had just blazed out in Europe. Most of America was amazed, mildly indignant that such a thing could happen in the Twentieth Century. The Perfesser reflected this frame of mind.

"It's a shame," he declared, "that those big nations of Europe have to fight as if

they were Mexicans. Why can't they live side by side like America and Canada have done for a hundred years, perfectly *embonpoint?*"

You may smile, as I did (behind my paper napkin), but that evening the waitress who had never heard of a *table d' hôte* dinner but who had heard the band play the Mayonnaise, that evening this girl and the Superintendent of Schools who wished that France and Germany could live *embonpoint* ("ongbongpong," he pronounced it) were both in the audience at the town Chautauqua to hear a lecture on "The Burning Issue of Alsace-Lorraine."

I might have known that I was in a good Chautauqua town. The prevalence of toothpicks was a hint. The canned food at that "eating place" in a region conspicuous for its fertile farms was another. The popularity of soggy pie and chicoried coffee was a third. The difficulty of getting a glass of fresh milk was a fourth. But best of all was the complete absence of olive oil. Some day a sociologist may explain to the world the connection between civilization and the use of olive oil. Count upon it, if ever you find yourself in a region of husbandmen where the town's hotel offers canned vegetables in Summer, if ever you stumble into a land of dairies whose inhabitants take their "cup o' cawfee" with condensed milk, above all, if fate ever leads you to where the rare (oh, very rare!) offering of fresh greens is seasoned with vinegar and sugar in place of olive oil, then, indeed *then*, you may know you are in the chosen pastures of Chautauqua.

Let figures tell the tale. Annually Chau-

274

tauqua carries its Message (mark the word) to some ten thousand hamlets of this great, brave land. Annually the attendance is about thirty-five million. Here, obviously, is a luscious opportunity for him who desires to gain the approbation, the esteem, the support and admiration of the multitude. No demagogue, no crank with a nostrum to sell, can afford to overlook the audience in the brown tent. Hark, now, to the testimony of the most eminent demagogue of our generation. The Honorable William Jennings Bryan is speaking:

> I know of no better audience than the Chautauqua audience . . . These meetings enable me to keep in touch with the People. I know of no better opportunity than they offer to present a Message worth presenting to those to whom it is worth while to present a Message.

Note that last sentence. It is in the true style of Chautauqua.

II

Now supposing that, like the Nebraska Medicine Man, one is eager to interest and inflame the plain people: how does one go about winning them? A clue may be found in the definition of Chautauqua bequeathed to us by Bishop John H. Vincent, the eminent Methodist *arriero* who founded the original annual roundup at Chautauqua Lake, N. Y.:

> Self improvement in all our faculties, for us all, through all time, for the greatest good of all people—this is the Chautauqua idea, a divine idea, a democratic idea, a people's idea, a progressive idea, a millenial idea.

What is here? Again the word-intoxicated, apothegmatic style of Chautauqua, but what else? Can't you detect beneath it the profound earnestness of tone? There, indeed you have it; there is our first pointer. Even though you be a Tyrolean yodler or a "polyphonic imitator," do not step out on the flimsy stage of the big tent unless you feel or can skilfully pretend to feel the sober purposefulness of human life. Even the telepathists and magicians pause in their rites to allude to the great lecturer who is to follow with his "inspiring elucidation of world problems." In brief, it is the fundamental assumption of Chautauqua that life is real, life is earnest, and that entertainment is distinctly secondary to instruction and edification. The lecturer must be more than merely informative or entertaining; he must also have a Message. The messianic delusion of the lecturer, plus the self-improvement complex of the audience—there is your Chautauqua equation.

One more proverb of the Methodist Fathers of Chautauqua is worth quoting: "Change of occupation, not idleness, is true recreation." There again you have the necessity of being *serious*. The gossoons who crowd the big tents have never entertained Stevenson's suggestion that the Differential Calculus and Hearing The Band Play In The Gardens are equally important chapters in the Book of Life. They have not heeded Masefield's remark that anything which makes men and women happy together, such as fox hunting, creates a permanent beauty. In fact, they have never heard of Masefield, and they are not consciously aware of such a thing as beauty. Bred in their bones is the Puritan instinct that Fun and Sin are two names for the same Devil. Hearing The Band Play In The Gardens is Fun, *i. e.*, Sin, whereas it is Change of Occupation, *i. e.*, Self Improvement, to sit on an unplaned board and hearken to Bryan.

Of course, the things that are serious are definitely categoried in Puritania. The gaudy dreams of such daring scientists as Lothrop Stoddard and Madison Grant are serious; good novels and good poetry are not. But Holy Writ, of course, is the most serious thing of all, and an ability to quote it copiously has enabled many a dull but deserving pastor or pedagogue to eke out the pittance of his profession with a goodly two or three hundred a week while the Summer circuits are open. *Be serious*, then, is the first rule. But the second rule is, *Be not too serious*. Don't count on much capacity for sustained thinking. Remember, your audience ranges in age from nine weeks to ninety years. Remember, experience has proved that the most successful method of delivery on all the great circuits imitates that of a machine gun. Bear in mind the sad experiences of some of our masters of after-dinner rhetoric, such as John Temple Graves and Irvin Cobb, when they tried their slow-reloading, Big Bertha style in the tent. Take to heart the advice of that sage magnate of the canvas circuits who says:

> Talk so fast they won't have time to think. For if they think at all it will not be about your words but about that pinochle game waiting in the back of the corner store or about that keg of hootch working under the cellar stairs.

Obviously, to maintain for an hour and a quarter a vocal imitation of the bark of the *mitrailleuse* is no slight strain on the vital parts. The platform is no place for a weakling.

III

From end to end of the Chautauqua belt there prevail certain widespread prejudices and *mores* which our young Machiavelli, "desirous of interesting and inflaming mobs," would do well to acquaint himself with in advance. He must heed these prejudices if he would gain access to the ear and purse of multitudes. The most staccato delivery, the strongest lungs and the most polished manner will avail him nothing if in the eyes of the local committees he does not demean himself, on *and off* the platform, like a "Christian and a moral gentleman." First of all, this means that whenever he speaks on the Sabbath, he will scrap his regular discourse for an amateur sermon or at least interlard his usual address with a few Golden Texts. Secondly, it means that if he values his weekly pay-check he will never permit himself to be familiar with the favors of the other sex, or with the juice that stimulates, or with dancing or cards. More than one good lecturer is now spending his Summers raking hay or tutoring

morons because he allowed a zealous committeeman to catch him in a dance hall or poolroom or at a game of casino. Let the word go through the underground channels of the righteous that so-and-so is a card player, and so-and-so's contract will be worth less than a busted flush. To the Baptist-Methodist-Presbyterian *bloc* which runs Chautauqua (and the United States) four of a kind are almost as horrifying as the eternal triangle.

Once, at a dismal railroad junction in Nebraska, a fellow Chautauquan and I, desperate at the prospect of a two hours' wait for our train, asked a citizen if he could direct us to a poolroom. The burgher drew back as if we had struck him.

"Gentlemen," he roared, "we'd as soon have a saloon in this town as a poolroom."

"Why not have both and be a real town?" I asked experimentally, but not a glimmer of a smile crossed that austere face, and our friend took himself off, as from a pair of lepers. Fortunately, I was not to lecture in this town, and fortunately my season was nearly ended. But the word did spread and at my remaining engagements on the circuit there were noticeably hostile faces in every audience.

Let the aspirant never forget that the Chautauquas are run by godly men. Even though he is booked to speak in a notoriously wide-open mining town, it is safe to assume that his appearance has been arranged by the minority of the pure, and probably, indeed, as pious propaganda against the heathen. Hide your spots as never before, for that evening you are to be the "sword of righteousness!"

So vital is this matter of private morals that the managers of the larger Chautauqua booking bureaus are wont to send form letters to their "talent," warning them to avoid as the pestilence anything falling within the bucolic definition of immorality. Official sanction for this attitude is given by the adoption of a uniform contract by the Chautauqua Managers' Association, stipulating that a lecturer's contract may be broken at the manager's will if the lecturer "conducts himself improperly," *i. e.*, in violation of agricultural *mores*.

IV

The Chautauqua movement, indeed, is a crusade against the Devil, and it shows all the intolerance of other crusades. A veteran of the tents, Dr. William S. Sadler, in addressing the last annual convention of the International Lyceum and Chautauqua Association, made the fact quite plain. He was trying to "impress the young generation of Chautauquans with the seriousness—may I even say, sacredness? —of their calling," and he declared that "lack of moral character and ethical standing may not always seriously handicap an actress, entertainer or musician on the American stage today, but such a lack of moral worth is, and I believe always will be, sufficient cause for disbarment from the platform of the American Chautauqua."

In such an environment one would not expect to find much regard for that mythical American institution, free speech, and one does not, in fact, find it. Mr. Paul M. Pearson, in his presidential address to the last convention of the International Lyceum and Chautauqua Association, said:

The pressure which is brought to bear on the system manager to allow nothing said from the platform which will be criticized by prominent persons in the community (most of whom are conservatives) is a great source of danger to the entire movement. . . . In my opinion, the criticism that we have too many "safe and sane" lectures is the most searching, the fairest and the truest criticism that is to be made against us.

Most successful lecturers, like most successful editorial writers, carefully try to cut their cloth both ways. In discussing so dangerous a topic as American relations with Europe at a time when a presidential campaign is on, one may be pardoned for a glow of pride if, after the lecture, one is complimented by different auditors both for one's "clear revelation of the knavery of Wilson's policy" and one's "brave appreciation of the splendid work of President Wilson." Such an experience was mine. On a later tour, the remnant of my conscience being sickened by this sort of straddling, I ventured to hint at a few personal convictions. One was that in view of the complexity of our population and the different social philosophies entertained in Nordic-Puritan Berea, Ohio, and Italian-Slavic Bridgeport, Connecticut, it might not be unwise to consider some modification of the Volstead Act. This neglect of the managerial admonition to be discreet created an uproar. One manager screamed that my *faux pas* had cost him much business, "in spite of the fact I made a special effort to go out there and apologize for what you had said on the liquor question."

I have preserved an interesting souvenir of this rash adventure. It is an official report on my Satanic work written on the bill head of a coal dealer, the chairman of the local committee. His counts were as follows (the italics are his own):

1. Audience not satisfied.
2. Admission 60 cents.
3. Weather good.
4. Not a strong speaker, deep thinker or instructive entertainer.
5. *His attitude on the liquor question very unpopular with our audience.*

It is always useful to commune with other lecturers who have spoken in towns where you are booked to go. Lecturers as well as hoboes have their fraternal, secret communications, and unfair practises, such as that, for instance of the Indianapolis Y. M. C. A., are soon known throughout the tribe. This Y. M. C. A. is famous for the censorship its officers apply to the men and women invited to its rostrum. Such speakers, of course, are booked several months in advance. But instead of finding out their religious views before booking them, it has been the custom of the Indianapolis Y. M. C. A. to send to each engaged lecturer, only a few days in advance of his scheduled appearance, a questionnaire intended to reveal whether or not he has a clean theological bill of health. Only a member of a Protestant church of the more evangelical type could honestly answer the questions in the affirmative. But if the speaker does not so answer them his lecture is apt to be canceled at the eleventh hour. A truly pious procedure!

I presume that it was owing to the illness of the energetic purifier who was secretary of that "Y" that I did not receive the usual questionnaire. When I reached the hall the acting-chairman asked me to omit the last part of my scheduled oration in order to exhort the audience of men to accept the Jahveh of the Old Testament. When I declined, protesting my conscientious doubts and pleading that all my advertising had shown my lecture to be non-sectarian, the chairman was furious and wanted to cancel the engagement. But, the hall being already filled, he confined himself to praying aloud for my pagan soul.

In return, I fear, every itinerant spouter prays nightly for the decease of all committee chairmen and professional introducers. There are a few who know how to combine felicity with brevity, but they are as rare as Baptists who prefer Beethoven to Irving Berlin. Painfully common are such bunglers as the Chautauqua Superintendent who introduced me in place of Colonel John Temple Graves.

"Folks," he drawled, "we were to have heard the message tonight of Colonel John Temple Graves, a man who, while a dwarf physically, is a giant intellectually. But there has been a last minute change and we are to have the pleasure of hearing Doctor Mason, a man who is a giant physically and . . . and . . . and . . ."

Someone tittered and I laughed. The Superintendent waved at me, muttered something incoherent, and fled.

V

Chautauqua audiences, by the way, are never men and women. They are rarely ladies and gentlemen, or even people. Nearly always they are folks. How that rustic term comes to grate on the ear of a veteran wanderer in the alfalfa! Nevertheless, not to use it freely is to handicap oneself as deliberately as if one put on a wrist watch or an Oxford accent.

These little things are half the battle— these little tricks which win the sympathy of your audience at the outset. Bryan is a master to be studied carefully by anyone who would be a Demosthenes of the steppes. When he issues from the wings he manages somehow to intensify the smugly pained lines in his face, the creases in his flapping and shiny habiliments. This suggests the noble suffering of one never far from Calvary, and the indifference to personal trivia expected in one who is a Bearer of Others' Burdens. When speaking on a hot day, he rubs one hand over a cake of ice on a table beside him, and clasps its frigorific palm over the opposite wrist. You or I would see in this simply a man sensibly trying to keep cool. But the Chautauqua fan sees a great Hero, a Folk-God, subject to noble but wasting emotions, who husbands his strength through no motive so selfish as personal comfort, but only to Serve Others by the delivery in entirety of his Saviour-like Message.

It will be a prodigious help on the circuit if, by cosmetics or otherwise, you can manage to achieve a death-mask pallor below eyes filled with tired kindness. When you reach the town of your engagement do not be seen eating, smoking or enjoying life, but preserve a mysterious retirement in your hotel room. Then, if time tables or fictitious obstacles of travel will bear it out, have your introducer allude to how "the speaker of the evening, forgetful of the gnawing malady that keeps him under a doctor's care, rode all last night in terrible discomfort because of his altruistic determination that you good folks should not be disappointed by losing his Message of Inspiration." Introducers lend themselves with a voluptuous joy to this sort of bilge.

The Chautauqua mob evinces a great readiness to work for the man who is supposed to entertain it. There are performers and chairmen who have an uncanny knowledge of how to use this amiable trait. I remember a Chautauqua in an Ohio town where the "concert company" ("song-birds and bell-ringers") which was to give the afternoon program (Chautauquas have two or three programs a day), had missed its connection and could not possibly arrive until forty-five minutes after the show was to begin. The resourceful Superintendent told the crowd just what had happened. But in a subtle way he made them feel superior to the tardy minstrels, he made them feel proud that *they* were here on time. Then he proposed that they sing "America," which he led in an oily, Methodist tenor. When they had sung it through twice, he proposed that the East side of the audience sing one verse and the West side sing the second. Then he had the men sing one verse and the women another. Some of the men looked sheepish at first, some of the women giggled self-consciously, but soon all were braying lustily, and they kept it up with obvious satisfaction till the missing entertainers arrived. I don't know why grown men and women like that sort of thing, but certainly in the Corn Belt they do.

There is danger that the novice, noting some of these childish traits of the congenital Chautauquan, will begin to resort to flattery. Here, strange as it may seem, the haranguer is on seismic soil. The cosy day when Chautauqua would rise to a crude compliment is past. It has been offered so much bait of this kind that it has learned to smell it from afar. Be subtle then, if you must flatter. "I cannot go on till I have told you what a pleasure it is for me to be in an up-to-date, enterprising town like this," will not get by. Even "I hardly need point out to an intelligent audience like this"—even that tried dart is apt to ricochet. Flattery by negation still goes occasionally—cataloguing the vices which an audience has *not*. But flattery by implication is safer—ridiculing boobish audiences you have addressed or uncouth towns you have visited and hinting *pizzicato* that the present audience or town is quite different.

VI

So much for the nature and habits of the fauna which our young Machiavelli is setting himself to interest and inflame. Now, for the nature of his own attack. He would do well to decide whether in any one hunt he will try mainly to *interest* or to *inflame*. For the fact is that the most successful practitioners incline to separate the two methods. Indeed, nearly all Chautauqua lectures today fall into one of two great classes, *i. e.*, those which are "informational" (the lectures which *interest*), and those which are "inspirational" (the lectures which *inflame*).

Formerly, nearly the whole field was filled by the inspirational lecture. But during the past decade, and particularly during the past half-decade, there has been a conspicuous development of the informational lecture. Travel talks come under this heading, of course, and so do health talks, "popular science" lectures, discourses of war correspondents, aviators and explorers, and narrations by the eminent of How I Did It and How You Can Do Likewise. The secret of the informational lecture is that it caters to the lust for self-improvement and to the desire to get something for nothing. This lust for self improvement, which is growing apace, is found nowhere in such intensity as in rural America. Does it spring in part from a hatred of environment? Certainly the most oleaginous prating about "self-betterment" is heard in states like Kansas, Nebrasky (pronounce through the nose) and Ioway, all of them conspicuous for the flat dreariness of their landscape and the flatter dreariness of their souls.

The peasant afflicted with this appetite sees Chautauqua as an agency through which he can gratify his longing for almost nothing. He is "sold" the idea that by paying $1.80 for five days of Chautauqua, he can get himself a liberal education, a whole carload of canned culture. It is cheaper than Dr. Eliot's sixty inches of printing and a darned sight easier. It is infinitely easier than trying to think.

The secret of the inspirational lecture is even plainer. This form of hypnotic self indulgence releases the obscure religious longings which lie in every looby. More than that, it warms the undeveloped feeling for poetry which exists in him no less, although he would be the first to deny it. Speaking broadly, the Mother, Home and Heaven lecture, even today, *is* Chautauqua. If we accept that generalization, then we may say that Chautauqua is the poetry of the American peasant. Religious poetry, tribal poetry. It expresses his *mores*, his taboos, his bewilderment at the mystery of the universe, his brute aspiration toward the stars. Chautauqua voices all these feelings and at the same time soothes the clodhopper and makes him contented. It assures him that he is right in preferring Gene Stratton Porter to Joseph Conrad, Eddie Guest to Robert Frost, the *American Magazine* to the *Nation*. It assures him that when he banned Chateau Yquem he lost nothing as good as his own corn licker.

Provided that you have a strong stomach and are able, figuratively speaking, to hold your own nose while you are orating, the Mother, Home and Heaven lecture is the easiest to master—far easier than the informational type. A certain amount of industry is necessary to acquire even enough *mis*information to fill an hour and a half, but any smart fellow with a flare for imitation who will study the more successful revivalists and Methodist pulpiteers can master the inspirational model. The patriotic note is useful here. Yokels who are resistant to flattery will follow the oriflamme to the heights.

VII

"But"—do I hear you shout?—"you have told me everything except where I am to get my *material* for lectures!"

Why, Sir, must I state in bald English that you may steal it? Yes, steal it. If you aim to be inspirational, dig up an old copy of "Getting On In Life," or of "Self Help," by Samuel Smiles, or, if you must be more modern, buy and study the collected works of Dr. Orison Swett Marden, Dr. Frank Crane and the Rev. Newell Dwight Hillis. If, on the other hand, your aspiration is to be informational, your task is equally simple—if you remember that in this field the fashion changes more frequently. Buy the latest book of H. G. Wells, rewrite a few chapters of it, deliver it in the pompous, rhetorically interrogative manner popular with women's clubs, and you will achieve much more than local fame as "a brilliant speaker, whose thought-provoking comment on world problems is a liberal education in itself." If you find the Wells wake already overcrowded, hitch your wagon to some lesser comet, such as Madison Grant or Lothrop Stoddard. Only, if you choose one of the latter, be sure you do it in a season when the Superiority of the Nordic Blond rather than Simple Living or Rhythmic Thinking is in the ascendancy. Eighty per cent of the success of the informational speaker is due to his ability to ride the latest fad a little before the other seers of rural Rotaria.

Let your conscience be at ease. The great majority of successful Chautauqua lecturers use these very methods. The vigor and forthrightness of an original thinker would be far too strong a dose for the folks in the tent. Better than I can paint it is the picture of them limned by William James after a visit to the original organization at Chautauqua Lake, New York. Thus he described the Chautauqua atmosphere:

> This order is too tame, this culture too second-rate; this goodness too uninspiring. This human drama without a villain or a pang; this community so refined that ice-cream soda-water is the utmost offering it can make to the brute animal in man; this city simmering in the tepid lakeside sun; this atrocious harmlessness of all things, —I cannot abide them. Let me take my chances again in the big outside worldly wilderness with all its sins and sufferings. There are heights and depths, the precipices and the steep ideals, the gleams of the awful and the infinite; and there is more hope and help a thousand times than in this dead level and quintessence of every mediocrity.

REFLECTIONS OF A BIBLE-READER

BY ARTHUR DAVISON FICKE

EVEN the most wordly mind would hardly deny that for centuries past the influence of the Bible has been incalculably great in establishing certain ways of thinking for the majority of men in Christian countries. The Bible is a tremendous fact. No matter whether we regard it as a bed-time story of our childhood days, or as an impressive text thundered from pulpits in the years of our prime, or as a consoling page to be studied though feeble eyes beside the flickering candle of old age, still from any point of view we must realize that the color of this venerable narrative has in some way affected most of the lives of Europe and America. But it is no easy matter to define in what manner it has affected them, or to say in what different degrees different types of men have been affected. I doubt whether enough attention has been given to this by no means irrelevant question.

One fact about the influence of the Bible is so obvious that it may be accepted as an axiom. It is this: that as the education of the individual increases, and as the scope of his reading and reflection widens, the Bible's influence upon him becomes diluted and modified by many other factors. And it is equally clear, conversely, that the simpler man, the peasant type, is likely to find in the Bible his most important and perhaps his only book. This simpler man is usually the chief concern of the religious organizations. For example, the New York Bible Society is taking pains that a copy of the Bible shall be placed in the hands of every steerage-passenger who comes through the gates of Ellis Island. A considerable proportion of these new-comers are naïve peasants, who will soon confront with some bewilderment the unfamiliar conditions of an amazing city. The Babylonian prodigality of upper New York will flash itself before their eyes; the roar of toil and social discontent in lower New York will resound in their ears; and they will have as their guide the Bible,— perhaps an old possession of their hearts, but certainly now held actually in their hands. A strange guide! May one be permitted to doubt whether the Bible is the best of text-books for such as these?

I ask the question because it was with great astonishment that I myself, a few weeks ago, rediscovered the Bible. I am now past my fortieth year; and except for purposes of literary reference, or to re-read the exquisitely sensual Song of Solomon, I had not opened the Bible once during the preceding fifth of a century. But when one night I found myself in a bedroom of a New York hotel, alone and without books, I took up the copy of the Bible which the New York Bible Society had placed on the table beside my bed, and began to read.

I turned deliberately to the Book of Esther; for the story of Esther was one that had haunted me ever since, as a child lying in bed at nightfall, I had heard my aunt half-read, half-narrate it to me; and my clear imperishable memory of her voice and of the shadowy lamp-lit room in which she read had ever since been no more vivid to me than the picture of the great court of Ahasuerus, and the figure of the noble and gentle queen who at the risk of her own life passed in stately presence down the long hall and into the forbidden throne-room, to demand from the king the forfeited lives of her people, the Israelites. The story had been, as I remembered it, a thing done in the grand manner, a heroic story. But that night in the New York hotel bedroom, I found that a somewhat different tale was the one actually recounted in the Bible.

The account opens with the scene of a great feast, and with Ahasuerus, monarch over India and Ethiopia, "merry with wine" on his throne. He lustfully orders "Vashti the queen" to be summoned before him, that he may "shew the people and the princes her beauty;" for, in a manner not uncommon in tyrannical men, he desires that the perfume of other men's lustful envy may be rank in his jaded nostrils. Vashti, upon receipt of the king's order, declines to come and exhibit her charms before the drunken feast. She is perhaps the one admirable figure in this extraordinary narrative; and her name should be kept always green as the name of the first feminist. But no one in that day, of course, believed that a woman might have some right to say when and where her own body should be displayed or enjoyed; therefore the wise men counseled the indignant king that her insubordination would set such an example to other wives that it might wreck civilization. So the king took their advice, and cast out Vashti—and we hear nothing more of this admirable woman.

But when Vashti was gone, the amorously inclined king was left rather at a loss; so it was necessary that "all the fair young virgins" of the land be corralled for his pleasure. Among these virgins was the Jewess Esther. Her kinsman, Mordecai, gladly let her go; for in all Eastern countries the road to preferment is considerably smoother if one has a female relative in the royal harem. Hence Mordecai, naturally eager that Esther should not lose the chance of so profitable a connection, warned her not to let anyone know that she was a Jewess; and she very carefully followed this prudent advice.

It required a year of cleaning, polishing and perfuming before a girl was considered fit for the king's bed; after these preparations were over "came every maiden unto the king" in her proper turn; "in the evening she went, and on the morrow she returned"; after that, "she came in unto the king no more, except the king delighted in her, and that she were called by name." Apparently Esther's performance in this competition was brilliantly satisfactory, for "she obtained grace and favor in his sight more than all the virgins; so that he set the royal crown upon her head." Esther had won. And naturally she still complacently pretended that she was not a Jewess; and the prudent Mordecai still kept careful watch outside the palace gates.

So much for the preliminaries,—this typical recital of the corrupt and servile intrigues that surround the harem of every Eastern potentate. It was the end that astonished me. I had remembered, from early childhood, how Ahasuerus rashly accepts the proposal of his chief counselor, Nathan, who is a Jew-hater, when Nathan offers to pay ten thousand talents of silver into the royal treasury in return for the satisfaction of being allowed to massacre all the Jews in the realm. But then comes the crisis of the story, much different from what I had remembered. Mordecai, wailing, beseeches Esther the queen to save her people, the Jews, by entreating the king's mercy for them. Esther replies that it is almost certain death for anyone to go to the king uninvited, and she declines to intercede at any such risk. Being a perfectly sensible oriental business-woman, whose only stock in trade is her body, she is not going to take any chances of having that body decapitated. But Mordecai, rising to the full stature of his nature, says to Esther: "Think not with thyself that thou shalt escape in the king's house, more than all the Jews." And then Esther sees that this is indeed no laughing matter; her own skin is in danger; and since, as Mordecai has convincingly pointed out, she is sure to be killed along with the other Jews if she remains inactive, she decides on a course of action. She invites the king to a beautiful "banquet of wine," and "finds favor in his sight," and eventually wheedles the silly old potentate into changing his mind about the destruction of the Jews. Thus Esther saves her race and herself, and Mordecai gets a fat appointment at court. Indeed, so prosperous does Mordecai become that he is finally strong enough to encourage the Jews to turn the tables, so that instead of being massacred they "smote all their enemies with the stroke of the sword, and slaughter, and destruction, and slew of their foes seventy and five thousand" within the realm. So all ends well.

But when I had read this story with the eyes of maturity, and recalled the legend as I had so long carried it in my heart, suddenly a noble and romantic figure, the great queen and heroine Esther, crashed at my feet into a pile of dust that smelled a little like the heaps of old clothes collected by Jewish rag-pickers.

I wandered on, that night, to other stories. It would be wearisome to detail them all; I may summarize by saying that they were all very depressing. As a man of letters, I admired their style, but as a human being, I loathed their content. I read of the good advice given by Moses, under God's direct guidance, which resulted in the Israelites thriftily borrowing from the trusting Egyptians much "jewels of silver, and jewels of gold, and raiment," in order that they might make off with these goods when they fled from Egypt. I learned that the Lord God deliberately "hardened Pharaoh's heart,—" and then with equal deliberation smote Pharaoh and his unoffending people with seven plagues, merely because Pharaoh acted according to the dictates put into his heart by God Himself. And I read of David's conception of what constitutes loyalty to one's subordinate officers in the army; and of the elaborate series of taboos and sacrifices which "the Lord spake unto Moses," according to the provisions of which the relatives of Moses were created a perpetual

hereditary priesthood and endowed with luscious perquisites, such as the "firstlings among thy cattle," and "atonement offerings" for all kind of imaginary sins. I perused frightful tales of corruption, cruelty, lust, bloodthirstiness: I saw a vivid picture of an old, horrible, superstition-ridden world, where the tribal security was the only social consideration of any importance, where God and man moved in equally barbaric disregard of common decency, and where the forces of ignorance, priestcraft, and unscrupulous selfishness mingled in a witches' dance compared with which the Devil's own Walpurgisnacht on the Brocken seems a mere innocent woodland-ballet.

After reading all these demoralizing tales, my mind went back to the type of man of whom I spoke earlier in this paper— the man to whom the Bible is the most important, if not, indeed, the only book,— the man who has little opportunity to correct by other reading the influence of these barbarous records, and almost no opportunity to see them set in their proper perspective. And I wondered why these shocking, evil Old Testament pages should be deliberately put into the hands of such a man,—who, by no great stretch of the imagination, may before many years be a soldier in the ranks of the Social Revolution in America. Hopefully as we may anticipate that America will escape such scenes as Russia has lately witnessed, still only an ostrich would dare to say that what I suggest is impossible. Therefore, I am wondering if the prosperous gentlemen who so eagerly subscribe great sums of money to Bible Societies have fully appreciated the possible effect of impressing sanguinary tales on simple minds. What may be the eventual result of keeping alive in men's hearts such wicked patterns of revenge and hatred, such examples of the satisfaction which comes from "smiting the oppressor with the edge of the sword," such sinister records of irreconcilable class-enmities? To what purpose are the cruel events that made up the history of an uncivilized little tribe in prehistoric Asia Minor so vividly perpetuated as a Gospel? I am wondering whether some of the quiet, respectable people who are now confidently spreading the Old Testament may not live to regret the day when they so recklessly urged an old-world barbarism upon the ignorant, superstitious hordes who come to America. If the hordes refrain from taking complete and despotic possession "with the edge of the sword," it will not be because of a lack of example by the God of Israel. I repeat, this is no idle fancy which I am expressing. Nor is it fantastic to visualize a clear and somewhat ironic picture of one of these Bible-spreading gentlemen hiding in terror under his bed, while in the surging streets outside a howling mob batters at his door,—a mob no more and no less fanatical than the one whose prophets cried, "Behold, the day of the Lord cometh, and thy spoil shall be divided in the midst of thee! For ye have sown the wind, and ye shall reap the whirlwind!" Such a thing may happen. For when you set an ignorant man to thinking of the injustices of our modern social order, and then put into his hands a holy book wherein he is readily able to identify his fury and his fate with those of God's long-oppressed chosen people, then you are not very far from creating a fanatic who will stop at nothing.

I do not suggest that the Bible should be altogether suppressed; for I am deeply opposed to the arbitrary suppression or even the censoring of any book whatsoever. But I do say that the reading of the Bible should be quietly discouraged; and that the ingenuity of our intellectual leaders should be directed toward that end. A few decades of intelligent coöperation among educators, publicists, writers, and the clergy could greatly diminish its circulation, and might happily result in leaving it stranded in the backwaters of Western life. I would not prohibit the reading of the Bible, but I would bend every effort toward putting it into the same class as such little-read books as the Iliad, the Koran and the Mahabaratta. There, among other reports of ancient and obsolete superstitions, among other somewhat inaccurate records of shadowy historical events, it would be readily available for the scholar; but it would not be likely to exert much pernicious influence on the man in the street. The decision to treat the Gospels in this manner was arrived at by a very wise religious organization a long time ago; one must view with admiration the sagacity of the Catholic Church in its long effort to keep the Bible out of the hands of the laity. Plato adopted a similar attitude toward the great sacred book of his time and race; he excluded the works of Homer from his New Republic because of the immoral superstitions in them.

I have been speaking so far of the Old Testament only; I must leave it to some other inquirer to determine whether the New Testament can conveniently be detached from the rest of the book, and given a breadth of circulation that must be denied to the Old. My own impression is that the division would be difficult, and would meet with much opposition. If the two parts are indeed inseparable, then it seems wiser that both should be allowed to sink into obscurity; for it must be gravely doubted whether the aggressive bellicosity preached by the Old Testament does not in the long run exert a far more powerful influence on men's minds than does the gentleness and charity preached by the New. The recent history of a Europe which has for ages been Christian makes argument on this point superfluous.

Thus the book cannot be regarded as anything but a vicious book. Reading it today with unprejudiced eyes, one sees mirrored in it precisely the kind of events whose recital one deplores when one sees them daily on the front pages of our worst class of newspapers. And it is not the leaders of social revolution, but the leaders of capitalism, who insist on flaunting before the new-come foreigner these ancient Jewish examples of class-hatred, bloody revolt, and the laying waste of cities.

SIX ORCHESTRAL CONDUCTORS

BY D. W. SINCLAIR

FROM the standpoint of a musician playing in the orchestra—and this article is written by and from the standpoint of a musician playing in the orchestra—the quality most necessary to a good conductor is simply the ability to inspire his men—to lift them out of the boredom that follows too much music, and fill them with enthusiasm.

Erudition alone cannot do this, and neither can mere temperament, so-called. The competent orchestral performer already has enough of both. Playing is his trade, and he is presumed to have mastered it. He knows all the traditions of the classical répertoire; he understands his own instrument; he is adept at all the devices of what is called routine. What he needs, now, to make him play divinely, as individual and as unit in the group, is contact with an arresting and dominating musical personality—in brief, with a conductor who, as a musician, is a great man.

Such great men are necessarily rare in music; they have been extremely rare among the conductors practising in America. In this paper I shall discuss six conductors under whom I have played myself: Stransky, Bodansky, Hadley, Damrosch, Monteux and Mengelberg. Among them there is but one who meets fully the test I have set up.

II

First, I consider Josef Stransky, for twelve years conductor of the New York Philharmonic. Succeeding one of the greatest figures in modern music, the late Gustav Mahler, Stransky maintained himself so long, not so much by his musical abilities as by his social charm and personal cleverness. He was one of the most astute opportunists ever seen in a like position; it is a pity, indeed, that abler conductors have so often lacked his genius to fortify his citadel. To be sure, his vogue did not depend solely upon his appeal to the powers behind the scene; he possessed, too, in great richness, that mock-heroic magnetism which wins large audiences. Given a superstructure imposing and ornate enough, and the interior can take care of itself: a national maxim. The Stransky façade was for a long time of the impregnable sort; his delicate hauteur and impassioned nobility were fully adequate to confound the unilluminate. And with an orchestra of able musicians always willing to do their best—which, by the way, was excellent—and a few older and more or less respected section-principals to offer counsel in perilous exigencies, no one but a few captious persons who remembered the Seidls, Weingartners, Toscaninis and Mucks so much as questioned his preeminence until his régime prepared to die gracefully of its own decrepitude.

So long as sufficient Beethoven, Tschaikowsky, Wagner, and Liszt is given, New York audiences seem to survive whatever else a conductor has the temerity to produce in a season. Stransky's reputation as a conductor of Liszt and Wagner undoubtedly grew out of the innumerable performances he gave to their works; it certainly did not come from the confused and unfinished performances themselves. He, of course, played many other composers. He offered Borodin, Rachmaninoff, Sibelius, Debussy, Mahler even. He was as kind to

285

Schubert and Mozart as any colleague has ever been. Haydn's "Military" Symphony was a special pet of his; also Dvořák's "New World." He was more than considerate of Americans. In short, he was wise enough to recognize the value of variety in pacifying those detractors who were wont to insist that he could give adequately only a limited répertoire. But few of his enthusiastic supporters, and perhaps fewer yet of the vast majority of musically untrained persons who made up his audiences realize even now that nearly all of the Philharmonic's concerts during his tenure were totally deficient in orchestral finesse, in grasp of the salient characteristics of the works played, and in ability to turn tradition to its proper account.

Such qualities could hardly be expected from one who scrupled not to alter dynamics, tempi and even instrumentation and notation whenever it pleased his whim, in the works of any and all composers, from Haydn to Tschaikowsky. Alterations of any sort may be used only with discretion by even the greatest of conductors. In fact, the only generally accepted ones that come to mind are the substitution of horns for bassoons in the restatement of the initial horn call in Beethoven's Fifth Symphony, and the like substitution of a horn for a clarinet in the "Egmont" Overture. Any musician can give the reasons for these alterations, which are nearly traditional today, but a hundred would be hard put to find a single reason among them for the wholesale butchery performed by the leader of the Philharmonic. Some conductors may know enough to aid inexperienced American composers; few are expert enough to correct the accepted masters of all time. And certainly Stransky was not.

But this particular intrepidity was, after all, but an accompaniment of other shortcomings that always characterize the second-rate conductor. Such a man, deficient in sure authority, must contrive to impersonate it as much as possible. In order to buttress his essential weaknesses, Stransky sought to convey an impression of supreme superiority. Yet in his gaudy armor the performer before him could detect frequent transparencies. It is impossible to delude musicians for long; equally difficult to gain and hold their respect. Therefore, having no other resource when it became evident that certain of his ventures in orchestration, in interpretation and in making cuts were producing grotesque effects and perhaps a mild humor among his men, Stransky took refuge in a febrile petulance that was often pitiful. A healthy, self-assured competence never flowed from him.

The inefficient conductor, alas, passes his career much more unpleasantly than is usually suspected. He is not responsible to the musicians in any artistic sense; if his employers are satisfied, nothing else matters. But his real troubles, no matter how much arrogance he may assume, are when working with his men. What he himself lacks must be made up from them, and usually is. Hence he often gravitates gently into a semi-detached reliance upon them, and manifests extreme displeasure if they do not perform with such perfection as to offset his own faults. If he would admit to them his dependence, all would be well enough, for musicians are unbelievably long-suffering, and congenitally loyal to the man with the stick. However, like other humankind they cannot be trusted to preserve diplomatic secrets; so that the second-rate conductor only too often tries to escape their babbling by grandly ignoring his weaknesses both in public and private.

III

The associate conductor of the Philharmonic, perhaps through no fault of his own, falls into the same category. Henry Hadley is one of the sincerest of musicians, well-schooled in almost everything but the technique of conducting. His knowledge of orchestration, composition and the routine of music in general is absolutely beyond question. As a musician he is head and shoulders above nearly all other contemporary conductors in America. But he has never had the good-fortune to get himself thoroughly entrenched as an orchestral conductor; his opportunities with the Philharmonic are confined to two weeks' concerts annually, during which he is expected to produce five or six American compositions. Hence it may be unjust to assume that his performances represent the highest ability he might develop. His rehearsals, which in fairness must be admitted to be insufficient, are too superficial to be memorable. Perhaps it is this very lack of time that often makes him irascible, inconsistent and provoking; but it must not be forgotten that the thoroughly equipped conductor seldom needs to invoke querulousness and obscurity. Hadley's instability before an orchestra is most regrettable in view of the fact that off stage he is one of the most ingenuous, unassuming, and comradely of men.

In Walter Damrosch is found another example of the accomplished musician deficient in conducting talent. The New York Symphony's performances are for the most part very tame. Despite a personnel as capable in most respects as that of any other major American orchestra, its conductor seems able to present little more than technically proficient renderings. It is not by his conducting but by other means that Damrosch has contrived to keep his security. He is an excellent pianist: for a conductor to step down from the stand and take the part of a performer is always a fillip for the audience. He has done much touring over the country as a missionary to the musical heathen: a glamorous reputation is thereby enhanced. He has fathered and nourished children's, young people's, and other educational concert series. He is thoroughly at home in professional controversy, as witness his ill-disguised denunciation of Mengelberg two years ago, directed ostensibly at claques. Therefore, he remains perennially a central figure. His standing is not questioned by the polite. By the impolite he has not been taken very seriously except as a basis of idle comparison with some of the Philharmonic's conductors. Thus it runs: He is better than Stransky; inferior to Bodanzky; more experienced than Van Hoogstraten, etc. The impolite, of course, do not essay the unkind comparison with Mahler or Mengelberg. As a sufficient commentary on the doctor's fitness to cope with such giants, it may be noticed that as soon as Mengelberg was engaged as a perennial guest-conductor by the Philharmonic, the New York Symphony began also to import guest-conductors. Thus, in 1921-1922 and 1922-1923 appeared Coates, the Englishman; this year there is Bruno Walter. Something must be done to keep the cognoscenti from migrating to Carnegie Hall.

IV

A conductor who has had but a limited career as leader of a symphony orchestra is Arthur Bodanzky of the staff of the Metropolitan Opera. Bodanzky, called to the New Symphony Orchestra in 1919-1920, after Edgar Varese had made a mess of his leadership, remained at the head of that organization, which became the National Symphony the next year, for two seasons. In 1920-1921 his orchestra was reorganized and except for a few incompetents compared favorably with any in America. But Bodanzky never brought it to the degree of achievement of which it was capable. It was not easy to determine the reasons for this at first. Only after Mengelberg had come, seen and conquered did the shortcomings of his predecessor become apparent. Bodanzky is a studious person, charged with a high degree of ardor, and straightforwardly, uncompromisingly idealistic. As a symphonic conductor, however, he gave an impression of being unfamiliar with what he was there to direct. There was a vast reserve of power, musical intelligence, and superior possibility in his orchestra that he did not seem even to suspect, let alone employ. A like criticism might be made of his readings. For one so imbued with the importance of the position he held, and displaying as he did in pre-Mengelberg days so ungrateful a superfluity of irritable *amour-propre*, those readings, conceived in what must have been a distinct belief in their worth and originality, constantly fell short of what was to be expected of the military discipline which bore them company. An exception might be made of Bodanzky's accompaniments for soloists, which, presumably because of his long experience in opera, were singularly careful and restrained.

In playing new scores, and in fact any music unfamiliar to the general répertoire, Bodanzky did considerably better th-n most of his contemporaries. This was because he worked hard at his calling, and where there was little tradition he had a good chance to show his musicianship. In such cases he often displayed an extensive grasp of orchestration and interpretation. An ornate symphonic poem of Gliére, for instance, he made to sound very solid and satisfactory. One remembers rehearsing Ravel's "Mother Goose" suite with him. The waltz-like "Beauty and the Beast" showed him extremely sensitive; he reminded the men that it was "Ravel, not Waldteufel." He also had the courage and knowledge to give Bruckner's rarely-heard Romantic Symphony a very illuminating performance. Lately, with his Friends of Music, he gave Mahler's "Lieder von der Erde"—and gave it a splendid reading for which he deserved nothing but praise. But in the ordinary répertoire his anxiety to create an impression of perfection often led him into stilted and unimaginative paths. Insisting on perfect technical precision, he contrived to vitiate a great deal of the lyricism and passion that certain composers, Brahms and Schubert for instance, offer. In effect, one felt that while the orchestra was playing very well it had only scratched the surface.

Relinquishing his baton to Mengelberg in 1921 seemed to have a definitely subversive effect on his conducting. When he returned to finish the last six weeks of the season the difference in him was immediately noticeable. He seemed to feel chastened, subdued; to have lost or mislaid the confident, authoritative bearing that had stamped him before. Mengelberg had made it impossible for any lesser figure to inspire the orchestra. Bodanzky's requirements seemed so simple after Mengelberg's that he and the men were unable to re-establish the harmony that had formerly prevailed between them. And when, a year later, Bodanzky conducted six Philharmonic concerts that the directors had thrown him as a sop for taking his orchestra away from him, he seemed an indifferent and disappointed man. He simply went through the motions, waving his baton over his score as if, in Toonerville parlance, he did not give a damn whether school kept or not. It was in truth a pity that he was not given the chance to continue as a symphonic conductor and to improve as he probably would have. For despite his defects, he was, when the musicians paid attention to business, a pleasant man to work with. He made his rehearsals short and not too onerous, and one detected a larger and more expansive nature in him than he was in the habit of showing.

V

Pierre Monteux, who is now finishing a four years' engagement as conductor of the Boston Symphony Orchestra, though not an outstanding personage, nevertheless merits the best that can be said of him. And that best may be immediately summarized by stating that Monteux is of that rare type: a conductor of elasticity and variety.

Nothing is more needed in America, where a limited symphonic répertoire is being run into the ground year after year. To be sure, the Boston position offers its incumbent *carte blanche* in the choice of programs; but even this apparent advantage can be misappropriated, as it was by Henri Rabaud, who, in 1918-1919, produced a nauseating succession of Gallic inconsequentialities. Monteux, however, has not abused his power. For four years he has given programs which have put his colleagues to shame and incidentally he has found hearings for more composers than any three of them. He has done this, moreover, in spite of the handicap of having to build up practically a new orchestra. The Boston program books of 1918 and 1924 show at least sixty changes from the personnel that existed before the trustees disrupted Dr. Muck's orchestra by expelling its unnaturalized German members in deference to the hysteria of wartime. The trustees were equally purblind in paying such wretched salaries that voluntary resignations and the strike of 1920 took away at least forty more. Monteux, therefore, deserves high credit for his reconstruction of the orchestra.

He is no gilded personage. In fact, he is so quiet and unassuming that he gives an impression of far less ability than he possesses. He has a better ear than any other conductor save Mengelberg, and is an exceedingly versatile musician. His performances lack, as a rule, the crystalline purity and flawlessness that characterized those of Nikisch and Muck, but they are far more satisfying and inherently musical than those of any of the contemporary crew of second-raters. His limitations proceed from the fact that he appears to care more for the music than for the performance. Unquestionably courageous in conception, he often showed in rehearsal deficiencies in detail. When he placed stress on one effect he was likely to leave two unnoticed. One came to the performance rather doubtful that the rehearsals had settled all matters of importance. Mistakes occurred (generally unnoticed, of course, by audiences and critics) which could have been avoided.

His classics—Beethoven, Schumann, Brahms,—seemed always incomplete, glossed over, hurried. The repose of reverence was not in him; it was simply a matter of one more symphony to be got through in order to clear the path for the modern intricacies that he dearly loves and in the playing of which he excels. If anyone can popularize the futuristic musical idiom Monteux is the man to do it. For he has a definite flair for discovering and emphasizing the bizarre, and he is a thorough enough musician to measure and reproduce whatever virtues the modern school contains. He has done much for Stravinsky, Ravel, Debussy, Florent Schmitt, Dukas, the entire crowd of curious Italian cacophonists, and a few Anglo-Saxons of talent, such as Bax and the late Charles Griffis.

His lack of greatness lies more in his personality than in anything else. He does not do himself justice. His beat is too rounded, his gestures too excitable, and he smiles too easily. With a discreet admixture of German precision he would perhaps attain to the importance that his energetic and excessive volatility cannot secure for him. It is a question, however, if in replacing him with Kussevitzky, the Boston trustees have not substituted for a broad and catholic musician a mere prima donna.

VI

Having thus disposed of a number of lesser lights, I come at last to the man who is undeniably the greatest not only of the men here discussed but of all men now conducting orchestras in America. Willem Mengelberg, since he performed the memorable achievement of transfiguring the National Symphony Orchestra in 1921, has no competitor to fear and no superior to yield to. Mengelberg has furnished the subject-matter for countless idiotic reviews and many absurd and childish controversies. But beside him his detractors are yelping pygmies; before his tremendous eminence they prove themselves little better than blind fools.

Mengelberg is the *ne plus ultra* of drill-masters; his knowledge of orchestral instruments and effects is microscopically complete. For another thing, he combines all sorts of temperaments in one: he has thoroughly assimilated the romantic, the precise, the energetic, the tender, the ruthless. Again, he has obviously devoted time to study as well as to conducting, for he is wonderfully acute and penetrating in getting the last drop of blood from the music before him. Further still, when he is free of hurry and irritation he simply radiates, almost exudes, a fine sympathy with his musicians, their capabilities and their problems.

Mengelberg has a decidedly individual musical aesthetic. It consists primarily of a unique conception of the extent and requirements of orchestral technique, which in rehearsal is exploited, taught and worked over to a high degree. The second and equally important part is the interpretive conception, which Mengelberg has developed to so fine a point that in his directions to his men he makes use of all possible analogies, constantly introducing the quaintest, drollest and simplest comparisons in order to explain his desires. He has always insisted on this dual purpose of an orchestra: to play perfectly is one-half, to make the audience understand the meaning of the music is the other. A performance failing in either way is to him no performance at all. Personally, I believe he is too sanguine in his hopes of blasé, miseducated and clique-ridden New York; but it cannot be denied that he has had a tremendous emotional effect there.

Once, preparing Strauss's "Don Juan" he failed to get from the orchestra the enormous power that rests in that superb score. He shook his fist in the air and burst out, "Don Juan is not weak—not an I-beg-your-pardon sort of man—he is strong—" here the fist shot upward to the consternation of the National Symphony's girl-harpist—"a new woman every day!" (Appropriate blushes from the harpist, but a cheerful response from the men). Rehearsing César Franck's delicate "Psyché" suite, he said: "Psyché is not a great, big—" here

indicating a female of washboiler proportions—; "she is a beautiful, sweet girl. If you have not all known a Psyché, you can't possibly play this music!" ("Known," in the Biblical sense, undoubtedly!) Brahms' "Academic Festival" Overture presented difficulties—it was too sweet to suit him. Quoth Willem; "Here are professors—dry old professors!"—accompanying his elucidation by making faces. For Berlioz' Scaffold-March in the "Symphonie Fantastique" he yelled: "You must play like devils!" Preparing Tschaikowsky's Fifth, he demanded herculean power. "Yes," he smiled sympathetically at the jaded orchestra, "Tschaikowsky is strong—*but I am stronger!*" No one who heard the performance could possibly doubt it.

The production in 1922 of Mahler's great Third Symphony furnished him with no end of opportunity. The flower movement was not played delicately enough. "No," said Mengelberg, "not so"—holding up a pitying forefinger—"but so—the poor little flower must die!" And, the E-flat clarinetist failing to achieve the needed raucousness in the ensuing animal-picture: "You are supposed to be a donkey— and you play like a *lady* donkey!" Of the first movement, with its introduction of sombre misery, and the succeeding march-movement, magnificent in its unsophisticated vulgarity: "This music tells of the future—*we are living in other times.* (Wir leben in andere Zeiten). Mahler understood these things!" Nothing is left out of Mengelberg's conceptions of art; everything is grist to his mill. How much ranting by critics about Mahler's apparent shallowness we might have been spared if these omnipotent preceptors of public taste had attended that rehearsal!

The real cause of the attacks that Mengelberg has had to contend with lies in his having been transplanted from the National Symphony to the Philharmonic, or as it might be expressed, from a free experiment to an established institution. The National Symphony was the ideal field for him because he had no rivals or deterrents in his own house. The National's audiences were not composed merely of *Bodanzkianer*. They included also the most enlightened orchestra patrons in New York—those who for a decade had been growing tired of the immovability of Stransky and Damrosch, and who came to the National's concerts because they signified a new venture. These audiences, very responsive to Bodansky, went completely out of their heads and senses when Mengelberg appeared on the scene. The enthusiasm of the 1921 National Symphony concerts has not been equalled since. It was spontaneous, uproarious, incredulous and delighted at once. When Mengelberg went to the Philharmonic after the merger, he found a far different setting. The Philharmonic subscribers were so befuddled with the notion that Stransky was a superman that they were not properly receptive and unprejudiced.

Mengelberg tried at first to win them. He could have done so, probably, if he had enjoyed a free hand. But he has had no such good-fortune. He must play largely what the majority of the directorate decides. To this handicap (wherever were any directors competent to supervise the operations of a genius?) is added the apparent necessity of catering to the sentimental ignorance of the established audience. An orchestra must show a reasonable

degree of financial success: Tschaikowsky, Wagner and Liszt pull in the mob. The critics, moreover, have forever disgraced themselves by snarling about Mengelberg's programs. Therefore the inevitable has come to pass; he has adapted himself in the past two years to New York, which is a terrible pity. But otherwise he would not be able to hold his own in the system of American musical politics.

No more Mahler; no Bruckner; Schumann's beautiful "Manfred" Overture received in myopic silence; no chance whatever, of course, for more than a superficial presentation of composers such as Monteux and Stock have played. American composers? My God, no; unless it be an instrumental star such as Schelling (no derogation implied), or a public figure, like the yeasty Goldmark. Why not? Because America refuses to countenance the free play of genius. It wants to buy its art as if it were ordering coal or potatoes; to stipulate the quantity and the quality. It will not be taught—it will not surrender its inferior, querulous egotism. It is so generally incompetent that it will not let anyone be magnificently competent. It will have no prophets. In Amsterdam Mengelberg is the national figure he deserves to be; New York is too shallow, too afraid of having to admit its own defects to accord him the freedom and power that are his due.

EDITORIAL

No country in the world, as everyone knows, is so fecund of political mountebanks as this, our great free Republic, the mentor and exemplar of Christendom. We not only produce the largest annual crop known to faunal statisticians, relatively and absolutely; we also produce the most lush diversity of species and the most copious multiplicity of strange, unprecedented de Vriesian mutations. So rich is this variety, indeed, that descriptive zoölogy is bankrupted, and the same banal, almost anonymous label has to be stuck upon specimens of the utmost unlikeness. What pair of messiahs could differ more harshly than Hiram and Magnus, the one a pedantic little fellow with a chelonian paunch and gold eye-glasses and the other a rough, shaggy, carnivorous revivalist from the dreadful steppes? Yet both are Johnsons, and the same ancient name had to do service, in an era now closed, for two prophets even more diverse, Andrew and Tom L. One is hard put, indeed, to find points of similarity between individuals so at odds. A Roosevelt and a Tom Watson, a Jerry Simpson and a Charles Evans Hughes seem to belong to different genera, even to different solar systems. Yet the patient scientist, laboriously examining and classifying these variegated and precious paladins of democracy, is suddenly struck with a likeness that runs through the pack from end to end, binding even the most bizarre and inordinate specimens into a compact brotherhood; nay, more, he finds *two* likenesses. The first lies in the fact that all are born hot for jobs, and never cease to hunt them until dust returns to dust. The other lies in the fact that all share the same passionate tenderness for the humble husbandman, the lonely companion of *Bos taurus*, the sweating and persecuted farmer.

A reader for years of the *Congressional Record*—which, in accuracy, is to all other American journals as an autopsy is to an Elks' lodge of sorrow—, I have encountered in its dense and pregnant columns denunciations of almost every human act or idea that is imaginable, from adultery to Zionism, and of all classes of men that the legislative mind is aware of, from Antinomians to Zoroastrians, but never once have I observed the slightest insolence, direct or indirect, to the farmer. He is, indeed, the pet above all other pets, the enchantment and delight, the saint and archangel of all the unearthly Sganarelles and Scaramouches who roar in the two houses of Congress. He is more to them, day in and day out, than whole herds of Honest Workingmen, Gallant Jack Tars and Heroic Miners; he is more, even, than a platoon of Unknown Soldiers. There are days when one or another of these totems of the statesman is bathed with such devotion that it would make the Gracchi blush, but there is never a day that the farmer doesn't get his share, and there is many a day when he gets ten times his share—when, indeed, he is completely submerged in rhetorical vaseline, so that it is hard to tell which end of him is made in the image of God and which is mere hoof. No session ever begins without a grand assault at all arms upon his hereditary foes, from the boll-weevil and the San José scale to Wall Street and the Interstate Commerce Commission. And no session comes to an end without a huge grist of new laws to save him from them—laws embodying the most subtle statecraft of the most daring and ingenious body of lawmakers ever assembled under one roof on the habitable globe.

One might almost argue that the chief, and perhaps even the only aim of legislation in These States is to succor and secure the farmer. If, while the bombs of goose-grease and rockets of pomade are going off in the two Chambers, certain evil men meet in the basement and hook *banderillas* into him— say by inserting jokers into the chemical schedule of a new tariff bill, or by getting the long-haul rules changed, or by manipulating the loans of the Federal Reserve Banks—, then the crime is not against him alone: it is against the whole American people, the common decency of Christendom, and the Holy Ghost. Horn a farmer, and you stand in contumacy to the platforms of all known parties, to the devout faith of all known statesmen, and to God. *Laborantem agricolam oportet primum de fructibus percipere.*

Paul wrote to the Bishop of Ephesus, at the latest, in the year 65 A. D.; the doctrine that I have ascribed to the Mesmers and Grimaldis of our politics is thus not a novelty of their contrivance, any more than their quest for jobs is a novelty of their contrivance. Nor is it, indeed, their monopoly, for it seems to be shared by all Americans who are articulate and devote themselves to political metaphysics and good works. The farmer is praised by Judge Elbert Gary and by William Z. Foster, by Judge Ben B. Lindsey and by Rabbi Stephen S. Wise, by John D. Rockefeller, Jr., and by the Rev. Dr. Newell Dwight Hillis; I have even seen kind words for him in the monthly circular of the National City Bank. Am I, indeed, the first to raise a murmur against him? If so, then let it be a murmur for ten thousand trombones *fortissimo*, with solid chords for bombardons and ophicleides in the bass clef. And let its text be the simple doctrine that the farmer is, for all his alleged woes, predominantly a fraud and an ignoramus, that he richly deserves nine-tenths of what he suffers under our economic system, and that any city man, not insane, who sheds tears for him is shedding tears of the crocodile.

II

No more grasping, selfish and dishonest mammal, indeed, is known to students of the Anthropoidea. When the going is good for him he robs the rest of us up to the extreme limit of our endurance; when the going is bad he comes bawling for help out of the public till. Has anyone ever heard of a farmer making any sacrifice of his own interest, however slight, to the common good? Has anyone ever heard of a farmer advocating any political idea that was not absolutely self-seeking—that was not, in fact, deliberately designed to loot the rest of us to his gain? Greenbackism, free silver, government guarantee of prices, bounties on exports of foodstuffs, all the complex fiscal imbecilities of the cow State John Baptists—these are the contributions of the virtuous husbandman to American political theory. There never has been a time, in good seasons or bad, when his hands were not itching for more; there has never been a time when he was not ready to support any charlatan, however grotesque, who promised to get it for him. Why, indeed, are politicians so polite to him—before election, so obscenely amorous? For the plain and simple reason that only one issue ever interests or fetches him, and that is the issue of his own profit. He must be promised something definite and valuable, to be paid to him alone, or he is off after some other mountebank. He simply cannot imagine himself as a citizen of a commonwealth, in duty bound to give as well as take; he can imagine himself only as getting it all and giving nothing.

Yet we are asked to venerate this prehensile moron as the *Ur*-burgher, the citizen *par excellence*, the foundation-stone of the state. And why? Because he produces something that all of us must have—that we must get somehow on penalty of death. And how do we get it from him? By submitting helplessly to his unconscionable blackmailing—by paying him, not under any rule of reason, but in proportion to his roguery and incompetence, and hence to the direness of our need. I doubt that the American people, as a whole, would submit to that sort of high-jacking, year in and year out, from any other necessary class of men. When the railroad workman attempted it, in 1916, there was instant indignation; when a certain small squad of the *Polizei* tried it, a few years later, there was such universal horror that a politician who put down the crime became President of the United States. But the farmers do it over and over again, without challenge or reprisal, and the only thing that keeps them from reducing us, at intervals, to actual famine is their own imbecile knavery. They are all willing and eager to pillage us by starving us, but they can't do it because they can't resist attempts to swindle each other. Recall, for example, the case of the cotton-growers in the South. They agreed among themselves to cut down the cotton acreage in order to inflate the price—and instantly every party to the agreement began planting *more* cotton in order to profit by the abstinence of his neighbors. That abstinence being wholly imaginary, the price of cotton fell instead of going up—and then the entire pack of scoundrels began demanding assistance from the national treasury—in other words, began demanding that the rest of us indemnify them for the failure of their plot to blackmail us!

The same demand is made almost annually by the wheat farmers of the Middle West. It is the theory of the zanies who perform at Washington that a grower of wheat devotes himself to that banal art in a philanthropic and patriotic spirit—that he plants and harvests his crop in order that the folks of the cities may not go without bread. It is the plain fact that he raises wheat because it takes less labor than any other crop—because it enables him, after working sixty days a year, to loaf the rest of the twelve months. If wheat-raising could be taken out of the hands of such lazy *fellahin* and organized as the production of iron or cement is organized, the price might be reduced by a half, and still leave a large profit for entrepreneurs. It vacillates dangerously today, not because speculators manipulate it, but because the crop is irregular and undependable—that is to say, because those who make it are incompetent. The worst speculators, as everyone knows, are the farmers themselves. They hold their wheat as long as they can, borrowing our money from the country banks and hoping prayerfully for a rise. If it goes up, then we pay them an extra and unearned profit. If it goes down, then they demand legislation to prevent it going down next time. Sixty days a year they work; the rest of the time they gamble with our bellies. It is probably the safest gambling ever heard of. Now and then, true enough, a yokel who plunges too heavily comes to grief, and is ingested by the county-town mortgage shark; now and then a whole county, or State or even larger area goes bankrupt, and the financial dominoes begin falling all along the line stretching from Saleratus Center to New York. But such catastrophes are rare, and they leave no scars. When a speculator goes broke in Wall Street it is a scandalous matter, and if he happens to have rooked anybody of importance he is railroaded to jail. But when a speculator goes broke in the great open spaces, there is a great rush of political leucocytes to the scene, and presently it is made known that the sin was not the speculator's at all, but his projected victims', and that it is the prime duty of the latter, by lawful order upon the Treasurer of the United States, to reimburse him his losses and set him up for another trial.

The notion that wheat would be much cheaper and the supply far more dependable if it were grown, not by a motley horde of such puerile loafers and gamblers, but by competent men intelligently organized is not mine; I borrow it from Henry Ford, a busted seer. Now that he has betrayed them to Dr. Coolidge for a mess of pottage, the poor Liberals, once so enamored of his sagacity, denounce him as an idiot and a villain. Nevertheless, the fact remains that Ford's discussion of the wastefulness of our present system of wheat-growing, in the autobiography which he didn't write, is full of a powerful plausibility. Ford was born and brought up on a farm—and it was a farm, as farms go, that was very competently managed. But he knows very well that even the most competent farmer is seldom more adept than a chimpanzee playing the violin. The Liberals, indeed, cannot controvert his judgment; they have been thrown back upon belaboring his political morals. What he proposes, they argue, is simply the enslavement of the present farmer, now so gloriously free; with capitalism gradually absorbing his fields, he would have to go to work as a wage-slave. Well, why not? For one, I surely offer no objection. All the rubber we use today is raised by slave labor; so is all the morphine consumed at Hollywood. Our children are taught in school by slaves; our newspapers are edited by slaves. Wheat raised by slave 'labor would be just as nutritious as wheat raised by men earning $10,000 a year, and a great deal cheaper. If the business showed a good profit, the political clowns at Washington would launch schemes to confiscate it, as they now launch schemes to make good the losses of the farmers. In any case, why bother about the fate of the farmer? If wheat went to $10 tomorrow, and all the workmen of the cities became slaves in name as well as in fact, no farmer in this grand land of freedom would consent voluntarily to a reduction of so much as one-eighth of a cent a bushel.

III

But the *Bauer* is more than a petty swindler; he is also the prince of political nuisances. I have said that the only political proposal he can grasp is one which offers him direct loot. It is not quite true: he can also imagine one which has only the effect of harassing and damaging his enemy, the city man. The same mountebanks who get to Washington by promising to augment his gains and make good his losses devote whatever time is left over from that enterprise to saddling the rest of us with oppressive and extortionate laws, all hatched on the farm. There, where the cows low through the still night, and the jug of Peruna stands behind the stove, and bathing begins, as at Biarritz, with the vernal equinox—there is the reservoir of all the nonsensical legislation which now makes the United States a buffoon among the great nations. It was among country Methodists, practitioners of a theology degraded almost to the level of voodooism, that Prohibition was invented, and it was by country Methodists, nine-tenths of them actual followers of the plow, that it was fastened upon the rest of us, to the damage of our bank accounts, our dignity and our ease. What lies under it, and under all the other crazy enactments of its category, is no more and no less than the yokel's congenital and incurable hatred of the city man—his simian rage against everyone who, as he sees it, is having a better time than he is.

Now he proceeds further. Not content with assaulting us with his degraded and abominable ethics, he begins trying to force upon us his still worse theology. In the cow States Methodism has already come to the estate and puissance of a State religion; it is a criminal offense to teach any doctrine in contempt of it. No civilized man, to be sure, is yet actually in jail for the crime; civilized men simply keep out of such bleak garages for human Fords, as they keep out of Congress and Franz Josef Land. But the long arm of the Wesleyan revelation begins to stretch forth toward Babylon. The mountebank, Bryan, after years of preying upon the rustics on the promise that he would show them how to loot the cities by wholesale and *a outrance*, now reverses his collar and proposes to lead them in a jehad against what remains of American intelligence, already beleaguered in a few walled towns. We are not only to abandon the social customs of civilization at the behest of a rabble of peasants who sleep in their underclothes; we are now to give up all the basic ideas of civilization and adopt the gross superstitions of the same mob. Is this fanciful? Is the menace remote, and to be disregarded? My apologies for suggesting that perhaps you are one of the multitude who thought that way about Prohibition, and only five years ago. Bryan is a protean harlequin, and more favored by fortune than is commonly assumed. He lost with free silver but he won with Prohibition. The chances, if my mathematics do not fail, are thus 1 to 1 that he will win, if he keeps his health, with Fundamentalism—in his own unctuous phrase, that God will be put into the Constitution. If he does, then *Eoanthropus* will triumph finally over *Homo sapiens*. If he does, then the humble swineherd will drive us all into his pen.

IV

Not much gift for Vision is needed to imagine the main outlines of the ensuing *Kultur*. The city man, as now, will bear nine-tenths of the tax burden (who ever heard of a farmer paying income tax?); the rural total immersionist will make all the laws. He makes most of them, indeed, even now; he is the reservoir from which issue Prohibition, Sunday Blue Laws, Comstockery, the whole insane complex of statutes against free speech and free thought. But with Genesis firmly lodged in the Testament of the Fathers he will be ten times as potent and a hundred times as assiduous. No constitutional impediment will remain to cripple and harass his moral fancy. The Wesleyan code of rural Kansas and Mississippi, Vermont and Minnesota will be forced upon all of us by the full military and naval power of the United States. Civilization will gradually become felonious.

What I sing, I suppose, is a sort of Utopia. But it is not the Utopia of bawdy poets and metaphysicians; it is not the familiar Utopia of the books. It is a Utopia dreamed by seven millions of Christian husbandmen, far-flung in forty-eight sovereign States. They dream it on their long journeys down the twelve billion furrows of their seven million farms, up hill and down dale in the heat of the day. They dream it behind the stove on Winter nights, their boots off and their socks scorching, Holy Writ in their hands. They dream it as they commune with *Bos taurus*, *Sus scrofa*, *Mephitis mephitis*, the Methodist pastor, the Ford agent. It floats before their eyes as they scan the Sears-Roebuck catalogue for horse liniment, porous plasters and Bordeaux mixture; it rises before them when they assemble in their Little Bethels to be instructed in the Word of God, the plots of the Pope, the crimes of the atheists and Jews; it transfigures the Chautauquan who looms before them with his Great Message. This Utopia haunts and tortures them; they long to make it real. They have tried prayer, and it has failed; they now turn to the secular arm. The dung-fork glitters in the sun as the host prepares to march. . . .

Well, these are the sweet-smelling and altruistic agronomists whose sorrows are the *leit-motif* of our politics, whose votes keep us supplied with Bryans, Bleases and Magnus Johnsons, whose welfare is alleged to be the chief end of democratic statecraft, whose patriotism is the so-called bulwark of the so-called Republic.

H.L.M.

JOHN MAROUFAZ AND HIS SONS

BY W. L. GEORGE

JOHN MAROUFAZ was born in a frame-dwelling in O'Connorville, Iowa. He was to carry with him as a birthright the memory of Main Street, cleaving its way through unbuilt lots, passing across the colored quarter, becoming for a moment august between the First National Bank and the United Cigar Store, reverting once more through brick and frames to bungalows. His father went every morning to Union Station, from which he wandered out upon the line to tap fishplates and secure bolts. His mother, who died during his boyhood, he remembered as rather pretty, rather dirty, shrill, overworked; she commonly appeared with her hair tied up in scores of little wisps of paper. In the house no books could be found, save the Bible and the fourth volume of a History of Scotland. But throughout the week the living-room was littered with scattered colored fragments of the Sunday supplement of the O'Connorville *Post*. In the Winter Maroufaz went to school in overshoes, through a morass of melted snow and flowing mud. In the Summer, when the wind blew from Chicago, it carried great quantities of dust. In a vacant lot near by, the crickets sang. Then beauty hung over the arid land, for in the Summer sky, that was purplish black, floated a harvest moon like a pan of fire.

John Maroufaz was fortunate in one thing. Being the only child of a family disposing of thirty-five dollars a week, he was fed. He was fed notably on canned beans, canned salmon, and canned peaches. He went to school, where the teacher was enthusiastic, but where only canned knowledge was available. There he was informed

that a dollar, invested at compound interest at five per cent, doubles itself in fourteen years; that England is the hereditary enemy of America; that the old masters, notably Rembrandt, improve the mind. Also he developed himself physically, first by hurling balls in an aimless manner, then by means of erratic base-ball, and finally by engaging in sanguinary fights with his fellows. In O'Connorville etiquette decreed that if a boy fell the victor finished him with his feet. John Maroufaz conceived gods: first came the chief engineer; then Abraham Lincoln; then his mother, for he was fourteen, and she had recently been deposed from a rank higher than even that of the chief engineer. He dimly suspected the possibility of a superior god, whom he worshipped in triumphant battle hymns. But he was not clear about that one. At fourteen he knew that woman is the inferior sex, that those who make good are always right, and that it is a wise child who knows his own father when the latter comes back from the saloon.

Since Maroufaz senior worked at Union Station, John Maroufaz was sent to work at Union Station. But as he had been educated he found himself, not upon the line, but in the office of the railroad. There, for two years, he filled in long statements showing the number of tons carried from O'Connorville to Grant, and from Grant to Shuswee. He did not understand the object of these statements, and did not realize that upon them depended the possible closing of the Grant station. Nor did he care. John Maroufaz, in those days, was thinking of linen collars, and wishing that his neck were long enough to allow him to

297

wear the fashionable three inch. Also, he was engaged in a continual contest with his mother to preserve for ice-cream and cigarettes a sufficient portion of his wage. This contest ended when she died.

At that time, John Maroufaz was a not unattractive lad. Very distant Syriac ancestors had left him a dark face, a slightly curved nose, a thick wave in black hair, and the noblest sombre eyes. Such persons as believe in the telling of character from features, looking down into those eyes, broad and liquid as those of the gazelle, would have thought that within the heart of John must stir a prisoned soul, that at opportunity another Shelley would speak from his lips in the accents of the skylark. But, in fact, John Maroufaz was not aware of any dreams other than his desire to save enough money to buy a rifle. His tastes were modest, for he did not know woman.

Not until he reached the age of sixteen did woman come to him. Then they came with such suddenness, in a manner so devastating, that the current of his life was turned awry. Since his birth, O'Connorville had developed, thanks to the new factory of the Consolidated Lamp Corporation. Upon the hill north of the town had arisen a settlement of large houses, which called itself Norton Heights. Following the rich people, a theatre came. One evening, as Maroufaz and his friend Pete Sawry were loafing outside the theatre, watching the people go in, a large blue automobile drew up. A small hand gloved in white kid fumbled at the brass handle. The polished door opened; then, very carefully, so as not to soil her shoes, there descended a creature who was to become visionary in the life of Maroufaz. She was very small, very slim, perhaps about seventeen. Her smooth fair hair lay coiled about a little round head. The soft blue eyes lay like sapphires upon a screen of white and rose velvet. The vision shimmered with silvery crepe, quantities of it, like the stuff of dreams.

A long time seemed to elapse until Pete jolted Maroufaz in the side and remarked:

"Some swell dame!" Then he drew back, surprised by the incomprehensible fury which had overspread his companion's features. He was still more surprised when Maroufaz turned and walked away so fast that it was not worth while to follow him.

Change had smitten Maroufaz. He was recreated in an agony equal to that of birth. He was not in love, for he could not be in love with anything so remote, with a being supernaturally glimpsed. It was not that. He did not think of the girl; he built no day-dreams where he flung treasure at her little feet. What she had done for him was with her frail hands to open a window upon life. She had shown him another world, where dust did not enter houses, where there was no screaming, no quarreling. The quality of his imagination threw up a suave, remote existence of broad spaces, deep carpets, soft voices, an atmosphere of refinement and of grace. He was intoxicated, as if from a high mountain he had seen the delicate lands.

Maroufaz very soon paid for his exultation. Little by little, this mood of glory, this perception of an airy realm, converted itself into the sensation that none of this was for him, that between him and the delicacy of life lay a gulf which only the wings of a bird could hope to span. He saw himself then as he had never seen himself before. He had been a boy, enjoying the vaudeville, and made a citizen of the world by fifty cents. Now he had seen a Canaan he might not enter. Quite seriously, filled with the pessimism of his years, he resolved to throw himself that night under the 11.42.

It was very dark upon the line. His eyes were fixed upon the signal that showed green. He was calm, having touched despair and become inspired. To die . . . why not? A little earlier, a little later, what did it matter? The signal changed to red. Far away he heard the train; he heard the cry of the brakes. He was without sensation. He was already as if dead. Then, automatically, he registered the start of the train. The dim sound grew loud. In the darkness he caught a glimmer of fire as the engine came near, louder and louder, closer and closer. Now to jump . . .

But he did not jump; as the engine towered above him, a strange thought had come to him: the engine was beautiful, so strong, so swift, so unrelenting, going irresistibly toward its goal.

Long after the train went by his slim body trembled, not with fear, but shaken by a sudden determination. Like the engine, he would go on strong and unrelenting, until at the end of his journey he by force penetrated the delicate lands.

II

John Maroufaz did not penetrate the delicate lands for twenty-one years. At the end of that time, the young man who stood trembling with ecstasy and ambition beside the thunderous train was a changed creature. He was much taller, broader. Indeed, the great hands sown with dark hairs, the thick neck, contrasted with the elegance of his blue serge suit and the negligence of his tie. You will imagine him, then, sitting at a broad desk almost bare of papers. He is president of the New York, Chesfield and Redway Railroad. He looks secure, and he looks strong. The dark face depends upon the massive jaw. He looks savage. The lips sit close upon the teeth: here is a man ready for all comers. About him the appointments are luxurious, for he is not a gross man. Though desk and filing-cabinet bespeak the business man, his feet rest upon a carpet olive and velvety. Upon the walls hang some Méryon etchings, and a Rubens which he will bequeath to the Metropolitan Art Museum. For Maroufaz at thirty-seven is in New York. He catches sight of himself in the mirror opposite, which enables him to watch people unobserved when he is dealing with them. He smiles. He is strong. He is pleased.

Twenty-one lives rather than twenty-one years separate the Maroufaz of the day from the ambitious boy who told himself: "Go East, young man, as do those who desire short cuts to power." The twenty-one lives were all of them filled with contest. When he decided to become, instead of being content to be, the secret energy of his nature led him to grasp at all instead of at a little. He was going to have power, money, houses, but also he would have culture. He would at once be what he would become. Maroufaz went to night-school and learnt about costing, about insurance, and about banking. He was ready for his day's work, also for overtime, yet fit to steal from the night hours that would enhance the day. He was capturing culture. At seventeen he ceased to speak the vernacular; he learned English from Emerson and Hawthorne. At eighteen he could for hours be seen standing outside an up-town club, watching the men go in and out, noting their boots, their ties, their gestures. Sometimes, in a vacant lot, he would try his voice, practise an imitation of the tones of the cultured. Maroufaz had time for everything, even for the arts, even for literature. Now, at thirty-seven, polished, tailored and calm, it was difficult to know him from the natural products of the class which he had broken into.

That afternoon represented perhaps the apex of his career, for his railroad had just taken over its rival, the New York and Netang: Maroufaz was president of the biggest railroad system in the United States. He was worthy, for he had learnt. Cost clerk, freight agent, district superintendent, local manager, superintendent of the line, vice-president, president . . . step by step, agony by agony, Maroufaz had learnt. He had learnt to hold his tongue and to let fools talk, because this pleased fools; he had learnt to avoid boasting, to avoid self-assertion; he had learnt to exchange humorous stories when his tongue ached to get to business; he had learnt to wait until a rival uncovered, and then to strike; he had learnt to say pretty things to women, and had succeeded in not meaning them; he had even learnt to say pretty things to men, and discovered them more susceptible to flattery than women; he had learnt to talk of golf, Bergson, and psycho-analysis as well as of freight rates. He was a complete man.

III

Love had occupied little time in the life of Maroufaz. It was the only thing for which he had no leisure. He was practically pure because woman appeared to him as a luxury, a self-indulgence, and therefore enervating. Thus he passed untouched through childish calf loves; later, when women strove to use him, he allowed them to use him and did not love them. But woman takes her revenges swiftly. Though he had long forgotten the shimmering apparition which descended from the automobile, though he had become familiar with equally shimmering apparitions in drawing-rooms, he had not hardened. He fell in love in a few minutes. This happened in an old drawing-room in a house on Murray Hill, where he had been mysteriously taken by a friend because the lady of the house was curious to see the new multi-millionaire. Set among their old Chippendale furniture and their old Chippendale traditions, the denizens of this house looked upon him with perplexity, some polite irony, and a measure of apprehension. Maroufaz did not realize this; thus, when he beheld their only daughter, Adeline, when he felt stir within him an unknown emotion which he at once called love because he did not know what to call it, he had a rapid vision of his wedding to take place within the week.

In the Maroufaz world things happened within the week. He was therefore surprised to find that it took him a year to win Adeline. In her own circle she was not called beautiful, but to Maroufaz she embodied everything of the delicate lands. She was very fair, to the point of colorlessness; even her eyes were pale. She was slight, rather silent. But she had a quality to him immensely appealing, a strange, easy grace. When she spoke it was without striving after effect; when she looked upon him, it was without evident curiosity, without embarrassment. The charm of Adeline resided in everything that she was not, in the refinement bequeathed to her by a family which had done no work for two hundred years. Maroufaz had never met a woman to whom self-assertion was unnatural. He had met triumphant beauty, famous wit, and practised charm. He had never met what he took to be divine modesty. He did not understand that this girl, in her perfect repose, in her mildness, represented an arrogance of class infinitely greater than even his personal pride.

Maroufaz proposed to Adeline four days after meeting her, and was rejected. Four times he offered himself in vain. Her father forbade him the house, but he entered it, sometimes threatening the servants, sometimes bribing them. The family hated and feared him. He became their preoccupation. Suddenly, after he had dragged her from a dance into his automobile, the consciousness of his strength found the heart of Adeline. She fell into his arms as a blossom drops from the branch that ripens.

IV

Maroufaz knew so little of women that the discovery of Adeline impressed him like a translation into another world. He had the good fortune to have stood aloof from love, so had no means of comparing his delights with others perhaps less sharp, but still delights. As he had lived for power, now he lived for passion. He surprised Adeline. She could not understand that a man might kneel at her feet, crying out incoherently, tortured as well as entranced. She did not understand that here was the final promotion. She laid her hand upon the thick black hair in a condescending caress. She was willing to be loved. Her husband was wholly happy; within four years two boys, Cedric and Edmond, were born to them.

It seemed that the cycle was complete, for now Maroufaz had discovered a joy which he had never expected: paternity.

He did not understand at first. He had assumed, as the boys were born, that here were interlopers, that they would intrude into the romance of his existence, that they would interfere between him and his pallid, his exquisite Adeline. Not until for the first time Cedric smiled up at him did he understand, did a tug, half of pity, half of enthusiasm, impress his bosom. The exaltation which had carried him so high bubbled in him, made him snatch up the child and strain it to him until it cried out. Now Maroufaz knew a new passion. He looked down upon his boys with a voluptuous joy. They had their being through him, they were his creation, they were the assurance that his essential spirit could never die. He still puzzled Adeline because he had forced himself into her life as a burning meteor through the heavens, but Cedric and Edmond looked upon him as a great natural fact, like sunrise and thunderstorms. By his mass, by his energy, he predominated in their lives. It was to him they came from their mother's skirt. Then, as he sat one upon each knee and told them fairy tales learnt especially from a book, while Adeline knitted with brown wool a garment for the poor, he felt that life had completed itself, that its curve was closed, that within sat he, John Maroufaz, master, ingeminator of all.

Time passed. He became more powerful. His wealth increased. His sons grew older. Maroufaz was handsomer at fifty-one than he had been fourteen years before. Age had taken from his grossness; the gray in his hair relieved its blackness, and he still had his splendid eyes; he looked a male, but his personality had evolved even more than his person. At last he had a quiet polish; he spoke almost without accent, with a slow gravity that suggested perfect poise. He could avoid indiscretion, inquisitiveness, comment on the affairs of others. He knew how to speak to women with calm and courtesy; he was not im-pressed by old families; he had met a king quietly. He had read that it takes three generations to make a gentleman, and he determined to add to his conquests the abbreviation of time.

One night, after dinner, he sat alone with Cedric. The latter, being fourteen and having just gone to a prep-school up-state, was promoted to the honor of dining with his parents. Now they sat together, the father with a cigar and a glass of port, the boy from time to time reaching out toward the fruit when he thought himself unobserved. Both the boys were akin to Maroufaz; both exhibited his darkness and his size, but it was a joy to him to find in each of them their mother's blue eyes. Cedric did not know that his father was watching him in secret amusement. But he could understand the look of passionate love which came to him from the eyes of Maroufaz a few moments later:

"Cedric," said Maroufaz. "Have you thought of what you're going to be?"

The boy considered, being of a quiet disposition. "Yes," he said. "I have thought a bit. I was thinking I'd like to be president of the N. Y. C. & R. Railroad."

Maroufaz said nothing; he was too moved. That his elder son should desire in life nothing more than to follow him was a reward indescribably sweet. All the same, he had to be fatherly: "I'm glad to hear it, Cedric. Only, you know, supposing you weren't clever enough?"

"Then," said Cedric, solemnly, "I shall be President of the United States."

Maroufaz nearly choked over his port, for Cedric was so serious and did not realize the bitterness of his implied criticism: "Well, my boy," he said, "you clearly want to be president of something, and you're quite right. It's only by wanting to be president that you become president. But one can't decide so quickly. I'd rather you went into the business, of course, especially, if you want to, but there's the law, or diplomacy, or anything you like."

"I'll think it over," said Cedric. "But I think I like the N. Y. C. & R. better than anything."

When Cedric had gone to bed Maroufaz went to the drawing-room and laughingly acquainted Adeline with the triumphant selection Cedric had made from among the occupations. Mrs. Maroufaz at forty was as pale and as sweet as she had been at twenty. Also, she was unhurried and reflective; she was inclined to ruminate. After a while she said: "Yes, I'd like him to go into your business, John. Then he could help Edmond."

"Edmond must help himself," said Maroufaz, fondly, though the words sounded harsh. Edmond was as foolish as Cedric was clever, but he had what was refused to his elder brother, great personal beauty. Everything that was strong in his father had in him become delicate. He was as subtle in design as a Neapolitan boy, and he intoxicated his father æsthetically.

"After all," Maroufaz went on, "they can do what they like. The world is open to them. They only have to choose."

Adeline did not reply. She continued to knit, while her husband took up an English novel and began to read. A few moments later it struck him as strange that the book should interest him so little. Funny! It began so well. He yawned, relit his cigar, resumed the book. Strange fellow, Cedric. Might do anything in life, with a brain like that. And he'd have his chance, bless him! Maroufaz read a few pages more, but the idea of Cedric oppressed him. He put down the book and allowed himself to think. Life was a queer thing. Here were these two boys with, as he himself said, the world open to them. They could do anything they liked. Their father could buy them a controlling interest in almost any corporation they fancied. He could use influence and make them senators, ambassadors, possibly bishops. They needed only to wish, and all could be done. Just because they were born sons of a multi-millionaire!

Because their father had collected millions, they had inherited the fullness of life: just because they were born. For no other service to mankind: just because they were born. And if they had no wish except to exist, they could enjoy abundant money in any way they fancied. Not only could they do what they wished, but they could do nothing at all: just because they were born. Maroufaz found himself thinking of his own boyhood, when he rose from his bed at five in the morning to walk through the flowing mud and melting ice to Union Station. He saw himself at the drug-store, the attendant girl contemptuous because she knew that ten cents was the limit of his expenditure. He remembered standing up to be insulted by his first chief, a youth of nineteen, who put his face close to his and breathed alcohol. A hot flush rose in the cheeks of Maroufaz as he remembered the bestial words, the filthy insults, which he had had to bear with an unmoved face. And the everlasting poverty, the collars with jagged edges which hurt his neck, the food served on tables stained with swill, the grossness and the dullness of it all. He had risen out of hell. His sons would know nothing of it, unless it amused them to visit the East Side, like Dante proceeding to Hades to call on Virgil.

"Thank God," he whispered to himself, "they'll know nothing of all that."

V

Time passed, and John Maroufaz led his ordinary life, making more money because thus only could he avoid losing any; entertaining because here was the evidence of his power; buying gifts for his wife because here was the evidence of his wealth. But now his life underwent a companionship; it was not so much a companionship as an undertone, like the sound of the second fiddle in an orchestra. He was thinking about his sons more often now. He was telling himself frequently how much he rejoiced that they would never understand what it means to eat just a little less than one wants. At the same time he was beginning to ask himself whether it is good, whether it is bracing never to have known how precariously all humanity lives. He was asking himself whether the boys would not grow up soft. Fatherly, he told himself that he would put them in the car works of the N. Y. C. & R. where they would learn to work with their hands. This bred with his wife one of those queer little disputes which signify so much more than they seem. One evening, Adeline told him that Cedric was short of pocket money. She would have given it him herself, only the boy, with a precocious sense of order, told her that he would rather have so much a week and know where he stood. He was going to speak to his father about it next day.

"More pocket money at fifteen!" said Maroufaz. "I give the boy five dollars a week."

"Well, it isn't much," said Adeline.

"You know quite well they don't like them to have too much pocket-money at school."

"I know," said Adeline, rather pettishly. "But the rule is broken. Cedric tells me that his friend Wilbur gets ten dollars a week."

"Five dollars a week is enough for any boy," said Maroufaz, in a tone so surly that it surprised him.

"If I'd known you'd take it like this I shouldn't have mentioned it at all. But he was going to speak to you himself, and I just mentioned it because I thought it would amuse you to hear that he didn't care to have money given him, except regularly. And I really didn't think that you'd be so mean . . ."

"Mean!" said Maroufaz, very quietly. "When have you known me mean, Adeline?"

"Oh, but I didn't intend . . ."

"Still, you said it," replied Maroufaz. "I ask you again: when have I been mean?"

"No, of course not," said Adeline, a little aggressively. "Only you've got

funny ideas. You think that Cedric ought to be kept short of money just because you . . . because . . ."

"Because I was poor," said Maroufaz suddenly. "Because five dollars a week once upon a time was enough to keep me, because I'm a common man who's risen. Say it, Adeline. I know you think it."

Mrs. Maroufaz had always been mild. It surprised him that now she should get up, refuse to answer, and go slowly to the piano, where she played to herself until he left the room.

When he was alone, Maroufaz asked himself what was the matter with him! Why hadn't he agreed to give Cedric ten dollars a week? a thousand dollars a week? anything? What did it matter? From what secret spring did the impulse come? He had just given Cedric an automobile. Edmond, at thirteen, had been allowed a private room at the Ritz, where he entertained his little friends at enormous cost.

"Why won't I give him another five dollars a week?" Maroufaz asked himself. He seized his head between his hands. "Why won't I give it? I love him. Why won't I?" He was in agony. He was confronted with something that he could not understand, with turbid impulses, with a conflict of emotions so intense that his eyes started forward, that he uttered a groan.

Then he understood. He did not love Cedric, nor Edmond. All these years he had been the victim of illusion. He had thrust gifts upon the boys, and they had been gifts to himself. He had never loved them. Indeed, there ran through him a lode of hatred which suddenly outcropped. It was like something that reared its head and forced him to look at it. He hated his sons because they were happy.

Now his brain was clearer and he could understand. He hated them because they went to a boarding-school up-state, while he had been content with the public school. He hated them because at eight o'clock in the morning they lay in soft beds, while he had risen early and gone out into a dark morning much akin to night. He hated them because they had money, while he had earned it. He hated them because it was unjust that they should be given everything, while he had been given only what he could take. Above all, he hated them because they were offered the one thing that would have been exquisite to him: opportunity. Here they were, at fifteen and thirteen, the savage, the beautiful world open to them. He went over the thoughts which he had pursued before, recalled the professions and functions they might indulge in. If that had been given to him! Perhaps he might not have had to push and scheme, sometimes to lie. It would have been easy, easy. He would have known pleasure as well as labor. He would have chosen. He would not have been thrust into the railroad business as an engine is placed upon the track and compelled to steam ahead. He would have known joyful days, enjoyed women, horses, cards, champagne, everything that he had snatched from a reluctant world when it was too late. And it was not so much that the lost delights mattered; it was the sense that such delights were given freely to his boys, that they owed them to him, that they had stolen them from him, that they owned them only because he had pursued virtue. He laughed aloud: Cedric and Edmond might be spendthrifts; they might indulge even in gentlemanly vices. He had paid the price of virtue which endowed them: courage, perseverance, thrift, clear-sightedness, justice, faith, hope, charity, all his life he had poured those out, making up the pile of virtue which could furnish his sons with the joys of vice.

VI

Maroufaz was a changed man, though he outwardly remained calm, courteous, and rich in virile charm. But now he was more merciless in his despair than he had ever been in his ambition. It was as if the world owed him revenge. Now he wanted the last cent; enemy of man, he wanted not only his money, but his pains. Maroufaz did not so much want to succeed as to destroy.

Time passed; all that his wife and children knew was that he seemed a little quieter, a little more determined. Under a polite mask he hid the hatred he felt for them, the hatred which was now becoming the motive power of his existence. By degrees his passion grew; he felt that he must gratify it, that something must be done to satisfy his craving. When Cedric reached seventeen he proposed to send him and his brother to the car works, where they might learn the feel upon their feet of cold stone floors. But the vice-presidents laughed at him. What was the good of giving technical knowledge to boys who were going on the financial side? Besides, Cedric practically refused to obey, and Maroufaz, his eyes red and congested, just avoided disowning him. He did not quite know how it happened, but the boys did not go to the car works. Indeed, out of this arose another conflict; both boys were destined for Harvard, and Maroufaz made a vague attempt to enroll them at the new university of O'Connorville. But Adeline wept; the boys were sullen. Reproaches came to Maroufaz from Murray Hill. He wanted the boys to rise at six o'clock in the morning, to know life. But Cedric asked him what he should do at six o'clock in the morning? Nothing happened, except that Adeline pondered her husband's new peculiarities, while the boys, unable to forget their old affection, treated him with surprise.

The solution of the problem did not come to Maroufaz until one night, as he lay awake. Why had he failed to convert the boys into workmen? Why had they gone to Harvard? Why were they now, during vacation, sleeping above his head in soft warm beds? Because he had arrayed himself against social circumstance, because the sons of men such as he did not pad through the night, because they had to go to Harvard, because sons of men such as he went to Harvard. He had proved his own enemy; he had given way to the social imperatives of his new class. Indeed his mouth was filled with Dead Sea fruit. He saw it now: he had labored and he had starved, just to force himself into a class which promised freedom and instead gave him new chains. He had to do what that class did, or in the arcanum of his mind be excluded from that class. Maroufaz sat up in bed; he was very hot, and his brain felt light. There was nothing he could do. There was no way out. He had gone on and gone on, presenting gifts to the unworthy, sparing them effort, sparing them disappointment, interposing between them and the hard life the effectual screen of riches. He couldn't stop it. He would have to go on, establish them, help them, see them marry young wives without waiting for success, see them enjoy children such as themselves, children not foreign to them. He did not understand that they would miss the greater delights: ambition, suffering, disappointment, fortitude. He saw only that he would envy them, envy them; envy the good breeding brought into their features through culture taken from the atmosphere, not torn from it; envy them their proficiency in games, for which they had time; envy them the light speech which they need not make profound; envy them all that he had given them, everything he had never had. He possessed nothing that had not come too late. They! They had arrived in time!

He rose from his bed. It maddened him to think that nothing could be done to redress justice, that he could not snatch back the years from the swiftly unrolling scroll of time, that chance had given him power, while chance had given them youth. His breath came quickly, his eyes stared: after all, one had only one life. Why should lives be different one from the other? Why must he assist at the reaping of the crop he had enriched with his own blood? Why should they enjoy? It is the fate of man to suffer; so was it ordained; by the sweat of their brow should they eat their bread. Not bread served upon a plate of gold. It was monstrous that they should lie there sleeping, awaiting the dawn of another radiant day.

He was trembling, almost weeping, as he went along the corridor, holding away from him the weapon he carried . . . It was too much . . . he couldn't help it . . . now the door . . . it opens easily . . . the sound of a shot . . . why, the boy hardly moved . . .

The tears running down his cheeks, he must go along the corridor . . . He heard voices. "I can't help it . . . I can't. Must finish the work . . ." Again the sound of a shot . . .

The patrolman on duty turned with surprise at this man in night clothes who ran past him. He did not see the revolver. Beside, if he left his post he would miss the relief that was coming in five minutes. He wanted to go to bed. So he turned his back upon the figure that disappeared up Park Avenue. In New York, each night brought something strange.

The patrolman soothed his remorse as he reflected: "He's got a bun on."

AMERICANA

CALIFORNIA

OBITER dictum of Hahn, J., a favorite jurist of Los Angeles, in the case of the State vs. Brown, Guthro *et al:*

> There is a line of demarcation between the spooning of persons not in love and the brand of affection displayed by young persons who have plighted their troth to each other. The first class of kisses more often precede a more serious offense, and therefore are a menace to the morals of society. The kiss of love has long been recognized by society as being on a legitimate and moral basis.

EFFECTS of the Volstead Act in the faubourgs of San Francisco, as reported by the *Examiner:*

> Scores of young girls and youths were found stupefied by liquor in San Mateo county roadhouses by Federal Prohibition agents yesterday. Some of the girls were only 14 or 15, the agents said, while in many cases their male companions were years older. Helpless under the influence of liquor, the girls were unable to resist the attentions of the men.

COLORADO

LAUDABLE development of politeness among Colorado job-holders, as reported by the *Rocky Mountain News:*

> Wayne C. Williams, a young Denver attorney, was sworn in yesterday as Attorney General of Colorado to succeed the late Russell W. Fleming. After the ceremony the new Attorney General requested each person present to pause a moment in silent prayer for his predecessor.

CONNECTICUT

PEDAGOGICAL dictum of Prof. Dr. William Lyon Phelps, of Yale, quoted in the advertising of the Moody Bible Institute:

> Everyone who has a thorough knowledge of the Bible may truly be called educated; and no other learning or culture, no matter how extensive or elegant, can form a proper substitute.

ILLINOIS

FROM a bulletin issued by the Illinois Bankers' Association:

> . . . the Bankers Mutual Fidelity and Casualty Company has been organized . . . to serve and insure Illinois banks against the risks of burglary, robbery, and fidelity.

PATHOLOGICAL effects of Prohibition in Illinois, as revealed by a news dispatch from Chicago, "the literary capital of America":

> Figures compiled by State Prohibition Director Moss show that 2,289,600 persons applied for, obtained and succeeded in having filled prescriptions for whisky, gin and other alcoholic "medicines" during 1922. The prescription blanks returned number nearly 500,000 more than the government issued. A majority of the reputable physicians of Chicago refuse to write any whisky prescriptions, but those who specialize in this branch of "medicine and surgery" made approximately $7,000,000 during 1922, while druggists who filled the prescriptions show a profit of $2,500,000.

LOUISIANA

PROGRESS of Methodist *Kultur* in the home of the Creoles, as reported by a press dispatch from New Orleans:

> The old Absinthe House, one of the landmarks in the old French quarter of New Orleans, where, according to repute, Jean Lafitte planned his piratical forays and boasted of what he and Napoleon Bonaparte would do to Messieures les Anglais, was badly damaged last night. Prohibition agents did it all for one quarter of an ounce of absinthe, according to their official report, filed today. In the old courtyard, a door, priceless relic of the old hotel, was smashed. The book in which artists, statesmen, writers and lesser or greater notables had signed their autographs was cast carelessly upon the wreckage littered floor. Because a few drops of absinthe was found in the place, charges of possession and sale of intoxicants were placed against the proprietor.

MASSACHUSETTS

FROM a public bull by Prof. Dr. Stanley Alden, of Smith College:

> American literary criticism needs above all else a stern father of Scotch Presbyterian ancestry and a Puritan conscience.

MINNESOTA

EFFECTS of the Harding literary style upon the native minstrelsy of Minnesota, as revealed by an ode by Miss Marianne Clarke, of St. Cloud:

Our Constitution is commemorated
　By Puritan Fathers who arbitrated
The grand ideals of our glorious past,
　May they inspire forever and cast
Abiding faith in our Declaration
　For United States seek ratification
Of Law and Order, Progress and Peace—
　Oh! heroes of old may thy spirit increase.

Our Constitution is the best that we know
　"Go To It," stand by it, as they did long ago,
Washington, Madison, Franklin so clever
　Fifty-six men were in council together;
John Marshall started the Supreme Court so
　great
　Now is there another Marshall to "fete"
To assemble the group of nineteen twenty-four
　A world Court of Justice from shore to shore?

Practical Peace in International Relations
　The power of man in Brotherhood of Nations
Strong, Righteous Service to the land of the free
　America first for you and for me.
Five Presidents arose and gave us their lives,
　Yes, including "Harding," all sacrificed,
The secret of life is "Be Just and Be True—
　To Our Constitution—and the Red, White
　and Blue."

MISSOURI

REVIVAL of beautiful letters in Missouri, as reported by a new publishing house in Kansas City:

If you enjoy *real* literature—a *Mental Feast*—a *Soul Banquet*—something that will make you bounce a little—a book that you'll call *Sweetheart* before you get half through it, you should read *The Fool-Killer's* new book, *"Warm Wireless Waves."* There's no book like it in human literature; it reaches mental heights of transcendent beauty and intellectual splendor that no other book ever dreamed of. It's the book you'll want to keep in the family and hand down to future generations. You'll want your wife and children to read it and *live* it. It shakes hands with your *heart* and calls you *pal.* Forty-five *sizzling* pages of *Soul-Music* and *Mental-Cream.* Contains the latest picture of the *Author.* Only 25c a copy or 5 for $1.00. Sent by mail, prepaid.

NEW JERSEY

PLANS and specification for a new religion lately launched by Carl H. Norbrom, 185 North Parkway, East Orange:

1. The church ritual shall be the same as the modern Jewish Synagogue. That of Rabbi Stephen Wise at Carnegie Hall, for example.

2. It shall elect its Rabbi and officers the same as the Christian Science Church.

3. The Old and New Testaments are to be used for texts along with modern science.

4. All members must be total abstainers. No booze.

5. No member of this church may personally sue to recover a debt, nor go into voluntary bankruptcy. He must diversify his investments and use forethought that will prevent his getting into financial difficulties.

6. He must never participate in warfare against another nation, of which 50% of the people are Christians. If conscripted, he must meet the penalty for evasion. He must take a passive attitude toward war propaganda. If a non-Christian country invades his nation, he must help drive them out, but not invade their land.

7. He shall not have a larger family than that which he can afford to raise and educate decently. He should do his utmost to keep his family free from charity.

8. Women to have equal rights with men in all church positions.

9. Owing to the unfairness to the children that follow, the members of one race (color) shall not marry into another, nor shall congregations be mixed in race.

10. No member of this congregation shall ever speak ill of another man's religion.

NEW YORK

REPLIES recorded by a *Sun* reporter who sought answers in lower Broadway to the question, Should Christianity be debated from a public platform?

1. Frank Mueller, M. D., 100 East Seventy-fourth Street—I am not in favor of any discussion of Christianity on any public platform, especially of the authenticity of the word of God. Modernism and materialism and even the old Babylonian philosophy are being taught in many places in this country.

2. H. Harris, retired business man, 56 Concord Street, Brooklyn—Absolutely no. The Bible, the living word of God, has stood the test of centuries.

3. Turner A. Monroe, accountant, 120 Broadway—I believe that instead of an argument on the truth of the Bible on a public platform the preachers should teach the gospel as it is written. The Bible will take care of itself.

4. J. C. Clark, restaurateur, 135 West Forty-seventh Street—Everybody has a right to his own opinion. Free speech is allowed in this country, but to discuss on a public platform the truth of the Bible is going too far. I do not approve of it.

5. P. De Fliese, banking, 120 Broadway—I see no occasion for any debate or discussion as to the truth of the Bible. It is the only record we have, and Christianity stands or falls on its authenticity.

THE next step in the Universal Uplift, as

revealed by an editorial in the estimable *Tribune:*

> So long as morons are permitted to remain at large there will be crime waves.

NORTH CAROLINA

RISE of an intellectual artistocracy in North Carolina, as reported by a Charlotte correspondent of the New York *World:*

> North Carolinians read the *World* and they even read the editorial, theatre and literary pages. A day or so ago I commented on the work of Mr. Heywood Broun in a column I conduct on a country newspaper, and immediately thereafter I was stopped on the streets by several of the townspeople, who discussed Broun with me. They read his column and his reviews and liked him. They also read "The Conning Tower" and the gardens of verses offered therein. Some of them go so far as to read Deems Taylor's talk about the music world. The sophisticates hereabout keep as close tab on the movement in the theatre district as do the smartest of New Yorkers. Then when they take their annual pilgrimage to the city they march down Broadway with a most supercilious air and are thoroughly entertained.

CHALLENGE to infidelity by a Tar-Heel Bishop Manning, from the Charlotte *Leader:*

> If the reports concerning Rev. Davis' remarks to the Brotherhood Class of the Congregational church are correct—namely "The Book of Jonah and the story of the great fish is but a myth, not worthy of credence"—as a preacher of the word of God and a minister of Christ, and pastor over a Bible-believing congregation, I take exception to such statement, and herewith challenge Rev. Davis to a public debate; time and place at his convenience.
>
> This undoubtedly would prove more interesting than his movie show, and perchance some people might learn a little more about the reliability and authority of the Bible.
>
> Yours respectfully,
> JOHN ZUIDERHOOK,
> Pastor Gospel Tabernacle.

OTTAWA

THE Rev. David Ness, of Glasgow, past president of the Imperial Orange Council of the World, in an address to Orangemen at Ottawa, as reported by the Ottawa *Citizen:*

> There is no story more interesting in the Old Testament than the story of the landing of Prince William of Orange.

PENNSYLVANIA

IDEAL of Service behind the recent military Vice Crusade in Philadelphia, as reported by the war correspondent of the Scripps-Howard newspapers:

> Philadelphia politicians ask why Mayor Kendrick put his head into this sort of a moral noose. The best answer they can give themselves is that he is looking beyond Philadelphia toward the governor's chair in Harrisburg and is willing to ditch the organization for the time being to win the rest of the State. Another and less flattering theory propounded out of the corners of their mouths is the suggestion that, after all, the inside organization men can sacrifice the perquisites of the police department so long as other departments are not interfered with. They have in mind Philadelphia's big construction program, running into many millions of dollars.

TEXAS

FROM the code of regulations for the Woman's Building at the University of Texas:

> The young ladies will be expected to consult invariably with the Director before making arrangements for going to entertainments or places of recreation; to regulate their conduct according to her decision, and to return promptly after night entertainments. Sitting on the steps or lingering about the door with escorts will be considered a violation of propriety.
>
> In conformity with the expressed wish of the Board of Regents, gentlemen visitors can be received on the first floor only.
>
> Each young lady is requested to procure for her bedroom windows sash curtains, which must be kept down at all times. At night, as long as the room lights are burning, the blinds must be down and closed.
>
> Negligeé costumes must not be worn on the first floor at any time.

FOLLOW-UP letter employed upon ungrateful patients by a medical man of Paige, Texas:

> NOTICE!
>
> I expect a prompt settlement of all accounts due me.
>
> If not possible to settle in cash, any of the following named articles will be acceptable, viz:
>
> Cotton Seed, Chickens, Ducks, Geese, Turkeys, Billy Goats, Live Cat Fish over 1 lb. each, Bull Dogs, Registered Bird Dogs, Live Wild Cats, Poland China Hogs, Skunk Hides (dry), Deer Hides, Shot Guns, Cedar Posts, Watches, Gold Teeth, Diamonds, Cream Checks, Pine Trees (2 ft. in diameter x 30 ft. long), Automobiles new or second hand, Peanuts, Black Eyed Peas, Liberty Bonds, Land Notes, Bacon, Lard, Country Hams, Clean Goose Feathers, Soft Shell Turtles over 5 lbs. each. Anything that can be sold for cash legally.
>
> I need the money.

EVERY SCIENCE AN EXACT SCIENCE

BY VILHJALMUR STEFANSSON

IT is said that Bacon considered all knowledge his province. But the sciences of today are so many and complex that a single Baconian view of them is no longer possible, and perversions of thought and action result because our intellectual horizon has been narrowed to a part of the field. From a realization of this have come various attempts to co-ordinate the sciences to permit a unifying view of the whole. The French philosopher, Comte, made one of these a century ago in his Positive Philosophy. There have been many since.

But if we pause to state clearly the case against the standardization of knowledge, the essential absurdity becomes so patent that we have to recall the numerous failures to convince ourselves that anyone was ever foolish enough even to try it.

Consider for instance the physiology of the human skin or the composition of a dust nebula. In these fields, among others, the accepted facts of a dozen years ago have become the error and folklore of today. You standardize knowledge, and while you are at the job the knowledge changes. Long before the thing can be adequately done it has ceased being worth doing at all.

Then why are we continually attempting this hopeless task? Partly, let us say, from irrepressible human optimism, which leads us to think that any desirable thing is possible. Partly, also, because of unclear analogizing from fields that seem related but are not. One of these analogies is from business. If you have on hand, on July 1st, a pair of socks, you will have them still on hand on August 1st, or else cash in your

till to correspond, assuming honest and successful management. But, in spite of unlimited honesty and efficiency, you have no guarantee that an idea on hand on July 1st may not have been simply removed by August 1st without any equivalent remaining on hand. You may have discovered that month, for instance, reasonable assurance that the moon is *not* made of green cheese, without being able to get any clear idea as to what it *is* made of.

The reader may here jump at the conclusion that we are arriving at a philosophy of pessimistic hopelessness. That is not the way of the true philosopher. His ideal is the *tabula rasa*. He sweeps away the systems of others, that he may build his own on a smooth foundation.

Realizing simultaneously the insatiable craving of the human mind for order and the impossibility of bringing order into the chaos of knowledge, we appear to be faced with a dilemma no less distressing than insoluble. But on looking deeper we find the dilemma apparent only. This will become clear when we consider the essential nature of knowledge.

The thoughtless among us may speak, for instance, of a red cow, and naïvely imagine we could prove our point with the testimony of a witness or two. But the philosophers have long ago made it clear that a cow would not be red but for the presence of someone to whom it looks red. Having established that point, the deeper of the philosophers go on to prove that the cow would not only not be red, but would not even exist, were it not for the presence of someone who thinks he sees a cow. In our argument the position is even stronger than this, for we have two lines of defense. First, we agree with the philosopher that you cannot prove of any given cow that it is red, or even that it exists at all; secondly, we insist that an idea is so much less stable than a cow that even were the philosophers wrong about the cow not being red they might easily be right about an idea not being right, or not existing. Take an example. The philosophers of the Middle Ages demonstrated both that the earth did not exist and also that it was flat. Today they are still arguing about whether the world exists, but they no longer dispute about whether it is flat. This shows the greater lasting power of a real thing (whether it exists or not, for that point has not yet been settled) as compared with an idea, which may not only not exist but may also be wrong even if it does exist.

II

We have now come in our discussion to the point where we see the absurdity of supposing ourselves to have any knowledge, as knowledge is ordinarily defined—or at least we would have come to that point but for lack of space which prevents us from making the subject really clear. However, it doesn't matter from a practical point of view whether you have followed this philosophical reasoning. Perhaps you are not a philosopher. In that case, and in the homely phrase of the day, I ask you, what's the good of an Englishman's learning first that all Americans speak through their noses and secondly why they do so, when he has to find out eventually that they do not? What's the good, again, of knowing that central Australia is a desert and that certain principles of physiography make it so, when you may have to listen to an afterdinner speech by some scientific traveler telling that it is not a desert?

Such things do not always go in triplets of (1) so it is, (2) why it is, and (3) it is not—but that is a common order.

The reader may here protest that we are not getting much nearer our promised emancipation from the dilemma between our passion for system and the impossibility of systematizing knowledge. We have hinted above that the solution lies in finding a new basis for knowledge, and this we now proceed to do.

So long as you believe in them, the nasality of American speech, and the desert nature of central Australia are fragments of knowledge capable of being arranged in a system. The trouble comes when you find them out, as it were—discover that they are "untrue." This gives the solution of our problem. We must have knowledge that is incapable of being contradicted. On first thought this seems impossible, but on second thought we realize that such facts do exist in the domain of mathematics. Two and two make four.

But why do two and two make four? Obviously because we have agreed that four is the name for the sum of two and two. That principle has been applied in mathematics to such advantage that it is rightly called the science of sciences, and this is the principle which, now at length, we propose to apply to all knowledge. Through it every science will become a pure science and all knowledge as open to systematization as mathematics.

The trouble with all facts outside the field of mathematics has been inherent in the method of gathering information. We call these methods *observation* and *experiment*, and have even been proud of them—not realizing their clumsy nature, the unreliability of the findings, the transient character of the best of them, and the essential hopelessness of classifying the results and thus gratifying the passion of the human intellect for order and symmetry in the universe.

Take an example. A man comes from out-of-doors with the report that there is a red cow in the front yard. Neglecting for the moment the philosophical aspect of the case—as to whether the cow would be red if there were no one to whom she seemed red, and also the more fundamental problem of whether there would have been any cow at all if no one had gone out to look—neglecting, as I say, the deeper aspects of the case, we are confronted with numerous other sources of error. The observer may have confused the sex of the animal. Perhaps it was an ox. Or if not the sex, the age may have been misjudged, and it may have been a heifer. The man may have been color-blind, and the cow (wholly apart from the philosophical aspect) may not have been red. And even if it was a red cow, the dog may have seen her the instant our observer turned his back, and by the time he told us she was in the front yard, she may in reality have been vanishing in a cloud of dust down the road.

The trouble lies evidently in our clumsy system of observing and reporting. This difficulty has been obviated in the science of mathematics. A square is, not by observation but by definition, a four-sided figure with equal sides and equal angles. No one has denied that and no one can, for the simple reason that we have all agreed in advance that we will never deny it. Nay more, we have agreed that if anyone says that a square has three or five sides we will all reply in chorus: "If it has three or five sides it is not a square!" That disposes of the matter forever.

Why not agree similarly on the attributes of a front yard?—making it true by definition that, among other things, it contains a red cow. Then if anyone asserts, for reasons of philosophy, color-blindness or the officiousness of dogs, that there is no red cow in the yard, we can reply, as in the case of the squares, "If it does not contain a red cow, it is not a front yard!"

III

The author feels at this point a doubtless unwarranted concern that he is not being taken seriously. Or perhaps the plan proposed is not considered practical. But the proof of the pudding is in the eating. The thing has been tried, and successfully—not in the systematic way now proposed, but sporadically. Some instances are well known and convincing.

Take the assertion that a Christian is a good man. If you attempt to deny this on the ground that Jones, a deacon in the church, ran off with some public funds, your stricture is at once shown to have been absurd by the simple reply: "If Jones was a thief, he was *not* a Christian." A Christian is, not by observation but by definition, a good man; if you prove that a certain man was not good you merely show that he was not a Christian. Thus we have established once and forever the fact that a Christian is a good man. It is like a square having four sides.

But if someone asserts that a Bolshevik, a Republican or a chemist is a good man, you can soon confute him; for the members of these classes have neglected to define themselves as good. Thus their attributes have to be determined by observation and experiment (after you have first run the gauntlet of the philosophers who ask whether the Bolsheviks could be good without the presence of someone who considers them good, and further whether any Bolsheviks would exist at all but for certain people who think they exist). It is highly probable that evidence could be brought against almost any given Bolshevik and even some Republicans to show that they are not good men. At any rate we have here no such clarity of issue as in things that are true by definition—as the four-sidedness of a square or the goodness of a Christian.

Through some experience of arguing this case in the abstract I have learned that its essential reasonableness can best be established from concrete examples. Let us, then, take cases at random from various fields of knowledge.

Consider first the ostriches of Africa. These birds have been studied in the wild by sportsmen and zoölogists, and as domestic animals by husbandmen who tend them in flocks like sheep. There are accordingly thousands of printed pages in our libraries giving what purports to be information upon their habits. Besides being indefinite and in many ways otherwise faulty, this alleged information is in part contradictory.

Having studied the bird of Africa, let us turn next to the ostrich of literature, philosophy and morals. Instead of the confusion in the case of the ostrich of zoölogy, we have clarity and precision. This is because the ostrich of literature exists by definition only. He is a bird that hides his head when frightened. You may too precipitately object that men would not accept universally this definition of the ostrich of literature if it did not fit also the zoölogical ostrich. The answer is that the definition has never received any support from zoölogists, hunters or the owners of the domesticated birds and yet it has been accepted universally throughout Europe since Pliny's time (about 50 B. C.). It has survived all attacks from science and from the bigoted common-sense of those who did not recognize its true nature. Like the definition of a four-sided square or a good Christian, it has survived because it was useful. Can you imagine any real attribute more instructive than the head-burying of the ostrich-by-definition? As a text for moralists, as an epithet that politicians use for their opponents, as a figure of speech generally, what could serve as well? Our literature is richer, our vocabulary more picturesque through this beneficent bird of hypothesis. He has many inherent advantages that no real bird could have. Since his habits are defined we need not waste time studying him first hand nor in trying to adjudicate at second hand between books about him that disagree. Since he never existed as a beast he is in no danger of the extinction that is said to threaten the lion and swan.

Consider next what trouble we should get into if we did not have the literary ostrich and wanted to convey picturesquely the idea of that sort of wilful blindness from which we ourselves never suffer, but

which curiously afflicts our opponents. In pursuit of suitable analogy we might vainly canvass the whole animal kingdom. The ostrich-by-definition is, therefore, not only less trouble to deal with than a real bird; he is actually more useful and instructive than any real bird or beast. When we consider how often he has been used in sermon and precept we must admit that this model creature has contributed substantially not only to the entertainment and instruction of nations, but also to the morality and general goodness of the world.

The ostrich is but one of several useful birds of definition. But we must be careful not to confuse these with real birds or their value is lessened. An example is the stork that brings babies. By a confusion of thought which identifies this stork with real storks, and through the pernicious birth-control propaganda which insists on rationalizing everything, this stork has ceased to be useful except in conversation with children, in the symbolism of the movie, and in the picture post-card industry.

The wolves of literature are among the most picturesque and useful of our definitions. Zoölogical wolves go in pairs or families, never above a dozen. It is obvious how inadequate this would be for modern movie purposes, where they should run in packs of scores or hundreds. Even in a novel or short story of Siberia or Canada you need packs large enough for the hero to kill fifteen or twenty, with enough left over to eat, or to be about to eat, his sweetheart. This is easily accomplished by employing a wolf of the general type we advocate—having no relation to the so-called realities but possessing by definition all the required characteristics (habit of running in packs of any desired size, willingness to eat, or attempt to eat, the heroine, etc.).

Another useful definition has long been that of Arctic, Canadian and Siberian cold. The danger and disadvantage of confusing this hypothetical with a so-called real climate are best seen if we compare the facility with which people who have never been in these countries use the weather in conversation, speeches and books, and contrast that facility with the awkwardness of travelers and natives. An example is a story by Tolstoi. Great as he was, he failed to realize the advantage in simplicity and vividness of postulating that Siberia is always cold, and actually allowed himself to be led into the artistic blunder of having the convicts in one of his novels die of sunstroke. An acquaintance of mine was filming this story. He realized the pictorial ease of "putting over" drifting snow as compared with heat waves—the snow could be managed with confetti and an aeroplane propeller, but how would one photograph heat waves? But he realized still more clearly that the public is wedded to the defined, as opposed to the "real," climate of Siberia and did what Tolstoi would have done in the first place had he lived in London—changed the scene from Summer to Winter and then froze to death as many convicts as the picture required.

IV

These few examples from among many will suffice to show not only that the method of knowledge-by-definition is and long has been in standard use, but also that it has the advantages of being easily grasped, picturesque and of a higher average moral value than the so-called "real" knowledge. It is inherent in the genesis and nature of defined facts that they can be made picturesque in proportion to the ingenuity of the one who defines them, and as moral as that one desires. This is a striking advantage over empirical knowledge, which cannot always be relied on to support the fashion of the time or even the moral system of the community. It is from this last point of view that there has grown up in many countries of recent years a profound distrust of "facts" and the theories deduced from them. In En-

gland they are dealt with by the simple and adequate way of paying little attention to the exposition of "new" things. In the United States it has been found that the public listens even to the newest views, and sometimes actually wants to act upon them. This has necessitated the expedient of passing laws prescribing what may and may not be advocated and believed. These laws are a step in the right direction, but inadequate because they do not have back of them any but specific moral considerations. Few people as yet realize the general reasons of expediency and broad sanity that lie back of the scheme we are here proposing.

Let us consider next a sample or two of knowledge-by-definition that could well be added to our present stock. Just as artificial tongues are built upon spoken tongues but avoid their mistakes, so may we conveniently base our knowledge-by-definition, or absolute knowledge, on what is already believed by some. Assume, for instance, that all Irishmen are peasants holding land by insecure tenure from grasping landlords, that each has a pig under his bed, that everyone carries shillalahs, that kissing the blarney stone is the chief national occupation. Having agreed on these things, we could teach them in the schools of all countries. We should then presently all agree (on the basis of common facts) as to what our attitude toward Ireland should be and the troublesome Irish Question would disappear from politics and history. Think, too, what a charm the new system would lend to travel in Ireland! So soon as you landed you would note the rarity or absence of all the things you had expected. You would meet surprise after surprise, which would not only delight you at the time but would give you material for endless letters home and for endless stories to tell when you got back. Thus would be built up an increasing tourist traffic, a source of revenue to Ireland itself and to the shipping and tourist companies of the various nations.

You may think such tourists, on coming home, would upset our system of facts-by-definition about Ireland. Not if that system is once thoroughly established. Consider in that relation the Greek pronouncement that at any time of year it becomes colder the farther North you go. North America is in language and civilization a homogeneous country in which one might think knowledge would therefore spread rapidly, and in which Atlanta, Richmond, New York and Montreal are and have been for a century large and well-known cities that are by observation about equally hot in July. Yet there is even today practically unanimous adherence in all these cities to the Greek definition ("the farther North the colder at any time of year") and each city believes those farther South to be hotter and those farther North to be colder, though thousands of travelers for a hundred years have found it to be uniformly otherwise. The ostrich with his head in the sand has survived two thousand years and is still going strong. No human being can retain oil, but the hypothetical Eskimo drinks it by the flagon in our books and belief and is none the worse for it. Then why should not all the world forever believe that every Irishman has a pig under his bed? All parties would benefit. It would be only the hypothetical Irishman that has the pig and we could by hypothesis arrange that he should thoroughly enjoy it. The real Irishman would get the benefit of the increased tourist trade and surely he ought to be grateful. The tourist would make facile discovery of the non-existence of the pig; that would please him and interest all his friends forever after as a sort of occult knowledge, like knowing privately that Indian fakirs are really no more clever than our conjurers, a pleasing secret now possessed and highly valued by many without detriment to the fakirs or to those who prefer to say they have seen them do marvels. Thus would everyone be the gainer.

V

It is obvious we could proceed along these lines to the development of a whole new system of thought and education. But we pause satisfied with having presented the germ of the idea. Once the point of view is attained, we feel sure the plan will develop in the reader's mind into a coherent philosophy helpful in solving the most difficult problems.

THE TWO TAFTS

BY CHARLES WILLIS THOMPSON

We have two Tafts, dear,
Two, and yet the same.—ROBERT BUCHANAN
forty years later.

IF WE hadn't, there would be no amiable Chief Justice expanding under the glow of newspaper approval, or, at worst, no more derided than other members of the Federal bench; there would be only the blundering politician who was hurled out of office by the greatest revolt his party had ever known, one that must have consoled the souls of Grant and even Blaine. The queer thing is that all his life Taft had wanted to be a judge, not a politician. Well, circumstances, in the form of Republican votes, as he himself would say, for he has a sense of humor and is honest with himself, decided that his ambition should be fulfilled at last, and there he is on the bench. If ever, on dull days, he hankers secretly for the fleshpots of politics, then he blunders again, for in politics Taft was ever all thumbs.

Taft the blunderer! It seems a strange epitaph for a President and Chief Justice of the United States; yet it is true, at least, of the politician and tells the story of his fall. The energy in him, that made him survive it, was of the judicial kind—and let no man doubt that there *is* judicial energy! Judicial history, in fact, is full of fists pounded on the table, including the Taft fist, which struck a table on the other side of which sat Medill McCormick. In nearly every case the pounding was a blunder, and meant the oversetting of the court, the judge, or, in the long run, the nation; but it must be observed that in the Taft-McCormick case the blow fell after Taft had left the bench and before he re-turned to it. Therefore, as a blunder, it belongs, like all Taft's blunders, to the political phase of him, not to the judicial. It was merely another proof of his essential sagacity when he used to say, "It's good of you, Theodore, but I'd rather be a judge." It would be going too far, perhaps, to say that that fist-pounding in 1909 turned the Middle West into the Democratic column in 1910 and elected Wilson in 1912, because no one thing did that; but the blunder which it symbolized did the trick, and more too. For example, it set Hiram Johnson at Coolidge's heels today.

In the era of his historic blunders Secretary and President Taft was a fat man; today, treading the primrose majority path of the Supreme Court he is only the size of every tall man. There was always something that gave promise of that reduction. He was never gross, even when he weighed three hundred pounds. He was always light on his feet; he liked to dance, and the girls said with surprise that he was a lovely waltzer; you did not hear the sound of his coming, as you did the sound of Billy Mason's. His pet amusement was skipping around the country in automobiles and Pullmans and off it in ships. Now he is no longer fat—not nearly so fat, indeed, as most other men of his height. But since Error dies only gradually, paragraphers and editorial writers will go on until the end of time, or of Taft, describing him as a second Daniel Lambert, just as they used to ascribe Roosevelt's misdeeds to the enthusiasm of youth long after he had joined, as he phrased it, the grandfather class.

315

II

But about those blunders, the celebrated blunders of the political Taft. First, it should be explained that politics was thrust upon him as an Ohio boy and the son of a man so deep plunged in the science as to be himself a Cabinet Minister, Judge Lorenzo Taft. Lanky and yet fat, young William Howard was mixing in politics before he was of age, and even encountered the majesty of the law for dealing pugilistically with a hostile partisan who made unseemly remarks about Judge Lorenzo. (He got out of it, they say, because the committing magistrate was of the Taft faction.) The judge interrogated the youth concerning his ambitions, and found to his sorrow that they lay toward the law rather than toward politics. Some minor judgeships therefore came his way, but in Ohio a judgeship is ever intricately mixed with politics, and so the two Tafts in one just naturally couldn't help running along together.

But gradually the judicial Taft came uppermost, and the judicial Taft, as judges go among us, is a good one—maybe no John Marshall, but that kind of talk tires me. There has been just one John Marshall in the whole world in the last hundred and fifty years. Those who know not what they speak of talk grandly of the dead days of Marshall, Story, Chase, and Kent, apparently unaware that those giants belonged to different eras and places, that Story's greatest fame was won elsewhere than on the Supreme Bench, that Kent is chiefly remembered in his capacity as a State judge, that Marshall was a builder of the Union and that Taney, whom it is heresy to mention at all, was the only other early judge actually in his class. Who knows that Chase was the anonymous plotter whom Drinkwater introduces in his play of "Abraham Lincoln" under an assumed name? Taft is as good a Chief Justice as the last decades have seen, for they are decades that have not required the talents of a Marshall any more than they have required the talents of a Samuel Adams or a Jefferson.

So, it being seen that Taft was a good judge, he was sent out to the Philippines, where he governed apparently wisely. His duties were quasi-judicial, and he came home with much kudos and became Secretary of War. In that office he also won kudos by doing just what the President, Roosevelt by name, wanted him to do. It is curious that both Roosevelt and Wilson used to require their Cabinets to do just what they, the Presidents, wanted; and that T. R.'s Cabinets used to find great joy in the same—even such dissimilar characters as John Hay, a second Van Bibber, and James R. Garfield, a John Drew in real life—whereas almost all the members of Wilson's Cabinets made mouths over it and mainly resigned, from Crown Prince Mc-Adoo to Garrison and Lansing. It wasn't because Wilson wanted them to do anything disgraceful, either. If Roosevelt had asked them they would probably have done it.

The rest of our hero's history is an open book. In opening it people generally point to the fact that when he ran for re-election in 1912 he carried but two States, Utah and Vermont. Considering that the American public was off on one of its periodical and unreasoning jaunts of hate that Autumn, I regard this as quite an achievement, and should be disposed to compliment Utah and Vermont if it were not that the Mormon machine and not reason pulled Utah through and that it's a capital offense to vote a third party ticket in Vermont. People elsewhere used language about Taft in that campaign that they would have been ashamed to use about the man who shot Petrosino. After the election some of them noticed that after all he was a human being, and said so. This led some newspapers to say that there was a visible reaction in favor of Taft. I was in New Haven during the following Spring, 1913, and mentioned this to Taft himself, with the design of cheering him up.

"Well," said he, with that sterling sense

which ever characterizes him when he is out of office, "you may have noticed that some 350,000 upright Republicans voted for me, even though I did run third. Now, Thompson, whenever I hear that somebody is visibly reacting toward me, I have a suspicion, I know not whence it comes, that the speaker is simply one of that upright and intelligent 350,000."

And as the same thought had passed through my own mind pianissimo before I spoke, I forebore to deny him; the more as he wore a judicial look, and pulled the cat's tail.

III

That general dislike of Taft, which seems so queer a thing when we look back upon it, and which was nowhere so strong as in his own party, rested upon the fact that "he cannot ope his mouth but out there flies a blunder." Often his blunders in those days were not blunders *per se*, but only blunders for a President. For instance, toward the close of his term a reporter asked him, as he got off his train somewhere, what would be the end or outlook of the labor situation, troubled then as now. Mechanically the President answered, as anybody but a President might have answered, "God knows!" This was the champion blunder of his administration. It flew over the United States, was reiterated and twisted, and became the text for a thousand indignant speeches. Yet anyone else might have said it without raising a ripple—save perhaps of approval. Perhaps, now that he is Chief Justice, Taft himself could say it with impunity. But it was one of the obvious, indiscreet things that a President just must *not* say.

He never could learn this difference between a President and a private person. He was for the Payne-Aldrich tariff bill, no doubt because it came from that wing of the party with which he had always been identified. This was bad enough, since the other wing was going to be in control of the party in the next congressional and presidential elections. But that was not

enough for Taft. The Payne-Aldrich tariff muddle was especially unpopular in the Middle West, but the disfavor with which the Middle West regarded it was applause compared with the sentiments which it engendered in the Northwest, and the Northwest might almost be counted as favorable to it compared with the sentiments it inspired in Minnesota. Speaking in favor of it was one of the few things for which a man might legally be lynched there, and the particular town in the State which disliked it most was Winona. Consequently, with unerring skill, when Taft went on his speaking tour in 1909, he chose Winona as the place in which to deliver his eulogy of it. The reaction throughout Minnesota, the Northwest, the Middle West and the United States came in the form of a reverberating roar. The Rocky Mountains stood on their heads, the Great Lakes turned inside out, and the Sierras danced like the hills of Scripture. Even the National Committee saw that something must be done, and so it hastily advised the President to say something that would calm the mountains down and restore the Mississippi to its bed. Taft hurriedly said it; and what do you think he said? What might have been expected. He said he had "dashed off the Winona speech hurriedly between stations!"

Now, you or I might say that, but the President of the United States is supposed to think thunderously, and his utterances are reckoned as revelations of God. Wilson loosed his "too proud to fight" aphorism in a moment of exaltation before he came to realize that fact. The greatness of Roosevelt largely consisted in the fact that although he appeared to speak impulsively, he actually never uttered a word publicly without having before him a mental vision of how it would look in type. "Makes up his speeches between stations, does he?" yelled the infuriated populace. "Is that the sort of President we've got? We've made up our minds how to vote!"

When Roosevelt started after his scalp

in 1912, Taft at first refused to take the stump against him. But as State after State loped into the Roosevelt camp, honking and tom-tomming—and he carried every one in which there was a presidential primary—the urging of Taft's friends led him finally to defend himself, and he fell upon the job. But he felt that such an unusual procedure on the part of a President needed explanation, and so, according to his nature, he gave the worst possible one. "Even a rat will fight when driven into a corner," he said, gloomily—and thus went the last chance he had of getting even a look-in in any presidential primary State! All the Republicans who could vote voted for Roosevelt, save only that gnarled knot up in Wisconsin which LaFollette never takes out of his pocket.

But how did Roosevelt happen to be against Taft? That was some more of Taft's statesmanship. The Lord, to save him, should have created him mute. Roosevelt had made Taft President. The convention which started the business wanted to renominate Roosevelt himself, and so did the party. For a year before the convention Roosevelt was engaged in strangling the Roosevelters. Whenever he heard that a State boss, such as John G. Capers of South Carolina, or Cecil A. Lyon of Texas, was going to bring a Roosevelt delegation to the convention, he would send for that misguided chief and say to him, "Let your delegation be for Taft, Cassio, or never more be officer of mine!" It was a bound and gagged convention, with Roosevelt's friend, Henry Cabot Lodge, running it— Lodge was at the end of a telegraph wire; the other end ran into the White House. At the White House end stood William J. Lee, the quickest telegraph operator in Washington. It was his duty to let Roosevelt know when the stampeders tried to put him over and to take Roosevelt's reply, which was to be an unconditional declination. Lodge was to read it. But Lodge worked the game without recourse to this device. When the Jonathan Bourne rooters started a stampede for Roosevelt, Lodge

began calling the alphabetical roll of delegates. Under cover of the uproar the latter voted for Taft inaudibly, and Georgia was being called before the Roosevelt rooters discovered what was going on. They stopped then, and Taft was nominated.

Having thus crushed all opposition and nominated Taft, Roosevelt carried him through the campaign and got him a majority up to that time unprecedented. After the election Roosevelt expected a word of thanks. He got it, somewhat in this form: "I owe a great deal to you, Theodore, and I want to take this opportunity of saying so." Proper expression by Roosevelt. "Yes," continued Taft, "in thinking over the whole campaign, I am bound to say that I owe more to you than to almost anybody else, *except my brother Charley.*"

I do not mean to say that this astonishing remark alone was what made Roosevelt go off to the Potomac meadows and bite his teeth till the blood came, but it was what started it. The finish was put on the business by what happened to Roosevelt's friends, especially Gifford Pinchot, after Taft was in office. Pinchot hurried across the ocean when Roosevelt emerged from Africa to be the first to tell him of all the things that had befallen Garfield, Loeb, and every other statesman whom Roosevelt had specially recommended. Roosevelt, who at that time still did not want to be nominated again, responded vigorously by announcing that he was a strong supporter of Governor Hughes. The rest is history. Taft was hurt and grieved. He did not know then, and probably does not know now, what he had done to break the friendship of a man whom he highly esteemed and, in his way, almost loved. Nor does he know that, human nature being what it is, nine men out of ten would have done exactly what Roosevelt did, though it may be a fact to be regretted.

IV

Practically all of Taft's bitter experiences in office were thus largely of his unconscious making. He was a good President at the wrong time. He was a far better President than McKinley, Harrison or Hayes, and in the eighties or nineties, where he belonged, he would have been reckoned an intelligent Progressive. As a judge his only fault is one which he shares with the majority of the Federal Bench: he believes a little too strongly in the existing order. It used to be said of District Attorney Jerome that he was a splendid prosecuting officer, except that his mind could not take in the idea that a rich man had done anything wrong. As a President, Taft showed something of the same fault. His pardon of Charles W. Morse, based on pleas and arguments that would never have deceived Roosevelt or Coolidge and might not even have deceived Harding, Wilson or McKinley, is a case in point. He fell too easily for such arguments; it was his blind side. On the bench he shows less of it, and certainly seeks to be impartial, though it

is possible to detect evidences of the old Adam still. It is, indeed, natural that his mind should unconsciously make him favor the old order, just as Justice Brandeis' mind unconsciously puts him in the position of a questioner.

He is thoroughly upright; in fact, the man who would question his honor would be laughed at. Even as a politician he always played square. But he should have gone on the bench early in life and stayed there. His incurable tendency to blunder ruined him as a politician. But, at worst, that tendency injured mainly himself. His blunders were disastrous only to Taft and the Republican Party, which needed a drubbing; whereas Wilson's blunders were disastrous to the United States, to Europe, and to remote communities not yet heard of. Taft's blunders are mainly forgotten. Wilson's will never cease to reverberate until the Resurrection morn.

MANSFIELD PARK AND AMERICA

BY ARTHUR BINGHAM WALKLEY

THE Clarendon Press at Oxford has lately done a fine thing. It has published a great edition of Jane Austen's novels, compared with which all other editions are naught but leather and prunella. The British Museum, old Directories of Bath—as Bath was a good quarter of a century before Mr. Pickwick and Sam Weller rediscovered it—Guides to the Ball-room, carriage-builders' catalogues, and even an early illustrated copy of Mrs. Inchbald's "Lover's Vows," have been ransacked for contemporary prints, fashion-plates and maps to elucidate the text. That text, hitherto remarkably corrupt, has been collated, emended and conjecturally reconstructed by the Clarendon editor, Mr. R. W. Chapman, with the ingenuity of a Bentley restoring the digamma to Homer or of a Verrall restoring common sense to Euripides. In short, an English classical author has at length been honored with an edition which is at once scholarly and, like Frank Churchill's letter to his stepmother, "handsome."

No doubt, these facts will leave what it is the fashion to call with fulsome flattery the English-speaking world comparatively cold. What, in the name of the Bodleian, asked Mr. Augustine Birrell, has the general public to do with literature? But there are Austenites, I suppose, in both hemispheres. Now that Howells is dead, how many are left in America? I hope my question, coming from an Englishman, is not impertinent. I know that there issue from American universities many learned monographs—diploma-pieces, they seem generally to be, theses or exercises for a degree—on far more rec-

ondite English topics than Jane Austen—for example, Coventry mystery plays, minor Caroline poets and the like. And I see that Mr. Harvey Eagleson, of Stanford University, has furnished the Clarendon editor with a tip about "Northanger Abbey." So there, at any rate, is one.

That there were fervent Austenites in America in our grandfathers' generation is clearly established by a letter (printed in "A Memoir of Jane Austen," by her nephew, J. B. Austen Leigh, 1869) to her brother, Sir Francis Austen, from Miss Quincey, "care of the Hon. Mr. Josiah Quincey, Boston, Massachusetts," asking for his sister's autograph, and dated January 6, 1852. "The influence of her genius," wrote Miss Quincey, "is extensively recognized in the American Republic, even by the highest judicial authorities. The late Mr. Chief Justice Marshall, of the Supreme Court of the United States, and his associate, Mr. Justice Story, highly estimated Miss Austen, and to them we owe our introduction to her society. For many years her talents have brightened our daily path, and her name and those of her characters are familiar to us as 'household words.'"

I have no warrant for supposing that the present generation has fallen from grace; indeed, I imagine (writing from a distance, one must speak with caution) that intellectual curiosity in the United States is keener and more catholic than ever. But this is a matter rather of tradition. Somehow, I mentally picture the tribe of Austenites, always "werry fierce," always thirsting for one another's blood over the choice between "Pride and Prejudice," and

"Persuasion" or the relative positions in the comic scale of Mr. Collins and Aunt Norris—I picture this savage tribe more readily in our British woad and skins than in moccasins and feather-dress. I can no more conceive an American reader getting excited about Highbury and Box Hill and Kingston market than I can myself about Appomattox or Old Point Comfort.

The fact is, Jane Austen was one of the most insular of English authors. She was as thorough a stay-at-home as Shakespeare, and her imagination never traveled further from Chawton in Hampshire than Bath or Exeter, on the one hand, and London on the other. That is one of her charms for us today: that she kept so still, that she contemplated only what was under her nose, that her color was so purely local. After all, it was not easy for a spinster lady of limited means to move about in those days. With the bad roads and the difficult traveling, the country towns and villages were far more self-centered than they are now, the squire and the parson more important figures in them, local gossip more violent from confinement, flirting with the militia officers a more regular employment. And where Miss Austen lived, the people of her novels must needs live also. "You are now collecting your people delightfully," she writes to a niece essaying a novel. "Three or four families in a country village is the very thing to work on." It must be as strange for an American to read about the people thus collected in an out-of-the-way village in Hampshire as it is for an Englishman to read about the people in Main Street.

Nor do I think that Miss Austen's mind had any sympathy with the democratic ideal. She was by temperament, like perhaps nine women out of ten, a devotée of the established order, and the established order, as she knew it, was uncompromisingly aristocratic. It was, to tell the truth, so far as home affairs were concerned, a rather dreary period in English history. For it was the period of blind reaction against the French Revolution, the Eldonine period, with its harsh penal laws, its bigoted worship of the *status quo*, its unawakened Church, its unreformed Parliament, its rigid class distinctions. That Miss Austen found this state of thing "all werry capital" I do not assert, but assuredly she never permitted herself to criticize it. Social etiquette in those days forbade ladies to talk politics. It is laid down in "Persuasion" that the concern of the ladies in a country family is restricted to housekeeping, neighbors, dress, dancing and music. In "Northanger Abbey" Henry Tilney's "short disquisition on the state of the nation" was received by the ladies in silence.

With politics, then, tabooed, we shall not be surprised to find that Jane Austen's novels make no comment on international affairs. She never mentions Nelson or Trafalgar (though she had two brothers in the navy) or Bonaparte, though she can record with minute accuracy the real names of a purveyor in High Street, Portsmouth, and a jeweler in Sackville Street, Piccadilly. The more important in world-history anything was, the less she was likely to notice it. It would have been natural, then, for her to ignore the vast continent of North America.

Yet she does mention America, just once, and in a very odd way. It was at the Bertrams' impromptu dance in Chapter XII of "Mansfield Park." Tom Bertram had drawn near Fanny Price, but, it seemed, to talk rather than to dance:

When he had told of his horse, he took a newspaper from the table, and looking over it said in a languid way, "If you want to dance, Fanny, I will stand up with you"—with more than equal civility the offer was declined;—she did not wish to dance. "I am glad of it," said he in a much brisker tone, and throwing down the newspaper again—"for I am tired to death. I only wonder how the good people can keep it up so long. They had need be *all* in love, to find any amusement in such folly—and so they are, I fancy. If you look at them, you may see they are so many couples of lovers—all but Yates and Mrs. Grant—and, between ourselves, she, poor woman, must want a lover as much as any one of them. A desperate dull life hers must be with the doctor," making a sly face as he spoke towards the chair of the latter, who proving, however, to be close at his elbow, made so instantaneous a change of expression and subject necessary, as Fanny, in spite of everything, could hardly help laughing at. "A strange business, this in America, Dr. Grant! What is your opinion? I always come to you to know what I am to think of public matters."

This is what Homeric commentators would call a remarkable *hapax legomenon*. Jane Austen's single reference to America is in a question hastily invented to hide what had been really said. No doubt Tom Bertram had seen the "strange business" mentioned in the newspaper he had just been looking at.

Now what was this strange business in America? The answer to this question would settle the "dramatic" date of the story of "Mansfield Park." ("Mansfield Park" was actually written between February, 1811, and June, 1813.) I turn for guidance to the Clarendon Editor's note, and what do I find? "It is probably hopeless to seek to identify the 'strange business' in America. Many strange things happened in those years." I call this a shabby evasion of responsibility. It was, surely, the editor's business to seek—or, at least, to compile a list of *all* the strange things that happened in America in those years. I am all the more vexed because I find myself unable to mention *anything*, strange or ordinary, that happened about that time in America. I have a vague idea that there was some little war on then between England and the United States about heavens knows what—I say a little war, because it must have been that by comparison with the big war with Bonaparte that England had on her hands in Europe. I remember a charming neighbor at a dinner some years ago in Washington, who first informed me about that little war; but she emphatically protested against the suggestion that it could have been, even by comparison, little; it was about the biggest and most important war, she held, in the history of the world, and what is more, the British were vanquished in it— "whipped," if I remember rightly, was her own word. She may have mentioned the date of this black page in English

history but, if so, I have forgotten it.

I apologized to her—as I apologize here to the readers of THE AMERICAN MERCURY —for my deplorable ignorance. It is all the fault of our English school-teaching of history; you go through a "period" and then you find yourself next term in another form, which is at an entirely different period; and you may never make up the gap. My gap, unfortunately, occurred in the period, early Nineteenth Century of American history, and these are omissions that can never be repaired in after-life. I can only guess how many Presidents of the United States there were between George Washington and Abraham Lincoln; I never knew their names. I missed them by being moved from the upper fifth to the sixth form. I daresay many American schoolboys have dropped some of their English Kings in much the same way, and I can only hope they were the bad ones. Such is our modern so-called education! *Pauvre et triste humanité!* But it was just as bad in Miss Austen's day, or even worse. The Misses Bertram, daughters to Sir Thomas Bertram, Bart., of Mansfield Park, had only learned their chronological order of the Roman Emperors as low as Severus.

Here then, is a very pretty problem for the American reader. What happened in America in either of the years 1811-12 that the son of an English country squire would be likely to remark upon as a "strange business" and about which it would be natural for him to ask the local parson's opinion? As it was a matter about which there could be two opinions, it can hardly have been an incident in the war—nor is it one of these "whippings" of the English which seemed to give my fair neighbor at Washington so much retrospective satisfaction. More likely, it was a political incident; but it must have had international bearings, for an incident of purely domestic American politics could hardly have interested either English squire's son or parson. I hope that an authoritative solution of the problem will be forthcoming, and communicated to the Editor of the Clarendon Press Jane Austen.

CLINICAL NOTES

BY GEORGE JEAN NATHAN AND H. L. MENCKEN

Give a Dog, Etc.—The moony college professors and hard-headed political shysters who now run what was formerly the Austrian crownland of Bohemia performed a very evil service for that fair land when they changed its name to Czecho-Slovakia. At one stroke they disposed of all the romantic associations that had hung around the old name for centuries. Bohemia, like Italy, was a name that slipped softly from the tongue, and left a pleasant flavor behind it; to its charm, indeed, far more than to any actual merit in the Bohemians, was due the good repute of the country. Nor was it charming only in English; the German and Swedish Böhmen, the French la Bohème, the Italian Boemia, the Dutch Bohemen and the Danish Böhmen were also charming, and so were the names for the Bohemian: Böhme, Böhmare, Bohemièn, Boemo, Bohemer and Böhmer, not to forget the Spanish Bohemo. Now he is a Czech—a word as foul and unlovely as any of the little four-letter Anglo-Saxon monosyllables that never get into respectable English dictionaries. A Czech, God help us!—and Bohemia is Czecho-Slovakia—in German Tschechoslowakei; in French something still worse! Who could admire a Czech, or dream sentimentally of Czecho-Slovakia? As well admire a Lett or a Serb, or dream of Harrisburg, Pa.

Criticism, Again.—It is one of the defects of the critical biology that criticism seeks to account for everything in the work of an artist, to plumb it thoroughly, estimate it and reason it out. In this, criticism often over-reaches itself. There are things in the work of the true artist, of the man of genius, that he himself cannot account for and reason out, that appear in his work unconsciously, bafflingly, without meditated cause, and they are often the finest things in that work. What is the human soul? No critic knows. What are certain of those elements that comprise the soul of a work of art? No critic can tell. It is not the duty of criticism futilely to explore such mysteries; it is the duty of criticism merely to announce them and venerate them.

Nostalgia.—If it be a crime, then lead me to jail: the fact remains that I long for the gaudy diversion of another war, and hope that it is not too long delayed. The last one provided a show that was precisely to my somewhat florid taste; I emerged from it profoundly thankful to Providence for letting me serve my term in the world in such an era—the most astounding and amusing since that of the Crusades. Now, on rainy days, I find myself pining for its incomparable entertainment. I long for the black, Gothic headlines on the front pages; for the romantic *communiques* of the French General Staff; for the photographs of German lieutenants feeding Belgian infants into sausage-machines; for the daily bulls and ukases of the eloquent Woodrow, with their uplifting, lascivious phrases; for the speeches by Charlie Schwab on America's cultural debt to France; for the subtle, Italian statecraft of the Hon. William Jennings Bryan; for the great days in War Babies on the curb; for the feverish manufacture of elliptical and rhomboidal shells for the poor Russians; for the yells for help from the sweating Motherland; for the heroic effort of T. R.

323

to horn into it by fair means or foul; for the tramp, tramp, tramp of scared clerks in Preparedness parades; for the daily bulletins from Plattsburg; for the majestic patriotic passion of Wall Street. I long for the draft and the struggle to get out of it; for the spy hunt and the slacker hunt; for the butchery of the Constitution by Palmer, Burleson and the Supreme Court; for the Liberty Loan drives and the wholesale blackmailing of stenographers, bookkeepers, waiters, yokels; for the gals collecting for the Red Cross; for the rush of consecrated men to enlist in the Y. M. C. A.; for the concentration of dollar-a-year men at Washington, within easy reach of the Treasury; for the patriotic effort of union labor to get a fair share of the loot; for the speeches of the three-minute men in movie parlors; for the thrilling bulletins of the Creel Press Bureau; for the romantic anecdotes about Joffre, Foch, Pershing; for the desperate struggle to save the conscripts from the scarlet woman; for the first dismayed days of Prohibition; for the war speeches of the Rev. Dr. Newell Dwight Hillis, the Rev. Dr. Henry van Dyke and the rest of the superior clergy; for the departure of the troop-ships; for the enchanting dawn of the Ku Klux Klan, 100% Americanism and the American Legion; for the bawdy stories that came back from France; for the endless French military commissions in their charming uniforms, and the growth of uneasy suspicions among American husbands; for the official movies showing the Kaiser made up as Desperate Desmond and the Crown Prince as a cannibal; for the editorials in the New York *Tribune* and the Russian news of the New York *Times;* for the heroic effort to canonize Woodrow and shove him into the Trinity; for the endeavor of the Senate to get a copy of the Treaty of Versailles from J. P. Morgan & Company; for the chance to pick up Liberty Bonds at 82; for the crash of drums, cymbals and *Blasmusik,* and one band playing "The Star-Spangled Banner" after another; for the first

alarms about Debs, the I. W. W. and the Bolsheviki; for the rush to build wooden ships, and the $20 a day jobs in the shipyards; for the attempt to put down Hearst; for the pleas of Otto Kahn, Adolph Ochs, Henry Morgenthau and Rabbi Stephen S. Wise for Anglo-Saxon unity; for the bellicosity of the Liberals; for the stampede of parlor Socialists to take the pledge and get under the table; for the high old time that the Aframerican doughboys had among the ladies of France; for the tall talk about self-determination, saving the world for democracy, breaking the heart of humanity; for the airship contracts and the $800,-000,000 that vanished; for the scares about ground glass in bread, strychnine in dill pickles and wireless plants in the halls of *Gesangvereine;* for Barney Baruch, "Hell and Maria" Dawes, Josephus Daniels, Lansing, Admiral Sims, Crown Prince McAdoo, Sergeant York, Newt Baker and all the other heroes of the time, now mainly forgotten; for—

But the list must have an end, though it is really endless. Those were happy, electric days—the dullest of them better than circus day, even than hanging day. I enjoyed them vastly. They sent me to bed in a glow and got me up in the morning with all the eager expectancy of a schoolboy entering a Museum of Anatomy. I say frankly that I hope they will return. I long to see the American Legion, bonus in pocket, marching off to another war.

A Score for the Comstocks.—The Comstocks are at least justified in their contention that the sincerity of an author means nothing if his book is, in their eyes, actionable. Morals aside, the much talked of sincerity of the artist is, as they rightly hold, very largely bosh. The most sincere American author of the last two years against whom the Comstocks proceeded produced a piece of work which, disregarding its morals, was third-rate stuff. The least sincere American author of the last two years against whom they proceeded produced a piece of work which, again disregarding its morals, was absolutely first-rate. It is further worthy of note that an all-righteous and accurately critical God let the Comstocks get the better of the sincere third-rater and let the insincere first-rater get the better of the Comstocks.

The Tolerance of Age.—The tolerance of age, as opposed to the intolerance of youth, has its genesis less in the experience and maturity of the mind than in a keen sense of age's diminished personal qualities. Youth is sure of itself; it is sure of its strength, its beauty, its ability to tweak the world by the nose, its romantic devil-may-care heart. Age, with its increased wisdom, knows that these rare attributes are no longer its own proud possession. Its tolerance is thus less sympathy for other men than sympathy for itself. It is tolerant because it is mistrustful of itself, and a trifle afraid longer to risk intolerance. Only the strong may be intolerant. Tolerance is a product of the self-perceived inferiority complex of the weak. And age, for all the power of its mind, is weak in all those things that form in combination the basis of the vanity of mortal man.

The Banker and the Artist.—Surely not the least of the numerous metropolitan drolleries is the spectacle frequently provided by the vainglory of those Wall Street bankers who take it upon themselves to invade gatherings of artists and speak their little pieces for the latters' delectation. There is hardly a public meeting, exhibition or banquet of artists that does not vouchsafe the juicy tableau of one banker or another making an address on a subject he understands nothing about to men of a species apart from himself about whom he similarly understands nothing. Artists are artists and bankers are bankers and never the twain shall meet. Yet these bankers not a little impertinently seek to push into a class to which they do not belong and cannot by virtue of lack of

aesthetic sensitiveness and perception ever belong. Invite a banker to speak to an assemblage of artists and he will jump to accept before the envelope is half open. Invite an artist to speak before an assemblage of bankers and he would let out a horselaugh that could be heard a mile away.

Studies in Boobology: A Survey of Current National Advertising Campaigns. First Series.—

1. Would you like to win the confidence, love, obedience and respect of your child? You can! Remember—no cost—no obligation—simply sign and mail the coupon below.—*Parents Association, Pleasant Hill, Ohio.*

2. No matter what your own particular difficulties are—poor memory, mind wandering, indecision, timidity, nervousness or lack of personality—Pelmanism will show you the way to overcome them. "Scientific Mind Training" is absolutely free. Simply fill out the coupon and mail it today. It costs you nothing, it obligates you to nothing, but it is absolutely sure to show you the way to success and happiness.—*Pelman Institute of America, 2575 Broadway, New York City.*

3. How to acquire a winning personality. How to become a clear, accurate thinker. How to be the master of any situation. Mail this free coupon. Send no money.—*North American Institute, 3601 Michigan Avenue, Chicago, Ill.*

4. How would you like to be a lawyer? To plead cases in court, handle big estates, occupy a position of importance in social, business and public affairs? You can—in two years—through our improved method in teaching by mail.—*American School, Drexel Avenue and 58th Street, Chicago, Ill.*

5. The power of Creative Thought is yours if you want it. This wonderful power can be yours. Send in the Free Lesson coupon today.—*Federal Institute of Psychology, 111 Federal Schools Building, Minneapolis, Minn.*

6. An evening with the greatest orator America has ever known will reveal to you how easily you can acquire a masterly,

persuasive and convincing manner of speaking English—the power of holding interest and making others see things your way. The first ten minutes spent with Col. Robert Ingersoll have convinced thousands how amazingly easy it is to acquire a poised, well-styled way of talking and an elegant polished flow of words. Can you persuade people to do what you want them to do? Do you know the secret of having your speech burn with feeling, flame with conviction? This great Master of Eloquence reveals to you how the magic power of thrilling with words is nothing more or less than a simple knack which is easily acquired. With the power of words, of eloquence, of force, of conviction, of persuasion, at your command, nothing is impossible for you—there is no position, either socially or commercially, that is beyond your reach. Can you afford to be without the works of this great Master? It is not necessary to send a penny in advance. Mail this free coupon now, at once.—*The Ingersoll Publishers, Inc., 3 West 29th Street, New York City.*

7. Want to overcome illness and poverty? You can do it! Send 10 cents for copy of "How to Go Into the Silence," which tells how to use Auto-Suggestion and get the most out of life.—*The Elizabeth Towne Co., Inc., Holyoke, Mass.*

8. Hobart Bradstreet Reveals His Method of Staying Young. The Man Who Declines to Grow Old. Here is his secret: *he keeps his spine a half-inch longer than it ordinarily would measure!* With all sincerity, he says nothing in the whole realm of medicine or specialism can quicker remake, rejuvenate and restore one. It costs nothing to try it. Fill out the coupon now.—*Hobart Bradstreet, 630 S. Wabash Avenue, Chicago, Ill.*

The Nordic Dolichocephalic.—After reading attentively and in trembling the works of Dr. Madison Grant, Dr. Gertrude Atherton, Dr. Lothrop Stoddard and all the other eloquent proponents of the thesis that the dolichocephalic or long-headed Nordic blond is the only truly human variety of *Homo sapiens* and that the brachycephalic or broad-headed Mediterranean, with his vague smears of Ethiopian blood, is a menace to the Constitution, Protestant Christianity and the American germ-plasm—after putting in two months with such terrifying literature, I happened to take down the volume of the *American Anthropologist* for 1898 and found therein, on page 347, the following startling words by Prof. Aleš Hrdlička, M.D., Sc.D., curator of physical anthropology in the National Museum at Washington, secretary of the committee on anthropology of the National Research Council, and member of a dozen learned societies at home and abroad:

> A pure American colored child almost always shows a pronounced dolichocephaly, while the normal white American child will show every variation from a markedly long head to a pronounced brachycephaly.

Epitaph.—To the Woodrow Wilson Foundation and the Roosevelt Memorial Association, Inc., each fertile in publicity for its promoters and offering comfortable jobs to their press-agents, now add the Harding Memorial Association. Just what this last proposes to do I don't know. Erect an equestrian statue of the Martyr in Marion, Ohio? Place hand-painted oil paintings of him in all the far-flung halls of the Benevolent and Protective Order of Elks? Endow a Brigadier General Charles E. Sawyer chair of homeopathy in the Johns Hopkins Medical School? I only hope that it is something bizarre and spectacular, something to arrest the attention and heat up the veneration of the plain people. Otherwise the late gentleman, twenty-ninth President of the United States, threatens to be forgotten before the ivy is green on his tomb. Already, he begins to seem as remote and vague as Garrett A. Hobart, Allen G. Thurman or Gum-Shoe Bill Stone.

At this moment, indeed, his funeral orgies remain more clearly in mind than any act of his own life. Certainly no man ever passed into the Eternal Vacuum to the tune of more delirious rhetoric. The Associated Press dispatches, printed in all the newspapers during the ghastly progress of the funeral train through that double file of village mayors, newspaper photographers, scared school children and anonymous morons, were not merely eloquent; they were lyrical, maudlin, heart-breaking. They gurgled; they snuffled; they choked and moaned. Who wrote them I don't know; if I did, I'd hire him as Obituary Editor of THE AMERICAN MERCURY, with the rank of archdeacon. I forthwith nominate him for the Pulitzer Prize. A supreme master of bilge. But probably not a very good prophet.

For I can see no evidence whatever for his thesis, maintained *fortissimo* every day while the train rolled on, that Dr. Harding was of immortal calibre, and will go down into history as one of the heroes of *Homo boobiens* in this land of the free. The simple fact is that *Homo boobiens* seemed to take very little interest in him until he fell ill and died, and that even then that interest was rather in his florid obsequies than in the man himself. The vulgar knocked off work, they went out to the railroad yards, they put pennies on the track to be run over by the fatal car, and that was about all. What was there in him, indeed, to set *Homo boobiens* a-frenzy? After Wilson, he seemed almost tongue-tied. After Roosevelt, he seemed only half alive. From first to last, indeed, he was an obscure man, even as President. No great and alarming Cause issued from his fancy. He invented no new and superior Bugaboo. Only once did he ever say anything that attracted attention, and then, I fear, he was laughed at. No one hated him, but no one worshiped him. Even the plain people, I believe, like to find something brilliant in their heroes. Dr. Harding was simply an amiable hand-shaker, a worthy fellow in his Sunday clothes, an estimable noble of the Mystic Shrine.

The editorial writers of the land, apparently unable to acquiesce in the theory of his greatness that lifted the Associated Press to its impassioned *vers libre*, fell back upon lavish praises of his honesty, as if honesty were rare in Presidents. The selection of this quality, it seems to me, was somewhat unfortunate. As a man, no doubt, Mr. Harding was the soul of honesty, as he was unquestionably the soul of amiability, but when one turns from the man to the politician it quickly becomes obvious that the definition of the term has to be humanely modified. I here allude obliquely to the chief plank in the platform upon which he was preparing to stand for re-election—the plank, to wit, declaring boldly and unequivocally for the Eighteenth Amendment. Is it maintained by anyone that Mr. Harding, personally, was a Prohibitionist by conviction and practice? If so, then it is maintained only by the sort of half-wits who still believe that the Kaiser started the war.

Nay, it was not a frank and candid man who stood on this plank—not even, indeed, a good actor. It was simply a politician of a depressingly familiar and dismaying species. The World Court scheme, I daresay, had sincerer conviction in it, but unluckily it was devoid of sense. The more one read and pondered the speeches in which it was set forth, the more hopelessly one searched for the substance beneath the words. Only a Chautauqua audience, long accustomed to the subtlest varieties of logomachy, could grasp the vision. The practical politicians of the Republican party found it too vague and so it got itself quietly shelved, to remain forgotten until Dr. Coolidge took it down again. First place was then taken by Prohibition, an old ghost in a new falseface. There was nothing else. The news that prosperity had been restored found the farmers plastered with mortgages and sending all sorts of preposterous dervishes from the Bad Lands to Washington. The foreign policy of the Feather Duster had irritated and disgusted both allies and foes, and piled up fresh enmities in Russia and Latin America. No war loot had been recovered; taxes had not been reduced; Daugherty still smelled like a tannery.

The wonder is, indeed, that a man so vastly lacking in the most elemental force and originality, a man so pathetically unfitted for the appallingly serious business that confronts the head of a great state, should ever have become President. It was, true enough, largely an accident, but nevertheless it was an accident that certainly did not do much violence to the ordinary political probabilities. The same machinery may throw up another such pale and incoherent Cæsar, and one, indeed, much worse. And, having thrown him up, it may keep him in office eight years, while things drift on to confusion worse and worse confounded, and the public policy of a great and puissant land is reduced to a mere series of empty phrases.

The gradual extension of democracy, by the direct primary, the widening of the franchise and other such devices will probably make it quite impossible, in the long run, for any man of genuine capacity, and particularly for any man of genuine dignity, to get into the White House. Only two varieties of statesmen will be in the running: first, unconscionable demagogues of the Roosevelt kidney, eager to embrace any buncombe that will inflame the proletariat, and secondly, inarticulate vacuums of the Harding-Coolidge type, too poor in ideas to be capable of arousing any serious opposition. Experience will prove that the latter are the safer, at least in ordinary times, and so it is likely that they will tend to be elevated oftener than the former. At the present moment, indeed, each of the great parties is preparing to nominate a safe and sane candidate— that is, a candidate who has never offended anybody, and may be trusted to stick to the same program hereafter. Both are afraid of all their more positive and forthright leaders. Both are especially afraid of such of their leaders as are obviously most competent by nature and experience to be head of the state, and most likely to discharge the office with courage and sagacity.

That the late lamented gentleman belonged to the second of these classes must be plain to everyone. He received the Republican nomination because all the more robust aspirants within his party had fought one another to a dogfall—because the need was manifest, if the expected victory was to be won, to agree upon a candidate who had no passions, no ideas and no enemies. And he was elected because the plain people were tired of a President from whom ideas radiated like quills from the fretful porcupine—because they were tired of being instructed and exhorted, and longed only for the return to normalcy that was promised them. The phrase pained grammarians, but it made votes.

Normalcy duly returned, but it was a stranger in a world no longer normal. Vigorous leadership, with some touch of bold imagination in it, was needed to reorient the nation, and disentangle it from its difficulties within and without. But instead of this vigorous leadership there appeared only a somewhat bewildered willingness, a great but ineffective diligence, an engaging urbanity that got nowhere—in brief, only the talents of a faithful bookkeeper or suburban clergyman. A few expenditures were cut off, but taxes remained high. The wicked were threatened, but continued to flourish. An idea was borrowed from a long-haired prophet out of the desert, got itself mellowed by hard-boiled men behind the door, and developed in the end ˙into an international entanglement that may one day bring down a national disaster.

Such was the reign of the Hon. Warren G. Harding, of Marion, Ohio. It slides into the shades with the reigns of Millard G. Fillmore, Franklin Pierce, Benjamin Harrison. It will probably mark, in the histories, a transition between the old traditions that blew up in 1917, and the new ways that none of us, today, knows the direction of. . . . The Associated Press professor of bathos had it that the deceased was done to death by overwork—a martyr to the complex and cruel demands of his high office. Perhaps. It was no place for an amiable and easy-going man, loving friendly contacts and a casual habit. But that he was engaged upon the duties of his high office at the moment he collapsed is certainly not an historical fact. He had actually put off the duties of his high office, and was engaged violently upon a canvass for renomination and re-election.

Form.—Too much emphasis, it seems to me, is laid by the critics upon form. Perfection of form is hardly the sine qua non of fine art. The old dime novel had almost perfect form; Joseph Conrad has none, or at best very little, in the currently accepted sense. Great art is often as formless as inferior art is sleek in form.

Reflections of a Bachelor of Forty.—1. Lucky the woman who can conceal her greatest and most secret defect from her rival.

2. It is not man's tragedy that his body grows old, but that his mind does. The arteries of happiness inevitably harden with the years. Wisdom and experience never yet have brought back the happiness of youth.

3. For a reason I have never been able to make out, General George B. McClellan has always seemed to me to be one of the most romantic figures of the Civil War.

4. When a man looks at a photograph of himself as a little boy, he sees there less himself than one who seems his own child.

Artistic Triumphs.—"It has taken me three years and it has cost $1,500,000, but I have at last succeeded in screening the masterpiece of my life!" said the great movie director.

"It has taken me three years and it has cost me my eyesight, but I have at last succeeded in engraving the entire Lord's Prayer on the head of a pin!" said the hermit of the Pyrenees.

From the Waste-Basket of a Critic.—1. It is significant that no New Englander has ever been able to write a beautiful love story.

2. The English artist is much more sensitive to criticism than the American. With negligible exception, the Englishman is extremely touchy when criticism steps upon his toes. Equally with negligible exception, the American gives the impression of not caring a continental.

3. Criticism in America has always suffered from ward politics.

4. Great art consists in the effort to express as completely as possible an inexpressible emotion.

The Greenwich Village Ball.—A ball is commonly accepted to be a large party devoted to dancing—but not any longer by anyone who has been to one in Greenwich Village. A ball in Greenwich Village is devoted solely and entirely to watching one young man baste another young man in the nose for venturing the opinion that former young man's green necktie is blue when the former young man insists that it is a rich maroon, to keeping one's self from being pushed headlong down the flight of stairs by the two excited officers of the law stationed on the job for the express purpose of seeing to it that no one is pushed headlong down the flight of stairs, and to hypnotizing one's imagination into believing that Miss Selma Goldfarb, stenographer in the Paramount Underwear Knitting Mills who is dressed up in pink and yellow cheesecloth, is Cleopatra of the Nile.

In the flush of the season, there is a ball in Greenwich Village almost every night. Whenever a couple of young men in the Village have to get the money to pay their rent right away or be booted out into the street, they borrow a few dollars from one of the waiters over at the Brevoort, have circulars printed on gilt paper announcing "The Gala Fête of the Nymphs and Satyrs," persuade some friendly newspaper reporter to print a piece saying that the whole "Follies" chorus will be on deck in the nude, and then lay back until the boobs duly appear on the scene at three dollars the boob. During the last month exactly nineteen balls have been held in Greenwich Village at which the whole "Follies" chorus was billed to appear in birthday clothes and at which the only person connected with the "Follies" who showed up even once was Florenz Ziegfeld fully dressed.

The gayety of the usual ball takes place on the dance floor. The gayety of a Greenwich Village ball is confined entirely to the advance advertising matter. This advance advertising matter is rich in deviltry and sin. There is never a plain ball in Greenwich Village. It is always "A Bacchanalian Revel of Lost Souls," "A Paphian Carousal of Imps and Demons," "A Saturnalia of the Sylphs of Satan," or "A Royal Carnival of the Priests and Priestesses of Passion." A perusal of the assemblages at these Revels, Carousals, Saturnalias and Carnivals would seem to indicate that the dismaying lost souls, imps and demons, sylphs of Satan and priests and priestesses of Passion bear an uncanny and disturbing resemblance to the nice boys and girls who work out in the packing rooms of one's own business offices. Yon bold and sinister sheik, for example, is surely Maxie Wanz, one's faithful office boy—surely one's own Maxie for all his false moustachios, his encircling bed-spread and his Aunt Mathilda's nightcap, while yon seductive Lorelei, for all her enveloping tennis net that passeth for a fishing net and her brother Gustav's cane with a pocket flash tied to the top (thus transformed into a magic wand), is surely none other than the estimable Miss Louella Dingle who, with her no less estimable mother, runs the Wee Winkle Tea Room around the corner in Tenth Street. Yet these, true enough, do not constitute the entire population of this sink of glamorous carmine sin. Yon ferocious hundred and twenty pound cave-man in tiger-skin is seen, upon coming closer, to be none other than Eustace Sprudel, the Greenwich Village poet who achieved undying fame in Greenwich Village a few years ago

by getting a poem, after years of assiduous devotion to his art, into *Snappy Stories*, while yon resplendent Don Juan with the two days' growth of beard is identified to one as the celebrity of the Village whose peculiar genius consists in fashioning ukeleles out of old cigar boxes and spittoons. Mingling with this gay crowd is a sprinkling of suckers from uptown, each nicked for an extra dollar for not appearing in costume. In this group one observes half a dozen cockeyed stock-brokers who have bought tickets in the fond hope of seeing the advance advertising matter come true and who sneak out considerably disgruntled when one o'clock comes around and the girls still have everything on but their nose powder, together with eight or ten college boys, more or less elegantly inebriated, who spend the evening trying to persuade the drummer to let them take his place in the orchestra, and two respectable dowagers who have come down with the fashionable young Willie Stuyvesant Hopfmüller to see the sights and who, after being razzed in turn by a number of the more stewed lost souls, sylphs of Satan and priests and priestesses of Passion, manage to sidle out of the door and make a bee-line for the Club Trocadero.

At many of these gala debauches, a prize is offered for the most beautiful girl present. The committee of award, it is generally set forth in the advance announcements, will consist of Charles Dana Gibson, Harrison Fisher and Penryhn Stanlaws, "who will judge the winner according to the strictest artistic standards." The committee of award, on the night of the ball, is more usually discovered to consist of one of the young men who are floating the ball, some stray but sufficiently well-dressed soak who has wandered into the ball and loudly announced himself to be Anatole France, and some lesser comic cartoonist from one of the New York newspapers who has been sent a free ticket and who has boredly dropped in on his way home to have a look at the shindig. From the looks of the last eight or nine hundred girls who have been awarded the beauty prize, it is evident that the voice and ballot of the comic cartoonist carry the most weight.

It is customarily announced that the prize-winning beauty will be awarded, in addition to the Crown of Beauty, one thousand dollars in gold, a leading rôle in George White's "Scandals," a painting of herself by the leading portrait painter of Italy, a free round-trip to Palm Beach, the entire front page of the New York Sunday *Times*' rotogravure section, a Rolls-Royce automobile, and a white Russian wolfhound with her name in full inscribed on the ruby-studded collar. Up to date, unless my private corps of statisticians is in grievous error, the most lavish prize that one of the winners of one of these beauty contests has received has been a ten cent celluloid badge inscribed with the words: "The Greatest Beauty in the World," supplemented with a copy of the circular announcing that the winner of the contest would get, in addition to the Crown of Beauty, one thousand dollars in gold, a leading rôle in George White's "Scandals," a painting of herself by the leading portrait painter of Italy, a free round-trip to Palm Beach, the entire front page of the New York Sunday *Times*' rotogravure section, a Rolls-Royce automobile, and a white Russian wolfhound with her name in full inscribed on the ruby-studded collar.

A leading feature of the Greenwich Village balls is the "pageant." Like the balls themselves, these pageants bear very flossy names. When they are not called "The Pageant of the Eunuchs and Courtesans of Ancient Egyptium" or something of the kind, they bear some such Macdougal-Alley-French title as "La Pageant Royale et Superbe des Demoiselles de la Maison D'Or." But whatever their names, the pageants are always the same.

They usually begin at twelve o'clock midnight. The band lets loose a flourish and through the door at the upper end of the floor bounds a fat young man clad in a cerise union suit, brandishing aloft a gilded broom handle, and yclept Apollo. Apollo waves the gilded broomstick in the air thrice and in a Robert B. Mantell voice summons forth from the shadows of the past the shades of Rameses, Agamemnon, Buddha, Madame de Maintenon, Du Barry and Lucrezia Borgia. The band now goes into a spooky tune and out come three male Greenwich Villagers in colored B.V.D.'s and three Village girls in white cheesecloth with green sashes of the same material. These are, respectively, Rameses, Agamemnon and Buddha, and Madame de Maintenon, Du Barry and Lucrezia Borgia. The sextet kneels on the floor, the boys facing the girls, and each section bows three times to the other. Then they struggle to their feet, join hands and do ring-around-a-rosy. This finished, Apollo again brandishes aloft his gilded broom handle and proclaims the rise of the Nubian moon. The band starts up a march, which with acute relevance to a "Pageant Royale et Superbe des Demoiselles de la Maison D'Or" usually turns out to be Sousa's "High School Cadets." Through the door now mosey forth in pairs about thirty or forty young men and women variously arrayed in homemade nondescripts representing individually everything from Mutt and Jeff to Titus Andronicus and from a Swedish peasant girl to Fannie Brice and representing collectively —if somewhat cryptically to the two sober persons out of the several hundred visitors present—the Demoiselles de la Maison D'Or. The parade marches around the floor twice, after which all the participants in it face the band, fall on their knees, lift up their hands to the ceiling and bend themselves in at the middle five or six times, chanting the meanwhile: "Allah, Allah, great is Allah!" Thus ends La Pageant Royale et Superbe.

The ball itself generally ends at half-past two with most of the men present trying to find out whothehell stole their overcoats.

PORTRAIT OF AN OLD MOTHER

BY ALICE MARY KIMBALL

I USED to wonder how divorces and murders could happen to law-abiding,
church-going folks with electric lights
in their nice, white houses, and holly-
hocks in their front yards, and money in
the bank—
Now—O God—I know!
An awful disgrace may happen to us this
morning—to us, the Stovers and the
Pillsburys, the oldest families in this
township and the best thought of.
I feel sudden death in the air like the smell
of a poison lily,
I feel divorce and suicide and the breaking
up of a loving family going through the
house in terrible red waves,
It goes in dizzy red waves like the waves
of thick heat on an August day.
O Lord, I've nothing to blame myself for!
That thought is a cup of cold water in the
midst of torment.
I brought Lucy up to be a good woman.
Why, she'd sooner hold her two hands
in the fire till they burned off than do
the things that Hawley girl has done!
I never talked to her of that which shouldn't
be spoken of.
She never kissed any man but the one she
was engaged to and married.
Her mind was a piece of blank paper when
she went to the altar!

II

That lovely wedding
When she walked down the aisle and prom-
ised to love and obey Lee Stover!
I can see her now—her long veil, her hair
like a shiny halo round the head of the
Virgin Mary,

Eyes that was modest blue posies looking
up at the sun—
The organ playing—the scent of the orange blossoms we'd sent away for—
And everybody buzzing about what a well-
behaved girl she'd always been, and saying "What a handsome couple!" and
"How nice that the groom has a steady,
well-paid job!" and talking of the wedding presents and the new oak parlor
set,
The sweet alto voice of Mrs. Doctor Busbee
singing "Oh, Promise Me!"
And I—the bride's mother—
Wiping my eyes, knowing I'd done my
duty.
I'd brought up Lucy innocent. I'd kept her
mind from evil things.

III

Fanchette Hawley! That half-French drab!
The Jezebel!
If I could have my way I'd drive her out,
Yes, if she starved and had to sleep in
gutters!
Oh, I knew when I came
To stay and help while Lucy had her baby
Just what *she* was—an adder
Glittering and coiling—lying in wait!
If I am sixty-nine, she didn't fool me—
I'd like to choke her dead. 'Twouldn't be
murder,
Killing a husband-stealer wouldn't be
murder!

IV

When she asked Lee to take her in his car
To Boonton Hills to pick some cherry
boughs

332

I saw the thoughts that crawled and squirmed behind her eyes.
I said: "I'll have my say," and so I says:
"Decent, self-respecting hired girls
Don't carry on with married men as you do,
Don't pull their eyebrows out or wear short hair
All frizzled like the insides of a mattress,
Don't wear silk stockings rolled below their knees so'st you can't tell where stocking ends and knee begins;
And those that sport bronze pumps to scrub the porch in
Ain't likely to be better than they'd ought to.
You might as well write love-letters to Lee
As cook for him the brazen way you're doing,
Courting him with maple cakes and custard pies,
And salads as immoral and outspoken as the mating-call of a low animal,
And his poor wife lying helpless in the hospital
With her week-old baby!"
She gave an uppish toss of the red hat she'd spent her last week's wages for,
And a saucy switch of the silk skirt that cost her a month of hard work,
And spit this out:
"Poor Lucy! I guess she ain't so bad off!
She's had Lee some time, ain't she? She's got little Emmy and Buddy and the new baby, hasn't she?
She's been kept soft and safe. She's had her living made for her and her hard work done for her,
She's had her new electric to drive, hasn't she?
Well, what about *me*, Mrs. Pillsbury?
Did that God you're always praying to make the world for married women?
Do you know there's ten girls to one man in Peacham Village?
And all the decent men are married and them that ain't are sticks?
And I ain't going to scrub and cook all day and lie awake nights half-crazy with lonesomeness,

Spring here—and them damn frogs a-hollering in the swamp!

"Look here, Mrs. Pillsbury,
I guess Lee has earned a spell off, what with sticking to the business day and night,
Nothing doing for excitement in this dead town,
Lucy melting out of shape over the children like a blob of butter on a hot day!

"Listen, Mrs. Pillsbury,
Peacham is full of old maids. God! I hate
Their squawking voices and dried-apple skins
The crabbed souls blinking out of their dull eyes!
And I ain't going to be one of them. Now smoke that in your pipe!"

V

It knocked me flat! That I should live to hear such talk
Out of a woman's lips! When Lee brought the car 'round
I tried to show him there'd be talk and scandal.
He said that I was old
And there was things I couldn't understand,
And they drove off. The May night swallowed them,
A treacherous night, it was,
With smell of apple-blossoms in the air,
And farmers' orchards on the far-off hills like small white handkerchiefs spread on bright grass,
There was a sky green as a gooseberry and a moon like a thin piece of pie,
Gold light acrost the fields and thrushes singing,
There shouldn't be such nights. They lead to sin.

VI

O God, this morning—
A month after that evening of wrongdoing—

Eight years after that sweet June wedding in the First Congregational Church,

There was Lee bent double over the wheel of his little speed car and racing up and down the road as though the devil was driving him. He stopped at the edge of the town dump where the selectmen ought to have put a high iron fence years ago. I saw him looking over the edge. He drove by slow and then came back, zipping along, a black streak, like a man possessed. He teetered along the edge. I shut my eyes and prayed. But he didn't kill himself after all. He came in to breakfast. His face was white and his eyes was bloodshot and I heard him mumbling: "I'm finished, too, and I belong down there. I belong there."

There was Lucy lying on the bed like a blessed angel of Heaven. Poor, poor dear, she doesn't know yet. There are things that can't be sensed by a woman that's been brought up as I brought Lucy up. Her yellow head was propped up on the pillows and Emmy and Buddy was gathered around her to take a peek at the new mite of a baby just back from the hospital—

There was Fanchette Hawley sulking in her room, and throwing things on the floor, and saying she was going to take carbolic acid because her appendicitis was worse—

Lord, she knows 'tain't no appendicitis, and I know, and Lee knows.

VII

I feel sudden death in the air like the smell of a poison lily,

I feel murder and suicide and the breaking up of a loving family going through the house in terrible red waves,

It goes in red waves like the waves of thick heat on a dizzy August day—

It is as real as the kitchen stove—

And I've had to get breakfast and find the leak in the ice-box and pick a chicken for dinner and get a sliver out of little Emmy's toe so'st she could go to school,

Mr. Babbitt, the vegetable man, poked his head through the door and said he had nice, fresh rhubarb this morning at twenty cents a mess,

The superintendent of the Sunday-school 'phoned in that the next lesson would be on Noah and the Flood,

Mrs. Hiram Bugbee, regent of the D. A. R., dropped in to say that the Daughters would go in automobiles to Butternut Centre next week a-Tuesday to present a silver spoon to old Mrs. Hiram Dodder, whose great-great-grandfather was a colonel in the Revolutionary War,

And the feeling of sudden death hangs in the air like the smell of a poison lily . . .

O God, I've nothing to blame myself for! I brought up my daughter to be a good woman!

BYRON IN AMERICA

BY SAMUEL C. CHEW

A HUNDRED years ago the news of Byron's heroic death at Missolonghi caused a sensation in America, as in Europe. Of that sensation there have come down to us records abundant and diverse, from the elegies which were printed in the poets' corners of obscure newspapers to the formal estimates which appeared in the influential reviews. As in England, France and Germany, the tributes in verse to the dead poet were almost innumerable; and the burden of all was similar. The poets were moved to their depths by the passing of a nobleman who was both a poet and a republican, for, as one elegist declared,

Though far from his home and his country he died,
Yet the loud voice of Freedom has hallowed his tomb.

There were not wanting, of course, moralists to pass harsh strictures upon Byron's career, but they seldom ventured to express their opinions in verse. To give a list of their forgotten diatribes would be pedantry worse than useless; two specimens will suffice. In 1824 there appeared in New York an "Inquiry into the Moral Character of Lord Byron" by one James W. Simmons. Glimmering through the mass of tedious philosophizing which makes up this tract there appears a ray of charitable understanding of the poet's nature, a tendency to condone his faults. But the author of the "Inquiry" passed unwitting judgment upon his own work, for one page is brightened by the remark: "It is the supreme consolation of Dulness to volunteer its strictures upon Genius." A year later a scathing attack upon Byron's memory was published in the *Atlantic Monthly;* and this anonymous onslaught was thought by someone in London to be worthy of republication in book-form. The English edition (1826) is entitled: "A Review of the Character and Writings of Lord Byron." The writer of a new preface assures us that "the poetical career of Byron is here traced by the hand of a master" and tells us that the book is an answer to "the ingenious and elaborate apologies which have been offered for [Byron's] aberrations and the specious glosses which have been drawn over his sentiments."

In American pulpits Byron's career was used as a text for denunciations of the atheist and libertine, the seducer of women and blasphemer of the Most High; and the estimable Lyman Beecher publicly expressed his regret that the poet had not come under his own particular surveillance and been led thereby to salvation. For a generation the press and pulpit continued to discuss Byron, and so spread knowledge of him and stimulated interest in his poetry. Though Bayard Taylor and a few others showed some appreciation of the greatness of Shelley and Keats, the literary history of America affords no parallel to the phenomenon which took place in England during the forties and fifties — the gradual usurpation of Byron's place by the posthumous renown of his two younger contemporaries. It was not till the sixties that Byronism in the Republic began to yield to the psychological subtleties of Robert Browning and the suave elegance of Alfred Lord Tennyson.

335

II

Byron admired America—or thought he did; perhaps what he really admired was American admiration of himself and his poetry. Of such regard he had abundant evidence. As early as 1813 the sight of an American reprint of "English Bards" gave him, as he said, "a kind of posthumous feel"; and in later years more fulsome transatlantic tributes inspired the sensation of "talking with Posterity on the other side of the Styx." In 1821, during his sojourn at Ravenna, he was visited by a young Bostonian, a Mr. Coolidge, who told the poet that he had bought in Rome a replica of Thorwaldsen's famous bust. "I confess," says Byron, "I was more flattered by this . . . than if they had decreed me a statue in the Paris Pantheon. I would not pay the price of a Thorwaldsen bust for any human head and shoulders, except Napoleon's or my children's, or some absurd womankind's." But he feared that his admirer from Massachusetts (who was, it would seem, his name to the contrary notwithstanding, a romantic, enthusiastic young man) was disappointed in him, finding him perhaps too much the man of the world, too little the inspired Bard. "I can never get people to understand," he explains, "that poetry is the expression of excited passion, and that there is no such thing as a life of passion any more than a continuous earthquake. Besides who would ever *shave* themselves in such a state?" One wonders whether the Thorwaldsen bust still exists among the lares and penates of the Coolidge clan.

A mere replica would not content the metropolitan admirers of the poet; and when, in 1822, a certain Mr. Bruen of New York asked Byron, on behalf of a group of compatriots, to sit for his portrait to the celebrated American artist, Benjamin West, the poet was flattered, and though he had "resolved to sit for no more such vanities," he consented, holding that this sign of popularity oversea was, as he told John Murray, "some compensation for your English native brutality, so fully displayed this year . . . to its brightest extent." He received various American visitors during these years. To George Bancroft, who brought him good tidings of his renown in Germany, he presented an autographed copy of "Don Juan" which afterwards passed into the Lenox collection. While he was at Genoa in 1822 an American naval squadron came into the harbor and he was invited on board the flag-ship. Byron's comment is that he was "received with the greatest kindness, and rather too much ceremony"—evidence of the antiquity of our national habit of too lavishly entertaining foreign literary celebrities. Byron records further that a lady from Philadelphia (whose name has not come down to us) "took a rose which I wore, from me, and said that she wished to send something which I had about me to America." He closes the incident at this point; but from Bancroft we learn that the following day the poet sent her "a charming note and a copy of 'Outlines to Faust' " (doubtless the famous series by Moritz Retzsch).

Americans were gratified by the noble poet's republicanism; they seem to have been unaware of the obvious fact that he wore his tri-color cockade with a difference. "Yes," Byron seems to say, "we are all brothers; but—ahem!—would you mind sitting a bit further down the table?" For he was no social "leveller" (to employ a word now passed from our vocabulary). Yet his political republicanism was sincere, and his hearty detestation of tyrants, foreign or domestic, dynastic or parvenu, led him to turn his gaze towards the New World. To the end of his life he remained of two minds towards Napoleon, in whom the elements of greatness were confused by cruelty and ambition, but he let his "weary eye" repose with satisfaction upon the modern Cincinnatus who

Bequeathed the name of Washington
To make men blush there was but one.

In "Don Juan" he declares that Washington's battle-fields, like those of Leonidas, are holy ground, for they "breathe of nations saved, not worlds undone." And his magniloquent "Ode to Venice" is redeemed from the commonplace by the concluding tribute to the land

> Whose vigorous offspring by dividing ocean
> Are kept apart and nursed in the devotion
> Of Freedom, which their fathers fought for, and
> Bequeathed—a heritage of heart and hand,
> And proud distinction from each other land. . . .
> Still one great clime, in full and free defiance,
> Yet rears her crest, unconquered and sublime,
> Above the far Atlantic!

Moved by the lethargic despair in which Italy lay (and to which Leopardi was then giving immortal expression), Byron declares that rather than exist where life creeps lazily along or rests in stagnation it were better to lie "in the proud charnel of Thermopylae" or to add "one freeman, more, America, to thee."—And then, presently, someone sends him an abusive American review of his poems; and repudiating these magnificent sentiments he turns with a characteristic gesture upon himself, saying, "In future I will compliment nothing but Canada, and desert to the English."

In 1822 and 1823, dispirited by the death of Shelley, bored by his blonde mistress, and conscious of the fact that his connection with Leigh Hunt had made him appear "low" in the eyes of Englishmen of the "better" sort, aware, indeed, that he was somewhat out-moded at home, Byron wished to leave Italy. There was some thought of emigrating westward; his idea was, however, to go not to the United States but to Bolivar's country. "I have many years had transatlantic projects of settlement," he writes to a friend. "I am told that land is very cheap there; but though I have no great disposable funds to vest in such purchases, yet my income . . . would be sufficient in any country (except England) for all the comforts of life, and for most of its luxuries. . . . As I do not go there to speculate, but to settle, without any views but those of independence and the enjoyment of the common civil rights, I should presume such an arrival would not be unwelcome." And he adds: "I speak of *South* America, recollect."

In Spanish-America, indeed, he might have been not far from content, for his temperament and way of life were Latin rather than Anglo-Saxon; and the cheerfulness with which, during both his visits to the Near East, he bore hardships, danger, squalor, and squabbling companions is warrant for the belief that he would have made no contemptible frontiersman, by no means requiring "all the comforts of life and most of its luxuries." For all its echoes of Rousseau, sincerity is patent in the well-known passage of "Don Juan" in which Byron describes the life of Daniel Boone. Boone had health, and long life, and children tall and fleet of foot. Crime, a stranger to solitude, came not near him; and when men followed in his tracks it was a simple matter to move further on, "where there were fewer houses and more ease." In contrast to this life of the frontier Byron points to war, pestilence, and despotism—"the sweet consequence of large society."

In the Kentucky of a century ago Byron might have been reasonably happy, finding in the rough and homely duties of daily life that "something craggy to break his mind upon" which in Italy he could find only in the study of Armenian grammar. In Kentucky—yes; but imagine the poet in the towns of the eastern seaboard: in Boston, not yet risen to intellectual pre-eminence; in Philadelphia, home of the most prosperous literary coterie; in New York, which was just beginning to contest Philadelphia's claim as the centre of culture! A giant among jealous dwarfs; a gorgeous exotic bird among blinking owls and chattering jays; a genius among literary *canaille;* Byron hobnobbing with Bryant and Freneau, and finding in Fitz-Greene Halleck his one sympathetic companion! Poe's martyrdom points the lesson.

III

Byronism appeared in America at an early date and struck root in the rank romantic soil, and was still flourishing long after it had withered in England and had become a weedy subterranean growth in France and Germany. Our older public libraries shelter, on high unfrequented shelves, a multitude of early off-shoots of Byron's poetry. Of most of them it is safe to say that if they are examined once every hundred years, on the occasion of Byron's centenaries, the conscientious critic will have done his duty by them. Knowledge of a certain monograph will lighten the critic's labors. In his early academic career, burdened with the necessity to produce a dissertation for the doctorate, an American poet of our own time, William Ellery Leonard, devoted himself to the lucubrations of the American Byronists, and spread them out in his thesis, "Byron and Byronism in America." I draw freely upon this fairly agreeable specimen of a disagreeable literary species; but I shall add some notes on a few productions that escaped inclusion in Mr. Leonard's catalogue.

In 1811, at a time when American periodicals borrowed most of their reviews from the English magazines, a twelve-page original notice of "English Bards and Scotch Reviewers" in the *Portfolio* of Philadelphia offered a noteworthy indication of the interest that was being taken in this country in Byron's career, then just opening. The anonymous reviewer was even aware of the fact that his Lordship was then on his travels in the East and he speculated upon the possibility of further encounters with Jeffrey and other foes on the poet's return. Byron, in this article, is spoken of as a disciple of William Gifford, a classification that is not astonishing, for in 1811 "The Baviad" and "The Maeviad" had not yet passed into limbo and the preface to "English Bards" in some measure justified the reviewer. In after years "English Bards" was responsible

for a numerous American progeny, all quite drab and deplorable. Earliest of these was Solyman Brown's satirico-poetic "Essay on American Poetry" (New Haven, 1817). In this work the debt to Byron is implied in a long note on the poet's domestic troubles, and among the minor poems in the volume is one pretending to come from the pen of Lady Byron, who is represented as upbraiding her faithless Lord. Somewhat better than this satire is J. L. Martin's "Native Bards" (Philadelphia, 1831). This attacks the Byronic vogue, then at its height. Among the external manifestations of that vogue were Byronic curls and open collars and lowering looks, all of which the satirist wisely characterizes as "nauseous tricks" that at most can but "deceive some foolish girl." Leave such antics, he counsels, and "go plough your fields." Another imitation, entitled "Reviewers Reviewed," was written by a Miss Ritchie to avenge the slighting reception of her metrical romance, "Pelayo." Romance, reviewers, and review are now all alike forgotten. Still another was L. A. Wilmer's "The Quacks of Helicon" (1841). This virulent and unjust performance has been kept faintly in memory by Poe's notice of it. In a pseudonymous satire called "The Poets and Poetry of America" (1847) imitation yields place to shameless plagiarism of Byron's ideas and tricks of phrase. This, too, is not quite forgotten, for it has been attributed, though probably in jest, to Poe. "Parnassus in Pillory" (1851) is of interest for its recognition of the extent to which contemporary American verse was under obligations to the leading English poets and for its expressions of contempt for the servile genuflections and prostrations which American men of letters executed before their British brothers:

Our country swarms with bards who've crossed the water
And think their native land earth's meanest quarter.

"Parnassus in Philadelphia" (1854) is replete with phrase and allusion and epithet filched from Byron; but the only lines that can attract any reader today are those lamenting the fact that Apollo's throne is no longer reared between the Delaware and the Schuylkill. Ten thousand lyres, the satirist declares, sound in New England, and the South wafts back a kindred song:

> But thou, O Philadelphia! Poesy,
> Though living yet, is almost dead to thee.

So much—it is a dry catalogue—for the offspring of "English Bards." Byron's other formal satires, "Hints from Horace" and "The Age of Bronze," awoke no echo in the United States. Nor did his plays receive the homage of imitation. During the decades which followed his death there were attempts a-plenty to revive the poetic drama upon the stage, but these abortive efforts were inspired by Sheridan Knowles, T. N. Talfourd, and the other "Elizabethanists," and not by Byron. One finds no direct imitation even of "Manfred" and "Cain," for American Byronism was so strangely crossed with pietism that the bold speculations and defiant blasphemies of these formidable protagonists were carefully avoided by the respectable Byronists of New York and Philadelphia. It is along three other lines that Byron's influence shaped itself in the main: Romanticism, with a slender but not insincere thread of Philhellenism interwoven; Melancholy, with just a hint of the cult of Satanism; and Irony, with a dash of Passion, seldom rude enough, however, to raise the blush of shame to the cheek of virginity.

IV

The giaours, corsairs and pirates who infest the Mediterranean of Byron's youthful imagination have their origins deep in the Eighteenth Century cult of the oriental and the exotic; and they have in them something of Rousseau. But they are also own cousins of Scott's barons and outlaws of the Border; and pirates and barons alike owe much to the example of the heroes of Mrs. Radcliffe's romances. It is difficult to separate these elements in the characters of the wild and self-willed heroes imagined by the early American poets. A rough but fairly sound distinction is this: that a plentiful dash of chivalry marks the derivation from Scott; a suggestion of the supernatural points to Mrs. Radcliffe; an inordinate amount of gloom and pride indicates descent from the Noble Poet. Analysis is made harder by the fact that the Republic contributed to the synthesis some native elements, notably the introduction of the Indian chief in place of the corsair or Border hero. Here the influence of Chateaubriand and the French cult of *l'homme sauvage* was at work. Moreover, the gentle pseudo-Byronism of Mrs. Hemans (a poetess immensely popular in this country in her day) combined with an indigenous strain to produce a strange concoction of Byronism and piety, of gloom and edification, of revolt and religiosity. The Byronic hero, American style, however disgracefully he may behave, is apt to leave behind him at home a dear old mother who prays for her wayward son.

At all events, there is plenty of Byronism to be found in our poetry between 1820 and 1860, however much contaminated and diluted. R. H. Dana's "Buccaneer" (1827) is a characteristic mixture of outlawry, diseased egoism, supernatural terror, and praise of the simple life. In the same year Poe began his literary career with "Tamerlane," which in its pride and gloom and remorse owes much to Byron, though through it there runs a vein of mysticism that is foreign to its principal source. In his mature work Poe shook off the influence of the English poet; but in his character and appearance and way of life there remained always certain traits which led people to associate his name with Byron's.

But far more definitely Byronic are the poetry and personality of James G. Percival, much of whose verse is sheer pastiche. His heroes are given to lonely contemplation of their disillusionment. In some of his poems he manages to suggest something of Byron's sense of the sublime in nature, and he has a certain feeling for the grand march of history. Of all the American Byronists, Percival is the one most sincerely touched by Philhellenism; in the case of the others one feels that their sympathy for suffering Greece is but an ephemeral fashion or literary convention, derived from the interventionist movement in London, or, at secondhand, from the strong current of Philhellenism in France and Germany, which so powerfully affected Victor Hugo, Adelbert von Chamisso, and other poets. Percival is representative, too, of those young romantics who fancied that by exposing their bare throats and glooming in dark corners they could ape the author of "Childe Harold." The writer of a series of articles on "American Literature" in the *Athenaeum* for 1835 says that "Percival looks the poet more absolutely than any man we ever saw; it is written on his forehead, and steeped in his eye, and wound about his lips." And his friend Samuel Goodrich thought that he "had been deeply injured —nay ruined by the reading of Byron's works."

This same Goodrich committed Byronism in his narrative poem, "The Outcast," in which Murder, Mystery, Sentiment, Asterisks, and other ingredients of the Byronic recipe are beaten up with Resignation and Piety into a characteristic early American mess, flavored with the theme of "Oh, where is my wandering boy tonight." And N. P. Willis, discarding temporarily the "nattiness" and "jauntiness" for which, through Lowell, we remember him, delivered himself in 1835 of "Melanie," an Italianate tale of an adulterous nun and a bastard brother, written in the manner of "Parisina." The insincerity of the Byronists is here caught *in flagrante dilecto*. The scholarly and (when his political prejudices were not aroused) gentle Bayard

Taylor combined in "Amram's Wooing" the oriental-passionate plot with the soothingly American happy ending. Mrs. E. Anne Lewis was, however, the most prolific of all those purveyors of narrative-romantic Byronism. I have no space to record even the titles of all the poems in which she pilfered from Byron. She was Orientalist, Italianist, Hispanist, Hellenist, and sentimentalist by turns—and all at second-hand. In the poem which has most significance for us she depicts the Indian Chief Kaughnawah, who is none other than our old friend the Byronic hero-villain, daubed with warpaint, festooned with feathers, and brandishing a tomahawk instead of the traditional scimitar. As stage-setting for this redoubtable figure obviously neither Sunium's marble steep nor the shore of an Isle of Greece is available; but Goat Island answers the purpose admirably; and from this spring-board Kaughnawah presently, to the reader's inexpressible relief, precipitates himself into the boiling cataract of Niagara. The European Byronists had no such mass of waters wherein to quench the fire preying upon their heroes' hearts and had perforce to content themselves with the only instruments at hand, the comparatively commonplace poison-vial and concealed dagger. Mrs. Lewis exploited to the full the advantages of her transatlantic situation.

V

The hero-villain of the Byronists presents a forlorn spectacle today. His tin sword is bent and battered; his sombre cloak faded and in shreds; his false moustachios meagre and awry. His ghost, ejected from its pristine poetic haunts, stalked for a while through the pages of the prose romance, gradually going down in the world and finding at last no refuge even within the covers of penny dreadfuls. Of late he has been analyzed and psycho-analyzed. A drop of his blood, perhaps, courses through the veins of Joseph Conrad's Peyrol, that

Brother of the Coast, that "man of dark deeds, but of large heart." But the unaltered and unadulterated Byronic hero-villain is a vanished literary type, dead and done with. Not so Byron himself; when I am told, as occasionally I am told, that "Byron is dead" I reply with the Scotsman: "I'd no bury him just yet—wait till he smells a wee grewsome." For in Byron there is something else than Violence and Crime and Fidelity to an Only Love, something by no means altogether histrionic. The Byronic despair and defiance are among the permanent possessions of the human mind. "Byron," said an anonymous critic some years ago, "sowed the spirit of questioning, and the courage of denial, deep in the hearts of men. . . . He is our deputy-rebel, and he has this advantage, that he speaks not as a croaker in a corner, but, with incomparable strength of utterance, as a man who had seen the kingdoms of the world and their glory." This advantage was not possessed by the paltry versifiers, the "croakers in a corner,"—English, French, German, Spanish, Italian, Polish, Russian, American—who turned the plangent rhetoric of "Childe Harold" into thin wailings or hoarse complaints. It is with a sensation akin to sea-sickness that one hears Willis Gaylord Clark lament that "man sinks down to death, chilled by the touch of time." Nor are we much impressed when Percival sighs—

> Life is made of gloom,
> The fairest scenes are clad in ruin's pall,
> The loveliest pathway leads but to the tomb....
> A moment brightens manhood's Summer ray,
> Then all is rapt in cold and comfortless decay.

Or when youthful Richard Henry Stoddard complains that

> buried hopes no more will bloom
> As in the days of old;
> My youth is lying in the tomb,
> My heart is dead and cold.

Or when the boyish William Winter (who lived to achieve a critical faculty that was exercised more than once upon Byron)

laboriously manufactures such lines as these:

> Pride wastes affection—what is Wisdom's state?
> The soul is void—the heart is desolate.

The extreme of this phase of Byronism meets us in the person of McDonald Clarke, who was, so Mr. Leonard tells us, "Byron-mad, even frontispiecing his works with his own portrait, having side pose, collar and locks almost identical with Byron's, and, save for the somewhat more angular features, hardly to be distinguished from his." There is no virility in the maudlin company. The lachrymosity in which Byron himself, in his weaker moments, indulged is here unrelieved by any touch of revolt. The American Byronists are not numbered among the "souls that dare look the Everlasting in his face and tell him that his evil is not good." They never impugn the Omnipotent. Nay more; there is often treachery in the Byronic camp, for the weapons of the poet's manner are turned to the uses of orthodoxy, as in this stanza:

> Doth gloomy fate with sullen frown
>   Consume thy soul with care?
> Hast thou the draught of misery known,
>   Whose dregs are dark despair?
> Art thou oppressed with sorrow's doom,
>   Thy heart with anguish torn?
> Oh, soon that sad and cheerless gloom
>   Shall make a brighter morn.

VI

But there is a greater Byron than the atrabilious and saturnine romantic who awoke these lugubrious echoes across the ocean. There is the writer of "The Vision of Judgment" and "Don Juan," the supreme satirist and ironist in English verse. It is interesting to observe the impact of "Don Juan," the most sophisticated of poems, upon a singularly unsophisticated society. In my book on "Byron in England" I have published an account of the no less than twenty-nine attempts that have been made to carry on the story of Byron's unfinished poem.

Four of these continuations were by Americans. Of the earlier two I need not speak again here; but upon the others (which are not mentioned in Mr. Leonard's monograph) a paragraph or two may be profitably spent.

In the Library of Congress may be found a stout volume entitled "The Rest of Don Juan" (1846). The author, one Henry Morford, seems to have made a specialty (like Sir Harry Johnston in our own day) of continuing famous works of literature; at any rate he lived long enough to seize the opportunity to write "John Jasper's Secret," one of the many attempts to complete "Edwin Drood." His "Don Juan" is inscribed "To the Shade of Byron"; and a captivating motto furnishes the assurance required by all American readers of the epoch: "If rough talk offend thee, we'll have very little of it." His poem is long—some six hundred and forty-five stanzas divided into seven cantos. The story, setting aside the tedious digressions, is of Juan's departure from England, his wanderings over Europe, and his arrival at Paris in time to witness various episodes of the French Revolution. A sweetheart there, whom he has cast off, murders a wealthy woman whom he is about to marry. The French capital becomes, not unnaturally, distasteful to him, and he returns to his native Seville where he settles down to a life of easy virtue and virtuosity. Dissoluteness is a prelude to dissolution, and one night, at a banquet, a tall dark stranger enters the room and beckons Juan away. The two depart together while the lights burn blue and the guests smell brimstone. On the morrow Juan's body is found in a cemetery. For such an ending Morford found a hint in Byron's poem.

Very different is the "Seventeenth Canto" which the talented and too-early lost Richard Hovey published in his volume, "To the End of the Trail," in 1908. This is one of the most convincing reproductions of the spirit and movement of Byron's verse that I have ever come across. It is supposed to be written by Byron in Hades. The poet refuses to take up the poem at the point at which Death had cut him short.—

Southey's forgotten; so is Castlereagh;
But there are fools and scoundrels still today.

In the sequel we hear nothing of Juan; the satire is expended upon current affairs. Byron is full of curiosity as to events on earth:

I've such a next-day's thirst for information,
I'd even be content to read the *Nation*.

So much for the few American continuations of "Don Juan." Turning now to the imitations of that poem, I note first Fitz-Greene Halleck's once-famous and still fairly readable "Fanny" (1819). Halleck's abilities are not sufficient to cope with the exigencies of the octave and he shortens the stanza to six lines; but he has a good store of deft rimes and he manages the anti-climax, a feature of the genre, amusingly. "Fanny" has been kept in memory by the characterization of it in the "Fables for Critics" as

a pseudo-"Don Juan,"
With the wickedness out that gave salt to the true one.

It is not quite that; for though there was no wickedness in Halleck or in his poem, there is a good deal of salt in the latter, and it is sprinkled with a liberal hand over the fashions and foibles of flashy New York society. But "Fanny" has nothing of Byron's cynicism; such a quality was not to be expected of the man whom Bayard Taylor characterized as "the brave, bright and beautiful growth of a healthy masculine race." Healthy masculine races must pay for their brightness and beauty by the loss of other qualities possessed by less fortunately endowed rivals; Halleck has nothing of Byron's range and profundity.

A quaint production (overlooked by Mr. Leonard) is a long anonymous poem called "The Pilgrimage of Ormond, or Childe Harold in the New World," which was published at Charleston, South Carolina, in 1831. This is a hybrid, for though a continuation of "Childe Harold" and written in Spenserians, the manner is that of "Don Juan." The Childe, thoroughly reformed, visits America and travels widely through the Southern States. His moderately diverting escapades are intermingled with descriptive and meditative passages and with tributes to leading Americans of the epoch.

Charleston engendered also one of the most ardent of the transatlantic Byronists, William Gilmore Simms, who, after pouring out a flood of lyric verse of a quality that betrays its model, gave to the world in 1843 his narrative poem, "Donna Florida." This he had left unfinished in his youth, and by the time that he decided upon publication he had developed doubts about it, and perhaps about Byron; for in a curious apologetic preface he speaks of his boyish presumption in having fancied that he could imitate the grace and felicity of "that unhappy production" (as he calls "Don Juan") "without falling into its licentiousness of utterance and malignity of mood." It was an English poeticule whom Byron had chastized good-naturedly for attempting to be "a sort of moral Me." Simms succeeded in this impossible attempt no better than Barry Cornwall had done.

Byron's more frivolous moods harmonize pretty well with the temperament of Nathaniel Parker Willis, whose "Lady Jane" (1844) had a success in this country surpassed only by "Fanny" and by "Don Juan" itself. Like Simms, Willis has a more definite and unified tale to narrate than Byron had or had wanted; but, unlike Simms, he indulges in long digressions, mostly mildly satiric; and occasionally he ventures into the domain of "high" poetry, only to fall thence into bathos. Greatly daring, he risks an infrequent racy passage, though with proper consideration of the so easily summoned virginal blushes against which our forefathers were constantly on their guard.

Then there is George Lunt's "Julia" (1855), which, like so many of the imitations, combines moods that are independent or differently mingled in the original, and in combining, spoils them. Lunt's satire is painfully feeble; his lyrics excessively mediocre; and when he tries to soar into Childe Harold-ish meditations upon the sadness of life and death's inevitability the result is dreary and depressing in a fashion that Lunt never intended. Yet "Julia" is an instructive performance, for to a fuller extent than any other product of its school it betrays the tendency to blend the Byronic gloom with a bourgeois sentimentality to which by this time Dickens was pointing the way, though to be sure there was no lack of native guides. In Simms and Lunt the tale's the thing, the digressions being few and unimportant. In "Cabiro" (1840-64), by the untiring George Henry Calvert, on the other hand, the narrative element is slim and the deviations have a more intellectual quality than one finds in other imitations or would expect from Calvert. His poem is still worth glancing at, if only for the light it casts upon contemporary American opinion of the English romantic poets. Nor are its passages of social satire altogether contemptible. In W. W. Western's "To Whom It May Concern: A Poem on the Times" Byron's manner and method are put to queer uses, for the poem tells in satiric vein of the authentic adventures of two Confederate officers who passed the blockade and made their way to Liverpool.

VII

In our own troubled and absurd era it has occurred to several writers that in Byron's Bernesque way of envisaging the serious and uncomfortable facts of life there are still weapons of irony and correction. Gilbert Cannan, in England, has attempted to revive the mood in his long epic, "Noël"; but far more successful are the two satiric poems by Gilbert Frankau which, though they do not sustain throughout a uniform level of interest and excellence (a feat which neither Byron nor Pulci, Casti and Berni before him had been equal to), are nevertheless arrestingly clever and full of pungent and penetrating satire and of shrewd observation of the curious phenomena of this sorry world. And here in America, in the midst of the Coolidge régime, a quaint, wise, far-traveled, experienced but not altogether embittered person who hides himself behind the pseudonym of "Autolycus" has very lately published his "epic, comic in intention" entitled "Ulug Beg," an adventurous tale of Turkestan and of Russian and Mohammedan politics in the East. The author's literary debt is gracefully acknowledged in a motto upon the title-page, drawn from "Love's Labor's Lost": "Nay, I have verses, too, I thank Biron."

In Frankau and "Autolycus" there are marks of lineal descent from the greatest of English satiric poets. Their work, indeed, is not unworthy of the illustrious original, howsoever far it falls short of "Don Juan" in the elements that insure an audience among posterity. These latest experimenters in the genre realize, as Byron realized, and make evident, as he made evident, that man

Plays such fantastic tricks before high heaven
As make the angels weep, who with our spleens
Would they themselves laugh mortal.

The splenetic is an element of the Bernesque; therefore those poets laugh. Yet, as Figaro said before Byron and as "Autolycus" might say today, "*Je me presse de rire de tout, de peur d'être obligé d'en pleurer.*"

With no more appropriate quotation, were I given to perorations, could I bring this survey to a close; yet the true moral of my tale lies elsewhere than in the *comédie larmoyante* of humanity. It is a practical one: the lesson derived from the example of the American Byronists is the same that is found in the many failures and half successes with which our national literature is strewn, namely, that the way to greatness in any of the arts lies for us, not in imitation of European models, but in the confident exploitation of the themes and moods and situations that are native to us.

AMERICAN PORTRAITS

II. The Washington Job-Holder

BY HARVEY FERGUSSON

OBSERVE closely the common middle-class American who has neither means nor any special talent, and you will find his life dominated by two desires: for security and for gentility. He yearns to be sure of bed, board and clothing, and he yearns to work sitting down, to wear a white collar, to feel superior to the men who sweat.

These, of course, are characteristics of *Homos sapiens* everywhere, but I believe they are especially marked in the Middle American breed. There is a tradition that restless daring is an American quality, but the reality of it has largely disappeared with the pioneering conditions that gave rise to it. The average American of today is no longer a man tempted by wide freedom and opportunity to bold enterprise. He is, on the contrary, a man whose political liberties have been restricted in every direction, who lives under a peculiarly ruthless economic system, and who is brought up to a hard and narrow social discipline. Most of his old individuality and enterprise have thus been squeezed out of him. He has acquired the longing of the cowed man for mere safety. When he goes hunting for a job, he always asks first, Is it permanent?

This man still believes, of course, in the traditional American freedom that he has lost. Although his government has been long operated by politicians who swindle him for the benefit of property-owners who exploit him, he yet believes with a childlike faith that he lives in a land of political liberty. Although his economic status often closely resembles slavery, he yet holds that America is the land *par excellence* of equal opportunity. Himself generally a snob and living under a complicated and preposterous caste system, he continues nevertheless to hold his faith in the democratic tradition of social equality.

His political liberty and his economic opportunity have become, for the most part, mere national myths, supported by no reality in his actual experience, but he is still able to achieve, at times, the caressing illusion that he is making social progress. Every farm boy and city workman who climbs out of his overalls and into an office job gets the glowing feeling that he has risen from one social class to the next higher, even though he has lost in comfort and well-being by the move. And so the majority of Americans go on aspiring, still with some hope of success, to what they believe to be a more genteel and elevated station in life. The typical common American becomes a man who is timid, cowed, ruthlessly clubbed into submission by his masters, asking above all for safety, and yet one who clings stubbornly to his social pretensions and ambitions. The fact accounts for a great deal in American life. It accounts perfectly for the Federal job-holder—for his characteristics as a man, and for his astonishing increase in numbers.

II

The government job is very nearly the ideal job for the young fellow who wants above all to be sure of an easy living, made in a genteel way. All of the posts under Uncle Sam, except a few held mostly by Negroes, are white collar jobs with high-sounding titles. The salaries are fixed by law and guaranteed by the government. A Federal employé cannot be dismissed except for the rankest kind of incompetence or misconduct, and in case of trouble with his superiors he can always appeal to his Congressman, to the Civil Service Commission or to the Federal Employés' Union. When he is superannuated he draws a pension. His whole life is arranged for him. He has nothing to do but sit down in his swivel chair and wait for death, with light and agreeable work to pass the time while he is waiting.

It is evident that to the bold and enterprising American of tradition and story— the American of Walt Whitman's dream or the typical hero of American popular fiction—a job of that sort would be intolerable. Yet the demand for such jobs grows faster than Congress can manufacture them, and it manufactures thousands of them at every session. And the greatest demand is for the lowliest jobs. There are always long waiting lists of common clerks, but the few positions that require skill and training are sometimes hard to fill.

Few Americans are aware of the rate at which this horde of job-holders has grown, is growing, and will continue to grow, unless checked by some unprecedented and inconceivable act of God. The records of the Civil Service Commission show that in 1821 there were 8,211 civilian employés on the government rolls. The population of the United States was then about 9,000,000, which meant about 3,500,000 persons gainfully employed. There was thus one Federal civil employé, approximately, for every 425 Americans gainfully employed. In March, 1923, there were 504,778 civilian employés on the Federal roster. Calculating in the same way, this means that one out of every seventy-five American breadwinners had a hoof in the Federal trough. It means that the army of job-holders had grown five times as fast as the population.

The population is growing more and more slowly, as each successive census, reveals, but the army of job-holders is increasing at a steadily accelerating rate. If both grow for the next hundred years at the same relative rates as in the past, there will be about 40,000,000 names on the Federal pay-roll a century hence, and one out of every twelve American wage-earners will have a government job. The roll has grown, not naturally, but by a series of rapid expansions, each of which involved stretching the Constitution to permit the founding of new bureaux. Every one of these bureaux began as a small office having from two to a dozen employés. But by a law which almost never fails to operate, each has grown until it now gives employment to dozens, hundreds, and in some instances thousands of job-holders.

The first additions to the simple governmental machine of the Fathers were the Interior Department and the Department of Agriculture, established under the constitutional power of the Federal government to promote industry and agriculture. They began as one-man or two-man offices. They grew quickly and each began to throw off branches. The second stage began with the era of government regulation of industry. The Interstate Commerce Commission was the first and remains a typical product of that movement. It began with less than a dozen employés and now has nearly two thousand. Its chief work has been the physical valuation of the railroads, upon which it has been engaged since 1917. This work is now generally conceded to be futile—but it has provided a thousand or more patriots with good livings for years.

The third stage in the expansion of the bureaucracy was begun by the brilliant political invention of the half-and-half plan, whereby the Federal government appropriates funds to be spent in States which raise an amount equal to the Federal allotment. By this ingenious device, which has just begun to work, the

Federal government has gone into road-building, vocational education, the care of infants and expectant mothers, and teaching housewives how to can beans, and has added many thousands of deserving incompetents to the Federal pay-roll. The fourth and last stage in the process now apparently impends. It will consist in the actual operation of industry by the government. Government ownership of railroads already looms ahead, and a project for the government manufacture and sale of fertilizer has strong support in both Houses. The Norris-Sinclair bill provides that the Federal government shall undertake the sale and exportation of food. The demand for the government operation of coal-mines is well known.

Obviously, all this shows a steady drift toward the most passionate variety of state Socialism. Yet no major party in the United States has ever specifically advocated Socialism. On the contrary, all of our politicians have declaimed against it, and the very word has become anathema to every 100% American. But as the public lands have disappeared, as the monopoly of all natural resources has tightened, as the processes of economic subjugation and social standardization have gone forward, a constantly increasing army of Americans has yearned for the safety and respectability of government jobs, and so the politicians have been forced into creating the jobs, and into all sorts of Socialistic adventures to provide the excuse.

Almost every politician, of course, declaims against this growth of Federal "paternalism" and against the burden of taxation which it lays upon the still active and industrious part of the population. But the proof of his insincerity, if any proof be needed, is found in the story of all the ostensible efforts of Congress to make the governmental machine more economical and efficient. Every move in this direction has resulted only in the creation of new commissions and bureaux; not one has ever reduced the Federal pay-roll in the slightest. The Civil Service Commission, established in 1883 to abolish the spoils system and put the merit system in its place, has itself grown into an enormous bureau, crowded with job-holders. Its chief function has become to protect the job-holder from his superiors, and so to promote inefficiency. But Congressmen have never had much difficulty in going over its head. It may keep out a few almost fabulous incompetents, but it has not kept the classified service from being primarily so much political patronage.

A few years ago, largely through the efforts of one influential Senator, the Commission was supplemented by a Bureau of Efficiency, which quickly grew from two or three employés to fifty. Its chief occupation is carrying on a civil war with the Commission. The history of the late President Harding's attempt to reorganize the government departments is well known. An expert was hired to draw up a reorganization plan, but it encountered so much opposition that it never got before Congress. Two bills designed to deal with the bureaucracy were long deadlocked in a Senate committee. Both were designed to classify the jobs in the Federal service and to fix salaries for the different kinds of work done. Both, incidently, provided substantial increases for most varieties of job-holders. One of them, sponsored by Senator Smoot, gave the chiefs of bureaux the power to discharge incompetents; the other, backed by the Federal Employés' Union, went to the opposite extreme. It provided a system of trial and appeal in case of dismissal which would have made it almost impossible to separate a job-holding moron from his job. It also provided much larger proportionate increases for the lower grades of employés than did the Smoot bill. In a word, the union bill was designed above all to make the government service safe and remunerative for the lowest type of man to be found in it. Despite the power of Senator Smoot, the bill reported to the Senate was substantially the union bill.

III

That the government service has become primarily a refuge for inferior men, and is run chiefly for their benefit, is seen in the way the lower class positions have been increased and fattened at the expense of those higher up. Just as in the reclassification bill just mentioned the smallest jobs were given the biggest raises, so in every increase of salaries since the government was founded the common clerk has profited at the expense of the executive and the technician. A stenographer, recently imported from some small town in Iowa where she would be lucky to make $15 a week, gets from the government about $1400 a year, while for highly trained technicians in some of its bureaux the government offers but $1800. The inevitable result is that the brains of this huge bureaucracy have dwindled while its bulk has swelled. Generally speaking, only the least able and ambitious of technical and scientific men now seek the government service; the best of those in it are on the lookout for a chance to leave it. At times the turn-over in a technical bureau has been so rapid as to disrupt the work, and almost always the man who leaves is better than the man who takes his place. This cumulative intellectual impoverishment of the service accounts for the pettiness and puerility which hang about the whole bureaucratic establishment.

The chief of the Bureau of Efficiency admitted to me that it would be easy to hire at $15 a week a large proportion of the typists and file clerks, mostly women, for whom the government pays from $1400 to $1600 a year,—that is, it would be easy if the government were allowed to buy its labor in the open market. But the positions are allotted by States, so many to each State in ratio to population, and to abolish this arrangement would be greatly to impair the value of these jobs as political patronage. The local politician's daughter who has come all the way from Iowa or Colorado to serve the Republic

must be paid enough to maintain herself in a fitting manner away from home and in a great city, regardless of her actual ability and diligence.

Congress, indeed, is especially tender in its attitude toward the thousands of women it has imported into Washington. An interesting proof of this is seen in the Plaza Hotel, which was built by the government during the war to provide housing for girl war-workers and is still caring for several thousand female employés at a considerable annual loss. Many of these girls draw from the government fifty to a hundred per cent more salary than they are worth, and are fed and housed by the government for about half what it would cost them to live otherwise. They are to all intents and purposes inmates of a charitable institution. They are provided not only with bed and board but also with entertainment and chaperonage. The government is especially careful of their moral welfare. At every session of Congress since the war, this Home for Virgin Bureaucrats has been loudly denounced, but the appropriations for its maintenance have always passed without serious opposition.

The way in which the so-called merit system works is too well known to need description here. Each applicant for a place in the classified service must pass an examination, very simple in the case of those applying for clerical positions. He then receives a rating on the roll of applicants from his State. In theory, his rating and the time of his application determine when he shall get the job, but in practice the support of an administration Congressman is of the greatest help. Almost every government position, with the exception of a few technical places that are hard to fill, is still a piece of political pie.

IV

The Washington spectacle then, as I see it, is that of a growing horde of decaying men and women, squeezed out of the industrial life of the country by their incapacity for useful and renumerative work, and running to the government for food and shelter. The government service outside Washington, of course, is largely a continuation of that spectacle, and all of the State, municipal and county employés must be added to the total of those who have given up productive work for job-holding. The principal and most necessary duty of every Congressman—indeed, of every politician—is to care for his share of this beaten and incompetent mob, which demands a living of the state as the Roman rabble demanded the Corn Laws. The Congressman who does not get jobs for all those who have claims upon him is doomed to retirement. Thus, what he always craves is more jobs to give away, and especially more jobs of the simple sort which any idiot can fill.

It is but little realized how many great reputations for statecraft and even patriotism are founded primarily upon a deft management of this trade in jobs. Senator Henry Cabot Lodge of Massachusetts, for example, generally regarded by the public as an aloof and chilly intellectual, far above all the lusts of the flesh, is a famous job-getter and has maintained himself in the Senate by that art and mystery in the face of the most formidable opposition. Not only is he diligent in obtaining easy jobs for his lieges of Massachusetts; but his interest in them never ends so long as they are in Washington. He is constantly recommending promotions and raises for the cohort of Massachusetts men who swarm in the capital. No Senator is more assiduous in his care of the intellectual vacuums who are dependent upon him.

The character of Washington as a city shows the lamentable consequences of thus making it a dumping ground for men and women marked principally by timidity, a cheap pretense to gentility, and lack of imagination and enterprise. Washington is a thousand miles of Main Street. There is a little fluff of pompous official society, with its millionaire hangers-on and bawdy pushers at the top, and a huge African

sub-stratum of menial labor at the bottom. What lies between is a miserable society of middle-class dulness and mediocrity, eighth-rate people. The town has been often described as unique among American cities. As a matter of fact, the bulk of its population shows only a selective intensification of the typical. Uniformity and dulness are its most striking characteristics. There is no enterprise in the place and no courage, and very little sense.

Go beyond the restricted area where the government buildings stand and the part of the Northwest section which has been preempted by the ambitious rich, and you will find endless rows of little houses, built wall to wall, all exactly alike, broken here and there by huge blocks of cheap apartment houses—the tenements of low-grade respectability. Farther out are sprawling miles of cheap bungalow suburbs. The town's leading newspaper, the *Evening Star*, is a village gossip-sheet almost incredibly stupid and trivial; every effort to publish an intelligent newspaper in Washington has failed. Its theatres are the poorest to be found in any city of the size in the country. Movies and vaudeville are what succeed in Washington, as do also cheap amusement parks and even cheaper dance-halls.

Food and games the Roman rabble demanded. The man who has ceased to struggle, whose work is merely an easy but tiresome way of making a living, suffers always from boredom and has an immense appetite for mere spectacle and diversion—for amusement which requires no mental or physical effort. Washington is a city of free shows and especially of parades,—of military drills and manœuvres, athletic contests, band concerts, speech-makings, fireworks, free movies, and all sorts of other blow-outs to which imbeciles go in mobs to gawk, listen and yell. Almost anything that is free will draw a crowd of the job-holding proletariat, and the huge public lawns and halls and the straight wide streets of the town are perfectly adapted to such gatherings.

V

The job-holder is generally an American of the old American stock; that is, he is not a product of the last two generations of immigration. He is most frequently of that Nordic strain whose imminent extinction has been so extensively lamented of late as a catastrophe to civilization. A look at the crowds that flood Washington's innumerable one-arm lunchrooms at noon will bear this out, and so will a reading of the names on any list of government employés. All this is to be expected. The old American stock still dominates the Republic politically. Congress might be described as a body of Nordic lawyers, with heads long and thick but not wide, and hair light or absent. It is natural that those of similar racial stock should be favored by congressional influence. This old American stock is being rapidly ousted from industry and commerce, and to a smaller but perceptible extent from the land, by people who have reached the United States during the last two generations. The job-holder is thus a dispossessed and beaten man, and many scions of our oldest families are in his ranks.

He owns little or no property, unless it is a home, in or near Washington, which he is buying on the installment plan. But a large percentage of his humble brethren once did own property, or else their fathers did. Many of them, indeed, are small farmers who have sold out in despair, or young men and women raised on farms who wanted to get to the city and live an easier and more genteel life. A typical Washington family consists of father, mother and three grown children, all holding government jobs, making about $6000 a year among them. They used to own a small farm in Ohio, where they probably seldom saw a thousand a year in cash.

But the job-holder is usually dissatisfied with his job and with himself. He is wont to say that there is no future in the service. He is often apologetic about being a government employé. He is fully aware that taking his job was a retreat and that keeping it is a surrender. Almost always he laments the dulness and monotony of his life. Very often he tells you that he is going to get out when the right time and the right opportunity come along. Sometimes he does so, of course, but usually Jefferson's saying holds good that "few die and none resign."

A characteristic figure is the man who came from some small town or farm to make a living while getting an education in Washington. Washington is full of night schools run for the benefit of such relatively ambitious fellows, and especially of law schools. The newcomer attends one of these and in three or four years he graduates. But meantime he has achieved an easy and comfortable living in some government bureau, doing some work that would be well within the capacities of a bright boy of twelve. In many cases he has married the stenographer or file clerk who sat across the desk from him. He has the responsibilities of a family man. The profession of law is crowded and difficult. Everything is difficult—except holding a job in Washington. He has dug himself into a deep little rut of security and routine. So he stays on, year after year, lulled by habit and ease, by Washington's curiously enervating climate, and by its atmosphere of dulness and indolence. He is a man lost in the battle—a man useless and forgotten.

THE SIRE OF KIWANIS

BY WILLIAM FEATHER

I BOUGHT a $280 time-clock from a salesman the other day. As we closed the transaction he said, "Mr. Feather, I don't want to sell you just a piece of machinery—I want to do you a great Service."

He was a dapper young man, trimly dressed, his upper lip decorated with a smart moustache. He smiled easily, and spoke incisively.

"I'm in business for Service and only Service," he continued. "You couldn't buy a clock from me if you didn't need it. But you do need it, and I'd be shirking my duty to you, to my conscience and to this great free Republic of ours if I didn't use all the eloquence at my command to make you one of our satisfied users."

And so we both knelt down and prayed, and when we arose and had sung "The Star-Spangled Banner" I looked into his honest blue eyes and saw that they were filled with tears. Then I called to the bookkeeper to bring me a blank check, which I signed and handed to my friend with these words: "Take this, brother! Fill in the amount yourself. Send the time-clock by airplane. How can I begin to thank you for what you have done for me? May the splendid Service of your wonderful company go on forever. Amen."

After he had left I sat alone for three hours and a half in an ecstasy of high resolve. How clearly he had pointed the way to success, achievement, glory! I felt myself in tune with the stars, with the planets, with the whole cosmos. This clock was to relieve me of all the depressing worries of business. It was to enable me at last to put my affairs on a scientific and idealistic basis. A monthly profit of a few miserable

dollars was to be swelled into a vast and ever-increasing fortune.

"Is it right, is it fair," he had demanded, "that for lack of a fully automatic, self-winding, nickel-plated time-clock your wife should be deprived of a fur coat and your son should be unable to go to college?"

He had showed me how the loss of a few minutes each day, multiplied by the rate of pay in our factory, and again multiplied by the number of working days in a year, leap years excepted, amounted to the difference between a stagnant, miserable existence and illimitable opulence for my family. Service had stretched out its long arm to me, and lifted me up.

II

This salesman was typical of scores who have called on me in late years, from whom I have only by extreme self-control resisted buying adding machines, lightning calculators, check protectors, filing cabinets, dictating machines, loose-leaf binders, wall maps, pencil sharpeners, trick ink wells, postage meters, envelope sealers and openers, typewriter duplicators, billing machines and addressing machines, not to mention thirteen methods of increasing production and nineteen ways of jazzing up the sales department.

The sales talk of all such agents and apostles of Service has been as accurately standardized as the parts of a Ford. What was the genesis of these modern talking machines? Where did they originate? Where did they learn the art of selling me a brass lead pencil for $5 by proving to me that without it Shakespeare could not

351

have written "Hamlet"—by showing me testimonials from users of pencils who say, "If I could not get another I would not sell the one I have for $10,000"?

I shall tell you in a moment. I shall tell you where the pilgrim of Service was conceived, hatched, educated, and developed to his highest perfection. I shall tell you, incidentally, the origin of the sales manual, the quota system, the guaranteed territory, the standardized demonstration, and the ninety and nine other great mysteries which engage the master minds at sales and advertising conferences and conventions. But first to the technique. Imagine you are being sold a machine to open envelopes. You don't want it, so you say you can't afford it. The answer is as follows:

"Sir, what do you consider a fair interest rate on money. Six per cent? What is the annual interest at six per cent on $870? Exactly $52.20. Now, sir, I have demonstrated and you have not denied that this device will save you $5 a week. Therefore, based on what this machine will earn I would be justified in asking you to pay 5 times $870, or $4350. Yet I offer it to you for only $297. Can you afford not to buy it? In justice to your family, to your wife, and your little children, can you afford to miss this opportunity?"

This argument, so unanswerable, so overwhelming, was the invention of the late John H. Patterson, of the National Cash Register Company, one of the boldest and most original fellows ever seen in American business, the discoverer of Service, of the Scientific Approach, of Pep—the high priest of Rotary, the sire of Kiwanis. Patterson standardized and romanticized the lowly office of the old-time drummer. He invented the Scientific Salesman. He invented the Sales Manual. He invented nine-tenths of the arguments that his disciples and imitators now play upon you when they seek to sell you automobiles, thermostats, wire lath, hail insurance, chicken wire, radio outfits, envelope lickers, cellarettes, dog collars, tungsten-steel safes, unbreakable wind-shields, towel

service. And he did the job completely; he overlooked nothing—no imaginable resistance, no conceivable emergency. A salesman who emerged from his seminary came out complete and perfect, ripe and irresistible. I quote some specimen strophes from his own Sales Manual. The prospect, a corner grocer, has objected to buying a cash register on the ground that it costs too much—that the company makes too much profit. The salesman *loquitur:*

I really don't know how much profit we make on this or any other register, and I do not believe that anyone could possibly ascertain with accuracy just how much it is.

For the sake of argument, however, we will admit that it is *all* profit; that this register which we sell for $500 costs nothing.

If this is true, our profit on this $500 register is $500. You will admit that it cannot be more.

That settles the profit the Company makes on the sale of this $500 register.

Now, let's see what *your* profit is:

If the register saves you $1 a day, it will save you, in round numbers, $300 the first year.

The Company's profit at the end of one year, therefore, is $500, and yours $300, the Company having made $200 more than you.

At the end of the second year, your profit is $600 and the Company's only $500.

You, therefore, are $100 ahead of the Company.

In ten years your profit will be $3,000, while the Company's profit still remains at $500, and you are $2,500 ahead.

As a matter of fact, then, it is not a question of how much the Company makes, but of how much *you* make.

III

John H. Patterson hoped to live more than one hundred years. He died in May, 1922, at seventy-eight. Even so, he lived too long. His contributions to American business science had been so widely applied by the time he died that their origin had been forgotten.

Patterson really did not get into action until he was past forty. He was in the full glory of his career at sixty-five, when the United States government placed him under arrest and convicted him of violating the Sherman Anti-Trust Act. Following the Dayton flood, this conviction was upset by the Supreme Court. By the time he was seventy his personality was already becoming a memory. His quota system, his Hundred-Point Club, his standard demonstration, his salesmen's conventions, his conferences, his training school, his endless tricks to excite vanity, competition, and hard-hitting among salesmen, had been taken over by all other Americans of his trade and calibre. Imitation Pattersons had sprung up like dandelions. Yet none ever equalled the father of the race. George F. Babbitt was one of the progeny, but he was crossed with a moron, and lacked his sire's daring and originality.

When Patterson first appeared on the business horizon the telephone was a rarity, the card index was still unknown, the adding machine had not been invented, the typewriter was still but little used. Business is said to move in cycles. During a period of falling prices, money is made by thrift, by tight-fisted economy, by saving pins and using the insides of envelopes for note-paper. On the rebound, when prices are moving upward, money is made by daring expenditures, by expansion, by quick action, by scrapping old machinery, by plunging. Patterson led the way through an era of rising prices. By temperament he was ideally suited to the spectacular. He spent money lavishly. His factory in Dayton looked like a university. His foundry was vine-clad. His smoke stacks glistened like a Childs' restaurant.

It was my privilege to be called to Dayton in 1915. I survived one year and was then returned to normal life as unexpectedly as I had been lifted out of it. In that year I had an opportunity to study Patterson at work, at play, at dinner, at breakfast, at luncheon, in the saddle, on foot, at conventions, and finally on the Battle Creek rubbing table. He was not the silent, uncommunicative millionaire of romance. He did not sit in his office and plot great coups. He was a man of action, action, action! He loved the telegraph. He liked fast automobiles, the Twentieth Century Limited, long-distance telephone calls, five-day liners. He worked on his feet. He could not think without a sheet beside him, to diagram his thoughts.

The cash register was the passion of his life, a monument in the building of which he took infinite delight. His interests never wandered; he kept his eye always on his own register. He had a newspaperman's instinct for building a story. He dramatized everything, even the dying wails of his competitors. He bought up their machines, heaped them into a huge mound, and labelled it "The Graveyard." When ground was broken for the present plant of the National Cash Register Company on the hill overlooking Dayton, John H. drove an ax into a fence post and announced melodramatically that it marked "the centre of population of the United States."

He made a romance even of his own life. He was born with a silver spoon in his mouth, was graduated from Dartmouth College, and in partnership with his brother, acquired extensive coal properties in southern Ohio, all operated successfully. In 1882 he heard of the cash register, the invention of one James Ditty of Dayton. According to his own story, he ordered two by telegraph for the coal company's store. Following their installation, the store showed its first profit; apparently what had been the clerks' gain had been Patterson's loss. Shortly thereafter Patterson the coal operator became Patterson the manufacturer through the purchase of the National Manufacturing Company. But in reviewing all this for visitors to the Dayton factory, the cash register king made a few changes. He was "born in a log cabin," "worked as a barefoot boy along the Ohio canal" and "was graduated from the university of hard knocks." That was as he would have liked it.

To understand Patterson and his philosophy it is essential to remember that he had absolutely no sense of humor. He did have a biting sarcasm, but to him nothing was funny. He never laughed. Long before the World War he bought American flags by the gross. Poles stuck out like porcupine quills from the buildings at Dayton.

"Today the flags are flying in honor of

our distinguished visitor, Dr. Frank Crane," the bulletin boards announced, and, looking up, one saw 30 or 40 flags waving in the breeze. The next day: "Today the flags are flying in celebration of the sale of the one-millionth cash register."

The crowning event of his career, perhaps, was the salesmen's convention held at the factory in the Autumn of 1915, to herald the return of good times after a bad year. All the salesmen—about 800—were called to Dayton by wire. Following a three-day revival in "The Schoolhouse," a Grecian temple erected for such gatherings, they were escorted to the railroad station by the 5000 factory employés. It took one hour and seventeen minutes for the line, marching four abreast, to pass the downtown N. C. R. City Club. Six bands and half a dozen drum corps were in the parade. Department heads and leaders among the selling force rode horses. President Patterson led the procession on foot, carrying a flag. Following him were the salesmen, in white trousers and white hats, also carrying flags. The factory divisions followed, each man waving a red torch, and each woman a sparkler.

This monumental exhibition of the go-get-'em spirit was duly chronicled in the company house-organ and in the local newspapers, marked copies of which were mailed broadcast. From my files I exhume the following encomiums, reported as "heard along the side line during the parade":

> This surely looks like old times again.
> This certainly ought to back up Mr. Patterson's "Business is Booming" talk.
> This is the finest, highest-grade, and most intelligent lot of men and women I ever saw in my life.
> This is the biggest commercial demonstration that was ever pulled off in any city—either here or anywhere else.

Of course, this was a big party, even for Patterson, but it was in no way unusual. He organized a Country Club for his employés at which huge entertainments were given throughout the Summer. Once each year he invited the entire population of Oakwood, a suburb of Dayton, to Far

Hills, his home, where all were served at a barbecue. Often he took a party of forty or fifty men to New York, renting an entire floor at the Waldorf. He sent men around the world and fired them by cable.

Firing men, indeed, was one of his chief delights. He liked new faces. If you had ambitions to keep your job it was fatal to attract the attention of John H. You might find yourself suddenly promoted from tutor in his household to vice-president of the corporation, as did an English schoolmaster. But you knew you couldn't last—and the schoolmaster didn't. He went to Australia on "company business" and never came back.

Patterson made cash register salesmanship highly theatrical. The machines he most fancied were ornamented like Luna Park merry-go-rounds, and then given a gold or silver finish. When the keys were pressed they made a noise like an automobile starter. A bell rang. The alarm made an instantaneous appeal to the saloon-keepers who for years had been robbed by their bartenders. Little salesmanship, in fact, was required in this market, but when the general retail field was entered special training became necessary. Patterson therefore opened a school for his salesmen. Here the art of exchanging a cash register for a merchant's notes became a science. So perfected did the sales talk become that in their off hours at conventions the star salesmen, for relaxation, would show the cubs how to sell a thousand dollar register to a bootblack. In those days a cash register was a certificate of prosperity, as an automobile is today, and Patterson made the most of it. He invented the quota system for salesmen and organized a Hundred-Point Club to which star salesmen elected themselves.

When he was well past middle age Patterson had serious trouble with his digestion. He heard of Battle Creek, bran, spinach, vegetarianism, olive oil, raw carrots, nuts, steam baths, coco oil rubs, horseback riding, no-breakfast diets. Always he reasoned, "What is good for

me is good for everyone." Once he had
quit meat he could not bear to see anyone
else eat a chop. He rode horseback one
morning at five and felt fine. *Ergo*, all
department heads must ride. The horses
were ordered and the stables built. For a
few months everyone, lean and fat, rode
horseback, the squadron being preceded
by a trumpeter. He canceled the order
as suddenly as he had issued it. One night
the horses and all trace of the stables
disappeared.

Although, as I have said, Patterson
did not use his own office at all, yet
he deemed it essential that his assistants
be housed in elaborate quarters. The
suite which I occupied was as spacious
as a western prairie. A glass partition
separated me from my secretary. Adjoining this office was a large private bathroom. However, I did not use this, for I
preferred another bathroom where three
men were regularly employed to assist us
in taking baths and to rub us down.

Every morning a man in white uniform
visited my office and spread a snowy white
napkin on a small table on which he
placed a large bottle of distilled water and
a glass, removing the unused bottle,
napkin and glass placed there the previous
day. I also was visited each day by a bootblack in white uniform. I was of an age
when it appealed greatly to me to dictate
to a secretary, answer the telephone and
have my shoes shined all at the same time.

Visitors were often aghast at the seeming extravagance, which was exactly the
impression he desired to make upon them.
They were told: "It pays." I suppose a
certain part of it did. It caused the cash
register company to be talked about.
Smart young men were attracted to the
ranks of its salesmen.

Patterson's neighbors in Dayton thought
he was "crazy." Most of his employés
were sure he was "crazy." Yet, when they
had been fired they found that it paid to
follow his methods, in whole or in part.
Whether it paid or did not pay, Patterson
could afford it, and he got the same thrill

from it that some men get from supporting
a musical comedy troupe. He believed that
business offered an opportunity for complete self-expression. For him it did. He
related everything to the making and
selling of cash registers. It was typical
that he should charge the entire cost of his
Dayton relief work to company expenses.
His expense accounts sent needles into the
spines of minority stockholders; he even
dismissed sales agents because their expense accounts were not large enough.
Nothing was so offensive to him as the
failure of a representative of the National
Cash Register Company to dress and conduct himself in a manner becoming his
chief, that is, extravagantly.

Life for him must move at a high tempo.
He was an idealist within the sphere of his
genius. He bred a race of near-Pattersons,
but none has ever risen to the heights
attained by this master of jazz.

IV

The New Business has sprung from his
personality. Pep specialists, sales engineers,
psychologists, statisticians, researchers,
laboratorians, surveyors and counsellors
now reach hundreds of thousands of business men each week with the Great
Message. Their audience is the membership of the Advertising, Rotary, Kiwanis,
Exchange, Lions, Gyro and Optimist
Clubs. This year the Associated Advertising Clubs of the World will hold its
convention in London, and thus its civi-
lizing influence will be projected overseas.
The program of a convention includes
parades, community singing, battles royal,
oratory, music, prayers, fireworks and
hula-hula dancing. Frequently the pulpits
of the convention city are assigned to the
visiting delegates on the Sunday preceding
the convention. The walls of St. Paul's
may reverberate with new echoes next July!

The program of the local clubs calls for
a weekly noonday talk. Some hold beauty
contests among their members, requiring
the candidates to do æsthetic dances and

356 THE AMERICAN MERCURY

pose as "The Dying Bootlegger." A committee of telephone operators and stenographers usually judges the contest. In the event that a speaker fails to keep his appointment a favorite form of recreation is for each member to lie on his back and kick a basketball with his feet. At Thanksgiving and Christmas the custom is for each member to bring a newsboy or an orphan to the meeting for a big feed— turkey an' cranberries 'an everythin', as the secretary says in his announcements.

The range of speakers at the meetings includes poets who recite sentimental verses, efficiency experts, Episcopal deans, trick artists, best-seller authors, Dr. Frank Crane, Charles M. Schwab, talking dogs, Roger W. Babson, Walter M. Camp (who discovered the great principle of the Daily Dozen) arctic explorers, and defenders of Hollywood. These meetings are designed to fit a man for an afternoon of hard work. They usually last from noon to 2 P. M.

Underpaid professors have found a lucrative source of income by talking to these groups on Service and Psychology. One professor has a speech in which he explains the favorable psychological effect of placing a needle and thread on the bureau in every bedroom in a hotel, of giving away a morning newspaper to every guest, and of providing signs which may be hung on the door, reading "Do not disturb." The professor shows how these little touches convert an unattractive $2 room into a $4 room. Another sure-fire talker is an eminent student of human behavior who "recently completed two years of research in Switzerland." His theory is that you can make people do anything if you understand the "principle of motivation." This speaker illustrates his talks with hand-drawn charts of the human brain and spinal column.

Often a "go-getter" is scheduled, some man who has increased his sales of leather vests from $33,000 to $526,455.12 a year by devising a mah jong contest. These fellows usually have hairy fists and punctuate every paragraph with a couple of "damns" and a "hell." Then there is the man who has formulated the scientific laws of advertising. He says that by testing your copy as he prescribes you can determine scientifically the number of suckers in each 1000 of the population that it will fetch. If the percentage is a paying one your copy is o.k., after which your problem resolves itself into deciding whether to spend the winter in Florida or on the Riviera.

Raising three or four million dollars for a community fund is a short morning's work for these live wires of the New Business. The old-fashioned minister and college president went out into the strange world and begged, accepting gifts humbly and gratefully. Under the new system charity and philanthropy are "sold" to "prospects" and each "salesman" has his "quota." "Hard nuts" are reported and are given special attention by a "wrecking crew." Years ago Patterson asserted that his methods could be applied to every field of human activity, including the ecclesiastical. "What is good for us is good for everyone," he argued. In a few hours, following the Dayton flood, he raised two million dollars for the rehabilitation of the city. As the dollars were subscribed they were rung up on an enormous cash register.

That he was a prophet is clear. The Y. M. C. A., the Boy Scouts and the Go-to-Church movement are merchandised today like breakfast foods. In an open letter, published in an advertising journal recently, Samuel Gompers was advised to modernize the labor movement by substituting advertising and up-to-date marketing schemes for the crude methods now employed to get higher wages. No one has yet suggested a Back to Common Sense Week but the proposal may be expected at any moment. It will be merchandised, when it comes, by means of brass bands, essays by school children, floats, lapel buttons, window displays, special movie films, four-minute speakers, and syndicate newspaper articles by Mary Pickford and Judge Elbert Gary.

SPANISH NIGHTS' ENTERTAINMENT

BY C. E. BECHHOFER

MY VISIT to the first of the theatres that I propose to mention was unpremeditated. I had not meant to go out that evening. It was a few weeks ago in Seville, and I was sitting quietly with an English friend and his wife in the lounge of our hotel, commenting on the sharp coolness of the air—the optimism of architects in Southern Spain is inclined to rule out heating appliances or to reduce them to almost purely theoretical proportions—and reading, as well as my primitive knowledge of Spanish allowed, a current copy of the weekly comic paper *Buen Humor*, in which I was delighted to find this illustrated variant of a witticism of earlier days:—

The Traveler: Hallo, Pascuala, where can one find your husband?
Pascuala: Well, he will be now in the *corral* with the pigs; he is the one who wears a little hat of straw.

A waiter came to our table and, asking us if we wished to visit the theatre, laid on our table the printed slips which in this part of the world do duty both as advance announcements of plays and as programs of them. It ran as follows:

Theatre of San Fernando

Official Company
of the Spanish Theatre of Madrid
of
Ricardo Calvo

Principal actresses:
Carmen Seco and Josefina Roca
Principal comedian:
Fernando Porredon

Program for Today
1. Symphony
2. First Performance of the fairy-tale in a prologue and three acts, divided into fourteen scenes, *original* of Don Jacinto Benavente,
LA CENICIENTA

Represented by this company, in the Spanish Theatre of Madrid, more than THREE HUNDRED consecutive times.

There followed the list of characters and scenes and the prices of seats, ranging from thirty pesetas (roughly five dollars) for boxes, and ten pesetas for stalls, to seventy-five centimos for "entradas de 2.a grada." The play, or rather the symphony that preceded it, was to begin at half past nine.

We discussed whether we should go. My friend and I were anxious to see an example of the work of one of the latest Nobel prize winners; neither of us knew more of his plays than was to be learned from the three volumes in English published by the Scribners. My friend's wife, a student of Spanish, declared that Benavente was sordid and cynical—did he not say, for instance, that "Art is the one subject on which aristocracy and democracy agree; both invariably vote for folly and vulgarity"?—and that she did not propose to ruin her evening by watching one of his dramas. It is true that neither she nor we had heard of his "La Cenicienta"—which we were careful to pronounce lispingly as *Thenithienta*—but when we discovered from some Spanish informants that this meant "something like Cinderella and the ugly sisters," she insisted that this was too sacred a subject to be profaned by sordidness and cynicism, and left us to put on our hats and coats and go to the theatre by ourselves.

We were directed through the Sierpes, the paved and winding street which, closed to all but pedestrian and donkey traffic, forms the centre of Sevillian life.

357

Little groups of Spaniards in dark suits and huge-brimmed Andalusian hats were standing there in talk or watching their more aristocratic fellows stare at them from comfortable armchairs behind the plate-glass windows of the clubs and the still more luxurious citizens who were being publicly shaved in the barbers' shops; the bars of "The Four Corners of San Juan" and the "Toro" taverns with the stuffed bulls' heads on the walls were crowded with customers; and an ambitious grocer, prepared for the anticipated invasion of an American tourist party and taking us for its forerunners, rushed out of his shop and thrust the following English handbill into our hands:—

HISPANO-AMERICAN SHOP

Best Old Wines

Americans! Americans! Malaga wine. Do not sail without it. When you are sorry or weary drink this gold wine and it will be your best companion. Keep some of it for your friends and family. The best wine for presents. Brought directly from Malaga. If you buy a bottle you will buy ten, so good you will find it.

We reached the theatre at last and, buying two stalls, entered the cool building. It was already half past nine, but there were few people present, although from the rattle of conversation and the rustling of the newspapers one might have thought the place full. On each side of the stage there was a large advertisement of a popular laxative, and the lowered curtain itself was covered with similar announcements. Even the footlights bore in huge letters the name of the electrician who had installed them. We were also warned against pickpockets. The orchestra's piano and half a dozen chairs belonging to the musicians were deserted, but on each side of them sat a fireman in his brass helmet, phlegmatically smoking cigaretts and throwing the burning stubs on the wooden floor. Little boys passed down the aisles, shouting "Caramels, caramels," or offering lottery-tickets; but they soon became weary and

put their wares down on the front row of stalls, immediately before us, and sat on them, the better to enjoy the coming spectacle. They kept their caps on to maintain their official position. At about ten o'clock two gentlemen in derby hats climbed over the barrier and sat down at the piano, talking to the firemen. A quarter of an hour later the audience began methodically to clap and stamp, with the result that soon three more musicians in derby hats entered the orchestra and, suddenly snatching off their derbies, played a dozen bars of music; then, the "symphony" finished, they rammed their derbies on again and rushed out of the building as the curtain went up. Whenever during the course of the play incidental music was called for, the musicians returned to their places in the same hurried manner, removed their derbies and took up their instruments at the latest possible moment, reversing the process even more quickly when they had done their work.

II

Everybody now said "Shhh!" to everybody else, and the prologue began with "The Three Magi," "The Sadness of the Prince," "The Fairy Fantasy" and "The Land of Illusion." My friend and I mustered our small understanding of Spanish and endeavored to appreciate the wealth of satire that we were sure lay behind the rather obvious awakening of Cinderella in her (double) bed by the spirit of Fantasy and the faded backcloths that portrayed the changes of scene. The strange thing was that we found we could understand almost everything that was said, and it appeared to us neither cynical nor sordid; nor, we noticed, did any of our heavily breathing neighbors or even the caramel-boys in front of us appear to be much moved by the speeches. True, there was one phrase we did not quite catch: it had something to do with liberty and drew a loud laugh from one of the boxes and two of the caramel-boys, but everybody else took it calmly. When the curtain fell on the last of the four scenes of the prologue, I suggested to my friend that probably this was only a cynically simple overture to the sordid satire that was to follow, and we discussed which of the characters might be taken to personify Spain, the Bourbon monarchy, the military *juntas* and the other political references that might reasonably be expected.

The first act was preceded by a *pas seul* of the electrician, who hung out of a stage-box and excitedly changed a couple of lamps in the footlights. He was loudly applauded. The curtain rose again after a long interval—the orchestra rushing for cover as before—and we were introduced to Cinderella again, her parents and her ugly sisters, who were described on the program as "Las Preciosas ridiculas." The third scene of the first act brought with it a finale by the whole company, including half a dozen small children dressed as monkeys, with tails and huge, grinning masks. These clasped hands and rushed 'round and 'round Cinderella until one of them let go and the rest of the half dozen piled themselves on top of him. This incident brought the house down in laughter until it was discovered that it was unrehearsed, the injured monkey arising in loud sorrow and running for comfort to his mother in the chorus. She soothed him and he returned after a short pause to his work, and the curtain descended for another interval. The audience calmly picked up its newspapers or went out for a drink, and my friend and I read astonishingly cynical meanings into what had gone before. To tell the truth, we were hopelessly befogged, but neither of us wished to confess it.

The second act carried on the story, still in the same obvious manner. The audience was roused to tremendous enthusiasm when Cinderella was shown in her pretty dress, off to the ball, under the supervision of the good fairy whom she had assisted to carry faggots in a previous scene and who now appeared to the weeping damsel out of a kitchen cupboard. I cannot hope to describe the sumptuousness of the ball itself, but it provided a very fine closing scene, after which the boys did a roaring trade in their caramels, a little warm and sticky from being sat on for so long, and my friend and I continued our discussion of the symbolism of the play over a glass of sherry in a neighboring bar. We were quite lost; we had understood practically everything that had been said, and nothing had shown any sign of the sordidness, satire or cynicism we had expected. The jokes had been simple; the episodes without subtlety; and the audience had shown no signs of reading a deeper meaning into them. But surely, we said to each other, Benavente, the satirical, sordid cynic, would never have written a mere English pantomime version of the Cinderella story; nor could this have been played for more than three hundred consecutive times in the Spanish Theatre at Madrid. Besides, "Don Juan" was down for the following evening; and nobody had ever called that a pantomime!

It was about half past midnight when we returned to our seats, anticipating the derby-hatted orchestra's devastating progress down the central aisle. At one o'clock the curtain rose on the final act. We saw "The Fatal Hour," with Cinderella (Mme. Carmen Seco herself) rushing in screams from the stage; then came the excruciating excitement of the Prince's attempt to find the owner of the crystal slipper. One of the ugly sisters (the charming Mme. Josefina Rosa) tried to cut half her foot off in order to get it on—although we could see that she could easily have put it on without this—and the other wanted to cut the slipper up. Cinderella's cruel stepmother also failed miserably in the test, much to the relief of the excited audience, which need perhaps not have worried very much, since she clearly could not marry the Prince when she was already in possession of Cinderella's henpecked father. Then amidst enormous applause Cinderella, the despised and browbeaten outcast, fitted her foot into the slipper as if it had been made for her, to be embraced by the Prince, his courtiers and her own long-suffering father. One of my neighbors who throughout the evening had been reading the reports of the Madrid and Barcelona exchanges, even put down his paper to clap loudly at this point.

The last scene of all was the Apotheosis, the wonders of which are not to be told with a Nordic pen. It wound up with a grand procession of all the actors and actresses through the theatre and up a plank bridge onto the stage. The only flaw to this triumphal ending was due to the same little boy who had been unfortunate in an earlier scene. The poor child tripped up on the planks and fell into the orchestra, fortunately alighting on the derbies of the musicians, who picked him up amidst much laughter and lifted him onto the stage. And so, with loud chords on the piano and the double-bass, Cinderella was joined to the Prince in marriage, and the other characters paired off matrimonially. The chief actors took their calls; the unlucky little boy was consoled by a special appearance before the curtain; and we all put our hats on and went home.

It was about two o'clock by now, and my friend and I walked back to our hotel, still anxiously discussing the possibility of the play's being satirical, cynical and sordid. We could reach no really satisfactory solution. But his wife met us in the lounge and showed us in the preface of one of the volumes of the English translation of Benavente that in 1911 he, with Porredon the actor, had founded a children's theatre in Madrid or Barcelona. She was anxious to know whether the "Cinderella" we had just seen belonged to the satirical style of the author or whether she could safely send her little son to see it at the children's matinée announced for the forthcoming Sunday. We reassured her, and a highly delighted English boy was among the audience on the next occasion that the play was produced. It started at half past six in the

evening, and he was able to get home by ten o'clock! His father and I gathered that the satirical symbolism had escaped him also.

III

My next adventures in the theatre in Southern Spain were not, I fear, quite on a level with what I have described. I did not go on the following evening to the representation of Tirso de Molina's "Don Juan," chiefly because it seemed likely to last well into the morning; and for art that is so long, life is surely too short. Instead, I betook myself to the Salón Imperial and saw the following spectacle:—

Grandioso Programa Artistico
A
Precios Populares

Orden del Espectaculo
1. *Sinfonia por el notable sexteto que dirige el maestro Emilio de Torre.*
2. *Gran Éxito de la elegante cancionista y ballarina LOLITA LIMARES.*
3. *Gran Éxito de la elegante y buena ballarina MATILDE USSONI.*
4. *Éxito de la bella y elegante cancionista CARMELITA CABALLERO.*
5. *Éxito Grande de la elegante cancionista JUANITA SAETA.* *artista enciclopédica*

It was added that the last performer had a *lujoso vestuario*—a luxurious wardrobe.

Quite apart from the delights of hearing a notable sextette, I looked forward to witnessing the carefully differentiated performances of an "elegant singer and dancer," an "elegant and good dancer," a "beautiful and elegant singer," and a merely "elegant" singer who would, however, be also an encyclopedic artiste. I was not to be disappointed.

It would be tedious to describe the theatre, the audience, the cigarette-smoking firemen and the rapid and perfunctory "symphony" of the notable sextette. These were all pretty much the same as in the theatre on the previous evening.

The curtain rose on an empty stage, but behind the scenes there was a rattling of castanets, and soon a graceful girl came out, dressed in white with a Spanish shawl flung round her and with a high white comb in her hair, through which the light shone upon the backcloth. She sang a song, wriggling her body and rattling the castanets and occasionally uttering the strange nasal notes that astonish the visitor to Spain. She finished her song and danced off, the audience showing no interest whatever in her, except for the small claque at the back of the hall, whose efforts were treated with indifference by everybody else. She soon returned, after signaling to the bored orchestra with her castanets, in a colored dress and a red comb. It may have been a better song this time, but the small boys selling caramels made more noise than she did; and again she moved off the stage unapplauded. But her third song, for which she wore a scanty dress of red frills, moved us all to enthusiasm. I do not know what it was about, but I could at least understand the first line of the chorus, which my neighbors occasionally interrupted their conversation to join in. It consisted of the stirring words—"Caramba, señore!" This time she had to return to bow her thanks for our applause; then after a pause she came back for her last appearance. She had changed into Andalusian dress, with a high, hard, full-brimmed felt hat and a blue-gray shawl. With a loud rattle of castanets and an accompaniment of "Olé, olé" from the audience, she danced vigorously, stamping with her heels and wheeling suddenly, all the time smiling proudly and enticingly at us. The curtain came down amidst much excitement.

The appearance of the "elegant and good" dancer was less successful. True, as became her goodness, she came out first dressed in white with a red rose in her girdle; but neither her song nor her dance was appreciated. As she left the stage for the first time, the claque applauded half-heartedly, but the more robust critics hissed heartily. Her two next dances went even worse; the orchestra, the notable sextette, chatted loudly to the firemen even while they played the tunes, and

the curtain fell a few seconds too soon, which pleased the audience more than anything that had yet happened. And when she danced a Red Indian dance, chasing and spearing imaginary animals in the wings, the audience hissed so fiercely that everybody had to go out for a drink during the interval that followed.

It was, I gathered, no accident that the next performer's name on the program contained no reference to her moral qualities. She sang four songs with a certain amount of success, won largely by a horrifying trick of raising her eyes until one saw the whites, and then dropping them with the opposite result. The louder she sang, the louder everybody talked, but she beat them all with her stamping, which was colossal. One song had an especial interest for a Spanish audience, which loves to be assured that Paris, Rome and even London are the seats of strange vices and frolics that the Spaniard knows nothing of.

And now came the star turn of the evening's entertainment, the encyclopedic artiste herself with the luxurious wardrobe. She proved to be a large lady, not unduly youthful, dressed in black with huge embroidered roses and with a veil over her bust and a large tortoise-shell comb. The orchestra greeted her with enthusiasm, but the audience fell into its habitual apathy. Only a few handclaps and hisses succeeded her first song. But she was waiting for us, just as we were waiting for her. Her next song was in the style of Marie Lloyd, whom she might have been studying; her clothes were the Parisian of the stage and her gestures the same. This went fairly well, but her next song, in which she played the part of a distressed young woman, was considered either not in good taste or not sufficiently well done. But when she came out draped with a huge Spanish flag of red and orange and sang a patriotic song with appropriately martial music, the audience rose at her, and one could hardly hear the hisses for the applause. The sextette played a few bars to see us out of the theatre; everybody cleared his throat and went out into the night. It had been an absorbing, if not very thrilling entertainment. As at the theatre, there were almost no women present; and I concluded from the attitudes of most of the audience that they had come in rather to kill time than to be edified or even amused.

I cannot say quite the same for the music hall I went to at Malaga a few days later. Two British cruisers lay out in the bay, and Malagan society had had a roisterous afternoon dancing on the deck of one of them; it had been possible to approach a Spanish lady in the midst of her family and ask her to dance with you without even having been introduced to her father and mother and aunts and married sisters. Naturally an orgy of this kind required a long period of recuperation, and I was not surprised to find the town exceedingly quiet in the evening. However, the proprietor of the "Theatre of the Vital Spark" was determined not to succumb to the prevailing tedium, and together with a hundred Malagans I found myself witnessing a program that consisted chiefly of a troupe of German ladies in "living pictures," preceded by single acts in which they appeared individually and sometimes boldly sang songs in what they imagined to be Spanish. To tell the truth, I could understand their songs better than I could the more correctly enunciated variety, but the audience, sternly patriotic in its at-titude to the language of its country, hissed them unmercifully. But when they appeared, much undressed, in classical, semi-classical and pseudo-classical groups, everybody took his cigar out of his mouth and murmured approval. But I did not find myself very appreciative.

If I found the Spanish music halls curiously restrained—for even the "living pictures" were discreet—I was to be still more surprised when I crossed the border and arrived in Rome a week or two later. For the Fascisti are engaged in a self-appointed mission to purify the dress, customs and spectacles of the Italian people. Ladies are not allowed any longer to appear in *décolleté* in a public place, and every music hall and theatre proprietor who wishes his entertainment to be a success seeks to arouse his audience by providing a lady who enters a box half an hour after the beginning of the show, takes off her wraps and discloses her shoulders and is then soundly hooted and driven out again. I saw this done on successive nights at two Roman music halls. The costumes of the artistes are also severely censored, and the only performer I saw who dared to show sufficient of the body to make possible the stomach dance—that unfailing attraction to a meridional audience—proved at last to be a boy disguised as a woman! He was, like most of the other turns, Arabs and all, a German.

THE AMERICAN VIEW OF POLITICS

BY JOHAN J. SMERTENKO

> If I write a learned article on chewing gum I find that I lose my clientèle of readers who are toothless, because they naturally are not interested in chewing gum if they have no teeth. Then, when I write on politics, I find that the honest people are not interested.

THUS Will Rogers, like every other popular humorist, uses a truism as the foundation of his joke, and, again like every other popular humorist, he uses one that is old enough to be familiar even to readers of the Sunday supplements, and hence one that is false as well as old and ugly. Nevertheless, his witticism has had the support, at one time or another, of authorities of no little weight and dignity. The Progressives in 1913 and the reformers in 1900 put the political indifference of Americans among the chief causes of the corruption of our politics, and twelve years before the latter James Russell Lowell, then near the end of his life, complained to his fellow independents that "the men who should shape public opinion and control the practical application of it" among us had left all political activity in hands "that are not too delicate to be dipped into the nauseous mess." He added as a clincher: "I do not believe that there is a man at this table who, for the past twenty years, has been able to embody his honest opinion, or even a fraction of it, in his vote." Thirty years before that, indeed, Lowell, like the Abolitionists, had cried out against "all the dirty intrigues of provincial politics" and bemoaned the fact that no educated man regarded them. And even so early as 1837 Abraham Lincoln had felt it necessary to explain why the forces which roused such zeal for politics during the Revolutionary period were dormant or dead.

But though it is thus justified by the opinion of the past, Mr. Rogers' joke is not substantiated by observation in the immediate present. Today the American has once more turned his attention to politics—not only the Ku-Klux-American Legion-Anti-Saloon League-American who has a gold brick to sell, nor the Irish-Jewish-German-Italian-American who has a special interest to protect, but also my honest country cousin-in-law who for more than two-score years has cast his Republican ballot on election day as proudly, as inevitably, and as arbitrarily as he has consumed his turkey on another day in November. Removed as he is in rural New York from the disquieting influences of the Farm Bloc, the Nonpartisan League, and the other progeny of Bad Times out of Progressivism, this septuagenarian seeks in his paper the news of political good works which will justify his unshaken faith in the Grand Old Party. And the signs are everywhere manifest that the natives of New York and San Francisco, Boise City and Covington, the Ozarks and Oshkosh have the same new and surprising interest in politics. The man in the street has added to his conversation on climatic mobility the equally profound discussion of congressional cachexias and presidential possibilities. In fact, this revival of interest is now so obvious that the press has detected and is recognizing it by devoting more columns to municipal, state, and national politics than to all the sports combined.

Hence we may expect to see the democrat, who has now and again denounced the people for renouncing in practise those Rights of Man which they most avidly accept in theory, jubilant because his faith in them is once more indicated, and we may hear the demagogue, who has always flattered the mob, prophesy another Golden Age because Agoracritus the Sausage-seller at last rules the realm. But what shall the skeptical spectator conclude from this reversion to the political fervor which accompanied the founding of the Republic?

II

Possibly an examination of the historical and psychological springs underlying the politicalmindedness of Americans will shed some light on the path they are likely to pursue, now that they are politically-minded again. Perhaps it may not be amiss to point out that although the American people are at last more exercised about politics than about the national pastime of baseball, yet the victory over baseball is not altogether complete. That our concern with politics differs from our enthusiasm for sports only in degree, not in kind, is contantly betrayed by the character of our party platforms and the inattention they receive from public and politicians, by the failure of candidates to offer any consistent, comprehensive policy regarding the local, national, or foreign problems which they must try to solve if elected, and by the absence of a distinct liberal or conservative attitude toward administrative problems. In this day of increasing and encroaching governmental paternalism there is not a single salient politician among us who champions state sovereignty or individual rights; at a time when every question of social, economic, and political adjustment is to the fore there is—Prohibition excepted—no coherent system of reform, no matured legal program, presented for public approval.

One could continue indefinitely piling up proof that politics in the United States, like horseracing, is still an individual competition for honors and stakes. But this has been done often enough by the critics I have mentioned and by others. Critical opinion is thoroughly agreed that politics, in the sense that Plato or Locke or Jefferson understood the term, we have not. We have not politics even in the sense that the contemporary European chancellors understand it. For over there the intrigues and enmities in which each nation is involved force every padishah to formulate and announce a genuine political attitude, at least on foreign affairs. Here, with two boundaries guarded by powerful oceans and the other two made secure by weak and outnumbered neighbors, we have troubled no more about a policy of international relationships than about a program of domestic legislation. Thus the American people have not even remotely associated politics with statecraft; they have confined it simply to competition for office.

Now, our valiant, if violent, defenders of democracy have pressed these points before; they incorporated them in their earliest attacks upon the American party system, which they regarded as the root of all our political and social evils. James Russell Lowell thus summed up the case: "The tricks of management are more and more superseding the science of government. Our methods force the growth of two kinds of politicians to the crowding out of all other varieties,—him who is called *practical*, and him of the corner grocery. Both parties have been equally guilty, both have evaded, as successfully as they could, the living questions of the day." And elsewhere he called the political bosses, "flesh-flies that fatten on the sores of our body politic, and plant there the eggs of their disgustful and infectious progeny." Charles Edward Russel put it more concisely when he coined the phrase, "Our invisible government." But the eloquence of such critics has been sterile, for it was directed against the tail which they believed to be wagging the dog.

The writer believes that the responsibility for the chaos of our polity rests directly on the character of the American people,—and that the factors which perpetuate in an empire the electoral and administrative conditions suitable to village government reside in a variety of politicalmindedness that is peculiar to our country. His aim, therefore, is not to repeat the ancient indictments against an ailing state but to chart the sources of infection, not to describe symptoms but to seek out the responsible germs, not to hawk aged specifics but to disclose the reasons underlying the constitutional vulnerability.

III

Temperamentally the American is a pragmatist. Latterly this turn of mind has been labeled single-track, but it may be more aptly likened to the local train which uses that single track. It is the one-station-at-a-time mind to which Coytesville is as important as Metropolis, and which has neither goal nor terminus, but simply a continuous oscillation. This mind is not concerned with vice and virtue in the abstract; it knows wrong only as concrete, demonstrable evils and right as concrete, probative benefits. It cannot focus on problems and programs, but it is quick to see grievances and advantages. It shies at visions, policies, and Utopias, but it rides triumphant over "practical" details, difficulties, and obstacles. Political philosophies, like those of Aristotle, Hobbes, or Marx, are indeed foreign to America—not because they were conceived on the other side of the Atlantic but because they predicate a mode of thought which has not yet crossed the ocean.

That this tendency to view the questions which incessantly confront life as particular and unrelated rather than as connecting links in "this sorry scheme of things entire"—that this habit manifests itself in our political misadventures is obvious. It is not too much to say that the temperament responsible for it is most evident in politics, whether in the perpetual fallacy of a "good man" vote or in the ephem-

eral issues which shut out the possibility of systematic reform, and that by virtue thereof no body of electors in the world is so constantly the victim of red herrings drawn across the trail of progress as are those of the United States. In other fields much may be said in favor of this attitude of mind. Science and industry, organization and invention bear witness to the value of an automatic psychological adjustment to life—but not politics!

In politics, the negative as well as the positive side of the passion for the palpable has effects that can only be detrimental. Everywhere the masses are susceptible to—in fact, are governed by—shibboleths and moral swear-words; in the United States, alas, this is not characteristic solely of the mob. By the otherwise reflective classes, too, all novel political theory is made part of that dreaded abstraction, radicalism. Here I do not refer to the propaganda, the perversions, and the forgeries that are consciously let loose to foment a senseless fear of and a violent prejudice against a particular bogey, such as Bolshevism or the I. W. W.; I mean simply the honest, conscientious, and well-meaning antipathy to any consideration of politics which implies the possibility of change along rational lines, that is constantly manifested on the editorial page of the Main Street newspaper.

For, in addition to the colorful plots to ruin the Republic, and turn it over to the Soviets which are featured in the metropolitan press, the Gopher Prairie *Intelligencer* prints diatribes of its own manufacture against a whole corps of "anarchistic socialists" who are alleged to be undermining American society. The sum of these is that all criticism of existing evils, no matter how well founded, is Bolshevism, that to insist on the rights guaranteed by the Constitution is unpatriotic, that to propagate the basic principles of the Declaration of Independence is treason. What wonder that the very word reform has become a red blanket to the populace and that the reformer is conceived as a mad mullah of fiendish purpose! As for the political theory attacked, let it be the life work of the best thinkers of a generation: it is condemned nevertheless as the vagary of a weak mind. Though it may be more antagonistic to other programs of reform than to the present social order, it is described in the same terms and denounced by the same epithets as the theories it supplants or opposes. Thus the man in the street learns that all protagonists of new theories, of whatever sort, believe in free love, wear dirty linen, carry bombs, and grow their hair in an immoral fashion!

It is impossible to overestimate the rôle of the bugaboo in the tragi-comedy of political evolution. *Ochlos* has always advanced like the swimmer, by pushing away what he fears will engulf him, save that the swimmer employs his energy purposefully and directs his course intelligently, whereas the mob flings its arms about in a frenzy, careless of its destination so long as it is beating off the waves. All American popular leaders, from Patrick Henry to Theodore Roosevelt, have been shrewd enough to recognize this phenomenon and to exploit it. The latter, in fact, was a very Dr. Faustus in conjuring up devils to frighten the mob. And now government by hysteria has become a political science, so that the people of the United States, once pioneers in democracy, have begun to dismiss in terror every new political theory offered to them.

How peculiar this attitude is to our politics may be seen by comparing it with our characteristic position toward reform in other fields. Whereas in Europe there is an enormous class of senile and sentimental persons who are troubled as much by the invention of a new loom or wine-press as by the formation of a new social organization, and upon whom the idea of innovation operates as a sort of moral and intellectual incubus, suspending all their faculties and awakening all their fears, in America there is none so old nor so sot in his ways as to cease his genuflections

to our great fetish, Progress. "Watch us grow!" is the slogan of town and church, trust and college, and the most radical innovations in airplanes and roach powders, breakfast foods and stock exchange manipulations are presented with pride and taken on faith.

This inconsistency in our point of view is undoubtedly due to the widespread ignorance of governmental machinery among us, an ignorance which amounts to a protective instinct. For your yokel dreads a thing of moving gears and pistons. He absolutely will not monkey with the works if the works throb and pulsate with life. Therefore, he eschews the investigation of our complex political apparatus as long as the mechanism is in action, no matter what may be its slackness, inefficiency, and expense. Americans have been content to wind the political clock every so often and to let the rest take care of itself. They have not dared to overhaul it when it was obviously out of order for fear of making a chaos of its wheels and balances. And they have resented the courage of those who offered to do the work for them.

IV

Unfortunately, this temperamental inclination to regard politics as complex and unintelligible has been abetted by the fact that until this generation the frontier and the wide open spaces knew government as something technical, superfluous, and far-removed. The social contract was not enforced by due process of law. When the crime against society was immediate and important, like horse-stealing, the community invoked the rope of Judge Lynch; when the sin was abstract or trivial, like denying God, the culprit was ridden out of town or treated to a round of drinks.

This conception of the inadequacy of a thing so remote and complex as government to enforce elemental and immediate law and order is even now illustrated by the Ku Klux Klan. After all, the pioneer went pioneering, not because he wished to found a new commonwealth but because he desired to escape the constraints of the old one. He went upon his quest in the spirit of the Irishman who, on learning that America also had a government, promptly declared, "Thin I'm agin it!" After the Revolution, inspired by the idealists who were intoxicated with the joy of creation, he took his politics seriously and enthusiastically, but not for long. The hatred of Bumbledom soon reasserted itself and has been carried on to the present day as a repugnance or indifference to or incomprehension of the administrative mechanism. Whether the present revival of interest in politics may resolve this obvious "complex" or whether it will simply spend itself in a campaign of more than usual strenuousness is a matter of speculation, but there can be no doubt that until this antagonism to the intricacies of government is dissipated, politics will not rise among us much above the level of a battle for office.

Similarly, our economic background perpetuates an indifference to political theory. People are moved "to alter their former Systems of Government . . . and to provide new Guards for their future security" less by the pabulum in their heads than by the absence of nutriment in their bellies. Compared to Europe, America has indubitably been a land of plenty as well as a land of promise. Its spaciousness and opulence have fostered a belief that El Dorado should be sought by change of place rather than by change of government. Although today the growing stratification of American society, due to the appropriation and exploitation of our virgin resources and the concentration of wealth, is constantly narrowing the margin of security for the future and widening the space between life on Primrose Avenue and that in Railroad Alley, the sense of well-being hangs over from the past and makes the American people as averse to action as a replete lion.

Moreover, "abstract liberty, like other mere abstractions, is not to be found.

Liberty inheres in some sensible object." In America, as in England, continues Edmund Burke, this object has ever been taxes. ". . . The great contests for freedom in this country were from the earliest times chiefly upon the question of taxing." Now, our system of taxation today is so skilfully indirect that those who, absolutely as well as relatively, pay most are least aware of it. This failure to recognize who is carrying the burden of our enormous administrative expenses is another cause for the general apathy toward systematic reform in administration. Incidentally, it is also the reason for the lack of responsibility revealed in the individual's relations with our institutions. In the army, in the civil service, in every department of government we find that the ethical sense is dulled. We daily learn of misappropriations and unwarranted expenditures with indifference. There is no sense of proprietorship in their government on the part of the people.

More subtle in its operations but no less effective in its results than the temperamental or economic prejudice against the view that the United States government is a living organism, and, hence in need of scientific culture, is the sublimed conception of America as something poured into a mould formed by the Declaration of Independence and the Constitution. This misconception gives to the political organization of the United States a fixity that is almost unknown elsewhere. The distinguishing marks of the American are the political concepts that he has adopted rather than the customs he has developed. The Frenchman remains a Frenchman whether his government be an absolute or limited monarchy, a directory or regency or republic, but the American is at present inseparable from the democratic dogma. But all this though it is true, is not one of your eternal verities. It is a truth simply because America is a nation still in the formative stage, because the American still lacks those qualities which are derived from immemorial custom and diuturnal habitation in a single land. And, as such, it is a truth growing less true every day.

The significance of this situation, and its bearing on American politicalmindedness, becomes apparent when we recall that nations are always wont to idolize and worship their own distinctive characters. But it is one thing to take abstractions like "English liberty," "*Kultur*," or "*esprit*," or delusions like "chosen people" or "Nordic blond" and make fetishes of them; it is another thing entirely to make idols of such pure instruments of service as are the two charters of Americanism. For in the first case the abstraction can always be reinterpreted and thus changed in accordance with the changing needs or ideals of its worshipers, whereas in the second the concrete documents must either be violated to conform with the actual life of the people or they must arrest the national development. That they are violated any schoolboy who has learned the Bill of Rights and the other amendments to the Constitution knows very well; that they also arrest political progress in America should be equally obvious.

Not merely the Declaration of Independence and the Constitution specifically, but democracy in general, so far as it is an institutionalized creed rather than an actuality, is prejudicial to sound political thought or action. It is characteristic of all institutionalized creeds, whether religious, aesthetic, or political, that their form and ritual tend to supplant their purpose and meaning. When an action or ceremony becomes traditional, the individual is apt to forget or ignore its original import and to attach that importance to the mere performance of the action or ceremony. The American people were lately on the point of making the exercise of the rights of citizenship a ritual pure and simple; in fact, the usual reason offered for party fidelity smacked suspiciously of an-

cestor worship. And it is a sufficiently sad commentary on the masses' use of the ballot that a few months ago Amos Pinchot repeated the ever-recurring proposal to organize a national campaign upon "one outstanding issue" because the nation's attention "cannot be concentrated on more than a single political idea at a time."

V

The difference between this attitude and the political alertness of the founders of the nation is illustrated in Burke's description of the Colonial mind. "In other countries," he said, "the people, more simple and of a less mercurial cast, judge of an ill principle in government only by an actual grievance; here they anticipate the evil, and judge of the pressure of the grievance by the badness of the principle. They augur misgovernment at a distance, and snuff the approach of tyranny in every tainted breeze." Today the change that has come with the years finds expression in the action of the Texas sheriff who sought a warrant for one Thomas Jefferson because he had written "some Bolsheviki propaganda," though it is seldom so truly revealed. Much more commonly the American idolater simply worships his country's Fathers, supremely unconscious of the ironic contrast between his demand for "practical" politics and their idealistic theory of popular government, with its rehashed philosophy of Locke, Rousseau and the radicals of the Revolution.

Whether he will ever become aware of this incongruity, and conform his ideas to his ideals or vice versa, is a matter for the future to determine. But at least we can be certain that America is not exempt from the tendency recognized by Machiavelli when he wrote: "All forms of human government have, like men, their natural term, and those only are long-lived which possess in themselves the power of returning to the principles on which they were originally founded."

THE THEATRE

BY GEORGE JEAN NATHAN

THE fact first. In "The Miracle," the combined talents of Max Reinhardt, Norman-Bel Geddes and Morris Gest have brought to the American theatre the most vividly impressive and thunderously beautiful spiritual spectacle, not that it has ever known—for it is too easy to say that—but, more, that it has ever dreamt of. These three men, the foremost active producing genius in the world, a young American scenic artist of rare talent, and a man who is the leading showman of his country, have realized, within the walls of what until yesterday was merely a millionaires' red and gilt dream of some transcendental bawdy-house, a super-theatre and in that super-theatre, imagined with a soaring fancy and made true with a remarkable panurgy, have lodged further what is beyond question the greatest production, in taste, in beauty, in effectiveness and in wealth of rich and perfect detail, that has thus far been chronicled in the history of American theatrical art. All the elements that go into the life blood of drama are here assembled into a series of aesthetic and emotional climaxes that are humbling in their force and loveliness. The shout of speech, the sweep of pantomime, the sob and march of orchestral music, the ebb and flow of song, the peal of cloister chimes, the brass clash of giant cymbals, the play of a thousand lights, the shuffle and rush of mobs, the rising of scene upon scene amid churning rapids of color, these directed by a master hand are what constitute this superb psychical pageant brewed from an ancient and familiar legend and called now "The Miracle."

The theatre that we have known becomes lilliputian before such a phenom-enon. The church itself becomes puny. No sermon has been sounded from any pulpit one-thousandth so eloquent as that which comes to life, in this playhouse transformed into a vast cathedral, under the necromancy that is Reinhardt. For here are hope and pity, charity and compassion, humanity and radiance wrought into an immensely dramatic fabric hung dazzlingly for even a child to see. It is all as simple as the complex fashioned by genius is ever simple. There is in it the innocence of a fairy tale, and the understanding of all the philosophers who ever were. There is the sentiment that is eternally implicit in gentle faith, and the sternness that one finds always in the heart of beauty. It is, in its pantomime, as silent and yet as articulate as a tune that haunts one in the far confines of the brain. For such a melody, as we all know, can be heard distinctly by the ear of the mind, for all its being a prisoner in the cells of silence. The only trouble with a thing like "The Miracle" is that it induces in the beholder an eczema of adjectives and other parts of speech. It converts the critic into a mere honkhonk, or circus press-agent. It makes him glow, like a reformed chillblain. It deprives him of a certain measure of cool sense, as does beautiful music; but what the need of cool sense on such occasions? So complete is the spell of illusion which Reinhardt works that critical penetration is considerably blunted. Where, in other circumstances, one might conceivably be dumfounded at seeing in the aisles a procession of nuns that appeared to include Al Woods and Archie Selwyn, it here matters not in the least. Belated seat-searchers, aye, even Dr. John Roach

369

Straton himself, fail for a moment to diminish the pervading air of sanctity and piety. The spectacle is too long; it might be cut down to two hours with much profit. But as it stands it is still a triumphant contribution to the theatre. Never before has this legend that Karl Vollmöller has retold, that Engelbert Humperdinck has veined with melody, that Geddes has framed, that Reinhardt has worked his wonder on and that Morris Gest has brought to life for the American theatre taken on such grandeur. Many a Sister Beatrice and Sister Megildis, in literature and in drama, has found her place taken in an old gray nunnery by the Mother of God since first the legend grew, but never until now has the legend itself found *its* place taken in the temple of Thespis by such artists as these. They have served the legend as only real artists of the theatre could hope to.

The vagrant nun of the American girl, Rosamond Pinchot, is a youthful, vital and dramatically picturesque figure. The Madonna of Lady Diana Manners is well-composed and of tender suggestion compact. The lesser rôles are handled without flaw.

II

Never having shared the tumultuous enthusiasm of certain talented critics for the stunning genius of Clemence Dane, I am unable to share their tumultuous surprise over the stunning mediocrity of her most recent play, "The Way Things Happen." This essential mediocrity, for all its occasional concealment in a deftly turned line or phrase, has been clearly discernible in her work from the first. As between "A Bill of Divorcement" and "The Way Things Happen," there is little to choose. Both are third-rate, the former but slightly less so than the latter. And "Will Shakespeare" is at best a good attempt at what is in general a comparatively poor accomplishment. It is not difficult to penetrate the reasons for the critical approval of the last named play, since there is a school of criticism that is ever hornswoggled by a play, however faulty, which treats of historical personages. All that one has to do to stir this school to high commendation is to take over some such old opera as "Mignon," cut out the music, rename Wilhelm Meister François Villon and the actress Filina Catherine de Vausselles, convert the gypsy chief Giarno into the priest Sermaise, make Mignon the daughter of the Duc Charles d'Orléans, have the estimable Deems Taylor compose a drinking song for the tavern scene, raise the height of the ceilings ten feet to give the necessary spacious air to the production, drop the curtain thirteen or fourteen times during the course of the evening (since a biographical play in the conventional number of acts would arouse the critics' suspicions), and craftily preface the whole business by sending to the critics, a week in advance of the opening and in plain envelopes, marked copies of the ecstatic notices from the London papers. It is true that there are several passages of excellent writing in Miss Dane's Shakespeare play. It is also true that there are several passages of excellent writing in the worst play of Percy MacKaye.

Clemence Dane, as I have once before observed, is a mild talent that postures a golden inspiration. Hers is the kind of playwriting that impresses one as being conscious and ever-mindful of its own importance. "A Bill of Divorcement" is nothing more than an ordinary play of commerce, of a somewhat remote vintage, given a contemporaneous feel by hitching it to a modern turn in divorce jurisprudence. "The Way Things Happen" is a mixture of Sardou and Henry Arthur Jones similarly given a contemporaneous feel by phrasing the passages concerning adultery with calm directness instead of in the old-time, roundabout, flossy manner and by causing the concupiscent villain to tell the heroine promptly and exactly what he is driving at instead of making him elaborately pave the way by having

Meadows serve a pâté and a magnum of Cordon Rouge and then chasing the poor girl around the table. Yet Miss Dane, for all the intrinsic banality of her materials, proceeds about her business with quite the same straight face and scholarly wrinkles that were affected by her fellow English genius of a decade and a half ago, the late Stanley Houghton. She appears to be as deeply impressed by her work as some of the rest of us are not. She is as intense as July heat, and frequently as enervating.

"The Way Things Happen," which is a fair example of the Dane craft, contains instances of adroit dramatic writing as do her other plays. But it is generally, so far as its dramatic materials and flavors go, a London Cohan Revue of 1895. She trots out all the favorite playwrights and dramatic stencils of the days when Shaw reigned and stormed in the pages of the *Saturday Review* and gravely—without the flicker of a Cohan smile—puts them once again through their paces. One by one they enter, under aliases that deceive no one, and go through their venerable parlor, drawing-room and bachelor-chambers tricks. Miss Henry Arthur Jones goes at midnight to the rooms of the wicked Sir Arthur Wing Pinero to get from him the papers that would incriminate the heroic young Sydney Grundy. She leaves behind her, in place of Oscar Wilde's pair of long white gloves, R. C. Carton's shawl, which is found by her jealous rival, the haughty Miss H. V. Esmond. Before, during and subsequent to this, the young juvenile in the blue serge jacket and white flannels, Hubert Henry Davies, bounces jovially in and out of the proceedings, the sweet, gray-haired Mrs. Augustin Daly, dear, kindly old soul, falls back in her chair and breathes her last even as she is smiling her happiness over the letter announcing that her son, absent these many years, is to return on the morrow, and the faithful old servant, Alfred Sutro, (in this instance a maid), offers with touchingly loyal lachrymation to stay on at the post for all the family's financial reverses. Nothing is missing. Yet sweeping into this refuse of another generation there comes the young American actress, Katharine Cornell, with the finest talent among the new women of our theatre, and into it with that talent and all its ardor and fire and flame she burns something that for the moment seems lively and vital and very true. A rare and beautiful performance, as clear and as eloquent amid the encompassing dramatic shoddy as the sound of a loud horse-laugh in the House of Representatives. Tom Nesbitt brings to the rôle of the cad-hero all the tremors of his anatomy. He plays his big dramatic scene at the conclusion of the second act for all the world as if it had been written by La Belle Fatima.

III

Pirandello's dramatic themes are ever more interesting than his thematic dramas. Possessed of a much more fertile and analytical mind than any other South European writing at the present time for the theatre, he finds himself in the embarrassing predicament of evolving themes that either escape the dramatic form or, perhaps more exactly, the particular dramatic form that thus far has eluded his ingenious but defective butterfly net. Another instance of this is vouchsafed to us in his play, "Henry IV," produced locally as "The Living Mask." While it may be utterly ridiculous to say that a man may be too intelligent to write good theatre plays, it may not be too ridiculous to say that Pirandello's especial kind of intelligence prevents him from achieving good theatre plays. The ideas which his intelligence gives birth to are often above the homely plane of drama. They are at times no more suited to the dramatic form than would be the ideas implicit in Kant's "Foundation of the Metaphysics of Ethics," Goethe's "Introduction to the Propylæa" or a treatise on the *Bibos frontalis*. A sound dramatic idea must be generically transitive; it must move, so to speak, even before the dramatist touches it. The dramatic ideas of Pirandello are essentially static. To make them seem to move at all, and in their moving produce a semblance of drama, it is necessary for him to have recourse to the propulsive agency of alien dramatic factors which in the very act of bequeathing a bit of slow motion to his undramatic ideas rob those ideas of much of their original power of static conviction. The effect is akin to making a moving picture out of Rembrandt's "Lesson in Anatomy." What remains is not composition, but de-composition.

A Pirandello play is less a play than a compromise with a play. It presents the picture of a group of actors in grease-paint hanging around a dissecting room. Actors give one the impression of being slightly out of place in the Pirandello drama. And not only out of place, but—sometimes—absurd. Pirandello thinks dramatically, it is clear, not in terms of a stage and footlights and performers, but in terms of an anomalous institution that is part clinic and part sideshow. The result, as I have said, is interesting, but chiefly if one closes one's eyes, listens attentively, and screws one's mind up the while to imagine that one is not in a theatre. "Henry IV"—with its theme of a man who in dementia believes himself to be head of the Holy Roman Empire and who, when once again after twenty years he regains his sanity, prefers to keep up the show of insanity as a refuge from the world that has grown harsh and ugly around him—is in this way infinitely more satisfactory to the ear than to the eye. The ear catches a neat-handed story of metaphysics and psychology; the eye sees only the mind of Pirandello trying grotesquely to hide itself in the body of a ranting and gesticulating actor. It is all very well to argue that the Italian is trying to fashion a new type of drama—actually, he is doing nothing of the kind—but before one sets out to fashion a new type of drama one must have known and forgotten the old.

Arthur Livingston's translation of the original text is a dismaying performance. In an unintelligible attempt to make the translation sufficiently lively, he has caused the Italian characters periodically to indulge in the Broadway vernacular and has introduced into the Tuscan dialogue allusions to Kalamazoo, Mich., and the like. Arnold Korff, an excellent actor, misses almost entirely the subtleties of the central rôle, playing it with so elaborate an orchestration of all the ham attributes and idiosyncrasies as to give one the picture of Paul Whiteman playing King Lear.

IV

There is much to admire in Sutton Vane's "Outward Bound." It is one of those odd plays that comes along every once in a while and that, by virtue of its general complexion of grace and skill, persuades one theatrically that even its failings, like those of a winning child, are charming. The story is of an assortment of men and women who find themselves somewhat puzzlingly aboard a strange ship bound for they know not where and who gradually awaken to the realization that they are dead and on their way to whatever heaven or hell may be like. With what seems to me to be as shrewd a sense of dramaturgic values as has come out of the popular theatre of England in many a day, Vane relates this tale with a constantly surprising and enviable aptitude for foretelling his audience's every momentary turn of mood. His melodrama, sentiment, comedy, burlesque, irony and fantasy are dovetailed with a very deft talent indeed; each falls into place with an exact click; each avoids the slightest suggestion of pigeonholing; the handling of each is perfectly timed and with a most blithe and captivating unstudied air. If I were a playwright, I should envy Vane his uncommon gift in this uncommon achievement of theatrical effect. At bottom, his technic may be as old as the hills, but his particular talent lies in making it seem fresh and hearty and engagingly new, like an old friend come back after a long absence. The pleasure of the evening is heightened by the knowledge that the job his theme offered him was anything but an easy one and by the further fact that he has triumphed over the difficulties that confronted him by taking the hardest road. The road of melodrama, the road of sentiment, the road of fantasy, the road of derisiveness, the road of comedy—each was open to him and each might have found a play at the end of it. But the road to a good play on this particular theme was not so smooth and straight, he appreciated. One would have to hoof them all, jump now and then from one to the other and again retrace one's footsteps as the theme elusively turned this way and that. This Vane has done. And out of the jigsaw he has evoked a sustained theatrical mood that marks a popular theatrical achievement of unusual quality.

The chief defects of the play, which actually disturb one very little while under its pleasant spell, lie in the author's Mother Goose point of view toward heaven and hell and in his strainful avoidance of dramatic climaxes. On the latter subject, I have already made discourse in another place. There I observed that the current prevalent fashion among dramatists of regarding a good, old-fashioned, rousing climax as something beneath dignity and artistic propriety is far from my own peculiar taste. When a dramatic climax has been foreshadowed and is rightly to be expected with high anticipation, it is thoroughly disturbing and disappointing to observe the playwright shush it off the stage and substitute for it a nonchalant, drawling allusion to the villain's spats. An effective climax is nothing to be ashamed of; the present-day practice of avoiding the realization of such climaxes to their full is the rankest affectation. In the matter of his heaven and hell, Vane makes the mistake not of failing to use his imagination, as his critics charge, but of using it. That imagination, like the imagination of most playwrights who

approach the same subject, were better left in peace. Its agitation is productive of dissent and dissatisfaction, and almost inevitably. Unless one be possessed of a very great poetic or ironic fancy, which Vane is not, philosophical explorations into the character of the hereafter may best be abandoned, especially in the theatre. When they are not abandoned, we are very likely to get such things as the Macphersons' "Happy Ending," which pictures heaven as a Pittsburgh millionaire's garden party, "Uncle Tom's Cabin," which pictures it as a German Christmas card, and Vane's "Outward Bound," which reveals it to be something like a William Hodge play. Had Vane left the subject to his audience's imagination rather than to his own, his play would have been a better theatre play. The production is extremely well made—William Harris, Jr., has never shown finer editorial taste—and the presenting company, with Alfred Lunt as its outstanding figure, is from first to last excellent.

V

Genius, in the case of Strindberg, is the capacity for dramatizing infinite pains. There is no major ache, whether of psyche or toe, that does not claim its moment of his enthusiasm. Life, to him, is the panorama of a great and encompassing colic. His tragedy does not so much purge the emotions and leave in its wake the beauty that is ever the residuum of profound sorrow, as constipate hope, and resolution, and human faith. Where Ibsen is the mocking dramatist of tragedy, Strindberg is the tragedian of mocking drama. He looks on the world as a child looks at the skeleton of some prehistoric monster, simultaneously beset by awe and disbelief and seeking relief from its bepuzzlement in a nervous and unconvincing laughter. Like Ibsen, a rebel against the established dramatic technic of his time, the liberator of that technic from its retarding ball and chain, and a pioneer whose brilliant path-clearing made free the way for the many who have followed in his steps, he is unlike Ibsen in that his technic is ever the slave-driver of his themes, beating down and weakening them with its tyrannical lash. The technic of Ibsen, to the contrary, is ever the off-spring of his themes, rising naturally and inevitably out of those themes as the only medium for their capture and expression. Strindberg, with few exceptions, super-imposes his technic arbitrarily upon his themes, where Ibsen permits his themes each to make up its own technic, so to speak, as it goes along. The close tech-nical resemblances in various Ibsen plays are often merely superficial. But, almost without exception, the fundamental tech-nical idiosyncrasies of Strindberg are visible in every one of his plays, sometimes to the complete confounding of the clar-ity of those plays.

Strindberg, on such occasions as his mind was still blessed with reason, wrote excellent drama, some of it of enduring life. On other occasions, after insanity had laid its grip upon him, he wrote what must frankly be set down as utter nonsense, the babbling of an idiot in whom one glimpsed pathetically but the distant rumors of a quondam genius. There are certain good-natured critics who cannot persuade them-selves that it is possible for a man once possessed of a sharp and luminous intelli-gence ever to go completely mad, ever to lose all of his antecedent rationality, and it is they, as sympathetic artistically as they are misinformed pathologically, who are in their charity responsible for much of the amiable rubigo that clings to the critical appraisal of Strindberg and his drama. These critics were here and there again observable when "The Spook Son-ata" was put on—admirably put on—not long ago in the little Provincetown Play-house. The play in point, save for one or two mild flashes of the author's left-over insight, is the mere raving of a stark lunatic, a burlesque of intelligibility, a caricature of all sanity. If it were signed with the name of some Broadway play-wright, even the waiters at the Algonquin Hotel would be seized with cramps from laughing. But because a celebrated name is attached to it, it is here and there viewed as being surely possessed of merit, how-ever much that merit may be concealed from the naked eye. Of merit, it actually has nothing. It is a symposium of all the deficiencies of the sane Strindberg raised to the peak of imperfection by the insane Strindberg. It is a dramatization of the profound pains of mortal man in terms of dialectic pink pills. And to answer all this, as answer has been made, by saying that a mad and inscrutable world is best to be dramatized thus madly and inscrutably, is to say that only the idiot is capable of realizing and transmuting the poetry that lies in the tale of an idiot dancing down the wind. The heart and soul of genius may be mad, but the mind of true genius is ever as clear as the heavens seen through pine trees. Strindberg is occasionally a genius. But Strindberg is also occasionally an absurdly unconscious quack.

VI

Zona Gale's Mister Pitt, in the play of that name broadly derived from her novel "Birth," is less the authentic instance of character drawing that certain of my colleagues claim it is than an authentic instance of character drawing so intensi-fied for theatrical purposes that its au-thenticity goes by the board before the play is half over. It appears to be Miss Gale's notion that, inasmuch as a play may run only two hours or so, everything that makes a character recognizable and convincing in a novel, all the little details and differences, all the little peculiarities and ramifications, must be packed tightly into one small bundle plainly marked on the outside with the character's one out-standing identifying trait, and the reductio offered to an audience, by way of getting the effect quickly and saving time, as the complete character. This procedure she has again followed in the case of her dramatized Mister Pitt as she followed it in her dramatized Lulu Bett, with the upshot that her stage character is a character that never was on land or sea. Her Pitt is not a character so much as a characteristic: a single idiocrasy in trousers. There is no change, no development or disintegration, no even trivial variation upon the insistent motif—and the span of the character covers a period of twenty years! In all the world, there probably has never been a single man as invariable as this stage character of Miss Gale's. He never lived outside of Bowery melodrama.

The trouble with Miss Gale is perfectly clear. She looks down upon the theatre. To her, the stage is the place where good novels go when they die. As an example of this conviction on her part, one need only consider the last act of her present exhibit. If ever there was an illuminating instance of happy ending bosh—the delusion of the condescending playwright—that instance is to be found here. It constitutes as shameless an affectation of superiority as a novelist turned playwright has shown. Walter Huston does all with the rôle of Pitt that the playwright permits him to, and Minna Gombel's Mrs. Pitt, save for a slight overzealousness in her obvious desire to get good notices from Alan Dale, Zit and other leading metropolitan critics, is a commendable creation.

VII

The Charlot revues in London, like the so-called Nine O'clock revues, have been built upon the principle that, in the music show, unlike in drama, the idea is more important than its treatment. Give the audience the idea and then ring down the curtain. Such is the theory, and, so far as music shows go, an excellent one.

The theory of the American revue producer, to the contrary, is that any comparatively fresh idea is worth at least a twenty-five minute sketch, the first three minutes of which are taken up with the idea and the last twenty-two of which are spent stalling until the stagehands have set up the fifteen thousand dollar set showing Hot Springs by moonlight and the girls have changed their South Sea Island costumes for costumes somewhat more relevantly Spanish. The Charlot revue at present on exhibition in New York follows the established London plan. It moves swiftly, lightly, amusingly, sprinkling agreeably under-developed fancies in its wake. It is as diverting in its contemptuous nonchalance as certain American revues are now and again tedious in their laborious overemphasis. And it enjoys, in the enriching persons of Beatrice Lillie and Gertrude Lawrence, two performers who are highly recommended to you for your more frolicsome moments.

VIII

The revival of Anna Cora Mowatt's "Fashion" at the Provincetown Playhouse is, save in the matter of such externals as costumes and scenery, not a particularly happy event. In addition to a direction that has burlesqued the old comedy to a point where even its original humors are often lost, there has been so desperate a slashing of the text by way of making the laughs follow quickly on one another's heels that much of the comic effect goes to pieces. "Fashion" is a cheap and tawdry play, but not so cheap and tawdry as this revival seeks superiorly to make out. If Sheridan's "School for Scandal" were cut with as deliberate and venomous a cruelty, it, too, would seem just as ridiculous.

Cheating the Mortician

PUBLIC HEALTH IN THE UNITED STATES, by Harry H. Moore. New York: *Harper & Brothers* .

THIS large and formidable work should be read in the light of Dr. Raymond Pearl's "The Biology of Death," for in general it is rather romantically optimistic, and the author shows little capacity for differentiating between public health measures that are scientific, effective, and above all, socially useful and profitable, and those that are merely sentimental and uplifting. That the death-rate in the United States is declining is known to everyone, but the rapidity of its decline, I believe, is popularly overestimated, and there is far too much tendency to give all of the credit to health legislation and to the various official and private agencies that operate under cover of that legislation. Many of the latter, it is probable, really accomplish nothing at all, and some of them do a great deal of harm. The unfit are preserved to reproduce their kind, and devices that might benefit the fit are not only neglected, but even opposed.

I point, for an example, to the case of the venereal diseases. These maladies, it must be obvious, are anything but selective. That is to say, they do not help to eliminate the unfit. The individual who has them and recovers from them transmits no immunity to his descendants; moreover, he is quite as apt to suffer permanent damage from them if he is otherwise perfectly healthy as if he is a half-dead weakling. If they select out a class for extermination, indeed, it is probably the best class of young men, at least physically. Yet little is done by any governmental agency to combat them intelligently. They are chiefly attacked, when they are attacked at all,

376

on moral grounds. The young are besought eloquently to avoid the wickedness which brings them on. This exhortation, as we all know, is usually ineffective. Nature, having no morals, sweeps aside the warnings of the sex hygienists. And meanwhile there are devices readily at hand that would, if systematically applied, diminish the incidence of these diseases by at least a half. Why are they not employed?

They are not employed simply because their employment, in the opinion of the sex hygienists, would encourage wickedness by making it safe. In other words, they are not employed because the sex hygienists are not really hygienists at all, but moralists. Their primary desire is not to dimish the venereal diseases; it is to lift the whole youth of the land to the degree of virtue that they advocate. Their horror at the spectacle of hundreds of thousands of young men wrecked by syphilis and gonorrhea is bogus. I believe in all seriousness that many of them take a positive delight in it—that it is somehow agreeable to their moral minds to see a sinner so ferociously punished. If I am wrong, then why do they oppose so violently every genuinely scientific effort to put down both diseases? Why is their literature so heavy with moral fulminations, and so bare of the news that a simple ointment, applied *after* exposure, is sufficient to prevent gonorrhea and syphilis—and if not invariably, then at any rate in 95 cases out of a hundred?

During the war these uplifters fell upon the Army and Navy with their warning pamphlets, their vice crusades and their pious lectures, and there followed a great plague of venereal diseases in both Services. In the Army the medical officers, after a hard struggle against the moralists, managed to apply scientific prophylactic measures on a large scale, and there ensued a sharp decline in both maladies; in some camps, indeed, they almost disappeared. In the Navy there was harder sledding, for the Hon. Josephus Daniels forbade the work on moral grounds. But all the more intelligent medical officers, I am informed, disregarded that prohibition, and so the jolly jack tars were also disinfected. This process of medical bootlegging rescued thousands of young men from invalidism and death. And now the moral hygienists claim the credit for saving them! The business was accomplished, it appears, not by the salts of silver and mercury, but by the evangelistic labors of Y. M. C. A. secretaries!

The Army medical records, though they have been attacked by moralists, prove conclusively that the prophylactic measures I have mentioned actually work—that it would be perfectly possible, applying them in an energetic manner, to reduce the incidence of venereal disease in any American city by at least a half in one year—that all such maladies might be made as rare as leprosy or cholera in America by ten years of concentrated and unsentimental effort. It is not done simply because any proposal to undertake it, in any American community, would be violently opposed by all Puritans—because any man undertaking it would be denounced as a promoter of sexual vice. The menace of syphilis is necessary, it is argued by these Christian publicists, in order to keep the young generation from emulating the morals of the barnyard. Is it so, indeed? They why doesn't the menace of syphilis work better now? Why is it that, in the face of warnings from every pulpit and every school-room desk in the land, the pestilence continues almost unabated?

The obvious remedy—the only one, in truth, that shows any sign of working at all—is to throw all the Pecksniffian literature of the sex hygienists overboard, and proceed against the spirochaetae and the gonococci as we proceed against the malaria protozoa—that is, with chemical agents, devoid of moral purpose. To withhold from the youth of the land the means of protecting themselves against venereal disease on the ground that such disease is usually produced by voluntary acts, and that such acts are immoral—this is as idiotic as it would be to abandon the war upon tuberculosis on the ground that many consumptives are brought to bed by drinking too much, by sitting up too late at night, and by consulting fashion rather than thermometry in the selection of their underwear. Preventive medicine should not concern itself with such considerations. The moment it ceases to be impersonal, that moment it ceases to be scientific, and becomes the sport of all sorts of quacks and fanatics. Its aim is not to punish the guilty, but to safeguard the innocent. If it cannot achieve the latter purpose without neglecting the former, then it must neglect the former. To argue otherwise is to argue that we should abandon science altogether and go back to priestcraft.

I note that Mr. Moore, in his discussion of venereal diseases, is careful to avoid specific mention of chemical prophylaxis. He ascribes their decline during the war to "a program of preventive measures in operation under the direction of the Commissions on Training Camp Activities, . . . and *subsequent* measures," but he very discreetly fails to mention what those "subsequent measures" were. The fact offers a very fair measure of his book.

A Modern Masterpiece

THE POET ASSASSINATED, by Guillaume Apollinaire, translated from the French, with a Biographical Notice and Notes, by Matthew Josephson. New York: *The Broom Publishing Company.*

WHATEVER may be said against the young literary lions of the Foetal School, whether by such hoary iconoclasts as Ernest Boyd or by such virginal presbyters as Dr. Farrar, the saving fact remains that the boys and girls all have, beneath their sombre false faces, a sense of humor, and are not shy about playing it upon one another. Such passionate organs of the movement as *Broom*, the Chicago *Literary Times*, *Secession*, and the *Little Review* print capital parodies in every issue, many of them, I believe, deliberate and malicious—parodies of Ezra Pound by the Baroness Elsa von Freytag-Loringhoven, of the Baroness Elsa von Freytag-Loringhoven by E. E. Cummings, and of E. E. Cummings by young Roosevelt J. Yahwitz, Harvard '27. Ah, that the rev. seniors of the Hypoendocrinal School were as gay and goatish! Ah, specifically, that Dr. Paul Elmer More would occasionally do a salacious burlesque of Dr. Brander Matthews, and that Dr. Matthews would exercise his forecastle wit upon the Urbana, Ill., silurian, Prof. Fred Lewis Pattee!

In the present work, beautifully printed by the *Broom* Press, there is jocosity in the grand manner. For almost a year past—a geological epoch among such neologomaniacs—the syndics of the movement have been whooping up one "Guillaume Apollinaire." When this "Apollinaire" died in 1918, they lamented, there passed out the greatest creative mind that France had seen since the Middle Ages. He was to Jean Cocteau as Cocteau was to Eugène Sue. His books were uncompromising and revolutionary; had he lived he would have done to the banal prose of the Babbitts of letters what Eric Satie has done to the art of the fugue. Such news was not only printed in the *Tendenz* magazines that come and go; it was transmitted by word of mouth from end to end of Greenwich Village. More, it percolated to graver quarters. The estimable *Dial* let it be known that "Apollinaire" was "a profound influence on the literature and perhaps still more on the art and spirit of this modern period." Once, when Dr. Canby was off lecturing in Lancaster, Pa., his name even got into the *Literary Review*.

This electric rumor was helped to prosperity by the fact that specific data about the New Master were extremely hard to come by. His books seemed to be rare—some of them, indeed, unprocurable—, and even when one of them was obtained and examined it turned out to be largely unintelligible. He wrote, it appeared, in an occult dialect of the modern *langue d'oïl*, partly made up of esoteric and pathological slang from the military and penal establishments of the Third Republic. He gave to old words new, mysterious meanings. He kept wholly outside the vocabulary at the back of "College French." Even returning exiles from Les Deux Magots and La Rotonde, specialists in French philology, were baffled by some of his phrases; all that these experts would venture was that they were unprecedented and probably obscene. But the Village, as everyone knows, does not spurn the cabalistic; on the contrary, it embraces and venerates the cabalistic. So "Apollinaire" grew in fame as he became inscrutable. Displacing Cocteau, Paul Morand, Harry Kemp, T. S. Eliot, André Salmon, Paul Valéry, Maxwell Bodenheim, Jean Giraudoux, Ezra Pound and all the other gods of that checkered dynasty, he was lifted to first place in the Valhalla of the Advanced Thinkers. It was "Apollinaire's" year. . . .

The work before us is the pricking of the bladder—a jest highly effective, but somewhat barbarous. M. Josephson simply translates "Apollinaire's" masterpiece, adds an *apparatus criticus* in the manner of T. S. Eliot, and then retires discreetly to wait for the yells. They will make a dreadful din, or I am no literary pediatrician! For what does "The Poet Assassinated" turn out to be? It turns out to be a dull pasquinade in the manner of a rather atheistic sophomore, with a few dirty words thrown in to shock the *booboisie*. From end to end there is not as much wit in it as you will hear in a genealogical exchange between two taxicab drivers. It is flat, flabby and idiotic. It is as profound as an editorial in the New York *Tribune* and as revolutionary as Ayer's Almanac. It is the best joke pulled off on the Young Forward-Lookers since

Eliot floored them with the notes to "The Waste Land."

M. Josephson, alas, rather spoils its effect by rubbing it in—that is, by arguing solemnly that "Apollinaire" was of romantic and mysterious origin—that his mother was a Polish lady of a noble house and his father "a high prelate of the Catholic Church"—that he was born at Monte Carlo and baptized in Santa Maria Maggiore at Rome. This is too much. "Apollinaire," I make no doubt, was, like all Frenchmen of humor, a German Jew. His father was a respectable waiter at Appenrodt's, by name perhaps Max Spritzwasser: hence the *nom de plume*. His mother, I venture, was a Mlle. Kunigunda Schmidt.

Art Criticism

CHINESE PAINTING AS REFLECTED IN THE THOUGHT AND ART OF LI LUNG-MIEN, by Agnes E. Meyer. New York: *Duffield & Company*.
WILLIAM GLACKENS, by Forbes Watson. New York: *Duffield & Company*.
GEORGES SEURET, by Walter Pach, New York: *Duffield & Company*.
A HISTORY OF ART, by Dr. G. Carotti, revised by Mrs. Arthur Strong, Litt.D., LL.D. Three volumes. New York: *E. P. Dutton & Company*.

THE book on Glackens by Forbes Watson and that on Seuret by Walter Pach belong to a series called "The Arts Monographs," edited by Mr. Watson. Their appearance simultaneously with Mrs. Meyer's searching and beautiful work on Li Lung-Mien, issued by the same publisher, must inevitably direct attention to their superficiality as criticism and their poverty as printing. Mr. Watson is so careless as an editor that in his own brief and vague essay on Glackens he permits himself a reference to a plate (page 16) that is not to be found where he says it is. But the printing in both of these monographs is far worse than the text. Any competent commercial engraver could make plates just as good, and any self-respecting printer, if he took the trouble, could print them better.

Mrs. Meyer's book, now appearing in a second edition, is immeasurably more workmanlike. Her plates, though they are unfortunately few in number, are carefully done in collotype, and her text is painstaking, accurate and extremely interesting. Li Lung-Mien belonged to the Sung period (960-1280), but she by no means confines her discussion to the Chinese painting of that time. Instead she attempts a study of the whole history of Chinese art, with particular reference to its grounding in Chinese culture. The relationship has been intimate from the earliest days. The painting of the West, especially in the modern period, has tended to isolate itself in an artificial world of its own creation. Painters are no longer citizens like the rest of us, interested in taxes, Teapot Domes, the price of wheat and the evidence for the Virgin Birth, but inhabitants of an Alsatia of their own, and highly disdainful of everything going on beyond its borders. Not so with the Chinese. Li Lung-Mien, like the great painters who went before him and those who followed after him, was primarily an interpreter of Chinese thought and the Chinese spirit—a social historian and philosopher even before he was a painter. His paintings thus retain the glow of life after eight hundred years. They are not merely pretty things; they are documents in the cultural history of a great race.

It is unfortunate that the Western world knows the art of the Chinese chiefly through its imitation by their intellectual poor relations, the Japanese. This is almost as if the architecture of the Greeks were known only through the parodies of it perpetrated by official architects at Washington. The Japanese owe almost everything they have to the Chinese, and they have debased and vulgarized everything. That they have surpassed their masters in mere technical skill is not to be gainsaid; even the worst of their work shows a great deal of cleverness. But they lack the simple dignity of the Chinese in the fine arts precisely as they lack it in life. They are an efficient but inferior people. The Chinese move less swiftly, but accomplish a great deal more. In almost every field of art, from architecture to painting and from the design of fabrics to gem-cutting, they can show work of the very highest quality. Nothing they attempt seriously is ever cheap and obvious.

The Carotti "History of Art" is probably the most useful handbook of the subject obtainable in English. Its three volumes proceed no further than the end of the Middle Ages, but from that period back to the dawn of architecture in Egypt they sweep the whole field in an extraordinarily comprehensive and satisfying manner. The present edition presents no less than 1257 illustrations. All of them, of course, are necessarily small, and in some cases their scale conceals or muddles detail, but in the main they serve their purpose admirably. Not one of them is superfluous; each actually illustrates and clarifies the text. That text is succinct, well-informed and well-arranged.

Three Gay Stories

THE HIGH PLACE, by James Branch Cabell. New York: *Robert M. McBride & Company.*
ANTIC HAY, by Aldous Huxley. New York: *The George H. Doran Company.*
THE BLIND BOW-BOY, by Carl Van Vechten. New York: *Alfred A. Knopf.*

THREE capital comedies for marionettes—that of Mr. Cabell, perhaps, showing the most adept workmanship and that of Mr. Van Vechten being the most novel in plan. "The High Place" is in the manner of the celebrated "Jurgen," and all the ground that the author seemed to lose in the first successor to "Jurgen," to wit, "Figures of Earth," is here recovered in a handsome style, with some gains further on. "The High Place," indeed, is far more competently put together than "Jurgen." The fundamental idea is simpler; the structure is less complex and dispersed. In brief, the melancholy story of a dream come true. Florian de Puysange has a vision in youth of the perfect maiden, Melior. Her beauty is beyond all other conceivable beauty; she is perfect as the seraphim are perfect. But not unattainable! Florian hacks his way to her through dragons and monsters;

he employs magicians to aid him; he is helped both by the Devil and by a holy saint. In the end he wins his Melior, and discovers—That she is a shrew? No; nothing so obvious. He discovers that she is an unbearable and incurable bore.

The tale has charm almost without measure. It is clear-running, it is ingenious, and it is full of truly delightful detail. Mr. Cabell was never more shrewd, sardonic, iconoclastic, daring. He has made a romance that is captivating in itself, and yet remains a devastating *reductio ad absurdum* of all romance. It is as if the species came to perfect flower in a bloom that poisoned itself. I praise it no more, but pass on to its defects, of which there are two. The first issues out of the fact that the author appears to be down with a bad case of pronounophobia; in particular, the pronouns of the third person seem to affright him. The result is a multiplicity of such sentences as this one: "Thus it was not until the coming of Spring that Florian rode away from the Hôtel de Puysange, wherein he had just passed the first actually unhappy period of Florian's life." Why not "his" for the second "Florian"? The sentence is botched as it stands—and a botched sentence in Cabell stands out as brilliantly as a good one in D. H. Lawrence. A worse defect comes at the very end of the book. Cabell brings it up to a logical and delightful finale, and then tacks on a banal chapter explaining that Florian's adventures in two worlds have been but the fancies of a dream—that he has never actually wooed, won and married the incomparable Melior, that he is still a romantic boy asleep under a magic tree. It is almost as bad as if he had added a moral chapter advocating the World Court and the Coolidge idealism. Still worse, he prints a second appendix hinting plainly that Florian has been called back to life and youth in order to open the way for a sequel. Such crimes against sense and decency are too gross to be punished in literary courts. If there is a secular arm in Virginia, let Cabell be handed over to it.

Messrs. Huxley and Van Vechten both suffer from the fact that the burlesque modern novel is very hard to write—that the slightest letting down reduces it to mere whimsicality and tediousness. Even Max Beerbohm, in "Zuleika Dobson," the best specimen of the genre yet produced, fell into that slough more than once. Huxley and Van Vechten do it whenever they try to be logical—whenever they abandon pure fancy for attempts to get an intelligible sequence into the events they deal with. Both start off better than they end—Huxley with his school-master who is inspired by the hard oaken pews in the school chapel to invent pneumatic panta-

loons—Van Vechten with his rich father who deliberately puts his son to learning all the things that other rich fathers devote themselves so futilely to keeping unknown. The Van Vechten notion is the more amusing, and makes what most readers will probably regard as the better story. But both tales are full of a fine gusto and neither ever grows dull, even when it grows thin. Human life is here depicted, not as a sort of continuous surgical operation, with overtones of Freudian suppression, as in the gloomy novels of the realists, but as gay, senseless and orgiastic. Is this realism, too? Is it, in fact, a more penetrating and accurate realism than that of the orthodox realists? There are days when I so suspect.

REVIEWS BY OTHER HANDS

The Popularization of Science

SOCIAL LIFE AMONG THE INSECTS, by William Morton Wheeler. New York: *Harcourt, Brace & Company.*
STUDIES IN EVOLUTION AND EUGENICS, by S. J. Holmes. New York: *Harcourt, Brace & Company.*

THE WRITINGS of scientific men, in the main, fall into two groups. The learned professor of palaeontology, for example, devotes himself regularly (*a*) to the production of profound tracts in which, with a minimum of literary grace and a maximum of technicality, he exposes to his peers the results of his conquests within the narrow field of his researches, and occasionally and by way of relaxation (*b*) to the composition of more lightsome essays for the public eye, in which the wider bearings of his subject are set forth with such rhetorical charm as has been vouchsafed him.

What can be the object of the man of science who tries to find readers beyond the circle of his colleagues? Certainly he cannot look for appreciation among the great masses of the people, the readers of Brisbane, Guest and Dr. Crane; all he may expect, if he makes himself intelligible to

them, are ridicule, opposition, and even persecution. Explain to a Kansas New Thoughter that a live horse, properly treated, will yield a cure for diphtheria and he will found an anti-vivisection society; argue to a Southern Congressman that he is a mammal and he will see that you are kicked out of the State University. It is clear, then, that the investigator of natural phenomena, in his effort to reach the lay mind, must address himself only to the more intelligent among the people, the civilized and cultivated minority, who, if they know little or nothing of biology or physics, are nevertheless accustomed to ordered thought and somewhat inured to the impact of novel ideas.

But just here a new difficulty arises. Such an audience is not content with incontrovertible facts; it demands literary quality, wit, a humane cynicism, a viewpoint at least as sophisticated as its own. It refuses absolutely to be bored with pedantry or tortured by bad style, however worthy of respect may be the ideas presented. These considerations serve to account for the numerous and conspicuous failures as well as for the occasional successes to be met with in the literature of scientific popularization, and they must be duly regarded in any appraisal of such writings. The two books under review are widely different in character but both are clearly intended to appeal to readers outside the limited group of the technically initiated. Granting their accuracy, how do they stand in the light of the requirements just set forth?

Dr. Wheeler is easily first among American students of the insect world. He is a professor, but his mind is clear, disciplined, and disillusioned, and in his writings the reader never fails to sense a background of intimate acquaintance with the culture of the ancient world, tempered by wide and well assimilated reading in all the fields of modern thought. Though his life has been primarily devoted to technical research he has retained a broad outlook and has known how to relate his specialty to the affairs of men in general. His literary style is clear and precise, of course, in passages of mere exposition, but it is always fluent and easy to read and often charmingly allusive. Here is evidently one anointed of God to preach the gospel to the scribes and Pharisees.

In this new book on social insects will be found a masterly survey of what is known about the subject, beautifully illustrated and organized with a rigorous regard for scientific exactness, well masked by an easy manner. The main topics discussed are the social beetles, wasps solitary and social, bees solitary and social, ants with their strange associates and degraded appetites, and the termites or white ants. A documentary appendix of world-wide scope provides an extraordinary array of references to recent publications of relevant bearing, calculated to delight the seeker out of original sources.

The fundamental attitude of the author in dealing with his subject may be described as philosophical. The facts are stated, and without sentimental or melodramatic nonsense, but always there is the search for the underlying principle, the unifying correspondence, revealing the evolutionary relation between the solitary insect which provides fully and in advance for offspring that it cannot live to see and the communal ant or bee, whose society is based upon parental longevity. In the inevitable comparison, moreover, human society is seen to be the same at bottom. "The whole trend of modern thought is toward a greater recognition of the very important and determining rôle of the irrational and the instinctive, not only in our social but also in our individual lives. The best proof of this is to be found in the family, which by common consent constitutes the primitive basis of our society, just as it does among the insects, and the bonds which unite the human family are and always will be physiological and instinctive." And it is further shown that even in the matter of social heredity, use of tools, employment of other animals, and communication between individuals there is a similar identity in general. In brief, Dr. Wheeler's book is a sound and readable introduction to one of the least familiar but most important fields of scientific research.

It is unfortunately impossible to give as high a place to Professor Holmes' disjointed work on human genetics. The contrast between this series of unequal and unrelated essays and the unified and satisfying Wheeler treatise is painful indeed. Nor can criticism be disarmed by the prefatory apology: "The present volume makes no claim to unity of treatment." Such a claim is always futile. One can only observe that if the reprinting of scattered scientific articles must result in such depressing incoherence, it would be far better to rework their material into an integrated form, or, if that be too laborious, to let it fade into oblivion. It is quite true that the ideas conveyed in Dr. Holmes' sketches are perfectly sound, but this, as we have seen, is not to the point; they have a certain value for the professionally interested, but they are hopeless for the layman. Their style is dull, pedantic, and often heavily obscure, as witness (page 117): "If we count so much upon nurture to carry civilization to greater heights, we should not forget that the primary condition of the greatest efficacy of nurture is afforded by a rich endowment of natural gifts." There is some elephantine playfulness in the essay on misconceptions of eugenics. But inelegance, stolidity, and a basic lack of integration form a combination too strong to be offset by such stray virtues as the book can boast.

H. M. PARSHLEY

Walter von Molo

AUF DER ROLLENDEN ERDE, by Walter von Molo. Munich: *Albert Langen.*

IN THIS, his latest novel, von Molo shows the ultra-modern side of his equipment as a novelist. It belongs, not to his series of historical romances, but to the category of his "Liebes-Symphonie," a collection of four searching novelettes on the subject of love and marriage. What interests him in the latter works is the enormous complexity of modern civilization, not only in its outward manifestations but also in its echoes in the tortured life of the individual. His hero in "Auf der rollenden Erde" (On This Rolling Globe) is one who, facing it, is not daunted by it, but strives to find in it a formula that man may live by. Man, in von Molo's philosophy is not good; on the contrary, he is selfish and bad. But he may yet *become* good; in his very selfishness there are possibilities of benefit to himself and others.

Walter von Molo, born in Austria in 1880 and partly of Italian origin, is one of the most successful and at the same time one of the most forceful and important novelists of present-day Germany. Trained as an electric engineer, he spent his early manhood as a patent expert in the Austrian government service, contributed extensively to technical journals, and wrote a text-book on automobile speedometers.

He began as a novelist with a story of the turf, followed it with a society novel, and then wrote "Klaus Tiedemann," a capital story about a business man. But his most popular work, and perhaps his best work, has been done in the field of the historical romance. His turning-point came when he discovered Schiller as a hero. In his two volumes the poet becomes the spirit of eternal youth. They are not history, but they are unquestionably literature.

From Schiller he turned to Frederick the Great. In "Fridericus," the first volume of a trilogy, he got far beyond mere hero worship and even beyond mere aesthetic delight in a great genius. What he had launched into, indeed, was more than an historical romance; it was a sort of vast epic of the German people, and especially of their struggle for freedom. The public response was stupendous; a Frederick cult was instantly established; the hero of the Seven Years' War moved over from history into German mythology. There followed "Luise," a human and appealing picture of the heroine of the War of Liberation, and after that "Das Volk erwacht" (A People Awakes), a sonorous and moving song to liberty. The hero here is no longer a king, but the people. This year the three volumes will be republished together as "Der Roman meines Volkes" (The Romance of My People). Later on, von Molo's collected works will appear in six volumes.

Von Molo stands clear of all the violent movements that now agitate German letters. His style is highly condensed and at times takes on an effect almost of breathlessness; it is wholly free from the usual German heaviness and intricacy. But his greatest merit lies in his fine intuitions as a psychologist. His portraits are absolutely living. At home he has already made a very brilliant mark; inevitably he is bound to be heard from abroad.

FRIEDRICH SCHÖNEMANN

THE AMERICAN MERCURY AUTHORS

C. E. BECHHOFER *is the author of "The Literary Renaissance in America" and of various novels and books of travel. He has traveled very widely. His home is in London.*

SAMUEL C. CHEW, *author of "Byron in America," is a Ph.D. of the Johns Hopkins and Professor of English Literature at Bryn Mawr. He is the author of important studies of Byron and Thomas Hardy.*

WILLIAM FEATHER *is a former newspaper man, now engaged in business in Cleveland, Ohio.*

HARVEY FERGUSSON *is the author of the Washington novel, "Capitol Hill." He is the son of a Congressman and has spent most of his adult life as a journalist in Washington.*

ARTHUR DAVISON FICKE *is the well-known American poet.*

W. L. GEORGE *is the English novelist, author of "The Making of an Englishman," "Caliban," etc.*

LELAND H. JENKS *is associate professor of history at Amherst. He is a Kansan and is a graduate of Columbia. For three years he was Amherst Memorial Fellow in London.*

ALICE MARY KIMBALL *was born in Vermont, and has done newspaper work in Vermont, Arkansas, Kansas and Missouri. She is now living in New York City.*

GREGORY MASON *is best known as a war correspondent and writer on foreign affairs, in which capacities he was for several years connected with the* Outlook. *During the intervals between his expeditions abroad he has lectured extensively.*

D. W. SINCLAIR *is an American musician who has been playing for years in orchestras in New York and elsewhere.*

JOHAN J. SMERTENKO *is a frequent contributor to the* Nation, *the* Literary Review *and other periodicals. He has been a lecturer at Hunter College and editor of the* Grinnell Review.

VILHJALMUR STEFANSSON *is the well-known Arctic explorer. He is the author of "The Friendly Arctic" and many other books.*

CHARLES WILLIS THOMPSON *has been a political writer for nearly three decades, and has represented the New York* World *and* Times *at Washington.*

ARTHUR BINGHAM WALKLEY *is the dramatic critic of the London* Times. *He frequently makes excursions into other fields of criticism.*

STEPHEN FRENCH WHITMAN *is the author of "Predestined" and other novels. He is a Philadelphian and has been writing since 1903.*

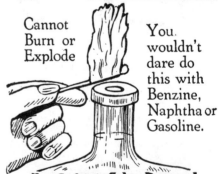

A Refreshing Bath Aid for Keen Out-of-Door Fellows

When you are sticky, hot and tired shift a little AMMO in the bath. In five minutes you'll feel as "fit as a fiddle."

AMMO gives water an added virtue and makes soap do double duty. Presto! Hard water is made as soft as rain water. With a little soap, AMMO creates a mountain of soft, creamy suds. Besides, it vanishes all odors.

Then too, AMMO in the water gives tired feet a new lease of life.

Refreshing—O'boy!

Enjoy this man's bath aid—unperfumed.

If your dealer cannot supply you, write us:
American Ammone Co., 1201 Times Bldg., New York.

A Suggestion

HAVE you had difficulty in securing from the newsstands your copy of THE AMERICAN MERCURY? Many readers have. So great has been the demand that it has been necessary to reprint both the first and second issues of the magazine. While we are endeavoring to meet this demand, the newsstand distribution can never be sufficiently large to serve the entire reading public. If you wish to be assured of receiving THE AMERICAN MERCURY regularly each month it would be well either to place a definite order with your local newsdealer or to mail us your subscription on the blank below.

The subscription rate is five dollars a year. Canadian postage fifty cents, foreign postage one dollar additional.

THE AMERICAN MERCURY, *730 Fifth Avenue*, N. Y.

Please send me THE AMERICAN MERCURY for one year, starting with the..........
issue. I enclose $........ (*check or money order*).

Name....................................*Address*...................................

Please send to the following names THE AMERICAN MERCURY for one year, starting
with the ....issue. I enclose $...... (*check or money order*).

Name....................................*Address*...................................

Name....................................*Address*...................................

Name....................................*Address*...................................

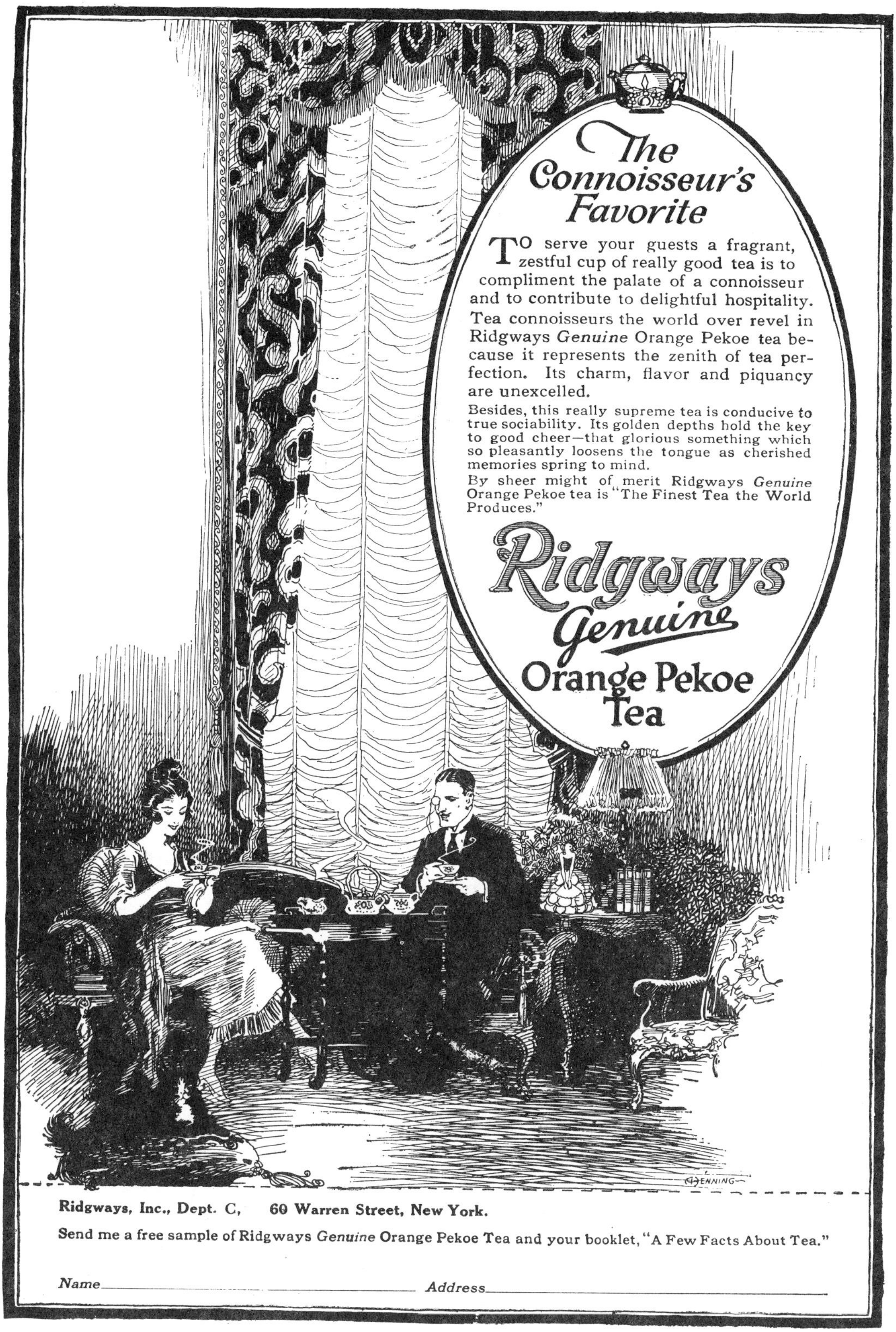
The Connoisseur's Favorite
TO serve your guests a fragrant, zestful cup of really good tea is to compliment the palate of a connoisseur and to contribute to delightful hospitality.
Tea connoisseurs the world over revel in Ridgways *Genuine* Orange Pekoe tea because it represents the zenith of tea perfection. Its charm, flavor and piquancy are unexcelled.
Besides, this really supreme tea is conducive to true sociability. Its golden depths hold the key to good cheer—that glorious something which so pleasantly loosens the tongue as cherished memories spring to mind.
By sheer might of merit Ridgways *Genuine* Orange Pekoe tea is "The Finest Tea the World Produces."
Ridgways
Genuine
Orange Pekoe
Tea
HENNING
Ridgways, Inc., Dept. C, 60 Warren Street, New York.
Send me a free sample of Ridgways *Genuine* Orange Pekoe Tea and your booklet, "A Few Facts About Tea."
Name ______ *Address* ______

The AMERICAN MERCURY

VOLUME I   April 1924   NUMBER 4

TABLE OF CONTENTS

HORACE GREELEY	Gamaliel Bradford	385
WHAT IS A STATESMAN?	Charles A. Beard	394
LILLIAN GISH	Joseph Hergesheimer	397
STELLA (*A Story*)	Thyra Samter Winslow	403
EDITORIAL		408
THE UPLIFT ON THE FRONTIER	James Stevens	413
APOSTLE TO THE HEATHEN	Ernest Boyd	419
IN DEFENSE OF THE PURITAN	Walter Prichard Eaton	424
AMERICANA		429
AMERICAN PORTRAITS, III. THE EDITORIAL WRITER	James M. Cain	433
THE INVASION OF AMERICA	Elbridge Colby	439
HYLAN	William Bullock	444
CLINICAL NOTES	H. L. Mencken and George Jean Nathan	451
MUSHROOM TOWN (*A Cycle of Sonnets*)	Muna Lee	459
THE ARTS AND SCIENCES:		
The Origin and Spread of Cultures	Robert H. Lowie	463
A Moratorium for Opera	W. J. Henderson	466
The Critical Realists	Woodbridge Riley	468
THE END OF A LITERARY MYSTERY	Frederick P. Hier, Jr.	471
WOODROW WILSON	Harry Elmer Barnes	479
THE GUARD (*A Story*)	Ruth Valentine	491
THE THEATRE	George Jean Nathan	497
THE LIBRARY	H. L. Mencken	504
THE AMERICAN MERCURY AUTHORS		511
INDEX TO VOLUME I		512

Unsolicited manuscripts not accompanied by stamped and addressed envelopes will not be returned and the Editors will not enter into correspondence about them. Manuscripts should be addressed to The Editors and not to individuals. All accepted contributions are paid for on acceptance, without reference to the date of publication. The whole contents of this magazine are protected by copyright and must not be reprinted without permission.

Published monthly at 50 cents a copy. Annual subscription, $5.00; Canadian subscription, $5.50; foreign subscription $6.00. . . . The American Mercury, Inc., publishers. Publication office, Federal and 19th Streets, Camden, N. J. Editorial and general offices, 730 Fifth Avenue, New York. . . . Printed in the United States. Copyright, 1924, by The American Mercury, Inc. . . . Entered as second class matter January 4, 1924, at the post office at Camden, N. J., under the Act of March 3, 1879.

Alfred A. Knopf   George Jean Nathan } *Editors*
Publisher   H. L. Mencken

These Are New Appleton Books

A Study of
OSCAR WILDE
from life

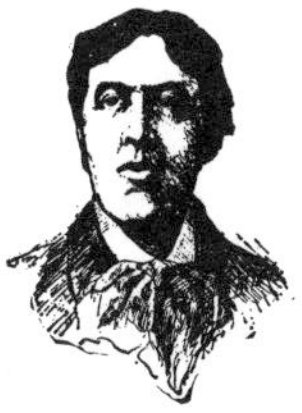

Echo De Paris

Taken right from life, this dramatic sketch portrays a striking scene from the career of Oscar Wilde. It tells of a luncheon in Paris which Wilde attended as a guest of honor. The conversation of this literary genius is here recorded with a skill that will be recognized by every reader of Wilde. $1.00

The six Hibbert Lectures of Felix Adler

The Reconstruction of the Spiritual Ideal

The Leader of the Ethical Culture Society deals with problems of marriage, labor, and a Society of Nations. $1.50

A Woman's Quest

The Life of Marie E. Zakrzewska, M.D.

By Agnes C. Victor. Partly autobiographical, this book creates a profound impression—the life story of the pioneer woman doctor of this country. Illustrated. $3.00

The Life of Anne Boleyn

Philip W. Sergeant's noteworthy biography of the hapless young wife of Henry VIII, the mother of Queen Elizabeth. Illustrated. $5.00

The Khoja: Tales of Nasr-Ed-Din

These folk stories, translated from the Turkish by Henry D. Barnham, C.M.G., offer a remarkable picture of the humbler folk of Turkey. Illustrated by Tony Sarg. $2.50

New Poetry

From the Song of France, French poetry early and recent translated by Grace Warrack. Illustrated, $2.50. **Collected Poems of Stephen Gwynn,** the well-known interpreter of Ireland, $1.50. **The Home Road** contains poems of home life by Martha Haskell Clark, $1.25. **Poems of Lord Byron,** selected by H. J. C. Grierson, $4.00. **The Aeneid of Virgil,** a line-for-line verse translation by C. J. Billson, $2.00.

Sunlight and Song

is the happy title of a delightful autobiography written by a Prima Donna of the Metropolitan Opera House who is known and loved throughout the world of music.

Maria Jeritza

Mme. Jeritza tells of her early years, her debut, her career at the Vienna Opera, her triumphs in America. A story full of glimpses of many of the world's famous people. Illustrated. $3.00

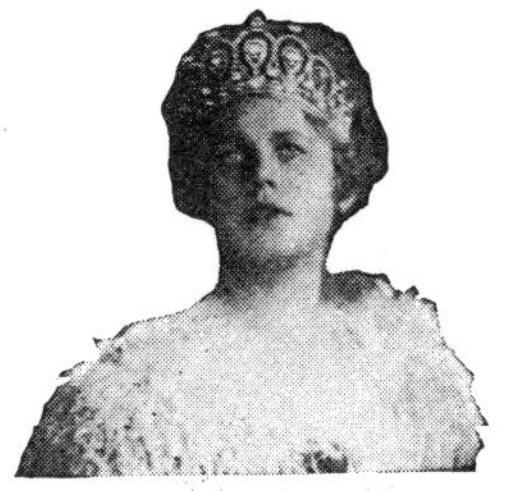

Blood Pressure:

Its Cause, Effect, and Remedy

A sound, non-technical explanation by Lewellys F. Barker, M.D., and Norman B. Cole, M.D., that covers the subject fully. $1.25

Religion and Natural Law

With sincerity and sound reasoning C. F. Russell studies the compatibility of the religious and the scientific points of view. $1.25

New Fiction

There is a Tide is a human and humorous story by J. C. Snaith ($2.00). **Mother of Gold** is the latest adventure romance of Emerson Hough, author of "The Covered Wagon" ($2.00). The Baroness De Knoop gives us the year's unusual heroine in **Pauline** ($2.00). Laurie Y. Erskine's **The Laughing Rider** is a dashing novel of the range ($1.75).

At All Booksellers

D. Appleton and Company will be glad to send free upon request their illustrated bulletin of new books and their authors

D. APPLETON & COMPANY
35 West 32nd Street New York

VOLUME I   NUMBER 4

The American
MERCURY

April 1924

HORACE GREELEY

BY GAMALIEL BRADFORD

HORACE GREELEY was all his life an intense and passionate worker. From his boyhood in the tens and twenties of the last century, until his death in 1872, it was work, work, work for him, and nothing else. As a child in school and on the farm he worked with his hands and with his brain. As a printer in New York he worked with his brain and with his hands. As editor of the *New Yorker* and the New York *Tribune* he worked with his brain, but still also with his busy fingers, till the fingers were weary and the brain worn to shreds and tatters.

Work was all of life that interested him. What would you do unless you worked? You worked all the time, except when you were asleep. He had a physique which, on the whole, admirably seconded all this intense activity. To be sure, his nerves were sensitive, played queer tricks with him, bothered him even as a child. But in general his body served him well, and he did not suffer from that physical drag which makes all work tormenting, if not impossible. Work, never tormenting to him, became such a habit that he could hardly conceive the attraction of idleness. He even extended his own passion to humanity in general, and could not believe that all men did not love to work as he did. "A lazy man, in my view," he said, "is always the pitiable victim of

miseducation. Each human being, properly trained, works as freely and naturally as he eats; only the victims of parental neglect or misguidance prefer hunger and rags with idleness, to thrift won by industry and patient effort."

To men of that temperament work seems sufficient in itself, a reward and a delight, quite independent of any ulterior motive. They work from mere restless impulse, from the mechanical instinct of nerves and muscles craving to be used, almost regardless of any definite aim or object to be attained. At no time in his life was the earning of money in itself an incentive to Greeley's efforts. He earned and saved because that was the natural accompaniment of his excessive work, and because his foresight and far-sight felt the power of protection in such saving. But money meant little to him, for he lived sparely and hardly and had no taste for spending. His youth was the homely, rugged youth of the New England farmer's boy in the first half of the century. The bare necessaries were all that Horace was ever accustomed to and apparently all he ever wanted. In the poverty of those early years were established the oddities of dress which became so peculiarly associated with him that men rarely think of him today without them. As a boy, even when he began to earn, he would spend nothing on clothes. He went into New York with the crudest country garments and he had no disposition to shed them even under the pressure of ridicule. All his life he dressed roughly, uncouthly, ineptly, wore trailing coats and trailing trousers and clumsy boots, and his slouch hat and white overcoat were objects of everlasting caricature.

Even with a family and a city household of his own it appears that Greeley maintained the same Spartan régime that had taken possession of his spirit in youth. No doubt the wife and children had the necessaries of life and many of the comforts, but they were trained to consider luxury as superfluous, if not wicked, and to believe that only the idle needed to spend money in order to be happy. Yet Greeley was fond of his children, devoted to them, and spoke of them with singular tenderness. The boy Arthur, familiarly known as Pickie, who was such a favorite of Margaret Fuller's, is described at length in his father's autobiography with a pathetic, lingering fondness, and his death was for the time a prostrating blow.

II

More and more, as I study the lives of men of mark, or of any men, for that matter, I feel curiosity about their wives. It is evident that Greeley's wife played a considerable part in his career, though we can get at her only very indirectly and obscurely. Here and there comes a touch that makes her stand out. For instance, we are told that, when Greeley married her, she was a teacher and was "crazy for knowledge." How clearly you see the type! You begin to understand how she could put up with her husband's oddities; perhaps she had plenty of her own. Her rigid family discipline is drolly illustrated in an account of Governor Seward's attempt to smoke on the Greeley premises: "Now Mrs. Greeley happened to be ill in a room just over that in which the gentlemen were, and her husband knew that

just so soon as the cigar-smoke made its way to her nostrils, through the flue of the chimney, she would descend upon them like an avalanche in whatever costume she happened just then to be." Wherefor Seward and his cigar were coaxed out into the street and kept promenading for an hour in astonished perplexity as to the cause of such inhospitable treatment. But, whatever Mrs. Greeley's oddities, she was a loyal and a helpful wife, and the loss of her, just as her husband had failed in his last great political struggle, was too much to bear. "In the darkest hour my suffering wife left me, none too soon, for she had suffered too deeply and too long. I laid her in the ground with hard dry eyes." But the memory that lingers with one most is that she was "crazy for knowledge." What a profound and pitiable epitaph!

Work and the domestic affections—these seem to have been all of Greeley's life. It is remarkable how the other common interests of mankind were slighted or left out altogether. All the references to his boyhood agree that he had no taste for play, never cared to join in childish sports or amusements. He was fond of fishing, but, as his biographer remarks, he fished not for fun, but for fish. He did like to play checkers. Also, he played cards occasionally, though never for money and never on Sunday. But such things were a waste of time and rather to be frowned upon, and "he advised persons of sedentary habits to shun them because of the inevitable tendency to impair the digestion and incite headache." Beyond question the people of that generation took life seriously!

It was the same with all the more elaborate distractions which are supposed to divert maturer age. Travel? Oh, yes, the man traveled, but it is clear that he was always in a hurry, and always accumulating copy for the *Tribune*. Social life? If you got him with people whom he liked and let him have all the conversation, he would talk and talk well. But he had no taste for ordinary social gatherings, and avoided them, and did not appear to advantage in them. His dress was inappropriate, his manners were uncouth. Alcohol he never touched, and he discouraged others from touching it. As for tobacco, you can't say much more against it than this: "The chewing, smoking, or snuffing of tobacco has seemed to me, if not the most pernicious, certainly the vilest, most detestable abuse of his corrupted sensual appetites whereof depraved Man is capable." Whew!

What are usually considered more refined pleasures had little better luck with such an instinctive Puritan. He tolerated the fine arts and filled his house with pictures; but I doubt if he ever looked at them. Even nature, from the aesthetic point of view, meant little more to this ardent farmer than it does to most farmers: crops and bugs and manure always loomed larger than sunsets. The same was true of books. Greeley had been an enormous reader from childhood. He was always at a book or a newspaper, read in the woods, or on his way from school, or by the fireside at night. But while in youth he read anything that came handy, literature proper or anything else, his taste was wholly practical, and the practical was all he got from all he read. He wanted education to be practical, and preached that it should be so, wanted it to turn out farmers and artisans who should understand their business and like it. Colleges, which he had never frequented, seemed to him to be dangerous, or at least greatly in need of reform. "We must have seminaries which not merely provide work for their pupils, but require it inflexibly from all." Work, work, always work! No doubt work is an admirable thing; but when you pack life too full and solidly with it, something is bound to explode.

III

Yet the work in Greeley's case was certainly not for himself alone, nor, though it was eminently practical, was it by any means always material in its nature or aims. His mind was constantly busy, and often in abstract thinking, but always with a practical bearing and purpose. His intelligence was almost preternaturally quick and active, a swift sequence of skipping, frisking, cavorting thoughts, which kept both the inner and outer cosmos in a perpetual whirl. At the same time, the thinking was not always very logical or very deep. It was that of the self-made, self-taught man, who acquires knowledge readily and widely, but without much system or much exact training in its use. Greeley did not gain control of his ideas; he lacked the capacity naturally, was erratic, easily led and misled, and duped by himself more often and more disastrously than he was ever duped by others.

In the more lofty regions of thought he counted for little or nothing. Religion did not trouble him much, or, in its higher emotional aspects, greatly concern him. When he was a child the darker phases of Calvinism repelled and distressed him. The old puzzle of an omnipotent God who made His creatures to suffer eternally would not let him rest. He finally solved the problem by adopting the comfortable doctrines of Universalism. The long and the short of it was that, as he said in later years, "I am so taken with the things of this world that I have too little time to spend on the affairs of the other." He was a faithful church-goer, but seemed to think that his bodily presence was the main essential, and allowed his mind to profit by the golden opportunity for sleep. "He generally stalked in rather early, the pockets of his long white coat filled with newspapers, and, immediately on taking his seat, went to sleep. As soon as the service began, he awoke, looked first to see how many vacant places were in the pew, and then, without a word, put out his long arm into the aisle and with one or two vigorous scoops, pulled in a sufficient number of strangers standing there to fill all the vacancies; then he slept again."

There you have the man: whatever benefits the church or anything else gave him must be shared with others, and the sharing was rather more important than the benefits. The side of religion that appealed to him was the practical, and the most fruitful field of labor for his vastly laborious spirit was work for others. His own personal benevolence was almost unlimited. He gave and especially he lent widely, freely—many persons thought, foolishly. Yet, if he was often duped, he was not fooled, that is, he fell into the trap with his eyes open, and knew that he was complying with Christian charity rather than with deserving need. And when a cause did not interest him or appeal to him, he could refuse with a decided petulance, and even with the curious coarse vigor of language which his wandering youth engrafted upon his age, as when he replied to the man who appealed for a subscription to "a cause which will prevent a thousand of our fellow-beings from going to hell," "I will not give you a cent. There don't half enough go there now."

IV

Greeley not only gave money, but advice, and in incredible measure. As a popular editor, the demands upon him in this regard were enormous, but he gladly spent his time and strength in meeting them. The advice was often roughly and broadly given, as in the celebrated "Go West, young man, go West!", or as in the more concrete story of the boy who had been living with his sister, had quarreled with her and left her, and came into the *Tribune* office to ask for assistance. Greeley kept on writing and did not even look up. "Is your sister married?" "Yes." "Is she respectable?" "Certainly, sir." "Go straight to your sister and tell her that you are ashamed of yourself, and ask her forgiveness. If she will take you, go back and live with her; and after this remember that if your own sister is not your friend, you will

not be likely to find any friend in New York City." The boy went and Greeley kept on writing. He was too busy for gentleness, but his advice was sound and wholesome, and those who took it profited.

He was just as ready to advise the world at large, and his editorial employment gave him a magnificent opportunity for doing it. He had the essential qualities of the born reformer: the immense energy, the quick and ready, if superficial, sympathy, the unfailing enthusiasm, the limitless confidence in himself. Various reforms appealed to him—in fact, all reforms did, so long as they were practical and could be felt and touched. He wanted Prohibition, he wanted a reorganized education, he worked with tireless zeal for the abolition of slavery. But perhaps he was most constantly and consistently interested in improving the conditions of labor and the general status of the poor. It is curious to see him trumpeting all the nostrums and panaceas of our own day—and of a thousand years ago—in the middle of the last century, with the same familiar and eternal confidence and undying hope. It is true that he was in some respects moderate. He never urged any fundamental attack upon the rights of property. But he was fascinated by schemes of association, long and ardently advocated Fourierism, and believed that if men of all types and classes would only meet each other and work together in good faith the worst of human evils might be overcome. On the practical side it may at least be said that he anticipated much of the coöperative tendency under which social reform has actually made its most decided gains.

As he had the zeal of the born reformer, so he had the superb unfailing optimism. You can see it written in his face. The author of the "Essays of Elia" proposed to hire a stone-cutter to set up a monument engraved, "Here Charles Lamb loved his fellow men." Greeley needed no stone-cutter: he carried his monument with him, in those benignant features from which even thirty years of New York journalism could not erase the delightful rustic candor, in that fringe of sparse white whisker which always leaves one doubting between an inverted halo and a tonsorial negligence. He expressed his immense belief in the future and in humanity not only with his countenance but also with his pen: "I see no reason why the wildest dreams of the fanatical believer in Human Progress and Perfectibility may not ultimately be realized, and each child so trained as to shun every vice, aspire to every virtue, attain the highest practicable skill in Art and efficiency in Industry, loving and pursuing honest, untasked Labor for the health, vigor, and peace of mind thence resulting, as well as for its more palpable rewards, and joyfully recognizing in universal the only assurance of individual good." When a man carries such sentiments in his heart, he may surely be excused for wearing optimistic whiskers!

V

It was unavoidable that Greeley's philanthropy should draw him into practical politics, though it would have been far better for his reputation if this had not happened. On abstract political questions he always had a definite opinion and an energetic one. He early devoted himself to the extreme protectionist theory and worked for it to the end. His opposition to slavery in the fifties probably made him more friends than anything else, as well as more enemies, and in that earlier period he was a useful and effective agent. But when the Civil War broke out it was too much for him. He was distracted between humanity, love of the Union, hatred of slavery, hatred of war, and his general disposition to dictate to everybody in everything. First he was for letting the South go, then for prosecuting the war and emancipating the slaves; then, when the struggle dragged on, he was for making peace, by foreign mediation if necessary; then, after it was all over, for forgiving everybody, especially Davis, whose bail-

bond he eagerly signed. Sometimes he pleaded with Lincoln, sometimes he bullied him, sometimes he rejected him as a poor creature. And always the *Tribune* was an enormous power in the country, which whirled millions after its vagaries, and forced the president to consider its editor, even when he could not agree with him. It is impossible not to contrast Greeley's flighty inconsistencies with Lincoln's deliberate and statesmanlike opportunism. Yet under all the inconsistencies we recognize the fundamental patriotic feeling and high-mindedness which Lincoln appraised when he wrote to Wilson, "I do not know how you estimate Greeley, but I consider him incapable of corruption or falsehood."

When it came to personal participation in political activity, Greeley was even less successful than in theorizing. It is clear that he was in no way adapted to direct political success. He had no magnetism at all, and it often seemed as if he had no manners. He irritated people and fretted them and rubbed them the wrong way. In those rough days this would often have resulted in personal conflict if he had been anything of a fighter. He was not. He had his courage, but it was of the passive order. When he was a boy, he would not stand up and fight. "When attacked, he would neither fight nor run away, but stand still and take it." And this was exactly what he did when he was attacked in Washington by a political enemy. He used his tongue savagely, without knowing it; he did not know how to use his fists, and did not care to.

Yet, with all these disqualifications, he was always eager for public office, always felt that he could be useful to his fellows there and always wanted the chance to prove it. His political desires and interests were much fostered by his association with Weed and Seward, the greatest political forces in the New York of that day. Weed early appreciated the value of Greeley's journalistic ability and made the most of it, but it soon became apparent that the qualities of a great editor were not necessarily those of a great administrator, and neither Weed nor his chief manifested any eagerness for getting their friend into office. Greeley resented this and finally broke off all relations in the well-known letter dissolving the partnership of Weed, Seward and Greeley; and his bitter opposition did as much as anything to prevent Seward from being nominated for the presidency in 1860. The episode as a whole did not make an agreeable phase of Greeley's career.

The only instance of his actually taking part in governmental work was when he was elected to fill an unexpired term in the House of Representatives in 1848. His brief activity in Washington was bustling at any rate, if not glorious. He at once started a furious investigation of the mileage allowances for members of Congress, which was no doubt well intentioned and beneficial to the public service, but did not increase his personal popularity. In his congressional career, as in everything, you see his vigorous self-assertion, his genuine desire to do good to everybody, and his complete disregard for what happened to anybody's feelings in the process.

In 1872 Greeley was nominated for the presidency. Grant was the regular Republican candidate, but there had been much disapproval of his first term, and the discontented Republicans got together at Cincinnati and nominated Greeley, who was also later nominated by the Democrats. There was something so ludicrously inconsistent about this procedure that it made the campaign almost a farce, though a bitter one. Greeley had spent his life abusing the Southern slave-holders, and the absurdity and hollowness of their supporting him could hardly be veiled by any pretext of shaking hands across the bloody chasm. The contest was cruelly personal in many respects, and the savage efforts of the cartoonists, notably of Thomas Nast in opposition to Greeley, gave it a vivid grossness which has rarely been surpassed. Greeley was not only beaten,

but overwhelmed. As he himself expressed it, "I was the worst beaten man that ever ran for high office. And I have been assailed so bitterly that I hardly know whether I was running for the presidency or the penitentiary." The strain, the fatigue, and the fierceness of the struggle were too much for nerves already overworked, and within a month after his defeat Greeley was dead.

The element of ambition in his character has been a great deal discussed and disputed. But it is evident that, like most of us, he wanted to succeed in whatever he undertook. He disclaimed political ambition, yet he felt that he had good ideas, great ideas, on governmental matters. The immense flattery that always waits upon popular editorship had to some extent turned his head, and he believed that he would make as good a President as another man, perhaps much better. What would have happened if he had been elected it is difficult to guess. High responsibility might have toned him down and made him practical and useful, but one has one's doubts. It is a familiar boast with our mothers than any American can get the presidency, and sometimes when one scans the long list of incumbents, one is tempted to think that any American *has* got it. Certainly many types have occupied the sacred chair, from genius to gentlemanly insignificance; but it is hard to think of any type, outside the State's prison, which is rather unfairly excluded, more incompatible with it than that of the fiery, versatile, garrulous, emotional, whimsical editor.

VI

All the same, he was a great editor. The cheap, popular newspaper came into prominence and power about the time he reached manhood, and he took to it naturally and completely. From childhood he wanted to be a printer, and he had a passion for reading the papers. As soon as he could get his elbows free from the fiercest necessity of self-support, he became an editor, first of the *New Yorker*, then of the political *Log Cabin*, then of the *Tribune*, which was the child of his effort and the mother of his reputation.

He grew as the paper grew, grew as journalism grew, grew as New York grew, developed daily and yearly in self-possession and self-assertion, if not in self-comprehension. On the merely business side of his undertaking he was not especially distinguished. I do not find his name associated with any of the mechanical discoveries which so greatly facilitated the dissemination of newspapers as the years went on, nor do I note that he was especially interested in them. Neither was he a great or successful financier. His magnificent thrift and self-control, his zealous and well-directed industry, enabled him to hold his own, even when unsupported. But the difficulties were enormous and almost overwhelmed him. He worked all day and nearly all night, drove everything and everybody about him. Yet even so, it was a struggle to keep the credit going and the bills paid. "I paid off everybody tonight, had $10 left, and $350 to raise on Monday. Borrowing places all sucked dry. I shall raise it, however." This, on a larger and larger scale, was the story, until McElrath came along and undertook the business management. It was the salvation of Greeley, and after that he had nothing to think of but his pen. The *Tribune* grew to be a vast investment, and its editor was always well provided for. True to his theories, he insisted on introducing coöperation, and the paper was early made into a stock company, with opportunity for all who worked for it to share in the ownership.

It does not appear that Greeley was particularly active in the advertising department, though he well understood the importance of it. What impressed him chiefly at the beginning was the danger of the advertising influence. Once allow yourself to be subsidized by rich and unscrupulous advertisers, what becomes of the independence of journalism? Godkin highly praises Greeley's earlier attitude: "He sacrificed everything, advertisers, subscribers, and all else, to what he considered principle." At a later date there came a change. The growth of business, the subtle and insinuating pressure of politics, forced Greeley to abandon his lofty position to some extent, never certainly in theory or in his own view, but distinctly in the unprejudiced opinion of others. His tolerance of the Tweed régime was as servile as that of the other papers, until the *Times* shook them all into unavoidable action. Here again, however, it is clear that Greeley was duped, partly by clever machinations, partly by his own ambition and enthusiasm.

The news in the paper was more in Greeley's province than the advertising. Here it is interesting to note his desire for and insistence upon accuracy. He was scrupulous as to form, emphasizing the importance of clear and readable English. He was scrupulous as to fact, at all times endeavoring to get a clear account of what really happened and then to stick to it. He condemned sensational journalism, even going so far as to say that the "violent hurt inflicted upon social order and individual happiness" by the lurid account of a murder involved greater guilt than that of the murderer himself, which is going pretty far, though perhaps not too far.

VII

But it was in the editorial columns that his main strength lay, and from the start he had an intense appreciation of the power that was just beginning to develop in the popular press and the future that lay before it. That power was completely a growth of the Nineteenth Century and it is doubtful whether anyone has yet analyzed its full nature and extent. To some persons its benefits and advantages must appear more questionable than they did to Greeley; there are certain evils which he was disposed to underrate or overlook. For instance, the American newspaper has been anti-religious, not so much by direct attack, which is not usual, as in a subtle undermining of the influence of the church. Again, it is anti-social. Before it came, men got the news by word of mouth and had to find and meet each other to get it. Now you learn more by staying at home in quiet and silence: the newspaper unites communities, but separates individuals. Little drawbacks like these, however, were nothing in the enthusiasm which Greeley felt for the newspaper as a universal, democratic, educative force. When he was invited to go before an English parliamentary committee and discuss the subject of journalism, he told the committee that he considered the newspaper "worth all the schools in the country. I think it creates a taste for reading in every child's mind, and it increases his interest in his lessons."

Another proof of the man's indomitable optimism! But he at any rate did his best to make the editorial influence what he would have had it, to use it to develop and educate and bring out what was best and noblest in the American people, whom he labored in his way to serve with all his heart and all his energy. Listen to his summing up of editorial requisites: "An ear ever open to the plaints of the wronged and the suffering, though they can never repay advocacy, and those who mainly support newspapers will be annoyed and often exposed by it; a heart as sensitive to oppression and degradation in the next street as if they were practiced in Brazil or Japan; a pen as ready to expose and reprove the crimes whereby wealth is amassed and luxury enjoyed in our own country at this hour, as if they had only been committed by Turks or pagans in Asia some centuries ago." This is a high ideal for a journalist, and if Greeley did not always live up to it, he could hardly be expected to. He carried it in his heart, at any rate, which was something.

To be sure, his methods seem to us to have been singularly at variance, sometimes, with his standards. He had heard too much of a rough and brutal style of speech in his youth, and he never got over it. Coarse and ugly terms applied to adversaries with careless inconsideration never really help a cause, and Greeley was too prone to them. He used profanity in his private talk and the equivalent of profanity in his editorials. These things made hard feelings, sometimes even resulted in legal proceedings, as in the case of the celebrated Cooper libel suit. They were a disfigurement which cannot be overlooked.

At the same time, they came partly from the man's very qualities of power. Words were natural to him, and he poured them out almost unthinkingly, ugly as well as graceful, bitter as well as sweet. His style has been extravagantly praised by excellent judges, notably by Godkin. It seems to me diffuse and by no means of the highest literary quality; but it is certainly vivid and energetic. He had no humor, because he never had the humorous, detached view of life: everything was too intensely and immediately absorbing to him. But he had a quick apt wit in giving things a mocking or satirical turn, after the somewhat exaggerated fashion of Mark Twain. His intellectual powers, while they were, as we have seen, not profoundly penetrating, were quick and agile, and ready to turn at any moment to any subject. Above all, he was inexhaustible in fertility of argument, and had that splendid confidence in human reason, especially his own, which some of us are born without, but which seems to be almost indispensable to the successful editor. He liked to argue, actually enjoyed it, would argue about anything. He liked opposition, liked to have people differ from him: it gave him a chance to show and especially to feel his own power. And he was reluctant to give up an opinion; he hated above all things to own that he was wrong.

With these editorial qualities he endeared himself to the vast masses of the American people and became perhaps the most notable of all the great personal editors of the middle of the Nineteenth Century. The personal element in the handling of a paper seems now, for various reasons, largely to have passed away. Curiously enough, the personal was intimately bound up with the impersonal. Beyond question what gave the editorial columns their singular power was chiefly their anonymity. You might laugh at Jones's opinion, or Smith's; but the editor's—that was different! The large type and the lack of signature somehow seemed to compel respect. So, though you knew it was Horace Greeley, he of the white coat and old hat, who was writing, his editorial words seemed to get a larger significance. And the impersonality at once developed egotism and was benefited by it. You could not help feeling yourself a big man when you were swaying the minds of millions; and the bigger you felt yourself, the more you swayed.

VIII

Some such feeling of almost godlike consequence certainly informed and inspired the soul of Horace Greeley, and he carried round with him in later years the sense of personifying one of the greatest forces and achievements of his century. This is clearly seen in the striking passage in which he describes his relation to his journal: "Fame is a vapor; popularity an accident; riches take wings; the only earthly certainty is oblivion; no man can foresee what a day may bring forth; while those who cheer today will often curse tomorrow; and yet I cherish the hope that the journal I have projected and established will live and flourish long after I shall have mouldered into forgotten dust:... and that the stone which covers

my ashes may bear to future eyes the still intelligible inscription, 'Founder of the New York *Tribune*.'"

It must be admitted, as Greeley himself admitted, that the glory belonging to his journalistic enterprise was of a somewhat ephemeral character; it was like that of the actor or the athlete, immense for the moment and immediately savored, but transitory and fast-fading as a dream. Yet when one looks about one at the enormous flood of literary production, and realizes how slight is the chance of any slow or careful work, or any hidden genius, ever making its way to permanence through such a throng of competitors, one wonders whether perhaps, after all, immediate renown, like Greeley's, is not better than the effort to create a masterpiece which posterity may or not worship. Only most of us would rather cherish the hope of the masterpiece!

At any rate, Greeley made the *Tribune*, and swayed America, and passed away. In his solemn and impressive funeral all antagonisms were forgotten. The New York papers, which a month before had been ready to put him in jail, united in eulogy, and the President, the Vice-President, and the Vice-President-elect rode in one carriage behind the hearse. It was only fair that these honors should be extended to his end; for the poor man was dead before the breath was out of his body, utterly and finally dead. Shakespeare tells us that

> The evil that men do lives after them,
> The good is oft interred with their bones.

Greeley had done no evil, or none to speak of, and the good he did, extensive and indisputable as it was, was not of a character to outlive him very long.

WHAT IS A STATESMAN?

BY CHARLES A. BEARD

WHAT are the qualifications or characteristics which mark the statesman off from the great horde of more commonplace persons who concern themselves with government? What is it that gives him distinction and enduring fame? This is a question which has received little consideration at the hands of those who have written on the evolution of political society. Carlyle, it is true, stormed a great deal on the subject and ended with the general conclusion that the statesman is a genius, a hero, a sort of divine messenger sent now and then to set the weary world aright. The Marxians at the other end of the pole dismiss the statesman with a scoff as a mere automaton produced by a complex of economic forces. But neither of these answers is an answer. Each is a sort of categorical imperative: believe or be damned. Neither satisfies the requirements of the scientific spirit any more than the Miltonic account of creation or the Japanese myth of the Sun Goddess.

Trouble begins when inquiry is made as to who are the statesmen of any nation. At the very outset many of Carlyle's heroes and statesmen are dismissed by the special and the general as no heroes or statesmen at all, but mere evanescent windbags. It also appears, if popular esteem be taken into account, that the same person is a statesman to some part of the public and a demagogue and charlatan to the remainder. Still more curiously, a man who is celebrated as a statesman by one generation is dismissed from the school books and biographical dictionaries with a scant bow by the next generation. Are there not times when Napoleon the Great is the hero of

France and other times when Pasteur receives the homage of the people? Was not John C. Calhoun the orator, statesman, and philosopher of the Far South and the incarnate demon of the Garrison-Phillips school? Bismarck, the Iron Chancellor, the maker of modern Germany, the successor of Frederick the Great, was a towering figure in the history books written between 1890 and 1914. He flouted the talkative members of the Frankfort Assembly—those loquacious professors, who sought to make a national constitution out of paper instead of iron and blood. He dismissed the windy Liberals of the Prussian Diet and built up a Prussian army in spite of their protests. He waged war on Austria and cleared that troublesome member out of the German Union. He made a constitution that gave Hans and Fritz a delusive representation in a national parliament. He outwitted Napoleon the Little in diplomacy and war; he created an Empire on the spot where Louis XIV once disported himself. Having launched the new state he guided its destinies until William the Small dismissed the safe pilot and ran the ship on the rocks. Surely here was a maker of great events out of his own wisdom and will. So it seems.

Yet there are many now who have grave doubts about the majesty of Bismarck, after all. If he had helped the Frankfort professors instead of kicking them down stairs, he might have made the transition to a constitutional democracy less tragic for the German nation. If he had picked no quarrel with Napoleon III, there would have been no *revanche*. With a characteristic gesture of omnipotence, he sought to si-

394

lence Socialists first by clapping them into jail and then by stealing their thunder with social legislation. In vain. When puny big men had run his ship ashore in the Autumn of 1918 it was only the hated Socialists who were prepared to take the hulk and keep her from pounding to pieces. In the light of cruel disillusionment, where does Bismarck stand?

Now take Gladstone. If all the school children throughout the English-speaking world were called upon to name two English statesmen of enduring fame, the Sage of Hawarden would be one of them. Yet how many who instinctively choose Gladstone could associate with his career one monumental achievement? What modern Liberal in England bases his appeal on the policies of Gladstone? In theological and scientific controversies he was a pigmy. In classical disputes he was approved principally by those who knew no Greek. He was a formidable debater, and yet to the Tories he was a man "intoxicated with the exuberance of his own verbosity." Liberal, humane, and evangelical, even when dealing with the Turk, Gladstone was idolized by those English bourgeois who refused to read a Sunday paper. Nevertheless in foreign and domestic policy, how far did he foresee the fate of England and prepare her for it? Even in his own sphere of Liberalism, it must be remembered, Disraeli dished him in 1867 by granting the suffrage to the working classes of England and later by formulating many enlightened measures of social legislation. The empire over the minds of men, which Gladstone built up in many long decades, vanished at his death. He left no heritage to his party, except that of defeat. And when the Liberal machine rose again to power in 1906 it was not his party but the party of the Welsh prestidigitator with his famous budget and his still more famous war. What and where is the Gladstone tradition? Even the friendly and facile Morley with three big volumes at his disposal could not create it. Read the speeches and books of young Liberals and see how few even refer to Gladstone,—much less take inspiration from him.

Those who have carried on a long flirtation with the changeful Clio can readily show how fickle is the fame of any statesman. An ingenious mannerist like Strachey can even make the non-conformist conscience crackle with merriment over the downfall of the choicest gods. Indeed, the process has been carried forward with such zeal in every historical quarter that the satirist, Philip Guedalla, is driven to the conclusion that the fate of a politician depends upon the character of his exit from the stage of his labors! If he goes off with banners flying, orchestra thundering, and crowds roaring, his niche in history is likely to be secure. If he is shot by the villain in the last act, and the curtain goes down to soft music, with the heroine bending low over him, then he is sure to take a place among the national gods. But if, after a thrilling display of the histrionic arts, he catches his toe on a torn rug and falls flat on his face amid jeers and tears—of laughter—he is promptly shot into the lumber room.

Illustrations of Mr. Guedalla's ingenious theory may be taken from any historical arsenal. One trembles to think of what would have happened to the gentle and majestic Lincoln if he had lived through the grewsome days of Reconstruction, the Credit Mobilier, and the Star Route frauds, and spent his declining years, toothless and bald, tottering around the streets of Springfield, Illinois. How much poorer in spirit the American nation would be! One is dismayed in trying to imagine Roosevelt, full of zeal and ambition at the age of seventy, beating his restless soul against the iron bars of circumstance and commonplace with Coolidge and Daugherty grinning in the background. Suppose the would-be assassin who shot at Clemenceau during the Peace Conference had done the victim to death; imagine the funeral cortege of the Tiger passing under the Triumphal Arch, the tears of a grateful nation, and the orations by the saints of the *Action Libérale!*

Still, it is well to remember that many politicians and princes have been shot without winning a place on the honor roll. A president of France was assassinated a few years ago. Who remembers his name? Could all the stage managers in the world, from the age of Euripides to the age of Charles Chaplin, fix up a more tragic setting for the exit of a political leader than the immortal gods arranged for Maximilian of Mexico? A scion of royalty who, under the tutelage of Napoleon III, was to restore the balance of the world by setting up an empire is shot by a firing squad and his unhappy princess is swept down the stream of sixty years a hopeless maniac! There is something in exits, but not much. Drums and funeral notes die away with unseemly haste and the rude janitor sweeps out the faded flowers.

If it is not the exit that makes the statesman, is it brains? Not brains alone. A man may be well equipped with powerful engines of logic and controversy and well stocked with knowledge, and yet, if he runs against the current of the long time, he passes away as grass that withers. How many read Bossuet now? And yet Bossuet was infinitely superior in intellect to Rosseau. Madison was one of the brainiest men in our Homeric Age; how many regard him as a statesman? In supercilious Boston he is more often remembered as the author of Mr. Madison's War which prevented business from going on as usual.

If not brains, then is it morals? Well, Mr. Bryan's character is above reproach. Would anyone put him higher in the scale of fame than Benjamin Franklin, whose morals, to speak softly, were marred by a certain carelessness? Is it ideals clung to unflinchingly until death? For every martyr who achieves fame there are a thousand cranks stoned by the mob and consigned to oblivion.

After this negative review, let me hazard a guess. The statesman is one who divines the long future, foresees the place of his class and nation in it, labors intelligently to prepare his countrymen for their fate, combines courage with discretion, takes risks, has good luck, exercises caution where it is necessary, and goes off the stage with a reasonable degree of respectability. He must have brains—some, at least. He must have morals—some at least. He must have ideals—but only those which are justified in the economy of Providence. He must be able to reconcile himself without complaining to the inexorable movement which the skeptical call the grand *pis aller* and the devout the divine plan. He must not only see; he must appear to be achieving in the current of things. Above all, he must be justified by events, that is, by good fortune. Perhaps beyond reason and understanding both Carlyle and Marx may be reconciled, a little bit. Meanwhile the mystery must not be entirely cleared up. Otherwise the game of politics would lose its savor.

LILLIAN GISH

BY JOSEPH HERGESHEIMER

IT occurred to me, gazing apprehensively at Lillian, that it might be wise to take a drawing-room on the New York train. We had been in West Chester, and we were standing on the station platform at West Philadelphia. Everyone who passed, or, rather, who approached, forgot what he might be doing, where he had been going, and regarded her from short distances. There wasn't a crowd, it was too bitterly cold for the casual; but no one on the platform was lost to us. Lillian had just been telling me that she hated a lot of clothes and was never cold. A fur coat, practically speaking, was almost all she needed between her and Winter; and she went on to explain how mistaken it was to refer to her as fragile. The fragility, it seemed, was more apparent than actual: I got the impression from her that when she was making "Way Down East" her favorite position was lying on natural ice with her loosened hair in the water of the river. An insurance company, called upon to protect Mr. Griffith against the risk of such scenes, would only chance its money on Lillian and her soundness. She told me this, more than once, I think, with a great deal of pride. As she said it she looked at me with the wistfulness, the drooping delicacy, of a young weeping willow at dusk.

The drawing-room to New York we got; and, finally, rid of the Pullman conductor and the train conductor, after assuring the porter once more that he had neglected nothing, I bolted the door on a public acting as though the car had been sharply tilted in our direction. I fastened the door, but, before I could sit down, a firm knock fell on it. I hope you don't mind, I said to Lillian; but I'll be damned if I hear it! She was a little startled at the damned, but at the rest she smiled. The knocking, however, grew continuous; and in the end, I was forced to recognize it. Two men at once entered as though they had been comically propelled from behind. The first was vaguely familiar, but there was nothing vague in his greeting of me: he had gone to school with me—thirty years ago, that would have been—his memory of those days held nothing happier than me, and he saw me again, after so long, with a deep pleasure. . . . . During this his intentness on Lillian was romantically complete.

The individual with this faithful friend of my childhood elbowed himself into view, and, prompted by their names, I introduced them to Miss Gish. I then explained that we were engaged in planning a moving, a very moving, picture, and they reluctantly withdrew. Lillian, sitting facing me, was turning over the pages of *Vanity Fair;* and I reflected that I was in a Pullman drawing-room, going to the city of New York, with, perhaps, the loveliest girl known. This surprised me in that I was surprised at my lack of surprise. If it had happened to me fifteen years before, if, at any time between twenty and thirty, I had taken Lillian from one place to another, I would have been in a state of incredulous delight. At the idea alone! But now— though no one in the world better appreciated her loveliness—I had a calm and very complete, almost a detached, view of her. The truth was that I was filled with the desire to use her beauty for my own very definite and selfish ends.

At that time my experience in moving, exceedingly moving, pictures had hardly begun: and I saw, in imagination, the picture I would, without a doubt in the world, make with Lillian Gish. I had described it to her: no one, I told her, who has worked with you, has had the slightest idea of what your charm really is. Two men, and not unsuccessfully, have written about it, about you, for years—James Branch Cabell and myself. James thinks it is Helen of Troy; and, if he is right, then you, too, are Helen. I mean that you have the quality which, in a Golden Age, would hold an army about the walls of a city for seven years. Helen might be different from you in every apparent particular, from the ground gold in her hair to her dyed feet, but you are one at heart. Listen, in this picture none will ever possess you, no arms will be caught about you, dragging you down to the realities of satisfaction. You will be, like the April moon, a thing for all young men to dream about forever; you will be the immeasurable difference between what men have and what they want.

How, she asked, could that be done on the screen?

Easily, I asserted—that, heaven is my witness, was what I said. The stories for you are endless; we can choose any period of the world's history, any place in the world: and there you'll be, perpetually young and always old, as eternal, almost, as the ice. Timeless. Her celebrated wistfulness, at this, increased. Looking back, now, I can see that she was thinking of the moving pictures as she knew them. But she was touched, pleased; my admiration was strong enough to persuade her, for a minute, that what I described might be accomplished.

But I hadn't, yet, made clear what, in her, the special power was that no one had publicly recognized. All men, I continued, young and old, have a longing for a perfection of beauty; they never possess it; and so their dream is uninterrupted. If this

happened differently, and the loveliest of ladies flung herself into the arms of a man cherishing her as a radiant vision, while he wouldn't consider himself defrauded, still the dream would escape. He would find it, a star, still undisturbed in the sky of his imagination. The loveliest of ladies he'd soon grow accustomed to. And you, dear Lillian, as I have already said, are the fragrant April moon of men's hopes.

I will make a picture for you that, a hundred years from now, will send young men away from it forever dissatisfied with reality. No one, seeing you, will ever again be deeply interested in other girls. I recalled to her the legend of Diana—how a countryman, hearing Diana's horn through the woods, lost in vague restlessness his familiar content. You will be the clear and unforgettable silver of the horn! She expressed a concern, for a moment pleasantly granting the incredible, for all those young men. It was then necessary to discover the outline of a suitable story; and, in a few minutes, I rapidly explained one which held the elements we were searching for. Lillian liked it, and a sense of triumph, of actual accomplishment, swept over me. Then, in a plaintive and musical murmur, she spoke of money. A great deal would be necessary. I knew that much, at least; but I was certain I could explain any sum from any source for the purpose of making deathless her charm.

And the director—

We could almost do it ourselves, I assured her; we might have a purely technical director, a mechanical director. Such a person, she admitted, she had never heard of. Perhaps I might find one. He would, I replied, be procured; and it would take me no time at all to clarify in his mind the Platonic theory of love. The end, she asked, hesitatingly, wouldn't it be unhappy? Of course not! Death isn't as tragic as the loss of a vision. If we could show that to the public . . . she lifted her gaze to me and left me—it invariably did—a little breathless. It will be as obvious,

LILLIAN GISH

and as remote, as an apple tree in blossom. An apple blossom and never the apple.

II

At West Chester Lillian had been reading, in manuscript, that part of "Cytherea" where Mina Raff, a moving picture actress delicate in beauty, had a part. I wanted her approval of Mina since, without Lillian, she would never have existed. One was not the other; it was just as I've said. I didn't want Lillian annoyed when the book appeared. She read before an open fire of hickory logs, in a characteristic delicate primness, the primness of a lily; and when she had finished we spent a long while trying to find a more satisfactory phrase for moving pictures than moving pictures. There was, we found, none other; and some people came in for one of those informal suppers where plates are carried to the stairs and to the corners of rooms.

There were drinks, but the one offered to Lillian she most firmly refused. She didn't, in this sense, drink; she never smoked. It dawned on me that she was a prude. By prude I meant a person convinced that the world and the flesh were the devil: she had an instinctive recoil from the thought of a cocktail and the implication of a cigarette. And that, as much as anything about her, delighted me; it was, for her, so exactly right; it made flawless her quaint rigidity of bearing, her withdrawn grace. She was, I thought, amazed at supper; and it occurred to me that the conjunction of undoubtedly nice people and drinking she found not without its novelty.

She talked very little—Lillian chattered not at all—and when she did it was in response to questions about what she called her work. That, naturally, was her passion, it was her religion, since it had accomplished for her the offices of a religion—it had raised her from the earth to the sky. Into her personal objective belief I didn't inquire. Yet, in whatever

she said, she was insistent on the debt owed to those who had helped her, who had, in a way, made her possible. I objected there, telling her that no individual was essential to her. You would have inevitably discovered what you needed and used it until the value was gone, and then you'd have taken the next step in your career.

She didn't agree with me, she even suspected my remarks for a lack of gratitude. The innate coldness, the self-preservation, of the creative spirit, she, in effect, repudiated. Her friends she adored. They were, in addition to warm actualities, symbols of what it was necessary to maintain. She could no more hold back her gratitude than—than deny her love for her mother. In Lillian's case, of course, it was possible that her mother was all she maintained for her; but I wasn't touched by the sheer idea, the word, of mother; and I admitted this. There are mothers who are only a nuisance, a fatality, I declared; and, of all her delightful looks, the one she gave me then was the most entrancing. It was during this that I happened to think of her eyes as butterflies fluttering softly to their object. Her breath was suspended: it was clear that a bolt from heaven, driving me down to the ultimate cellar, would not have astounded her.

I went on, not too seriously, in an attack on the most celebrated objects of veneration, including home, the lamp in the window, loud patriotism, charity; and, as I progressed, she positively looked for the bolt from above; she regarded it as dilatory, a bolt not about its avenging business. Lillian had never before heard the coolness of logic applied to the figures of emotion, and I wondered how it was affecting her. I wondered if it were possible to add to her loveliness a mind liberated from the tyranny of mob sentimentality. And, in this connection, I repeated perhaps the most beautiful phrase ever conceived, the truth shall make you free. I wanted this, I am afraid, more for myself than for her—wasn't she to act in the picture I had mentally projected for her, for us . . . for me!

The trouble with her was slight—she hadn't associated with the people and ideas that would have given a clear and aesthetic form to her thoughts. She hadn't the relative calm, the superiority, of an intelligent background. Lillian, God knew, was wholly superior; but the surroundings chance, and her needs, had led her into were not those to encourage a tonic hardness of mind. The acting profession, for example, was notoriously sentimental, generous with money and tears and sympathy and promises; loving its mother—why, practically, was its father never mentioned?—and declaiming the beauties of conventional curtains transferred from a stereotyped stage to informal reality. Inherently Lillian was infinitely better than this; but it had imposed itself on her willingness to believe good of everything that wasn't bad. That, however, was not her fault; it was the failing generally, of America.

It was, in particular, the weakness of moving pictures. The men who—no better presenting themselves—really had them in charge were without aesthetic background. They had been, in many cases, actors; with the stoutest of hearts their minds weren't tough enough to encounter life, now out of the theatre, and set it down with even a relative truth. They carried into the new suspended possibilities of moving pictures the stupid terms of the stage—a heavy, the lead, the juvenile; and into those tin moulds they forced, well—Lillian. I was thinking rather less about Mr. Griffith than of others; but when, in a picture that held Lillian's utter grace, he persuaded a hen to drop an egg on the head of the immemorial fat boy, I began to see that we couldn't turn to him for a visual legend silver like Diana's horn and tender like the veiled moon of Spring.

Some of this I said to her on the train and some through dinner at the St. Regis.

We began the latter promptly, a few minutes past seven; I made what seemed to me a few remarks, and a dining room captain told me that it was time to close. It was past midnight. A waiter gave me my account: on it there were charged six plates of raspberry ice, three English double corona cigars, and an alligator pear salad. The table cloth was traced with red lines —the raspberry ice—which formed the pattern of a moving picture; the cigars had vanished . . . I suspected Lillian of eating the salad, and it was time to go. I didn't remember the details of our talk, but I did know that she had grown enthusiastic: for us, then, our plans were complete. What remained was inconsiderable. Did she tell me that she was then rehearsing a moving picture over Keen's Chop House? It seems to me that, in addition, she described how every night, conferring with the author, a new ending was written. Or was it the entire picture? There was a bother about money, too. More promises. It appeared to me that Lillian had been imposed on.

Yes, she did tell me such an unhappy story: the author of the stationary picture was the daughter of someone famous— was it on the Paris stage or in French letters? Anyhow, for that reason, principally, she had been retained. Again that wide willingness to accept everything as for the best! The romantic misconception. She secured the fur coat, and, in her automobile, we returned to our several hotels. The automobile, at least, was a reality, a fact; that much she had spun out of the intangible film of her charm; she had materialized, from a magic lantern, a solemn and correct chauffeur and a perfumed spray of flowers in an engraved glass cone.

III

I was the last person in the world to deny the solidity of her accomplishment there: a limousine and maiden-hair fern, flowers, for a Winter night were more than admirable; they were indispensable. I left her, at the Savoy, I think it was, and returned to the Algonquin; and it was a long while before I saw Lillian again. The brightness of our imagined picture grew dim; it flickered and went out; since, among other things, I had been unable to discover a director willing to hear the Platonic theory clarified for the purpose of Lillian on the screen. Money and plans widely different from mine took possession of her. During this time I became better acquainted with the actualities of moving pictures. I met other stars, mostly clusters of electric lights, a number of directors, and some pictures were made from my stories. Now, a moving picture was a very large pan indeed, but not, by many diameters, large enough to hold all the fish it was required to fry. There was the star, the director, the author of the story, the author of the scenario, the whole technical battery, the distributors, the public, and the investment—visible, usually, in the persons of one or even two reassuring beings standing, on the locations, in an apart and distinguished calm beside the cameras. Every one of them had to be satisfied. The author of the scenario, for example, was almost invariably an exceedingly attractive and forceful woman, a woman, safe in the chair of authority, whose general attitude was one of benevolence together with a total lack of any spare moments. I liked them very much, but I always had the feeling that they heard what I had to say exactly as they heard the running clicking of the cameras, a necessary but not insuperable noise.

There could be no doubt about where the authority, the unquestioned power, should be—with, of course, the director. The quality of being Lillian Gish, the difficulties of that accomplishment, made practically impossible the gathering of the other widely separated and indispensable requirements for a successful moving picture. Here, again, was the question of background—an enormous knowledge of what had and what could be done. The directors I met were insistent on the difference of moving pictures from other formal methods of expression, but that was, except for technicalities, mere nonsense. The essence of their occupation, like the base of mine, was a story: that was, a logical and convincing arrangement, the clearest arrangement possible, of facts and emotions for a given emotional result.

The parallel between themselves and me they wouldn't admit; what I called a successful picture they regarded as a sum of money up to a half million dollars dropped magnanimously into the bottomless cavern of art. The word art was theirs; I detested and never repeated it. They suspected me of a melancholy nobility which I was willing to discharge at their expense. In the meantime, though, in momentary burning nobilities of their own, they produced ideals of art; with, financially, the result that their suspicions, where I was concerned, were solidified.

Yes, the director, and not Lillian, should control every aspect of a moving picture woven out of her; and in that, miraculously, she was entirely willing to agree. She had a wonderful temperament, plastic and strong, and with an inhuman capacity for work. I watched her in "'Way Down East"; and, thoroughly sophisticated to the mechanics of exhibited feeling, when her baby died I had a most naïve contraction of the heart. She wasn't, there, a shining and unattainable moon; but she was absolutely satisfactory . . . when she was allowed to be. The picture as a whole was a vaudeville, nothing more; its parts had no more essential relationship to each other than the varied acts of an evening at a vaudeville theatre. The sole difference was this—that, fortunately, Lillian came upon the stage more than once.

When she appeared what had been dead took life, what had been meaningless took meaning, that contraction of the heart occurred. A story had to have movement and direction, it had to be composed to a centre, and the centre never, under any circumstance, lost sight of. Lillian was, it turned out, the centre of "'Way Down East"—the part Richard Barthelmess had was not, I thought, interesting to Richard —but her story was more blurred than focused on. What there was of it was admirably arranged by Mr. Griffith; but she was continually neglected for the laugh which, in moving pictures, is supposed to be the required support of a tear. Laughter, of course, could be quite all right, but it must be laughter in the tone of the whole, it must be the same voice, the same purpose, the single purpose—the story—speaking.

The trouble with that, it might be urged, lay with the censors—a force I had neglected to mention—for "'Way Down East" was the story of a betrayal. But that, then, was a fault in selection; better that it should have been, with me, Platonics. If you couldn't have the picture of the stork winging downward burdened with his special errand then, obviously, you couldn't make the betraying of innocence sufficiently real. This, under the circumstances, was carried as far as might be, and the rest left to the accommodating and domestic hen. The photography was as fine as possible; and the river choked with ice, the crumpled figure at the frozen edge of death, were as stirring as the inevitable rescue permitted. Good vaudeville, but not Lillian.

In Lillian moving pictures had a miraculous possibility—the perfect medium of expression; but they were, so far definitely, unable to realize her. I didn't see "The White Sister"—I had no wish to see Lillian's pale charm against the rigid whiteness of a nun's headdress—but I heard rumors of earthquakes and terrestial disaster, and of extraordinary machines. Damn it, I wanted Lillian! I wanted a screen quiet and composed, out of which her magic would reach and touch all hearts with tenderness and longing and memory, with hopes. I wanted her to fill America with the illusion of the beauty of love. Instead of that a *terremoto*.

IV

Just before she left for Italy I saw her in a little private reception room of a hotel in New York. Her loveliness was more potent than ever. I had grown older, and, instead of talking, planning pictures never to be a reality, I wanted to sit as silently as possible and hold her slender hand. But, naturally, she was concerned with "The White Sister"; and, as usual, I couldn't hide from her that I disliked what she was doing. Anyone who cared to was free to deduce from this that I was merely self-seeking, impatient with developments that had no place for me. They could go to the devil!

She talked in little eager cool rushes; and again, it seemed to me, she had a belief in what I said. It was almost like the dinner at the St. Regis—time was obliterated. The April moon, the fragrant April evening, in a reception room at the Ritz-Carlton; an evening with a stir among the new maple leaves and the dim whiteness of early apple blossoms. She smiled, torn with doubt; a smile never to forget. I left her, and another phase of her career began, a new stardom in electric lights of a potential argent planet.

STELLA

BY THYRA SAMTER WINSLOW

As she dressed, Stella thought about Frank Simmons. He was coming to call in half an hour—it was half-past seven—and Frank was always on time. He would probably say something definite about getting married. Oh, he wouldn't propose in so many words, really. Men didn't do that. But they were to be alone for the evening and it would be easy enough to have him say something that would settle things. He had said a lot the last few times they had been together. She could have snapped him up if they had been alone. There had always been someone around, Margaret or Rita or Rita's Laurence. Well, she'd be alone with him tonight.

Stella dressed slowly so as to take up all the time, so that she would just be finished when Frank arrived. That was best. She hated that few minutes of waiting, after you've finished dressing, that interval when you sit with a book or play a Victrola record or run back and forth looking into the mirror, adjusting a stray hairpin, adding a little more powder.

She put on her best underthings, peach colored *crêpe de chine* with little scolloped lace edges. They wouldn't show, of course, but it sort of gives you confidence if you know you are looking nice underneath. She put on her newest, next-to-best dress. Her best dress was too formal for a casual call. This dress was brown satin with nice big chiffon sleeves. She could raise her arms and let the sleeves fall softly away. Nice sleeves. A nice dress. It had a big silver ornament at one side and made her look slender. It had been expensive but she could wear it all winter—after she was married, even. It pays to buy a really good dress once in a while.

Stella ran the comb through her hair again and stuck in a few invisible hairpins. She wore her hair bobbed and it curled just a trifle. She knew the myth about bobbed hair being so much easier to take care of but she knew it took more time to keep her hair nice looking than it had ever taken when it was long. Still, it did make her look younger. That was the main thing.

Stella looked in the dressing-table mirror. No, she didn't look her age. She felt sure of that. Twenty-seven! What an awful age! Frank thought she was twenty-three. She hadn't told him that, actually, but Rita was twenty-three and he thought her just a little older than Rita. Would she have to tell him? Maybe. Oh, she could smooth that over all right.

She examined her face closely. Yes, there were wrinkles. Little ones at the corners of her eyes and rather deep lines from her nose to her mouth. Her cheeks were a little thin, too. She didn't have any gray hair, though. Of course she had found a few gray hairs from time to time, but if you pull them out when you first see them . . . That's all rot about ten coming in for every one you pull out. Twenty-seven wasn't old, these days. Being small kept Stella from looking her age. She knew that. Wasn't there an old German proverb about "*Alle kleine Hünde . . .?*"

What would it matter, once she was married to Frank? She wouldn't let herself go. Of course not. She hated women who actually slumped. But it would be nice to relax, sort of. Even a good job,

403

the kind Stella had, being a private secretary, isn't easy work. Long hours and getting up early in the morning when you've been out late the night before. How do men keep it up, year after year? Stella felt pretty tired nearly all of the time. Well, Frank didn't believe in women working—a woman's place is in the home. That was something. He had a good position, too. Really good. They'd get an apartment not too far up town—maybe in the East Sixties if they wanted to be really sporty—well, anyhow, near the park, West, and not as far out as the hundreds. A nice little apartment—and have the girls in to dinner to show how well she'd done. She'd look up the girls she knew who had got married— get in with nice married couples. Frank had a lot of fine business friends, too. He'd introduced her to some of them. They could have them to the house, too. Maybe a maid, even, in cap and apron, always neat and ready to answer the doorbell. Not like this . . .

Stella looked around at the apartment she shared with Rita Lewis. Not bad for two girls. A living room with a davenport in it. Rita slept on the davenport. An alcove, called by courtesy "the bedroom," with Stella's bed and the dressing-table for both of them. A kitchenette off the living room. A telephone on a little table in the hall. Two big chairs in blue velour to match the davenport. Orange silk curtains and lamps. A gray rug. The Victrola. Not at all bad for two girls. Certainly not. If she'd only had more opportunities to meet men Stella knew she could have made them awfully comfortable when they called. It was hard to meet men in the city. Business acquaintances never really meant more than a stray dinner now and then. Other men were always tied down, permanently, had a mother to support or were married or didn't want marriage—like Kenneth. She wasn't going to think of Kenneth any more. Of course not. Kenneth was out of her life. Completely. Here she was, all ready to marry Frank.

Did she love Frank? Of course. How silly! She wasn't the sort of girl who'd marry a man she didn't care for. Everyone knew she loved Frank. She had talked him over with the girls.

"I think he's a perfectly splendid man" . . . "Good looking, too, I love that type, sort of honest and dependable . . ."

There were few enough men she liked at all. Of course she loved Frank. A lot. Lucky to get him. She didn't love him as much as she had loved Kenneth, perhaps. This was different. But nicer. Much nicer. More comfortable. She'd be happy with Frank. He didn't interest her to talk with, the way Kenneth had. Things he said didn't have wonderful, mysterious, heart-stopping meanings. Why should they? Wouldn't it be silly having things like that happening all the time? Frank was nice and comfortable . . . and . . . and comfortable. She wouldn't have to talk with Frank, entertain him, after they were married. They both liked to read. They could read, evenings, instead of talking. She wouldn't have to think up conversations when they were married. Of course not. Comfort! That was the main thing. Even thinking about Frank was nice and comfortable. He always telephoned her exactly when he said he would. She always knew where he was, where he was going to be. She could get him on the telephone any time she wanted him. Frank never looked at another woman, hadn't really ever cared for other women. Oh, there had been a woman or two. She was glad of that. It made him appreciate her more. But he hadn't had a lot of affairs— like Kenneth. Years ahead—nice comfortable years—new clothes and a nice place to live and friends in and the theatre once or twice a week. Not the way she had imagined life once upon a time—a few years ago. What did that matter? This was life, really—comfort and pleasant years stretching out ahead.

The doorbell rang. Another dab of the powder puff. Stella hurried to the door. Frank.

"Hello Frank. For me? You are a dear to bring me these . . . oh, you spoil me. You remember my favorite chocolates. Sit down here. Comfy? I was just thinking about you. I cut a clipping out of the morning paper — thought maybe you hadn't read F. P. A."

Frank! This was nice—the one shaded light and sitting next to Frank on the blue davenport. His arm was around her. It didn't mean a great deal, his arm or the touch of his fingers. It didn't mean thrills, that is. It did mean peace and . . . and comfort.

And Frank said,

"I was looking forward to tonight. We never get an evening together. You know, the evenings with you are the most important things in my life. Other evenings just seem marking time . . ."

He was nice—a dear! She liked his arm around her, his kisses. His kisses weren't like—like Kenneth's. Why should they be? That was an episode, breath-taking, unreal. This was lasting contentment, serenity.

The telephone bit into their completeness. Stella jumped to answer it, smoothing her hair unconsciously as she took up the receiver. A woman's voice:

"Hello, Stella. Guess you'll be surprised to hear from me. It's Ruth—Ruth Morris."

Ruth Morris—a little flash of days with Ruth and Alex Morris and—Kenneth. Stella shivered just a little.

"Hello, Ruth," she said.

"Guess who's here?" Ruth went on. "He insists on seeing you—just got back to America today—Kenneth. Uh, huh, right here with us! He came up to dinner with Alex. He won't come to the 'phone. Wants to know if you're still sore at him."

"Of course I'm not angry," said Stella. "Not a bit. I never was. Tell him I'm not angry at all. In fact I'm awfully glad," she tried to make her voice smooth and cool. "I'll—I'll be glad to see him sometime soon."

Ruth giggled.

"Oh, you know Kenneth. He isn't going

to wait. Asked about you the first thing. Said to get you on the 'phone and if you're home and not angry he's going to run in tonight—right away—to say 'hello' for a minute."

"He—he can't come tonight," said Stella. "I've got company. Frank Simmons. You ever meet him? Tell Kenneth to—to come to the telephone."

A wait, then, little noises over the telephone. Stella turned to Frank,

"A man I used to know last year—two years ago. He just got back from abroad—he wants to come in for a little while."

"Why, of course," said Frank, courteously, "why not let him come in for a while, if you like—a friend of yours . . ."

"He won't come to the telephone," said Ruth, and giggled again, "and he said to tell your new boy friend to go to hell. He'll be there in half a minute, he said. He's been drinking all through dinner—brought some stuff with him. You know Kenneth. He hasn't changed a bit . . . same old Ken. Ring me up in the morning and tell me what happens. Goo' bye."

II

Stella went back to the blue davenport. Everything in the world had changed. She didn't know what to do. Should she get Frank away—before Kenneth came? Should she go out with Frank and have Kenneth find the apartment deserted? She could visualize Kenneth ringing the bell of the empty apartment. Should she just wait—with Frank—and let Kenneth call?

Why not? Nothing would happen. How silly! She wasn't really engaged to Frank —in words. Of course she could get Frank to think that they were engaged—Frank wanted matrimony—was willing for matrimony, anyhow. Still, what could happen? Kenneth didn't want to marry her. Kenneth wouldn't do anything. He would just come in and say "hello" and leave again. That was all. Why—it was two years since Kenneth had gone away. He probably wouldn't mean anything to her any more—would mean nothing at all.

She explained, in little sentences, to Frank:

"Yes, he used to be a good friend of mine. Ruth Morris, she was Ruth Sterling, then, and Alex, the man she married and Kenneth Hendricks and I used to trail around together. I haven't seen him in ages. You won't mind—if he comes in. He may not even come. He won't stay long. A nice chap, splendid. But odd. Awfully odd. I'm anxious to see what you think of him. Says all sorts of odd, peculiar things. Everyone likes him though. Ruth said he'd been drinking a lot . . ."

The atmosphere of peace—of Frank and the lamp-lit room—was gone. Stella's heart began thumping a little. She sat stiffly, waiting.

Kenneth back again—and she'd thought of him only tonight. Tonight—why, there hadn't been a night she hadn't thought of Kenneth. To think that he was coming—tonight. Why not tonight? Wasn't this just a night, a night that she was having a caller? Frank had called lots of nights. Kenneth hadn't come those other nights. Kenneth and Frank—together. Like a play. Why was it like a play? How silly! Nothing to get nervous about—just Frank—whom she—might marry—and Kenneth, an old friend.

Kenneth would never marry—would never have married her. He said that. He didn't believe in marriage. Why bother about Kenneth?

She got up, slipped into the bedroom, powdered her face, added more rouge and lip-salve, touched up the corners of her eyes with her pencil. She puffed her hair softly around her face. She was glad she had on the new brown dress. Kenneth would see she hadn't mourned for him. He'd see her —having a caller, candy, a new dress— Kenneth was clever—he'd see she didn't care at all any more.

Talking with Frank again. She listened with only a part of her consciousness. The rest went to the telephone, the door, the street. Would Kenneth come—or tele-phone? How would he look? What would he say? Kenneth!

"Yes," she said earnestly to Frank, answering something he had said, "yes, I think so. I agree with you absolutely. I really think that—"

The doorbell rang. Stella jumped up, ran to the door. She had intended going slowly. She forgot all about that. She opened the door. There—why there was Kenneth—dear Kenneth—the Kenneth of year-before-last, of her nights of sleeplessness and sobbing, of her wasted days of dreaming . . . Kenneth . . .

"Hel-lo, Kenneth," she said. "Enter, my son. The—the prodigal back home! Kenneth Hendricks, I want you to meet Frank Simmons, my—my 'jump-man friend'." Giggles, then.

Kenneth was cool and amused—and taller than she had remembered him. Taller than Frank. She hadn't thought of him as that tall. He put down his hat and his stick, lounged over to Frank, then to the largest chair, took out his pipe— Kenneth's pipe . . .

"Hum, home-like," he said, "this *is* worth coming back for. Still the one sentimental light, I see. Turn up another one, old dear." Then, to Frank,

"Isn't she the greatest girl for sentiment? Give Stella one rose-colored light or a mushy novel or a movie with a sad ending and she'll cry happily for hours. I remember one time . . ."

That wasn't right. That wasn't what Kenneth should have said! Stella wanted to tell him so, give him a cue. Why, here was Frank, who didn't think she was sentimental, who was going to marry her . . .

"Did you miss me?" asked Kenneth. And "those were the great days. Oh, well, now that Papa's back again . . . Stella's the greatest kid. Can't tell you how glad I am she's not all married and everything. I'd hate to have to break up a home. Not that she'd fall for me or anything like that, eh sweetie? She always was hunting around for something permanent and I was sort of afraid she'd be married by now. I don't see why women are always hunting for husbands. It beats me. Over in Paris I ran across a girl I'd known here in New York—you remember that little Finch girl, Stella, the one who was up at Lakewood that summer . . ."

A long anecdote, one of Kenneth's anecdotes—bitter, hard, cynical—and unbelievably interesting. How could she have forgotten him? Had she forgotten? Not for one minute all of the time. Kenneth . . . Kenneth . . .

She looked at Frank—Frank who had grown curiously aloof, curiously a stranger, Frank in his neat blue suit with his serious, peering, kind eyes behind thick glasses. Frank was wondering, was uneasy about the stranger with his easy knowledge of Stella, of women. She looked at Kenneth, relaxed, sprawled in the big chair, his hair mussed and a bit shaggy as always, his light eyes narrowed, lean of jaw, his mouth perhaps just a trifle soft.

Kenneth held the floor as he always held the floor, with anecdotes just a trifle risqué and yet showing a peculiar knowledge of life and of women. ". . . you'll meet her, Stella, a Miss Picard, a beautiful girl. She came back on the boat with me. I've a date to take her to dinner on Tuesday. When we were in Paris she told me about this Giovanetti . . . "

Miss Picard—Kenneth was going to take her to dinner on Tuesday! A sudden hot jealousy—a jealousy she had not felt in two years, came to Stella. Miss Picard! He'd seen her in Paris. Stella had been a bit jealous of Frank one evening, months ago —but nothing that Frank could do could have mattered, really. Tuesday—dinner with Miss Picard—a beautiful girl— Kenneth knew a beautiful girl when he saw one—always knew beautiful girls—

"I—I'm afraid I must go," said Frank, hurt, puzzled. Stella knew that and knew why. She knew how all of Kenneth's little personalities had offended him, how it had annoyed him when Kenneth, passing to turn on an additional light, had rubbed his hand across Stella's hair, "my—the girl's

gone and got a bob. Get it cut shorter in back, sweet thing, that's the way they wear it in Paris now . . ."

"It's early," said Stella. She knew that she ought to say something, explain. She knew that Kenneth ought to offer to go, that Kenneth wouldn't. She would have fought, somehow, if he had tried to go.

"Yes, I know, but I was up late last night," Frank answered. "I'll telephone you later in the week, if I may. I'm glad to have met you Mr., oh, yes, Hendricks."

The door slammed. Frank was gone. It would be hard to get him back again. Frank—peace—contentment . . .

Kenneth stood up.

"Come and kiss Papa," he said. "Gee, I'm glad the chief mourner had brains enough to beat it early. Just brains enough, I'd say. What a cheerful individual! Is that who you've used as a pinch-hitter while Papa was away? Gee, Baby, it's good to get back again. You and I are going to put on some of the prettiest parties this winter, eh, sweet thing . . ."

His arms were around her—his kisses on her lips . . . Kenneth's kisses. Had she forgotten them even for one moment? Kenneth—back again! Across Stella's mind there surged a hundred things—unhappiness, the memories of hours she had waited for telephone calls that had not come, the memories of Kenneth making love to other women, treating her with studied—and with unconscious—indifference . . . unrest—tumult—fever. . .

"Love me?" asked Kenneth, "love Papa?"

How silly—"love Papa?"

She could have pushed him away, now— she could have told him to leave—while Frank was still there. Here he had come in—spoilt everything—her peaceful winter, her contentment, her life. Here he was— back again—for a little while—a little while . . . Kenneth—her Kenneth—who cared enough—to come back. What did anything else matter—the future, peace, anything! Kenneth was back, now. Stella gave a little prayer of thankfulness.

"Of course I love you," she said.

EDITORIAL

HALF the sorrows of the world, I suppose, are caused by making false assumptions. If the truth were only easier to ascertain the remedy for them would consist simply of ascertaining it and accepting it. This business, alas, is usually impossible, but fortunately not always: now and then, by some occult process, half rational and half instinctive, the truth gets itself found out and an ancient false assumption goes overboard. I point, in the field of the social relations, to one which afflicted the human race for milleniums: that one, to wit, which credited the rev. clergy with a mysterious wisdom and awful powers. Obviously, it has ceased to trouble all the superior varieties of men. It may survive in those remote marches where human beings go to bed with the cows, but certainly it has vanished from the cities. Asphalt and the apostolic succession, indeed, seem to be irreconcilable enemies. I can think of no clergyman in any great American city today whose public dignity and influence are much above those of an ordinary Class I Babbitt. It is hard for even the most diligent and passionate of the order to get upon the first pages of the newspapers; he must make a clown-show, discreditable to his fraying cloth, or he must blush unseen. When bishops begin launching thunderbolts against heretics, the towns do not tremble; they laugh. When elders denounce sin, sin only grows more fashionable. Imagine a city man getting a notice from the ordinary of the diocese that he had been excommunicated. It would trouble him far less, I venture, than his morning *Katzenjammer*.

The reason for all this is not hard to find. All the superior varieties of men—and even the lowest varieties of city workmen are at least superior, in information and experience, to peasants—have simply rid themselves of their old belief in devils. Hell no longer affrights and palsies them, and so the sorcery of those who profess to save them from it no longer impresses them. That profession, I believe, was bogus, and its acceptance was therefore a false assumption. Being so, it made men unhappy; getting rid of it has delivered them. They are no longer susceptible to ecclesiastical alarms and extortions; *ergo*, they sleep and eat better. Think of what life must have been under such princes of damnation as Cotton Mather and Jonathan Edwards, with even bartenders and politicians believing in them! And then compare it to life under Bishop Manning and the Rev. Dr. John Roach Straton, with only a few antediluvians believing in them! Or turn to the backwoods of the Republic, where the devil is still feared, and with him his professional exterminators. In the country towns the clergy are still almost as influential as they were in Mather's day, and there, as everyone knows, they remain public nuisances, and civilized life is nearly impossible. In such Neolithic regions nothing can go on without their consent, on penalty of anathema and hell-fire; as a result, nothing goes on that is worth recording. It is this survival of sacerdotal authority, I believe, and not hookworm, malaria or 100% Americanism, that is chiefly responsible for the cultural paralysis of the late Confederate States. The South lacks big cities; it is run by its country towns—and in every country town there is some Baptist mullah who rules by scaring the peasantry. The false assumption that his pretensions are sound, that he can actually bind and loose, that contumacy to him is a variety of cursing God

—this false assumption is what makes the yokels so uneasy, so nervous, and hence so unhappy. If they could throw it off they would burn fewer Aframericans and sing more songs. If they could be purged of it they would be purged of Ku Kluxery too.

The cities got rid of that ancient false assumption half a century ago, and have been making cultural progress ever since. Somewhat later they got rid of its brother, to wit, respect for law, and, in particular, respect for its visible agents, the police. That respect—traditional, and hence irrational—had been, for years, in increasingly unpleasant collision with a great body of obvious facts. The police, by assumption austere and almost sacrosanct, were gradually discovered to be, in reality, a pack of rogues, and but little removed, save by superior impudence and enterprise, from the cut-throats and purse-snatchers they were set to catch. When, a few decades ago, the American people, at least in the big cities, began to accept them frankly for what they were—when the old false assumption of their integrity and public usefulness was quietly abandoned and a new and more accurate assumption of their roguery was adopted in its place—when this change was effected there was a measurable increase, I believe, in the public happiness. It no longer astonished anyone when policemen were taken in evil-doing; indignation therefore abated, and with it its pains. If, before that time, the corps of Prohibition enforcement officers—*i. e.*, a corps largely composed of undisguised scoundrels—had been launched upon the populace, there would have been a roar of wrath, and much anguished gnashing of teeth. People would have felt themselves put upon, injured, insulted. But with the old false assumption about policemen removed from their minds, they met the new onslaught calmly and even smilingly. Today no one is indignant over the fact that the extortions of these new *Polizei* increase the cost of potable alcohol. The false assumption that the police are altruistic agents of a benevo-lent state has been replaced by the sound assumption that they are gentlemen engaged assiduously, like the rest of us, in finding meat and raiment for their families and in laying up funds to buy Liberty Bonds in the next war to end war. This is human progress, for it increases human happiness.

II

So much for the evidence. The deduction I propose to make from it is simply this: that a like increase would follow if the American people could only rid themselves of another and worse false assumption that still rides them—one that corrupts all their thinking about the great business of politics, and vastly augments their discontent and unhappiness—the assumption, in brief, that politicians are divided into two classes, and that one of those classes is made up of good ones. I need not argue, I hope, that this assumption is almost universally held among us. Our whole politics, indeed, is based upon it, and has been based upon it since the earliest days. What is any political campaign save a concerted effort to turn out a set of politicians who are admittedly bad and put in a set who are thought to be better? The former assumption, I believe, is always sound; the latter is just as certainly false. For if experience teaches us anything at all it teaches us this: that a good politician, under democracy, is quite as unthinkable as an honest burglar or a virtuous harlot. His very existence, indeed, is a standing subversion of the public good, in every rational sense. He is not one who serves the common weal; he is simply one who preys upon the commonwealth. It is to the interest of all the rest of us to hold down his powers to an irreducible minimum, and to reduce his compensation to nothing; it is to *his* interest to augment his powers at all hazards, and to make his compensation all the traffic will bear. To argue that these aims are identical is to argue palpable nonsense. The politician, at his ideal best,

never even remotely approximated in practise, is a necessary evil; at his worst he is
an almost intolerable nuisance.

What I contend is simply that he would
be measurably less a nuisance if we got
rid of our false assumption about him, and
regarded him in the cold light of fact. At
once, I believe, two-thirds of his obnox-
iousness would vanish. He would remain
unpleasant, but he would cease to be a
fraud; the injury of having to pay freight
on him would cease to be complicated by
the insult of being swindled. It is the
insult and not the injury that makes the
deeper wounds, and causes the greater
permanent damage to the national psyche.
All of us have been trained, since infancy,
in putting up with necessary evils, plainly
recognized *as* evils. We know, for example,
that the young of the human species
commonly smell badly; that garbage
men, boot blacks and messenger boys
commonly smell worse. These facts are
not agreeable, but they remain tolerable
because they are universally assumed—
because there is no sense of having been
tricked and cozened in their perennial
discovery. But try to imagine how distressing fatherhood would become if prospective fathers were all taught that the
human infant radiates an aroma like the
rose—if the truth came constantly as a
surprise! Each fresh victim of the decep-
tion would feel that he had been basely
swindled—that his own child was somehow bogus. Not infrequently, I suppose,
he would be tempted to make away with
it in some quiet manner, and have another
—only to be shocked again. That procedure would be idiotic, admittedly, yet
it is exactly the one we follow in politics.
At each election we vote in a new set of
politicians, insanely assuming that they
are better than the set turned out. And at
each election we are, as they say in the
Motherland, done in.

Of late the fraud has become so gross
that the plain people begin to show a
great restlessness under it. Like animals in
a cage, they trot from one corner to

another, endlessly seeking a way out. If
the Democrats win one year, it is a pretty
sure sign that they will lose the next year.
State after State becomes doubtful, pivotal,
skittish; even the solid South begins to
break up. In the cities it is still worse.
An evil circle is formed. First the poor
taxpayers, robbed by the politicians of one
great party and then by those of the other,
turn to a group of free-lance rogues in the
middle ground—non-partisan candidates,
Liberals, reformers, or what not: the name
is unimportant. Then, flayed and pillaged
by these gentry as they never were by the
old-time professionals, they go back in
despair to the latter, and are flayed and
pillaged again. Back to Bach! Back to
Tammany! Tammany reigns in New York
because the Mitchel outfit was found to
be intolerable—in other words, because
the reformers were found to be even worse
than the professionals. Is the fact surprising? Why should it be? Reformers and
professionals are alike merely politicians in
search of jobs; both are trying to bilk the
taxpayers. That either has any other motive I expressly deny. If any genuinely
honest and altruistic politician had ever
come to the surface in America in my time
I'd have heard of him, for I have always
frequented newspaper offices, and in a
newspaper office the news of such a marvel
would cause a dreadful tumult. I can recall
no such tumult. The unanimous opinion
of all the journalists that I know, ex-
cluding a few Liberals who are obviously
somewhat balmy—they believed, for example, that the late war would end war—
is that, since the days of the national
Thors and Wotans, no politician who was
not out for himself, and for himself alone,
has ever drawn the breath of life in this
vast and incomparable Republic.

The gradual disintegration of Liberalism
among us, in fact, offers an excellent proof
of the truth of my thesis. The Liberals
have come to grief by fooling their customers, not merely once too often, but a
hundred times too often. Over and over
again they have trotted out some new

hero, usually from the great open spaces, only to see him taken in the immemorial malpractises within ten days. Their grave-yard, indeed, is filled with cracked and upset headstones, many covered with ribald pencilings. Every time there is a scandal in the grand manner—such as the Teapot Dome business, for example—the Liberals lose almost as many general officers as either the Democrats or the Republicans. Of late, racked beyond endur-ance by such catastrophes at home, they have gone abroad for their principal heroes; losing humor as well as hope, they now ask us to venerate such astounding pala-dins as the Hon. Bela Kun, a gentleman who, at home, would not only be in the calaboose, but actually in the death-house. But this absurdity is only an offshoot of a deeper one. Their primary error lies in making the false assumption that some politicians are better than others. This error they share with the whole American people.

III

I propose that it be renounced, and contend that its renunciation would greatly ration-alize and improve our politics. I do not argue that there would be any improve-ment in our politicians; on the contrary, I believe that they would remain substan-tially as they are today, and perhaps grow even worse. But what I do argue is that recognizing them frankly for what they were would instantly and automatically dissipate the indignation caused by their present abominations, and that the disap-pearance of this indignation would pro-mote the public contentment and happi-ness. Under my scheme there would be no more false assumptions and no more false hopes, and hence no more painful sur-prises, no more bitter resentments of fraud, no more despairs. Politicians, in so far as they remained necessary, would be kept at work—but not with any insane notion that they were archangels. Their rascality would be assumed and discounted, as the rascality of the police is now assumed

and discounted. Machinery would be grad-ually developed to limit it and counteract it. In the end, it might be utilized in some publicly profitable manner, as the insen-sitiveness to filth of garbage men is now utilized, as the reverence of the clergy for capitalism is now utilized. The result, perhaps, would be a world no better than the present one, but it would at least be a world more intelligent.

In all this I sincerely hope that no one will mistake me for one who shares the indignation I have spoken of—that is, for one who believes that politicians can and ought to be made good, and cherishes a fond scheme for making them so. I believe nothing of the sort. On the contrary, I am convinced that the art and mystery they practise is essentially and incurably anti-social—that they must remain irrecon-cilable foes of the common weal until the end of time. But I maintain that this fact, in itself, is not a bar to their employment. There are, under our perfected Christian civilization, many necessary offices that demand the possession of anti-social tal-ents. A professional soldier, regarded real-istically, is much worse than a politician, for he is a professional murderer and kid-naper, whereas the politician is only a professional sharper and sneak-thief. A clergyman, too, begins to shrink and shrivel on analysis; the work he does in the world is basically almost indistinguish-able from that of an astrologer, a witch-doctor or a fortune-teller. He pretends falsely that he can get sinners out of hell, and collects money from them on that promise, tacit or express. If he had to go before a jury with that pretension it would probably go hard with him. But we do not send him before a jury; we grant him his hocus-pocus on the ground that it is necessary to his office, and that his office is necessary to civilization, so-called. I pass over the journalist delicately; the time has not come to turn State's evidence. Suffice it to say that he, too, would prob-ably wither under a stiff cross-examina-tion. If he is no murderer, like the soldier, then he is at least a sharper and swindler, like the politician.

What I plead for, if I may borrow a term in disrepute, is simply *Realpolitik, i.e.,* realism in politics. I can imagine a political campaign purged of all the current false assumptions and false pretenses—a campaign in which, on election day, the voters went to the polls clearly informed that the choice between them was not between an angel and a devil, a good man and a bad man, an altruist and a go-getter, but between two frank go-getters, the one, perhaps, excelling at beautiful and nonsensical words and the other at silent and prehensile deeds—the one a chautauqua orator and the other a porch-climber. There would be, in that choice, something candid, free and exhilarating. Buncombe would be adjourned. The voter would make his selection in the full knowledge of all the facts, as he makes his selection between two heads of cabbage, or two evening papers, or two brands of chewing tobacco. Today he chooses his rulers as he buys bootleg whisky, never knowing precisely what he is getting, only certain that it is not what it pretends to be. The Scotch may turn out to be wood alcohol or it may turn out to be gasoline: in either case it is not Scotch. How much better if it were plainly labeled! For wood alcohol and gasoline both have their uses—higher uses, indeed, than Scotch. The danger is that the swindled and poisoned consumer, despairing of ever avoiding them when he doesn't want the , may prohibit them even when he does want them, and actually enforce his own prohibition. The danger is that the hopeless voter, forever victimized by his false assumption about politicians, may in the end gather such ferocious indignation that he will abolish them teetotally and at one insane swoop, and so cause government by the people, for the people and with the people to perish from this earth.

H. L. M.

THE UPLIFT ON THE FRONTIER

BY JAMES STEVENS

THE pioneer outlaws and harlots of the Golden West and that glorified farmhand, the cowboy, have been so vastly celebrated in American legend that every schoolboy knows about them, and the pioneer farmer, trader and missionary have had their shares of glory too, but the pioneer laborer remains unhonored and unsung. Yet it was his sweat that really won the West—his strong and untiring muscles that cleared off the primeval forest, bridged the rivers, tunneled the mountains, and laid the shining lines of rail. For one argonaut butchered by the Indians or lost in the deserts, for one cowboy trampled or frozen on his lonely vigil, there were a thousand loggers done to death in the woods, and a thousand miners sacrificed under the earth, and a thousand "savages" wrecked and wiped out in the railroad construction camps.

"Savages" is what they called themselves. It was, indeed, a savage life out there at the edge of civilization, and they delighted in the fact. They were men of primitive impulses and desires—barbarians thrown off from the docile herd. They were cynical of the benefits of democracy and scornful of its laws, but fearful of its confinements. Regimentation was loathsome to them, and seemed impossible. They preferred rough camps to houses, the open trail to paved streets, liberty to security. Worked cruelly hard, more often than not ill-used, they yet felt themselves to be free men and rejoiced in their freedom.

That was fifteen years ago, ten years ago, even five years ago. The wild West lingered among these savages long after the last argonaut had become a town boomer, and the last cowboy had gone into the movies. But the savage, too, is now only a memory. The uplift has reached out its long arm and brought him to grace. He is "civilized." He lives in a house. He has gone on the water-wagon. He wears store clothes. He reads the newspapers. He goes to see Douglas Fairbanks and Bill Hart. A few short years have completely reformed him. He is no more the outlaw that he was. He has been reduced to the common level of American workingman.

I myself have shared his transformation with him, for I have been a common laborer in the Northwest for fifteen years, and remain a laborer today. I had behind me a boyhood amid gentler scenes when I took to the wilds, and its influence, perhaps, is strong upon me now, but while I worked and roistered with the savages I was genuinely one of them. I lived in grading camps, box-cars and jungles, and liked it. I was a team-hand, a muleteer. I graduated from the gay-cat class, and won my tribal name: Appanoose Jimmie. Now I set down some memories of those old days, and some notes upon the new ones.

II

One April night in 1909 I crawled from the trucks of a dining-car in Pocatello, Idaho, and joined a band that was headed for a railroad job in Montana. We gathered in a saloon, and the ones who had money bought amusement for us all. I knew some of them; the others had rambled in from the East and South, where they had wintered.

The bar was in a squalid room, but I would not have traded it for a palace

413

chamber. The smoke-grimed ceiling, the spotted and streaked walls, and the rows of kegs on the floor made the glitter of the bar itself seem only the richer and warmer. There the swaying, gesticulating, stamping mass of muleteers in dark suits and round-topped, curly-rimmed hats—the uniform of the tribe—bawled out news, stories and plans. I, the youngling, was silent, of course. I stood at the end of the bar, downing foul whisky with the rest and pridefully dispensing with any chaser. The alcohol added a crimson flame to the glory in my soul. I was among heroes! In this band was Hard Line Billy, who could crack a bottle with a leather line flung twenty feet, and Poker Tom Davis, the champion poker player of all the camps. Also there was Red Grabby, who, as a walking-boss, had commanded camps of two hundred men. These were of the nobility. But Paddy the Devil, I thought, was the king of them all. He was hammer-chinned, light-footed, powerful. His piratical countenance—all sinister shadows of thick eyebrows, Indian eyes and twirled moustachios — and his fame as a battler gave me an impression of heroic personality. I had heard tales of riots in camps, jungles and saloons, where good men fell or fled before his passionate attack, his shattering fists. He wore a twenty-foot lash wound around his waist. And the tribe called him Paddy the Devil.

While I worshiped I snatched what sense I might from the racketing talk. As I remember, there was little that was vile spoken. They talked rather of wars with John Yegg, roving thief and enemy, with John Law and John Farmer, and with the scissor-bill, the settled laborer of the towns. I caught bits of history about the building of the Milwaukee, the Midland Valley and the North Bank, where they had helped grade the road-beds. . . . The glasses clinked, the smoke thickened, the voices became an unintelligible roar. . . .

Paddy the Devil had gripped my arm. "Not 'nother shot, Appanoose; you gotta keep your legs to make the three o'clock

rattler." And then he bawled to the others, "Come on, you savages; let's perform!"

Here haziness intervenes, and I recollect but dimly a parade through the redlight district, where I heard a shrill of female voices and saw painted faces and thrilling eyes. Then the railroad yard.

I was awakened at dawn from my slumber in a gondola-car loaded with coal. The train was on a siding in a sagebrush desert. Paddy the Devil heaved me to my feet, shaking me roughly, "Yay, Ned," he growled. "Ditch the sleep! The shack's fixed, and we ride an empty to Lima."

We all left the gondola and crawled into an empty box-car. Bottles were passed around, and we stretched out for another sleep. When I awoke again beer and food had been procured at some town, and the savages were eating lustily. When the bread and canned salmon had been consumed there were many bottles of beer left, and with the emptying of these came stories and songs.

Songs of toil and stories of toil, of wanderings, sprees and battles without rules, of hardships, privations and persecutions that marked the lowest range of life's miseries. But even these were told for laughter. I remember most clearly Jailhouse Whitey hoisting his shirt to display the hideous scars made in a Southern prison camp—"Got a 'riginal tattoo, I has, b'god—," Paddy the Devil describing a battle with five loggers who had assailed him with beer bottles, and Memphis Fogarty telling of the murders of Negroes in Mississippi levee camps, and their burial with dead mules in the dumps of levee fills.

We reached Lima, the division point, at sundown. We bought supplies and went to the jungles—always a sheltered spot by some stream, where crude cooking-ware was used and left by various bands. There we prepared the "call." This, a strictly jungle dish, is composed of mashed potatoes, bits of bacon and onions. On call, coffee and bread we feasted. We drank the coffee from old tin cans and ate the call from cans or boards, using whittled-out paddles for spoons. I remember that the last two savages to eat sat facing each other—the can in which the call had been cooked between their legs—and solemnly took turns in scooping up mouthfuls.

The night was spent in the back room of a saloon, where we had drunk enormous quantities of beer earlier in the evening. The next day we proceeded to Armstead, the headquarters for the new railroad. Armstead, then a village of many brothels and saloons, one hotel and one store, was built at the junction of two narrow valleys. There were new warehouses and sidings by the main line, and alongside them were great piles of material for the building of the railroad. Dust from freight wagons rolled all day up the slopes of the bald, wrinkled hills. The streets streamed with men, and as soon as we left the yards we met other members of our tribe. Now we felt the excitement of the enterprise, and as we jammed into the first saloon the talk was all of the work before us, of the wages to be made, of the virtues of the various camps. Gamblers and yeggs worked through the saloons, seeking possible victims, and on the fringes of the mob cowboys stood marveling at the rushing, violent life that left them without honor in their own country.

The hard-rock men, or dynos, and the team-hands ruled for the moment; their hard labor of ten hours a day would in time thrust twin rails of steel ninety miles up a valley and into the heart of a region rich in metals. For this they would receive a wage, but the reward they claimed was a short day or so of riotous drinking, brawling and primitive amour, and then a free ride to a new job. If they considered their souls at all they thought them as useless as neckties; they had no politics, nor any religion; they were as remote from the amenities of civilization as a tribe of Neanderthals. But they had a sharp instinct for the drama and color of their violent life, and a sense of the simple usefulness of pioneer labor. So they lived greatly in their own light. They did not want salvation or betterment. And as they had only contempt for the prosperity of tamer people and were wary of the law they did not tamper with others.

Considering them austerely I might admit that the savages were detestable fellows and that the suppression of their old life has been a noble work. But the memory of my experiences with them flashes on my mind in hot streaks of light. I knew them when I knew the fresh fire of youth, and this fire is ecstasy of the flesh. Even now I do not shudder at their brutalities, or at the blood on their hands from knifings, clubbings and fist-fights. No, I still feel a thrill of elemental passion in the memory of the pickhandle duel between Paddy the Devil and Keen Heel Sam at Leyden Brothers' camp on the Armstead road.

That was the hey-day of the savages and I was in the thick of it, and happy every hour. Squalor and dirt were in the camps, of course, and the work was hard and the hours long. But the savages themselves, for all their brutality, were amusing and amiable fellows, and life among them went with a rush. The day-ends were for stories and songs around the fire—vast, heroic, incredible epics that have yet to find their poet. At that time I had read nothing save an occasional newspaper for a year and a half; when I began reading again, a year later, I had almost forgotten how. So the tales that I heard were literature to me, and I took them in with immense satisfaction. "Blow-ins" came on pay-day—colossal, barbaric revels, but short, and, I believe, not harmful. It was the life of overgrown boys. It was hooky every day.

III

It was, of course, doomed to perish. The frontier kept sliding back; civilization kept sneaking in. Every time they finished a new line of rail or cleared a new section of woods the savages were pushed further into the wilderness, and soon or late they were bound to come to its end.

But it was not natural forces working from within but a spirit working from without that broke up the old life and converted the care-free savage into a sober workingman. I believe that it was none other than Henry Ford who made the first inroads. Ford's ideas, put into practice in his automobile plant, penetrated to the camps very quickly, and there they seemed to arouse discontent in men who had been quite unaffected by the prodding of radicalism. One began to hear strange doctrines preached, some of them subversive. The savages began to be class-conscious, to consider their woes, to demand relief. The men of the crafts and the common laborers joined forces "for the common interest"; there was talk of unionism, of one big union. Newspapers appeared and ideas were mulled in the evenings. The old songs and stories were heard no more; the savages began to learn shame and aspiration.

Then came the war, and with it the uplift —and the end was in sight. The camps began to be penetrated by the prophets of all sorts of new gospels—preachers of patriotism, sacrifice, service, order, morality. The bordellos were closed; the saloons came under a strange and disconcerting ban; silence fell upon the once loud and happy savages. It began to appear that almost everything that had made the old life charming to them was wrong—that it was wrong to go on a bust on pay-day, wrong to get drunk and fight, wrong to squander money. The camps began to grow decorous and dull. It was a tremendous change, and there was something unnatural about it. But it lasted.

In 1917 after spending some seasons in the woods, I returned to the construction camps. I rode the freights to Kansas City, and from there I shipped out to a tunnel job in Wyoming. Then I worked in the Utah copper mines and on a reclamation project. I was driving mules on California highway work when I was snared in the draft. I found the life of all the camps profoundly changed. Everyone was covered with the scum of city labor, and its tribal traditions and vitality and the innocence of its old spirit were smothered by the aggressive righteousness of the towns. In camp the savages complained; in the jungles they were surly and depressed. Everywhere I heard: "I'm goin' to get the hell outta this an' join the Army." Most of them did. With the halting of development work others drifted into the new war enterprises. Troops guarded the railroads and there was a general suspicion of all strangers. The savages settled down. The saloons were finally closed and the last tribal bond was broken.

Few of the old team-hands have returned to construction work. The grading camps are now simply places of labor. In the logging camps and sawmill towns the old spirit breathes only feebly. Ancient loggers keep alive the memory of Paul Bunyan, their legendary hero, and stories and songs survive from the primitive days, but the younger loggers are all of a much different stamp. They still have the instincts that make them scorn the duller trades and usually they are hard-muscled and exuberant of spirit, but they were not yet men when the new regimentation began and they have been moulded and guided by its influences. They are no longer savages. They are simply laborers.

IV

I am writing this paragraph after eight hours of work, loading lumber. I am writing it, as I have written the preceding ones, mainly because I have nothing else particularly interesting or exciting to do. My labor did not weary me, I am full-fed, my room has cheer and comfort, and the devising of phrases is an intriguing sport, though a tame one. So I shall write. But first I must consider my ideas and get them in order. I turn off the light and settle comfortably in my chair.

Through my window I see the mill lights and the glowing domes of the burners, and beyond these the darkness of a great forest that reaches to the snows of the Cascades. Lofty peaks, hundreds of sections of giant pines, a river roaring down a canyon which cleaves a desert of lava ridges and buttes. To the South there is a hundred miles of cattle range. Surely a grand setting for a roaring, tumultuous life of freedom-loving men, . . .

An idea: I shall go exploring, and on my return write of the men and life I have found. . . .

I descended the stairs and saw two of my fellow-roomers, husky mill-workers, solemnly conversing over a table heaped with magazines and newspapers. I stopped to listen. Perhaps a spree was being planned, or a joust with a crew of loggers. The voices were argumentative.

"What the hell y'see in Fairbanks, anyway? He's a swift guy, all right, but he can't pull half the stuff Tom Mix does. He was a real cowboy, too, that bird was."

"What I'm trying to get at is Fairbanks has the *art*, see? He's there with the real he-actin', too, but he puts *art* in his picshers, an' that way they's somethin' to his actin', see? For what the newspapers say is, the picshers need more *art*. That way they's a real force of progress an'—"

I passed on. Art has enchanted the savage; his soul ripples and gleams under its airs and stars!

I left the boarding-house and turned up the street that led by the mills. After passing the American Legion building I reached Main Street, but ere I struck out for the bon-bon district I paused for respectful consideration of the 4-L Hall. The Loyal Legion of Loggers and Lumbermen was a creation of the tyranny of holiness; the good folk used it to oust the I. W. W. from spruce operations during the war. The organization persists now as a petting party between the lumberman and his employés. It is not greatly different from other company unions. A fair fraction of the workers belong to it because they consider it a guardian of the eight-hour day. It provides means to settle disputes between the employer and the workers, guarantees a very minimum wage and

stands staunchly for American Ideals. It opposes rum-drinking, hell-raising and unrestricted immigration, and its members must vow allegiance to the land of milk and honey and, incidentally, declare against strikes. The president of this loyal legion of brawny loggers and hard-headed lumbermen is an ex-professor of English! In this hall the safety and efficiency experts punch out their ideas and the ecstatic sociologists deliver themselves of profundities and appeals. Citadel of the New Freedom! I saluted it gravely and passed on.

I reached the first business block and passed a grocery store, a cobbler's shop, a confectionery, a meat market, a poolroom and confectionery, a temple of art, another confectionery and a clothing store. I turned into the side street and the light of Ye Sweete Shoppe threw its glitter into my eyes. I retreated to the poolroom. I entered, sauntered past the big show-case crammed with candy, and stopped by three men who were drinking pink milkshakes.

As I sipped my near-beer I contemplated the trio. Good men, all three, still representing the best stuff of the nation, because they were still the least pretentious. They had strong frames for hard and perilous living, and eyes—alight with vitality even now—that could be dancing stars in a free and stirring environment. At their labor of felling trees or skidding logs, their faces sweat-streaked and dusty, their rough-clad bodies turning, twisting, lunging, stiffening in shifts of action, they stir admiration. When in the woods I have fancied that the loggers have the blood that beat in the legions of Rome and the sailormen of old England and Spain. In physical energy and vitality they are superior to any class of American labor. But what a transformation when their hours of leisure come and they remember their duties as members in good standing of Our Civilization! For them, too, there are now pure and refined pleasures, docile behavior, modish apparel, consideration of public matters . . . !

My friends were dressed in the latest from Rochester; they were barbered and bejeweled, and talcum powder whitened their cheeks. The players of cards and pool were quiet; they simply played and smoked and munched candy. The suppressionists had conquered and tamed their race; their spirits were caged, their instincts drugged. Small wonder that the simpletons among them are lured by the childish excitements of the Ku Klux Klan!

We took a few chances on a punch board, and K. C. won a box of candy.

"We got some high-school women dated," said K. C. as we ate the sweets. "We got plenty of room in the car. Come along."

"Got something else on tonight."

"I ain't keen on goin' myself. Them damn goofy kids give me a pain. But what else you got to do 'round this hind end of creation but chase 'em, that's what."

"What else anywhere in the whole damn country?" growled P. L.

Having no intelligent reply, I plucked an answer from the national catechism.

"America's the best country in the world. How'd you like to live in Europe? You got eight-hour jobs, all you can eat, clothes and automobiles. Still you kick!"

"Well, I s'pose that's true enough," P. L. agreed reluctantly, and the others nodded.

"But just the same," declared K. C., "I want to get a kick out of life sometimes, an' I feel all haywire, for I can't somehow. Moonshine ain't worth a damn the way you have to drink it, sneakin' around alleys or lockin' yourself up, an' I 'bout got a bellyfull of gasoline an' women. But they's all they is. I wish I could go hog-wild an' raise hell just once an' do it right. Oh, well; let's have some more pink belly-wash."

V

These men belonged to the tribe whose calked boots once crashed on the floors, and whose bellows once rattled the glasses of the bars on Burnside Street and Yesler Way! In mackinaws, stagged overalls and logger boots they came to town for their blow-ins, and in this garb they returned to the camps, their rough life brightened by the memory of short but wild and thrilling days of revelry. They toiled fiercely at dangerous labor, and they were violent in every activity. When the uplifters began to burn away the weeds and briers of evil in the West the loggers terrified the missionaries by starting the I. W. W. forest fire. This organization had courage and imagination in its beginnings, but the campus radicals devitalized it. Its pungent by-words were bundled into sober tracts, and the shrewd and wary labor policies of the employers soon left it to the mercy of the intelligentsia—and it began to disintegrate. Now it is an earnest and active ally of the Prohibitionists, and during the strike it called last Summer in Portland and Seattle it played the rôle of stool-pigeon!

Such is the new laborer of the frontier, the heir of the old-time savage. He has many material comforts undreamed of by his predecessor. In the section where I am working our condition is almost Utopian. We have the eight-hour day, respectable wages, insurance, health protection, safety-guards, sheets and showers in the camps, democratic association with our employers. But we also have a large measure of boredom, which, like a wet fog, breeds rust wherever it falls. The new laborer has leisure and nothing to do with it. He reads desperately the chief newspapers and fiction magazines. He has discovered duties and ideas, and they have made him sober and right-minded and a little ridiculous, Consider the spectacle of a paw-handed. anvil-shouldered toiler declaring the faith to a gang of equally Gothic listeners! The new rival of the barber! Behold his hairy paw fumbling among the ribbons and lace of a box of chocolates! Hearken to his basso giggles as he rides down the highway with a gang of spooners! The suppression of his old spirit has brought him into a sugar age. The bulge in his pocket is a box of candy instead of a bottle. And the pamphlet he is reading is not the *Police Gazette*, but a work on etiquette!

APOSTLE TO THE HEATHEN

BY ERNEST BOYD

IN THE high and far-off days of splendid isolation he would have been merely incredulous if it had been suggested that America would ever open a lucrative career for his talents. He had then just come down from Oxford and was hardly aware that the North American colonies existed. Fabian Socialism was his creed, more or less, but he was an aristocratic radical and had shunned the plebeian society of such Rhodes scholars as might have too sharply reminded him of the overseas dominions. On his arrival in London he had inevitably been caught up in the orbit of those now dimned stars, then blazing comets of post-Victorian radicalism, for whom what is now euphemistically known as the British Commonwealth was simply imperialistic propaganda designed to further the tariff schemes of Joseph Chamberlain. Clean-limbed Englishman though he was, the battles which he won on the playing-fields of Eton were not of the kind that give promise of Waterloos. England, he used to say, was good enough for him, and it was his ambition to be accounted one of the gallant band of Liberal warriors of peace who wished to restore that demi-paradise to its once high estate by means of Fabian social reform. With Wells and Shaw as pillars of fire in the night of industrialism he came to London to place his pen, his perfect manners and his classical education at the service, not of the People, for he despised them, but, at the service of a vague monster whom the early Fabians had christened Social Democracy.

To see him on the lecture platform, or lunching at a women's club, in his morning-coat and well creased trousers of Bond Street elegance, his wing-collar catching the light on its all-British gloss, was a sartorial reminder of changed times. In the early days he affected a brown velvet jacket, the baggiest of trousers and a monstrously gnarled stick. It was in this garb that he adorned the editorial office of a weekly review in which his unsigned editorials on the nationalization of mines and kindred topics were hardly less admired than the poems and sketches which he contributed over his own name to the literary section. The latter were collected and appeared as his first book, in a small edition which he has so successfully suppressed that his American admirers cherish the few copies obtainable at a price exceeding his total monthly income at this period. His wife still has a file of the review containing those anonymous political writings which eventually secured him an important post on a London paper. It was then that he acquired the leisure in which to write the books upon which his claim to fame—and eventually to American royalties—was to rest. At the same time, owing to his position as literary editor and the innumerable ramifications which he gradually established in the English press, he also acquired a network of influence which materially assisted his career as an established author. It became impossible for an unfavorable review of any book of his to appear, because almost every possible reviewer was under obligations to him, or entertained hopes of him, in his editorial capacity. The clippings from the London papers which accompanied the offer of his works in America naturally impressed the colonial mind, and in due course he achieved the dignity of a New York imprint.

II

Even then, however, it cannot be said that his American public more than vaguely existed in the background of his consciousness. For one thing, he was too busy consolidating his home defences to trouble about so distant a front. For another, he really had no public in this country, as his too confiding publisher discovered when the books about which so many nice words were said in London were jobbed off to the second-hand dealers in New York. Subconsciously he reacted to the discouraging half-yearly statement of his American sales by reinforcing his conviction that this was a barbarous country, which produced no literature of its own and could not be expected to appreciate a genuine work of art when confronted with it. His reviewing staff had a free hand where American authors were concerned, and the patronizing or abusive articles that resulted were some compensation for injuries received. Not that this matter very seriously concerned him, for by now his position in London was assured, and Prime Ministers' week-ends knew him as a welcome guest. He moved in the smartest society, where literature was never sordid shop but always the natural adjunct of the well-educated English gentleman or lady, and here he was privileged to assist at the first flutterings of authorship in young women whose social graces covered a multitude of literary sins. This was vastly more amusing than his relations with a few survivors, now repentant feminists, from the remote period when these ladies had begun to live their own lives by sharing in the great adventure of his beginnings as a man of letters.

As he said to himself, it was rather a bore when the war came and disturbed this pleasant existence. Fortunately, his social success was such that it never became necessary for him to contemplate actual service. Like all his friends, he had to adjust his vocabulary to the changed situation, and he did this so effectively that he soon found himself attached to a propaganda department. Innocent as he was of any language but his own, he seemed peculiarly equipped to undertake journalistic missions to the heathen of neutral Europe, who could never, unaided, have realized the true significance of the great struggle. Thus he passed those hectic years armed with no weapon more lethal than a diplomatic passport, but with this he carried many a difficult position and fought the good fight to such purpose that decorations descended upon him almost as if he were an important profiteer. He guided the pens of foreign editorial writers; he organized bureaux of information, and acquired such an intimate knowledge of European sleeping-cars and first-class Continental hotels that his novels, to this day, are proof that travel broadens the mind. His brochures and pamphlets were masterpieces of the kind, and it was generally felt in official circles that his combination of literary skill and good form was worth the bones of a hundred temporary gentlemen in uniform. He was especially skilful in his treatment of the problem of American intervention, possessing just that mixture of contempt and condescension which is the heritage of the true Briton in his relations with the Colonies. At the same time, he knew how to appeal to a sentimentality which he perfectly understood but did not share. When America finally answered the call of the Mother Country his feelings were comparable to those of the country squire when the tenants have voted as his Lordship wished—dignified rather than exuberant approval.

It was a fitting reward that he should experience in his own person a revelation analogous to that which he had labored so patriotically to effect. He, too, became aware of the existence of These States as a source of help in time of trouble. When the lull of the Permanent Peace came, he was no longer the insular Englishman. He had traveled and lectured and preached to the barbarians, and it occurred to him that he might turn his war-developed talents to his own account. His London publisher concurred in the view that his American public would like to see him, and with admirable resolution he decided to go over and find out what those weird Americans were like in their natural habitat. In Europe they had affected him as unpleasantly as the Anzacs, but the time had come to face the hardships imposed by his sense of duty to himself and to English letters. After certain delicate tests had been made by his New York and London publishers, news paragraphs began to percolate to propitious places announcing that this distinguished man of letters was about to visit America on a lecture tour.

III

His British reserve was a little strained by the first terrific impact of the New World upon his consciousness. The reporters who met him on the steamer extracted from him the inevitable words of admiration, tempered with advice, which he had been prepared to utter. He declared modestly that he had read nothing of American literature since Poe, but he added that America could not expect to make any real contribution to the arts so long as her attention was concentrated on the sordid business of making money. The pursuit of the dollar, he felt, should be left to other and older races, peculiarly fitted for the task by ties of kinship and centuries of cultured tradition. He added a few words concerning the dire need of American idealism to help in the rebuilding of Europe, and hinted that, with the coöperation of the two great branches of the Anglo-Saxon family, the League of Nations could achieve those ideals for which England and America had fought in the Great War.

He languished only a night or two in a New York hotel, for he soon discovered that a host of cultured women had planned to provide him with the lavish Transatlantic equivalents of those house-parties which he enjoyed so much at home. As he never failed to remark, he was overwhelmed by American hospitality. Cars, wives and daughters were placed at his disposal, and within a week he was calling several prominent Long Island hostesses by their Christian names, and had seen more copies of his works on drawing-room tables than he could ever hope to see at home, where his books flourished chiefly amongst the nondescript fiction which the circulating libraries purchase with an altogether admirable catholicity of taste. He secretly conceived an immense respect for these charming people, who actually bought his books instead of promising to ask for them at the library. When eager young things pressed him to write an appropriate sentiment in a treasured volume, he autographed it with a gracious seriousness which persuaded all but the most skeptical that he had done this sort of thing before for privileged people and knew the value of his signature. In a letter to his London publisher he made arrangements to have a limited, large-paper edition of his forthcoming book signed by the author. "The Americans will take it off your hands," he said reassuringly.

His public appearances were a huge success and his agent soon had mapped out a tour which covered the whole country and brought him in a sum in excess of anything he had dared to hope. He looked so distinguished that the women just adored him; he was so unlike the crude type of their own men, who never really looked like creative artists. His subjects, too, were so illuminating. At the P.E.N. Club he addressed an appeal to all concerned for closer relations between America and England, and dwelt upon the bond of language as the greatest factor in establishing an Anglo-Saxon peace. His lecture on "Is There an American Literature?," which he repeated in every place he visited, was particularly stimulating. After an appreciative reference to Emerson and Longfellow he would discuss with real feeling the danger to American literature of straying from the straight path of Anglo-Saxon tradition, and without mentioning individuals he would deprecate the rise of a school of writers whose very names betrayed their alien outlook. By audiences composed of the loveliest daughters of Zion, for the most part, this Nordic aesthetic was as warmly welcomed as by the professors of literature who presided, and who wrote appreciative studies of the man and his work in the Sunday supplements.

He could be relied upon for any occasion, from a Wanamaker Book Week to a Book and Play Luncheon, from an address to the Sulgrave Institution to a reading at the Thanatopsis Club of Davenport, Iowa; he could even carry off a debate with a rival from England at the National Arts Club without mishap, but he never talked without a fee, in accordance with the terms of his contract. For a time he found it possible to evade specific questions which would reveal his complete indifference toward current American literature and his unalterable conviction that, with the possible exception of O. Henry, this country had nothing to offer. In due course, however, he came into contact with some of his American contemporaries, and with truly British acumen set himself to exploit them for his own ends. The art of publicity, as understood in this country, being now familiar to him, he realized the importance of cultivating American authors who would advertise him by word of mouth or in print. Thus he would allow himself occasionally to become interested in a work whose sales could never be large in England, or whose success could in no wise clash with that of his own work. For such he would write a preface, or, more frequently, a commendatory paragraph in a London paper. With the writer personally he

would, in a few hours, achieve a degree of affectionate intimacy utterly at variance with his practice at home. I have known him to write letters to a casual American acquaintance in such terms of friendliness as he would be ashamed to betray to his oldest friend in England. His reserves, as a strong, silent Englishman, vanish under the stress and urge of this very personal Anglo-American friendship, which is the goal he has substituted for the wider and more disinterested service of war time.

IV

In this fashion the new type of literary visitor was evolved from his—in every sense—rude forbears, whose harsh strictures on American life belong to the classical literature of Anglo-American relations. The voice has changed, but the hand is still the same that held the pen of Mrs. Trollope and Mr. Dickens. The pilgrim, modern style, keeps to himself the thoughts which his predecessors ingenuously committed to print. He hitches his wagon to the League of Nations, or to Sulgrave Manor, and proceeds to feed the national appetite for ideals while his own energies are concentrated on more realistic aims. He reserves for the private ear of his own people his impression of Colonial manners and customs and, instead of becoming facetious about cuspidors and ice water, he will now write an essay entitled "American Poetry of Today," which proves on examination to be merely a sniffish review of a book of verse by some minor New England poet. This revised form of the old condescension is irresistible evidence of the dawn of a brighter day in the literary relations of the two countries. The incorrigible persistence of the American language is still, however, a delicate subject, and even the most tactful English commentators cannot refrain from pointing out that it is "incorrect" to say trolley when one means tram. When faced with an American translation of colloquial speech the conviction still surges up in the British mind that it is blasphemous to write: "Say, kid, how do you get that way?" when the slang of the original text demands it, but that the laws of God are obeyed when it is rendered: "I say, you priceless old bean, aren't you rather going in off the deep end?"

The unpleasant emotions aroused by the harsh dissonances of the American idiom are something more than a mere philological protest. Amongst the heathen a certain barbarism, linguistic and otherwise, is inevitable, but the strident yawp of the American language is symptomatic of deeper heresies. It is the outward and visible form of the revolt against colonialism which is finding expression in literature and art that are quite outside the line of apostolic succession. This naturally complicates the task of the missionary visitor, and, what is more important, threatens his prerogatives. The old patronizing attitude was plausible when challenged by nothing more substantial than the well-bred provincialism of a literature that knew its place and was humble in the presence of its superiors. Nowadays American writers actually arise in public meeting and disturb the proceedings with defiant scepticism and the irreverent queries of an aesthetic agnosticism which knows nothing of the childlike faith of its forefathers. The apostle has felt decidedly uncomfortable during these encounters, and with genuine alarm he foresees the day when such uncouth fellows will set out to conquer new worlds and perhaps expect, in their turn, to make a little money out of their missionary enterprise. So far, with exquisite British tact, he has succeeded in keeping the visiting American author within the bounds of a rare show, allowing him to exhibit his eccentricities privately and without profit. But the time will inevitably come when Americans in London will refuse to perform for less than the terms specified in their contracts. They will insist upon a treaty of literary reciprocity, and will abrogate the existing policy of the (one way) Open Door. Of such dire changes is the American language the sign and portent. In anticipation whereof a far-sighted zeal, an otherwise inexplicable sensitiveness, are noticeable whenever the hegemony of the King's English is disputed.

Out of the sorrow and suffering of the Great War, however, the Island Race has emerged with a wider and deeper sense of the infinite possibilities of this great Republic. The literary pilgrim has a mission to do for himself what his country did in her hour of need. He has mastered the technique, and if here and there his natural inhibitions and prejudices peep out, his willingness for closer coöperation and mutual service is wholly admirable. With what graciousness he submits to the frank democratic friendliness of his American hero-worshippers, he who shuns the common herd at home and is rather proud of the fact that most of his colleagues are personally unknown to him! In New York, it is now possible for one English author to meet another in a spirit of the purest human camaraderie, so perfectly do they adapt themselves to the freer atmosphere of the New World. The lesson of Armageddon—as they used to call it in the old propaganda days—has not been lost upon them; they realize that sweet are the uses of publicity. Pinning their faith in a few platitudes to carry them through the intellectual wilds of America, the literary pilgrims set out for the land that promises royalties and lecture fees. And each time they turn eastward, with their income tax returns skilfully adjusted and duly stamped at the Custom House, their hearts are filled with gratitude. They depart with tangible evidence that the pursuit of the dollar in America is not incompatible with the liveliest interest in the arts. It all depends upon who does the pursuing.

IN DEFENSE OF THE PURITAN

BY WALTER PRICHARD EATON

BEING myself a descendant, on both sides of my family, of the earliest settlers in the Bay Colony, I have a certain personal reaction when the adjective Puritan is contemptuously applied. (It is never, of course, applied except contemptuously.) I have been puzzled frequently to discover why Bryan, Volstead, the Reverend Dr. Straton, should be Puritans, and Charles W. Eliot (whose ancestor translated the Bible for the salvation of the Indians), Henry Adams, Amy Lowell, should not be. John S. Sumner, the famous smut-hound, is, I am told, a Puritan, but Charles Sumner evidently was not. A Puritan, it would appear, is anybody who assumes an I-am-holier-than-thou attitude, is afraid of the truth, shrinks from change, from speculation, even from honest doubt, and endeavors to compel all of his neighbors to live and think as he does. A Puritan is a bigoted, petty moralist, and there is no joy in him. That is what, I gather, he is today. If that is what he always was, the settlement and early growth of America is certainly the most extraordinary phenomenon in the whole history of mankind.

But that, of course, isn't what he was, and the current critical usage of the word Puritan is a degradation, if not actually a perversion. The Puritans had descendants, both bodily and spiritual. Some at least must still exist. And certain it is, to me at any rate, that they are not named Volstead nor Bryan nor Straton. It may be they are not numerous; it may be that the thing, Puritanism, is not potent in our midst any longer. But that I regard as a pity, not a cause for rejoicing. We need

424

more Puritanism, not less, in our life and our letters; and we need to recognize it when we see it, and not go on confusing sometimes dubiously historical accidentals with the fundamental virtues of the Pilgrim breed.

The Puritans in England closed all the theatres; but they also cut off the head of a king. The Puritans in America endeavored, with a passionate sincerity no sane person can doubt, to live, and to make everybody else in their communities live, according to the necessities of a terrible theology; but meanwhile they conquered a wilderness, flung ever westward, over rivers and mountains, the thin frontier of empire, and prepared the soil for what was to be the Eighteenth Century's great contribution to history, the ideal of democracy, of government as a contract with the governed. The Puritan theology, by which, as we now envisage them, those ancestors of ours lived, bleakly and sternly averting their countenances from all the joys of this life and in the interests of salvation forbidding others to be joyous, we may truthfully say had little to do with Eighteenth Century political ideals. In fact, the revolt of a too rigidly repressed human nature from this theology was in America at least a much more contributory cause. But the spirit in which that dread and dreary religious philosophy was at first accepted had everything to do with the Eighteenth Century, because it was a spirit of intense faith in the worth of the individual and of assertive independence of individual conscience. The Puritan conscience (one hesitates now to employ the emasculated and belittled phrase) was a consciousness of the individuals responsible to his Maker alone, and most awfully responsible, since his consciousness included a strange awareness, hardly since possessed by any peoples, of this as a moral universe. For his faith he was quite willing to be, and frequently was, a martyr. But being also an Elizabethan Englishman, for it he was quite ready to fight. Either way, he regarded his faith, his way of feeling, his individuality, much more highly than he regarded any existing customs, conventions or laws. In other words, he was a true revolutionist. What was Puritanism in its very inception but a revolution? What was the *Mayflower* compact but a revolution?—though those who signed it, no doubt, were unaware in their truly superb self-sufficiency of the seed they were sowing in the world. People don't revolt, we are told nowadays, unless driven to it by hunger and misery. But the Puritans did. They revolted when somebody told them they should not believe thus and so, which happened to be what they did most intensely believe. They were not in the least afraid of change in customs, in the very fundamentals of society, if thus they could secure their own way. Their trust in God seems, indeed, to have been considerably mixed with an Emersonian "Trust Thyself."

"Trust Thyself—every heart vibrates to that iron string"—thus the Puritan Emerson, from Concord, more than two centuries later; Emerson, renowned as a good neighbor who "kept his fences up" and interfered with nobody, Emerson who refused to administer the Communion in church because the ceremony "didn't interest him." Not every heart, in spite of Emerson, vibrates to an iron string. The seductive catgut is more to the taste of many. But they do not make revolutionists, and they do not make Puritans. When the *Mayflower* was on her way to the "stern and rockbound" sand dunes of Cape Cod and Plymouth, many of the passengers were seasick and excited the profane mirth of the sailors, who frequently added low-lived abuse to their jibes. The Pilgrim fathers and mothers bore this meekly, and naturally gained no respite by that scriptural method. But when, later, after the arrival, the crew were stricken with disease, and from fear of infection and hardness of heart refused aid one to another, it was the Pilgrims who cared for them. Self-trust and self-interest have little or nothing in common. The heart that vibrates to the iron string is always warmer than the heart of the sensualist. Self-trust, too, breeds trust of others. Self-trust, and self-trust alone, can create and keep alive the dream of democracy.

II

The Puritan's apparent distrust of himself, meaning his natural man, was an accident of his theology. That he dared defy Church and State, that he braved the stake, that he hazarded the wintry Atlantic in a cockle shell and pitted his lone ax against a virgin forest, that he cut off a king's head and told the world he knew more about where the authority for government came from than all the traditions of a thousand years, isn't exactly to display a conspicuous lack of self-assurance. But the Puritan knew also that he lived in a moral universe. He was not afraid of duty, and to him virtue was beautiful. Embracing a religious philosophy which imposed rigid and narrow duties, and severely constricted the virtues, he found himself faced by a well-nigh insoluble problem. He was confronted by all the bodily instincts of mankind, by youth and love and music and the rhythmic loveliness of the world. He took exactly the step you would have expected him to take, knowing both his intense belief in his religious philosophy and his supreme confidence in his powers. He set out rigidly to suppress all that his philosophy declared to be evil.

Of course it didn't work. In Bradford's "History of Plymouth Plantation," his entry for 1642 begins as follows: "Marvilous it may be to see and consider how some kind of wickednes did grow & breake forth here, in a land wher the same was so much witnesed against, and so narrowly looked unto, & severely punished when it was knowne; as in no place more, or so much, that I have known or heard of; insomuch as they have been somewhat censured, even by moderate and good men, for their severitie in punishments. And yet all this could not suppress ye breaking out of sundrie notorious sins, (as this year, besids other, gives us too many sad presidents and instances,) espetially drunkennes and unclainnes; not only incontinencie betweene persons unmarried, for which many both men & women have been punished sharply enough, but some maried persons allso. But that which is worse, even sodomie, and bugerie (things fearfull to name,) have broak forth in this land, oftener than once. I say it may justly be marveled at, and cause us to fear & tremble at the consideration of our corrupte natures, which are so hardly bridled, subdued and mortified; nay, cannot by any other means but ye powerful worke and grace of Gods spirite. But (besids this) one reason may be, that ye Divell may carrie a greater spite against the churches of Christ and ye gospell hear, by how much ye more they indeaour to preserve holynes and puritie amongst them, and strictly punisheth the contrary when it ariseth either in church or comone wealth; that he might cast a blemishe & staine upon them in ye eyes of ye world, who use to be rash in judgmente. I would rather thinke thus, then that Satane hath more power in these heathen lands, as som have thought, then in more Christian nations, espetially over Gods servants in them.

"Another reason may be, that it may be in this case as it is with waters when their streames are stopped or damed up, when they gett passage they flow with more violence, and make more noys and disturbance, then when they are suffered to rune quietly in their owne chanels. So wickednes being here more stopped by strict laws, and ye same more nerly looked unto, so as it cannot rune in a comon road of liberty as it would, and is inclined, it searches every wher, and at last breaks out wher it getts vente."

It would appear that the good governor was not without a realization alike of the difficulties of the task the Pilgrims had set themselves, and of the true causes of their failure. Ensuing years in Puritan America saw a fairly steady breaking down of the artificial dykes of restraint against the natural man, a fairly steady increase of recognition for the normal instincts. This, of course, was constantly and bitterly opposed by the clergy, who felt their powers slipping, and the legislators continued to legislate against nature. But unless it can be shown that the clergy, carrying Calvinism by remorseless logic to even greater depths of monstrosity, alone remained true to the Puritan spirit (not alone the Puritan theological creed), while the people lost their self trust, their consciousness of a moral universe, creed or no creed, their spiritual independence, then it is impossible in fairness to brand as Puritan today only this temper of unnatural restraint, this hang-over of Calvinistic theology.

Nothing of the sort can, of course, be proved. Quite the contrary is the case. What James Truslow Adams calls "the pessimistic passivity and determinism of Calvinism" was not a creation of the Puritans. It was imposed upon them by theologians, and accepted by them not because they were the only peoples dour and sour enough to accept it, but because they were the only ones with the moral stamina, the concentrated purpose, and the scorn for worldly consequences necessary to give this theology the trial which history demanded. It is absurd to suppose that what qualities made the Puritans effective in the world vanished when they ceased to accept a dogma. To suppose that they did is to yield to the common failing of all timid men grown old, accusing the new generation of every manner of iniquity because of its new beliefs. In 1701 an elderly observer remarked sadly that many boys in Harvard College "differ much in their principles from their parents." So "the stock of the Puritan" was dying even before "Fair Harvard" was written! But it didn't die immediately. Its interests were diverted into other channels than the theological, to be sure, but those men and women of the Puritan stock who retained their sense of a moralistic universe, and their consciousness of individual responsibility and integrity, led the world to its next great historic experiment—led it, of course, through revolution. In 1776 the little town of Ashland, Mass., in the frontier of the Berkshire wilderness, passed in meeting assembled a resolution that is open to criticism for its spelling, but hardly for its adherence to the Puritan spirit. "We will take the Law of God for the foundation of the forme of our Government," Ashland resolved, and "it is our opinion that we Do not want any Govinor but the Govinor of the univarse, and under him a States Gineral to consult with the wrest of the united States for the Good of the whole."

I am confident that the people who are called Puritans today would regard this perfection of Puritanism as sheer anarchy, and would have the perpetrators in jail if they could.

III

It chances that more than a century later, Ashland, no longer a frontier village but a community left far behind and forgotten by the westward march of empire, sprang into notice again because there a latter-day Puritan followed his conscience and defied the mob. He was a delicate and gentle spirit, a lover of sensuous beauty, of art and poetry. His name was Charles Eliot Norton, and he reminded his excited countrymen that we had taken the law of God for the foundation of our Government, and that law did not sanction the ruling of alien peoples against their wills,

even if they were brown-skinned Filipinos. America was just then donning its imperialistic diapers, and was in no mood to be told that it shouldn't play with this new rattle. Professor Norton, and the little band who stood with him, were roundly abused. They weren't running with the mob. They were standing steadfast by their consciences, by their belief in a moralistic universe, by their faith in the individual.

Nothing could well be farther from Calvinism than Unitarianism, considered as doctrine. But when, a century and more ago, the church in Rowe, Mass., was burned, and the covenant destroyed, every member, including the pastor, Preserved Smith, forgot it and refrained from asking for a new copy, so for twenty years more the Reverend Mr. Smith continued to preach liberalism to his flock, till the people down Boston way finally heard of the scandal, and tried the poor old parson for heresy or some other crime. However, that church remains Unitarian to this day, a quaint little witness, far up in the hills, to the independence of the Puritan frontiersman. The Unitarianism of Channing, of Theodore Parker, was no less intensely aware of a moralistic universe than the Calvinsim of Cotton Mather. And it was no less ready to defend the individual conscience and defy traditional authority. The temper of Parker and Channing in the pulpit was their temper, also, in the anti-slavery contest. It was the temper of Garrison. It was the temper of nearly all the early Abolitionists, who were concerned, and only concerned, with the dignity of the individual, with the supreme importance of right principles. Cotton bales and factory dividends were a later and quite unpuritanical issue.

Wendell Phillips, defying the Boston mob in Faneuil Hall, was a Puritan. He was no less a Puritan many years later when he delivered his famous Phi Beta Kappa oration at Harvard. Having seen the dignity of the individual Negro vindicated (or so he then believed), he dared to tell the Harvard graduates and overseers that individual working men also possess dignity in God's sight, yea, that even women do. It was the voice of the Puritan speaking—a very eloquent voice, to be sure, so eloquent that it is recorded that one Brattle Street gentleman was seen to applaud vigorously, at the same time exclaiming, "The damned old fool—the damned old fool!" But still, the voice of the Puritan, of the revolutionist for right.

And the Puritans today—who are they? If you care to say that some of them have rather recently, and reluctantly, been let out of Leavenworth prison, I shall not take the trouble to dispute you. They are certainly not the men and women who run with the mob; they are not the men and women who wrap about them as a garment the mouldy husks of a dead theology and seek to impose their traditions and inhibitions on all their fellows in the name of a petty morality which, even to them, has no living force because it is not the fruit of their own revolt, and has no connection at all with the higher moral law; and neither are they the men and women who, in the name of individual liberty, recognize no moral force in the universe, or those who have not the courage or the fibre to be either for God or against Him. Mr. Volstead is not a Puritan. But no more is the man who is fired by a passion for individual liberty merely because he wants a drink. Let us have done with such shameful belittling of the word.

The Puritan was a revolutionist for the right. He instinctively placed principle above expediency, his trust in himself above his trust in tradition, and possessed the fibre to put his convictions to the hazard of any necessary experiment, however daring. Show me a man today, and I care not what his theological creed may be, if he has one (the chances are at least equal that he hasn't), who views the world and society as something more, and something deeper, than a jumble of trade, politics and pleasure, as something which should step with the march of moral law and who himself looks for this moral law, in his own heart and his own intelligence, and determining it there trusts the verdict though kings or mobs or editors or parsons or all tradition be against him, that man I will call a Puritan. He will speak or write with force and conviction. He will not belong to any pretty-pretty, or pee-wee school of life or literature. But he will respect the integrity of all other honest individuals. He will hate sham, and cant, and timid shirking; he will insist that life has duties, and he will rejoice in doing them. He will be a man most men respect, and many admire. Not so many will follow him, because to follow him will require character, purpose, spiritual integrity, the moral bravery which dares revolt.

It does not seem to me that this characterization outlines a portrait of our current smut-hounds and Sabbatical Leaguers. It seems to me to outline the portrait of a man I could wish for a leader in these troubled and unconfident times, hoping greatly that his integrity to principle will be to the principle of scientific truth, that the light he follows will be the light of reason, not of faith—a word we of the Twentieth Century should regard with the utmost suspicion.

AMERICANA

ALABAMA

FIELD sports in the home State of the Hon. Oscar W. Underwood, candidate for the presidency, from the archives of the Committee on the Judiciary of the House of Representatives:

Helena, Ala.: After protecting himself against a mob for six hours John King, employed in the mines, was lynched by men whom he had accused of taking money from his pay-envelope.

Adamsville, Ala.: Will McBride, 60 years old, was taken from bed by a mob and beaten to death. He had been arrested on a charge of assault but dismissed by the judge. Some school children had become frightened at seeing him walk along the road.

ARIZONA

FATE of the First Amendment to the Constitution in the Arizona Free State, as reported by a Nogales dispatch to the Tucson *Daily Star:*

George L. Patrick, of Seattle, Wash., a civil engineer, will probably spend the next 200 days in the Santa Cruz county jail, as a result of getting all het up at the international line, and proceeding to say unkind words about President Coolidge. Patrick arrived here several days ago with the intention of crossing the border with two burros on a prospecting trip down the west coast of Mexico. He tried to get a permit from the Customs Service to take a rifle across the line and when shown a telegram from President Coolidge stating that an embargo had been placed on firearms and advised that he would have to get a permit from Washington, he is alleged to have replied: "To h—— with Coolidge; it's only an accident that he is President." A complaint was filed against the man and Justice of the Peace Charles Hardy gave him his choice of paying a $200 fine or serving 200 days in jail. He chose the latter.

CALIFORNIA

PROGRESS of the Higher Learning at Stanford University, as reported by a press dispatch from Palo Alto:

Yell leading has been made a subject in the curriculum at Stanford and credit will be given to sophomores trying out for assistant yell leader who register in the new course. "Bleacher psychology," "the correct use of the voice," "development of stage presence" and "what a coach expects of the yell leader" will be topics of lectures by members of the faculty and by Prof. Andrew Kerr, football coach.

FROM a list of acts forbidden by city ordinances in Los Angeles, prepared for the use of visitors:

Shooting rabbits from street cars.

Throwing snuff, or giving it to a child under sixteen.

Bathing two babies in a single bathtub at one time.

Making pickles in any downtown district.

Selling snakes on the streets.

CONNECTICUT

DÉBUT of a new crime in the land of Blue Laws, as reported by the Waterbury *Republican:*

Amelia Moses, eighteen, was arrested yesterday by Lieutenants Timothy Hickey and Milton MacMullen of the Detective Bureau, charged with *being in danger of falling into vice.*

FROM the platform of the new board of editors of the *Yale News:*

The Eighteenth Amendment should be strictly enforced throughout the university.

Compulsory chapel should be retained.

There should be a course on the Bible as literature.

There should be a course in dramatic art.

DISTRICT OF COLUMBIA

CONTRIBUTION to a new Gesta Romanorum by the current *Hofprediger*, as reported by the Washington *Herald:*

Jiggs, hen-pecked husband of Maggie, one of the comic strips appearing in the Washington *Herald*, served as an example in the sermon yesterday at the First Congregational Church. The Rev. Jason Noble Pierce, pastor of the church, speaking of the unhappiness of the rich, said: "Money does not always bring happiness. Mr. Jiggs knows this. Of course you all know Jiggs of the 'Bringing Up Father' cartoon. Recently Jiggs lost his fortune. Sitting on the steps of the pretentious residence from which he had just been evicted, Jiggs remarked,

'Oh well. You got to be poor to be happy anyway!' And that's the truth."

President and Mrs. Coolidge were among the congregation.

FROM a public bull by the Board of Temperance, Prohibition and Public Morals of the Methodist Episcopal Church:

No representative body in the world surpasses the American Congress in intelligence or character.

FLORIDA

APPEARANCE of a new and fantastic heresy in the swamps behind Miami and Palm Beach, as reported by an alert correspondent of the Florida *Baptist Witness:*

I am not seeking a controversy, but would like to say that the custom that some Baptist churches have fallen into of oyster crackers and cubes of bakers' bread in the Lord's Supper is to my mind unscriptural and a digression from our Master's example and Apostolic usage.

ILLINOIS

FROM an interview with Mary Garden in the Boston *Herald:*

"I often discuss spiritualism and future existence with my friends and—"

"You believe in spiritualism?" she was asked.

"I can't tell. I only know that when I die I shall be cremated and that my ashes will be thrown into a lake."

"Why not the ocean? It's not as apt to be muddy."

"No. It must be Lake Michigan, in front of Chicago. Think of how thrilled some of the bathers would be to have the ashes of Mary Garden swept up against them."

FROM an address by Col. R. R. McCormick, co-editor of the Chicago *Tribune*, to the advertising staff of that great newspaper:

There is no one—be he priest, or preacher, or rabbi; be he poet or editorial writer—there is no one whose calling is more exalted than yours!

IOWA

EFFECTS of Prohibition, vice crusading, laws against cigarettes, wars upon the bunny hug and other Christian moral measures in Des Moines, the Western capital of the uplift, as reported by the estimable *News* of that city:

Criminals are running wild in this city!... The people of this community, with their lives and property in constant jeopardy, and fearing to venture from their homes after nightfall, have known for a month that crime was rampant and unbridled in Des Moines. . . . The criminals who infest Des Moines are robbing banks, beating up helpless women and becoming more daring, more brutal in their operations.

FROM a trade journal for life insurance go-getters published in Kansas City:

An Iowa agent for a western company, who has two and a half millions in force in his county, makes a point of attending practically every funeral in his county and invariably sings at the service. He makes a note of all those present at the funeral whom he considers as prospects. He also finds out whether the deceased carried life insurance and the amount.

As he sings at the funeral all who are present must see him there and that fact justifies his discussion of the insurance affairs of the deceased with them and opens the way for a consideraton of the prospect's own insurance needs.

Perhaps you can't sing at funerals, but if you are RESOURCEFUL the story of this Iowa agent may stimulate you to think of original and effective methods of your own.

KENTUCKY

TRIUMPH of human enterprise by Blue Grass disciples of the Wilson idealism, as reported by the Louisville *Herald:*

Within seven minutes after receipt of the news that former President Wilson was dead, the Louisville *Herald* was on the street with a bona fide extra announcing the news and giving the exact time of Mr. Wilson's death.

The other morning newspaper (i. e., the *Courier Journal*) also issued an alleged extra in which it was announced that President Wilson had died on February 2 (Saturday). No time was given. A bulletin carried by that newspaper credited the news to the Associated Press, as follows:

Washington, Feb. 2 (A. P.)—Former President Wilson is dead.

The actual text of the Associated Press bulletin read as follows:

Washington, Feb. 3 (By the Associated Press)— Former President Wilson died today at 11.15 A. M.

The question naturally arises: Was the "extra" issued by the other morning paper printed Saturday night? The date given on the alleged Associated Press dispatch would indicate that.

The moral, of course is, When in doubt, buy *Herald* extras! Then you get the REAL NEWS first.

MARYLAND

LINGERING effects of the late war for democracy upon jurisprudence in the Maryland Free State, as revealed by an advertisement in the Baltimore *Sunpaper:*

LAWYER WANTED
To Enter Suit Against a
PRO-GERMAN CONCERN
Address Purchasing Agent, 5870, Sun.

MASSACHUSETTS

THE New Thought method of snaring a husband, as described in the *Nautilus Magazine*, of Holyoke:

> Make up your mind that God knows the right man, that God *now* brings you and the right man together IN SPIRIT.
>
> Now, the only way that the right man can find you is for you to so express yourself that all men looking upon you may see your good work, your radiant spirit, and may *glorify the loving Father within you*.
>
> In short, begin to *express yourself*, instead of sitting around and praying or affirming or longing to have God hand you this particular man on a silver platter!

MISSISSIPPI

FROM the archives of the Committee on the Judiciary of the House of Representatives, in charge of the Dyer anti-lynching bill:

> Ashland, Miss.: An unnamed colored man, charged with stabbing a white man, was taken from jail by a mob, hanged, and his body riddled with bullets. The white man, who had charged the Negro with stealing, attempted to search him.
>
> Pickens, Miss.: An 18-year-old colored girl was shot by a mob which was in search of her brother, who was said to have borrowed 50 cents from a white man and refused to pay him 10 cents interest.

NEW YORK

THEOLOGICAL dictum from an article in *America* by the Rev. Wilfrid Parsons, S. J.:

> How do we know that this particular miracle of the Virgin Birth happened? We know that it happened *because the Catholic Church teaches that it happened*. This is in itself complete, absolute and final proof of the truth of this doctrine.

THE theatre's tribute to the late Dr· Wilson, from a memoir in *Variety* entitled "The Draped Proscenium":

> During the bitter days of the grim war he was a steady attendant at the lighter amusements. Each Monday found him in his box at Keith's. The players gloried in his presence and he smiled upon them. . . After the war he modestly declined to use the box he had so long occupied as President, but came each Monday and sat in extra seats behind the last row. A sincere patron of the stage arts, a figure almost divine who lent the glamor of his person to heighten the effulgence of an institution so frequently shadowed by the intolerance of the soulless, Woodrow Wilson glorified the history of the theatre as he glorified the history of his country and his world.

NORTH CAROLINA

UPWARD sweep of the Fundamentalist wave from the steppes of Texas toward the line of the Potomac, as revealed by a dispatch from Raleigh, home of the Hon. Josephus Daniels:

> The North Carolina State Board of Education, headed by Governor Cameron Morrison, today voted to bar from the list of biologies to be adopted by the State high schools all books which in any way intimate an origin of the human race other than that described in the Bible. "Evolution," said Governor Morrison, "means progress, but it does not mean that man, God's highest creation, is descended from a monkey or any other animal. I will not allow any such doctrine or intimation of such doctrine to be taught in our public schools."

OHIO

SPORTING offer of the Hon. Norman E. Tully, of Youngstown, O., in the esteemed *Vindicator* of that city for January 16 last:

> I will lay a small wager that the long-looked-for Second Advent of Jesus will occur within five years.

CURIOUS contribution to American history by the Rev. C. Jeffres McCombe, D.D., pastor of the Broad Street Methodist Episcopal Church of Columbus:

> Before going to Washington to take the oath of office the late President Harding said to Bishop William F. Anderson, of Cincinnati: "My prime motive in going to the White House is to bring America back to God."

OREGON

EXITUS of an ancient legal maxim, as recorded in a dispatch from Portland:

> Speaking before the District Attorneys' Association of Oregon here last night, Governor Walter M. Pierce declared time has modified the old adage that every man's home is his castle and sanctuary, and in the future Oregon homes must be kept in such condition that a visit from an inspector of the State Prohibition forces will be welcomed at any time.
>
> "The laws and customs have changed vastly since first was announced the right and doctrine that every man's home was his castle and sanctuary," the governor said. "The law clearly makes it your duty as district attorneys to cooperate with the Prohibition commissioner. We claim the right to go into any place in the State at any time as secret agents and to discover, if possible, law violations."

PENNSYLVANIA

AMENDMENT of the First Amendment in Pennsylvania, as reported in a dispatch from Wilkes-Barre:

> Mayor Daniel L. Hart today supported the action of members of the American Legion in breaking up a meeting called to honor the

name and memory of Nicholai Lenin. To members of the Workers' Party of America, who protested that their right of free speech had been abrogated, he declared that in the future the city will not issue a license for any public meeting *unless such a meeting is approved by the American Legion.*

FROM a communication by the Hon. William B. Yeakel, of Coopersburg, Pa., in the *Farm Journal:*

Mr. William S. Hallman wants to know if life insurance is a good investment. I say, absolutely no! In what way is it right for a man, made in the image of God, to walk around with a price on his head, payable after death?

SOUTH CAROLINA

TRIALS of the Fundamentalists, as revealed by a letter to the *Baptist Courier*, the leading organ of Christian thought between the Peedee and Tugaloo rivers:

The South Main Street Church of Greenwood is again without a pastor. It came in such a short time after we had gone through with the trials of securing one to whom the church was devoted and whom it had hoped to keep for years, but it seems that it had to be; for that Earle Street, Greenville, crowd just kept working until they got us in this fix. Personally, I have no censure for any one of them, because I must love my brethren, but they had better mind, and keep away from Greenwood the remainder of their days. Trying to locate a pastor is no little job. Our prayer is for a message from heaven, naming the man upon whom the Lord has laid his hands to do this blessed work.

TEXAS

PROGRESS of Fundamentalist jurisprudence in the great Republic of Texas, as reported by the National Association for the Advancement of Colored Peoples:

At Bishop, Texas, one Smith, a colored physician, was burned to death after his hands and feet had been cut off. It was alleged that Dr. Smith, while riding in his automobile, collided with a car occupied by whites.

NOVEL contribution to the American language by Texas Baptists, as revealed by news notes in the *Baptist Standard* of Dallas:

Work starts well on the Carlton-Olin field. Within the last three weeks a brand-new six-room *pastorium* has been built, insured for three years, pastor's family moved in and graciously pounded, and salary paid to the end of the year . . .

Dr. McHenry Seal is leading the San Saba Church in a beautiful way. The spiritual life of the church is good in spite of the fact that it has just built an excellent *pastorium* and a two-story annex to the church building.

FROM a circular distributed by Nordic Blond evangelists at a recent revival in Dallas under the leadership of the Rev. Dr. Bob Jones, an eminent pastor of those remote steppes:

I am a Searchlight on a high tower.

I run my relentless eye to and fro throughout the land; my piercing glance penetrates the brooding places of Iniquity. I plant my eyes and ears in the whispering Corridors of Crime.

Wherever men gather furtively together, there am I, an austere and invisible Presence. I am the Recording Angel's Proxy.

When I invade the fetid dens of Infamy there is a sudden scampering and squeaking as of rats forsaking a doomed ship.

I am the haunting dread of the depraved and the hated Nemesis of the vicious.

The foe of Vice, the friend of Innocence, the rod and staff of Law, I am —

THE KU KLUX KLAN.

EFFORTS of this subtle espionage on the native Christians, as reported the next Sunday by the estimable Dallas *News:*

An employé of one of the largest bookshops in Texas recently managed to get hold of a copy of an obscene book, paying about $5 for it. He offered it to a prominent business man in one of the prominent towns of Texas, and the man immediately paid $20 for it.

VIRGINIA

DECAY of the spoils system and rise of the technical expert in the Old Dominion, as reported by the Roanoke *Times:*

William F. Drewry, M. D., for 37 years in the service of the State caring for the insane, has accepted an appointment as city manager of Petersburg.

STATE of the enlightenment in the same State, as reported by the worthy *Nation:*

Two hundred excited persons, gathered before Magistrate Bell in Princess Anne County, Va., accused 70-year-old Annie Taylor of witchcraft. Whether convinced or not that Annie could kill a mule by waving a cane at him, queer the rising of good corn bread, or put snakes in a woman's stomach, the court banished her to North Carolina.

WEST VIRGINIA

GROWING appreciation of the bozart in West Virginia, as revealed by a banner over the main automobile entrance to Parkersburg:

Parkersburg, W. Va.—Birthplace of Harold Tucker Webster, artist, writer, humorist. Entertains the nation with his "Poker Portraits," "Life's Darkest Moment" and "The Beginning of a Beautiful Friendship." Is married, loves the great outdoors and plays a keen game of poker.

AMERICAN PORTRAITS

III. The Editorial Writer

BY JAMES M. CAIN

You are, I shall suppose, a cub reporter on a newspaper. Life is a bleary maze of thick green pencils, skew-cut copy paper, busted typewriters, round sergeants, coroners, near-beer saloons, corpses, patrol wagons, and three-alarm fires, with a cacophonous accompaniment of whoops from Saturday night drunks, the *clack-clack* of telegraph instruments, the rumbling of presses, *cop-e-e-e-!* —and over all the majestic chant of the city editor: Gimme a new lead on it . . . Better get on that right away . . . Cut it to two sticks . . . Work it up from that angle . . . Smoke him out, make him come clean . . . Well, it's worth a feature, anyway . . . Check up on that before you go . . . Get the low-down on it . . . Hell, we should worry if he wants it in or not . . . !

It is all terribly confusing, and your head aches: it is so hard to tell appearance from reality. For instance, the old gent frowning so portentously in the swivel chair, the one you thought it would pay to stand in with, is nothing but the head copy boy; and the kid chewing tobacco with his feet on the desk, that you thought was the janitor, is the news editor, with authority to tell even the city editor where to head in. There doesn't seem to be any way of going by looks. They all mooch about in waistcoats, without coats, all have prematurely gray hair, all have the same funny look about the eyes.

You start in your chair. There is that man again, over by the city editor. Who is he, anyway? You have seen him around a lot, and intended to ask about him. But —*is* he the same man? They all look so much alike, and this one in particular looks like a synthetic portrait of everybody in the shop, from the make-up man to the anemic copy reader who sits on the other side of the copy slot. It must be the same man, though. He always wears a green eye-shade, and his shirt makes a little soft pillow where it rolls out from under his waistcoat over his belt. Yes, it is the same man. Come to think of it, his face has lurked in the background all through these first awful days. Who is he, anyhow? You prepare to make covert inquiries.

Well, well, save your breath. Pull up your chair and I shall tell you who he *is*. The man is a Priest. He is Keeper of the Soul of the American People. He sits alone in his office, high above the madding crowd, and as he sits, soft voices rise from below. When he hears them, he passes into a long, long dream, and as he dreams, his hand (which holds a pencil) begins to write and write and write. . . . The voices are so soft that few could hear them at all, but the man hears them because hearing them is his trade. They are the Voices of the People, the Voice of God. And they go into his ear while he dreams, and in his head they become thoughts. Not ugly, naughty thoughts such as you and I have, but thoughts that Nobody Will Deny— Beautiful Thoughts that the People think, about Rights of the Taxpayer; Do Your Duty, Mr. Mayor; Our Grand Old Man, the New Parking Plan, Five Years of Peace, and Mr. Tchitcherin's Latest Treachery. And as the thoughts pass out again, through his hand, they become renewed, purified, transmogrified, until they become the very soul of the American People. . . . In brief, this fellow in the green eye-shade is the man who writes the editorials.

Like yourself, he started as a cub. He too had a terrible time finding his way around, and he too soon developed that weary wisdom, that precocious cynicism about life—Well, hardly that. But a veneer of wisdom, a posture of cynicism. On $22 a week, cynicism was about the only luxury he could afford. It helped a lot when he had to eat in one-arm hari-coteries. . . . He had his derisive names for some of the certified prominent citizens. For instance, Mr. Littleton Thomas Tits-comb, president of the Second National Bank, who made 972 four-minute speeches during the war, he called Little Tom Tit, and boasted that he never had to go hear Tom Tit's speech, for he already knew it by heart. Mrs. Bertha Willoughby, of the School Board, he called Bertha Krupp. His Excellency, Oglesby A. Adams, governor of the State, he called Old Up-And-At-'Em. Sometimes his wisdom reached lyrical heights as he argued with his fellows: he made glib references to the City Hall Crowd, and cynical predictions about things: They're not going to let Nick Beal walk off with that nomination. Don't fall for that stuff. They know who they're going to put in there, and when it gets too late for anybody else to file, they'll put him up, see? Hell, all this talk about Nick Beal just hands me a laugh.

So his early years. He passed through the stage where he said: Ain't this a hell of a life for a white man? Where he called the telephone girl Sweetie. Where he said: They got a hot way of running things around this joint; *I'll* say they have. Where he called the theatre managers by their first names, ordered gin by telephone, clapped the mayor on the back, corresponded for *Variety*. He saw the staff change completely as men came, saw, and got the gate. He held his job, though. After a few years the city editor called

him by his first name and relied on him whenever a *big* story broke, such as a suicide, love-nest, or murder, or a bad wreck up on the P. B. & R. Oh, he had come to know the business, all right. According to the life line in his palm, a Great Big Change was just about due in his life.

II

And sure enough, it came. He had been covering the big McGinnis murder case, wherein the bandits jumped out of the car, shot the bank messenger, and scuttled off with $5426 in good hard cash— BANDITS SLAY RUNNER, GET $5426 LOOT, ESCAPE IN AUTO. The case had been on for two days, and not a trace of the jolly *banditti* had been found. He had been up two nights on the story, and came down the next afternoon ready for more heavy work. But a surprise was in store. He was called into the managing editor's office.

After a preliminary compliment about the story, the managing editor got down to business:

"You know, I think it's about time we went aboard the police department in this town and went aboard them right. This is the eleventh murder this year where they haven't even made an arrest. Gosh, that's rotten! . . . But we don't want to be unjust, and that's what I wanted to see you about. You're in pretty close touch over there. Do you think we're justified in jumping on them with both feet?"

Is Our Hero flattered? He is. Consulted by the managing editor! On a question of *editorial policy!*

Indeed, his mental processes at this point give the whole key to his subsequent development, and throw a bright white light on the whole business of writing about public affairs in these United States. First, about his cynicism (by now he doesn't think of himself as cynical— simply hard-boiled). Does he come out and tell the managing editor that all this crusade stuff is the bunk and the police department will go on running the same old way until the end of time, crusade or no crusade? He does not. His cynicism evaporates faster than the clouds in the last verse of "Anchored." Cynicism! Why, you dumbbell, how do you get that way? The managing editor doesn't want to know his *personal* feeling about the police department. So far as that goes, a lot of those boys over there are friends of his;—no better bunch in the world;—and he and Sweeney, captain in the Eleventh Precinct (where the murder was done) are right down buddies. No, nothing like that. What the managing editor wants to know is whether the police department needs reorganization (shake-up) for the public good. When a crime like this is committed, it concerns the whole community. . . .

So he looks solemn and tells the managing editor he has been wondering why the paper didn't take up that angle. Of course, he's no authority on police systems, but it stands to reason when their Bertillon bureau is away out of date, and they haven't any system for keeping track of suspicious characters, and they have no men available for special assignment, no "flying squad". . . . "You've said enough," says the managing editor. "Now let's handle it this way." So the upshot is that he is sent off on a trip to New York, Philadelphia, Baltimore, Pittsburgh, and Cleveland, and makes a study of police systems in those cities. He draws $250 expense money (feeling pretty important), stays away a week, and writes a series of articles under the caption: HOW OTHER CITIES COPE WITH CRIME. For the first time since he has been on the paper he sees his name signed to what he writes. . . . And Sweeney loses his job.

It has been a turning point in his life. As a result of his articles, he gets a $10 raise. He is frequently consulted by the managing editor. He finds it pays better to be Constructive than Cynical, or even Hard-Boiled. Oh, the devil; he hates to

think what a fool he was once. So he begins to orient things with a view to the Public Interest involved. He takes them seriously. The police department gets into the limelight again, and he is asked to write an editorial about it. By now he is a real expert on all public matters: the taxable basis, the City Hall crowd, the school situation, the police department, the merit system, vice, the health department, the city Federation of Labor, the flying squad of the Prohibition enforcement bureau, the State police, the situation in the counties, the attitude of the women voters, and the date of the birthday of Rufus P. Higgins (president of the Consolidated Foundry Company and Our Grand Old Man). . . . So he gradually comes into his own. One day the editor dies unexpectedly, the assistant editor is promoted to be editor, and Our Hero is made assistant editor. At last he is an Editorial Writer. He is to write the local editorials (and foreign editorials too on Tuesday, the new editor's day off).

So the next day he shows up at 9 A. M. instead of 2 P. M., hangs his coat in the editor's office, and sits down to work. He has quite a day ahead of him. There are two columns of editorials to get out, and editorials don't grow on trees. Then a dozen or so of breezy sayings must be composed, to sandwich between the editorials and relieve the tedium a bit. Then other papers, magazines, etc., must be clipped for novel tid-bits, and these must be captioned. Then the letters to the editor must be read and captioned (But, Sir, If You Were Governor, Would You Compel All Dry Law Violators To Drink Prussic Acid, As You Propose?). Then most likely a number of people will be in, to see about something or other. . . . Well, to work, to work!

First off the bat: What to write an editorial about, heigh-ho, heigh-ho? He skims through the paper. The first story he spies is this: MAYOR PLAYS HORSE—FOR KIDS AT NEW—PLAYGROUND OPENING. Well, well, well! This surely must have an editorial. So he hitches up to the typewriter.

But mark you: In the old days, when he was a cynic, his own honest reaction to this story would have run about like this:

"Say, that there is a hot sketch, ain't it? Playground for the kiddies. You heard about that playground, didn't you? Nick Beal had three acres out there he couldn't sell to the P. B. & R. and dam if he didn't wish it off on the city. 'S a fact. Say, what do you know about Nick riding the totties around on his back? How does he get that way? Does this town hire that fat mope for a mayor or a mule, I'd like to know."

Not exactly lofty, but incisive, in its way, and possessed no doubt of a certain interest to the public, if published. But does it occur to him to write it? Or to paraphrase it into more orthodox prose? Or to ignore the whole performance, on the ground that such monkeyshines are not worth writing about? Not on your life!

Great guns, no! Of course, everybody knows about Nick and the P. B. & R. deal, but nobody has ever brought any charges against him, and if you went on putting things like that into the paper you would have the worst libel suit on your hands you ever saw in your life. As for Nick putting in his whole time at the City Hall, why it has come to a pretty pass when the mayor of this town can't spend a few hours at a playground opening that cost the city $75,000, and he got half of that! As for not writing anything about it, why, man, remember that a whole lot of people are interested in that playground. There were 5000 children out there, and everyone of them has a father and a mother, or most of them have, anyhow. Besides, it's a community affair, and it's up to the paper to take an interest in everything of that sort.

So—to the editorial. He captions it: "The New Playground." The first paragraph:

Every resident of the city must rejoice at the opening of the Evergreen Park Playground. Coming as it does at the beginning of the warm weather, it means that thousands of little tots will have the opportunity for fresh air and play all through the Summer. Wholesome frolic in such surroundings means that when school opens in the Fall, thousands of sturdy, sun-burned scholars will be on hand to take up the more serious business of life with renewed vigor.

And so on. A paragraph on the need for sturdy bodies. A paragraph on fresh air as the best Road to Wellville. A paragraph on the hitherto inadequate playground facilities of the city. Then to His Honor, the Mayor:

Happy the official who can spare an hour or two during a busy day to romp with the kiddies at a time like this. *Parva leves capiunt animus.* It is well so, and it would be well for us all to realize it more often. We salute you, Mr. Mayor, as one who has not forgotten the happy days of childhood. And we freely confess that our salutation is slightly colored with envy.

This graceful tribute out of the way, he picks up the paper again. The next story he spies is: MERCURY SETS MAY 14 RECORD. To the machine again. Does he pull down the side of his mouth and say: "Well, hell, it's supposed to be hot in May, ain't it?" Nay, nay. He hops off this way: "At the wedding feast men may be seated according to high or low estate, but before Old Sol all men are equal." On to the next story: CITIZENSHIP SCHOOL —GRADUATES 31 ALIENS. He writes: "One reads with a sense of civic pride of the work which the Citizenship School of the Chamber of Commerce is doing toward qualifying aliens for the complex duties that will confront them after they become citizens." On to the next: TO PUSH CONSTRUCTION—ON SCHOOL NO. 78. He writes: "The School Board is to be congratulated on its determination to lose no time in the completion of School No. 78; and if its action comes rather late, the patrons in that section, served so poorly by the present structure, at least have the satisfaction of knowing that it has been taken at last." And so on and so on. Next Tuesday, when the editor is off, he will write: "The decision of M.

Poincaré to make drastic cuts in expenditures, in order that the budget can be balanced and the downward course of the franc arrested, will be read with satisfaction by all who realize the far-reaching implications of the present fiscal situation in France." And on June 22, birthday of Rufus P. Higgins, he will write, under the caption "Our Grand Old Man":

> How chastened and humble most of us must have felt yesterday when we learned that Rufus P. Higgins had passed the seventy-fifth milestone of his life. Serene and untroubled as the years march slowly by, this Grand Old Man of industry and public affairs spent the day at his desk as usual, a simple private soldier in the ranks of productive effort.

And so on, and so on, and so on. Day after day, week after week, month after month, year after year. Take up any provincial paper in the land and turn to the editorial page. If you find a single editorial that rises above this general level cut it out and paste it in your hat. You won't find it again.

III

Why is such stuff written? Why is its tone so uniform, from Portland to Portland, and so feeble? I think its hollowness is the hollowness of an echo; it is *not* the genuine thought of the man who writes it. Certainly he never talks any such ponderous blatter. Mostly his conversation consists of long anecdotes about what Bill Murphy said up at the State convention back in 1912. . . . Rather it is his notion of what the great multitudes of plain men think. Often, of course, he gets as low as plain fawning, and that may be because he is afraid if he doesn't stay on the right side of Bill Murphy he will lose that place on the Board of Police Examiners that has been promised him for next year, after Pete Humphreys gets out. But even if he is of comparatively high spirit, he soon comes to regard himself as a sort of tribune of the people, rather than as one speaking in his own right. Thus he becomes an inverted horn, a

recording instrument, tuned to catch the slightest murmur from that great throng milling about below. In very few instances does he write what he himself thinks. He takes a sort of pride in having voted the Republican ticket for 22 years, all the while writing Democratic editorials; and a sort of pride by inversion in his paper, that was so broadminded it never even thought of discharging him for it. . . . He writes what the upper end of that great horn tells him to write—what the people think. Often he erects what the people think into transcendental verity: "The opinion of so eminent an artist as Mr. Jan Humperdinck as to the location of the Robert E. Lee statue should be weighed carefully before a decision is made; *yet in the face of so overwhelming a popular demand"* . . . So, his writings attain their unbelievable flatulence and blowiness; they are permeated throughout with the greasy smell of voting booths and assessors' notebooks, for it is these things that the people are primarily concerned with.

But, you say, sometimes he does get really heated up—assails the mayor and police department, wages crusades, demands complete and searching investigations. Yes, but always within the compass of the horn. If he writes for a Democratic paper, he assails a Republican mayor bitterly; but he says only what all Democrats think about the mayor, and what all Republicans would think of a Democratic mayor. He never calls attention to the odd fact that all mayors somehow contrive to look alike. That is an octave above the range of the horn. He subscribes, by the rules he imposes on himself, to all the notions that the people hold: that it is a civic duty to vote (he may not have voted for 20 years himself); that foreigners ought to become naturalized (his own mother may be a citizen of the Irish Free State); that girls ought not to use paint (his own daughter may put it on with a feather duster). The sum total of these notions makes a fairly definite philosophy, a stew in which all ideas must be dissolved before they may be promulgated—and any idea not therein soluble is ruled out of the paper. . . .

The characteristic flavor of this *potage mondain*, I believe, is supplied by the moral judgment, the judgment that includes an ought or ought-not, that assesses blame or credit: The mayor ought to take action. . . . The police department is to be praised for its efficiency. . . . The dancer should not be permitted to land. . . . All good citizens of the community must have been shocked to hear. . . . No man is more truly entitled to the epitaph, *Requiescat in Pace*. . . . A complete investigation of the scandal should be demanded by Congress. . . . All of us might learn a lesson from the example of the girl who. . . . The warmest co-operation should be extended the Health Department in its effort to. . . . The action of the City College trustees will meet the approval of all who. . . . The deficit in the State budget is a matter that should be explained and explained at once. . . . Before Germany presents this plan formally to England and the United States she must first convince the world she is really at work. . . . Most thoughtful citizens will condemn these trips on the *Mayflower*, feeling that the President of the United States might better occupy his time than by courting the favor of politicians. . . . Nicholas R. Beal is an official who, most thinking citizens will agree, should be supported for re-election. . . . It does seem, however, that the Weather Man, after giving us 16 rainy days in succession, might vary his répertoire a bit. . . .

If, as an editorial writer, you hoist the *fasces*, you will dissolve your ideas in the soup willy-nilly, no matter how brilliant you may be, and write just such silly stuff as this. There are many men on the big Eastern papers who are vastly informed in their fields; they are perambulating encyclopedias on foreign affairs, on city, State, and national government, on labor questions—not all of them got their posts by the same route as Our Hero, who is the Average Case. But do their writings show any vitality? Would you re-read their editorials? Hardly ever. They succumb to the limitations of their depressing trade. It would seem, indeed, that *any* man must succumb. The minute EDITORIAL appears over what he writes, that minute what he writes ceases to be worth reading. Composing in his own right, his tempo may be sizzling fast, but his editorials will move at a decorous *andantino*. Composing in his own right, he may thrust sharply at the truth, scale high pinnacles of fancy, unloose flashing wit—but not in his editorials. Do the people thrust at truth? Scale pinnacles? Wax witty? Then neither does he. He has become a Spokesman. His writing is the writing of the Committee on Resolutions.

IV

This seems to be a story without a moral. I have racked my brains for one, and the only one I can think of is not original, but I give it:

When he dies the Press Club buries him.

THE INVASION OF AMERICA

BY ELBRIDGE COLBY

EVERY nation is in danger of invasion. This is true in spite of the fact that no nation is ever an invader. No nation, indeed, ever attacks another nowadays; everyone is always the innocent party. No nation ever declares war; everyone waits for an assault to be made upon it and then recognizes reluctantly that a state of war exists. No army is ever maintained for offensive purposes; the object of every government is simply to provide for the national defense. Such is the state of international thought in the world today. But the fact remains that some nations are stronger than others, that some have bigger armed forces than others—forces better provided with rapidly available reserves, well-trained and ready to march to the sound of the drums. Whatever the theory, such facts survive. A nation with a large army may be pacific; nevertheless, it may *possibly* become the aggressor. A nation with a small army will certainly be on the defensive, at least in the opening days of hostilities. Thus each nation in the world today tries to maintain armed forces for its national defense, in proportion to its wealth, resources, population, and the degree of exposure of its frontiers. There is the question: the question of the frontiers! The whole problem of national defense in the United States depends initially upon the protection of our sea-coasts.

The first defender on whom we count to protect them is the sailor lad in his wide-bottomed trousers swaggering along the deck of his dreadnaught. The Navy has a set strength, defined and established by the Disarmament Treaties. We are even on a parity with Great Britain, so-called "mistress of the seas," as to our paper strength—which, by the way, is not at present maintained. But our Navy, alas, is divided. An enemy navy, or group of navies, would not have to go to the trouble of trying to obey the first portion of the time honored precept: "divide and conquer!" We have already done that for them, putting half our fleet in Pacific waters and half in Atlantic waters, and so making it easy to defeat the whole piecemeal. The Panama Canal is essential to the union of the two halves—and the Panama Canal is certainly not invulnerable. With that short-cut waterway out of service, the Navy might as well not exist. We could not concentrate our ships on the eve of a possible war, any more than we could start mobilizing reserve officers and training new drafts. Such conduct, when war threatens, becomes a precipitant of war; and no government can afford to countenance it. So with a weak fleet, and whatever helter-skelter army we could muster, we would have to meet our enemy.

Under these conditions the burden of the first big clash would fall upon the coast defenses. After the frantic days of the Spanish War, when every little seaport feared it might be bombarded by the ranging cruisers of Cervera, the Coast Artillery Corps came into its own. Every shore-line congressional district shouted loudly for its share of the appropriations. New forts were laid out. Newer and bigger guns were mounted. Increases in personnel were authorized, enough to make votes and provide a few contractors with work, yet scarcely enough to last for twenty-odd years. Down in Panama, during the recent

439

maneuvers, we heard that even with the assistance of infantry,—infantry unaccustomed to the manipulation of big weapons,—Fort Sherman was able to operate only four of its disappearing guns. Doughboys, cavalry, ordnance experts, food dispensers, military lawyers, and pill rollers rushed to cover the threatened coast. A single battalion had to be spread out to protect forty-five miles of shore. Naturally, the enemy landed. He simply could not be stopped. Army beans and rolls of bandage could not do the work of rifles and of big guns adequately manned.

According to the War Department, "of the twenty-five harbor defenses which have at great expense been installed and equipped for the protection of our coasts, fifteen have been turned over to caretaking detachments sufficient only to keep these valuable installations from becoming useless through deterioration." These include such important posts as Philadelphia, Wilmington (Delaware), Charleston, Savannah, Key West, Mobile, and San Diego. "It has not been possible to assign to even the most important harbors more than sufficient coast artillery personnel to operate approximately twenty-five per cent of the major armament." We have a nice new railroad artillery developed during the late war, big guns mounted on railway trucks ready to run up and down the coast with the same ease that a wheeled-chair glides from end to end of Atlantic City—but not so fast! We have a few guns in actual steel and we have the rest in India ink on drafting paper. Have you ever, going up and down the coast, seen any railway tracks or any concrete emplacements where the guns might be stopped to do their firing? You have not. They do not exist. Even the bottle-ships of the bootleggers penetrate our territorial waters with impunity. The Chief of Ordnance in his last annual report tells of one project after another for new and up-to-date defenses—all at a standstill for lack of funds, lack of material, and lack of personnel.

II

But are the coast defenses really undermanned? Don't the picture papers show us, every now and then, a nice concrete emplacement and a large weapon belching smoke, with heroic troops standing by? Well, let us look at the coast defenses of Boston, seven forts in all. They have less than two hundred coast artillery troops to man them! Here are the coast defenses of Delaware with less than forty at four forts. Here are the important defenses of Narragansett with about two hundred and fifty and the defenses of Southern New York with fifty. At one of the coast forts not long ago a visiting inspector was highly pleased to see a handful of less than two hundred artillerymen first operate the guns at one of the forts and then sail across the harbor and operate entirely different guns at another fort! Very nice for peacetime inspection; in due course a letter of commendation came down from higher authority. But could this be done in war? The batteries, alas, would have to fire simultaneously in war; an enemy would not wait until the troops went from one fort to another; shell and shrapnel would come down instead of letters of commendation.

There are other troops at some of these forts. But these other troops are chiefly infantry, infantry belonging to tactical divisions which, in the event of war, would have to be withdrawn and concentrated wherever the main enemy attack might develop. They are even today carried on the lists as part of the projected covering force for the imaginary "national position in readiness." The famous Sixteenth Infantry, for example, is in New York harbor. The efficient Eighth Infantry is occupying Fort Screven outside of Savannah. But these troops are merely housed there to keep the rains of Summer and the storms of Winter off their heads in time of peace. They would be urgently needed elsewhere in time of war, to meet the invading enemy and prevent him interrupting and shattering our plans for mobilizing men and munitions. A year ago General Pershing made a formal report to the Secretary of War in which he outlined what he called "the national position in readiness." If a war came, he explained, the regulars and the National Guard would be rushed to the frontiers, to the danger points. They would be placed at appropriate places along the coast, and behind them would be the reserve divisions, gradually filling up with men, materials, weapons and clothing, and slowly approaching an efficient condition of training. A good plan. A clear plan. Yet only a plan nevertheless. Suppose that the guardsmen and the regulars were not sufficient to hold the line? Suppose the "enemy" of the Panama maneuvers became an active enemy instead of merely a simulated one? Suppose he landed on the coast? He would disrupt the entire scheme—and we'd have a problem of National Defense indeed!

To what extent can the regulars be counted upon? With a third of their regiments on the inactive list, with but a single regiment at all fully trained and equipped for war, and that one a demonstration regiment down in Southwestern Georgia, our regular army would be in a difficult position from the start. Could we depend upon the World War veterans to fill the ranks quickly and take up the combat they dropped in 1918? The World War veterans are gradually approaching the age where they will no longer be of use for military service. In 1925 there will not be 40 per cent available. Could we depend upon the generality of loyal American patriots to resist the foe? We could not so depend upon them in any effective sense at Bladensburg. Could we depend upon the Air Service to bomb an enemy away from our coasts? Our planes deteriorate rapidly and are not being replaced.

Let us resign ourselves, then, to the conclusion that an enemy *could* approach our coasts and attack our ports, our important concentration points, and our industrial centers. The fleet appears off New York with its big caliber, long range guns—and its airplane carriers. Our aviators are swept from the sky in tangled masses of flaming wreckage. Our coast defense guns are outranged and outshot, and many do not even get an opportunity to fire at all, for lack of men to operate them. Over the tops of the skyscrapers comes a fleet of hostile planes. Peering over the fuselage and down through the broken clouds the enemy aerial leader picks his targets. There are the Grand Central Station and the Pennsylvania Station. A few bombs will disrupt transportation and the bringing in of re-enforcements. There are the Post Office building, the telephone exchanges, the *Times* Building above a network of subways. A few bombs there will confuse the communications and transportation system of the whole city. The bridges may as well go too. The railway tracks down the Hudson shore, across the Jersey meadows, and above Hell Gate are essential to the assembling of more troops. They go too.

Don't say that all this is hypothetical and imaginary. I am not trying to follow in the wake of H. G. Wells. Taking into account our actual strength and the known actual strength of a possible enemy, a group of officers down in Washington played a war game last year. They figured that we would have so many planes in the air, and that the enemy would have so many. The number of enemy planes was so much superior to ours that, even with allowance made for American superiority in courage, for American desperation in defense of the homeland,—even then, our planes would have been dashed to the ground, the Capitol would have been destroyed, the Treasury demolished, the White House bombed, the State, War and Navy Building smashed. The government would have been so disrupted that an infinite military advantage would have been gained. Because such an attack would result in that vast military advantage, such an attack may be expected.

III

This war game was not played as a piece of big-army propaganda. It was an exercise given to high officers of our army as a serious part of their training. Another similar problem was set not very long since out at Fort Leavenworth. It also was hypothetical, and yet it was surely not fanciful. The procedure was in accordance with the so-called applicatory method, whereby general principles of war are applied to specific, concrete, probable situations. Such problems must hold fast to facts; they must include only possible contingencies. The topic this time was "a group of armies in defense." The general region to be defended was the mid-Atlantic area. And with the primary object of study, indeed with the sole object of study, and not at all with any alarmist motives, not with any purpose of impressing the people of the country, this is the analysis that preceded the problem:

The plans for the national defense had originally contemplated a covering force composed of nine divisions of the regular army and eighteen divisions of the National Guard. The scheme contemplated that behind this covering force there would be mobilized and concentrated the units necessary to complete the first three field armies of twenty-seven divisions.

Since this policy had been inaugurated, however, legislation had materially reduced the size of the regular army until it was so small that only two incomplete divisions could be hurriedly extemporized in an emergency. Because of lack of popular interest in matters connected with national defense, and consequent lack of legislative aid, it had been impossible to recruit the ranks of the National Guard even to "reduced" (65 per cent) strength, or to bring the cadres of the organized reserves up to the required 10 per cent of peace strength.

From the moment war was declared, the enemy was able to land an average of 300,000 men per month. From the moment of the enemy appearance at the entrances of Chesapeake and Delaware Bays, considerable confusion existed in the executive departments of the government. It was not known where the enemy would strike, and such small forces as could be gotten together were divided.

Events succeeded each other rapidly. Our weak air forces took the field, but being practically unprovided with pursuit aviation, they were obliged to relinquish control of the air. The enemy overpowered the coast defenses and landed near Wilmington and Baltimore. There

was fighting in which the enemy was victorious. The capital was hurriedly moved from Washington to St. Louis. Public clamor demanded that the enemy be driven out of the country at once. Recruiting offices for the regular army, National Guard, and organized reserves were swamped, but many applicants were physically deficient, and practically all were untrained.

Public sentiment would not countenance delay, but ran so high that it was necessary to combine all available forces into the existing regular and guard units. Some officials desired to preserve the existing cadres of the organized reserves as moulds into which the raw man-power, obtained by voluntary enlistment, and by a draft law hurriedly passed, could be incorporated. But the government could not withstand the popular demand that the enemy be stopped, and almost all men of the organized reserves were amalgamated with regular and National Guard units in order to bring them up to a reasonable strength. These forces opposed the enemy. In a series of engagements they were badly defeated. They withdrew; the bulk of their forces concentrating in Northern New Jersey to prevent an advance from the Delaware on New York; the remainder concentrating and observing the enemy in Northern Ohio.

Weak cordons were formed around the regions occupied, and we carried on at the same time a harrying warfare with small forces against isolated enemy detachments, and conducted raids against enemy communications. In the meantime the government launched a diplomatic drive on neutral countries to secure allies.

All this is not fanciful. Every government with a modern, organized army has what is called a General Staff, a group of officers devoting themselves to the careful study of what might probably happen in time of war. These gentlemen know the male population of every country in the world, the number enrolled in the standing armies of the world, the number listed as reservists, the number of reservists that have adequate military training and not mere paper obligations, the facilities for assembling those reservists and fitting them out as military forces, and the ability of each country to supply immediately shells for its guns and food for its men. Potential power and powerful resources are not enough; there must be organization, and organization that can go into action immediately. We have an organization in this country, but it is a paper organization. We have a regular Army, but it is too small even for the work it is called upon to do in peace time, and could not furnish a force adequate to oppose an enemy in war. We have, the Secretary of War's annual report says, over five hundred thousand men in this country taking military training or holding reserve commissions, but most of these are of officer caliber; they are the training elements only, and after the war started we would have to do the training. In 1917 we had been through the throes of a Mexican border mobilization, which should have attracted attention to the state of affairs; nevertheless in 1917 we went to war unprepared. The war lasted, for us, something over one year and seven months; and the year was a year of preparation. During that year we were training.

IV

We have plans now for something better, but plans merely, untried plans subject to test and revision, yet plans that might conceivably eventuate in the smooth mobilization of which a young army captain has just written in a book. He has said that units will assemble locally, and then move off to join their higher headquarters in succession along military channels, until finally an imaginary adjutant general addresses an imaginary commander-in-chief with "Sir, the Army is formed!" This officer has a lively imagination and looks far into the future. There may now be sixty-odd thousand reserve officers with reserve divisions— but there are only two thousand enlisted reservists for them to command! Imagine a regiment of a hundred officers and three soldiers! With an army like that of Mexico we could fight no better than does Mexico. The rest of the soldiers would have to be gathered from the highways and by-ways. The rest of the soldiers would be green. They might think their light mortar a glorified umbrella rack, their one-pounder a saluting gun from a private yacht, and their automatic rifle a

new type of dentist's drill. The cadres provided for the organized reserves are weak enough, but even those cadres are not complete. A skeleton army is frail and fragile enough, and yet there are bones missing even from the skeleton army!

The Leavenworth description of the general situation is true to fact, as can be seen by anyone who will go over the reports of the chiefs of the various branches of the army for the last fiscal year. Examine the comparative strength of our air force, the weakness of our coast defenses. Remember the scattered regulars now engaged in care-taking, the reduced strength of units upon which we would have to depend to hold the first line of defense. All of these things are not set forth by the chiefs of bureaux in characteristic army growl. They are plainly stated, but the definite achievements of the troops are likewise stated, to show how well things are being done under adverse conditions. No one, however, seems to have noticed these things save perhaps the President of the United States, who, in a message to Congress, remarked that army reductions must stop and that the air service must not be weakened. But within a week the budget cut in half the funds the air service requested—so much, indeed, that the increase over the previous year amounted to only about $9,000—perhaps enough to buy a new nose for the *Shenandoah*, if the *Shenandoah* were an army instead of a navy airship.

We do not notice these things in time of peace. We do not think of war until we want to go to war. But if a war should suddenly come to us these things would be brought home to what Bacon called "the businesses and bosoms of men." "There is a rank among nations," remarked our greatest President, and our first, "that is due the United States, that will be lost by the reputation of weakness." With that weakness, we try to arrogate to ourselves that rank.

HYLAN

BY WILLIAM BULLOCK

HYLAN himself says that he is a follower of Grover Cleveland, and in the fact his followers find an occult and encouraging significance. On the night six years ago when he left the County Court bench in Brooklyn and crossed the Brooklyn Bridge to enter New York's musty old City Hall—at that hour of fate, when the votes of New York's embattled freemen, piling mountain-high, were crushing the eternal daylights out of John Purroy Mitchel—at that precise moment, 'mid the rockets' red glare and the huzzahs of the multitude, the Hon. David Hirshfield, LL.B., as good a Man Friday as the game of politics ever saw, rubbed his hands together and exclaimed, "Next Albany! And next the White House!"

So far, alas, it has not come to pass, but Hylan, despite his long illness, may yet live to put David among the prophets. Cleveland, McKinley, Roosevelt, Taft, Wilson, Harding, Coolidge: we seem to be going down hill. In another decade—who knows?—we may actually reach the Hylan stratum. Meanwhile, here he stands waiting—big-boned, fleshy (though now illness has pulled him down), with reddish hair, heavy features, and eyes with craft in them. A man of ambition, but apparently afraid or unable to stand alone; and so leaning on others, and so attempting to mask himself behind a stony reserve, and so hesitant to meet and fraternize with his fellows; slow and stumbling in his talk, and indecisive, on his own account, in action, and even in his walk; timid to the point of refusing a gesture when on the platform; coming before his audience like a man on stilts; standing there a bulky,

444

seemingly inanimate figure, reading off in a sing-song monotone the words that others have written for him, and never venturing a word more. A queer hero, indeed. But there is Coolidge—

II

How did Hylan happen? How do the Hylans rise over brains and personality, and honest, solid worth, in our public life?

Hylan was born on a farm near Hunter, Greene County, New York, on April 20, 1868. He did chores, went to the Hunter public-school, and otherwise led the lucky outdoor life of the American country boy. He didn't like farming, so he went as brakeman on the Stony Cove, Catskill Mountain and Kaaterskill Railroad. He was a fireman on the same road for a time, but in 1887, when he was nineteen, he went to live with a relative in Brooklyn. He soon got work on the Brooklyn Elevated Railroad, and for ten years, or until June, 1897, he ran a locomotive for that line. But he saw little ahead on the Elevated, and so he decided to enter the law. He pursued his studies, it would seem, back on the home farm, in Greene County; in October, 1897, he was admitted to the bar. He returned to Brooklyn, and opened a law office at Gates Avenue and Broadway.

Even at that early date Hylan had his eye on politics. He had made one capital discovery—that the first real step in politics in New York City is to become a lawyer. Lawyers in New York practice politics as a close corporation; they look on all others seeking places at the trough as outlanders; there is not a lawyer in the town, no matter how hard put to pay for the shingle outside his desk-room door, who is not ready and willing at a moment's notice to step into any public office within the gift of the plain people, from the Mayoralty to the Presidency. Hylan became a member of the Democratic organization of the Twentieth Assembly District, Brooklyn, and from the first showed the prime talent needed for progress in politics: he played up to the leaders.

The rule in Democratic politics in New York is that a man, to arrive anywhere, must not show a mind of his own. Hylan never made any mistake in this respect. From his first day in politics he was always on hand at the Democratic Club when needed, ready to do what he was told to do; and in time he became recognized as one of the regulars, or, to put it in political parlance, one of the boys. Meanwhile he tried hard at the law, but rose to no distinction. There is no record of him in a case of importance. He had to do mostly with petty criminal cases, and bill collections.

One of Hylan's clients was Charles A. Purcell, a cousin of his wife. Purcell held a judgment for $3,780 against the Mutual Brewing Company, of College Point, Long Island. Hylan collected it, and wanted a fee of $2,280. Further he proposed to sell Purcell some stock in a company he was promoting. Purcell could not see it, and the two fell into a lawsuit. Hylan paid over an additional $1,280, and the suit was abandoned. The stock Hylan wanted Purcell to buy was in the Black Diamond Automobile Company. He had organized the company with a capital of $500,000, but of this very little was paid in in cash. The Black Diamond met rocky going from the start. Hylan was an officer, and in time filed suit against his own company. He claimed $5,772 for legal services. He assigned the claim to his clerk, Frank H. Herbert and then himself prosecuted the suit.

He tried other things outside the practice of the law. The records of the Patent Office show him taking out a patent, in 1893, for a bicycle whistle. He also lent himself to the promotion of a mail-order course in public speaking. None of these enterprises made him rich, neither did the law. After nine years of struggle, he decided to go out for public office. Here his somewhat lame plodding in his profession didn't count against him. His regularity, his standing as one of the boys formed the needed asset. He was marked as tractable, amenable, willing to take orders. He was nominated for judge of the Municipal Court. He was far down on the ticket and was left to do his own campaigning. He was defeated.

This was a set-back, but Hylan was not done. If the voters wouldn't have him, there was another way. He again got machine endorsement, and George B. McClellan, at the time a good Tammany Mayor, appointed him a magistrate. This is the lowest judicial post in New York City, and Hylan served in obscurity from 1906 to March 28, 1914. Then, again backed by the machine, he was named to fill a vacancy as County Judge, in Brooklyn, by Governor Martin H. Glynn. At the general election in 1915 he stood for the same office, and was elected for a seven-year term. This was his real political start. But the County Court is not of much account, as courts go in New York, and there was then no thought, not even among politicians, of Hylan as a possible candidate for Mayor.

III

But he *did* bob up as candidate for Mayor. More, he and his friends stepped in and literally walked off with the office.

These friends were three in number— the aforementioned Hirshfield, Joseph A. Solovei, and Francis P. Bent. Hirshfield was another lawyer. Solovei was a third. Bent, however, did not follow the law: he was a vaudeville entertainer. These three men were John F. Hylan's political promoters, his intimates, his cronies.

When he was County Judge, Hirshfield and Solovei enjoyed refereeships and receiverships. Solovei was one or the other nine times; Hirshfield in eighteen months earned $11,810 in Hylan's court.

The headquarters of the whole movement was a rusty, battered letter-box, No. 3, in the hallway of No. 1028 Gates Avenue, Brooklyn. This was the place where Hylan had had his law office; where he had had a branch office of the Black Diamond Automobile Company. Hirshfield, Solovei and Bent ran this letter-box. Hylan also carried a key, and dropped in and opened it occasionally.

It was the office and headquarters of an organization with a high-sounding title —the Allied Boards of Trade and Taxpayers' Associations of Brooklyn. But the only real alliance behind this board of boards was made up of Hirshfield, Solovei, Bent, and Hylan. But no one ever thought of looking up the Allied Boards of Trade and Taxpayers' Associations of Brooklyn; no one ever so much as cast a curious eye on letter-box No. 3 until Hylan was the Tammany Mayoralty nominee, and within a few days of election. Then it was too late, or as one of the remorseful backers of Mitchel put it, "The beans are dumped!"

The Mayoralty fight was in 1917, with Mitchel up for a second term. The Hylan attempt to land the Tammany nomination began just twelve months earlier. The plan was simplicity itself, but none the less effective. From letter-box No. 3, and in the name of the Allied Boards of Trade and Taxpayers' Associations of Brooklyn, Hylan began to send out caustic criticisms of the Mitchel administration. In addition, he began a constant and ever-increasing round of genuine taxpayer's organizations. There are more than 2,500 of them in the five boroughs of New York, and they find it hard to get speakers to give novelty to their monthly meetings. Most of them are under Democratic control, but at the same time they are all supposed to be non-political. It was not a question with Hylan and his three promoters of waiting for invita-

tions, which probably never would have come; he simply listed what bodies he wanted to appear before, and presented himself. The taxpayers were glad to see him. They heard his pious objurgations against Mitchel.

But here at the start, unluckily, Hylan and his trio encountered a rather formidable obstacle. None of the four knew the first thing about the city's government; they were at a total loss for actual facts and figures against the Mitchel administration. So Hylan conferred with one of his old Black Diamond associates, James P. Sinnott, and Sinnott paid a call on Charles F. Murphy, boss of Tammany Hall. Sinnott and Murphy were friends, and members of the same club. It was a small request Sinnott made. Were there any facts and figures not complimentary to young Mr. Mitchel that could be supplied to Judge John F. Hylan, to be used in the right way when accepting calls from taxpayers' organizations? Murphy was delighted. He would attend to it. Anything that would spell trouble for the anti-Tammanyites holding forth in the City Hall was the very thing to interest Charles Francis. He might, being a wise politician, suspect Judge Hylan of an ambition not confined to the bench, but what of that? Any stick is good enough to beat a dog with. So he sent word to his publicity bureau, engaged day in and day out in digging up facts discreditable to the Mitchel administration. The order was that it should give prompt aid to the friend of good government, Judge Hylan.

When the word was received by the bureau, it asked, "Who in hell is Hylan?" Murphy's own bureau didn't know him! It had to look up the *World* Almanac to find out just what Brooklyn bench he was adorning! But he got copies of all the reports that had been given to the press, or circulated in pamphlet form, by the bureau, and Hirshfield, Solovei and Bent went to work on the stack. From that day there poured out a steady stream of warmed-over denunciations of Mitchel from letter-box No. 3, and the Allied Boards of Trade and Taxpayers' Associations of Brooklyn. If the big New York newspapers recognized old stuff they did not seem to care, for about every day they printed paragraphs, and always they ran in Hylan's name—which was the important thing. And when Hylan found that he couldn't get publicity from certain of the smaller newspapers, circulating locally here and there, or limited to a single borough, there was space to be had at timely intervals at so much an agate line. This bought space, of course, was set out as legitimate reading matter. Hirshfield, Solovei and Bent were now in earnest. In six months Hylan was getting a headline now and then; in nine months he was getting headlines every day.

IV

But he was not yet a candidate. Nor would he ever have been a candidate if a certain bankruptcy had not come at the wrong moment. Tammany was not only willing but eager to let Hylan have his fling. It wants as many would-be candidates in the field as can be made to feel the urge. The more there are the better for Tammany; it likes to give the public the impression of an over-supply of available timber. If real timber is scarce, Tammany orders picked men from its ranks to "go out and make a noise!" It gives these men "citizens'" committees to support them, though they well know it is all a fraud, and that the lightning is not going to strike them. But in that year there were others beside Hylan seriously making the great bid. William P. Burr, who had been ousted from the Corporation Counsel's office, was one; Thomas W. Churchill, former member of the Board of Education, was another, and, to name a third, there was Bird S. Coler.

Coler was the man Murphy had secretly decided to make Mayor. He was a Brooklyn man, and it was believed at the time that the election would turn on Brooklyn. He had come within 8,000 votes of being

elected Governor when he was only a political infant—the pet of Hugh McLaughlin, Brooklyn boss in his own right before Tammany crossed the Bridge. Coler fitted Murphy to a T. He was one of those men who can laugh over a joke till tears course down their cheeks; he was a personality in his way, a pleasant, likeable man; and, better still, he trailed along docilely, and wasn't at all of the build to ask bosses the reason why. Coler had proved himself a voter-getter a second time when he ran off with the Borough presidency of Brooklyn some years before. In every way, from the Murphy standpoint, he was just the man. And then at the last moment, just when all was, so far as the Tammany boss could see, cut and dried, Coler, in the business of selling municipal bonds, and attempting to run a small Southern railroad on the side, had to go to smash.

There was something akin to consternation in the faded old red-brick home of Tammany that day. The boss believed that there was only a small chance of defeating Mitchel; he believed that that small and only chance lay in Coler. But it would never do to take a man in financial difficulties and offer him to the voters to manage their $300,000,000 budget. Murphy had a sad vision of the collapse of his campaign before it had fairly begun. He did the next best thing for himself: he took Hylan.

Murphy could readily have found a Brooklyn man of substance, but he didn't want a man of substance. He had had one experience along that line— when William J. Gaynor, in 1909, forced his hand, and grabbed the nomination. Gaynor was a man of substance; he was a Mayor who *was* Mayor; and the four years that ensued were so painful to Murphy that he was determined the like would not happen again. Hylan was the sort of man he wanted—no Coler, of course, but vastly better than another Gaynor—the best substitute, in fact, in sight.

Letter-box No. 3 had thus done its job. It had spread Hylan's name, given Hylan his chance when the chance came. There the situation was, and there Hylan was! Tammany would rather lose with a Hylan than win with a Gaynor. Tammany had to have a man that the voters had heard about; Tammany was fixed in the idea that only a Brooklyn man would do; and the one man in Brooklyn filling all these Tammany requirements was John F. Hylan.

So he was nominated, and the tragedy of it for Murphy was that, if only he had foreseen, he might have taken any old horse he pleased out of the stall. For with the naming of Hylan, the luck broke so that John Purroy Mitchel suddenly found himself in no end of trouble. His closest friends, with their fingers in his political pie, were indicted for fraud against the city; the very next week, mainly by reason of these indictments, he was beaten in the Republican primary. Thus he was forced to an independent renomination, and was in the race against not one candidate but two. There was no longer any doubt of the outcome. A three-cornered fight means handing the city over to Tammany—John F. Hylan was given what the politicians picturesquely term a walkover.

V

But there were yet some alarming incidents before the campaign was over. For one thing, a shiver passed over the Hall when it was discovered just what kind of candidate John F. Hylan was. Tammany naturally assumed that any man aspiring to sit in the City Hall would know something about the not difficult art of handling himself in a political campaign. It had nominated a learned judge; a man who had appeared before many highly intellectual taxpayers' associations; a man who had got himself a lot of newspaper space; a man who was backed by the Allied Boards of Trade and Taxpayers' Associations of Brooklyn. In view of all that,

was it too much to suppose that this man was a discreet, clever and eloquent fellow?

Tammany thought so, but Tammany was mistaken. It quickly found out that it had to get under its candidate and support not only his arms but his whole body, including his head. It appointed three trustworthy and experienced men to this task. It buried them in a bridal suite in the Manhattan Hotel. They proved equal to the job, and they had a good assistant; John F. Hylan never interfered with them. He took what they handed him, and never offered a suggestion, and never asked a question. His speeches were written for him by these professors, even to the "Ladies and Gentlemen," or "My Fellow Citizens." At first the phrases of salutation were not put in, but later they always were—lest the candidate would forget to use them. Scarcely a syllable, scarcely a vestige of a thought, of John F. Hylan's own was used by John F. Hylan during the campaign.

It was a strange and somewhat new situation; Tammany had never confronted it before, and Tammany was nervous. It had reason to be, for it knew the opposition knew just what kind of candidate Hylan was. There was speculation as to what the fighting Mitchel would do. He did just what he was expected to do: he challenged Hylan to a debate. This was on October 11, 1917, and Mitchel went into Brooklyn and repeated the challenge at four meetings. One of these challenges was close by Hylan's doorstep. Hylan was alarmed by this development, but his three Tammany secretaries met the emergency. They wrote:

No mere oratorical contest with this petulant young man, who is smarting under deserved and almost universal condemnation, will meet the situation or satisfy the people. This is the case of the City of New York against the Mayor and his administration, and his answer must be made to the people.

And so on, to the flat refusal of Hylan to engage in any kind of debate with so trashy a fellow. Hylan was to read these solemn words in Hunt's Point Palace, in Bronx Borough, but he almost spoiled everything. The packed audience didn't

know why he hesitated and mumbled;
why he halted nervously over his type-
written sheet. The reason was that he had
forgotten his glasses! But he somehow
muddled through, and the newspapers
next day carried his brave and solemn
words to the whole city.

Mitchel kept on repeating his challenge;
he offered to meet Hylan in Tammany Hall.
But Tammany was taking no such chances;
it would have burned down the old Hall
itself before permitting its candidate to be
led away from his manuscript. So alarmed
and watchful did it become that it sprinkled loud-voiced adherents through every
one of Hylan's meetings; and at the first
sign of heckling they raised the cry,
"Throw him out!" or otherwise shouted
the hecklers down. Not a single heckler
ever got so much as half a chance at the
Tammany candidate.

When the campaign was nearing a close,
Mitchel tried another tack. He charged
that Hylan was a member of an organization called the Friends of Peace, formed
by a German agent. Mitchel produced a
letterhead with Hylan's name listed as
vice-chairman. He bellowed, "I accuse
John F. Hylan of being an associate of
paid agents of Germany." Hylan was in
a stew over this attack; he didn't know
what to do. But when he took up his
paper the following morning, there were
these thunderbolt words of the other John
F. Hylan—the three-headed one in the
bridal suite at the Manhattan Hotel—,
running side by side with the Mitchel
charges:

The use of my name in its present association and
significance is a dastardly eleventh hour attempt by
Mr. Mitchel in his effort to prove that all opposed to
him are traitors, and to distract the voters from the
issues of the campaign. No one ever has had the right
to use my name for any purpose hostile to the interests
of my country. I now distinctly say and solemnly avow
that I am informed for the first time and by Mayor
Mitchel alone, of the existence of the letterhead of the
Friends of Peace with my name upon it. I know nothing of this society and its propaganda. What I do
know is that as vile and ignoble as has been the
Mayor's attempt to hide the corruption of his official
acts behind the flag, he has tonight outdone himself,
in mendacity and indecency.

Hylan's campaign reached a climax in
Prospect Hall, in his home borough. Here
he was advertised for a most important
speech: to tell exactly what he would do
as Mayor, to sound his keynote. There
were brass bands and marching clubs and
an overflow. The stage was all set; Hylan
was plucking his sleeves all ready to go
on, when a terrible disaster fell upon him:
his speech was pilfered from his pocket!
Someone, supposedly in his opponent's
camp, had hired a light-fingered gentleman,
and there was the Tammany candidate,
and there was the expectant audience, and
there was no speech. And it was half-way
across Brooklyn, and across the East River,
and all the way up to the Manhattan
Hotel, to get another copy—a matter of
an hour there and an hour back. Hylan
was flabbergasted. The audience was stamping and roaring; the cause seemed lost.
But then, unexpectedly, one of the three
professors who had spent all afternoon
writing the speech happened around to see
how the mass meeting was going—and he
chanced to have a carbon copy in his
pocket. So Hylan went out, made his
speech, and had his revenge on fate a
short time later by being triumphantly
elected.

VI

In the Mayor's chair Hylan has done just
what Tammany knew he would do. He
has been complacent; he has been sub-
servient; he has been willing to let Tammany run him. At the start, true enough,
he did attempt a few gestures of his own.
Once, for example, he wrote a letter to his
heads of departments, warning them that
they must spend their appropriations for
the year in twelve equal parts, or a twelfth
each month. He said in this letter:

It is gross or culpable neglect to spend more than
one-twelfth of the money provided for in the budget
for any purpose or object in any one month and any
violation of these Charter sections by the head of
the department, or any of his subordinates, will be
sufficient cause to make necessary a change in the department, as well as being subject to criminal prosecution.

Hylan cited Sections 1542 and 1551 of the City Charter as requiring this, which, of course, the sections did not. If they had it would have been necessary for the city, in the market, say, for a horse, to buy that horse in twelve pieces, one a month. Likewise, Hylan's commissioners would have to expend as much on band concerts in Winter as in Summer, and as much on coal in July as in February. One of the commissioners had a horse to buy, and, showing the Hylan letter, went about the City Hall asking if he should buy the tail in January or December. But he didn't go near His Honor asking that. So peculiar a man is Hylan that one and all of his commissioners were afraid to approach him on the subject; they just went ahead spending their money as before, and in all likelihood he is unaware to this day of his joke on himself.

Hylan dictated and signed a few more letters. Here is one of them:

CHARLES NORRIS, M. D.,
Chief Medical Examiner.

Dear Sir: Your letter of September 3, [1918] requesting permission to increase the salary of Mr. Archibald Fulton to $1,800 is received. I understand that this man was not entitled to the increase until he passed an examination. I wish that those who are employed by the City would use their great ability in suggesting how to render better service to the city instead of scheming how much they can get out of the city.

It is too bad that the people on the payroll of the city have only one desire and that is to see how much they can get out of the city. Ask those in your department to forget the clock and to forget the questions of their salary and try to serve the city to the best of their ability, and who knows but that one of them might become great and possibly Mayor of this city.

Very truly yours,
JOHN F. HYLAN.

This letter took wings; it came in quick time to Tammany Hall. Boss Murphy is a practical man. He decided it was time to take Hylan in hand again. And he did.

CLINICAL NOTES

BY H. L. MENCKEN AND GEORGE JEAN NATHAN

Sine Qua Non.—In every thoroughly charming and effective person, one finds a suggestion and trace, however small, of the gutter. This trace of finished vulgarity is essential to a completely winning manner. The suavest and most highly polished man or woman becomes uninteresting save he or she possesses it. In the soul of every fetching man, there is a streak of ingratiating commonness; in the heart of every alluring silken woman, there is a touch of calico.

The New Galahad.—My agents in attendance upon the so-called moving pictures tell me that persons who frequent such shows begin to tire of Western films—that they are no longer roused to clapper-clawing by the spectacle of actors in patent-leather boots murdering Indians and Mexicans. Several of the astute Ashkenazim in charge of the movie industry, noting that slackening of taste, have sought to find a new hero to replace the scout and cowboy, but so far without success. The children of today, young and old, seem to take no interest in pirates, nor are they stirred by train-robbers, safe-blowers and other such illicit adventurers. It can't be that the movie censorship is to blame, for the same thing is visible in the field of *belles lettres*. The dime novel, once so prosperous, is practically dead. The great deeds of the James brothers, known to every literate boy in my youth, are now forgotten. And so are the great deeds of Nick Carter and Old Sleuth: the detective has fallen with his prey.

What is needed, obviously, is a new hero for the infantry of the land, for if one is not quickly supplied there is some danger that the boys will begin admiring Y. M. C. A. secretaries, crooked members of the Cabinet and lecturers on sex hygiene. In this emergency I nominate the bootlegger—not, of course, the abject scoundrel who peddles bogus Scotch in clubs and office buildings, but the dashing, romantic, defiant fellow who brings the stuff up from Bimini. He is, indeed, almost an ideal hero. He is the true heir, not only of the old-time Indian fighters and train-robbers, but also of the tough and barnacled deep-water sailors, now no more. He faces the perils of the high seas in a puny shallop, and navigates the worst coast in the world in contempt of wind and storm. Think of him lying out there on wild nights in Winter, with the waves piling mountain-high and the gale standing his crazy little craft on her beam! Think of him creeping in in his motor-boat on Christmas Eve, risking his life that the greatest of Christian festivals may be celebrated in a Christian and respectable manner! Think of him soaked and freezing, facing his exile and its hardships uncomplainingly, saving his money that his old mother may escape the poor-farm, that his wife may have her operation for gall-stones, that his little children may be decently fed and clad, and go to school regularly, and learn the principles of Americanism!

This brave lad is not only the heir of Jesse James and Ned Buntline; he is also the heir of John Hancock and of all the other heroes who throttled the accursed Hun in 1776. All the most gallant among them were smugglers, and in their fragile craft they brought in not only rum but also liberty. The Revolution was not merely against the person of the Potsdam tyrant, George III; it was also, and especially, against harsh and intolerable laws—the worst of them the abhorrent Stamp Act. But was the Stamp Act worse than Prohibition? I leave it to any fair man. Prohibition, in fact, is a hundred times as foul, false, oppressive and tyrannical. If the Stamp Act was worth a Revolution, then Prohibition is worth a massacre and an earthquake. Well, it has already bred its Hancocks, and soon or late, no doubt, it will breed its Molly Pitchers, Paul Reveres and Mad Anthony Waynes. Liberty, driven from the land by the Methodist White Terror, has been given a refuge by the hardy boys of the Rum Fleet. In their bleak and lonely exile they cherish her and keep her alive. Some day, let us hope, they will storm the coast, slit the gullets of her enemies, and restore her to her dominion. The lubbers of the land have limber necks; their blood runs pale and yellow. But on the roaring deep there are still men who are colossally he, and when the bugle calls they will not fail.

Here are heroes—gallant, lawless, picturesque, adventurous, noble. Let the youth of the land be taught to venerate them. They make the cowboys who linger in the movies look like puny Christian Endeavorers; they are the only Olympians left in a decayed and flabby land, or in the seas that hedge it 'round. Who will be the first poet to sing them?

Observation in Passing.—One of my books was recently published in England. I observe that it has been highly praised by those English critics who like America and Americans and vigorously damned by those who do not like America and Americans. The book itself, so far as I am able to make out, has been dealt with by only one man.

Trio De Luxe.—The contention that, so far as a man is concerned, the pleasantest of all parties is the twosome, that is, one composed of a fellow and a girl who like each other, is no longer maintained save by professors of the orthodox and banal. The true masculine connoisseur of pleasure knows from long experience that the most amusing party ever devised by the angels on high is the one that is made up of one man and two girls, and that its amusement qualities are not particularly much interfered with one way or the other whether the attendants like one another or not. In fact, the less they like one another the more likely the party is to be to the taste of the man, assuming him, of course, to be a member of what may be called cultured society.

The twosome generally repeats itself. One such party is as much like another as the soup stains on a Congressman's waistcoat. The man who can still find gratification of the spirit in sitting around with a girl, holding her hand under the table, gazing lovingly at her ear and whispering sweet emptinesses to her is either a recent college graduate, who hence knows nothing, or a vain old idiot of a bachelor making a gallant and futile stab at youth and romance. The man of any intelligence who spends an evening at a table with a fair creature may, true enough, enjoy the first half hour, but he is a liar who would seriously maintain that thereafter the party does not descend to the time-worn stencils and rubber-stamps. Recall, if you will, that it is the amusement-power of such parties of which I am speaking—nothing else. And with this in mind, consider the relative pleasure to be derived from the triangular party, the one composed of one man and two girls. Here is humor in its fullest promise! Where, in the case of one man and one girl, both the man and the girl feel a certain amount of reserve, and conduct themselves accordingly, this reserve, as everyone knows, promptly disappears when an extra girl is on the scene, and to the establishment of the necessary gala note. What one girl will talk about with a man isn't worth listening to, save perhaps by young boys and adult mushheads. But what *two* girls will talk about with a man is worthy the attention of the savant. No man who has experienced the joys of the mixed threesome will for a moment debate its tremendously superior humorous horsepower. The conversation at such an affair has life, salt, gayety, wit, searching truth, and the charm that lies ever in the heart of frankness. The conversation at the party made up of a fellow and a girl is usually fit only for the ears of imbeciles, already full-blown or potential.

After 1900 Years.—At the end of one millennium and nine centuries of Christianity, it remains an unshakable assumption of the law in all Christian countries and of the moral judgment of Christians everywhere that if a man and a woman, entering a room together, close the door behind them, the man will come out sadder and the woman wiser.

Memorial Service.—If he were still alive today, the late James Harlan, LL.B., of Iowa, would be 104 years old. In 1865 Abraham Lincoln, whose son had married his daughter, appointed him Secretary of the Interior. One day he was informed by spies that a clerk in the Interior Department, Walter Whitman by name, had written a book of poems, by title "Leaves of Grass." Sending for a copy of this book, he read it with indignation, and at once fired the author. Let us pause a moment to remember this dreadful and almost forgotten ass: James Harlan, of Iowa, Secretary of the Interior in the Cabinet of Abraham Lincoln.

More Reflections at Forty.—1. It is only the amateur of feminine loveliness who believes that a woman looks more beautiful in an evening gown than in day dress. As a general thing, a woman is not half so physically attractive in décolleté as in the habiliments of afternoon.

2. With the possible exception of Abraham Lincoln, every one of our really great Americans was by nature and in private

life a light-hearted and even waggish man.

3. Nothing grows tiresome so quickly as an interesting talker.

4. There is one thing, at least, that age is not successful in deceiving itself about. It may lie convincingly to itself about a hundred different things, but it stubs its toe embarrassingly when it is met with an invitation to toboggan. A man and woman become definitely old in their own consciousness the moment the toboggan sled begins to seem risky and uninviting to them.

5. No woman, in the highest moment of her happiness, thinks of marriage. She begins to think of it in her moments of misgiving, self-doubt and misery. Marriage is generally a craft that backs quickly out to sea from a shaky and partly condemned dock.

6. Nothing is so ruinous to the success of a dinner party as good food.

7. Few things in this world are so thoroughly boresome as a professional entertainer doing his stunt after midnight.

8. A policeman who feels that he is growing old—there you have the essence of pure tragedy!

Revolt.—It is frequently said that revolt is ever the distinguishing characteristic of the Younger Generation. This is only half true. The Younger Generation in any double decade or of any century merely talks of revolt. The actual revolting is generally done by the Older Generation. The Younger Generation may be found atop the soapboxes, but the loaded guns are usually found in the hands of their elders.

Vanished Hobgoblins.—In the days before the Nineteenth Amendment one of the chief arguments against the extension of the suffrage to women was this: that the act of voting would bring them unpleasant and contaminating contacts, that going into polling-places peopled by low ruffians would offer them indignity. This argument was heard chiefly from ladies of an elder school; almost all of us had aunts who voiced it. The instant they got the vote they voiced it no more. What they found in the polling-place was not a horde of assassins from the waterfront, but half a dozen humble and harmless fellows from the neighborhood—the corner delicatessen dealer, an apartment-house janitor, a bookkeeper from a lumber-yard, a retired plumber, and so on. It surprised them, I daresay, but they said nothing; women are far too intelligent ever to admit their errors specifically.

Some worse ones flourished in those ancient days, and now, thanks to the progress of moral endeavor in the Republic, it is impossible to dispose of them by evidential means. Thus they probably continue to hold credit in camera. I offer, as specimens, the general feminine notions of what went on in saloons, in men's clubs, and in what used to be called mellifluously disorderly houses. The saloon, seen from the outside, probably bore an extremely sinister and romantic aspect. It was the place where father acquired his hiccup, where improper anecdotes originated, where politicians, burglars and other criminals met to plan their rogueries. In most American States women were forbidden by law to enter its doors; in all States their entrance was frowned upon by the communal *mores*. Yet they passed those doors every day. They caught whiffs of its ethereal aromas; they heard echoes of its occult ribaldry; they nursed, on occasions, the victims of its sorceries. No wonder they were curious about it, and ready to believe fabulous tales about it!

It is a pity that, at least in its more gaudy and romantic forms, it disappeared, along with the old-time men's club, before the communal *mores* had been abated sufficiently for them to go see it for themselves. Their inspection, of course, would have given them a surprise vastly greater than that they suffered when they began to vote. For the saloon, in actuality, was even more banal than the polling-place. Its charm, to a sober visitor, was scarcely beyond that of a hardware store or a Pullman wash-room. Like the barber-shop—also mysterious and sinister in its time, but now invaded by flappers of ten and twelve—, it was simply stupid. I frequented bar-rooms, in the days before the Wesleyan Reformation, pretty steadily; my constitution, then as now, required an occasional dram. Yet I can't remember ever having met any man in one who was worth meeting, or having heard anything that was worth hearing, or having seen anything that might not have been set before an audience of grandmothers. I seem to remember a few florid paintings of the nude, but the nude certainly would not shock grandmothers. Once I saw a man black another man's eye, but I have seen precisely the same thing in a cemetery.

The old-time bordello, nine times out of ten, was quite as innocuous. Its reputation for thrills was kept up, not by those who had ever actually examined it, but by sensational clergymen who viewed it from a range of 1000 yards. In reality, it was commonly run almost as decorously as the Lake Mohonk Conference. The instant gayety went beyond a mild *mezzo forte* the bouncer emerged from the cellar, the piano-player jumped out of the window, and the police reserves arrived. Save in the lowest dives, improper dress was forbidden the internes, and profane or Rabelaisian language was severely punished, often by heavy fines or suspension from the faculty. The music, true enough, was vulgar, but it was never so vulgar as the current music of Broadway; always there was some simple sentiment in it to mitigate its cacophony. Nor was drunkenness countenanced, save perhaps by the higher functionaries of the gendarmerie. A police captain, on his day off, was permitted to drink beyond the seemly and lie snoring on the floor, but that was out of respect for his office. A private citizen who essayed to imitate him was kicked out without ado, and his hat and stick thrown after him.

This institution, as I say, passed out of existence before the recent relaxation of the old pruderies permitted any woman of any social dignity to inspect it for herself. The result is that the romantic view of it lies embalmed in amber. It still figures in Sunday-school stories as a place of levantine debauchery—the scene of revels that would have staggered even Offenbach or Heliogabalus. Suburban clergymen, in their Sunday-night discourses to bored victims of the laws against Sunday movies, depict it as a sort of moral slaughter-house, and speak of its suppression as one of the greatest triumphs of Ku Klux Christianity. But was it actually suppressed? I often doubt it. I believe, rather, that it died of inanition—that the dance craze, the vast extension of boozing under Prohibition, and, above all, the increasing bawdiness of the theatre, simply drove it to the wall, as the old-time leg shows were driven to the wall by the universal exposure of the female calf.

Definition.—Christendom may be defined briefly as that part of the world in which, if any man stands up in public and solemnly swears that he is a Christian, all his auditors will laugh.

A False Prudery.—It is less than two hundred years since the art of the surgeon was definitely separated from that of the barber, but already its practitioners have developed a great corpus of professional hocus-pocus and a high sense of their own dignity. If it were not for the remedies for malpractise that equity offers to their patients many of them would be operating in dress suits today, as all of them did down to Lister's day. Not a few of the more pretentious of them, I believe, still refuse to finish an operation that they have begun. The patient is sewed up, not by the virtuoso who gets his money, but by an apprentice who gets nothing. This results, I suppose, in more stitches, but perhaps in fewer stitch abcesses. All the auxiliary work, of course—boiling instruments, counting sponges, shaving the field, and so on—is done by menials, many of them of the female sex and some of them beautiful.

But against all this I do not protest. If a clergyman deserves an altar-boy to open his missal for him and hand him his censor, then certainly a surgeon deserves an assistant to hand him his instruments and prepare his patient for the embalmer. What I object to is the professional sniffishness that has handed over one of the most important departments of surgery—that of cosmetic repair—chiefly to quacks. Nine out of ten surgeons of the first rank, I believe, refuse to engage in it—that is, when it is not a necessary sequel to traumatic or operative mutilation. They will help a soldier who has had his nose shot off in the wars or even a pugilist who has lost an ear in the ring, but they will not help a poor working girl who is lovely in every particular save that her mouth is six inches wide. If she would have it reduced to normalcy by the surgical art, she must resort, usually, to a practitioner who is somewhat below the salt, and not infrequently the net result is that she gets a tremendous bill and two bad scars, and sees her boss' son married to some other girl.

It is difficult to detect any sense in this professional prudery. If the Hippocratic Oath obliges a surgeon to trephine the skull of a Prohibition enforcement officer who has fallen a victim to the just wrath of a *posse comitatus*, then why should it forbid him to relieve the agony of a young woman whose nose, in saggital section, is like a clam shell, or whose ears stick out like studding sails? The girl is obviously more worthy than the enforcement officer and her malady is more dangerous to her success in life. Moreover, her relief and improvement are of infinitely greater value to society in general. To save a Prohibition agent's useless and degraded life is to carry humanitarianism to the verge of pedantry; to convert a homely and unhappy girl into a pretty and happy one is to increase the general store of joy in the world. She is herself lifted to the heights of bliss, and the rest of us are made easier in mind, for nothing, it must be obvious, is more depressing than the spectacle of a human virgin without physical charm. She is a walking futility; a tragedy in one long, lugubrious act. Surgery, three times out of four, could help her. So long as it fails to do so it is recreant to its trust.

Nearly always her relief presents a trifling problem, surgically speaking. She is not homely all over; she is simply homely in one salient feature, and repairing it is seldom as complex a business as repairing a broken knee-cap. The worst nose imaginable yields very readily to the plastic surgeon's ingenuity. He can shave it down if it is too big; he can shrink it if it bulges; he can correct its lines if it is offensively Socratic. Ears, too, are easy for him, and so are double chins. He can make dimples. He can reconstruct necks. He can enlarge or diminish mouths. He can correct bow legs and knock knees— and often, in fact, does so, though always on some specious "ethical" ground. But, in general, he appears to dislike these humane offices. It is his theory that it is *infra dig* for him to aid the beauty doctors, so-called—that he must confine himself to the repair of injuries and the cure of disease. Well, bad ears are injuries to any young girl, and a mouth like a ferry slip is a disease far worse than Asiatic cholera.

On the medical side I detect something of the same prejudice. So long as it may be reasonably argued that a female patient's bad complexion is due to some definite malady, the skin specialists and professors of internal medicine labor diligently to relieve her. But the moment the fact appears that she is quite well otherwise— that her muddy color is simply an act of God—then they desert her. No scientific investigation of complexions *per se* has ever been made; there is absolutely no literature on a subject at least twice as important as, say, color blindness or writer's cramp, both of which have been studied so laboriously that the records fill whole shelves. Medicine is an art as well as a science, and as an art it should be concerned with beauty. To increase the

general sightliness of the human race, to augment the number of pretty girls in the world and diminish the number of homely ones—this is an enterprise quite as respectable and ten times as important as ridding infants of the *Oxyuris vermicularis*. It is, indeed, an enterprise that should be one of the first concerns of every civilized people. One can only deplore the fact that the pruderies of the only men scientifically capable of it should stand in the way of its undertaking.

More on Divorce.—In the many learned and eloquent treatises on divorce that have appeared in the various public prints, including this department of cosmic wisdom, it seems to us that we and our colleagues in philosophy have at times laid too much stress on important things and too little on trivial. The adjectives are used, of course, in their generally accepted sense; hence there is no paradox. What we mean to say, specifically, is this: that the causes of divorce are doubtless infinitely more insignificant, as such things go, than the majority of investigators and examiners believe. The real causes, that is. The reasons that appear in court are generally as far from these real causes as the human eye can reach. Long before a husband has committed adultery, for instance, the divorce germ has entered his consciousness; long before a wife actually runs away from her husband, the seed of divorce has begun to take root in her mind. A hundred little things preface a husband's beating his wife, and so giving her grounds for divorce in certain States, as a hundred little things, which the investigators dismiss as negligible, preface a wife's running off to Paris with the first available bellhop. What are these little things? Let us guess at a few.

Perhaps one of the chief causes of divorce, or, more exactly, leading up to the act or acts legally recognized as grounds for divorce, is a trivial physical blemish in one or the other of the parties to the marriage. This defect, in the husband's or the wife's person, may be comparatively insignificant, yet no matter. Such a blemish, when lived with for a period of time, has a cruel and devastating habit of burning itself into the eye and consciousness of the other person; it gradually becomes almost a visual phobia; its image will not out. It colors the one person's entire picture of the other; it grows to dominate that picture completely. In time, if the other person is at all sensitive—and four out of five persons are extremely sensitive in this regard—it becomes unbearable. The husband, if it is the husband, begins, almost unconsciously, to look around him at other and theoretically more immaculate women. The look grows steadier . . . Atlantic City . . . the divorce court. Or he deserts his wife, or treats her with cruelty. The wife, on the other hand, if it is the wife, simply gets to the point where she cannot endure the marriage relation any longer, and leaves her husband's bed and board. And the newspapers, in due course, print the grounds of divorce, but fail to print the reason.

Another reason for the act or acts leading to divorce may be found in the inability of the married parties to stand the aesthetic jars that propinquity forces more or less upon them. This is particularly true of men and women who marry after the twenties have passed into the thirties. Such men and such women have grown so accustomed to physical and emotional independence that the habit is not easy to break. It is much more difficult for them to endure the invasions upon privacy that marriage brings with it than it is for younger persons. For every couple that have been put asunder by adultery, or lack of support, or a carpet-beater, there are two that have been split by being compelled to use the same bathroom, or by a bathroom that was too disconcertingly close to their bed-chamber.

There are dozens of other such reasons, each and all overpowering in their superficial triviality. The two that have been set down are sufficient to suggest many of the rest. A marriage that has weathered stormy seas all too often goes to smash on a pebble.

Consolation.—A sense of moral superiority, as everyone knows, is very comforting. Personally, I find myself unable to indulge myself in it very often, chiefly, I suppose, because most of the things I like to do are forbidden by the *mores* of my time and nation. Yet even I have my virtues and it is very agreeable to think of them. I would not invite a guest to dinner and then give him bad gin; I would not, if I had been shoved into the trenches, accept a bonus in satisfaction of the injury; and I would not do what Mr. Fall did. At the moment that is as far as I can go. If I ever think of anything else I'll resume the subject.

Studies in American Boobology: A Survey of Current National Advertising Campaigns. Second Series.—

1. "I can show you how to rise quickly above the mass in business, how to jump into prominence and become an important part of board meetings, how to become a leader, with the poise and assurance to plunge right into any subject and convince your hearers of your point of view, to sell any number of people, from one to a thousand, on the idea you want to put over. This is the wonderful ability I can and will give you."—*North American Institute, 3601 Michigan Ave., Chicago, Ill.*

2. "The most astounding power ever discovered! So says the man who has startled America. Fear—Poverty—Sickness—Sin—all have vanished before the amazing power this man has demonstrated to thousands in America's great cities—a new and wonderful way to success and health and happiness. What is this mysterious force? Dr. David V. Bush, who, in poverty, wrestled many years with the problems of life and death, finally struck the gold vein of living Truth—a simple secret that has lifted thousands from mediocrity to health, happiness and suc-

cess. Thousands have crowded great auditoriums in America's largest cities to learn the secret of the tremendous force Dr. David V. Bush has so successfully applied and taught to others. Those who suffer the pangs of poverty—the blight of failure —the pain of sickness—the agonies of mental depression find relief. He has swept before him everywhere all doubting, all unbelief, as chaff before the amazing power he proves the rightful heritage of every living person. In Chicago—Denver—San Francisco—Seattle—Salt Lake—Boston— Washington, D.C., and scores of other cities he has given throngs his own wonderful secret—a secret that can be easily grasped and applied by everyone."— *David V. Bush, 225 N. Michigan Ave., Chicago, Ill.*

3. "For years the mistaken idea prevailed that writing was a 'gift' miraculously placed in the hands of the chosen few. People said you had to be an Emotional Genius with long hair and strange ways. Many vowed it was no use to try unless you'd been touched with the Magic Wand of the Muse. They discouraged and often scoffed at attempts of ambitious people to express themselves. These mistaken ideas have recently been proved to be 'bunk.' People know better now. The entire world is now learning the TRUTH about writing. People everywhere are finding out that writers are no different from the rest of the world. They have nothing 'up their sleeve'; no mysterious magic to make them successful. They are plain, ordinary people. They have simply learned the principles of writing and have intelligently applied them. I have shown hundreds of people how to turn their ideas into cash—men and women in all walks of life—the modest worker, the clerk, the stenographer, bookkeepers, salesmen, reporters, doctors, lawyers, salesgirls, nurses, housewives—people of all trades and temperaments. I believe there are thousands of people like yourself who can write much better stories than we now read. Just fill out the coupon. All the secrets are yours."—*The Authors' Press, Auburn, N. Y.*

The Backward Art.—In all the numerous fields of human ingenuity and enterprise, none shows so small a measure of progress as that which concerns itself with the artificial thatching of the male mammal's bald dome. Human imagination and skill have triumphed over fire and water, the air and the land, the sea and the jungle; they have chained electricity and water falls; they have defied the flight of birds and the very passing of time. But the wig in this Year of Our Lord 1924 is still the melancholy looking and completely obvious dingus that it was in the Sixteenth Century. It is reasonable to believe that thousands upon thousands of men in the last five or six centuries, and particularly in the last, have labored to perfect a wig that would be at least partly deceptive, that would seem to belong where it was put. And yet with what result? With the result that the wig looks today exactly like—a wig.

There never has been a wig or a toupé that could deceive even an onlooker with a violent case of astigmatism. One can spot the spurious covering on a bald head a block away. It is approximately as successful in concealing the fact that a man hasn't any of his own hair left as a bustle is successful in concealing the fact that a woman is deficient in what need not further be described. The wig or the toupé, in fact, does not so much conceal baldness as loudly announce it. The only person it fools is the man who wears it. Yet why should this be? Why should one of the apparently most simple things in the world thus baffle human ingenuity? No prize will be given for the correct answer.

Footnote.—The difference between a moral man and a man of honor is that the latter regrets a discreditable act, even when it has worked and he has not been caught.

MUSHROOM TOWN

By MUNA LEE

THE DRUG-STORE

A DOOR *with blurred panes swung aside to show*
The cavernous room, across whose muffled scents
Came sudden drifts, volatile and intense,
Of pennyroyal or tansy. A smeary row,
Cases of soaps and notions stood before
Long, gleaming shelves of jars in sapphire glass,
Below were drawers—salts, sulphur, copperas.
The soda-taps dripped sirops by the door.

And pent in every jar, a bewildering djinn:
Linden—*among whose crackling light-brown leaves*
Still clung small blossoms from a foreign tree;
Sesame—*flat seeds known to the Forty Thieves—*
A child for hours could peer and find within
Spoil of far lands and islands of the sea.

II

ELECTORS

T HE *drug-store was a club, in whose talk took part*
Tall men, slouch-hatted, neither old nor young—
Men who had failed elsewhere, and who had wrung
Stakes from scant capital for another start.
Not hopeless men: here was a junction which
Ensured a Harvey Eating House; next year
Congress would pass the Enabling Act; right here
Would be a metropolis: they would all be rich.

These consummations meanwhile they awaited
In the drug-store, talking politics till night.
Texans, farmers, and carpet-baggers they hated;
Feared the Negro—"This state should be lily-white,"
And arguments to damn whatever scheme
Were the epithets "Utopia" and "dream."

459

III

AUGUST

*D*AY *after day the treeless street was baked*
  By intolerable sun.   The moulded wagon-tracks
Were rayed and rifted by the widening cracks.
Through wavering blurs of heat the red bricks ached.
Drouth made the plain stretch flatter and more wide.
There was no dew in August, there was no shade.
Upon the lake the Commercial Club had made
Hundreds of dead fish floated on their side.

Walking the sweltering street, "wet leaves," one said.
"Rainy leaves," "drenched leaves"—oh words like rillets stealing
Amongst the tortured brain's heat-tangled mazes.
"Drenched leaves," "wet leaves"—savouring the words of healing
For crisp forgetful moments the spirit fed
Upon cool freshness of the cress-like phrases.

IV

MURDERERS

*O*N *Landau's corner, the loafers saw them fall.*
  Meeting, each drew with an oath; they fired together,
And each fell dying without knowing whether
His enemy fell too.   And that was all.
The town threshed through the story, nothing loath—
Simple enough, they told it over and over:
How Billy Ascham was the woman's lover,
The Doctor's wife's; the Doctor had warned them both.

Afterwards, when the town forgot at last,
Not nudging nor whispering even when the woman passed
With that hard, veiled look of hers, one child still thought
With dull, perplexing pain, for a long while,
Of a trick with matches that Mr. Ascham taught,
And of the red-haired Doctor's freckly smile.

V

THE CARNIVAL

*T*HE *carnival came late to town that year,*
  Tents pitched forlornly in the baseball park,
Where a cold wind extinguished every spark

Of merry-making.   A ferris-wheel, austere
In skeleton loneliness, viewed vacant grounds.
It rained continuously, a dreary, chill
September drizzle.   The merry-go-round was still;
Half-hearted spiels and catcalls the only sounds.

My brother and I, small, shivering wretches beneath
Our papery coats, stood with chattering teeth,
Drinking in pleasure desired through arid days
As we watched a draggled woman lift to our gaze
Grisly tentacles of the octopus, and explain,
"This one killed three sailors off the coast of Spain . . ."

VI

MRS. HASTINGS

AROUND Mrs. Hastings' house, verbena grew.
She coaxed her roses from reluctant earth,
And tenderly nursed jessamine to birth,
And through long drouth, her iris-plot was blue.
She told of an Irish childhood; of hopeless hours
Waiting tables in Dallas; of how the saints one day
Had sent Sam Hastings to snatch her far away
And build the yellow house amid the flowers.

Sam and her boy—coarse as the hides they tanned,
Gamblers and drunkards and foul-mouthed fools—no less—
Were tinged with romance by her tenderness.
"I would not die before them!" the soft voice said.
"How could I bear that an unloving hand
Should bathe and tend the bodies of my dead!"

VII

METHODIST REVIVAL

WHEN the throbbing drums of the opening hymns were still,
The preacher shouted, "Brethren! let us pray!"
And ardently he pled that God that day
Might bend an hundred sinners to His will.
The prayer ended, he touched a lighter note—
Joked with the choir, and merrily mocked the Devil;
Then flung God's curse at the drunken nation's revel
With a voice that sobbed and fluted in his throat.

"Oh, my beloved . . . . !" he launched his passionate pleas.
A woman stood. "Praise Jesus!" shrieked another,
A girl ran sobbing and knelt beside her mother.
At a sudden word, again the music swept
The tent with thunder. Quivering, one wept,
Wretched, and shamed, and groveling on one's knees.

VIII

PRAIRIE SKY

SOMETIMES for days one can forget the sky
*   That god-like, indifferent, never fails to bless*
With unflawed beauty our huddled littleness.
One can forget—the meddling breeze goes by
Piling vacant lots with waste to catch the eye;
Or mud, or dust, or merely the heat that shows
In quivering air, can make the senses close
To everything that is far or vast or high.

Then a scrap, a bird, the casual glance beguiles
Up, up, up!—till once more, swiftly, surely,
The clean, keen blade of ecstasy stabs purely:
Oh, glorious blue across which clouds are blowing,
Or lucent gray the far rain-tempests showing,
Or sunset blazing for ten thousand miles!

Anthropology

THE ORIGIN AND SPREAD OF CULTURES

By Robert H. Lowie

On one of his jaunts through Germany Goethe fell in with a droll pair of panacea-mongers,—Lavater, the mystic and phrenologist, and Basedow, the reformer of education and Christianity. The poet thus found himself one day at an inn with Lavater on one side holding forth to a rustic parson on the meaning of Revelation, while Basedow was demonstrating to a dancing-master that the rite of baptism was a superannuated custom; and the experience evoked the oft-quoted lines,

Prophete rechts, Prophete links,
Das Weltkind in der Mitte.

American anthropologists find themselves nowadays in somewhat the same position as Goethe at the Coblenz tavern. The British historical school is bullying them on the one side, while the German-Austrian *kulturhistorische* school is cajoling them on the other, both serenely certain that they have found the solution of the anthropological riddles of the universe; yet the calm commonsense of the American *Weltkind* somehow manages to withstand alike the hectoring of Professor Elliot Smith's disciples and the soft wooing of Fathers Wilhelm Schmidt and Wilhelm Koppers.

What is it all about? That part of the science which on this side of the Atlantic is called ethnology attempts to study the whole of mankind's social heritage,—to determine what it is in each particular case, and by what means each people obtained their share. Now it is obvious that any part of a people's culture may have originated on the spot or it may have been imported from without; and so whenever the same mechanical device or game or belief turns up in two distinct regions the question arises, which of the two logical possibilities applies? A classical writer of the old type like the illustrious E. B. Tylor was content to judge each case on its merits, and the majority of American ethnologists have followed in his wake, though on the whole rather more strongly impressed than their predecessor with the frequency and extent of cultural borrowing. Not that an actual migration of peoples is deemed necessary for the spread of a custom or invention; mere friendly or even hostile contact is often sufficient to carry an idea or an object hundreds of miles from its starting-point. What is more, this sort of thing goes back to, nay far beyond, the pale of written history: yellow-amber beads from the Baltic, where alone such material occurs, have been unearthed in ancient Greek graves, and in Dakota mounds seashells from the Atlantic mingle with those from the Pacific coast. Yet in this country this notion of diffusion has not been carried to extremes; while a very large portion of any particular culture may be admitted to come from an alien home, it is generally recognized that occasionally, even though rarely, a new idea arises spontaneously and that such a lucky chance may be repeated.

It is quite true that such duplication is not nearly so common as might be supposed. A layman is likely to point to the records of the Patent Office and ask whether the same discovery has not been frequently repeated. But he forgets that the conditions are very different now from

463

what they were in early and primitive days. First of all, every single modern investigator starts with the same stock of ideas and has access to identical instruments, mathematical aids, and what not. But the primitive inventors of two different areas lacked this identity of cultural background, and so it certainly was less easy for one of them to repeat the other's achievement. Secondly, modern scientists usually deliberately set themselves a definite problem and work systematically toward its solution, whereas the inventions of their savage colleagues were undoubtedly casual and often accidental. There is thus no genuine parallel, and the modern instances do not prove anything for the dim past.

All this may be readily conceded. But the historical schools of both Germany and England go further. The very idea that anything should ever have been invented twice seems to them ridiculous twaddle; and accordingly members of both have constructed complete schemes for the culture-history of the world on the assumption that every element of culture goes back to a solitary place of origin and was thence diffused to wherever it may have been found since. This harmony between two groups of workers in different countries might be a splendid argument for the correctness of the conclusions reached were it not for a trifling circumstance, to wit, that though they are completely at one in insisting that diffusion is the key to all the mysteries of culture history, the two schemes are alas! in utter disagreement as to every other point; they differ as to the time, the place, the combination of traits associated with the spread of culture. That little circumstance, given the *Weltkind's* Missourian frailty, somehow tends to cast doubt on the certainty of their conclusions.

It must not be assumed that the two schools represent the same level of scholarship. Both, indeed, present a curious twist that well merits psychological, not to say psychoanalytical, study. But the Aus-

trians, biased as they may be, not only envisage culture as a whole but are bending every effort to keep abreast of modern thought. Not so the British diffusionists, who for that very reason present a rather more amusing spectacle for popular entertainment,—especially in their latest pronunciamento, Mr. W. J. Perry's five-hundred page volume on "The Children of the Sun." These Britons form very much of a close corporation. For some occult reason the theoretical arguments of writers outside their group are largely ignored. Does insular etiquette perchance demand that one must not quote men whom one has not met socially? On the other hand, there is constant appeal to comrades-at-arms. The late Dr. Rivers quotes Professor Elliot Smith and Mr. Perry; Professor Elliot Smith recites the tentative hypotheses of Dr. Rivers as though they were geometrical propositions derived from basic axioms; and Mr. Perry determines moot-questions by an appeal to Professor Elliot Smith and Dr. Rivers.

The essence of their theory may be put into a few words. The only place where any worth-while evolution of culture has taken place, they contend, is Egypt; the remainder of the world represents progressive stages in the decay of an "archaic civilization" that started globe-trotting some time subsequent to 2200 B.C. Do the women of New Guinea make a crude kind of pottery? Then it shows only the degenerate form of an ancient technique evolved on the Nile. Does any tribe anywhere worship the sun? Then that notion could only come to them from the same source and has of course suffered the usual sea-change. And what is asserted for the solar cult is suggested as highly probable for all belief in the supernatural: "prior to the coming of this [Egyptian] civilization the native peoples were devoid of any magical or religious practices or ideas." There is thus a complete reversal of the customary point of view, inasmuch as the culture of such rude peoples as the Australians is defined as not primitive at all, but as merely part of the Egyptian wreckage. Consistently with this general scheme, Central American civilization is conceived as an importation ultimately traceable to the Nile, while all the North American cultures represent merely fragments of the "archaic civilization" derived from Mexico.

It is not easy to criticize this structure of theory because from whichever direction one blows upon it the house of cards collapses forthwith. For one thing, students of the Near Orient are not yet by any means agreed as to whether the seat of the earliest civilization is to be sought in Egypt or in Babylonia, and even if it were true, as Mr. Perry asserts, that agriculture originated on the Nile, to decide the antiquity of all other inventions by this one is a most naïve form of economic determinism. Still less acceptable is the summary refusal to grant any kind of inventiveness to the ruder peoples of the world. It is true enough that there is no mysterious impulse in the human psyche to progress *ad infinitum;* yet wherever we look we find very neat adaptations to local conditions. Did the Eskimo derive their snow-goggles from Egypt via Mexico, as Mr. Perry's theory implies? How is it that the California Indian, otherwise so simple in his mode of life, is second to none as a plaiter of basketwork? And from whom could the tropical forest-dwellers of South America learn to prepare their staple diet by removing the poisonous principle of an *indigenous* plant?

The obvious fact is that creation is not restricted to one favored portion of the species but that its mental prerequisites are widely, even though sparingly, distributed. When different peoples with their respective inventions come into contact, there is a chance for the exchange of ideas, and the resulting enrichment of both cultures, itself a stimulus to men of genius, leads to still greater achievements. The notion that when two peoples of varying culture meet, the simpler plays a purely passive part is demonstrably false, and demonstrating its falsity lays the ax to the root of the pan-Egyptological mania. Again and again we find that "higher" peoples borrow from "lower." The Caucasian discoverers introduced metal tools and horses into America, but they borrowed maize, potatoes, and tobacco. China has been a remarkable agency for spreading civilization in the East, but her records show one case after another in which the Chinese adopted the devices of lower cultures.

If this is true on the material side, where the more completely organized people manifestly enjoy a definite advantage, it obviously holds at least equally true in the realm of belief and fancy. An African witch-doctor or American *shaman* is certainly not badly handicapped in a race with Egyptian hierophants when the goal is some theory of the universe, let al·one when it is not a matter of theory at all but of emotional reaction to the ever-present crises of everyday existence. Not a few Egyptian religious ideas and rites, indeed, may have been adopted by the Egyptians through association with simpler peoples; others undoubtedly antedate the historic civilization of the Nile valley and are merely survivals of notions going back to dim antiquity, to a period when all humanity shared a limited stock of simple cultural elements.

There is, of course, something fascinating about a scheme of such simplicity as that propounded by the pan-Egyptians, just as there is about the quest for the philosopher's stone and the mystery of perpetual motion. But Nature and History alas! are not *simplistes*. It is also an agreeable exercise for leisure hours to thumb one's nose at Commonsense, to look at the world while standing on one's head; we all like to do that from time to time. But it is perilous to turn a somersault while walking the tight-rope of scientific argument.

Music

A MORATORIUM FOR OPERA

By W. J. Henderson

Cannot a patient but weary world be rid for a term of that beaten bladder called opera which is now tied around its neck? Why not let us indulge, in New York at any rate, in the bliss of a five years' moratorium of lyric drama, that real music may be free to stretch her glorious limbs and chant her hymns that need no painted faces or scenic gauds to help them?

Why is so much solemn and apparently philosophical criticism wasted on this limping hybrid of the arts? Its origin was respectable enough, to be sure, for Angelo Poliziano, a real poet, fathered it, and the famous old marquisate of Mantua was its cradle. But though it came into the world with the peplum of Minerva streaming from its shoulders, its chastity was soon debauched by the passionate sensuousness of the Italian mind. It declined through the whole Sixteenth Century and was rescued from total destruction only by the reform movement started in the Palazzo Bardi. No sooner had the young liberators, led by Rinuccini and Peri, given it a second chance at an honest existence than public opera-houses began to be opened and the rescued victim of spendthrift princes was dragged from her narrow path and made common again in the streets of Venice and Rome.

A creation which had started in life as the entertainment of the most intelligent aristocracy the world has ever known found its late Seventeenth Century triumph in furnishing tunes for gondoliers to shrill through the *canali piccoli* after male sopranos had fluted them in the dozen opera-houses of Venetian alleyways. The dullards who came in the early Eighteenth Century to sit in the seats of the Baglioni, the Gonzaghe and the Medici took their lyric pleasures just as the gondoliers did. It was no wonder that in the late years of that cycle D'Alembert scoffed at the arbiters of fashion in Paris when they loosed what they called opinions about opera!

"Such people," he wrote, "when they talk about melodious music simply mean commonplace music which has been dinned into their ears a hundred times. For these people a poor air is one which they cannot hum and a bad opera is one of which they cannot learn the airs by heart."

Did he live now, he would thus blaspheme the sacred "Pagliacci." Away with all such men to the Tower! Let the curtain rise on the picture of the interior of Saint Andrea della Valle. Let Mario paint and sing. Let Tosca be furious with jealousy. Let Scarpia be black as his inky robe. As statesmen, philosophers, men of the world and persons of superior taste, we shall take it each according to his humor. And the hopeless old globe will go ringing down the grooves of conventionality just as it has done since Adam ate the apple.

The opera of today is in a sorry state, indeed, and the opera going public of New York is in a condition to excite pity. If Wagner's greatest works had to come newly before this public as novelties and ask for favor, they would be incontinently damned by a Society which at this hour secretly abhors them and usually gives away its subscription tickets on the evenings of their performances. If even so recent a reincarnation of the splendid soul of the Italian Renaissance as Montemezzi's "L'Amore dei Tre Re," which was new here only ten years ago, had now to gain its place on the New York stage, it would be thrust into outer darkness to make way for Giordano's "Fédora" and Massenet's "Thaïs." For of such operas, with their lollipop music and their jugglery of gestures and posings, the ideal répertoire of the patrons of "the greatest opera house in the world" is constituted.

But Society, with all its petty peccadillos and traditional sins, cannot be burdened with the chief blame for the state of opera in New York. It keeps its platitudinous comments to itself; what parades as public opinion is the vociferation of a small army of standees. The thunders of applause following the strident emission of banal tunes into the Metropolitan auditorium come from connoisseurs whose taste is equally ravished by the floating serenaders of the Venetian lagoons or the traveling bands on the Capri steamers. Watching the frantic demonstrations of these standees, agitated by the stentorian shoutings which they call singing, one is driven to a sudden recollection of words of Nietzsche which seem vaguely to apply to the case:

> Must they needs have their ears beaten to pieces before they will learn to hear with their eyes? Must one rattle like a kettle-drum or a fast day preacher?

For the conditions which exist in the Metropolitan Opera House, the glass of American operatic fashion and its source of form, we undoubtedly owe some gratitude to the present administration. Twenty-five years ago the Metropolitan was famous for its matchless assemblage of singers, its inferior chorus, its negligible ballet and its unmentionable scenery. All this has been reformed. Today we have scenery of excellent quality, a competent chorus, an excellent ballet, a tolerable orchestra and a large company containing perhaps half a dozen artists, of whom possibly two would have been admitted to the first rank in that earlier day. As a distinguished personage remarked in Milan last summer, "All that is needed to make a successful opera institution in New York is two good singers and the press."

For the daily newspapers bravely uphold the standards of art as they are now flaunted at the opera. The reasons for this attitude ought to be clear to any careful newspaper reader. The Metropolitan is regarded as a fashionable place of amusement, not as a temple of artistic ideals. It necessarily caters to Society and secondarily to that vociferous proletariat which

nightly shakes the rafters with its approval of musical rant and fustian. A struggle to create a body of artistic ideals among such patrons would be inevitably futile. No newspaper desires to make itself obnoxious to the general public by assuming the habit of a common scold, and as such it would be certainly viewed if it kept on, week in and week out, mercilessly exposing the shortcomings of the Metropolitan and its presentations. Thus the chroniclers of the press have fallen into the practise of treating the routine performances as casually as possible, inviting consideration only to whatever may be of passing merit and saying little about permanent defects. That there is frequent opportunity to praise is due to the individual efforts of certain members of the organization, and to Mr. Gatti-Casazza, whose untiring search after a répertoire commands admiration.

The standards of criticism now full-masted in the press-room of the Metropolitan Opera House flutter gently under the influence of the subtle system of education which has existed there for years back. Oscar Hammerstein invented the expression "educational opera," by which he meant operatic performances by merely acceptable singers, given at prices intended to bring into the opera-house persons previously debarred from its joys by the limitations of their pocket-books. It cannot be said that the pocket-book has played the same part in the system of education which now operates at the Metropolitan. As the quality of the performances has gone down the price of orchestra stalls has gone up. The public has simply been educated to pay the prices and to believe the performances to be the best in the world. The older newspaper critics have not been able to escape the process of education. They take their pleasures modestly. The younger ones never heard any better opera.

But the blame for operatic decay cannot be all laid at the doors of the Metropolitan. The seed of disease is in the blood of opera itself. It is an art form suffering from anaemia. The suggestion that it be sent into retirement for five years is not an idle jest. Such a moratorium would immeasurably benefit musical art. All the unmusical people in the City of Shams would be compelled to seek their true level, the vaudeville theatre, and those who really hungered for music could satisfy their appetites with real works of art, the symphonies of Beethoven and Brahms, the piano music of Chopin, the vast and amazing tone pictures of Stravinsky. Instead of joining in the vehement *bravi* evoked by the still more vehement bawlings of Signor Stridolini or the anguished shrieks of Mlle. Morbidezza they would begin to acquire some insight into the true beauty of musical performance. They would listen to the piano playing of Josef Hofmann, the violin playing of Fritz Kreisler, the singing of Frieda Hempel. They might even soar so magnificently above their own dusty level as to go to a concert of the Flonzaley Quartet. In the course of the five years some of them might learn that watching the silly antics of some ponderous basso as *Don Basilio* in a soporific representation of Rossini's "Il Barbiere di Siviglia" is not half so much fun as attending a Sunday evening concert of the International Composers' Guild and studying the futile struggles of Darius Milhaud and Arnold Schönberg to raise themselves by their boot straps to the shoulders of Stravinsky.

Philosophy

THE CRITICAL REALISTS

By Woodbridge Riley

The essence, or logical (neutral) entity, which is my datum in a given case of perception or conception, may be identically the same essence that is your datum, and even the very essence, or character, of the existing object perceived or conceived by us both. This essence may be said to have being or subsistence independently of my, or your, consciousness of it, and of its embodiment in the object. . . . Suppose, *e.g.*, that my perceptual datum is the character-complex a round-wheel-about-three-feet-in-diameter-moving-away-from-me-and- now- between-this-house-and-the-next . . .

THESE are not quotations from the very blank verse of Gertrude Stein, but passages from a treatise on the latest invention of American philosophers, Critical Realism. In darkest Dewey and his Instrumentalism there are paragraphs that are hard enough, and yet worse are in the New Realism in the original, but for uncouth words and a style as technical as that of Thomas Aquinas, without his clarity, I commend the works of the Critical Realists. Dewey uses technical tags such as "things experienced as" and charges the Presentative Realist with "substituting for irreducibility and unambiguity of logical functions (use in inference) physical and metaphysical isolation and elementariness," and the New Realists have their strange slogans, such as "neutral mosaic" and "ego-centric predicament," but all these may be worked out with the aid of an unabridged dictionary and the midnight oil. What however, is one to make of such strophes as in this in the tomes of the Critical Realists: "When we see faces, we do not see our seeing of them, but only the faces . . . That which we feel, when we feel, *i. e.* distinctly attend to a sensation, is capable of existing when it is not felt."

It is no wonder that William James complained of the absence of the polishing process in the younger generation of American philosophers. Their obscurity has now reached such a pitch that they do not even understand one another. Thus, one of the Critical Realists declares that the Pragmatists say that ultimate reality consists of experiences—"meaning by this, only God and Professor Dewey know what." Another exclaims that he cannot get the faintest notion of what is meant by this passage on mental activity: "Instead of acting on the world, we so act upon ourselves as to place ourselves where we see things in an order and combination different in the case of illusion from the actual."

So much for the style of the Realists, whether they call themselves New or Critical. Several of them were pupils of James, but whereas he preserved his thoughts in amber they preserve theirs in mud, like the Chinese with their eggs of ancient vintage. From the list, however, one should make one notable exception, and that is George Santayana. It is he who has furnished his colleagues with their main doctrine, that of "essences," or universals which may be given directly to the mind, data which are not existing things, nor states of mind, but ideal. He has done this in a manner so precise and plausible that he has been able to put forward as a novelty a notion that is as old as the Middle Ages, if not older.

This doctrine of the possibility of cognition by means of essences or universals was prepared for by the New Realists, and in two ways: by their notion of "subsistents," and by their theory of the "extension of consciousness." They had the notion of subsistents as "facts," capable of being held before the mind; actual and possible objects of thought, independent realities like the relation of the radius to the circumference or even the square root of minus one. They also had the theory of the extension of consciousness. This meant that consciousness takes unto itself a "new" dimension into which it protrudes and thus becomes a part of that "neutral mosaic" which is neither matter nor mind, but the realm of pure being, a realm which may explain, for example, why "the algebra in our mind also exists in nature."

Such are some of the technical terms which must be learned by the player in this new game of metaphysical mah jong. But the game is really not new. It is the ancient philosophical amusement called reification, the turning of thoughts into things. In Western philosophy it began with what has been well described as the olympianization of ideas. Just as among the Greeks men became heroes, heroes demigods, and demi-gods the gods themselves on top of Olympus, so things, terms, classes, universals, were gradually raised up into heaven. Thus Plato's empyrean has been brought back again, and propositions, relations and universals have become realities, subsisting not in the space and time of ordinary things, but in the "non-spatial extension" of the New Realists.

Such are the subsistents which, by the Critical Realists, are identified with essences—data hovering between the individual and outside objects, in a peculiar world of their own. It is one thing to postulate these essences; it is quite another to know them. Thus the problem of the possibility of knowledge is raised. How is the mind to reach out into this strange realm of subsistents, data, essences? The English Realists achieve the feat by means of their doctrine of awareness or compresence, which posits a situation in which thought and thing overlap. This superposition, which recalls placing a triangle of solid lines over an identical triangle of dotted lines, seems to be identical with the "neutral mosaic" of the New Realists; and consciousness becomes that "cross section of the infinite realm of being to which the organism specifically responds."

But all this speculation carries no conviction. It turns the brain into a kind of telautographic machine whose signatures are not honored. Anyone can fill out and sign a mental check, but who will accept it? Some of the New Realists try to wriggle out of the dilemma by speaking of a nonspatial extension of consciousness, but into what realm they project or protrude their thoughts they do not tell. At times they seem forced over into a hypothetical fourth dimension, but to call the things they put into this dimension "real" is not acceptable even to the mathematicians. The latter, if a lay reader can understand them, do not utilize the fourth dimension as "non-spatial extension," but as fourfold space. This space they use as a postulate, not as a place. It is simply mental room in which to carry on mental gymnastics. However, the Critical Realists appear to have borrowed it from the New Realists, just as the latter borrowed it from Bertrand Russell. At any rate, it gives them elbow-room in which to practise their speculative jiu-jitsu. By it they are enabled to manipulate their entities, which they describe as neither psychological nor physical but of a peculiar type belonging to logic. Thus, in reading a book, what is presented to the mind, they say, is the significance of the ideas set forth and not the mere printed characters, and this significance is not an existence and not in time and space, but a purely logical entity; or to put it in another way, "a sensation is capable of existing when it is not felt, and does so exist."

Now, what does all this mean? It is, in fact, nothing but an exploded theory which pretty well passed away in the Middle Ages. In other words, all these precious essences are nothing but the old Scholastic "quiddities," slyly injected into the skulls of his colleagues by Santayana. When Sherlock Holmes exclaimed "Quick, Watson, the needle!" he knew precisely what he was going to get. The Critical Realist evidently does not, but a casual reference to Thomas Aquinas and his quiddities will discover the true source and character of the drug. Santayana is a past master at persuasion, and as a Thomist he has a training in clearness and precision of statement that has enabled him to put across what another Thomist has called "a wild hypothesis of Scholasticism." This hypothesis assumes the possibility of cognition by purely intellectual "species." Being interpreted, that means that as our senses perceive objects by means of an impression on the sense organ (for example, the image on the retina, communicated to the brain) which impression is not itself received by the mind, but is simply the medium by which we perceive the object, so our intellect knows by means of impressions, which are the media by which it knows ideas. Now, impressions are but attributes of material objects, abstracted, that is, considered apart from the objects. Hence, by means of these impressions the mind directly knows abstract qualities or quiddities which exist individually in material objects, but it knows them, not as existing individually, but as potentially universal.

Thus Thomas Aquinas in the first book of the "Summa." This doctrine of an underlying reality Santayana puts forward as self-evident and then he runs through the whole gamut of Scholastic Realism. By its aid he so charms his audience that they become enraptured even of essences, just as the lady at the court of Louis XIV did of the vortices of Descartes. Thus, American philosophy, in this, its latest phase, is little but a revival of outworn mediaeval Realism, with its intellectual species, quiddities, essences, call them what you will—entities ever hovering between subject and object, outside space and time, with about as much to do with real life as the smile of the Cheshire cat after the cat itself has faded away.

THE END OF A LITERARY MYSTERY

BY FREDERICK P. HIER, JR.

WHEN John Burroughs died the way was opened for publishing a curious story which had lain in secret since 1867, when Burroughs published his first book, "Notes on Walt Whitman as Poet and Person." This story, involving Whitman and Burroughs in one of the strangest literary ventures on record, would never have become known but for a series of accidents. For the book itself dropped out of print in 1871 and Whitman's instruction to one of his literary executors, to write the story after Burroughs' death, survived that executor only by the narrowest margin.

My curiosity was aroused by this book, when, on reading it in conjunction with Burroughs' "Whitman, A Study," published in 1896, I was struck by the marked difference in their styles. The greater vigor of the former I at first attributed to Burroughs' youth, but after maturer reflection the difference did not seem explicable on any theory of natural development. At the time I left the question open, but with the conviction that the first book, contrary to what might be expected, was much stronger and more original than the later one. Subsequently a more careful analysis convinced me that "Notes on Walt Whitman as Poet and Person" was not what it appeared to be on its face, the veritable first book of John Burroughs, but that it was something else—that the strange circumstances surrounding its first publication and unexplained disappearance sufficed to make it one of the mystery books of American literature.

It became clear to me, for example, that the author of the "Notes" had not only an accurate knowledge of the general facts of Whitman's life, but also an uncanny grasp of the undercurrents of his personal growth and integration and an attitude too familiar and nonchalant to have been acquired in the three years of Burroughs' acquaintance with him. The unmasking aptness of the quotations, unimprovable after half a century's study, argued too great a perception in a beginner. The sure extravagance of certain statements about Whitman, which brought down on Burroughs immediate criticism in some quarters as hopelessly prejudiced, made it look doubtful if Burroughs himself would have put things so abruptly. Most significant of all was the manner of expression. There was a vigorous breadth and sweep and a native, poetic feeling, arriving at an orchestral total effect, which was not the manner of Burroughs at all.

These hints led to an extended search. It was found that Burroughs' style during the same period was characteristically different from that of the 1867 "Notes." There was a gentle, contemplative moderation in it, like a ship under easy sail, as, for example, in his Whitman piece written for the *Galaxy* in 1866, quite in contrast with the bluff vehemence of the Whitman book. Burroughs had a meandering touch, part of his attraction, whereas the flight of the "Notes" was that of the eagle. "Wake Robin," published in 1871, which Burroughs had written from 1863 onward, during the very period of the "Notes," announces in the second paragraph of its preface:

Though written less in the spirit of exact science than with the freedom of love and old acquaintance, yet I have in no instance taken liberty with facts, or allowed my imagination to influence me to the extent of giving a false impression or a wrong coloring. I have reaped my harvest more in the woods than in the study; what I offer, in fact, is a careful and conscientious record of actual observations and experiences, and is true as it stands written, every word of it. But what has interested me most in Ornithology is the pursuit, the chase, the discovery; that part of it which is akin to hunting, fishing and wild sports, and which I could carry with me in my eye and ear wherever I went.

In the preface to the Whitman "Notes," the second paragraph is in the same general form, but note the difference:

In History, at wide intervals, in different fields of action, there come (it is a thrice told tale,) special developments of individualities, and of that something we suggest by the word Genius—individuals whom their own days little suspect, and never realize, but who, it turns out, mark and make new eras, plant the standard again ahead, and in one man personify vast races and sweeping revolutions. I consider Walt Whitman such an individual, I consider that America is illustrated in him; and that Democracy, as now launched forth upon its many-vortexed experiment for good or evil, (and the need whereof no eye can foresee,) is embodied, and for the first time in Poetry grandly and fully uttered, in him.

Here in the latter quotation, is the barbarous and elaborate interpolation unmistakably characteristic, not of Burroughs surely, but of Whitman himself. The words genius, history, and democracy are capitalized, as was Whitman's practise with these and other words he considered important—and not Burroughs'. The punctuation is singularly his, especially in the two parentheses, for as Emory Holloway observes in his recent work, "The Uncollected Poetry and Prose of Walt Whitman," "his system of punctuation was unique... A parenthesis seldom sufficed, but must be reinforced with commas." Practically all the parentheses in the book are thus reinforced.

In fact, the style of the "Notes" is like Whitman everywhere. His personality underlined his commonest utterance, and in his more deliberate efforts, especially those pronouncing his deeper purposes, it assumed the peculiar forms which have become known as Whitmanesque. His first three articles about himself (to be regarded

further), his explanatory projection of the poet's mission in the introduction to his first edition of "Leaves of Grass," the reply to Emerson in 1856, and, in fact, the full course of his collected prose, are one in blood, bone, body and soul with the "Notes." Here, for example, is a quotation from page 39:

We have swarms of little poetlings, producing swarms of soft and sickly little rhymelets, on a par with the feeble calibre and vague and puerile inward melancholy, and outward affectation and small talk, of that genteel mob called "society." We have, also, more or less of statues and statuettes, and plenty of architecture and upholstery and filigree work, very pretty and ornamental, and fit for those who are fit for it.

In precisely like measure and voice, Whitman said in his "Democratic Vistas" (1871):

Do you call those genteel little creatures American poets? Do you term that perpetual, pistareen, paste-pot work, American art, American drama, taste, verse? I think I hear, echoed as from some mountain-top afar in the west, the scornful laugh of the Genius of these States.

One native and exclusive Whitman phrase, "spinal marrow," occurs throughout his writing. He used it typically in his Shakespeare essay (Collected Prose, page 283), and again in his last explanation of his meanings (Collected Prose, page 527): "If I am to give impromptu a hint of the *spinal marrow* of the business." He wrote of "my *spinal* and deliberate request," in a letter to Dr. Bucke in September, 1888. Very indicative therefore is the appearance of this phrase in the "Notes," where, on page 119, one reads: "This is the *spinal marrow* of the various poems."

As a result of all this intrinsic evidence, here only partly represented, I concluded that "Notes on Walt Whitman as Poet and Person," alleged to be John Burroughs' first book, was really his only in very small part,—that it was mostly written by Walt Whitman himself.

II

External evidence bearing upon this conclusion soon added to its weight. Whitman's essay on Burns, first printed in 1882 (Complete Prose, page 395), is called, "Robert Burns as Poet and Person"; the same peculiarity of title. The only other extended piece on Whitman during the 1867 period, O'Conner's "The Good Gray Poet," was, like the "Notes," published under the name of one of Whitman's closest friends during a time of continual association; yet every line is as different from Whitman as could be. Whitman's letters to his mother during 1866-67-68, contain references to Burroughs' *Galaxy* article on himself, enclose a special copy to her, talk of his forthcoming 1867 edition of "Leaves of Grass," but never once mention the 1867 "Notes on Walt Whitman." Recall that this was the first book about him, 108 pages in length, and that Burroughs' 9-page magazine piece was referred to in at least three separate letters. Very curious, too, is the letter Whitman wrote to A. K. Butts on February 8, 1874, referring to copies of his books:

> O'Kane has undoubtedly sent you *all* the copies of my books remaining in his possession—he received originally—239 Leaves of Grass, 100 As a Strong Bird, 92 Democratic Vistas, 45 Notes by John Burroughs, etc.—You now have *all* my books in the market.

It is not so important, perhaps, that in a list of what Whitman twice called "my books," "Notes by John Burroughs" should appear. But it is very notable that this was the only book about himself that Whitman ever handled and sold personally. Why was not Burroughs, the supposed author, or Redfield, the publisher, in possession of and engaged in the sale of the book? In 1871, Whitman brought out three books; a new "Leaves of Grass," "Passage to India," and "Democratic Vistas"; and Burroughs two, "Wake Robin" and the second edition of the "Notes on Walt Whitman." All the Whitman volumes *and the* "*Notes*," were published by Redfield, Whitman taking personal charge; whereas "Wake Robin" was put into the hands of another house, which has printed all of Burroughs' subsequent

books and continues to publish them to this day.

Among the scores of conversations about Burroughs recorded by Traubel there is not a single definite averment by Whitman regarding the "Notes." There is one, however, in a little-known book, a highly pointed, personal fragment, which to those acquainted with Whitman's method of production will come as an intimate disclosure. It is known that he made notes beforehand in which he projected roughly and in the largest suggestiveness the general drift of a poem or article. These notes often contain in a few lines the germ and scope of an elaborate piece. After his death these notes were divided among his executors. The share that fell to Dr. Richard M. Bucke was edited and published by him in a volume entitled "Notes and Fragments" in 1899. In his preface Dr. Bucke says that "every word printed in the body of this book is before me in the handwriting of Walt Whitman." On page 64, in the section relating to the meaning and intention of "Leaves of Grass," appears the following:

CURRENT CRITICISM

Notes on Walt Whitman as Poet and Person. By John Burroughs. New York: American News Co., 1871.

It seems as if the debate over Walt Whitman and his "Leaves of Grass" were not only going to be kept up with more and more animation and earnestness every year, but that the discussion is to bring (and indeed has so brought already) an examination unwonted among us, of the very bases of the art of poetry, and of the high original laws of ethics and criticism. These bases—how do they refer to our social age and country? These laws—what are they, as applied to the poets and artists of the first class, for America and for the wants of the American people? Such are the questions which the advent of Walt Whitman has evidently roused and of which these notes are attempts to at least suggest the answer.

This might have been a forenote or an afternote to the book (the date, 1871, was evidently filled in later) but in either event it is certainly one of Whitman's musing notes on one of his *own* productions, containing in a single paragraph the fundamental design of the whole so-called Burroughs book!

III

Now let us see what was Burroughs' overt reaction to the situation. Happy at the time in getting the publicity of association with the greater name of Whitman and of saying something for the man he loved, he would no doubt in maturer years repudiate, in his consciousness at least, the book that was not wholly his own. That is exactly what he did. For the 1871 edition of "Notes on Walt Whitman" was its last one. That year, Burroughs' authentic first book, "Wake Robin," came out. It has gone through innumerable editions since then, but the Whitman book was allowed to fall out of print and sight and has never reappeared. It is the single and only title in Burroughs' long list of twenty-one volumes which was never and is not today included in his collected works. He would never consent to another edition after the second of 1871, though strongly urged to do so in the eighties and after Whitman's death.

But even this fact might not be conclusive if Burroughs' "Walt Whitman, A Study," published 25 years later, in 1896, was an enlargement of, or superseded the earlier and smaller work. In that case it would be only natural for one to wish his mature work perpetuated and his early attempts forgotten. But such is not the case and Burroughs knew it, as we shall presently see. The 1896 "Study" is written on an entirely new plan, which does not resemble that of the early book. It is in no sense an augmentation of the original scheme, corrected and amplified in the light of more complete knowledge. In fact, the "Study" does not even refer to the former book, directly or indirectly. To my knowledge there is no other case in literature where an author has written (to all appearances) two books on the same subject or person, and in the second book completely ignored the first. Some explanation or hint is always given, in a preface or introduc-tion, as to why the second book is necessary and how it adds to the first or provides a more deliberate judgment. To cite a former book, in matters it is not desired to repeat, is a natural and common practise. But Burroughs, in his "Study," says on page 7 that he has no apology to offer for making another addition to the growing Whitman literature without breathing a word about his previous book. More, he told W. B. Harte in 1896 that "he had for some time cherished the idea of writing a book upon Whitman"—as though he had held a project in his heart which he had never yet accomplished!

As the evidence indicating Whitman's authorship of the "Notes" piled up, my astonishment grew that the masquerade should not have been discovered long ago. It would be inexplicable were it not for the fact that the book is so rare and diffi-cult to obtain; most of the writers on Whitman, I presume, have never seen a copy. At any rate, the assumption that the book was Burroughs' own has been prac-tically universal, and both Whitman and Burroughs fostered it. Burroughs, nowhere that I have found, makes the out and out avowment that the book was his, but he allowed his biographer and close personal adviser to call it his first volume. And we find Whitman writing to W. M. Rossetti on December 3, 1867: "I sent you hence Nov. 23,—a copy of Mr. Burroughs' Notes," and on May 9, 1868, to Charles Hine: "I send you by same mail as this—a little book, written by Mr. Burroughs (a second Thoreau)—the book—all about my pre-cious self."

Whitman's closest friends repeat the same thing. O'Connor wrote to Whitman, May 9, 1867: "He (Allen) doesn't say a word about John Burroughs' book, etc. I have written to him saying that John will at once put the book to press himself." Dr. Bucke in his "Walt Whitman," 1883, quotes the "Notes" as Burroughs's. The standard biographies and studies are no exception; Perry, Platt, Kennedy, Car-penter, all credit Burroughs with the book.

All the bibliographies which include biographical material, save that of Wells and Goldsmith (1922), list the book in like manner. But elsewhere there are hints at the truth, usually somewhat guarded. Whitman's literary executors—two of whom knew the facts—speak in the introduction to the ten-volume Camden edition of his works (page xxxiii) of "John Burroughs, in his book about Whitman—a book to which Whitman himself contributed invaluable features in advice and revision . . . ," and again (page lxiii) of: " 'Walt Whitman as Poet and Person,' a biographic and philosophic statement of the case of the 'Leaves' by John Burroughs—who had the advantage in the project mention of Whitman's counsel and endorsement . . . " and Emory Holloway, in the "Cambridge History of American Literature" says that "the substance if not the phrasing" of a passage he quotes "was supplied by Whitman himself." But that is all.

IV

Before, however, all of this evidence and corroboration had been assembled, positive information came to me unexpectedly from Horace Traubel, one of the executors. We were speaking of the books about Whitman and I remarked that Burroughs' first book appeared to me abler than his lengthier work of 1896. Traubel incisively agreed. I continued and said that the manner of the early book was really more like Whitman than Burroughs and that if Burroughs wrote it he had duplicated Whitman with marvelous success. Traubel ejaculated a characteristic short "Yes!" and for some time sat silent. Then he looked up and said:

I want to tell you something. But I don't want you to say anything till the time comes. You deserve to know because you guessed it. Walt wrote Burroughs' book for him; maybe not all of it, but most of it. Bucke told me and I asked Walt and he said it was so. We thought the book was invaluable and ought to be reprinted and Bucke approached Burroughs on the subject but Burroughs wouldn't consent. It was then that Walt told Bucke that he wrote the book and that that was the reason Burroughs didn't want it republished. When I talked to Walt he said he wrote most of the book and wanted me to tell about it some day to get things straight, but not to do it till after Burroughs died. Now I guess Burroughs is going to live longer than I am and I want you to do it.

I suggested to Traubel that owing to the nature of the information, my say-so might be questioned, and asked him to make a written statement. He signed the following declaration:

"Notes on Walt Whitman as Poet and Person," which was published in its first edition in 1867, was mostly written by Walt Whitman. Dr. Richard Maurice Bucke got this information first from Whitman, and Walt himself told me that it was true. This is probably the reason that Burroughs never allowed an edition of the book to be printed after the second one of 1871, though he was several times approached for the purpose. I do not want this information used till after Burroughs' death, but whatever anyone says, it is true.

(*Signed*) HORACE TRAUBEL
Literary Executor of Walt Whitman.

Dated June 10, 1919, New York City.

Only four men had known this, Whitman, Burroughs, Bucke and Traubel, and the latter's death in 1919 left Burroughs alone surviving. The case was complete except for his word; consideration convinced me that perhaps it was unfair to hold such information while he was alive without giving him a chance to be heard. He was the only person who knew at first hand the original facts and his word would add the final authentication. In reply to an inquiry he wrote to me as follows on October 15, 1920:

Roxbury, N. Y.

Dear Sir:—I have received your letter of the 10th relative to my little book, "Notes on WW as Poet and Person." There is a modicum of truth in what you have been told. Whitman's mark is on several of my books and magazine articles which were written during the Washington days. He was a great critic, and I was in the habit of submitting my MSS. to him for his strictures.

The first thing I wrote about him was in the *Galaxy* in the late sixties, and was called "Walt Whitman and His Drum Taps." This was written while Whitman was absent in N. Y., and he never saw it till it was in print. My next piece was called "The Flight of the Eagle," (in "Birds and Poets"). This he named, and there are a few sentences scattered through it from his pencil.

Page 197 was written by him. He told me the incident and I asked him to write it out, which he did, and I put it in.

I have not a copy of my "Notes on WW" here, and I have not looked in it for years, but I know it abounds in the marks of Whitman's hand. I had a more ambitious title, I forget what, and he renamed it, and pruned it, and reshaped many paragraphs. The most suggestive and profound passage in it is from his hand, nearly a whole page, but I cannot refer you to the page. Whitman named my first volume, "Wake Robin," for me. I took a number of titles to him and he held me to that one. It is certain that my "Notes" would not have been what they are without his help. If I remember rightly the supplement to the last edition was entirely written by him.

My volume, "Whitman, A Study" would have been of much greater value could he have pruned it. It is too heady and literary.

When I go back to West Park I will look over the "Notes," and if I can throw any new light on the subject, I will write you again.

Sincerely yours,

John Burroughs

This statement is so candid that it shames criticism. Certainly if it was the first time Burroughs had ever been confronted with the facts, he came through with that high punctilio for which he was distinguished. And it must not be forgotten that he was an aged man, over half a century away from those facts and without the documents at hand.

It is notable, however, that he writes, "my *first* volume 'Wake Robin,'" and, referring to his Whitman writing after the *Galaxy* article of 1866, skips over the "Notes" and calls "The Flight of The Eagle" of 1877, "my next piece." It is probable that Whitman's part in this "next piece" has never been known before. Burroughs admits, what is evident upon examination, that the eighteen-page supplement in the second edition was entirely written by Whitman, though the introductory note to this edition, signed "J. B., June, 1871," says: "The Supplementary Notes commencing page 109 present what I have to say of the book 1871-2."

Further query followed concerning the "most suggestive and profound passage" mentioned in the letter's third paragraph and Mr. Burroughs replied, this time with the "Notes" before him:

West Park, N. Y.,
Nov. 6, 1920.

Dear Sir:—I have been looking over my little booklet "Notes on Walt Whitman as Poet and Person" & am a great deal at sea about it. I find it hard to separate the parts I wrote from those he wrote. The fine passage I referred to by him begins on p. 37, chapter xxi, & includes the whole of that chapter. In other places I see where he has touched up my work, leaving the thought my own. The chapters on Beauty, & on "Drum Taps" are all my own. The Biographical Notes he enlarged and improved in the proof, from notes which he had given me verbally. I have no doubt that half the book is his. He was a great critic & he did me great service by pruning and simplifying. The title, too, is his. I had a much more ambitious title.

Very Respy.

John Burroughs

Putting the two letters together, we get the following results. Burroughs wrote unaided the chapters on "Beauty," pp. 50-57, and on "Drum Taps," pp. 97-108, a total of nineteen pages. Whitman provided the title and wrote chapter XXI, pp. 37-39, and the supplement, pp. 109-124, and supplied the personal sketch, pp.77-96; a total of thirty-nine pages. About half the book, 58 out of 124 pages, is thus accounted for by Burroughs. Whitman's hand is so spread over the remainder that he could not separate the parts. There will never be perfect agreement, I suppose, as to all the parts exclusively Whitman's but in view of the entire data, it may be said fairly that the book is virtually his.

V

There are delicate implications in the matter which may cause misconstruction unless the whole thing is placed in its natural setting among the forces and elements out of which it grew. The most potent of these were Whitman's tendency to mysterious concealment and the public's early antagonism, which together gave birth to his anonymous self-advertising; and the psychology of the Whitman-Burroughs friendship in its relation to their personal dilemmas and the outward events of 1867.

Whitman's hiding of things, which continued throughout his life, began in his earliest boyhood, when his own family was perplexed by it. His mother testified that he came and went as he pleased, taking everything for granted and accounting for nothing. He always had reticences, and however we lift the curtains the residue of mystery is great. Set the man and his great book side by side. "Leaves of Grass" is probably as naked and complete an expression of a total man as was ever written, but Whitman's own intimate life is almost unknown. He not only thought and acted behind the scenes, but often wrote anonymously in favor and defense of his book. This sly advertising began about two months after the ill-fated first edition of "Leaves of Grass" was placed on sale, with a long piece in the *United States Review* for September, 1855, entitled, "Walt Whitman and His Poems." Then followed a short notice in the Brooklyn *Daily Times* on September 29, with the ingenuous heading, "Walt Whitman, a Brooklyn Boy " The third was a review of "An English and an American Poet" in the *American Phrenological Journal* for 1856; Tennyson's "Maud" and "Leaves of Grass" being the subject matter. The three pieces were reprinted as part of a supplement added to the second issue of the first edition of "Leaves of Grass" in 1856, and two of them reappeared in the appendix to the second edition later in the same year. When the third edition was published in 1860-61, the publishers, Thayer and Eldridge, distributed gratuitously a little brochure of sixty-four pages, "Leaves of Grass Imprints," containing a number of criticisms of "Leaves of Grass," including Whitman's three articles. It is now known that Whitman arranged and edited the booklet, though his name did not appear.

In 1883, "Walt Whitman, a Brooklyn Boy" was included in Dr. Bucke's book on Whitman, still with no hint of its authorship, in spite of the fact that Whitman himself revised and authenticated the whole volume. Not until 1893, the year after Whitman's death and thirty-seven

years after the articles were written, did it become generally known that Whitman himself wrote them. His literary executors then published a miscellaneous collection, "In re Walt Whitman," and the first three articles were these early attempts of the poet to justify himself, then printed under his name for the first time. Whitman's last venture of this kind, entitled, "Walt Whitman in Camden," appeared in the *Critic* for February 28, 1885, under the pseudonym of "George Selwyn." This painstaking exposition of himself, begun in 1855, did not end till the posthumous volume of 1893, but it is notable that Whitman did no extensive anonymous writing during the later years, but confined himself to suggestion, counsel and revision. What then, were the earlier causes, which pulling and pushing "Leaves of Grass" through its many vicissitudes, induced him to advocate his own work?

The first edition of 1855, stepping out imperious and magisterial, met with almost unanimous scorn and mockery. Of the one hundred and twenty copies placed on sale in New York and Brooklyn, only one was sold, and the dealers, after two months' display, insisted upon the book's withdrawal. Complimentary and review copies were burned or thrown away. Whitman was driven into solitary contemplation at the far end of Long Island. The second edition of 1856 had a slightly larger sale, but the howl of the critics increased. All of the arrogant disdain in Whitman was aroused and this, together with his profound confidence in the ageless truth of his book, set him at work, not on virulent attacks upon his calumniators but on lusty and sinewy expositions of himself. He thought that his book was being not only assaulted but misunderstood, and with indefatigable diligence he tried to direct attention to the actual issue and to shift the battle to his own ground.

The palpable success of the third edition in 1860, for the first time in the hands of good publishers, was interrupted by the Civil War. After these three successive attempts had all been frustrated, it is small surprise that Whitman stirred himself. He said later: "I was then in the struggle, fought desperately for my life." And when he consented to the publication of his three early pieces in "In re Walt Whitman," he told his executors, "that in a period of misunderstanding and abuse their publication seemed imperative." Of the "In re" book itself, Whitman observed that it "seemed necessary to the fuller elucidation of the critter and his cause." The "Notes on Walt Whitman" was simply the most elaborate of Whitman's early justifications, and it is necessary, if we would understand it, not only to appreciate Whitman's cryptic tendencies and the reasons for his propaganda, but to conceive his environment and his relationship to Burroughs at the time.

In 1858, when he was only twenty-one years old, Burroughs had become acquainted with Whitman's work. Whitman then gave him, as he wrote later, the broadest outlook of any poet of his time. The two men did not meet, however, until the Autumn of 1863, when Burroughs, crushed by the events of the war, went to Washington to enter the ranks, but instead became Whitman's fellow clerk in the government service. An immediate intimacy sprang up, for Burroughs had, besides his enthusiasm for "Leaves of Grass," strong, outdoor qualities and sanities which Whitman felt and responded to. It is not strange, therefore, to find Whitman speaking of "the high lasting quality of John's best work," which Whitman considered to be in those regions where the best of the man was: outdoors. But he did not give unqualified adherence to Burroughs as a writer. Amidst Whitman's more remote creative imaginings, Burroughs felt uneasy and bewildered, and he admitted that "Leaves of Grass" itself had left him uncertain, until he had experienced Whitman's personal reassurance. Whitman saw this and while he was quick to grasp Burrough's fine and vital enthusiasm, he himself drew the horizon and main outlines of Burroughs' picture of "Leaves of Grass" and its author when the time came.

It did come four years after their first meeting. They were then in the nervous midst of the after-strain and turbulence of the war. Whitman, the discouraging difficulties of his first three editions behind him, was preparing his enlarged fourth edition of 1867. Only two years before he had been discharged from his government position through "dastardly official insolence," as he later described it. The time was critical for him, and with the impress of the terrible struggle just past in hot scars upon his spirit he projected a rounded and final fabric of his song. He was forty-eight years old and in grand maturity. Burroughs, on the other hand, was in his commencement days. He was only thirty years old and not yet on his own or established in the literary field. He had published little except miscellaneous essays and verses and his *Galaxy* piece on Whitman. Both men were natural writers, suddenly released from the war's engrossment. Burroughs looked to Whitman as a friend and master; Whitman to Burroughs as a friend and helper. "Notes on Walt Whitman" was the spontaneous fruit. It gave Whitman the needed push and it gave Burroughs the needed pull.

WOODROW WILSON

BY HARRY ELMER BARNES

THE vast amount of anecdotal and eulogistic material which appeared after the recent death of Mr. Wilson suggests the desirability of attempting a preliminary estimate of his personality, achievements and place in history. Many would urge that we must wait for years before making any effort to pass even a tentative judgment upon his career, on the familiar ground that no one who has lived in a period can write about it intelligently —that to get sound history we must delay until someone entirely ignorant of the passions of the era discussed can study the documents embodying its dead enmities and biases; and thus construct an adequate, penetrating and absolutely impartial exposition and interpretation of it. This position is based on two errors. The first lies in the assumption that a later generation will never share the prejudices of its predecessors. If you believe it, try to imagine a Boston aristocrat of 1924 writing fairly of Thomas Jefferson, or Maurice Barrès of Bismarck or Moltke! The second is found in the theory that a person living later will have a better perspective and keener insight than a contemporary. This implies a tacit acceptance of a theory of historical causation long ago disproved by Hume— that subsequent events are necessarily results of earlier ones—and also of the notion that a consideration of the remote results of a period is more valuable for estimating it than a clear view of its actual events. It is the writer's contention that while contemporaneity may possibly intensify hatreds and affections, yet the type of person likely to show a reasonable impartiality under any circumstances at all will make better use of the same evidence if he has lived through the period he deals with.

In this article there is little space for description. Some effort will be made to suggest plausible explanations and interpretations, but there will be no attempt at personal praise or blame. The writer does not pretend to any finality of estimate. He merely claims to be free from a few of the more atrocious distortions of the Drool Method in regard to the subject chosen, and to have canvassed a great variety of written and oral estimates of the late ex-President as scholar, writer and public figure.

II

The extreme divergence of opinion as to Mr. Wilson's personality and achievements, and the intensity of the apologies and accusations launched by his friends and foes have astonished many impartial observers, but all of them are probably adequately explained by the luxuriating of the herd instinct during the World War. The passions of the Civil War produced like results. We are apt to forget that Congressmen wrote home in April, 1865, that Booth had been an instrument in God's hand, and that clergymen in the North thanked God publicly for the nation's deliverance from Lincoln. It may, however, be instructive to reproduce typical examples of the encomium and the indictment in the case of Mr. Wilson. I shall choose those which are made impressive by reason of their extreme deviation from plausibility and by the fact that they are the product of distinguished historical scholars—the late Dr. William Roscoe Thayer, fresh from the presidency of the American Historical Association, and Professor William E. Dodd, who, on the basis of his professional work, was far more deserving of that honor. Professor Dodd, normally a highly intelligent and progressive historian, the biographer of Mr. Wilson, and even beyond Ray Stannard Baker the chief historical architect of the Wilsonian Epic, has given us his most concise delineation of his hero in an article, "Democracy's Great Triumvirate," in the New York *Times* for January 29, 1922. Typical sections follow:

Forty-eight years after Lincoln another, and the last of our three great leaders, came to the Presidency. It was Woodrow Wilson, sprung from the loins of Lincoln's broken South. He found the masters of industry, after half a century of untrammeled power, confronting him. . . . Lincoln had succeeded in one thing: the saving of the unity of the country. Jefferson succeeded in two things: the widening of the area of democracy and the marvelous revival of the democratic spirit of the people. Wilson in two or three short years carried through more, and more important, legislation than any other President ever made into law. . . . It was a great, unprecedented program, and it was successful beyond all expectation. But Wilson was marked for defeat. He was hated by many who were called great or eminent; they resolved that his career must be halted. . . . I shall not retell the story of the great conflict, of the high hopes and the great performances of those great years, 1917-18. It was a high tide in American history, a great day for all who knew and felt the impulses of the time. Over all presided the spirit of Wilson, too fair to be unjust even to the German people; too democratic and too Christian to indulge in the language of hate. At the close of the struggle . . . he promulgated his peace of reconciliation and then his famous Fourteen Points. . . . He would make a peace the like of which men had never before known. But he was still marked for defeat. . . . Men could not forgive him for being the world's acknowledged leader. He must go. It was the ancient spirit of privilege which had warred upon Lincoln, which had hurled its anathemas at Jefferson. . . . Thus came the bitter end to him, as to Jefferson and Lincoln. It was American industry, ancient privilege, fighting for a strangle hold upon the world, that mobilized all the hostile elements in 1920. . . . Industry, American industry, won at Paris.

Now for the other side. Perhaps the most bitter arraignment of Mr. Wilson ever printed is that contained in an estimate of his personality and career published by Mr. Thayer in the *North American Review* for March, 1921. I quote:

The American election day of November 2, 1920, may well remain a most conspicuous landmark, not only in the chronicles of the United States but in the history of democracy. Never before had American democracy reached so vital a crisis. An egoist who happened to be President of the country under abnormal circumstances, freed alike from precedents and moral bonds, saw the way to assemble in his own hands extraordinary powers which made him a despot of unlimited reach, and the United States a docile despotism.

Probably President Wilson did not deliberately plan to attain this result. He was an opportunist, even in his guilt. By nature stubborn, self-satisfied, and self-reliant, he was a most fertile soil for the seeds of ambition to grow in. He did not create favorable chances, but he quickly discerned and seized them when they arose. . . . This stage of egomania is, of course, very common. The peculiarity in Mr. Wilson's case is that he was able to delude many persons into asserting that his disease was the highest wisdom. I have heard him extolled as a modern Messiah, and the persons who so extolled him were unquestionably sincere. . . .

He had "kept us out of war," as long as it served his purpose. Now he spoke proudly of being in the war: "I, too, come of fighting blood," he said jauntily. More remarkable still was his ingenuity in finding reasons for our joining the Allies, or "Associates," as he preferred to call them. We took up arms "to make the world safe for democracy," he explained. . . . The war had not progressed long before thoughtful men of every nation, shuddering at its horrors, set to thinking how all war could be abolished and peace be made permanent. Various plans were suggested. One of them, the League to Enforce Peace, seemed to many Americans the most popular and feasible. President Wilson did not initiate this . . . but when he found that it was gaining in favor, he openly espoused it, and, as chance often plays freaks of this kind, he came at last to be revered as its starter by persons who did not take the trouble to inform themselves as to the origin of the project. . . .

He saw in the League of Nations a marvelous opening to his own aggrandizement. If any league should be agreed upon when it came time to make peace, who would be more likely to be chosen its President than himself? This suggestion became an obsession, and to it he sacrificed all other considerations. . . . Having scorned to take counsel with anyone, having reduced his Cabinet ministers and other officials to the status of servants, he threw off all pretense of being bound by the Constitution. . . . Whatever blocked his ambition was bad; consequently the Senate was bad. So blinded by egomania was Mr. Wilson that he imagined that the people of the United States were on his side—the very people who had defeated him by more than a million votes in 1918. Accordingly he planned to stump the country in behalf of his scheme for a League of Nations. . . . November 2d came. Inexorable as fate, the Great and Solemn Referendum turned out to be the Greatest Repudiation in American history. . . . A majority of more than seven million and a half Americans repudiated Woodrow Wilson, his ways, his régime, and his visions.

In an effort to arrive at something like a valid interpretation of Mr. Wilson and his achievements, I shall first consider his scholarly standing and productions, and then briefly discuss the facts of his political career.

III

It has been very commonly assumed that because of his having been a college professor and president he necessarily possessed a highly superior intellect and could boast of a scholarly record of unusual merit. As a matter of fact his scholarship was only average, and distinctly lower than that of the normal college professor, who is well-nigh universally embellished with a Phi Beta Kappa key earned as an undergraduate. As a student his record proves him greatly inferior to his immediate predecessors in the presidency. Mr. Roosevelt was in the first eighth of his class at Harvard and Mr. Taft graduated second in a class of 121 at Yale, but Mr. Wilson finished only thirty-eighth in a class of 106 at Princeton. As there is no evidence that any of the three was given to wildness at college, it may be safely assumed that these facts offer a fairly accurate reflection of their relative native intellectual endowments. Certainly no one will hold that the scholarly requirements of Princeton were more severe at the time than those which prevailed at Harvard and Yale.

I need not spend any time discussing Mr. Wilson's purely academic career. The facts are well-known and they may be allowed to stand at their face value. Let us turn instead to his literary and scholarly achievements. In his professional work Mr. Wilson was primarily a political scientist rather than an historian. In this field his work was creditable if not distinguished. His most important book was his earliest, "Congressional Government," published in 1885, which was the first considerable American treatise to move in the direction of James Bryce and Mosei Ostrogorski, and, leaving the sterile classificatory political science of Bluntschli, Burgess and Woolsey behind, to describe the chaos and depravity in the actual operation of our party system. Unfortunately, the early promise of this essay was not fulfilled. Mr. Wilson's later writings on politics became more stereotyped and formal, and, in the light of subsequent work along lines he suggested by Bryce, Ostrogorski, J. A. Smith, Bentley, Weyl, Brooks, Beard, Merriam, Kales, Young and others, "Congressional Government" now seems a product of the Mesozoic age of American political science.

Another idea worthy of note which we may ascribe to Mr. Wilson was that to the effect that it would be a good thing to let the youth of America know that there were civilized peoples being governed passably well outside the confines of the United States. This conviction produced his well-known book, "The State." Though embodying no original research, pathetically erroneous in its theory of political origins, exhibiting little power to penetrate beneath external forms into the processes of actual government, based very largely on a formal German manual, and, because of its detachment from the facts of government in action, one of the most difficult books to teach or learn from ever offered as a textbook in political science in an American university, it deserves the credit of having first really introduced the American academic world of the last quarter of the Nineteenth Century to the study of comparative government. No other work from his pen possesses any real merit as a contribution to political science, but his "Mere Literature" throws a significant light on his deeper attitude toward that science and its cultivation. After legitimately calling attention to the sterility of most professorial lectures and formal treatises on the subject, he recommends "poets and sonneters," as the best source of political information and inspiration. "There is more of a nation's politics to be got out of its poetry than out of all its systematic writers upon public affairs and constitutions." These are surely not the words of a realistic observer and penetrating student of politics. They give us, I believe, a clue to his real methods and preferences, and show that as a political scientist, as well as in the rôle of politician, he was a rhetorician first and always. One does not need to read Dr. William Bayard Hale's "Story of a Style" to discover that words were ever Mr. Wilson's chief stock in trade.

The most scholarly and persistent of his apologists has been recently reported as saying that in 1912 he was the foremost of American political scientists, but a careful perusal of all the competent written opinions on the subject and a fairly thorough canvass of oral judgments have failed to disclose a single authoritative confirmation of that estimate. As an original thinker he will not compare for a moment with such men as Pound, Beard, Bentley, Weyl, Croly, Holcombe or Shepherd, nor as an assiduous compiler with F. A. Ogg, or W. F. Willoughby, nor as a penetrating delineator of governmental systems with President Lowell, nor as a master of the juristic side of political institutions with Goodnow, Freund, McIlwain, Powell or Corwin, nor as an interpreter of the actual processes of modern government with Merriam, Bentley, H. J. Ford, Beard, Brooks, Ray or Kales. Unquestionably, his success in the field of academic political science was due far more to his stimulating teaching than to his writing, and here it was chiefly the impressive rhetoric, and often keen dialectic, of his lectures that gained him popularity. Painstaking interrogation of his former students fails to disclose any evidence of their having been overwhelmed by any such combination of analytical

power and erudition as that which characterizes the lectures of Roscoe Pound on jurisprudence, or brought spontaneously to their feet by any such realistic interpretation of political life and exposure of contemporary political abuses as that which thrilled Professor Beard's students for a decade, or given any such practical insight into contemporary political situations as that which has been the reward of Professor Merriam's students.

As an historian his concrete achievements were even more slender and less impressive than his feats as a political scientist. It was doubtless assumed by many that his election last December as president of the American Historical Association was convincing proof of his eminence as a devotee of Clio, but this illusion may be easily dispelled by having recourse to a printed list of ex-presidents of the Association. At least half are men whom even the most heroic imagination could not place in the front rank of contemporary historians, though it is true that in some cases distinguished scholars have been chosen. The greatest scholar American historiography has produced, Herbert Levi Osgood, was never seriously considered for the presidency, though he lived to the relatively ripe age of sixty-three. Likewise, only one of the men who have placed American historical scholarship a generation ahead of that of any other nation in modernity and vitality of outlook,—such men as Robinson, Breasted, Turner, Shotwell, Beard, Becker, Dodd and Farrand—has been honored by this office.

Mr. Wilson's historical works consist of a brief book on the history of the United States from 1829 to 1889, entitled "Division and Reunion," published in 1893; a biographical study of George Washington, of interpretative and literary, but scarcely of historical, significance, published in 1896, and a popular history of the United States in several volumes, published in 1902. Of these, only "Division and Reunion" has ever attracted any favorable attention from historians. While this work is but a slender manual brought out in a textbook series, and gives no evidence of any mastery of, or particular reliance upon, source-material, it was in its day, like "Congressional Government," rather a novelty, in that for the first time it told the story of the Civil War and Reconstruction in a spirit as free from the savagery of Thaddaeus Stevens and Charles Sumner as it was from that of Ben Tillman. If it now seems puerile, when compared with the volumes of McMaster and Oberholtzer, James Ford Rhodes and Professor Dunning and his students, that fact should not obscure its value at the time of its publication. Yet a hundred volumes of more merit have appeared since 1893 on various phases of American history without having incited reviewers to suggest the authors as candidates for the presidency of the American Historical Association.

The "George Washington" is not history, whatever one may think of Mr. Wilson's intuitive and literary gifts, and in fifteen years of daily contact with university departments of history I have heard the "History of the American People" mentioned but once, and that was when a venerable professor warned a seminar of undergraduates that it was not to be regarded as an authoritative work on any period of our national development. At the same time it may be conceded that it is of high literary merit and one of the best popular histories of our country that has been brought out by a single author. A wide-spread perusal of it would doubtless be beneficial to the majority of Americans. It is equally fair, however, to point out that it shows scarcely any use of the new scholarship that has revolutionized American history in the last twenty-five years, and that more of substantial value can be discovered in many a single volume by other men—for example, Willis Mason West's "American Democracy," S. E. Forman's "Our Republic," Frederick Jackson Turner's "The Frontier in American History," Max Farrand's "Development of the United States," or Carl Becker's "The United States." It is quite evident, then, that no informed person would think of suggesting that Mr. Wilson was qualified to rank as one of our leading historians. In sober fact, he failed to rank with even Mr. Roosevelt in actual achievement.

IV

Probably the best way to reach some estimate of his place in American political life is to rehearse his contributions to progressive thought and sound legislation early in his administration, then enumerate the phases of his débâcle, and finally endeavor to discover some credible, if not always adequate, explanation of his apparent inconsistencies.

While his achievements as governor of New Jersey were not epoch-making in any sense, he did certainly make some slight progress in positive legislation and in temporarily improving the public tone of that trust-ridden and machine-controlled State. And during the first two years of his administration as President of the United States his bitterest foe must concede that he got through more externally impressive legislation than can be claimed for any like period of years since Alexander Hamilton's unparalleled achievements at the opening of the Washington administrations. We may agree with the judicious estimate of Professor Farrand that "his first administration as President of the United States will probably long remain an unequalled record of legislative achievement, for which the greatest credit must be given to Mr. Wilson himself. Merely to mention a substantial reduction in the tariff rates, a revision of the banking and currency system, the strengthening of the Interstate Commerce Commission, the bolstering up of the anti-trust laws, and the creation of a Federal Trade Commission would be sufficient to indicate his accomplishments." To these should be added the beginnings of federal provision for rural credits, and the passage of the Adamson Law, probably the most forward-looking act of Mr. Wilson's political career, however much it may have been purely opportunist. Coming to the war, it may be said that whatever the sordidness of the actual preparation and administration, of which he was probably only imperfectly conscious, he did certainly manage to keep our ostensible reasons for participating with the Allied Powers on an unprecedentedly high, if largely illusory, moral and rhetorical level. Finally, while not the originator, he was certainly the foremost practical sponsor of the most discussed plan for international coöperation in the long history of such proposals.

There are, of course, some qualifications which should be appended. Not a single new policy was involved in any of the above acts, unless it was in the Adamson Law, which can scarcely be regarded as an outcome of a well-considered philosophy of government or political program. Tariff revision had always been a basic policy with the Democrats and progressive Republicans; the banking laws were but a modification of the Aldrich plan, and have certainly failed to ward off all the evils which were alleged to be inherent in that scheme; and the legislation relating to the curbing of trusts and the strengthening of the Interstate Commerce Commission was strictly a part of the Rooseveltian heritage which had been side-tracked during the Taft defection from "my policies." And anyone who thinks this last legislation has been effective should consult the statistical exhibit of Senator LaFollette in the *Congressional Record* for March 14, 1921. For this failure, however, we must assign the responsibility to what Herbert Spencer called "the great political illusion" rather than to any special lack of wisdom on the part of Mr. Wilson.

Turning now to the case for the prosecution we may pass over at once the silly villification of Thayer and George Harvey, and consider the allegations made by those whose criticisms possess enough objectivity and pertinence to entitle them to a hearing. They may be summarized about as follows. In his legislative policy from 1913 to 1916 Mr. Wilson did not touch the real issues involved in the reconstruction of American economic, social and political life, but was only a Bryan sixteen years delayed. "The New Freedom" was but the cocked-hat transformed into printed paper. We did not actually go into the World War to protect ourselves from imminent German invasion, or to make the world safe for democracy, but to protect our investment in Allied bonds, to insure a more extensive development of the manufacture of war materials and to make it possible to deliver our munitions to Allied ports. Serious infringements of international law by Allied Powers were passed over with mild protests; our inability to trade with Germany or Austria was never seriously resented. Even assuming that we did enter for the sake of advancing the cause of democracy, Mr. Wilson sanctioned during this crusade for Demos the most serious inroads upon democratic practice and human liberty in the history of our country, wiping out in three years most of the solid gains of a century and a half of struggle against arbitrary power. When the war ended the United States—the alleged apostle of freedom—was the most reactionary state in Christendom.

Again, during the period of formal rhetorical idealism and of great coöperative sacrifice on the part of the masses of the people, there was being carried on an orgy of profiteering and corruption, any approximation to which had never before been known among mankind. Much of Mr. Wilson's idealizing about the war to end war, it is further argued, and about the right of national self-determination, and a peace of justice and fair-dealing, was but the grossest form of compensatory, if partially sub-conscious, hypocrisy to assuage him for his unpleasant knowledge of the Secret Treaties. He gave the signal for the disintegration of the non-partisan devotion to the national welfare by his notorious appeal for a strong and partisan Democratic Congress in the Autumn of 1918, on the eve of his departure to negotiate a just peace as the delegate of an undivided nation. His Fourteen Points were not the product of his own thought but a summary of the work of a commission, and perhaps written by a member of it. They were never understood or assimilated by him in their true implications, and were violated in spirit and letter alike in the Treaty of Peace. Though constantly speaking of a peace of charity and justice, he permitted it to be negotiated in an almost unprecedentedly arrogant manner, without allowing the vanquished to be represented, and forcing them at the point of the bayonet to deny the obvious facts of history and sign a document confessing their sole responsibility for the great conflict. The outcome of this procedure was "as harsh a product of the ruthless spirit of victory as is recorded in history."

Not satisfied with this betrayal of the trust and faith of the peoples of the world, he insisted upon wedding this hideous offspring of chauvinistic hate and greed to his plan for the ending of national enmity and cupidity. The League of Nations, a scheme to which he had been converted in 1918 by a group of progressive Republicans, was interwoven with the nefarious peace pact in such a manner that neither could be accepted or rejected without the other. But even under such circumstances and in the face of expressed executive contempt, Congress would have accepted both, had it not been for the arrogant demand of Mr. Wilson for the "whole hog or none." Had he been able to act as a realistic and conciliatory statesman, instead of as an inflexible zealot, we might five years ago have been a member of a far stronger international organization than that which the contemporary Wilsonians are urging upon Congress in the form of the Bok Peace Plan. The most sinister and potent cause of the current European confusion, misery and chaos has been the reparations sections of the Peace Treaty, and, while Mr. Wilson was not accountable for their initiation, he was responsible, it is argued, for allowing their inclusion through his silly and notorious defiance of logic and the advice of the American economic experts. Finally, though incapacitated for office in one of the most crucial periods in our history, his egotism kept him from resigning, and prompted his curt dismissal of the one Cabinet member who was doing his best, however unimpressive that may have been, to maintain some semblance of existence in the executive branch of the government.

V

A number of considerations will naturally occur in extenuation or explanation of various phases of this bill of indictment. In so far as he proposed a millennial utopia his failure was simply one more addition to the museum of age-old testimonials to the inadequacy of one "righteous soul" in the face of the cussedness of mankind. Hence, probably the chief reflection on him lies not in his defeat, but in his colossal mistake in believing that it could be done at all— that it might be magically realized in a few weeks times and in the face of the momentum of a half million years of human savagery and hunting-pack ferocity. And though the reasons assigned for our actual entry into the World War by John Kenneth Turner may be approximately the correct ones, it can be safely held that Mr. Wilson never realized that this was the case. The most probably hypothesis is that the pressure of patriots and investors, with an eager newspaper service at their disposal, became so heavy as to wear down his resistance, during which process he built up the justification, defense and compensation mechanism which was given oral expression in his declarations and speeches from April, 1917 onward. His mind was of such a sort that if he once *said* that we entered for purely idealistic reasons such became the indisputable and permanent fact so far as he was concerned.

The phrase, with him, always vanquished the reality. He was not a hypocrite; he simply lived in an unreal and ethereal world of rhetoric and metaphysics. In complete consonance with his philosophy, he sought an interpretation of the facts and issues of the war in Luther's speeches and Milton's verse rather than in the statistics of American industry, the income-tax reports, the investments of American bankers abroad, or the shipping records of American ports. Only once, and that after the Paris Conference had ended, did he give evidence of a realistic attitude towards the war. This was exhibited in his St. Louis speech of September, 1919, when he offered the same interpretation of the genesis of the war which had brought Eugene Debs four years at Atlanta.

His apparent acquiescence in administrative inefficiency and corruption is to be explained in the same way. As the late Frank I. Cobb pointed out in a fine and discriminating apology in the New York *World* for March 4, 1921, Mr. Wilson's interests were in principles, not in men. Appointments were distasteful to him; they were distracting concrete realities. He rarely considered the subsequent efficiency or even the existence of an appointee unless the man ran counter to the Wilson program, in which case the examples of Bryan, Garrison and Lansing are instructive. Nor should he be too severely blamed for the decrease of liberty and tolerance during the war period. There is invariably a tightening of the social or herd machinery in times of great crises. Such a situation was inevitable, even though the American manifestation was more than necessarily atrocious, perhaps because of the unreality of the alleged group danger and the unusual necessity of artifically inflating the illusion and preventing disconcerting criticism. Those who had never lived through a period of war might have been excused in 1917 for believing in its potential ennobling impulses, but now that we have an opportunity to view the thing in its bald futility and baseness, those who

still cling to the illusion should seek admission to a salubriously situated colony for the feeble-minded.

Wilson was defeated at Paris primarily because he was in no sense fitted to meet the situation. His ineradicable traits of mind were his chief handicap. Even though he employed experts to amass a vast body of information, he believed the matter practically settled when he had enunciated his attractive abstractions as to the future disposition of the world. While we can scarcely believe Mr. Baker's absolutely damning assertion that his detachment from fact was so pathological that he had never read the Secret Treaties before leaving for Europe ten months after their publication in what was then America's leading evening daily, yet he certainly continued to dwell primarily in the world of words and *a priori* concepts and expedients. And when he found gradually and too late that the crimes of two thousand years of European diplomatic and military chicanery could not be effaced in a few weeks by the therapeutic influence of fourteen moral principles, he attempted to enter the diplomatic game himself, with the results that would normally attend the entrance of a rural clergyman into a poker game on a trans-Atlantic liner. Professor Carl Becker, in a judicious review of Mr. Baker's voluminous work, concludes that Mr. Wilson failed primarily because of the rapid collapse of "idealism" upon the close of hostilities—the rapid revulsion of feeling from the noblest heights to the most sordid depths, so characteristic of mankind. There is doubtless much in this, but it cannot be denied that Mr. Wilson himself fired the pistol which gave the signal for the release of the psychic toboggan when he made his appeal for a Democratic Congress in the Autumn of 1918, a month before the armistice.

One phase of this Wilson program has often escaped notice, namely, the problem of its fundamental wisdom. It has usually been assumed that the principle of complete national self-determination was both wise and inevitable. But much good opinion can be adduced on the other side, for the path of historical progress has been accompanied by the erection of larger and larger states. To a certain extent the creation of a great number of artificial political entities based only on national aspirations was in reality a reversal of the process of history. It should be remembered, however, that some of the evils attendant upon the creation of such states might have been eliminated by a thoroughgoing adoption of the League of Nations, though only a very naïve person would hold that the League at best could be more than a feeble first step in the campaign against the savagery of nations.

Mr. Wilson lost out at home upon his return because he was a Democrat first and foremost, and because of his inflexible spirit and his eschatological interpretation of personal opposition. He had been a Democrat first, last and all the time from 1913 to 1917, a perfectly natural, defensible and fruitful attitude; he had been somewhat of a Democrat throughout the war, as was evidenced by his attitude towards Roosevelt and Wood and his unwillingness to create an able non-partisan Cabinet; and in the autumn of 1918 he once more openly caressed the donkey. Few could hold the senior Senator from Massachusetts in lower esteem than the writer, who regards the characterization of him in "The Mirrors of Washington" as a eulogy, but it seems unfair to criticize him for accepting the challenge which Mr. Wilson threw down to him. But even the opposition of Mr. Lodge might have been overcome had it not been for Mr. Wilson's impossible method of dealing with opponents. Looking upon himself as the delegate and instrument of cosmic good, the Logos of the new internationalism, he held his opponents to be wilful servants of the spirit of evil and darkness. There was no intermediate ground, no basis for compromise.

Mr. Strunsky believes that Wilson

might actually have retrieved his fortune, so sadly damaged at Paris, "if he had consented to barter with Lodge as he bartered with Lloyd George and Clemenceau." There seems no doubt that his adamant rigidity on the matters of separating the Treaty from the League and the revision of the latter was compensation for his knowledge of the weaknesses, inconsistencies and broken promises embodied in the former. He seemed to feel that he could purify a document containing endless hate, arrogance and oppression by linking it up with the mystic philological key to the new international Apocalypse.

VI

After all allowances and extenuations are made, however, one sombre fact remains and defies all apology, namely, Mr. Wilson's defection from Liberalism. It is difficult to contemplate a more striking irony of fact and fate than the circumstance that at the trial of the Boston Communists, in 1920, under the notorious espionage legislation sanctioned by him, the government expert on radicalism unwittingly branded a section read from "The New Freedom" as good Communist doctrine and just cause for the deportation of the author. It is Chafee and Post, rather than Keynes and Turner, who have dealt the death blow to the Wilsonian Epic. He may be forgiven for falling before the superior adroitness and unscrupulousness of Lloyd George and Clemenceau in diplomacy, but nothing can remove the blot of the Palmer degradation. To be sure, many of Mr. Wilson's apologists have urged in his defense that Lincoln indulged in nearly as atrocious conduct in repressing dissent during the Civil War. But they fail to point out the fact that Lincoln quickly forgave his enemies. He would never have permitted the debauch to run on for over two years after the war had ceased. One can scarcely hold that Mr. Wilson would have prevented Charles Sumner from having Jeff Davis's head on a platter. Some have contended that he was never an apostate from Liberalism, but simply insisted upon administering it to unwilling subjects in allopathic doses by means of the maul and ramrod. Doubtless Mr. Debs would hold that this amounts to the same thing, and Senator James A. Reed is probably right when he argues that it was the Wilsonian forcible feeding of his own brand of Liberalism which made it unpalatable some time before his retirement, and rendered the name of Liberal one which is today everywhere in disrepute among us as never before in a half century.

The greatest problem in the complex career of Woodrow Wilson is held by some to be that presented by the transformation of the Wilson of "The New Freedom" into the sponsor of the Palmer Inquisition. But its solution is really relatively simple if one looks over his career as a whole. When this is done, the Wilson of 1910-1917 appears to be the anomaly and the Wilson of 1918-21 the normal man. His writings reveal him to be primarily an aristocrat and a conservative, whose Liberalism was abortive and opportunist. One does not need to have recourse to chapter II of Hale's "Story of a Style" to be convinced of this. His philosophy was that of the benevolent *laissez-faire* school, and his ideal the aristocratic gentry of England and the Old South. About his only conspicuous expression of practical political opinion prior to 1910 was his wish that Bryan, the crusader against privilege in 1896, might be knocked into a cocked hat. But in his unquestionably laudable effort to make over Princeton University into a genuine educational institution he came into conflict with the alumni of that university, who happened to be the very back-bone of the most rock-ribbed American conservatism and standpatism. In this battle he came to hate the class which opposed and ultimately ousted him, and so he eagerly accepted the opportunity offered by a political career to hit back at it effectively.

No one can understand the divergence between the "Constitutional Government" and "The New Freedom" who does not see in the latter his economic and political challenge and defiance to his enemies of the Princeton battlefield. In the reform legislation of the first two years of his administration he had, as he felt, dealt them a good wallop, and so his animus was considerably deflated. In office and society he was thrown in more and more with them and their class, and they began to seem rather decent and tolerable after all, especially now that he was their acknowledged superior and they came to him for aid and favors. This trend was greatly magnified and hastened after the entry of the United States into the war. He depended very largely upon the group of financiers and industrialists for encouragement and guidance, and it flattered him to have them at his beck and call. In a few months the Wilson of 1912 had completed his reversion, and was his old self once more before the year 1917 had ended. When to this is added the fact that he felt himself to be the moving force and guiding angel in the greatest moral crusade in the history of humanity, one can understand his impatience at opposition and criticism —why he should feel that the bottom of the Atlantic Ocean constituted quarters altogether too comfortably appointed for Rose Pastor Stokes, Eugene Debs, Bill Haywood and Victor Berger. There is no conscious hypocrisy or overt diabolism here, merely the normal evolution and oscillations of a personality unconsciously adapting itself to changing circumstances and surroundings. The psychological mechanism known as "projection" sufficiently explains his invective against the Kaiser, against the "little group of wilful men" of 1917, and against the Republican senatorial group of 1918-19.

All these facts constitute an adequate rejoinder to Professor Dodd's thesis that Mr. Wilson was overthrown by capitalistic reactionaries. This is pure nonsense. The most vigorous of his critics from 1918 to the present have been the Liberal periodicals, especially the *New Republic* and the *Nation*, a few progressive and independent dailies, and such Liberal writers as J. K. Turner, Chafee, Keynes, Weyl, and Post. Even the partisan opposition which integrated the Republicans in the opposition following 1918 was by no means limited to, or directed by, the reactionaries. Hiram Johnson and Borah were much more vocal than paleolithic party-horses like Henry Cabot Lodge and George H. Moses. The League was defeated primarily because Mr. Wilson alienated the progressive group, who had praised his idealism and internationalism in 1918, through insisting upon linking it up in an inextricable manner with a monstrous and reactionary Peace Treaty. The atrocious assaults against the very foundations of American liberty executed under his *aegis* by Palmer and his dragoons endeared Mr. Wilson to the reactionaries more than the acts of any other president since Grover Cleveland, and established a popular and fatal precedent for dealing with dissident groups in a republic. Whatever ousted him, it was not the hatred, animosity or activity of the American Bourbons. The attempt of reactionary Republican Wall Street lawyers, led by Austen G. Fox, to secure the dismissal of Professor Chafee from Harvard University for revealing a small portion of the Palmer atrocities is a fair proof of how little actual hatred of the Wilson régime of the period after 1917 prevailed among the vested interests. The allegation that he was destroyed by the Morgan firm after having let himself be exploited to protect the bonds of the Allies is preposterous. The Morgan firm, in common with most other great banking houses, was strongly in favor of the League. The reparation clauses of the Treaty were approved by Mr. Wilson against sound financial advice.

VII

The task remains of considering the actual Wilson personality. The problem has been well stated by the *Nation:*

If history deals gently with Woodrow Wilson it will portray him as one who wrought mightily by proclaiming ideals and painting them in moving terms. If it deals with him in the truth of justice it must also point out how universally he failed to achieve those ideals. . . . Today one can but recall his words and marvel how little has been the actual achievement for peace of the man who uttered them, how colossal the opportunities lost, how staggering the defeated idealism, how limited the sum total accomplished.

The solution, it seems to me, lies in the fact implied from time to time above, namely, the flight of his mind from the reality of concrete situations into the illusory world of abstractions and rhetoric. Walter Weyl, in a profound and brilliant characterization, has admirably described this escape:

The simple faith of Mr. Wilson in his Fourteen Points, unexplained and unelaborated, was due, I believe, to the invincible abstractness of his mind. He seems to see the world in abstractions. To him railroad cars are not railroad cars but a gray, generalized thing called Transportation; people are not men and women, corporeal, gross, very human beings, but Humanity—Humanity very much in the abstract. In his political thinking and propaganda Mr. Wilson cuts away all the complex qualities which things possess in real life in order to fasten upon one single characteristic, and thus he creates a clear but over-simple and unreal formula.

Mr. Simeon Strunsky, in an interpretation published recently in *Foreign Affairs*, has defended the opposite thesis, namely, that Mr. Wilson was actually far greater as a realistic statesman than as a phrasemaker. His argument is based chiefly on the fact that he often made speeches which contain phrases ill-suited for the moment, as, for example, the famous "too proud to fight' speech delivered three days after the sinking of the *Lusitania*. But it would seem that this fact is open to exactly the opposite interpretation, namely, that he was so detached from reality and so absorbed in phrases that he became wholly unconscious of the circumstances of the moment and was often guilty of most unfortunate, if unintentional, indiscretions. Definite proof of Mr. Wilson's capitulation to the seductiveness of phrases wholly divorced from fact and conviction is to be found in the appendix to J. K. Turner's "Shall It Be

Again?" Here there are concrete exhibits proving that on every important issue connected with the war he directly contradicted himself, on occasion in the same speech and frequently on the same day.

There still remains, of course, the deeper and more fundamental problem of why and how he came to possess this type of mind. For this we should doubtless have to fall back upon the psychiatrist, with his conception of the introvert and the extrovert and his theory of the mechanism of compensation and of the flight from reality. We should need to know all the details of Mr. Wilson's personal life from his earliest childhood, purged of all rationalizations and defensive resistances and justifications. Perhaps a clue is to be found in his early failure as a practising lawyer. That failure may well have impelled him to seek compensation in legal and political cobwebspinning. The writer, however, does not regard this theory as sufficiently explanatory. The truth is that Mr. Wilson's basic traits seem to have been fixed in childhood on a narcissistic pattern. It is, perhaps, not an insignificant fact that, from his earliest recorded days, he was the recipient of uniform, persistent and extensive adulation from women. I here hint at nothing improper; I merely state a fact, itself certainly not discreditable. But every astute person knows the effect of such adulation upon masculine character, attitude and conduct. It makes for cockiness, self-assurance and intellectual exhibitionism.

One other fact may throw some light upon Mr. Wilson's penchant for regarding well said as well done. He was for twenty years a lecturing professor in political science. Now, as we all know who are in the profession and are honest enough to admit it, the professor, particularly in the fields of philosophy, literature and the social sciences, tends toward a dictatorial attitude and the utterance of a vast amount of careless spontaneous opinions and dicta —impulsive generalizations prompted by the circumstances of the moment, passed out unchecked and soon forgotten. We are faced with little probability of being interrogated or asked for proof, partly because of the general state of psychic intimidation in which college students are held, and partly because a large portion of the class, normally in various stages of somnolence and distraction, is not likely to be following the lecture or digressive remarks very attentively. Further there is little danger, even if someone in the class detects an erroneous or dubious opinion, for we may safely assume that he will have forgotten it before the next session. The looseness and arbitrariness in the use of words permitted to a professor, as compared with a doctor, lawyer, manufacturer, engineer, or stock-broker, is enormous. This tendency towards carelessness in thinking and expression becomes more apparent in proportion as one is possessed of rhetorical gifts, and Mr. Wilson was admittedly one of the most rhetorical of lecturers.

But there is one thing concerning which no wise professor will make rash and ill-considered remarks, or indulge in loose talk and that is the promise of a vacation. His class is sure to wake up, take notice and demand fulfillment. Woodrow Wilson promised mankind a vacation from the most horrible scourge now afflicting it— war. And the peoples of the world bestirred themselves and remained around to watch him make good. Having promised the impossible and having even failed to obtain much that was within the scope of human achievement, he collided with a universal disillusionment and discontent. It is an interesting but perhaps futile and insoluble question as to who is the more dangerous—he who promises much and produces little, thus begetting a great crop of disillusioned cynics, or he who promises nothing and achieves nothing, thus failing either to arouse hope or to produce dejection. I pass this problem on to John Dewey or Stanley Hall, but no fair-minded person can well deny that Woodrow Wilson produced more cynics than any other figure in modern history.

THE GUARD

BY RUTH VALENTINE

FRANCIS XAVIER RANEY, the guard, leaned against the high desk at which a trusty filled in prisoners' names on printed slips of paper. An olive drab uniform and cap matched too well the color of his face and hair to give them any distinction by contrast. Under pale lashes his yellow-gray eyes bulged slightly and his thin-lipped mouth was a downward slash in his narrow face.

It was Saturday, Visitors' Day, at Stanton prison and as each bus from the station stopped before the towered entrance its occupants crowded into the small office of the Captain of the Guards, where Raney was lounging. The trusty, a pensive-faced young man, needed no supervision, but Raney liked to stand there, aware that he made the visitors nervous. Those among them who came for the first time often stammered under his suspicious stare as they gave the names of the prisoners they wished to see. The nervously friendly visitors, particularly the women, who approached him with questions or offered harmlessly unnecessary remarks about the weather, he looked at blankly for a few seconds, then asked in a flat menacing voice, "What?" Nothing more than that, but they repented of the weather and usually moved away to the chairs lined up against the opposite wall without repeating their questions. Raney regretted this for he liked saying "No" whenever he could.

On this Saturday in May the sunny weather brought more than the usual number of people, and the office chairs and the long green bench outside were so soon filled that several men and boys and a young woman with two little girls were left standing. Back of the bench was a railed-in garden, a bit of lawn, a maple tree and a small bandstand fringed with red geraniums and bushes of marguerites. Through the gateway went the two children and started chasing each other around the bandstand. Out of the office door came Raney and, raising a threatening arm, yelled,

"Come out of there, you!"

There was something in his voice that spoke to the children of punishment and they ran, terrified, from the garden to their mother. Though trusties who had the limited freedom of the grounds outside the prison sometimes smoked their Bull Durham on that garden lawn there were none there that day. The rule painted on a sign said "No Visitors Beyond Here," and Francis Xavier liked rules.

An old gray-mustached Mexican sat on the end of the bench, corded brown hands folded between dusty black serge knees. He had been there an hour and his son's name had not yet been called. When it was called he would go into the close packed "reception room," seat himself at the guard's direction across a high desk-like partition from his son and try in that confusion of voices to ask him questions and hear the low answers. He got up slowly, for his bones ached with rheumatism, and went to Raney.

"I see Ramon Sepulveda soon?" he asked timidly.

Raney looked at him, then beyond to a boat on the bay.

"You can't see him, he's in the hospital."

"Hospital? "repeated the old man and moved his lips, trying to seek some answer to the confused terror that made him stupid.

"Yeh, he's sick, you can't see him."

Raney stared at the old Mexican coldly.

"Please, what sickness has he?" This like a begging child.

"You can't see him, I tell you—that's all!" Raney turned back to the office and looking over his shoulder as he went up the steps, saw the old man once more humped on the bench. "Old fool," he announced, spat neatly across the walk into the gutter and went inside.

There he found MacKenzie, another guard, talking to the trusty at the desk. None of that for him, Raney's contemptuous look said. The superintendent of the prison was his model—if he needed one— a man who had had his training in the good old days when you could beat up a con when it was good for him. Partridge, the "supe," had fallen in with this prison reform junk (for so Raney considered it) to keep his job, but he had some tales of what they did to the cons in the old days that warmed Raney with pleasure.

Raney had been a guard at Stanton for almost twelve years. He had got the position through the influence of Belle's uncle, who was a county sheriff. He and Belle were engaged to be married and as his wages as driver of a delivery wagon in a small town could never have supported a wife, the sheriff's offer to get him a place as prison guard made possible his marriage and seemed a great step up in the world.

At first he had been restive under the monotony of prison routine, but the habit of watching men work yet not working with them and the growth of a capacity for bullying them gradually made him into an excellent prison guard. His development was not influenced by the presence of a "reform" warden at the head of the institution, for had these two ever conferred over the question of prison discipline, the warden would have found in Raney a large

contempt for his policies. Fortunately for Raney, the actual supervision of the prison was in the hands of the callous superintendent who had seen several wardens come and go and who, though he saw to it that the guards for the most part obeyed the letter of the rule that forbade them to lay hands on the convicts, observed with satisfaction the brutalizing ingenuities of their evasions of its spirit. Raney had perfected many ways of provoking in the men the insubordinations necessary to send them to "solitary." To the newcomers even his sneering stare was unbearable.

There was a fly in Raney's ointment. He was tired of his small salary. He felt that after twelve years he was the victim of shabby treatment because he could not afford an automobile. So his thoughts had been turning for the past year toward some vague but well paid occupation in the world outside the prison walls. He preferred one of a get-rich-quick nature. This pleasant prospect slowly obscured in his mind the advantages that went with a small salary at Stanton—the easy monotony, the many perquisites, the authority. His wife, eager for the change (she hated the prison) talked always of her brother's success in the city, of this and that friend of his who had done well, without, so she said, being any smarter than Raney, until he believed he was a fool to stay where he was.

II

As Raney walked to his cottage on this Saturday evening, smoking a cigarette, cap pushed comfortably back from his forehead, he breathed in with disgust the rotten egg odor that came from the mud flats of the bay below the road. Low tide had left them gray and slimy, pock marked by the bubbling up of air. He saw a lumpy gunny sack a few yards from the edge. Probably a dead dog in it . . . no wonder the place smelled worse than usual . . . was he going to spend the rest of his life in this cheesey place? . . . like hell he was . . . a swell chance for promotion with a captain of guards and a supe who couldn't be pried from their jobs . . . he was worth a lot to them . . . he knew how to put the fear of God into the cons . . . nobody slipped anything over on him either . . . if he had another job in sight he'd quit tomorrow.

So went his thoughts as he climbed the curving road to the row of six yellow frame cottages, all alike, and turned in at the one with calla lilies growing along the inside of the picket fence. He hoped Belle was home from the city and had his supper ready. Yes, he heard her moving about in the kitchen as he went around to the back door. He walked in, gave her a muttered greeting, and sat down at the table.

"See Henry today?" Henry was Belle's brother and should be useful in finding work.

"Yes, I did," answered Belle, "he took me to lunch and then I took the children to a movie."

"Did you say anything about a job for me?" Raney was as nearly eager as it was possible for him to be.

"I said you were thinking of making a change and he said he was glad to hear it and maybe he could help you. Say, why don't you give notice when you get your pay next week and that'll give you a month to find something and I'll look for a flat next time I go to the city?"

Raney grunted, ate in silence for a minute, then said,

"All right, I'll do it. I'll write Henry tonight and ask him to get busy."

The letter was written and after its completion, the sporting page, a cigar and his favorite patent rocking chair lulled him to peaceful stupor. Belle watched him from the less comfortable chair in which she sat crocheting with intent energy. She was a little dark woman with eyebrows that were forever nervously twitching. Twelve years of trying not to give offense to a husband she could never seem to please made her look older than her thirty-eight years. She wanted to move to the city so that she could be near Henry and his children.

III

Henry found work for his brother-in-law with two friends who were starting in business for themselves as manufacturers' agents for automobile accessories. These men, Dustin and Kent, employed Raney only as a favor to Henry, for the vague business experience he fabricated for his brother-in-law could not otherwise have stood their scrutiny. Kent did comment to his partner after their interview with Raney,

"Pretty quiet sort of fellow. Maybe too bashful to sell."

But Dustin, who had recently read with credulous patience a book titled "How to Tell Character at a Glance," said with assurance,

"Not him. Nobody with that stare is bashful. Anyway, if he's no good we don't have to keep him."

Raney, the salesman of new and patent devices designed for the further complication of the business of running an automobile, started out in the fog of a June early morning carrying in his pocket a memorandum book of the firms he was to visit, and in his hand a heavy sample case of imitation patent leather. On the ferry he found a seat and sat down to read the morning paper. As he finished a column at the bottom of the page his glance moved away from the paper and was caught suddenly by a familiar pair of shoes across the aisle. Broad and bulging of toe, clumsy soled, of thick lustreless black leather, they were noticeably unlike ordinary shoes. Raney knew them well. They were the product of the prison shoe factory, worn by the convicts, and a pair of them was supplied to every man discharged from prison. The feet across the way moved uneasily. The man was conscious of the stare and Raney knew it and stared on. The man got up and walked to the forward end of the boat with a step he tried to make leisurely. Raney recognized him as a man who had recently finished his sentence. The man knew Raney too, and only by an agonized effort kept from looking back to see if Raney followed him. Raney amused himself by following the man in his frantic dodgings about the boat. The terror he was causing pleased him enormously.

For the rest of that week Raney carried his sample case in and out of stores, but found himself on Friday evening with only two small orders. He returned to his employers with a grievance. It was impossible, he told them, to sell anything in the towns to which they had sent him. There were too many other fellows selling the same line. Why, most of the places he went they didn't even give him a chance to show his stuff. His employers asked him with surprise if he expected to sell without competition and at his surly "I suppose not" gave him a talk on salesmanship, as they conceived the art, full of advice to him in such terms as "get the psychology of the man you are selling" that were meaningless to him. "Get your man" was current in his vocabulary, but not this other.

He started his second week of effort with cheerful assurances from his employers that this week he would surely bring in a lot of business. But the merchants he visited showed no eagerness to become his customers. This in spite of the fact that he used on them almost the same methods of verbal persuasion that had always been so successful with his charges at Stanton. The week ended with an incident that completed Raney's distaste for salesmanship as his approach to wealth. He had on his list the name of a large garage in a prosperous country town, one of several in the county owned by one man, and to this he went first on Friday morning, told the first mechanic he met what he wanted and was directed to the accessories department, which he found was a store in itself. As he entered the door, the place was empty. He lifted his case to the counter and was unfastening the snaps when a vigorous voice behind him said,

"Good-morning, sir, what can I do for you?"

Raney turned around, but forgot his customary opening speech that had been the result of his ruminations on Kent and Dustin's talk on salesmanship. For he looked into the alert brown eyes of young Clark Rogers, a dark, powerfully built boy of twenty-two who had been his particular enemy in prison. Clark had served a sentence of a year. A drunken ride of his had ended in a smashed store window, and an indignant judge, exasperated by too much reckless driving in the community, had sent him to prison as an example to alcoholic and thoughtless youth. Clark took prison as lightly as he had taken all else in his life and his irrepressible cockiness had made him the object of Raney's dislike and consequent persecution. Raney had not been able to cow him into the prison pattern of submission and hated him for that.

When Clark saw who his visitor was, he rubbed his hands together and laughed joyfully.

"Well, well, *Mister* Raney, this is a pleasure. Can it be that you have left poor old Stanton flat? What will the brothers do without their dear old chum Raney!"

He noticed the sample case. "So you are a little salesman now. Well, it's a strange world with you in it. That's a tricky hat you're wearing but your little tan cap suited you better. What are you selling, *Mister* Raney, handcuffs for bad babies?"

Raney turned to close his sample case with a savage,

"Shut up, or I'll fix you!"

"Tut, tut, Mister Raney, that's not the way to sell your toys."

Raney shook a finger at him. "In ten minutes you'll be out of a job here. I'll tell them you're an ex-con!"

Clark strolled to the counter and leaning provocatively near Raney said, softly,

"My boss knows all about me. I was paroled to him and he happens to be my uncle. So beat it, Raney, before we kick you out. You can't sell a nickel's worth of stuff to anybody in this county. I know everybody in this business around here and I'm going to pass along the word to them to give you the gate if you show up. Go on back and bully the poor devils in prison, that's your meat. Gee, I'd like to beat you up, but you're not worth the trouble. Better get out before I change my mind about doing it."

Raney, cursing, got out. The next day he walked into the office of Kent and Dustin and resigned, to their relief. They had decided to discharge him, but were putting it off because of their friendship for Henry.

The obliging but somewhat annoyed Henry found another job for his brother-in-law. This time Raney put on the white duck uniform of an operator at a gasoline filling station and functioned for a month. Then he was discharged. The sales at his station had decreased alarmingly. The other operator at the station reported that Raney "made everybody sore" and that he "ordered the customers around too much."

"Frank," said Henry, "you can't hold a job where you meet the public unless you act friendly to people, and I guess you got out of the way of that up at Stanton."

"I'll be damned glad not to meet 'em," Raney answered, "and I'll get a job where I don't have to."

He did not ask Henry to find this job, but he did have to borrow fifty dollars from him to meet his bills. After a two weeks' search he found what he wanted. A construction company hired him as boss of a gang of pick and shovel men working on a road in the mountains. Raney traveled all day on the train to reach the construction camp and when he reported for duty found that he had charge of a crew of fifteen men and that he was under the superintendent of construction, Blake, a young engineer. Blake's instructions to him were brief, to keep the men at work and to keep them satisfied, for they were a long way from any source of labor supply. Raney had had experience keeping men at work in the prison mill and this seemed an easy task.

He stood watching his men the first day; saw them sweat and strain as they swung their picks in the hot sun high up on the side of a canyon whose bottom-most pines wavered in the heat; heard the rattle of chains as the scraper crews cleared away the loose earth and rocks; breathed in the odors of dust, sweating horses and manure. He was more content than he had been for many weeks. This kind of work he understood.

"No loafing there!" he called to a young Italian who had straightened up to rest his shoulders and looked with empty dreaming eyes over the canyon. The boy scowled, spat on his hands and swung his pick in slow monotonous rhythm again. It was hot and the water bucket was soon emptied by the frequent parched gulps taken from it. One of the men picked it up and started down the road to refill it at a nearby spring.

"Come back and get to work!" ordered Raney. "You can fill that at noon."

He was angry that the man had not asked permission. The man paused, sullenly, dropped the bucket where he stood, and came back.

At the end of that first day the men hated Raney and showed it by ignoring his orders as much as they dared. Raney knew of their hatred and gave the only answer of which he was capable, more bullying. Saturday night when the men were paid they swore openly at Raney and left for the nearest railroad station. The superintendent telegraphed for a new crew and asked Raney to go easy with the men. Raney privately decided that he had been too easy with the first bunch. They were a lot of bums. He'd show the new ones who was boss when they started. He showed them so well that they lasted only two days and all work on the road was held up until a third crew came from the city. With them came a new boss, and the superintendent gave Raney his fare back to the city, telling him that they could not afford to be changing men all the time. Angry at the dismissal, Raney tried to pick a quarrel with the new boss, but met only patient good nature.

IV

When Raney reached home the next evening he told Belle that he had been fired, but added that he was going to quit anyway because he was damned if any company could pay him to be an easy mark for a lot of wobblies. If he had them up at Stanton, where they belonged, he'd show them. Belle knew from experience that this was no time to annoy her husband with questions, but the troubling uncertainty of the future forced from her a worried,

"What *are* you going to do now? We've got to pay our bills and how we're going to do it when you can't keep a job is more than I can see."

"Don't I know that?" agreed Raney. "It's not my fault. If I could get a chance at a decent job, I'd keep it all right. So for God's sake quit jawing me."

He was discouraged but could not admit it to Belle. When he left Stanton nothing seemed easier nor more sure than that he would be successful. There were no obstacles in his imaginings. Here was the reality, confusing and insoluble. He woke Belle that night to talk to her. Never a reflective man, the frustrations of the past weeks had begun by angering him and then bewildered him into a state of jumbled self questionings that was a new experience. For the first time in many years he sought advice from Belle.

"What you think I'd better do?" he asked when his repeated "Belle" had wakened her. "Partridge would be darn glad to have me come back to Stanton."

"Well, I don't know," Belle considered, raising herself on an elbow as if to lift herself above the problem. "We could keep going if you'd let me go to work until something turned up."

"Nothing doing on that," vetoed Raney. "I'm not going to have Henry say you're supporting me. I don't see anything to it myself but to go back to Stanton, but I don't want you saying I made you go to work."

Belle subsided on her pillow.

"All right, Frank," she said patiently, "you do what you think's best."

In a short time the Raneys were back in the yellow frame cottage. Belle looked down the hill at the gray group of stone buildings with bitter dislike as she watered the dusty calla lilies inside the picket fence, but Raney found them an exhilarating sight. He had been back three days when the jute mill where most of the convicts worked shut down for five days while worn out machinery was being replaced. The men who usually worked there spent that unwonted time in the enclosed mill yard. Lest they should consider it a holiday they were forbidden to take any games or reading matter into the yard. Raney was one of the guards detailed to duty there, charged with the carrying out of this order which included the confiscation of forbidden material and the reporting for "solitary" of any convict who offended twice. Everytime his "hand those over, you!" was obeyed, the annoying memory of his encounters of the past weeks became soothingly dimmer. He was able to report two men for solitary. The first day he found them with a pack of cards, and the second he discovered them flipping small wads of cigarette papers at a line in the dust. He altered this pastime in his verbal report to the more heinous crime of pitching pennies and produced six from his own pocket as evidence. His word was better than the men's so they paid a penalty for having faces that reminded him of two members of his pick and shovel crew.

His homecoming was complete when he learned that there were eighteen I. W. W.'s in the dungeon for refusing to work. This news caused him almost to burst from his uniform with satisfaction.

"Those dirty wobblies," he said to his friend Bowers, a hard-boiled guard, as they smoked their cigarettes in the sun at the noon hour, "they're a bunch of soreheads that haven't got the guts to get along in the world like the rest of us. I'd hang every damn one of them."

THE THEATRE

BY GEORGE JEAN NATHAN

Zoë Akins' "The Moon Flower," an adaptation of Lajos Biro's "The Last Kiss," is, like her "Déclassée" and "The Varying Shore," servant girl drama written for ladies and gentlemen. That, at least, is the design, although in the present instance there is need for the ladies and gentlemen to be either under twenty, in which event the play may conceivably impress them as at once fresh and poignantly romantic, or over seventy, in which event it will serve wistfully to recall to them their early days of theatregoing. To those of an age between, Miss Akins' exhibit will be merely an overly bedight and gilded copy of the ancient fable of the celebrated courtesan, the wealthy protector and the young lover, made considerably idiotic by the author's apparently ineradicable relish for what is known in the vernacular as spending names. It is Miss Akins' idea of elegance and rich dramatic atmosphere casually to mention a king, a grand duke or a duchess every third minute, and to embellish the intervening spaces of time with allusions to champagnes of rare vintage, *plats* of infinite *aux* and *à la's*, million dollar yachts, priceless strings of pearls, Monte Carlo, the Riviera and the various royal families of Europe. As further evidence of her recognition of *bienséance* and intimate acquaintance with the refinements of exclusive *milieux*, she fills her plays with tony French waiters, of whom there are at least three to every person at table and who elaborately bow themselves in and out at the nose-in-air beck and nod of a super-tony *maître d'hôtel*, baccarat, pools of goldfish, Dimitrino cigarettes with gold tips, lace napkins with the morning chocolate, imperial suites of thirty or forty rooms, and casual references to those personal peculiarities of the kings and queens of Europe that have come to her personal notice while she was hanging out for the week-ends at their palaces. Miss Akins is a talented playwright—one of the most talented that has thus far shot across the American scene—but she is rapidly corrupting that talent with her absurd backstairs affectations. Her plays begin to remind one of nothing quite so much as a winsome little country girl in calico and black cotton stockings who pins a portière to her rear, struts majestically through the old family parlor with a brass curtain pole and assures her elders, upon their somewhat puzzled but still amused interrogation, that she is the Queen of Sheba.

"The Last Kiss," from which Miss Akins has derived her latest play, represents the modern Hungarian drama at its most shopworn and conventional. Hungary has it jitney Pineros and its Pierre Frondaies as well as its Molnars, although it is only fair to Biro to record that this is the poorest of all his dramatic efforts. Upon Biro's ground plan, the American adaptor has reared a play that in the matter of *clichés* goes back to the 1890's: a thing full of such delicatessen as "I would gladly give my life for one night in her arms," "Let us leave this place with all its false glitter and sham and go away together to some quiet little village where we can love and dream away our days," "She is the most mercenary courtesan of Paris and he is the richest and most powerful duke in all Europe," "Buck up, my lad, twenty years from now you'll look back at it all and laugh," "He has killed men for doing no more than you have done," "You are very rude, but (*with a twinkle in her eyes*) I like

497

you," and "Take me, hold me close; I am yours to do with what you will!" They are all here, either literally or in essence. And they contrive in the aggregate, what with the backdrop painted to represent the Côte d'Azur, with all the doggy waiters backing in and out and with barons, dukes and the like lounging around promiscuously and democratically, to produce just such an evening as is hugely enjoyed by the maid on her Thursday night out. Miss Akins' control these days is evidently Elinor Glyn, with Emily Post and the late Ward McAllister ringing the bell and banging the tambourine inside the cabinet.

In the rôle of the cocotte, Miss Elsie Ferguson, due perhaps to the intrinsic nature of a character which imposes upon its expositor no necessity for the finer shadings of emotion but only emotions that have been calloused by long and hard usage into a, b, c, manages her share in the proceedings satisfactorily. The grand duke of Frederick Worlock, though it would be a ridiculous performance in a more intelligent manuscript, fits the present servant girl scheme accurately. But the performance of Sidney Blackmer in the rôle of the dashing, daring, young romantic is the worst piece of acting that this Algonquin Salvini has thus far, with all his compelling virtuosity in the way of bad acting, vouchsafed his admirers. If there is a poorer young actor on the American stage at the present time, my astigmatism must be much more acute than my oculist says it is.

II

It is always something of a shock to a reviewer to come upon a performance of a classical rôle which grossly violates all of his preconceived notions, laboriously harmonized out of long antecedent experience, and to find to his horror that this latest performance is apparently just as right about it all as he previously would have believed it to be wrong. It is with something of this unpleasantly agreeable sensation that Jane Cowl's Cleopatra affects me. It is intelligent in a conception that I had hitherto doubted as intelligent; it is variously and accurately registered in keys that previously I would have held to be faulty; it is shrewd in various emotional shadings which, had they been outlined to me by some august professor, would have elicited from me some very superior snorts. It is, in brief, a Cleopatra critically sound in every particular, carefully and sagaciously studied, and wisely and adroitly projected—that never for a moment is possessed of the theatrical effect that Shakespeare strove for and that never for a moment holds one, persuades one and moves one as have Cleopatras infinitely less critically sound.

The fault with Miss Cowl's Shakespearian Egyptian is, it seems to me, precisely the fault of Walter Hampden's Shakespearian Dane. Its obvious carefully modulated and painstaking rationality takes the essential warmth out of its theatrical effectiveness. Hampden's Hamlet is ever less a prince of Denmark than an intelligent actor reciting the rôle of a prince of Denmark. Miss Cowl's Cleopatra is ever less the serpent of the Nile than an intelligent actress playing the rôle of a snake-charmer. She is the master of a rôle which persists in remaining outside her person and which obeys her, as it were, at something of a distance. There is illusion in her own mind, but she does not impart it to her audience, as she did in the instance of Juliet and Mélisande. As a person she has thought out a Cleopatra that as an actress she is unable to force convincingly over the footlights. Miss Cowl has conceived the best criticism of her various sister actresses' Cleopatras that I have encountered; but her sister actresses still paradoxically remain the more vital theatrical Cleopatras. It is all much like a play by, say, Percy MacKaye and one by, say, Austin Strong. The former is indubitably the more sophisticated, intelligent and well-written, yet the latter is the more auspicious in the matter of necessary theatrical power.

The production of "Antony and Cleopatra" sponsored by Miss Cowl suffers, first, from an Antony in the best high school graduation-exercises tradition and, secondly, from a perspirational effort to put into the production what is known to certain scholars as pep. The Antony of Rollo Peters is an amazing creation. For eloquence, we have violent waggings of the head; for decision and defiance, the left foot thrust far forward and the right leg set to quivering with every spoken syllable; for despair, the head dejected and face cupped in palm after the technique of the more fashionable Sixth Avenue photographers; for exaltation, the shoulders thrown back, the eyes raised to heaven and the right index finger pointing toward the heart, as in a Nathan Hale statue; for passion, a mere making of bedroom eyes and an excessive impetuosity of breath. The actor's enunciation and articulation contrive out of the Shakespearian line something as follows:

> There's a great spirit gone! Thus did I desire it;
> What our contempts do often hurl frumps,
> We wish it ours again; the present preasure,
> By revolution lowering, does become
> The opposite of itself; she's good beingawne;
> The hand could pluck her back that shov'd herron.
> I must from this enchanting queen breakoff:
> Ten thousand harms, more than thills I know,
> Midleness dothatch. Ho, Enobarbus!

The quest for life and speed has led the producer frequently to run off the speeches as if the play were a George Cohan music show. One momentarily expects a troupe of Tiller girls to come on. Of majesty, there is no more than in the Majestic Hotel; of romantic glamor and Egyptian passion hardly more than one finds in a Weber and Fields act.

III

"The whole enterprise," says the reviewer for the New York *Herald*, writing of the Messrs. Kaufman's and Connelly's "Beggar on Horseback"—"beginning with the purchase of a German original by Winthrop Ames, who read it and then threw it into the scrapbasket—is a fine achievement." What we have here, however, is a much more commendable and thrilling display of 100 per cent Anglo-Algonquinism than an acquaintance with the facts, for Mr. Ames threw much less of Paul Apel's "Hans Sonnenstösser's Trip to Hell" into the scrapbasket than the *Herald's* comradely booster and patriot believes. It is true that the American adaptors have put several original and diverting scenes into the play, but that play, for all their embroideries, remains in theme, structure, intimate plan, characters, climaxes and numerous details considerably like the play that was produced in Berlin twelve years ago. The adaptors have Americanized the characters in the matter of externals, have brought up to date and localized satirically portions of the dream-body of the manuscript, have made their young composer hero play a composition by Deems Taylor instead of Chopin's Prelude in C minor, as in the Berlin production, have converted Apel's gramophone into a hurdy-gurdy and caused it to play a jazz tune instead of Paul Lincke's appallingly popular "Give Me a Little Bit of Love" from the then current musical comedy success, "Berliner Luft," and have contrived a number of other such patent alterations, but, though they have done their job dexterously, they have brought little sound humor and fancy to the text that were not in it originally. Their deletion of the parrot, a highly comical device of the original; their conversion of the ear-torturing orchestra of the original into a singing jury; their mere suggestion of the nerve-racking phonograph that drives the young composer to distraction—these are as unfortunate as their literal adherence to the amusing murder scene at the end of the first act, to the manner of the epilogue and prologue, and to the device of the irksome heiress and the dancing waiter is the opposite.

The best elements in the local version of the play consist in the adroitly humorous touches with which the adaptors have tricked out the ends of several scenes in the original which, had they been left as they were, would doubtless have trailed off somewhat ineffectively for an American audience, as well as in a thoroughly charming pantomine incorporated into the play by Deems Taylor—the most delicately lovely thing of its kind I have seen since Madame Donnet's little ballet, "La Pomme d'Or," and a vastly hilarious Kaufman-Connelly burlesque of an American newspaper which is peddled among the audience during the entr'acte. Roland Young has the rôle of the young composer whose nightmare of what life would make of him, were he to marry money at the expense of artistic happiness, brings him back into the arms of a waiting Cinderella. His performance is generally well managed, although one might wish that, inasmuch as he cannot play the piano, he would at least learn the relative positions of the keys so that his digital manoeuvers might less drolly fail to follow and synchronize with the off-stage playing.

IV

When the curtain went up on George Kelly's "The Show-Off" and disclosed the suburban sitting-room with the walnut centre table draped with a fringed tidy, the armchair upholstered in nondescript velvet and the cheap brass chandelier, I said to myself: here is still another of the attempts to duplicate Craven's "The First Year," and prepared myself for the worst. There was nothing in the first fifteen minutes of the play to make me change my prefatory attitude. These minutes were given over to a recitation by two characters of a series of usual and immediately recognizable bromides which, according to the next morning's newspapers, constituted remarkable powers of observation on the part of the author. (In New York, a remarkable observation consists merely of the talent for hitting off the more obvious and superficial characteristics of a

dramatic character. Thus, any old woman who keeps on mouthing such familiar sayings as "What a small world it is, after all!" or "My rheumatics is troubling me again; it's a-going to rain," is uniformly greeted as a well-rounded character made sharply photographic by the playwright's "observation.") A few more minutes went by, and down the hills of Angostura still the tide of perceived stencils rolled. Then something happened. There was a loud, reverberating, barbershop laugh off stage and a moment later it entered in the person of a character named Aubrey Piper, and a moment later Kelly's play took on life and shrewd humor and some very real observation. Did I say the play? If I did, I am foolish, for the play did nothing of the kind. But the character of Aubrey Piper did, and in the doing caused the play to fade gracefully and unnoticed into the background, after the manner of an oil painting in a window full of tin-types.

This Aubrey of the belted overcoat and the latest Kuppenheimer modes, with his Mr. Simms of Seattle handshake, oppressively expansive nature, egregious prevarications and glowing regard for himself, is, for all the leaven of burlesque which the author has injected into him, as authentic and honestly entertaining a character as the native drama has given birth to. Jimmy Gilley in "Bought and Paid For," the fat boy in George Cohan's "Broadway Jones" who won't smoke cigarettes because they soften the brain, the coon in George Ade's "Country Chairman" objecting to certain cigars because they are rolled "too severe," the young boy in Tarkington's "Intimate Strangers," this Aubrey Piper—in such as these flows some of the best blood of American drama. If our dramatists were as expert in drama as they frequently are in dramatic character, the American theatre would be rich indeed. Kelly, for example, has achieved this excellent Aubrey, but not much more. His dramatic method is largely the method of the vaudeville sketch: five minutes of jokes followed by five minutes of drama, and repeat. There is no get-together. Again, his invention is crude. When, for example, a father dies in the hospital and the family rushes off to his bedside, he keeps the more loving of the daughters at home for no other reason save that he *has* to keep her at home or stop his play. Still again, he rings down on nothing more tangful than the ancient E. E. Rose-Winchell Smith success of the million dollar invention. But the Mons. Aubrey thumbs his nose derisively at his creator's other shortcomings and blinds the audience to them. A thoroughly amusing figure. And played by a vaudeville actor, Louis John Bartels, to perfection.

V

When the curtain went up on the Messrs. Gropper's and Hammerstein's "New Toys" and disclosed much the same sort of middle-class sitting-room as Kelly's, with much the same sort of centre table and uphol-stered armchair, I said to myself: here is *still* another of the attempts to duplicate Craven's "The First Year," and prepared myself, as in the former instance, for the worst. Unlike in the case of "The Show-Off," there was nothing in the first two and one-half hours of the play to make me alter my preparations. All that the Messrs. Gropper and Hammerstein have succeeded in capturing of "The First Year" are a few minutes, and these few minutes, that might have been developed into first-rate comedy, their talents have been insufficient to bring to flower.

The effort of the authors has been to show not what happens in the first year of a married couple's life, as Craven showed, but what happens in the second. They have brought nothing new to Craven's idea. All that they have done is to take "The First Year," rewrite it badly, and palm it off as a study of the second year of marriage by sticking a baby into it. This baby actually has no more to do with the theme of their play, for all they seem to believe it has, than the baby had to do with McGuire's "It's a Boy." But even if it did, the common dodge of the theatre which asks an audience to work up its sympathies for a baby that all too obvi-ously is actually nothing but a long bag of oatmeal tied with pink ribbons would work to the play's undoing. When, in that scene of a play wherein the audience is asked to get wet in the eyes over a lonely baby's plight, the audience can plainly see that the lonely little baby being hugged to the bosom of the desolate father was certainly never brought by the stork but was very much more likely dragged in by the cat, and when further its plaintive little cry emanates less from the bundle that represents the baby than from a stage-hand hidden behind the window twenty-five feet away—when this happens, Haupt-mann himself, to say nothing of the Messrs. Gropper and Hammerstein, find that they have cut out a tough job for themselves. I surely am not ass enough (Cries of "Hear, hear!") to urge that realism be carried so far in the theatre that real one-year-old babies be begot, or merely hired, as the dramatic occasion may require, but I feel, as the skilful pro-ducers of "Baby Mine" and many another play that has depended largely for its effect upon the verisimilitude of the infant protagonists have well appreciated, that at least a satisfactory compromise with realism should be arrived at. It may be that the babies in "Baby Mine," though fashioned with an extreme ingenuity out of wax, did not look exactly like real live babies, but it is certain that, at their worst, they looked a whole lot more like babies than like so many sofa pillows in diapers.

Ernest Truex was the star of the occa-sion. He is a comedian whose technical equipment permits him to give a good account of himself in the initial portion of an entertainment, but whose equipment is so limited that thereafter he repeats himself to the subversion of the effects he strives for.

VI

Abby Merchant's "The New Englander" is simply a George Broadhurst play with the scene laid in Boston. It is no more the study of the New England character and viewpoint that it aims to be than a Drury Lane melodrama is a study of British naval warfare and horse-racing. Its characters are New Englanders only by the grace of gray wigs, lavender tea gowns and a slightly whiter makeup than is commonly used. Miss Merchant appears to have gained her ideas of New Englanders chiefly from attending the Boston theatres: her characters are less Puritan stock than Puritan stock company.

By way of reflecting the New England character and viewpoint the playwright has selected a plot that is a cross between Jules Eckert Goodman and Ibsen: a *smörgasbord* of sweet and loving ingénues, slangy low-comedy juveniles, stolen bonds, hereditary criminal impulses, suddenly restored memories and suicides off stage left. It is entirely possible that a genius, or even a person of some talent, might contrive successfully to reflect the New England character and point of view with a groundwork of such materials, but all that the present author has succeeded in reflecting is the dramatic character and point of view of a household made up of Charles Klein, Rachel Crothers, Owen Davis and Bertha Kalish.

The Equity Players, after a critically praiseworthy beginning with "Queen Victoria," seem to have made a sorry mess of their season, both financially and artistically. What they plainly need is a commercial theatrical manager with experience in combining the artistic and the profitable, of which species there are several who might be willing to undertake the job. If such a manager is, by reason of their organization's doctrine and the overwhelming conceit of the genus actor, objectionable in their sight, they might at least get hold of some gifted outsider to pick their plays for them. With char-

acteristic modesty, I offer my own services gratis, at least to the extent of suggesting the following plays, most of which are possessed of authentic merit and, doubtless, of box-office possibilities: 1. Rostand's "Last Night of Don Juan"; 2. Porto-Riche's "The Old Adam"; 3. Eugene O'Neill's "The Fountain" (an arrangement might be effected with Arthur Hopkins, who, as I write, holds the script); 4. Rittner's "En Route," an amusing Don Juan play which, while not to be mentioned in the same breath with Rostand's, might be put on for much less money if the Rostand outlay was deemed too heavy for the Equity Players' treasury; 5. Paul Apel's grotesque tragi-comedy "Love," though it would need careful translation and adaptation; not an important piece, but an entertaining one; 6. Aristophanes' "Lysistrata"; 7. Freksa's "The Fat Caesar"; 8. W. Somerset Maugham's "The Critic," which might lose money but not any more than was lost by "Neighbors" or "The New Englander," and which, unlike these other plays, would be worth taking a gamble on; 9. Sacha Guitry's trivial but jolly "Nono," with Equity member John Drew in Papa Lucien's old rôle, or Sacha's immensely funny "The Prestidigitator," though not in the heavy adaptation that went the rounds of the managers' offices a few years ago; 10.—but what do the Equity Players want for nothing?

VII

The considerable talents of H. G. Wells and St. John Ervine, working in combination, have produced in "The Wonderful Visit" an inconsiderable play, one which, indeed, —so far as imagination, humor and merit generally are concerned—is hardly to be compared even with William Le Baron's boob-bumper on a similar theme, called "Back To Earth," and presented here six or seven years ago. In it are visible no evidences of the skill of either man; from first to last it is completely tame and bare. Founded on an early novel of Wells', the exhibit takes the form of the stereotyped dream play. The dream in this instance is of an angel who comes to earth and who, instead of being able to elevate the soul of man, finds itself slowly pulled down to man's own low level. The characters selected to further this fable are the standard personages of modern British drama: the soft-hearted and imposed-upon vicar, the vicar's chatty old gardener, the seduced young housemaid, the gallant lover who is killed in the war, the fat and puffy housekeeper, the timid little bald-headed curate, the mannish Englishwoman of title who snaps out her pieces of mind, and the villainous Sir John in riding boots who periodically flicks them with his riding crop and, glancing over his shoulder to make certain that no one is within earshot, bends over the housemaid and tells her with a leer that he deems her a pretty wench. Thus do the Messrs. Wells and Ervine divulge themselves in the rôles of label leaders. Nor do the sentiments and philosophies which they lodge in the mouths of these stock dummies depart greatly from what in the last twenty years has come to be formula. They make their points very largely after the manner of amateur checker players: watching their game, one can foretell their every move; and their little triumphs are all too anticipatedly easy. They put up no imaginative hazards and barriers in the path of their theme. They play a bowling game in which they use tissue paper cones for pins, and against them roll large medicine balls. They have made their thematic job too childishly simple. Their angel faces less the grim problems and hard hearts of men than the drawing-room problems and soft hearts of the popular London playwrights of the 'Nineties. And the production vouchsafed their play by the Lenox Hill Theatre company is surely of no assistance to it. Miss Margaret Mower's angel has all the spiritual qualities of a book-agent selling Van Loon's "Outline of the Bible."

VIII

Miss Eva Le Gallienne's idea of "The Assumption of Hannele," by Gerhart Hauptmann, was produced recently at a series of special matinées. Miss Le Gallienne's idea of the play, unfortunately, seems to be somewhat at variance with the author's. The result, on the stage of the Cort Theatre, was the Grand Transformation scene of "Uncle Tom's Cabin" stretched out to two hours and interrupted every now and then by what appeared to be selections from Gorki's "Night Refuge." The most remarkable result of the production, however, was the criticism of the play itself published in the New York *World*, a portion of which I append, for lovers of the rich and juicy, without comment:

> It was the year 1924, but to one sitting in the theatre it seemed as if the drama had, by ukase, been suddenly turned over to the brightest girl in the graduating class of a parochial school. One would expect that this play was written by just such a person, or at least the chief salesman for a manufacturer of church windows, altar cloths, and the pictures which have been long associated with a mail order heaven. The production of a play like this can mean only one thing. The name of a Hauptmann is too much for managerial judgment. If this play had been submitted by a child of thirteen, the producer, we have no doubt, would have patted her upon the head and sent her to the Sunday School superintendent with a letter of recommendation. Naturally enough the actors and actresses found nothing to grasp, and their performance, even taking into consideration that it was hurriedly rehearsed for special matinées, deserves to be excused.

I said that I would make no comment. But after transcribing the above, I have changed my mind. I wish to make comment. My comment is as follows:

Great God Almighty!

The Little Red Schoolhouse

THE GOSLINGS: A STUDY OF THE AMERICAN SCHOOLS, by Upton Sinclair. Pasadena: *Upton Sinclair.*

THIS volume is a sort of continuation of the author's previous work, "The Goose-Step," and is devoted to the elementary, grammar and high schools of the Republic, chiefly but not exclusively those maintained at the public cost. It presents an engrossing, instructive, and, if allowance be made for the author's indignation, highly amusing record of chicanery and imbecility—a vast chronicle of wasted money, peanut politics and false pretenses. The theory behind the public schools, which cost the taxpayers hundreds of millions every year, is that they manufacture hordes of enlightened and incorruptible voters, and so safeguard and mellow democracy. The fact is that they are mainly manned by half-wits and bossed by shysters, and that their actual tendency is to reduce all their pupils to the level of Kiwanis.

Mr. Sinclair proves all this by an immense accumulation of facts. He not only toured the country, inspecting innumerable schools himself; he also entered upon relations with many rebellious schoolmarms, male and female, and so heard the details of the sad story from the inside. Furthermore, he threw himself into a scientific study of the inner operations of the National Education Association, the trades union of the higher pedagogical functionaries, and digested whole shelves of reports, statistical tables, volumes of graphs, and other such fearful documents. The result is a tale that lacks nothing in the way of circumstantial corroboration. It is, in truth, overwhelming in its plausibility, and I doubt that anyone will ever challenge successfully any essential feature of it. But under the telling of it, alas, there is an erroneous assumption, and there springs therefrom a great deal of false reasoning and vain indignation.

That erroneous assumption is to the effect that the aim of public education is to fill the young of the species with knowledge and awaken their intelligence, and so make them fit to discharge the duties of citizenship in an enlightened and independent manner. Nothing could be further from the truth. The aim of public education is not to spread enlightenment at all; it is simply to reduce as many individuals as possible to the same safe level, to breed and train a standardized citizenry, to put down dissent and originality. That is its aim in the United States, whatever the pretensions of politicians, pedagogues and other such mountebanks, and that is its aim everywhere else. If any contrary theory is cherished among us it is simply because public schools are still relatively new in America, and so their true character and purpose are but little understood. The notion that they were invented by American patriotism and ingenuity, and go back, in fact, to the first days of the New England Puritans—this notion is, of course, only hollow nonsense. The early Puritan schools were not public schools at all, in our modern sense; they were what we now call church schools; their aim was to save the young from *theological* heresy—the exact aim of the Catholic parochial schools and the Jewish *Cheder* schools today. The public schools, which originated in Prussia during the Eighteenth Century and did not reach the United States, save sporadically, until the middle of the century following—even in Masachusetts there was no Board of Education until 1837—, have the quite different aim of putting down *political* and *economic* heresy. Their purpose, in brief, is to make docile and patriotic citizens, to pile up majorities, to make John Doe and Richard Doe as nearly alike, in their everyday reactions and ways of thinking, as possible. How they succeeded in Prussia is well known to every student of the war papers of George Creel, Woodrow Wilson, Newell Dwight Hillis, Owen Wister and other such eminent experts. How they are succeeding in the United States is archly revealed by the current bulls of the American Legion, the National Security League, the Rotary Club, Kiwanis, the Chamber of Commerce of the United States, and the Ku Klux Klan. These great organizations are all made up of their graduates, as are, in fact, the Independent Order of Odd Fellows and the United States Senate.

Thus Mr. Sinclair is contumacious to the Holy Ghost when he protests against the harsh intransigence, the organized stupidity, the Tammany discipline that he finds everywhere in the public schools. He seems to believe, Liberal that he is, that every schoolmarm should be free to handle her little flock of morons in her own way, and teach them whatever she happens to believe, congenitally or transiently, herself. He even goes so far as to argue that what is taught in the schools in general should be largely determined by schoolmarms sitting in congress—that they should have a voice in fixing the curriculum, and even in fixing their own salaries and promotions. This is Bolshevism in its most extravagant and accursed form. The schoolmarm actually has no more right to her own ideas than a deacon in holy orders has to his. She is sworn to propagate only such ideas as happen to be official, and no others. When she departs from that oath in the slightest way, if only *in petto*, she deserves to be handed over to the American Legion for punishment according to its chivalrous rites. Her prime duty is not to serve the enlightenment, but to serve the Republic, which is to say, to serve whoever

happens to be running it at the moment, and deciding what it shall think.

I thus find it impossible to share Mr. Sinclair's ire. What he sets forth so wrathfully was already known to me before I read his book, and I had got used to it. He is, as usual, on the wrong track, and pursuing a chimera. The Liberals have many tails, and chase them all. But I'd be recreant to my vows at ordination if I did not commend his volume unqualifiedly as excellent reading. It is, in fact, one of the most interesting books I have got through for months. It presents a vast mass of scandalous and amusing facts, it sorts them out very deftly, and it is very well written. Why he has had to publish it himself I can't make out. Are all the regular publishers idiots?

Provincial Literature

THE STORY OF DETROIT, by George B. Catlin. Detroit: *The Detroit News*.

THE OUTLAWS OF CAVE-IN-ROCK, by Otto A. Rothert. Cleveland: *The Arthur H. Clark Company*.

OUT OF THE DESERT, by Owen White. El Paso: *The McMath Company*.

MEN OF MARYLAND SINCE THE CIVIL WAR, by Paul Winchester. Baltimore: *The Maryland County Press*.

IT is a genuine pleasure to encounter such books as these, all of them local histories, written by resident authors and printed by publishers on the spot. Mr. Rother's stately volume deals with the river pirates and other outlaws who infested the lower Ohio between the years 1795 and 1820, when the coming of the steamboat drove them out; Mr. White's, even more impressive in size, recounts the brief but highly melodramatic history of El Paso; Mr. Catlin's deals with the founding and growth of Detroit, and Mr. Winchester's is chiefly devoted to a critical discussion of the career of the late Arthur Pue Gorman, for four terms United States Senator from Maryland, and one of the shrewdest, boldest, most unconscionable scoundrels ever seen in the upper house.

That no full-length biography of Gorman has ever been written is really quite remarkable, for he was not only a man of complex character and interesting career, but also a figure of great importance in the political history of the United States between the Civil War and the end of the Nineteenth Century. For two decades he was one of the leaders of the Senate, and for half of that time its undisputed boss. It was he, and not Nelson W. Aldrich, who perfected the Senate machine; Aldrich, after his passing, merely imitated him. He managed Cleveland's campaign in 1884 and gained the narrow victory by a magnificent display of all the arts of the political manipulator. He defeated the Lodge Force Bill of 1890. He fought off tariff reform during both Cleveland administrations. In 1892 and again in 1904 he was a formidable candidate for the Democratic presidential nomination. All the while, of course, he was really a Republican at heart, like so many other salient Southern Democrats, including Oscar W. Underwood. Bryan, in the late 90's, had no more bitter and relentless enemy, and Aldrich had no more faithful friend.

Cleveland distrusted and disliked Gorman, but unquestionably owed the presidency to him in 1884. The popular vote in that year, as everyone knows, was very close; Cleveland's plurality over Blaine was but 62,683. In the crucial State of New York it was but 1,149. In the last days of the contest Gorman, whose headquarters were in New York, sent for some of his Maryland henchmen, including a veteran ballot-box stuffer named Eugene Higgins. On election night Higgins went to the town of Oneida, where the Democrats were in control of the election machinery, emptied the ballot boxes, stuffed them with Democratic ballots, and so carried the State and the country. After Cleveland's inauguration he was rewarded with a job in the Treasury. One day an Oneida acquaintance came down to Washington and told the President the story of Higgins' exploit. At once Cleveland sent for the latter, denounced him as a rascal, and

ordered him to resign his post. "Mr. President," said Higgins unperturbed, "if what I did was, as you say, criminal, and bad enough for you to demand my resignation, don't you think it was bad enough to make you resign too? You were counted in when I burned those ballots, and as a direct consequence are now President of the United States!" But Cleveland stuck to the White House, and poor Higgins had to get out.

Mr. Winchester's account of this and many other such transactions is straightforward and convincing; he was intimately acquainted with most of the men he deals with, especially Gorman himself. He gives a curious account of Gorman's final downfall. It was due mainly to the ferocious assaults of two Baltimore newspapers, the *Sun* and the *News*. Both postured as public benefactors when the battle was over, but neither, in point of fact, went into it with clean hands. The *Sun* after supporting Gorman for years, turned against him overnight when he incautiously advised Cleveland, in 1893, against appointing George W. Abell, its managing owner, Postmaster General. Abell didn't want the office, but he wanted the chance to refuse it. Gorman's objection to his appointment was that it would give him too much Maryland patronage, and so damage the Gorman machine. When the facts leaked out they cost Gorman his hide, for the *Sun*, then as now, was extremely powerful in Maryland.

The *News* had been hammering Gorman for a year before the *Sun* took a hand. Its editor, the late Charles H. Grasty, always took credit in after years, in fact, for the old war horse's destruction. But Mr. Winchester shows that Grasty was actually ready and willing to take service under Gorman but a few months before he began to attack him. The arrangements, in fact, were all made for Grasty to buy the *News* and convert it into a Gorman organ, when a rich politician named Jackson, who was to supply the money in return for the junior Maryland senatorship, decided to wait until the senatorship had been delivered. Grasty, growing impatient, then began negotiations with a group of wealthy Baltimore reformers, and they quickly bought the paper for him, and he launched it against Gorman. If Jackson had not been suspicious, Gorman might have stayed in the Senate, got the presidential nomination in 1900, and beaten McKinley. Jackson's suspicions, in point of fact, were well founded. Gorman always betrayed his friends. He had a favorite motto: "There can be no sentiment in politics." Maybe that is why he is so soon forgotten. The *privat dozent* in history who essays to exhume him will strike a goldmine. Mr. Winchester's modest but instructive volume shows the way to it.

The history of Detroit by Mr. Catlin is a conventional compilation by a man without much apparent imagination, but it at least presents the main facts in an orderly manner, and through its pages flit some extremely interesting figures, among them Potato Patch Pingree, Tom L. Johnson, Embalmed Beef Alger, Henry Ford and the Dodge brothers. The book on El Paso by Mr. White covers less time, but is richer in picturesque incidents. So recently as 1873 El Paso was a sprawling cow town, and its mayor and principal citizen was the Hon. Ben Dowell, proprietor of a celebrated saloon and gambling-house. All the more eminent residents of that era carried artillery, drank like Kansas Prohibitionists and lived with Mexican women. Today El Paso is as orderly, refined and forward-looking as Bayonne, N. J., or Youngstown, O. It is a stronghold of Fundamentalism, has five large tanks for ducking Baptists, supports a country club, a little theatre and a thousand bootleggers, and is the episcopal seat of a Catholic bishop, a grand goblin of the Ku Klux Klan and a provincial superior of Kiwanis. Twenty-five years ago, when a traveling troupe played Ibsen's "Ghosts" in the town, there were riots; today the flappers smoke Lucky Strikes, laugh at God, and read Marie C. Stopes and Guillaume Apollinaire. Mr.

White is no virtuoso of prose, but he tells the story of the struggle upward with considerable charm, and to it he appends a number of biographical sketches, with portraits, of the principal El Paso Babbitts. I commend to connoissuers of ripe American manhood the group showing the three Coles brothers—A. P., Otis and Frank. If Bridgeport, Conn., can show three such handsome realtors, then it has improved vastly since I was last there.

Why are there not more such books? I know of no American town so dull that its history would not make an interesting volume. And every great highway of the land, as Mr. Rothert's work on the Ohio shows, is full of the ghosts of old adventurers.

God's Country: Exterior View

AMAZING AMERICA, by H. M. Somer. Sydney: *New South Wales Bookstall Company.*
DAS LAND GOTTES, by Herman George Schefauer. Hannover: *Paul Steegemann.*
EIN FRUEHLING IN AMERIKA, by Roda Roda. Munich: *Gunther Langes.*
AMERIKA VON WASHINGTON BIS WILSON, by C. A. Bratter. Berlin: *Ullstein and Company.*
AUSLANDSRAETSEL: AMERIKANISCHE UND SPANISCHE REISEBRIEFE, by Friedrich Dessauer. Munich: *Josef Kösel and Friedrich Pustet.*
NEW YORK UND LONDON, by Alfred Kerr. Berlin: *S. Fischer.*
DER AMERIKANISCHE MENSCH, by Annalise Schmidt. Berlin: *Deutsche Verlagsgesellschaft für Politik und Geschichte.*

BOOKS on these States, of course, are common, but two-thirds of them, unfortunately, are written by visiting English literati, and so they tend to run in a groove. What one such visitor says is what all of them say, with immaterial variations. They are all entertained at the Coffee House, they all get drunk on what they learn with surprise is regarded as Scotch, they all meet Johnnie Farrar and Otto Kahn, and they all go home determined to come back next year and take another look at that girl in blue who mixed the cocktails at the tea-party after the lecture before the women's club at Ypsilanti, Mich. The reader who has pursued a course in their

books will turn with some relief and curiosity, perhaps, to works on the same subject
by less practised hands. Here are seven of
them, and no two of the authors have
precisely the same equipment. Mr. Somer
is an Australian agricultural expert and
came to America, not to gape at the Wool-
worth Building, but to study cattle and
sheep raising in the West. Mr. Scheffauer
is a Californian who has lived so long
abroad that the United States is now almost
a foreign country to him. Mr. Roda Roda
is a South German humorist who came
here to lecture, but mainly to have a good
time. Mr. Bratter was for many years a
newspaper correspondent in New York
and is now one of the editors of the *Vos-
sische Zeitung* in Berlin. Prof. Dessauer is a
distinguished German physicist, specializing in radium, and came on a scientific
mission. Dr. Kerr is a dramatic critic, and
came merely for the sea voyage, staying
in New York only a fortnight. Miss
Schmidt is a teacher who left America in
1915, and who thus deals chiefly with the
days before the war.

Of all these books Prof. Dessauer's is
the most romantically gushing and Mr.
Roda Roda's is perhaps the most searching
and amusing. Who served as guide for the
learned professor I don't know, but I am
strongly tempted to suspect that it was
his colleague in radiography, Dr. Howard
A. Kelly, professor of Christian apologetics in the Johns Hopkins Medical
School. At all events, the man who steered
him around New York must have been a
Prohibitionist, for his account of what he
saw reads almost exactly like a pronunciamento by the late William H. Anderson
selig. I quote a few strophes:

*In diesen fünf Wochen sah ich—in Dutzenden der
verschiedensten Gaststätten, niemals offen, einen Tropfen
alkoholischen Getränkes, und nur zweimal im leeren Lokal,
versteckt in später Nachtstunde. Sehr viele sind jetzt
gegen das Prohibitionsgesetz, wollen Bier und Wein
weider zulassen. . . . Aber solange das Gesetzt gilt, wird
es respektiert; es würde nicht verstanden, alles würde sich
dagegen wenden, wenn einer versuchte, es öffentlich zu
verletzen.*

This on page 58. On page 67 the professor says that all Americans pay their income tax willingly, and that it is not
regarded as nice here *die Steuerbehörde zu
überlisten*. On page 69 he says that all
varieties of honest labor are equally respected, and that a boss, when he has to
issue an order to a workman, slaps him
on the back and exchanges witticisms
with him. On page 70 he says that no
American ever works his wicked will upon
a maiden, or keeps a mistress. On page 94
he says that—but I refuse to put it into
English; you must have the original:
*"Die Waschfrau kommt mit ihrem Ford
angefahren."* . . . Turn now to Roda Roda.
He describes an evening party that he
attended on Riverside Drive, among the
newly rich of the second class. He lays it
on, I fear, pretty thickly, but the essential
facts are all there. It is burlesque, and yet
it is fundamentally true. Roda Roda is
under no illusions about Prohibition. He
got as far West as St. Paul and as far South
as Washington, and nowhere did he lack
lubrication for his educated Bavarian
whistle. He is known at home as the man
who lifted the anecdote to the dignity of
an art form. His book is made up of very
short chapters, some of them half a page.
But every one is amusing.

Mr. Somer's book, as I have said, is
chiefly devoted to animal economy in the
West. Alone among all the foreign visitors
that I have ever heard of, he was not much
impressed by the Chicago stock-yards.
They seemed to him to be dirty, and, inferior in many respects to the killing-pens
at home in Australia. Mr. Bratter's book
is devoted exclusively to politics, and contains a long and well-informed discussion
of the American elections system. It stops
with the year 1916, but not a dozen changes
would be needed to bring it down to
today. Dr. Kerr, Mr. Scheffauer and Miss
Schmidt are more concerned with the
intellectual life of the Republic. The first-
named gives special attention to the
theatres, the second to literature and the
general trade in ideas, and the last-named
to social questions, including feminism.

Mr. Scheffauer's book, in places, makes rather curious reading. He is an American by birth and education and he has remained in constant contact with Americans; nevertheless, his long residence abroad gets a touch of foreignness into his discussion of his own country. He sees it most clearly as it was before the war; the vast changes that have come during the last decade sometimes to leave him rather bewildered. But of all the books in the present list, his is the one most likely to be of value to a foreign reader, for its fundamental judgments are based, not upon superficial observation but upon solid experience, and so they are seldom inaccurate. He should come home and then write another book. The America of today would surprise him, and perhaps appall him.

The Husk of Dreiser

ARLIE GELSTON, by Roger L. Sergel. New York: B. W. Huebsch.

THIS novel, the first by the author, a young journalist of the Middle West, seems to have made a very powerful impression upon the Young Intellectuals. Within a week after its appearance I began to receive letters from them, urging me to read it and enclosing encomiastic reviews of it. Unluckily, I was engrossed at the time in legal business of a nightmarish variety, and so I had no appetite for prose fiction. But of late, delivered by Providence, I have gone back to the vice of reading it, and, among other highly commended volumes, I have got through "Arlie Gelston." I can only report that it seems to me to be a respectable, but entirely undistinguished work. The story it tells is dull and often actively unpleasant, the people it depicts are mainly stiff and unplausible, and the English of the author seldom gets beyond the obvious. A palpable follower of Dreiser, he misses completely the quality which gives Dreiser most of his solid dignity and significance as a novelist.

That quality, of course, is the capacity to enlist the emotions of the reader—to make him feel for and with the people of the fable. The notion that Dreiser is a mere representational realist, which is to say, a mere photographer, is utterly absurd. It is held, to be sure, by his chief academic opponents, and it seems to be held, too, by some of his imitators, but it is absurd nevertheless. The virtue of such a book as "Jennie Gerhardt" does not lie in the fact that it is accurate and life-like as representation; it lies in the fact that, in some way that is hard to analyze, Dreiser manages to make us see the world through Jennie's eyes, and so gives us an understanding of her pitiful tragedy. Superficially, she is simply a girl of loose morals, living in contempt of the Mann Act. But actually, in Dreiser's highly skillful hands, she becomes a representative of the agony of all womankind. The last scene of the book, with Jennie looking through the train-gate as Lester's carcass is loaded into the baggage-coach, is surely not mere photography; it is poignant and unforgettable tragedy. To argue that it cannot be tragedy because Jennie is a poor simpleton—in other words, that simple folk cannot know disaster and despair—is to argue plain nonsense.

This evoking of emotion is the essential business of the novelist, as it is of any other artist. A novel that neglected it, however brilliantly done otherwise, would be a bad one, and doomed to a swift forgetting. There is, of course, such a thing as lifting mere representation to such heights of skill that the lack of emotional substance is momentarily overlooked, but on second thought the reader always notes that something necessary is lacking. Thackeray discovered this fact when he published "Barry Lyndon," unquestionably the best of all his novels as representation, but now so far in the shadows that I seem to be the only man left alive in the world who still reads it. Sinclair Lewis came near going over the same precipice in "Main Street." "Babbitt" shows how he discerned his danger, and took measures to remove it. "Babbitt" is certainly not all mocking;

there is also pity in it, and one touch of that pity is worth all its humor. For when art ceases to reach the feelings it ceases to be art and becomes science—and a book of science cannot be a novel. If only H. G. Wells could take in this simple fact, his sales would be vastly greater than they are today, and a public alienated by a long succession of thinly disguised tracts would be wallowing again in such charming things as "Tono-Bungay" and "Mr. Polly."

Mr. Sergel, it seems to me, fails on all counts. His people are not competently represented, and he is quite unable to project their feelings into the reader. His Arlie Gelston is stupid and dull without being pathetic; her story has the impersonal emptiness of a series of fractions. One gets the feeling constantly that it is all one with her whether she does or she doesn't— that she moves through life in a sort of idiotic haze. Such persons exist, and they are of great interest to the psychiatrist. But they are as hopeless in novels, *i. e.,* in art, as persons without faces.

Brief Notices

ANTHROPOLOGY, by A. L. Kroeber. New York: *Harcourt, Brace and Company.*

An excellent introduction to the subject, designed for the general reader and chiefly based upon American material.

LETTERS FROM W. H. HUDSON, 1901-1922, edited by Edward Garnett. New York: *E. P. Dutton and Company.*

Obviously, a "made" book. Three-fourths of the letters are trivial, and only once or twice does Hudson say anything worth hearing.

TENNYSON, by Harold Nicolson. Boston and New York: *Houghton Mifflin Company.*

An extremely amusing and instructive account of the Poet Laureate—in his later days as much one of the noble ruins of England as Stonehenge. The first purely literary biography in the Strachey manner.

TRAVELS IN ARABIA DESERTA, by Charles M. Doughty. Two volumes. New York: *Boni and Liveright.*

A stately and dignified edition of this most curious and baffling work, for years almost unobtainable. There is no need, at this late date, to review it. Its partisans regard it with almost fanatical reverence; its critics find it tortured and dull. I can only report that I dislike its innumerable affectations intensely, and yet find myself reading it.

SAM SLICK, by Thomas Chandler Haliburton; edited with a critical estimate by Ray Palmer Baker, Ph. D. New York: *George H. Doran Company.*

"Sam Slick" is an important work to the student of early American literature. It introduced the Yankee to fiction, it was one of the first American books to become popular in England, and it founded that American school of humor which culminated in Artemus Ward and the early Mark Twain. But reading it today is not unlike reading the debates in Congress during the Pierce administration.

MONETARY REFORM, by John Maynard Keynes. New York: *Harcourt, Brace and Company.*

A vigorous argument against the gold standard by the author of "The Economic Consequences of the Peace." It would be more convincing if it were less cock-sure.

REFLECTIONS ON THE NAPOLEONIC LEGEND, by Albert Leon Guérard. New York: *Charles Scribner's Sons.*

A charmingly penetrating and ironical reconsideration of the known facts about the Corsican. An iconoclastic but extremely valuable contribution to history. Who will do Lincoln in the same way?

THE AMERICAN MERCURY AUTHORS

HARRY ELMER BARNES *is professor of historical sociology at Smith College and* ad interim *professor of economics and sociology at Amherst. He is a member of the American Historical Association, the New York State Historical Association, the American Sociological Society, and the Academy of Political Science.*

CHARLES A. BEARD, PH.D. (Columbia) *was formerly professor of politics at Columbia. He is the author of "An Economic Interpretation of the Constitution," of a history of the United States, and of many other books.*

ERNEST BOYD, *author of "Apostle to the Heathen," is the well-known Irish critic and essayist. He is the author of "The Irish Literary Renaissance" and numerous other books.*

GAMALIEL BRADFORD *is the author of many character studies of distinguished Americans. His books include "Lee, the American," "Confederate Portraits," "Union Portraits," "Portraits of American Women" and "Damaged Souls."*

WILLIAM BULLOCK *is a journalist with much practical experience in politics. He had an active hand in the Hylan campaign.*

JAMES M. CAIN, *author of the study of the American Editorial Writer, is a newspaper man of long and wide experience.*

WALTER PRICHARD EATON *was born in Malden, Mass., in 1878. He was educated at Harvard. He was for a time on the staffs of the New York* Tribune *and New York* Sun. *He is the author of a dozen or more books on various subjects, among them "Plays and Players," "The Man Who Found Christmas," "The Idyl of Twin Fires," "Green Trails and Upland Pastures," "In Berkshire Fields," and "On the Edge of the Wilderness."*

W. J. HENDERSON *has been music critic of the New York* Sun *(now merged with the* Herald) *since 1902. He is the author of a standard work on Wagner and of many other musical books.*

FREDERICK P. HIER, JR., M.E., LL.B., (Syracuse) *is a member of the American Society of Mechanical Engineers and of the New York Bar. He is a practising lawyer in New York City. He has made a special study of Whitman for many years and has published a number of articles dealing with the poet's life and work.*

MUNA LEE (Mrs. Luis Muñoz Marín) *has printed one book of poems, "Sea-Change," and is a frequent contributor to the magazines. She is an Oklahoman.*

ROBERT H. LOWIE, PH.D. (Columbia) *is associate professor of anthropology in the University of California. His specialty is the anthropology of the American Indians and he has done much field work. His book, "Primitive Society," published in 1920, was very widely read and discussed.*

WOODBRIDGE RILEY, PH.D. (Yale), *is professor of philosophy at Vassar. He has specialized in the history of American thought and is the author of "American Philosophy," "Le Génie Américain" and "American Thought."*

JAMES STEVENS *has worked as a laborer in the Northwest for fifteen years. He is now employed in a lumber mill at Bend, on the Oregon coast.*

THYRA SAMTER WINSLOW *is the author of "Picture Frames," a volume of short stories, and is a frequent contributor to the magazines. She was born in Arkansas and now lives in New York.*

INDEX TO VOLUME I

American Portraits:
   I. The Labor Leader 196
   II. The Washington Job-Holder 345
   III. The Editorial Writer 433
Americana 48, 177, 306, 429
Anderson, Sherwood: Caught 165
Arts and Sciences, The:
   Anthropology. 463
   Architecture. 89
   Biology. 213
   Book-Collecting 215
   Medicine 91
   Music 466
   Painting 218
   Philology 94
   Philosophy 468
Authors, The American Mercury: 128, 256, 384, 511
Barnes, Harry E.: The Drool Method in History 31
   Woodrow Wilson 479
Beals, Carleton: Carrying Civilization to Mexico 227
Beard, Charles A.: What is a Statesman?. . . . 394
Bechhofer, C. E.: Spanish Nights' Entertainment 357
Boyd, Ernest: Aesthete: Model 1924 51
   Apostle to the Heathen 419
   Review of "Main Currents in Nineteenth Cen-
   tury Literature" by George Brandes and
   "Poesia e Non Poesia" by Benedetto Croce 125
Bradford, Gamaliel: Horace Greeley 385
Bullock, William: Hylan 444
Cabell, James Branch: Review of "Fantastica:
   Being the Smile of the Sphinx and Other
   Tales of Imagination" by Robert Nichols . 123
Cain, James M.: The Labor Leader. 196
   The Editorial Writer 433
Chew, Samuel C.: Byron in America 335
   Mr. Moore and Mr. Chew 39
Cline, Leonard Lanson: Sweeney's Grail 99
Clinical Notes 75, 201, 323, 451
Colby, Elbridge: The Invasion of America . . . 439
Dreiser, Theodore: Four Poems 8
Eaton, Walter Prichard: In Defense of the Puritan 424
Editorial 27, 161, 292, 408
Eglington, Guy: The American Painter. 218
Feather, William: The Sire of Kiwanis 351
Fergusson, Harvey, The Washington Job-Holder 345
Ficke, Arthur Davison: Reflections of a Bible-
   Reader 281
Fishbein, Morris: Osteopathy 190
George, W. L.: John Maroufaz and His Sons . . 297
Goldberg, Isaac: Review of "Patria Nova" by
   Mario Pinto Serva 126
Henderson, W. J.: A Moratorium for Opera . . 466
Hergesheimer, Joseph: Lillian Gish 387
Hier, Frederick P. Jr.: The End of a Literary
   Mystery 471
Holloway, Emory: More Light on Whitman . . 183
Huneker, James Gibbons: Huneker on Huneker 22
Hussey, L. M.: The Pother About Glands . . . 91
Jenks, Leland: The John Brown Myth 267
Johnson, Gerald W.: The Ku-Kluxer 207

Kellner, Leon: A Note on Shakespeare. 237
Kimball, Alice Mary: Portrait of an Old Mother 332
Krapp, George Philip: The Test of English . . . 94
La Farge, C. Grant: The New Sky-Line. 89
Lee, Muna: Mushroom Town 459
Library, The, by H. L. Mencken . 120, 248, 376, 504
Lind, John E.: Review of "Luther Nichols" by
   Mary S. Watts. 255
Lowie, Robert H.: The Origin and Spread of
   Cultures 463
McClure, John: Panorama 212
   The Weaver's Tale 85
Martindale, Miles: Two Years of Disarmament.. 62
Mason, Gregory: Chautauqua: Its Technic . . . 274
Mencken, H. L.: The Library . 120, 248, 376, 504
   Editorial 27, 161, 292, 408
   Clinical Notes 75, 201, 323, 451
Münsterberg, Margaret: Santayana at Cambridge 69
Nathan, George Jean: The Theatre 113, 241, 369, 497
   Clinical Notes 75, 201, 323, 451
Oneal, James: The Communist Hoax 79
O'Neill, Eugene: All God's Chillun Got Wings 129
Owens, John W.: The Tragic Hiram 57
Parshley, H. M.: Heredity and the Uplift . . . 221
   Review of "Social Life Among the Insects" by
   William Morton Wheeler and "Studies in
   Evolution and Eugenics" by S. J. Holmes . 381
Pearl, Raymond: Alcohol and the Duration of
   Life 213
Pennypacker, Isaac R.: The Lincoln Legend. . . 1
Riley, Woodbridge: The Critical Realists. . . . 468
   The New Thought 104
Robinson, W. F.: Review of "Revolutionary New
   England" by James Truslow Adams 254
Sapir, Edward: The Grammarian and His
   Language 149
Sargent, George H.: Modern First Editions . . . 215
Schönemann, Friedrich: Review of "Auf der
   Rollenden Erde" by Walter von Molo . . . 383
Sinclair, D. W.: Six Orchestral Conductors . . . 285
Smertenko, Johan J.: The American View of
   Politics 363
Stefansson, Vilhjalmur: Every Science an Exact
   Science 309
Stevens, James: The Uplift on the Frontier. . . 413
Suckow, Ruth: Four Generations 15
Sykes, Howell: The Part-Time Missionary . . . 156
Theatre, The, by George Jean Nathan
                  113, 241, 369, 497
Thompson, Charles Willis: Pinchot 180
   The Two Tafts. 315
Valentine, Ruth: The Guard 491
Van Doren, Carl: Stephen Crane. 11
   The Comic Patriot 234
Walkley, Arthur Bingham: Mansfield Park and
   America. 320
Whitman, Stephen French: Cretheus and the
   Lions 257
Winslow, Thyra Samter: Stella 403
X——: On a Second-Rate War. 109

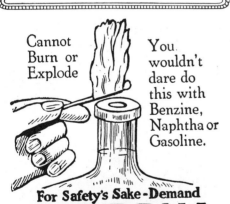

"~a mystic braid was wove"

Sir Walter Scott

A D'ARTAGNAN—One of the best families of Virginia—Known on the Avenue, the Mall, and the Champs-Élysées—The immediate announcement—. A hundred happy thoughts flashed in quick succession. Yet he had not appeared to notice her before tonight.

Yesterday, it must have been true! "You are becoming such a 'drab little thing.' Won't you take a hint?" Those were Marie's very words.

Little did she think that her *confrère's* advice would enlist such a magic wand. What a radiance it gave to her natural charm. Falling across her shoulders, her hair looked like clustered rays of finely spun sunlight. *How different!*

It was he who said only an hour ago, "Tonight, your hair puts me in mind of the gold of Autumn in Versailles!"

If she had given the *raison d'etre,* she too would have said, "Thanks to that Parisienne genius, Dr. Charles Marchand!" [*Graduate Ecole Centrale Des Arts et Manufactures de Paris.*]

Marchand's Golden Hair Wash is specially prepared to bring back the golden tint of girlhood, or to transform black or dark hair to chestnut, auburn or golden shades. Charming results attained, easily, quickly and safely.

Used by French coiffeurs, especially in New York, for over twenty years.

MARCHAND'S
GOLDEN HAIR WASH

Concerning Subscriptions

THE AMERICAN MERCURY is now four months old. Not a great age certainly. Still, enough time has passed to enable you to tell whether you are going to like it or not. If you do enjoy reading it, and we believe you do, or you would not have this copy, why not become a regular subscriber? Avoid the trouble of having to remember to get it each month from the newsstand.

If you are already a subscriber, you can insure yourself against your copy being borrowed by that enthusiastic friend by giving him this subscription blank, and suggesting that he fill it out and mail it.

The subscription rate is five dollars a year; Canadian postage fifty cents, Foreign postage one dollar additional

---

THE AMERICAN MERCURY, *730 Fifth Ave., New York*

Please send me THE AMERICAN MERCURY for one year, starting with the.........
issue. I enclose $...... (check or money order).

Name................................Address...................................
Please send to the following names THE AMERICAN MERCURY for one year, starting

with the..........issue. I enclose $...... (check or money order).

Name................................Address...................................

Name................................Address...................................

Name................................Address...................................